KEEPING THE TABLETS

KEEPING
THE TABLETS

Modern American Conservative Thought

A REVISED EDITION OF

American Conservative Thought in the Twentieth Century

EDITED BY WILLIAM F. BUCKLEY, JR.

AND CHARLES R. KESLER

Harper & Row, Publishers, New York
Cambridge, Philadelphia, San Francisco, Washington
London, Mexico City, São Paulo, Singapore, Sydney

This work is a revision of a book originally published in 1970 under the title *American Conservative Thought in the Twentieth Century*. It was published in a trade edition as *Did You Ever See a Dream Walking?*

KEEPING THE TABLETS: MODERN AMERICAN CONSERVATIVE THOUGHT. Copyright © 1970, 1988 by William F. Buckley, Jr., and Charles R. Kesler. All rights reserved. Printed in the United States of America. No part of this book may be used or reproduced in any manner whatsoever without written permission except in the case of brief quotations embodied in critical articles and reviews. For information address Harper & Row, Publishers, Inc., 10 East 53rd Street, New York, N.Y. 10022. Published simultaneously in Canada by Fitzhenry & Whiteside Ltd., Toronto.

Designer: Sidney Feinberg

Copyeditor: Ann Finlayson

Library of Congress Cataloging-in-Publication Data
Keeping the tablets.
  Revision of: Did you ever see a dream walking?
  1. Conservatism—United States. 2. United States—
Politics and government—20th century. I. Buckley,
William F. (William Frank), 1925–   . II. Kesler,
Charles R. III. Did you ever see a dream walking?
E743.K39   1988   320.5'2'0973   86-46049
ISBN 0-06-055128-3   88 89 90 91 HC 10 9 8 7 6 5 4 3 2 1
ISBN 0-06-096285-2 (pbk.) 88 89 90 91 HC 10 9 8 7 6 5 4 3 2 1

Contents

KEEPING THE TABLETS

Preface

Some years ago, I published a collection of essays under the title *American Conservative Thought in the Twentieth Century.* (I entitled the trade book edition *Did You Ever See a Dream Walking?*) The study was one part of the extensive American Heritage Series put out by Bobbs-Merrill under the general editorship of Professors Leonard Levy and Alfred Young.

Almost two decades have gone by since the book's appearance, and few would deny that during that time much has happened that explicates conservative thought. No one would deny that political action of historic consequence has issued from such thought. It did not surprise me when, a year ago, I was asked by Harper & Row to bring out a new edition of the book.

To do this competently, I needed the help of a scholar in whom I had confidence, who had spent time during recent years studying the relevant literature. I was lucky to have discovered Charles Kesler while he was still in high school as something of a prodigy. He graduated magna cum laude from Harvard in 1978 and got his Ph.D. there in political science in 1985, having written a dissertation on Cicero and the Natural Law. He agreed to collaborate with me.

To my surprise, what grew out of a fresh scholarly investigation was a book substantially new. Only 30 percent of the essays published in the 1970 volume survive. It isn't that the discarded material is less interesting now than then. But perspectives change, new authors write, and old authors whose work was neglected sometimes reappear with fresh relevance. And, of course, there is the problem of space. It became necessary, at the end, for us to discard eight essays we had intended to include.

Along the way, I suggested that Kesler take primary responsibility for the volume, given his more recent experience with the material. We agreed that the book should retain much of the introductory material I provided in the original volume, including material I wrote to introduce the discrete sections. (They remain substantially the same: The Quest for a Tradition; the Status of Freedom; the Critique of Rationalism; Political Economy and the Welfare State; Contemporary Challenges and the Social Order; Foreign Policy and the Communist Threat; The Spiritual Crisis.) I also agreed that it would be useful to include substantial sections of the introduction I wrote for the first volume. It is, we judged, of continuing historical and intellectual interest, dealing as it does with some of the definitional struggles undertaken by *National Review* during the years it was serving as the crucible of modern American conservatism. I thought it important that readers should know something of that day-by-day struggle against heretical accretions, minor and major, that a journal as clearly associated as *National Review* with the development of modern conservative thought needed to fight its way through, to think its way through.

We proceed then, with Charles Kesler's own Introduction to *Keeping the Tablets: Modern American Conservative Thought.* It is followed by my essay, "Did You Ever See a Dream Walking?"

WILLIAM F. BUCKLEY, JR.

Introduction
Charles R. Kesler

Between the overwhelming defeat of Barry Goldwater in 1964 and the reelection of President Ronald Reagan in 1984, American politics was turned upside down. In those two decades, American conservatism came of age, passing from an unsteady dissenting faith to a dominant political creed. In a single generation the American conservative movement advanced from critic of public policy to executive of public policy.

Although electoral success does not require the abandonment of political principles, more often than not it requires their attenuation. Accommodations need to be made in order to assemble a working coalition. For that reason, the time is appropriate to reacquaint ourselves with the paradigms of conservatism, to revisit the insights that first gave rise to the conservative movement and that have guided the public rhetoric of the Reagan administration. The enterprise is all the more useful as a means of informing a new generation of young conservatives, who cannot reasonably be expected to know the intellectual provenance of their own convictions.

But the point is not simply to remind ourselves of what conservatives have thought, or to measure how much—or how little—they have achieved politically, but to reflect on what they *ought* to be striving for. Keeping the tablets implies a duty not only to transmit the principles that American conservatism holds sacred, but to think them through, to keep them vivid, alive.

This book is an effort to aid that rediscovery. In their foreword to the 1970 volume, *American Conservative Thought in the Twentieth Century*, Professors Leonard Levy and Alfred Young wrote, "Mr. Buckley is the foremost expositor of rational, humanistic conservative thought in America today." Working closely with my old friend, I have tried in the present volume to maintain that emphasis on rational, humanistic conservatism. What I have sought to do, consistent with space limitations, is to place before the reader a representative selection of the best of American conservative thought, taking care to display its range and profundity (and occasional cussedness). Disputes among conservatives are treated at greater length than in the earlier book, in order to spur the rethinking and crystallization of conservatism's first principles.

A vital element in the shaping of conservative rhetoric and policies that I do not discuss is the influence of right-wing journals of opinion. But that story is brilliantly told by William F. Buckley, Jr., in respect of *National Review*, in "Did You Ever See a Dream Walking?," an essay that further illuminates the criteria that have governed our selection of contributors to this volume.

In this introduction, I shall attempt to say something about both the principles and practice of American conservatism, keeping always in mind the intimate relation between the two. In particular, I want to sketch the development of conservative ideas within and between the various strands of the movement, essaying their gradual, though by no means uniform, democratization—a circumstance that is perhaps insufficiently understood today. This leads finally to a consideration of conservatism's relation to America, and to the political forms by which conservative principles ought to be advanced.

Those principles came to be popularly identified with the term "conservatism" only in the years after the New Deal, beginning particularly in the mid–1950s. The upsets in public policy that recently have become associated with the conservative cause—reductions in income tax rates, lowering of inflation, increased defense spending, a reinvigorated foreign policy, the appointment of federal judges pledged to judicial restraint— all this, the achievement of the Reagan years, would have been impossible without nearly four decades' intellectual preparation. That preparation was multiform and in some respects even contradictory, as are the constituent parts of the conservative movement today (about which more anon). But even so, conservatism from the beginning possessed a remarkable unity of tone, which derived from a unifying concern: the crisis of the West.

It was not simply the inordinate expansion of government power that triggered the awakening of conservatism. However much the New Deal increased the size and appetites of the federal government, at bottom it was not the multiplication of government agencies, or the increase in federal spending and indebtedness, that mobilized the incipient conservative. It was the *moral* dislocation involved. Although Big Government has always been the *bête noire* of right-wing rhetoric, especially between the 1930s and the early 1950s conservatives typically saw Big Government as a corollary of Big Society, or rather of "mass society." This theme was popular with both liberal and conservative critics, who regarded the unprecedented size and scope of modern democratic, industrialized society as the breeding ground for conformity, mediocrity, and passivity in its citizens. Indeed there was no room left for republican citizenship, for independence of judgment and will, in this view of mass society. Individuals seemed doomed to become "organization men," whether imprisoned within the hierarchies of corporations (the liberals' angst) or of unaccountable, and therefore malevolent, government (the conservatives' complaint). In either case, individualism was thought to be no more than the plaything of what Churchill called the "mass effects of modern life." At its heart, the predicament of modern man was thus not just a problem of overgrown governmental or industrial bureaucracy but of a wrong turn in Western life as a whole—the problem identified by Spengler as the *Untergang,* the going down of the West; the fall of the West.

In one respect, the decline of the West was obvious after World War II. The territory controlled by the Western powers shrank dramatically. Senator Robert Taft noted in his 1951 book, *A Foreign Policy for Americans,* "In 1945, when Mr. Truman became President, the Soviet Union was exhausted. Much of its industry was destroyed. It had no atomic bomb, no long-range bombing planes, no serious navy. Its hold on eastern Europe was shaky. China was our ally and the Chinese Communists were hemmed into a small area. President Truman held such power as no man had ever held before. . . . Today Stalin has atomic bombs and long-range bombers capable of delivering them on the United States. . . . He has riveted an iron control on eastern Europe. China is his ally. . . . In 1941 Stalin ruled 180 million subjects and was not sure that he or his empire would survive. In 1951 Stalin directs 800 million people." James Burnham depicted the same retreat in his first book on American foreign policy, *The Struggle for the World,* excerpted herein. There followed a stream of books assessing the blame for Western weakness and sounding the trumpet of advance, including, at the popular level, Barry Goldwater's *The Conscience of a Conservative* and *Why Not Victory?* Yet the West's strategic superiority, which its initial monopoly on atomic and hydrogen bombs and its later preponderance in nuclear weapons and delivery systems had ensured, was steadily slipping away.

But the most ominous sign of the decline of the West was intellectual and spiritual. History could record that the West will go down, as Leo Strauss used to put it, with flags flying and guns blazing, a heroic sacrifice to a noble cause that, however powerless it found itself, deserved victory. The philosophical danger—as conservatives saw it—was that the West would simply go down, unsure of itself, unresisting; and therefore unlamentable.

This was the real crisis of the West: the looming possibility of intellectual and moral self-destruction. Today the same danger is often traced to the West's loss of nerve or lack of will; but conservatives were aware from the beginning that the failure of Western nerve or will was symptomatic of an underlying and more serious disorder—a tragic failure of understanding.

American conservatism was always radical, going as it did to the root of the problem. It was a movement of ideas—moreover, of ideas that could move people. How else explain the innocuous, almost ludicrous title of Richard Weaver's little book, *Ideas Have Consequences,* becoming the watchword of thousands of conservative activists across the country. Most prominently among the political movements of the past fifty years, conservatism confronted the intellectual crisis within the West. But it did not overcome that crisis, partly because it could never agree on its cause.

American conservatism is divided into three parts, each with its own interpretation of the contemporary crisis. The alliance of these parts into the conservative political movement required the emergence of a consensus, always a little ragged around the edges, against government encroachments on personal freedom and individual character, and against the sansculottism of the 1960s. What conservatism's parts had in common above all, however, was a commitment to vigorous anti-Communist policy, i.e., a recognition of the common enemy. Conservatives have always found it easier to identify what they are against than what they are for, more congenial to be in opposition to government than in government. It is fair to say that all the factions of conservatism thought the Communist phenomenon reflected the fundamental internal crisis of the West, but just exactly how (raising the question "why was anti-Communism itself justifiable?") was unclear.

The *traditionalists* saw Communism as only the latest and most radical form of the deracination of man in the modern world. Wrenched from the traditional communities for which his nature and heritage suited him, modern man was rootless, alienated, adrift; stripped of the decent drapery of custom and religion, he stood before the centralized state as a pitifully weak mass man, able to find meaning for his life only by being aggregated with other, characterless human beings.

One by one these etiolated individuals added up to a society, to mass society, even as two, three, four grains of sand eventually become a pile. The traditionalists deployed several explanations for man's dehumanization: Twelve Southerners, in their manifesto *I'll Take My Stand,* declared the industrialized, commercial society of Northern capitalism to be at fault. Russell Kirk and Robert Nisbet, among others, while expressing sympathy for the Agrarian viewpoint, found the roots of the problem in the Enlightenment rationalism unleashed in the French Revolution, and its solution (or at least its keenest diagnosis) in Edmund Burke's defense of the prescriptions of the British Constitution against the universalistic, ahistorical "natural rights" of the French revolutionaries. Ever since, American conservatives have tended to view the Bolshevik, as well as subsequent Communist revolutions, through the lenses of Burke's *Reflections on the Revolution in France.*

The *libertarians* concurred in seeing the evil of Communism in the light of the French Revolution, but for them the specific evil of the latter was neither its rationalism nor its universalism but its attempt to found "the republic of virtue." In this hubristic attempt stirred the noxious egalitarianism, the contempt for liberty, the pious cruelty that characterized every scheme by tyrannical governments to enforce morality. The only morality worth the name was voluntary, not coerced; and this morality of free choice—libertarians argued—is immanent in the network of transactions and exchanges that free men make in the marketplace, whether of ideas or of economic goods and services. Any transcendent or objective ideological morality is an imposition on human freedom, depriving man of the possibility of genuine moral choice. That left out of account the morality of the marketplace itself: does morality include the freedom to decide against freedom? to reject the market? But for that question libertarians had at least two answers.

In one camp, among whose adherents are Milton Friedman, James Buchanan, Friedrich A. Hayek, and (in the field of law and economics) Richard Posner, the justification for the market is its efficiency and utility in distributing scarce economic resources and goods. No overarching moral theory was possible, or necessary, to justify it. Freedom worked, and the value of such efficient work, even if it could not be established objectively or philosophically, was apparent to any intelligent man who understood that scarcity was an inescapable fact of life.

In the other camp, the morality of the market was validated by reasoning deductively from the rights of man, which are superordinate to any duties the state may legitimately impose. Utilitarianism was not enough; and in fleeing moral skepticism, many libertarians made this version of the natural rights argument flat out, among them Murray Rothbard and Tibor Machan; but in the hands of Robert Nozick and Richard Epstein, perhaps today's most influential libertarian moral and legal theorists, the rights argument is merely hypothetical (i.e., *if* man has certain rights against the state, then it follows that government has no higher purpose than to secure them). In any case, for the libertarians the crisis of the West consisted not in the eclipse of community but in the growth of collectivism, of the interventionist state distributing rewards and punishments according to abstract standards of virtue (or need, which in the welfare state becomes a kind of virtue).

The latecomers to American conservatism (they arrived on the scene toward the end of the 1960s) were the *neoconservatives*. Besides being "liberals who've been mugged by reality," as Irving Kristol once defined them, the neoconservatives tended to be academically trained social scientists (even as traditionalists tended to be trained in literature and history, libertarian theorists in economics or philosophy) whose movement toward conservatism was prompted by the New Left's open insurrection against American middle-class democracy and the American university. Some neoconservative intellectuals wrote widely on foreign policy (Norman Podhoretz, Richard Pipes), some on domestic issues (Nathan Glazer, Daniel Bell, James Q. Wilson), some on both (Irving Kristol, Jeane Kirkpatrick). Insofar as they exhibited a common intellectual method, it consisted in the acknowledgment of the unreliability of the fact-value distinction, accompanied by the study of social facts, from which emerged qualified but nonetheless bold value judgments.

On foreign policy, their conclusions were relatively unqualified, and such writers as Norman Podhoretz and Richard Pipes found themselves at the cutting edge of conservatism's resistance to the military and diplomatic offensives of the Soviet Union in the 1970s and 1980s. The earlier conservative critics of American foreign policy, alongside apostles of "the god that failed" school—James Burnham and Whittaker Chambers, to name the most prominent—had made many of the same analytical, moral, and geopolitical points. But the neoconservatives' emphasis on *Realpolitik* separated them from the sublime religious fervor of Chambers' interpretation, and their strategic thought was less audacious than Burnham's.

For the neoconservatives, the febrile spirit of ideology was *the* enemy of freedom at home and abroad. The distrust of ideology, indeed of rationalist political theory in general, has been common ground between them and the traditionalists, but the latter's nostalgic, or merely imagined, enthusiasms for the *respublica Christiana* and the Old South separated them from the (mostly Jewish) neoconservatives, for whom these enthusiasms were themselves forms of ideology.

As these three intellectual strands were brought together in a political movement—as conservatism began rallying from Barry Goldwater's defeat and Richard Nixon's protracted humiliation—the imperatives of politics asserted themselves. The necessity of appealing to the American public, of speaking as a citizen to other citizens, helped soften and combine the discrete elements into a recognizable public message. By far the most striking change, as conservatism became a serious political force, was the virtual abandonment of the mass society analysis that, in the beginning, had colored both traditionalism and libertarianism. Both Russell Kirk and Albert Jay Nock, for example, had endorsed the idea of a saving elite (the "Remnant," Nock called them—see his essay "Isaiah's Job" in this volume), who constituted the enclave of human excellence in a mass society. But today a kind of conservative populism has largely taken the place of the dichotomy between mass and elite; conservatism has to that extent been democratized, a process that began as long ago as the Hiss-Chambers case, the McCarthy crusade—and the struggle against Communism in general. What is new is the thorough domestication of that democratic impulse and its reification in the career of Ronald Reagan. Indeed, the long-term influence of Reagan's example on the rhetoric and political strategy of the conservative movement is bound to be enormous, even though it remains largely unstudied.

Another factor in the popularization of conservatism has been the controversies generated by the Supreme Court—especially in *Roe* v. *Wade,* the abortion decision. These have energized millions of citizens, formerly apathetic, now a mass constituency of the conservative movement. The concerns of the traditionalists have been both sharpened and broadened: broadened by the accession of millions of new conservatives who wish to resist the judiciary's inroads on traditional morality, in place of restoring an idyllic communalism; sharpened by the need to make hard political choices (busing or abortion? constitutional amendment or new appointments to the Court?) rather than indulge in complaints against modernity.

Libertarianism, too, has changed. Faced with correcting the legacy of the past few decades' monetary, fiscal, and social policies, it has undergone a creative evolution of exciting dimensions. The rise of monetarism (Milton Friedman's special contribution) and supply-side economics has not only exposed the shortcomings of Keynesianism, but has cast new light on entrepreneurship and production as decisive economic categories, thus rehabilitating the *morality* of productive activity and investment, thrift, and even what Schumpeter called the "creative destruction" wrought by free competition.

Still, perhaps the most important change brought about by the political demand that economics and morality should intersect has been the rediscovery of the family as an economic and social unit, alongside the "individual." George Gilder, Charles Murray, and Bruce Chapman have argued persuasively that the well-intentioned programs of the welfare state have damaged poor families, particularly black families, almost beyond repair; and have sent the economy of the inner city, and the welfare system itself, spiralling downward out of control. Nor should it be forgotten that on all of these fronts—libertarian as well as traditionalist—the contribution of neoconservative thinkers and analysts has been crucial to the development of coherent conservative public policy.

And yet, and yet, despite the victories of the past twenty years, the American conservative movement cannot claim to be successful. Its revolution in public policy is incomplete and will stay that way because its political revolution is incomplete. I do not mean to counsel perfection, or to flatter younger conservatives by citing the tasks remaining for them to accomplish. I mean simply to observe that the Reagan Revolution is not yet a revolution, and barring dramatic changes will not be one. At least not if by the Reagan Revolution is meant a Republican realignment, and the equation of the two is, so I shall argue, both reasonable and necessary. It is necessary because the policies of the Reagan administration cannot be held up against its Democratic opposition, much less sustained and enlarged over the next two decades, as they need to be if, like FDR's legacy in the New Deal, they are to become a permanent part of American politics, absent the building of a genuine conservative majority among the electorate. And the equation is reasonable because the logical home for that majority is the Republican party, whose task is to bring virtues of its own to the American conservative movement.

The paramount goal of conservative politics over the past forty years, though seldom articulated, has been to build a conservative Republican majority. This goal is paramount precisely because without it all the other things that conservatives have sought to accomplish—the specific domestic and foreign policies on which conservative politicians and research institutes lavish so much attention—cannot be accomplished over the long run. If conservative policies are to work their slow, inspiriting, transformative work on the country, then they must have a deep and secure basis in American public opinion. Abraham Lincoln expressed the thought memorably: "In this and like communities, public sentiment is everything. With public sentiment nothing can fail; without it, nothing can succeed. Consequently he who molds public sentiment goes deeper than he who enacts statutes or pronounces decisions. He makes statutes and decisions possible or impossible to be executed."

While this is not the place to unfold the theory and practice of American elections, much less to review the Reagan administration's electoral record in detail, the character of the American conservative movement bears on its destiny in at least two major ways. First, there is the relation of conservatism to America, and second, the relation of a political "movement" to a political party. To understand the contemporary position as well as the prospects of the American conservative movement, a brief review of these matters is in order.

American conservatism has never been, except perhaps in temperament, particularly American. It has, in a strange way, been thoroughly cosmopolitan, ever since Russell Kirk sought its distinctive principles in Edmund Burke's defense of the British Constitution, and Friedrich Hayek located the principles of liberty primarily in the Whig (not the Republican or Democratic) tradition. True, in his seminal *The Conservative Mind,* Kirk celebrated some American figures—John Adams, John Randolph of Roanoke, John C. Calhoun, Orestes Brownson, Irving Babbitt—but they played second fiddle to Burke, who was the compleat conservative. And missing from the conservative pantheon were the major figures in the mainstream of American political life, e.g., George Washington, Thomas Jefferson, James Madison, Abraham Lincoln. This was in a way understandable, inasmuch as conservatism arose in response to what it perceived as a civilizational, not simply a national, crisis. But it was odd that the traditionalists (of all people) would so easily pass over their own immediate tradition. On the other hand one would not expect the libertarians—the great champions of the universal principles of free choice—to bother with the American tradition of freedom or of political economy, and by and large they did not. Aside from an occasional reference to William Graham Sumner, it would be difficult to find many American influences on their thought. It was to Austria and to English classical economics that they turned.

What exactly is at stake here? My point is not that it is illegitimate to venture outside the American tradition, but that the riches and subtleties of the American political tradition are, regrettably, not being exploited. Conservatism presupposes that there is something worth conserving, and what is most our own, and most in need of conserving, is the American tradition itself. It is, after all, difficult to cast the spell unless you know the magic words, and in American politics it has too often been the liberals who have known the magical words needed to unlock our highest traditions. In the process, those traditions have been transformed and appropriated, with the result that it has become easy for modern liberals to seize the moral high ground on virtually any issue. Why? Because all the minor issues lead back to what Abraham Lincoln called the "central idea" of our political tradition, and that idea—"that all men are created equal"—no longer means what it meant to the signers of the Declaration of Independence or to Lincoln himself. In liberalism's mouth it has tended to become an imperative call for some far-off, visionary equality of condition, to be reached by gradually bloating the definition of "rights" until there is a so-called right to anything, and everything, pleasant or useful. And then, adding insult to injury, they attribute these ginned-up doctrines to Lincoln and the Founding Fathers.

So successful is this Orwellian rewriting of America's principles that conservatives now believe it. Many of them—conspicuously, not Ronald Reagan—denounce the Declaration as positively un-American, by which they mean that it does not seem to comport with American life as it has actually been lived, and with how most Americans still desire to live. Rather than fight to restore the authentic meaning of equality, they have acquiesced in liberalism's gloss on it, rejecting the heart of our political tradition in favor of some ersatz version of it. But there is no substitute for the faith of our fathers. If the Declaration of Independence is not American, then nothing is. The most notable conservative politician of this century has known better than to allow the liberals to seize this moral high ground, to let them set the terms of political debate. Reagan's victories and defeats correspond to his success or failure in seizing those heights.

Whether invoked rightly or wrongly, then, the great proposition enshrined at the heart of the Declaration, so touched with the majesty of

Jefferson and Lincoln, so alive with the history and destiny of the American people, can still cast a spell on an American audience.

Which brings us to the most important consideration of all: the abiding truth of the principles of our political tradition.

The American republic claims to be based on self-evident truths, first among them that "all men are created equal." Properly understood—meaning an equality of rights, not of virtue, wisdom, or talents, an equality reflecting man's humanity, i.e., his place in nature and the universe—this *is* self-evidently true. But it has not fared well with the majority of conservative thinkers over the past few decades, as several selections in this volume will attest. Indeed, on this question, the traditionalists, libertarians, and neoconservatives stand virtually united. Russell Kirk, Friedrich Hayek, and Irving Kristol would agree that a healthy nation cannot really be dedicated to any proposition or abstract truth, because a nation is a kind of spontaneous social order emerging from historical experience and the unguided evolution of market and cultural forces. Therefore, each is in his own way a Burkean, understanding the United States Constitution (following Burke's description of the British) as "grown" rather than "made." But the U.S. Constitution was "made" by fifty-five or so men in Philadelphia and ratified by special conventions called by the states, on behalf of a people that had declared its independence from Great Britain in 1776. The American Revolution was not made to asseverate the rights of Englishmen, but the rights of Man. No one thought the two mutually exclusive, but the American founders regarded the former as valuable only insofar as they secured the latter. When the Americans' unalienable rights were no longer considered secure under the forms of the British Constitution, then those forms and the rights appertaining to them had to go.

Plainly, conservatives have tended to depict the American Revolution as Burke interpreted the Glorious Revolution of 1688, opposing a native tradition of political moderation to the bloody French record of ideological fanaticism. But there is a difference between principled politics and ideological politics: The one acknowledges universal principles but recognizes that, in practice, they must be mediated by the dictates of prudence; the other insists on both universal principles and universal practice. American conservatives have tended to obscure this distinction, and in the interest of healthy politics, they have read universal principles out of the American Revolution and by implication out of contemporary conservative rhetoric and politics. They tend to regard the real American Revolution—or at least its proclamation of rational, universal principles in the Declaration of Independence—as suspiciously, well, French. ("Jefferson's Declaration of Independence," a prominent traditionalist wrote recently, ". . . carried the American cause into the misty debatable land of an abstract liberty, equality, fraternity.") They would prefer to think of the Declaration as a distillation of the rights of Englishmen, and of Americanism as merely the continuation of English politics by other means. But the political teaching of the Declaration is neither ideological (French) nor prescriptive (English). It neither absolutizes nor eschews universal doctrines. Rather, it is principled, openly declaring that "prudence indeed will dictate" how the natural rights of men ought to be secured and honored in practice. It is, in short, American.

Without moral principles for prudence to serve—and recalling that for Aristotle and Aquinas prudence is the virtue of deliberating well on the *means* to moral ends—prudence is left on its own, like the pilot of a ship whose orders are to sail, but without any prescribed destination. The result is that the wind and currents take the helm. This is the predicament of traditionalism, libertarianism, and neoconservatism insofar as they deny the first principles of the American founding. In some matters, to be sure, experience may be a better guide than reason; but politics at this level is not one of them. Experience is an indispensable part of practical wisdom or prudence, but it is neither a substitute (a) for prudence nor (b) for the ends of prudence. Experience includes, or can include, the good and the bad, the just and the unjust, the noble and the base. To render it useful we must make the elementary moral and intellectual distinctions that experience per se cannot pronounce. The failure to do so places conservatism in the same boat with liberalism, debating whether to sail cautiously or boldly—all the while, the wind and waves fixing and unfixing our course.

This is the reason for the failure of American conservatism, so far, to bring about a genuine political realignment. To realign means both to switch sides and to put something back into line; and in American politics, political realignment means that significant numbers of the American people switch parties—or, having been apathetic, enlist in a party—in order to bring the country back into line with what they regard as its true principles. Thus every major realignment involves reopening the question of the meaning of the American Revolution, the public understanding of which sets the boundaries of the orthodoxy (the "middle of the road") that will prevail in our national politics for the next couple of generations. The difficulty is that conservatism seems to have no clear commitment to those principles or, more precisely, that it does not seem to understand why they are so important. It has not yet learned the vernacular of American politics, despite its great and numerous successes.

Just because the political world has been turned upside down, does not mean that it is now right side up. One sign of this is that conservatism has remained a "movement." Now, all kinds of exotic movements have flourished in American history—"temperance," "labor," "abolitionism," "women's suffrage," and so forth. The movements organized around a single issue have tended to die out after either losing big (e.g., bimetallism), stagnating (the single tax), or threatening to become so successful that one or both of the major political parties had to co-opt them (temperance, women's suffrage, etc.). But conservatism is not a single-issue movement. Its closest analogue would be the Progressive movement, which spanned many different issues and at various times controlled its own and half the Republican party, before settling down to run the Democratic party. The term "conservatism," in fact, is more nearly the antonym of "progressivism" than of "liberalism"; both are defined more with reference to change or history than to any abstract principle of justice. (John Stuart Mill called them "the party of change" and "the party of order," Emerson "the party of hope" and "the party of memory.") One might say that conservatism is fighting a rearguard action against the huge advances made by the forces of progressivism in this century.

But in keeping with its preference for the advance, progressivism had a clear-cut theory of party, articulated by Woodrow Wilson and other progressive political scientists around the turn of the century. According to their doctrine, the political party was the vehicle by which strong presidential leadership (in the best of cases—sometimes one of the other branches would have to take the lead) would mobilize the country for the long march into the future. Wilson's presidency was the first major application of this theory to the Democratic party, which did not wholeheartedly adopt it until the New Deal. Conservatism, however, never developed a theory of party because its concern was with the past, with society's salutary and gradual evolution—for which rational or political leadership was unnecessary and even dangerous.

To put it differently, conservatism has not been very good either at understanding or practicing democratic statesmanship. It has been peculiarly difficult for conservatism to envision the relation between the people and their representatives, beginning with the mass-society analysis of the 1940s and 1950s. Having assumed that democratic citizens were undistinguished and rather soulless, it was hard to see how anything but government by the few could be good. The people were at best short-sighted and at worst corrupt, materialistic, depraved. As this form of analysis gradually was superseded by conservative populism, the tables turned, and the conviction grew that the people possessed quite enough political good sense already, thank you, and did not therefore need instruction from any elite. Whereas the danger of majority tyranny had once loomed large in conservative thought, it was now replaced by the potential depredations of Supreme Court justices and know-it-all social engineers. Willmoore Kendall, the most profound theorist of this conservative majoritarianism, emphasized that only a virtuous people could rule itself; but he stubbornly resisted defining these virtues, or delimiting the power of majoritarian governments, perhaps because he believed that the people carried their political virtue "in their hips" rather than in their souls or on the tip of their tongues.

Thus politics as the art of the democratic statesman was either impossible or unnecessary, depending on whether conservatism was in an elite or a majoritarian mode. To progressivism this was not a problem, inasmuch as the leaders and the people were supposed to vibrate to the same historical wavelengths; the leaders' antennae were, simply, more sensitive. But conservatives were torn between conceiving themselves as the beleaguered "Remnant," or as "We the People." President Reagan is a virtuoso of the majoritarian or consensus school, but has been unable to translate his personal popularity into a permanent conservative—i.e., Republican—majority in the electorate. Part of the explanation of this is the consensus theory itself, which declines to raise fundamental questions about the country's principles. Before there could be a new Republican majority—one that would establish Republican control over the House and Senate as well as the presidency—there would need to be a sharp division of the country around such questions, even as there had been in the prior, decisive realignments of 1800, 1860, and 1932.

For example, the case for reducing marginal tax rates and flattening the progressivity of the income tax—both major achievements of the Reagan administration—was made entirely on economic grounds: the measures would bring in as much if not more revenue than the old system, discourage tax shelters, stimulate GNP, and so forth. Hardly anything was said about the fairness, the justice, of taxing income at different rates. To have argued (in addition to the economic claims) that progressive taxation is *unjust* would have tended to take the whole issue out of the administrative, fiscal realm and into the political. The debate would suddenly have taken on a new character, involving fundamental questions of equity and rights. (To be sure, liberal Democrats would have denounced conservatives as oligarchs; but that is liberal boilerplate, the kind of thing they say routinely, anyway. It is only conservative Republicans who are loath to call their opponents unfair.) As it happened, however, the salutary reforms were enacted without a sharply partisan debate; many Democrats climbed aboard the bandwagon, and any political advantage accruing to conservative Republicans was soon lost. What is more, the chances that tax rates will be raised in subsequent administrations were greatly increased.

On affirmative action, too, the issue could have been posed much more starkly to the American people. Discrimination by race and ethnicity raises a fundamental challenge to a Constitution based on the principle of human equality. Moreover, it is emblematic of liberalism's intention, articulated in the Progressive era and pursued ever since, to replace constitutional politics with a system of interest group (and racial) competition, of bargaining for government benefits within the administrative or welfare state presided over by activist judges, policy "experts," and bureaucrats (in collusion with congressional committees). Far from being an issue of interest only to white males, affirmative action goes to the heart of the equality underlying the rule of law, and could justly have been exploited as a danger to every citizen's legitimate rights. But it was not, and when it was trotted out at all, it was as either a legal question to be decided in the courts—not as a question that the American people had to make up their mind about—or as a kind of litmus test that black conservatives had to pass.

To take a third example, the Strategic Defense Initiative—certainly a breakthrough for conservative strategic thinking and for the administration—could have been presented not as a way to make nuclear missiles obsolete (thus playing into the hands of the pacifists), but as the only conceivable way, under present circumstances, to fulfill the United States government's constitutional responsibility to protect the nation. Do we desire to leave hundreds of millions of American citizens hostage to the designs of our enemies? Do we wish to be able to prosecute a liberating foreign policy at least at the margins of the Soviet empire (which is the real meaning of the Reagan Doctrine)? If we do, then we must have the ability to defend our country and Constitution, because no other foreign policy is credible—not the Reagan or the Carter or the Truman or even the Monroe Doctrine—so long as the American mainland is utterly exposed to attack. A full and free discussion of these matters in all their strategic and moral gravity would go far toward awakening a strong, prodefense majority in the American public.

The examples could be multiplied, but the point is that any important issue opens up onto the fundamental questions of justice and the common good that are at the heart of politics. Virtually any one of them could have been prudently exploited to inform the American people of liberalism's comprehensive, though disguised, challenge to the principles of the Declaration and Constitution. Such questions are in one sense abstract, because they depend upon universal principles, but they are also terribly concrete, because the salvation of the country depends on them and others like them. These kinds of question—urgent, critical, volatile— could have been raised in the past few years. But President Reagan, like American conservatism as a whole, has preferred to run on his record.

Perhaps the chief reason for this is that he, and the conservative movement, have presumed that a conservative majority already exists in the American electorate. What President Nixon dubbed the Silent Majority had, after all, spoken out loudly for Reagan, twice electing him by landslide margins, not to mention preferring Nixon over McGovern in 1972. Indeed, the tradition of electing Republican presidents by huge majorities goes back to Eisenhower in the 1950s. It was not thought necessary, therefore, to persuade the American people that conservatism is better than liberalism and so ought to be adopted by them; it was not even necessary for conservatives to clarify their own first principles. The people are *already* conservative. The only thing required—conservatives decided—is to let the people know that you are on their side.

But the public mood is changeable; it responds to arguments and events, to passions and caprices. The same electorate that chooses Republican presidents by landslide proportions also—routinely—returns Democratic majorities to the House of Representatives and Senate. Although a latent, diffuse conservative majority may exist, it must still be activated, and not merely for particular questions but for broad and noble purposes.

For the public to be persuaded to enlist in the conservative cause, in short, they have to be given strong reasons not simply for voting conservative but for becoming Republican. They must understand that the choice of a party is a constitutional choice, and that in becoming Republican they are subscribing to what Lincoln called "our ancient faith," as over against the constant epiphanies of Democratic politics. To ask them to join the conservative movement is not enough, because for a political movement to be serious it must have a fixed destination, and some enduring structure of authority to keep it on course. This is not a problem for liberalism, which asks only that its political leaders be ready to conduct the people into "the future." There is, so far as liberalism is concerned, nothing special to teach the people, no tablets whose laws and truths must be inculcated, because the people will learn whatever they need to know soon enough. The future has its own lessons, and their revelation is imminent.

Convictions about the nature of man and the unchanging content of justice, however, deserve to be embodied in the aims and structure of a political party, which functions not only to win elections but to form citizens by educating their opinions. Parties are the link between the Constitution, democratic statesmen, and the people, the crucial meeting ground of wisdom and consent under our form of government. Despite the fact that conservatives have dominated the Republican party since 1964, they have been unable to make it the majority party, largely because they themselves have regarded it as an instrument of convenience having no special constitutional significance or historical resonance. So long as conservatism considers itself primarily a "movement," the American people will reciprocate, tending to regard it as one more constituency of the administrative state, an ideological pressure group to be played off against others in calculating the historical vectors, nothing more. The conservative movement therefore runs the risk of looking like liberalism in reverse—an unprincipled commitment to the past instead of the future. It does not appear to raise any comprehensive claims, to be willing and able to stand for the whole country and hence to be worthy of the American public's wholehearted support.

It is true that parties are not always, or ever, simply bastions of principle. In party politics one must accommodate many different interests and often compromise on particular measures. But the point of party politics—and of republican politics in general—is to control the grounds of compromise, to set the terms of debate, to convince one's fellow citizens of what is just and prudent. The very effort to persuade is a token of respect, an act of intelligent patriotism. The peculiar utility of the party of Lincoln, under present circumstances, is that it offers a political form that should allow conservatives to rediscover what they are, or at least ought to be, trying to conserve. Through it, the American conservative movement can rediscover the American political tradition, and, one hopes, restore the principles that, for more than two centuries, have constituted and preserved us as a free people.

Did You Ever See a Dream Walking?
William F. Buckley, Jr.

The idea of this book was obvious enough. Notwithstanding efforts, some of them greatly ingenious, either to make American "conservatism" go away or to deprive it of substantial meaning, it was still very much with us. Sometimes it seemed as if half the academic and journalistic communities were engaged in demonstrating that the term "conservative" is meaningless while the other half engaged in attempting to define its meaning. Neither camp succeeded. Nor will this book succeed in so forbidding a venture in taxonomy as to fix forever the meaning of an elusive and glamorous term. This doesn't mean that the idea ("conservatism") is empty of structural content, merely that people disagree about what the content is. And there is, of course, no final authority on the matter, qualified to act as arbiter, nor should there be. The purpose of this volume is not, therefore, to vouchsafe that content. Merely to say: here is a single student's understanding of what is the flesh and blood of conservatism in America, and here are a few essays by contemporaries of whom one or two understand themselves as engaged in the very act of distilling the essence of conservatism. The others are merely saying what they want to say, and it is the exclusive responsibility of the editor to have corralled them into a single volume that attempts to describe the conservative position: its attitudes, its tones, its—to use a word I loathe but which we are no longer permitted to live without except in self-conscious essays concerning its objectionability—its "ideology."

There are several points to be made here briefly. One is that reasonable and well-informed men differ in their understanding not merely of what conservatism is, but of what are its provenances, political, historical, and philosophical. Another is that, notwithstanding such disagreements, the term is practically useful; that is to say, the term does communicate sufficiently to keep it in use, which would not be the case if it were regularly used to mean contradictory things. Another is that every student of conservatism charged with putting together a book containing quintessential samplings of conservative thought would come up with different and differing selections, though not, I think, with totally dissonant selections. Whereas it is predictably the case that the conservative who reads this book will wish that Mr. Jones had been left out and Mr. Smith included, he is not, in my judgment, likely to think of Mr. Jones's presence here as anomalous. Not, at least, the conservative whose views are generally accepted as "conservative" on the American scene. Confusion tends to arise less on account of disagreements about this emphasis or that than from categorical objections by anticonservative militants who either insist (a) on illegitimizing the entire enterprise (on the grounds of its intellectual inexactitude); or (b) on identifying contemporary American conservatism with altogether eccentric political modalities (a dissociation from which is a ritual form of self-elevation, particularly in the academy).

The original volume was an honest effort to transcribe one American conservative's understanding of some of the recent sources of the illumination he lives by. The discipline of the book (as set down by the master editors of the series) was both constricting and reasonable. We are concerned with *American* conservative thought. The authors (the rules continued) must have written in the twentieth century (exit Burke, and Adams, and Burckhardt, just for instance). On the other hand, I ruled (and got away with it) that an individual who figured seminally in the formation of twentieth-century conservative attitudes was not necessarily to be preferred, notwithstanding his traceable personal-intellectual influence, over one of his disciples who speaks to us more idiomatically. This liberty I took licentiously. Not merely because I know better the works of the very contemporary conservatives, some of them younger than myself, but because I am attracted to their way of saying things in preference to that of some of our venerable elders (I can't, for instance, read Santayana, even though I know he is beautiful), a personal preference I certainly should not undertake to defend by the use of purely conservative arguments.

One's own experience is of course relevant in such a selection as I have here attempted. Unlike most of the editors of the other volumes in the series, my experience has been not in the academic world but in the more agitated outside, as editor of the conservative journal of opinion, *National Review.* I think it prudent under the circumstances to highlight some of my own experiences as an editor, insofar as they shed light on the crystallizing definition of contemporary conservatism.

I am asked most frequently by members of the lecture audience, "What is conservatism?" Sometimes the questioner, guarding against the windy evasiveness one comes to expect from lecturers, will add, "Preferably in one sentence." On which occasions I have replied, "I could not give you a definition of Christianity in one sentence, but that does not mean that Christianity is undefinable."

Usually that disposes of the hopes of those who wish a neatly packaged definition of conservatism which they can stow away. Those who are obstinate I punish by giving, with a straight face, Professor Richard Weaver's definition of conservatism as "the paradigm of essences towards which the phenomenology of the world is in continuing approximation"—as noble and ingenious an effort as any I have ever read. The point is, of course, that we are at the stage dangerously close to mere verbal gambiting. I have never failed, I am saying, to dissatisfy an audience that asks me the meaning of conservatism.

Yet I feel I know, if not what conservatism is, at least who a conservative is. I confess that I know who is a conservative less surely than I know who is a liberal. Blindfold me, spin me about like a top, and I will walk up to the single liberal in the room without zig or zag and find him even if he is hiding behind the flower pot. I am tempted to try to develop an equally sure nose for the conservative, but I am deterred by the knowledge that conservatives, under the stress of our times, have had to invite all kinds of alien people into their ranks to help with the job at hand, and the natural courtesy of the conservative causes him to treat such people not as janissaries, but as equals; and so, empirically, it becomes difficult to see behind the khaki, to know surely whether that is a conservative over there doing what needs to be done; or a radical; or merely a noisemaker, or pyrotechnician, since our ragtag army sometimes moves together in surprising uniformity, and there are exhilarating moments when everyone's eye is Right. I have, after all, sometimes wondered whether I am myself a true conservative. I feel that I qualify spiritually and philosophically; but temperamentally I am not of the breed, and so I need to ask myself, among so many other things, how much does it matter what one is temperamentally?

There are other confusions.

Whittaker Chambers, for instance, distinguished sharply between a conservative and a "man of the Right." "You," he wrote me on resigning as an editor of *National Review,* "are a conservative, and I know no one with better title to the word. But I am not one, never was. I call myself, on those occasions when I cannot avoid answering the question, a man of the Right." I reflected on that letter, needless to say, as would you if you were the editor of a journal from which Whittaker Chambers had just withdrawn, and remarked an interesting thing: In the five-year history of the journal, Chambers was the only man to resign from its senior board of editors explicitly because he felt he could no longer move within its ideological compass; and yet he never wrote a piece for us (or, in the last dozen years of his life, that I know of, for anyone else) that was out of harmony with the thrust of *National Review*'s position.

Oh yes, people withdraw, and write and denounce you, and swear that green grass will never grow over your grave on account of this or that offensive article or editorial or book review; but these losses are merely a part of the human attrition of outspoken journalism. They prove nothing, in our case, that has anything to do with ideological fecklessness. What I am saying is that notwithstanding the difficulty in formulating a conservative position, and the high degree of skepticism from our critics before *National Review* was launched, *National Review*'s political carriage was, I believe, instantly intelligible from the very first issue.

He would probably say that anyway (the skeptic will charge), *it being in his and the journal's interest to say so.*

But I make that statement on empirical grounds, as I propose to make others in this introduction on the meaning of conservatism, which will reason *a posteriori* from facts to theory—and which will be based on my own experiences as editor of *National Review.* Since I shall not refer to it again, let me say it now unambiguously: This part of this essay is about the experiences of *National Review,* and their bearing, by the processes of exclusion, on the formulation of a workable definition of contemporary conservatism. I do not by any means suggest that *National Review* is the only functioning alembic of modern conservatism, merely that it is the only one whose experiences I can relate with any authority.

The magazine, founded in 1955, found instantly, and expanded, an audience that seemed intuitively to grant and to understand the happy eclecticism of the magazine's guiding ideas. The critics, whose delighted line at the beginning was one or another variant on the theme, "This country needs a conservative magazine and, having read *National Review,* we *still* say what this country needs is a conservative magazine," finally gave up and began to refer to *National Review* as, plain and simple, a "conservative journal."

Since this is an empirical probe, based on my experience as editor of *National Review,* I speak about people and ideas with which *National Review* has had trouble making common cause between 1955 and 1970. In 1957, Whittaker Chambers reviewed *Atlas Shrugged,* the novel by Miss Ayn Rand wherein she explicates the philosophy of "Objectivism," which is what she chose to call her creed. Man of the Right, or conservative—or whatever you wish to call him—Chambers did in fact read Miss Rand right out of the conservative movement. He did so by pointing out that her philosophy is another kind of materialism—not the dialectical materialism of Marx, but the materialism of technocracy, of the relentless self-server who lives for himself and for no one else; whose concern for others is explainable merely as an intellectualized recognition of the relationship between helping others and helping oneself. Religion is the first enemy of the Objectivist and, after religion, the state—respectively, "the mysticism of the mind" and "the mysticism of the muscle." "Randian Man," wrote Chambers, "like Marxian Man, is made the center of a godless world."

Ayn Rand's effective exclusion from the conservative community was, I am sure, in part the result of her desiccated philosophy's conclusive incompatibility with the conservative's emphasis on transcendence, intellectual and moral; but also there is the incongruity of tone, that hard, schematic, implacable, unyielding dogmatism that is in itself intrinsically objectionable, whether it comes from the mouth of Ehrenburg, or Savonarola, or Ayn Rand. Chambers knew that specific ideologies come and go but that rhetorical totalism is always in the air, searching for the ideologue-on-the-make; and so he said things about Miss Rand's tone of voice which, I would hazard the guess, if they were true of anyone else's voice, would tend to make it *eo ipso* unacceptable to the conservative. "The book's [*Atlas Shrugged*] dictatorial tone . . . ," Chambers wrote,

is its most striking feature. Out of a lifetime of reading, I can recall no other book in which a tone of overriding arrogance was so implacably sustained. Its shrillness is without reprieve. Its dogmatism is without appeal . . . resistance to the Message cannot be tolerated because disagreement can never be merely honest, prudent, or just humanly fallible. Dissent from revelation so final can only be willfully wicked. There are ways of dealing with such wickedness, and, in fact, right reason itself enjoins them. From almost any page of *Atlas Shrugged,* a voice can be heard, from painful necessity, commanding: "To a gas chamber—go!" The same inflexibly self-righteous stance results, too, in odd extravagances of inflection and gesture. . . . At first we try to tell ourselves that these are just lapses, that this mind has, somehow, mislaid the discriminating knack that most of us pray will warn us in time of the difference between what is effective and firm, and what is wildly grotesque and excessive. Soon we suspect something worse. We suspect that this mind finds, precisely in extravagance, some exalting merit; feels a surging release of power and passion precisely in smashing up the house.

As if according to a script, Miss Rand's followers jumped *National Review* and Chambers in language that crossed the *i*'s and dotted the *t*'s of Mr. Chambers's point. (It is not fair to hold the leader responsible for the excesses of the disciples, but this reaction from Miss Rand's followers, never repudiated by Miss Rand, suggested that her own intolerance is easily communicable to other Objectivists.) What the experience proved, it seems to me, reaching beyond the unacceptability of Miss Rand's ideas and rhetoric, is that no conservative cosmology whose every star and planet is given in a master book of coordinates is likely to sweep American conservatives off their feet. They are enough conservative—and therefore anti-ideological—to resist totally closed systems; those systems that do not provide for deep and continuing mysteries. They may be proideology and unconservative enough to resist such asserverations as that conservatism is merely "an attitude of mind," as one contributor to this volume once asserted. But I predict, on the basis of a long association with American conservatives, that there isn't anybody around scribbling into his sacred book a series of all-fulfilling formulae which will serve the conservatives as an Apostles' Creed. Miss Rand tried it, and *because* she tried it, she compounded the failure of her ideas. She will have to go down as an Objectivist; my guess is she will go down as a novelist or, possibly, just plain go down, period.

The conservative's distrust of the state, so richly earned by it and so energetically motivated in this volume, raises inevitably the question, How far can one go? This side, the answer is, of anarchism—that should be obvious enough. But one man's anarchism is another man's statism. *National Review* will never define to everyone's satisfaction the tolerable limits of the state's activity, and we never expected to do so. We got into the problem, as so often is the case, not by going forward to meet it, but by backing up against it.

There exists a small breed of men whose passionate distrust of the state has developed into a theology of sorts, or at least into a demonology, to which they adhere as devotedly as any religious fanatic ever attempted to adhere to the will of the Lord. I do not feel contempt for the endeavor of either type. It is intellectually stimulating to discuss alternatives to municipalized streets, even as it is to speculate on whether God's wishes would better be served if we ordered fried or scrambled eggs for breakfast on this particular morning. Yet conservatives must concern themselves not only with ideals, but with matters of public policy, and I mean by that something more than the commonplace that one must maneuver within the limits of conceivable action. We can read and take pleasure in the recluse's tortured deliberations on what will benefit his soul. Bernanos's *Diary of a Country Priest* was not only a masterpiece, it was also a best-seller. And we can read with more than mere amusement Dr. Murray Rothbard's suggestion that lighthouses be sold to private tenants, who will then chase down the light beam in speed boats and collect a dollar from the storm-tossed ship whose path it illuminates. Chesterton reminds us that dogmas are liberating because the damage they do when abused cannot compare with the damage that might have been done had whole peoples not felt their inhibiting influence. If our society seriously questioned whether to denationalize the lighthouses, it would not question at all whether to nationalize the medical profession.

But Dr. Rothbard and his merry anarchists wish to *live* their fanatical antistatism, and the result is a collision between the basic policies they urge and those urged by conservatives who recognize that the state sometimes is the necessary instrument of our proximate deliverance. The defensive strategic war in which we have been engaged over a number of years on myriad fronts cannot be prosecuted by voluntary associations of soldiers and scientists and diplomats and strategists, and when this obtrusive fact enters into the reckonings of our state-haters, the majority, sighing, yield to reality, while the minority, obsessed by their antagonism to the state, refuse to grant it even the powers necessary to safeguard the community. Dr. Rothbard and a few others have spoken harshly of *National Review*'s complacency before the twentieth-century state in all matters that have to do with anti-Communism, reading their litanies about the necessity for refusing at any cost to countenance the growth of the state. Thus, for instance, Mr. Ronald Hamowy of the University of Chicago complained about *National Review* in 1961: ". . . The Conservative movement has been straying far under *National Review* guidance . . . leading true believers in freedom and individual liberty down a disastrous path . . . and in so doing they are causing the Right increasingly to betray its own traditions and principles."[1]

Mr. Henry Hazlitt, reviewing enthusiastically Dr. Rothbard's magnum opus, *Man, Economy, and State* for *National Review* in 1962, paused to comment, sadly, on the author's "extreme apriorism," citing, for instance, Dr. Rothbard's opinion that libel and slander ought not to be illegalized, and that even blackmail

"would not be illegal in the free society. For blackmail is the receipt of money in exchange for the service of not publicizing certain information about the other person. No violence or threat of violence to person or property is involved." . . . When Rothbard [Mr. Hazlitt comments] wanders out of the strictly economic realm, in which his scholarship is so rich and his reasoning so rigorous, he is misled by his epistemological doctrine of "extreme apriorism" into trying to substitute his own instant jurisprudence for the common law principles built up through generations of human experience.

"Extreme apriorism"—a generic bull's-eye. If *National Review*'s experience is central to the growth of contemporary conservatism, extreme apriorists will find it difficult to work with conservatives except as occasional volunteers helping to storm specific objectives. They will not be a part of the standing army, rejecting as they do the burden of reality in the name of a virginal antistatism. I repeat, I do not deplore their influence intellectually; and tactically, I worry not at all.

We ran into the John Birch Society—or, more precisely, into Mr. Robert Welch. Mr. Welch's position was once, however briefly, very well known. Scrubbed down, it is that one may reliably infer subjective motivation from objective result. If the West loses as much ground as demonstrably it has lost during the past twenty years to the enemy, it can only be because those who made policy for the West were the enemy's agents. The *ultima ratio* of this position was the public disclosure—any 300-page document sent to hundreds of people can only be called an act of public disclosure—that Dwight Eisenhower was a Communist (to which the most perfect retort—Russell Kirk's—was not so much analytical as artistic: "Eisenhower isn't a communist—he is a golfer").

In criticizing Mr. Welch, we did not move into a hard philosophical front, as for instance we did in our criticisms of Miss Rand or of the neoanarchists. Rather, we moved into an organizational axiom, the conservative equivalent of the leftists' *pas d'ennemi à gauche.* The position has not, however, been rigorously explicated or applied. Mr. Welch makes his own exclusions; for instance, Gerald L. K. Smith, who, although it is a fact that he favors a number of reforms in domestic and foreign policy which coincide with those favored by Mr. Welch (and by *National Review*), is dismissed as a man with an *idée fixe,* namely, the role of Perfidious Jew in modern society. Many rightwingers (and many liberals, and all communists) believe in a *deus ex machina.* Only introduce the single tax and our problems will wither away, say the followers of Henry George. . . . Only expose the Jew and the international conspiracy will be broken, say others. . . . Only abolish the income tax and all will be well. . . . Forget everything else, but restore the gold standard. . . . Abolish compulsory taxation and we shall all be free. . . . They are called nostrum peddlers by some; certainly they are obsessed. Because whatever virtue there is in what they call for—and some of their proposals strike me as highly desirable, others as mischievous—no one of them (or dozen of them) can begin to do the whole job. Many such persons, because inadequate emphasis is given to their pandemic insight, the linchpin of social reconstruction, are dissatisfied with *National Review.* Others react more vehemently; our failure to highlight *their* solution has the effect of distracting from its unique relevance and so works positively against the day when the great illumination will show us the only road forward. Accordingly, *National Review* is, in their eyes, worse than merely useless.

The defenders of Mr. Welch who are also severe critics of *National Review* are not by any means all of them addicts of the conspiracy school. They do belong, however inconsistently, to the school that says that we must all work together—as a general proposition, sound advice. Lenin distinguished between the sin of "sectarianism," from which suffer all those who refuse to cooperate with anyone who does not share their entire position right down to the dependent clauses, and the sin of "opportunism," the weakness of those who are completely indiscriminate about their political associates.

The majority of those who broke with *National Review* as the result of our criticisms of Mr. Welch believe themselves to have done so in protest against *National Review*'s sectarianism. In fact, I believe their resentment was primarily personal. They were distressed by an attack on a man who had ingratiated himself with them and toward whom their loyalty hardened in proportion as he was attacked. So their bitterness ran over, and now it is widely whispered that *National Review* has been "infiltrated."

The questions we faced at *National Review* were two. The first, to which the answer was always plainly no, was whether Mr. Welch's views on public affairs were sound. The editors knew from experience that they were not. Enough of us had recently been to college, or were in continuing touch with academic circles, to know that the approaches to the internal security and to foreign relations that have been practiced by successive administrations after the Second World War were endorsed by the overwhelming majority of the intellectuals in this country. Therefore, any assumption that only a communist (or a fool, as Mr. Welch allowed) could oppose the House Committee on Un-American Activities or favor aid to Poland and Yugoslavia must deductively mean that the nation's academies are staffed, primarily, by communists (or fools). It is not merely common sense that rejects this assumption, but a familiarity with the intricate argumentation of almost the entire intellectual class (who, of course, are not fools, at least not in the sense in which Mr. Welch uses the word).

The second question then arose—whether it was necessary explicitly to reject Mr. Welch's position as an unrealistic mode of thought. And that had to be answered by asking whether at the margin it contributed to the enlightenment of rightwing thought. The answer was not as obvious as one might suppose. Ironically, the assumptions that reason will prevail and that logic and truth are self-evident—the constituent assumptions of those who believe that that syllogism is correct which says, "(A) We were all-powerful after World War II; (B) Russia is now as powerful as we are; therefore, (C) We willed the enemy's ascendancy" (the essence of Mr. Welch's methodology)—argued in favor of leaving Mr. Welch alone. Thus might one reason if one believed that the truth will triumph: If Mr. Welch merely succeeds in drawing people's attention, which otherwise would not be drawn, to public events, if he scourges them to read about and think about public affairs—then those same people, though introduced to public concern by Mr. Welch, will by the power of reason reject, upon examination, Mr. Welch's specific counsels and graduate as informed members of the anticommunist community.

But reason is *not* king (and many of those who have shrunk from Mr. Welch have done so less because on reflection they repudiate his analysis than because public scandal of a kind has in fact attached to discipleship in a movement dominated by a man with a very special set of views that reality rejects). And so it seemed necessary to say what one hoped would be obvious: that the Welch view is wrong, that it is wrong irrespective of the many personal virtues of Mr. Welch, and wrong irrespective of how many people who were otherwise politically lethargic are now, thanks to Mr. Welch, politically animated.

In consequence, *National Review* was widely criticized for "throwing mud" at Mr. Welch (a curious way to refer to the act of throwing at Mr. Welch his own statements), and some battle lines (and some necks) were broken. Whom did we actually alienate? A body of people? A body of thought? I tend to think not, for the reasons I have suggested. If we alienated those who genuinely believe in *pas d'ennemi à droite,* why do these same people (a) applaud Mr. Welch's exclusion of Gerald L. K. Smith, and (b) proceed to exclude us? It is no answer to the latter inconsistency that the penalty of turning against someone on your side excuses the turning away against the offender; and Mr. Welch, although failing to be consistent on point (a) above, *was* consistent in respect of (b). Aside from a few aggrieved references to *National Review*'s naïveté and to the Communists' need of conservative frontmen to implement the smear of the John Birch Society, he never did exclude us from the anti-Communist community, and in a very few years, the John Birch society was moribund.

In the midsixties, Mr. Max Eastman, the author and poet, wrote sadly* that he must withdraw from the masthead of *National Review:*

There are too many things in the magazine—and they go too deep—that directly attack or casually side-swipe my most earnest passions and convictions. It was an error in the first place to think that, because of political agreements, I could collaborate formally with a publication whose basic view of life and the universe I regard as primitive and superstitious. That cosmic, or chasmic, difference between us has always troubled me, as I've told you, but lately its political implications have been drawn in ways that I can't be tolerant of. Your own statement in the issue of October 11 [1958] that Father Halton labored "for the recognition of God's right to His place in Heaven" invited me into a world where neither my mind nor my imagination could find rest. That much I could take, although with a shudder, but when you added that "the struggle for the world is a struggle, essentially, by those who mean to unseat Him," you voiced a political opinion that I think is totally and dangerously wrong. . . .

Can you be a conservative and believe in God? Obviously. Can you be a conservative and not believe in God? This is an empirical essay, and so the answer is, as obviously, yes. Can you be a conservative and despise God and feel contempt for those who believe in Him? I would say no. True, Max Eastman is the only man who has left the masthead of *National Review* in protest against its proreligious sympathies, but it does not follow that this deed was eccentric; he, after all, was probably the only man on *National Review* with that old-time hostility to religion associated with evangelical atheism—with, e.g., the names of Theodore Dreiser, Upton Sinclair, Henry Mencken, and Clarence Darrow, old friends of Eastman. If one dismisses religion as intellectually contemptible, it becomes difficult to identify oneself wholly with a movement in which religion plays a vital role; and so the moment came when Max Eastman felt he had to go, even while finding it difficult to answer the concluding observation I made to him: "I continue to feel that you would be at a total loss as to what to criticize in the society the editors of *National Review* would, had they the influence, establish in America."

*A letter to the editor.

Mr. Eastman's resignation brought up an interesting point, to which I also addressed myself in my reply to my old friend:

You require that I take your letter seriously, and having done so I must reproach myself rather than you. For if it is true that you cannot collaborate formally with me, then it must be true that I ought not to have collaborated formally with you; for I should hate for you to think that the distance between atheism and Christianity is any greater than the distance between Christianity and atheism. And so if you are correct, that our coadjutorship was incongruous, I as editor of *National Review* should have been the first to spot it and to act on it. All the more because my faith imposes upon me more rigorous standards of association than yours does.

I know now, several years after this exchange of letters, that my point here, that the reciprocal of the proposition that a God-hater cannot associate fully with a Christian, is not in fact true—for reasons that are not easy to set down without running the risk of spiritual or philosophical condescension. But the risk must be taken, and I choose the Christian rather than the secular formulation because, although the latter can very handily be made,[2] it remains debatable in a way that the Christian formulation does not. The reason why Christian conservatives can associate with atheists is because we hold that, above all, faith is a gift and that, therefore, there is no accounting for the bad fortune that has beset those who do not believe or the good fortune that has befallen those who do. The proreligious conservative can therefore welcome the atheist as a full-fledged member of the conservative community even while feeling that at the very bottom the roots do not interlace, so that the sustenance that gives a special bloom to Christian conservatism fails to reach the purely secularist conservatism. Voegelin will argue on purely intellectual grounds, taking as his lesson the Socratic proposition that virtue can be taught, but only if virtue is defined as knowledge. Socrates defined knowledge, Voegelin reminds us, as transcendental cognition, as, in fact, requiring the ability to see far enough into the nature of things to recognize transcendence, a view he elaborated in *Protagoras*.

The God-hater, as distinguished from the agnostic (who says merely that he doesn't know) or simply the habitual atheist (who knows there is no God, but doesn't much care about those who disagree), regards those who believe in or tolerate religion as afflicted with short-circuited vision. Their faith is the result of a combination of intellectual defectiveness and psychological immaturity, leading to the use of such analysis and rhetoric as Max Eastman "can't be tolerant of."

The agnostic can shrug his shoulders about the whole thing, caring not whether, in his time, the conflict between the proreligious and antireligious elements within conservatism will be resolved. There are so many other things to do than think about God. "Are you anything?" a lady flightily addressed at her dinner table a scholarly gentleman and firebrand conservative who has always managed to nudge aside questions or deflect conversational trends that seemed to be moving into hard confrontations involving religion. He smiled. "Well, I guess I'm not *nothing,*" and the conversation went on pleasantly. Max Eastman *was* nothing; and he could no more resist the opportunity to incant his non-belief than the holy priest can resist the opportunity to proselyte; and so the tension.

Mr. Eastman, like many other programmatic conservatives, based his defense of freedom primarily on pragmatic grounds. Mr. Erik von Kuehnelt-Leddihn once remarked that Friedrich Hayek's *Constitution of Liberty* seemed to be saying that, if freedom were not pragmatically productive, there would be no *reason* for freedom. It appears to be the consensus of religious-minded conservatives that ordered freedom is desirable quite apart from its demonstrable usefulness as the basis for economic and political association. The research of the past fifteen years on Edmund Burke appears to have liberated him from the social pragmatists by whom he had been co-opted. Not to stray too far from the rules of this discussion, I cite a poll a few years ago which showed that the great majority of the readers of *National Review* think of themselves formally as religious people, suggesting that conservatism, of the kind I write about, is planted in a religious view of man.

Though, as I say, only a single resignation has been addressed to *National Review* in protest against the magazine's friendliness to religion, there is much latent discord, particularly in the academic world, centering on the question not so much of whether God exists or doesn't (only a few continue to explore the question consciously, let alone conscientiously, and most of the latter are thought of as *infra dig*), but on the extent to which it is proper to show toward religion the intellectual disdain the God-haters believe it deserves. Russell Kirk was not allowed inside the faculty of a major university in which, *mirabile dictu*, conservatives (specifically, libertarians) had control of the social science department—because of his "religiosity."

Although I say the antagonism is here and there seen to be hardening, I have grounds for optimism based not merely on *National Review*'s own amiable experiences with all but the most dedicated atheists, but on the conviction that the hideousness of a science-centered age has resulted in a stimulation of religious scholarship and of all of those other impulses, intellectual and spiritual, by which man is constantly confounding the most recent wave of neoterics who insist that man is merely a pandemoniac conjunction of ethereal gases. The atheists have not got around to answering Huxley's self-critical confession that neither he nor his followers had succeeded in showing how you can deduce Hamlet from the molecular structure of a mutton chop.

I repeat what is obvious: These are merely notes, though not, I hope, altogether desultory, suggesting where are some of the confines of contemporary conservatism, the walls it runs up against and bounces away from. The freeway remains large, large enough to accommodate very different players with highly different prejudices and techniques. The differences are now tonal, now substantive, but they do not appear to be choking each other off. The symbiosis may yet be a general consensus on the proper balance between freedom, order, and tradition of the kind to which Mr. Frank Meyer alludes in his contribution to this volume.

To the student who may at this point be saying that he now has some idea of what conservatism is not but very little idea of what it is, I say: Be patient. Not only because at this point there are so many unread pages in this volume, each one of which, I am confident, he will find suggestive of something that conservatism is. But patient even after finishing this book, patient especially throughout the course of his academic experience because there he will find that the general assumption is that conservatism is the habit of mind of the heavy people who make up the bourgeois order and the intellectual plaything of here and there a dilettante writer or poet whose idea of chic is sort of perverted.

I think of one student who graduated recently from Exeter, which is one of our finest preparatory schools, and matriculated at a venerable Ivy League college where, after two months, he approached the local conservative professor—most colleges tolerate one (1)—and told him that forsooth he was the first intelligent conservative he had ever met. Now of course by "intelligent" one must understand that the boy meant somebody who could do his academic arpeggios; said boy, almost surely, would have said the same thing even if he had grown up next door to Henry Ford the Elder. America is teeming with highly intelligent conservatives who, however, aren't thought of as "intelligent" because all *they* do is build bridges, develop cyclotrons, understand the national budget, argue before the Supreme Court, or fathom the will of God. Because they are, in general terms, well integrated into a part of the national culture.

Now I take it that one of the reasons why academicians tend to be liberals is that many of those who choose to take up scholarship are also rejecting alternative professions, the professions which are tied in to the existing culture. That is to say, they are influenced in part by the desire to learn and to teach, and in part by the desire to dissociate from their culture and, up until now, the politics of dissociation have been liberal, even as teaching has been the vocational form of dissent.

What then does the student do face to face with the minds he will encounter in this volume? Obviously he will not agree with all of them (they do not agree among themselves). But he will not doubt that most of them speak with considerable intellectual force, will not doubt that all of them speak competently, that some of them express themselves brilliantly, some with great beauty. That will come as something of a surprise to many readers, and the more they are surprised, the more they need to acquaint themselves with some of the literature, the existence and the scope of which is suggested by these essays.

To conservatives, I would say that this volume at least suggests that the struggle availeth, having said which I hasten to add that the struggle is also permanent. Surely Mr. Weaver's intricate definition of conservatism seems to suggest the twin conservative concerns for advance and prudence. A conservative is properly concerned simultaneously with two things: the first, the shape of the visionary or paradigmatic society toward which we should labor; the second, the speed with which it is thinkable to advance toward that ideal society with the foreknowledge that any advance upon it is necessarily asymptotic—that is, we cannot hope for ideological home runs and definitive victories. What American conservatives have achieved is not only the dismay of local radicals but of European intellectuals, who find the rise of conservative thought in America utterly baffling.

To be sure, it is quite widely believed in Europe that the principal contribution America can make to Western thought is not to think at all. I grant the generality that the world would probably be better off, not worse, if a lot of people who are currently hard at work thinking, should desist from doing so, and spend their time, instead, cultivating the elevated thought of others. I remember an occasion not long ago when an editor of *National Review* remarked, on hearing the news that $600,000 had been allocated to bring together in seclusion for one year a dozen top American philosophers at Santa Barbara just to think about thinking, that the expenditure of $60,000-odd per year apiece toward the withdrawal of the average modern philosopher from public life was a price America could ill afford not to pay.

It is quite widely thought in Europe that America, in the modern era, has taken the place of Rome in the ancient era; that it is we who have successfully organized the resources of nature, in order to guard the peace, and who have produced the greatest share of the world's material goods, in order that others might indicate how best they might be enjoyed in usufruct. But unlike Ancient Rome it is said sadly—truthfully—America has not acquired the mien, let alone the habit, of great power. We have not even acquired *gravitas*. Nor has America shown a proper veneration for the values of the Old World, to compare, for instance, with the Romans' humility before the civilization of Greece. America, it is generally agreed, can contribute to Western thought only the physical shelter under which Westerners can continue their dialogues; to that extent, it is believed, America can be useful. But even then—hark the dissent—the danger lies that in an excess of zeal, out of a fatuous idealism which distinguishes our exuberant moralism, it is altogether possible—altogether likely in the opinion of some—altogether predictable, if we are to listen to the school of Bertrand Russell—that we will end up triggering a conclusive holocaust, which would forever interrupt that purposeful intercourse between the blither spirits of the West, the continuing hope of an upward-mobile mankind, the dialogue between C. P. Snow and Yevtushenko.

The existence of much conservative scholarship, and of the conservative movement in America, is a phenomenon concerning which European intellectuals—most particularly I would charge the English, since it is their ignorance I am most educated in—are in a state of innocence so total that one might be tempted in earthier circumstances to regard it as vulgar, which, under the present circumstances, we had better merely call distracting. They do not know that there is growing in America a spirit of resistance to the twentieth century, and it is just possible that that development will prove the most significant of our time.

I grant that I am involved in an uneasy figure of speech. It is hardly possible to "resist" the twentieth century, as the term is commonly used, any more than it is possible to "resist" gravity or death. But the figure is useless only insofar as it invokes a mechanistic view of history, which presupposes that it is the inescapable destiny of the twentieth century to codify certain trends, social and philosophical, economic and organizational, trends that are irresistible even as the passage of time is irresistible—trends which issue out of the very genes of history.

It is a common epithet to say of a man whose views are deemed out of fashion that he "resists the twentieth century." There are any number of lively polemical variations on the theme. Senator Goldwater, it has tirelessly been said, entered the twentieth century kicking and screaming. Russell Kirk, it has been said one thousand times, though to be sure mostly by those who are unfamiliar with the Middle Ages, "has a brilliant fourteenth-century mind." And so on.

The friction arises, of course, when two essentially different attitudes toward history are rubbed together. We of the Right do not doubt that history is in fact tendentious, that the vectors of social thought and action nowadays point to monolithic government and the atomization of norms. And it is certainly true that most of the intellectuals in America appear to be disposed to submit to the apparent imperatives of the twentieth century. Apocalypse is in the air; and the cost of hitchhiking along with the century, in Europe, in Asia, in America, is tacitly acknowledged to be the surrender of one's potty little self (the New Left, to its credit, gags). The older intellectuals in America grew into a world that seemed to be headed inescapably toward social self-destruction, and then, when the Bomb came, toward physical self-destruction. In 1960, Whittaker Chambers drew my attention to a note in the *Journal of the Goncourt Brothers,* one of whom had been taken that day by Madame Curie to see radium in the laboratory in which she had discovered it and had intuited where it would all leave us: "I thought I heard the voice of God, ringing out as clearly as the doorkeeper's at the Louvre at five o'clock every weekday afternoon, and uttering the same solemn words, 'Closing time, gentlemen!' "

Indeed no one of those who would resist the twentieth century would be so foolish as to say that it is the ideal arena in which to make the struggle. "If you wish to lead a quiet life," Trotsky said to a contemporary, "you picked the wrong century to be born in." "And indeed," Chambers commented, "the point was finally proved when a pickaxe mauled the brain of the man who framed those words."

So it is not an escapist's ignorance of the distinctive darkness of this century's shadows that makes possible the traces of whiggish optimism which are here and there discernible in this book. The spirit of defiance doesn't issue from a romantic American ignorance of the gloomy composure of the times we live in; but it does, I think, issue from distinctively American patterns of thought, from the essence of the American spirit. In America it is quite true that a substantial number of people are dragging their feet, resisting, kicking, complaining, hugging on to our ancient moorings. Consider:

(1) It is essentially the modernist view that only the state can negotiate the shoals that lie ahead of twentieth-century man. We are accordingly urged to believe in the state as the primary agent of individual concerns, a belief that is embedded in the analysis and rhetoric of socialism. Yet we are resisting, in America, the beatification of the state, most particularly in the past few years, when American conservatives have been joined by prominent liberals in expressing skepticism for the capacities of the state. Even though the statists did lull the general public into accepting the state as a genial servant, the state was never truly integrated as a member of the American household. The native distrust the majority of Americans hold for the genus state has not, I am suggesting, completely dissipated. We are still reluctant to accept the state as a sacramental agent for transubstantiating private interest into public good.

Consider the course of postwar American history:

—The call for the nationalization of basic industries, so insistent in the immediate postwar years, is still, utterly stilled, droning away only in the fever swamps of the dogmatic Left.

—With all its power, the ideological Establishment has failed in its efforts to ease over to the federal government the primary responsibility for education, or health, or even housing.

Through inertia we might indeed end up, as de Tocqueville predicted we would, as minions of an omnipotent government; but it may yet be that American resistance by the minority is nowadays more remarkable than American acquiescence by the majority. At any typical gathering of Americans there are members in the audience who know prescriptively what you are talking about when you warn of the danger in relying on the state. Something, somehow, kept us from accepting the state, as the trend of the twentieth century seemed to dictate that we should do, as the sanctifying force in political affairs.

(2) Probably no country in the history of the world was ever so devoutly secularist as our own in its practical affairs; and yet the spiritual side of life, which the twentieth century is here to anachronize, is an unshakable part of us. The worst failure in America is the man who aspires to true cynicism. Let the lushest bloom of the twentieth century stand before a typical nonacademic American audience and declare his fidelity to materialism, and the audience will divide between those in whom he has aroused pity and those in whom he has aroused contempt. It is as fashionable in America as in Europe to declare that truth is not knowable, that the freedom of inquiry is the nearest we can hope to come to the truth. And yet, although the American people tolerate and even support universities dedicated in effect to the proposition that no truth is knowable, still, the majority of the universities' supporters and alumni organize their lives with reference to certitudes, certitudes which for reasons sometimes of humility, sometimes of laziness, sometimes of awe, they decline to identify. But that these certitudes are there, underlying human experience, they do not seem to doubt; and that—the faith of our fathers, it is sometimes called—gives the cast to our—to be sure equivocal—foreign policy: relieves us of tortured doubts over the question whether we had rather be dead than red, or red than dead. The utter failure of the collaborators in our midst to engage the public in a trauma of self-doubt over the issue of Red or Dead finally suggests that adamant resistance of the American people to submission to the twentieth century.

And finally, (3). There is what this book is about. There is an American renaissance of thought, a grinding of wheels, an on-going commotion. What is coming is the intellectualization of the spirit I speak of. Modern formulations are necessary even in defense of very ancient truths. Not because of any alleged anachronisms in the old ideas—the Beatitudes remain, surely, the essential statement of the Western code—but because the idiom of life is always changing, and we need to say things in such a way as to get inside the vibrations of modern life.

For years Americans seemed woefully incapable of speaking for themselves. The great apostles of the twentieth century are not American. With perhaps the exceptions of Oliver Wendell Holmes and John Dewey, no matter how hard they practise in the American idiom, our own intellectuals for the most part speak a derivative speech, speak in European accents. Adlai Stevenson was for reasons perfectly clear to me a greater hero in England than in America. So is John Kenneth Galbraith and David Riesman. So—dare I say it?—was Franklin Delano Roosevelt, notwithstanding the genius with which he seemed to be fashioning indigenous American ideals, though all the time he used an alien clay. In the past fifteen years in America a literature has emerged which taken together challenges root and branch the presumptions of the twentieth century. The intuitive wisdom of the founders of the American republic and of the European giants from whom they learned the art of statecraft is being rediscovered. The shallowness of the nineteenth-century social abstractionists has been penetrated, and their followers are thrown on the defensive. The meaning of the spirit of the West is being exhumed; impulses that never ceased to beat in the American heart are being revitalized.

Will we all be saved then? "Whom knows," as Leo Durocher once thoughtfully put it. I hope so, caring as I do that we shall be saved from this dreadful century, whose name stands for universal ignominy in the name of equality, and, in the name of freedom, a drab servitude to anonymous institutional idealisms. I hope and pray that, as time goes by, the twentieth century will shed the odium that clings to its name, that it may crystallize as the century in which the individual overtook technology—the century in which all the mechanical ingenuity of man, even when fired by man's basest political lusts, proved insufficient to sunder man's essential reliance on his Maker, the century in which we learned finally (no, not finally; we never learn finally), or at least for a period, how useless it is, how dangerous it is, to strut about ideologizing the world when we need to know that it was born intractable and will die intractable.

1970

NOTES

1. Ronald Hamowy, "National Review: Criticism and Reply," *New Individualist Review,* I, no. 3, 1961.
2. See, e.g., Eric Voegelin's "On Readiness to Rational Discussion," *Freedom and Serfdom: An Anthology of Western Thought,* ed. Albert Hunold (Dordrecht, Holland: D. Reidel, 1961), pp. 269–284.

PART I

The Quest for a Tradition

SCRATCH A CONSERVATIVE and you will find a patriot, albeit an irritated one. Modern American conservatism grew out of a profound irritation with the main currents of what Henry Luce dubbed the "American Century"—paradoxically, as it turned out, because on the whole this has been a most un-American century. Conservatives, to their credit, discerned that early on. With the triumph of the New Deal at home and the rise of Communism abroad, the threats to American liberty seemed unprecedented, the victories won against its foes merely stopgaps. But in the breathing space carved out by victorious American arms in World War II—backed up now by the atomic and hydrogen bombs—and secured domestically by the resurgence of the Republican party, a rethinking began.

However much the external and internal threats to the American way of life in the postwar years seemed to conservatives to parallel one another, there was an obvious difference between them. The New Deal had not been imposed by force of arms; it had been authorized by millions of American voters, over and over again. Those enormous majorities had been persuaded that President Roosevelt's relief and reform measures were not radical departures from the country's first principles, but prudent applications of them. Didn't FDR put Thomas Jefferson on the nickel, after all?

The first problem confronting American conservatives was therefore to decide what to conserve, to figure out the meaning of the American founding and the grounds of proper American patriotism. This proved harder to do than one might think. Not so much because of the elusiveness of the founding, but because the New Deal was seen by most conservatives as the third or fourth act of a worldwide revolutionary drama that had begun in France in 1789, as the Introduction explains. To oppose this revolution, therefore, American conservatives turned to the great nemesis of the French Revolution—the most acute of all analysts of the phenomenon of total revolution—Edmund Burke.

If Russell Kirk was not the first, he was certainly the most influential writer to point to Burke as the quintessential conservative. Kirk may well be the best known "professional" conservative in America, by which adjective is meant that he launched his extraordinary career by an act of conscious apostleship to a social and historical and philosophical order which he denominated as "conservative." His first spectacular was *The Conservative Mind* (1953), a book that traced a high-toned tradition of conservative thought running from Burke through prominent English and American statesmen and intellectuals of the next two centuries. Liberal reviewers were stunned by his command of intellectual history; conservatives discovered that they had a philosophical pedigree, indeed quite a respectable one—and the ball was rolling. We present an excerpt from the first chapter of the book, in which the author distills the essence of Burkean conservatism into a short list of propositions, which he contrasts with those characteristic of liberalism.

Jeffrey Hart, professor of English at Dartmouth and a senior editor of *National Review,* places Burke's insights in the larger perspective of Continental philosophy and contemporary social science. Burke knew that the French Revolution was not only a political, but a spiritual, cultural, and psychological event, and this essay depicts him as initiating a great conversation about the nature of man and society, and especially about the role of prescription, prejudice, and history in the definition of man. Professor Hart is himself an expert practitioner of cultural reconstruction, being the author of two acclaimed reveries on America, *From This Moment on: America in 1940* and *When the Going Was Good: American Life in the Fifties.*

Which brings us, however, to the difficulties that Burke's thought poses for American conservatism. The British Constitution, which Burke celebrated precisely because it was prescriptive, because it had existed time out of mind and had adapted freely and gradually to the changing circumstances of British life, is not easily assimilated to the American Constitution, which was written at one stroke and intended to be permanent, i.e., so far as possible unchanging. The dynamics of American society, particularly our robust economy, are also not amenable to the prescriptive theory, which emphasizes the dignity of Britain's "establishments"—its ancient class structure, its noble families, the established Church. In fact, perhaps only one section of the United States could come close to fitting Burke's celebration of a traditional political and social order—namely, the South.

Although the Southern criticism of Northern society as unchivalrous and money-grubbing is older than the republic, it achieved a new intellectual coherence with the revival of interest in Burke. One could not classify Richard Weaver's work as a simple application of Burke to America—it was much more than that, a subtle and profound investigation of the place of rhetoric and humane letters in civilized life—but his doctoral dissertation, written for Cleanth Brooks at Louisiana State University, helped to set the stage for conservatism's questioning of the American founding. *The Southern Tradition at Bay* was written in 1943 but first published in 1968 in a posthumous edition by Professors George Core and M. E. Bradford. As a cerebration on the meaning of the Southern experience, it is scarcely less important than the famous manifesto of the Agrarians, *I'll Take My Stand* (1930), whose contributors included John Crowe Ransom and Donald Davidson, under whom Weaver had studied at Vanderbilt University, and Robert Penn Warren, then an editor of *The Southern Review,* whom Weaver greatly admired.

In Russell Kirk's essay, he warns against the "consumption-society," adjuring conservatives to "rake from the ashes what scorched fragments of civilization escape the conflagration of unchecked will and appetite." It was Weaver's (and the Agrarians') achievement to channel that injunction into a vindication of Southern traditionalism, a defense of what Weaver called "the last non-materialist civilization in the Western world." Against the rationalism and science of the North, he invoked the "fourfold root" of Southern tradition: "the feudal theory of society"; "the code of chivalry"; "the ancient concept of the gentleman"; and what he termed the "older religiousness." The essay reproduced below stands as the introduction to his compelling inquiry into the Southern mind.

Any apology for the South must, sooner or later, bump up against the question of slavery. Weaver himself did not pursue the political implications of his argument; his was a literary and philosophical conservatism. "The Old South may indeed be a hall hung with splendid tapestries in which no one would care to live," he acknowledged in the final sentence of *The Southern Tradition at Bay,* "but from them we can learn something of how to live." Thus his appreciation of the South was not apparently incompatible with a respect for Abraham Lincoln. (See the admiring essay, "Abraham Lincoln and the Argument from Definition," in Weaver's *The Ethics of Rhetoric* [1953].)

The implications of the traditionalist argument for the issues of slavery and civil rights are taken up in the remaining essays in this section. "Equality and the American Political Tradition" is both an important contribution to this debate, offering a synopsis of the views of one of the most important conservative political theorists of the past generation, and a rollicking display of a unique style of argument. Willmoore Kendall remains, almost twenty years after his death, something of a legend. Not only because he made a lasting impression on his students and colleagues, some of whom adored him, some of whom despised him, but because of the workings of his extraordinary mind, which brought a huge theoretical talent to the organization of political problems. He wrote very few books, and his professional reputation rested on his doctoral dissertation, *John Locke and the Doctrine of Majority Rule.* But he translated several works of Rousseau, and wrote many articles for the academic quarterlies.

His essay ranges over almost the whole field of equality's relations to American political life, appealing to the Declaration of Independence (emphatically *not* a revolutionary document, he insisted), the Constitution, and the Bill of Rights to prove that the Supreme Court and its champions in the academy err in linking the cause of civil rights to basic American principles. Equality as an abstract principle, as a reformers' goal, has nothing to do with the American founding, he argues, or with American life as it had in fact been lived, at least until Lincoln transformed our political tradition. Kendall's prose, by the way, is as controversial as his politics. There are those who dismiss it as plainly impossible. Others differ. For instance, Garry Wills, while still a conservative (even as an apostate, by the way, he remains touched by Kendall's influence), reviewing Kendall's *The Conservative Affirmation* in *Modern Age* in 1963, called it "a literary masterpiece."

For it is one of the best-kept secrets of our age that one of the best prose stylists of our age is Willmoore Kendall. The long sentence that argues with itself down one page and around the next did not, we find, go out with William Morris wallpaper. Professor Kendall has given the suspect Victorian periodicity, which *disciplines* the reader while delighting him, a new lease on life; and this by three means. First, he introduces slang into these staid surroundings. Then, he follows speech rhythms—not the lecturing cadences of a pulpit age, but the lunge of two voices contrapuntally going at each other. Last, he makes fun of his own grammatical arabesques, elaborating them in the most arch fashion. The result is a combination of the colloquial and the baroque that is invariably exciting. His sentences hover somewhere between a ballet and a rumble.

Harry V. Jaffa is ready for that rumble, and in "Equality as a Conservative Principle" he challenges Kendall to defend his deprecation of Abraham Lincoln and his depreciation of the Declaration of Independence, both of which are elaborated on in Kendall's posthumous book *Basic Symbols of the American Political Tradition* (written with and completed by George W. Carey, a distinguished Georgetown University political scientist). In the past decade, Jaffa, the Henry Salvatori Research Professor of Political Philosophy at Claremont McKenna College and Claremont Graduate School, has built upon his reputation as one of the premiere authorities on the American political tradition—brilliantly established by *Crisis of the House Divided* (1957), his interpretation of the Lincoln-Douglas debates—to become the leading advocate of conservatism's rededicating itself to the principles of the Declaration. He is, like others of the most able students of political philosophy, a former student of the late Leo Strauss, from whom he obviously inherited his relish for philosophical combat. In *How to Think About the American Revolution* (1978), from which his essay in this section is drawn, and in *American Conservatism and the*

American Founding (1985), he subjects the opinions of many prominent conservatives and neoconservatives to dialectical criticism, arguing that if the conservative enterprise is to have any meaning at all, it must be grounded in the tradition of Washington, Hamilton, Jefferson, Madison, and Lincoln—who are united by their recognition of the self-evident truth "that all men are created equal." This equality, Jaffa maintains—not slavery, feudalism, or a crude faith in popular sovereignty—is what Americans have to conserve; what American conservatism is all about.

The reader should know that Jaffa's essay gave rise to a spirited rejoinder by M. E. Bradford, a professor of English at the Unviersity of Dallas. In "The Heresy of Equality" [reprinted in his book *A Better Guide Than Reason* (1979)], Bradford reviews and in some respects radicalizes Kendall's argument against equality as a conservative principle. Jaffa's surrejoinder is contained in his *How to Think About the American Revolution*—the entire Kendall–Jaffa–Bradford exchange forming one of the most important, and engaging, debates in the history of American conservatism.

RUSSELL KIRK

The Idea of Conservatism

"The stupid party": this is John Stuart Mill's description of conservatives. Like certain other summary dicta which nineteenth-century liberals thought to be forever triumphant, his judgment needs review in our age of disintegrating liberal and radical philosophies. Certainly many dull and unreflecting people have lent their inertia to the cause of conservatism: "It is commonly sufficient for practical purposes if conservatives, without saying anything, just sit and think, or even if they merely sit," F. J. C. Hearnshaw observed. Edmund Burke, the greatest of modern conservative thinkers, was not ashamed to acknowledge the allegiance of humble men whose sureties are prejudice and prescription; for, with affection, he likened them to cattle under the English oaks, deaf to the insects of radical innovation. But the conservative principle has been defended, these past hundred and fifty years, by men of learning and genius, as well. To review conservative ideas, examining their validity for this perplexed age, is the purpose of this book, which does not pretend to be a history of conservative parties. This study is a prolonged essay in definition. What is the essence of British and American conservatism? What system of ideas, common to England and the United States, has sustained men of conservative instincts in their resistance against radical theories and social transformation ever since the beginning of the French Revolution? . . .

Only Britain and America, among the great nations, have escaped revolution since 1790, which seems attestation that their conservatism is a sturdy growth and that investigation of it may be rewarding. Conscious conservatism, in the modern sense, did not manifest itself until 1790, with the publication of *Reflections on the Revolution in France.* In that year the prophetic powers of Burke defined in the public consciousness, for the first time, the opposing poles of conservation and innovation. . . . If one attempts to trace conservative ideas back to an earlier time in Britain, soon he is enmeshed in Whiggery, Toryism, and intellectual antiquarianism; for the modern issues, though earlier taking substance, were not yet distinct. Nor does the American struggle between conservatives and radicals become intense until Citizen Genêt and Tom Paine transport across the Atlantic enthusiasm for French liberty: the American Revolution, substantially, had been a conservative reaction, in the English political

From Russell Kirk, *The Conservative Mind* (Chicago: Henry Regnery, 1953), pp. 3–10. Reprinted by permission of Regnery Gateway Company.

tradition, against royal innovation. If one really must find a preceptor for conservatism who is older than Burke, he cannot rest satisfied with Bolingbroke, whose skepticism in religion disqualifies him, or with the Machiavellian Hobbes, or that old-fangled absolutist Filmer. Falkland, indeed, and Clarendon and Halifax and Strafford, deserve study; still more, in Richard Hooker one discovers profound conservative observations which Burke inherited with his Anglicanism and which Hooker drew in part from the Schoolmen and their authorities; but already one is back in the sixteenth century, and then in the thirteenth, and this book is concerned with modern problems. In any practical sense, Burke is the founder of our conservatism. . . .

Any informed conservative is reluctant to condense profound and intricate intellectual systems to a few pretentious phrases; he prefers to leave that technique to the enthusiasm of radicals. Conservatism is not a fixed and immutable body of dogma, and conservatives inherit from Burke a talent for re-expressing their convictions to fit the time. As a working premise, nevertheless, one can observe here that the essence of social conservatism is preservation of the ancient moral traditions of humanity. Conservatives respect the wisdom of their ancestors (this phrase was Strafford's, and Hooker's, before Burke illuminated it); they are dubious of wholesale alteration. They think society is a spiritual reality, possessing an eternal life but a delicate constitution: it cannot be scrapped and recast as if it were a machine. "What is conservatism?" Abraham Lincoln inquired once. "Is it not adherence to the old and tried, against the new and untried?" It is that, but it is more. Professor Hearnshaw, in his *Conservatism in England,* lists a dozen principles of conservatives, but possibly these may be comprehended in a briefer catalogue. I think that there are six canons of conservative thought—

1. Belief that a divine intent rules society as well as conscience, forging an eternal chain of right and duty which links great and obscure, living and dead. Political problems, at bottom, are religious and moral problems. A narrow rationality, what Coleridge calls the Understanding, cannot of itself satisfy human needs. "Every Tory is a realist," says Keith Feiling: "he knows that there are great forces in heaven and earth that man's philosophy cannot plumb or fathom. We do wrong to deny it, when we are told that we do not trust human reason: we do not and we may not. Human reason set up a cross on Calvary, human reason set up the cup of hemlock, human reason was canonised in Nôtre Dame." Politics is the art of apprehending and applying the Justice which is above nature.

2. Affection for the proliferating variety and mystery of traditional life, as distinguished from the narrowing uniformity and equalitarianism and utilitarian aims of most radical systems. This is why Quintin Hogg (Lord Hailsham) and R. J. White describe conservatism as "enjoyment." It is this buoyant view of life which Walter Bagehot called "the proper source of an animated Conservatism."

3. Conviction that civilized society requires orders and classes. The only true equality is moral equality; all other attempts at leveling lead to despair, if enforced by positive legislation. Society longs for leadership, and if a people destroy natural distinctions among men, presently Buonaparte fills the vacuum.

4. Persuasion that property and freedom are inseparably connected, and that economic leveling is not economic progress. Separate property from private possession, and liberty is erased.

5. Faith in prescription and distrust of "sophisters and calculators." Man must put a control upon his will and his appetite, for conservatives know man to be governed more by emotion than by reason. Tradition and sound prejudice provide checks upon man's anarchic impulse.

6. Recognition that change and reform are not identical, and that innovation is a devouring conflagration more often than it is a torch of progress. Society must alter, for slow change is the means of its conservation, like the human body's perpetual renewal; but Providence is the proper instrument for change, and the test of a statesman is his cognizance of the real tendency of Providential social forces.

Various deviations from this system of ideas have occurred, and there are numerous appendages to it; but in general conservatives have adhered to these articles of belief with a consistency rare in political history. To catalog the principles of their opponents is more difficult. At least five major schools of radical thought have competed for public favor since Burke entered politics: the rationalism of the *philosophes* and Hume, the romantic emancipation of Rousseau and his allies, the utilitarianism of the Benthamites, the positivism of Comte's school, and the collectivistic materialism of Marx and other socialists. This list leaves out of account those scientific doctrines, Darwinism chief among them, which have done so much to undermine the first principles of a conservative order. To express these several radicalisms in terms of a common denominator probably is presumptuous, foreign to the philosophical tenets of conservatism. All the same, in a hastily generalizing fashion one may say that radicalism since 1790 has tended to attack the prescriptive arrangement of society on the following grounds—

1. The perfectibility of man and the illimitable progress of society: meliorism. Radicals believe that education, positive legislation, and alteration of environment can produce men like gods; they deny that humanity has a natural proclivity toward violence and sin.

2. Contempt for tradition. Reason, impulse, and materialistic determinism are severally preferred as guides to social welfare, trustier than the wisdom of our ancestors. Formal religion is rejected and a variety of anti-Christian systems are offered as substitutes.

3. Political leveling. Order and privilege are condemned; total democracy, as direct as practicable, is the professed radical ideal. Allied with this

spirit, generally, is a dislike of old parliamentary arrangements and an eagerness for centralization and consolidation.

4. Economic leveling. The ancient rights of property, especially property in land, are suspect to almost all radicals; and collectivistic reformers hack at the institution of private property root and branch.

As a fifth point, one might try to define a common radical view of the state's function; but here the chasm of opinion between the chief schools of innovation is too deep for any satisfactory generalization. One can only remark that radicals unite in detesting Burke's description of the state as a divinely ordained moral essence, a spiritual union of the dead, the living, and those yet unborn. . . .

In a revolutionary epoch, sometimes men taste every novelty, sicken of them all, and return to ancient principles so long disused that they seem refreshingly hearty when they are rediscovered. History often appears to resemble a roulette wheel; there is truth in the old Greek idea of cycles, and round again may come the number which signifies a conservative order. One of those flaming clouds which we deny to the Deity but arrogate to our own employment may erase our present elaborate constructions as abruptly as the tocsin in the Faubourg St. Germain terminated an age equally tired of itself. Yet this roulette-wheel simile would be repugnant to Burke (or to John Adams), who knew history to be the unfolding of a Design. The true conservative thinks of this process, which looks like chance or fate, as, rather, the Providential operation of a moral law of polarity. And Burke, could he see our century, never would concede that a consumption-society, so near to suicide, is the end for which Providence has prepared man. If a conservative order is indeed to return, we ought to know the tradition which is attached to it, so that we may rebuild society; if it is not to be restored, still we ought to understand conservative ideas so that we may rake from the ashes what scorched fragments of civilization escape the conflagration of unchecked will and appetite.

JEFFREY HART

Burke and Radical Freedom

As everyone knows, an enormous revival of interest in Edmund Burke has taken place during the past twenty years or so, the period, roughly, since the end of the Second World War. Scholars, to be sure, have always been

Jeffrey Hart, "Burke and Radical Freedom," *The Review of Politics*, XXIX, No. 2 (April 1967), 221–238. Reprinted by permission of *The Review of Politics*.

interested in him, and he was widely admired for his style, and by some for his "practical wisdom," during the nineteenth century. But the point is that in our time he has come to be read not merely as one among a large number of other important figures in the history of political thought, but as a thinker of intense, of special, contemporary relevance. Burke is our contemporary, he is an *issue,* in a way that Locke is not, and Leibniz is not, and even Mill is not. Burke has not receded into what Lovejoy called the pathos of time, by which he meant that benign and even tender feeling we have for thought that is now completely, forever, a part of the past—and so neither defines us nor menaces us.

In part, of course, Burke is a beneficiary of the revival of critical and scholarly esteem for eighteenth-century writing generally, and especially for eighteenth-century writing on the conservative side. Like Dryden and Pope and Swift and Johnson, he speaks, we see, for civilization, for a high and elegant and traditional civilization, and this is a welcome voice to us in our age of cultural democratization, and corruption of manners. In part, too, Burke is a beneficiary—as is conservative thought generally—of the fact that in the world arena today America is irreversibly a conservative nation; with everything to gain from the maintenance of order and nothing from its dissolution. Yet neither of these reasons quite accounts for the atmosphere of passion and polemic that surrounds the subject of Burke. Attitudes toward him among otherwise sober-seeming scholars tend to suggest total commitment—for him, or against him. Individuals whom one would never suspect of much capacity for feeling transform themselves when the question of Burke is up. And this, I will maintain, is because Burke was the first to recognize the deep moral division of the West, which was just then opening up, and which today, across the board, is decisive for our moral, political, and metaphysical opinions, and because Burke, having recognized the division and defined its doctrinal grounds, took sides.

Burke's break with Charles James Fox in 1791 may be taken as a kind of symbol of the division then opening in the West itself, and I think that Burke himself so understood it. Burke, of course, had always been known as an advocate of reform. He had urged a moderate and conciliatory policy toward the American colonies. A recently uncovered note among his papers at Sheffield in England demonstrates that Burke actually had a good deal of sympathy with the American Revolution. "The Americans," he noted,

as I have and do repute them the first of men, to whom I owe eternal thanks for making me think better of my nature—tho they have been obliged to fall down at present before the professional armies of Germany, have yet afforded a dawning hope by the stand they have made, that in some corner of the globe, at some time, or in some circumstance or other, the Citizen may not be the slave of the Soldier.

In his parliamentary career Burke had fought for the independence of Parliament against what he thought to be the unconstitutional influence of the Crown. In economic matters, Burke was reformist as against the older mercantilist economic theory; he inclined to the theories of Adam Smith, who said, indeed, that Burke was the only man in England who really understood him. Burke's reformist politics even involved him in some friendly friction with his associates in Dr. Johnson's circle, who were very largely Tories. (Dr. Johnson, you will recall, remarked only half-playfully that the first Whig was the Devil, and that Patriotism—by which he meant the so-called Patriot political group, that is, the critics of George III, and not what we mean today by patriotism—was "the last refuge of a scoundrel.") Burke was the friend of Dr. Johnson, but he was the friend and political ally of the reformers—of Sir Philip Francis (the probable author of the Junius letters), of Sheridan, of Charles James Fox. Jeremy Bentham had read with approval and copiously annotated his reformist speeches; and Burke was admired from afar by Tom Paine. If we could transport the pre-French Revolutionary Burke to our own times we would consider him a moderate and a reformer, humanitarian in his sympathies; he was, as against politics, half in love with philosophy and literature; but the French Revolution did occur: and it changed all this. Burke's principles did not change, but the deep transformation of the world cast him into an entirely different role.

Dramatically, Burke found himself separated from his former allies, who sympathized with the Revolution—and separated from them not only politically but personally, so far-reaching and decisive did the issues seem to him. In the spring of 1791, during a parliamentary debate on matters unrelated to France, Charles James Fox, well known to be an admirer of the Revolution, interpolated into a speech some comments favorable to it. Burke decided to reply to Fox at the earliest opportunity, and on May 6, during a debate on the Canada Bill, Burke rose to speak on the Revolution. As he spoke, Fox's followers repeatedly interrupted him and created an atmosphere of general disorder in the House. Irritated by this, Burke commented angrily on Fox's eulogies of the Revolution, and finally spoke these irrevocable words: "It is indiscreet," he said, "at any period, but especially at my time of life, to provoke enemies or give friends occasion to desert me. Yet firm and steady adherence to the British Constitution places me in such a dilemma; I am ready to risk it, and with my last words to exclaim, 'Fly from the French Constitution.'" Charles James Fox eagerly called to him that there need not be any loss of friends. "Yes, yes," replied Burke, "there is a loss of friends. I have done my duty at the price of my friend. Our friendship is at an end." Aghast at these proceedings, the members watched Burke stalk from the Chamber. This was an unexpected and dramatic but by no means fortuitous event: only a few months before, after a sharp argument over the *Reflections on the Revolu-*

tion in France, Burke's long friendship with Sir Philip Francis came permanently to an end.

No doubt Fox and Francis, worthy enough men, but certainly not thinkers of the first order, were perplexed by Burke's behavior. They were men of generous spirit, they wished well to the people of France. Fox in particular was a sympathetic and colorful character. He was fat, he gambled for enormous sums in the front window of Brooks', he stabled a string of racehorses, he kept a mistress, and after relentlessly attacking Lord North for years he reversed himself, in the genial manner of the time, and formed a coalition with him. But men of this sort, good men though they were, possessed we might say of all the Dickensian virtues— the very creatures, indeed, of the old order—were not equipped either imaginatively or intellectually to understand the implications of the revolutionary threat to the European order, or of the doctrine that informed the threat.

Burke was. The focus of the *Reflections* is on final political things. We do not go to it for a definitive account of the economic conditions of France in 1789, or for a character sketch of Marie Antoinette, or for an apt account of the members of the Assembly. We do go to it for Burke's insight into the intellectual and spiritual issues. For the French Revolution seemed momentous to Burke not because of its violence, or because it threatened the peace of Europe; these things were derivative. Burke was, as he says, "alarmed into reflection" by what he considered a "revolution of doctrine and theoretic dogma," by emotions which, it seemed to him, would render impossible any stable and settled condition of society, and which would issue, indeed, in *permanent* revolution. As he says, near the beginning of the *Reflections,* in a sentence which reverberates in the mind like the opening bars of a great and dark symphony, this was "a great crisis, not of the affairs of France alone, but of all Europe, perhaps of more than Europe."

I think the best way of stating Burke's fundamental objection to the Revolution would be to say that it turned on a definition of "freedom"— that for Burke, freedom was a concrete and historical thing, the actual freedoms enjoyed by actual Englishmen: They enjoyed the historic rights of *Englishmen.* What revolutionary theory proposed, he thought, was a freedom that was abstract and unhistorical, not the rights of Englishmen but the Rights of Man. For Burke, there was no such thing as an abstract man, and to evoke one, as Rousseau had done in the famous first sentence of *The Social Contract,* was to construct a battering ram against all normal social relationships: "Man is born free," said Rousseau, "but everywhere he is in chains."

I do not mean to suggest, idiotically, in the remarks that are to follow, that Rousseau caused the French Revolution. That is not the role of ideas in relation to historical events. In addition, I know very well that there is a good deal of discussion among Rousseau scholars today on the precise intention behind that sentence. Nevertheless I think it remains true that in the *rhetoric* of that sentence we may find articulated the longings that were at the heart of the Revolutionary ethos, and continue, today, to inform the modern revolutionary spirit.

In what sense was man "born free"? we might well ask with Burke. The infant does not look free; he seems completely dependent. And the violence of the statement is suspicious: *everywhere* in chains? *Everywhere?* And it is significant that the chains—man's social circumstances "everywhere"—are concretely imagined in Rousseau's metaphor, but that the "freedom"—man is "born free"—remains hypothetical, abstract, a mere proposition, whatever its rhetorical authority as the opening statement of the sentence. Just what is this freedom? It evidently is not the concrete, historical *freedoms* which Burke has in mind, but rather the hypothetical, indeed mythical, freedom of a presocial self. It is the freedom of man as an essence, not as an existence. Traditional thought—and this is the real reason why religion is necessary to any viable conservative politics—envisioned man as achieving essential being (that is, being as an essence) only outside of time, in eternity. Obviously this is logically consistent and intellectually respectable. But what Revolutionary theory sought, and this was the source—is the source—of its deep appeal in the West, was the experience of *essential freedom,* the freedom of man as an essence, *within* time. And that is why it proved, and has proved, to be so powerful a weapon. Any concrete circumstance standing in the way of *that* freedom—and any concrete circumstance would have to stand in the way of that freedom—would at best be regarded as a bothersome and interim thing, and at worst as contemptible and intolerable, something to be spat upon and smashed.

The theoreticians of the Revolution proposed, as Taine put it, to strip from man his artificial garments, all those fictitious qualities that made him "ecclesiastic or layman, noble or plebeian, sovereign or subject, proprietor or proletarian." Only when these supposed fictions had been stripped away could "natural man," man *qua* man, make his appearance in history—man liberated from false appearance, and so spontaneous, innocent, and free. The actual results of the French Revolution did not diminish the vitality of this hope; nor have the results of subsequent revolutions done so. There is, indeed, a sense in which the revolutionary hope cannot *be* defeated historically, since it is fundamentally unhistorical. By the time Shelley wrote *Prometheus Unbound* the French Revolution was part of history, and it had not transformed human nature. Yet the revolutionary vision retained all of its original vitality, and Shelley longed for another revolution, a final and successful one, which would liberate man at last from the "masks" of actual social existence:

> The loathesome mask has fallen, the man remains
> Scepterless, free, uncircumscribed, but man
> Equal, unclassed, tribeless, and nationless,
> Exempt from awe, worship, degree, the king
> Over himself; just, gentle, wise; but man
> Passionless? no, yet free from guilt or pain.

But if Shelley is a poet of the revolutionary vision, Burke is a poet of man conceived of as a social being, man as we have actually known him *in* history. He identified the revolutionary vision with great precision, and in the *Reflections* launched a powerful attack upon it. In a passage reminiscent of *Lear,* and employing the traditional metaphor of *clothes* to signify—as in Shakespeare or Swift—man's social aspect, Burke describes the informing impulse of the Revolution:

All the decent drapery of life is to be rudely torn off. All the superadded ideas, furnished from the wardrobe of a moral imagination, which the heart owns and the understanding ratifies as necessary to cover the defects of our naked, shivering nature, and to raise it to dignity in our estimation, are to be exploded. . . .

In Burke's metaphor, clothes—what he calls "the decent drapery of life"—correspond to Shelley's "loathesome mask" and to Rousseau's "chains"; that is, they are our actual social roles. When they are stripped away, there remains "our naked shivering nature"—or in Shelley's terms, "man . . . scepterless, free"; or in Rousseau's terms, man "free" as he supposedly was when he was born.

At the center of the *Reflections,* then, is this issue: if indeed that "self" does exist, can it really be divested of its "artificial" attributes, and if it can be, will its nakedness be productive of joy? Burke was one of the first to understand that the spirit of the Revolution—and, as I wish to insist, the spirit of revolutionary modernity (which is not here a merely chronological concept)—was at its roots characterized by a hatred of the very idea of *society*. He knew that the defense of what the *philosophes* called "appearances" or "masks" is the defense of society itself, that the reality of society consists of appearances, of "roles." The natural man of revolutionary theory is only a myth, though a powerful one, and a destructive one—for the critique of roles, of forms, the assault upon Rousseau's "chains" (an element of his sentence which I will explicate shortly) has issued, precisely because natural man is a fiction, not in a more intense experience of selfhood but in the experience of emptiness, disgust, and alienation, in a deep hatred of the actual circumstances of social life, in a deep hatred, indeed, for historical existence itself; that is to say, in the special anger of the revolutionary spirit, which we daily feel all around us.

This spirit, as Christopher Dawson has remarked, is characterized by

a disgust with the concreteness of man's being. Jean Paul Sartre, a very great man in my view, conceives of himself, quite correctly, as a continuator of the Revolutionary tradition, as the heir of the *philosophes,* and he has made immense contributions by way of deepening and expanding that tradition intellectually. He is certainly a much more formidable figure than Camus, whose sensibility, much more traditional in character, surely strikes many as more attractive. Now it is characteristic of the Sartrean hero as we meet him in, say, Roquentin of *Nausea,* that he feels a deep revulsion in the presence of what he regards as "absurd" limitations on his freedom. "I see," says Roquentin in a moment of illumination, "I recall better what I felt the other day at the seashore when I held the pebble. It was a sort of sweetish sickness. How unpleasant it was! It came from the stone. I'm sure of it. It passed from the stone to my hand. Yes, that's it, that's just it—a sort of nausea in the hands!" Mere things seem to Roquentin simply to be there, without reason or purpose, devoid of consciousness. "The world of *Nausea,*" as Francis Jeanson has said, "is the world as it threatens to appear to us when we look at it passively, when we refuse to project a future for it. It becomes a petrified consciousness." The man of Sartrean sensibility, as he moves away from consciousness toward the unconscious, experiences increasing "viscosity"—we hear of "the stickiness," "the rising triumph of the solid over the liquid," "thoughts made sticky by their own objects," as well as, even more frequently, of "bloatedness," "insipid flesh," "pink flesh," "clammy flesh," and so on. Consciousness for Sartre is freedom, experienced as complete lucidity, while unconsciousness is a prison of "facticity." And the emotion includes his own body: "a dull and inescapable nausea perpetually reveals my body to myself."

This polarity between freedom and imprisonment is the reality of human experience for Sartre, but against it men of bad faith, whom Sartre calls "salauds"—stinkers—and who are principally to be identified with the middle class, erect the barriers of habit, conventional assumption, social role. All these constitute refusals of consciousness and freedom. Thus, in a characteristic gesture the Sartrean hero (Roquentin, Mathieu, Goetz) asserts his freedom from facticity by actually stabbing himself: "My saliva is sweetish, my body lukewarm; I feel insipid. My penknife is on the table. I open it. Why not? In any case it would change things a bit. I place my left hand on the writing pad and dispatch a good knifethrust into the palm." It is by asserting himself against all forms of facticity and unconsciousness that the Sartrean hero becomes a free and spontaneous individual. "Sartre's essential philosophical trend," observes Wilfrid Desan, "is one of *negation,* a negation of all limitations to freedom, all hampering of man's free movement." Surely Desan is correct in this, for the attitude in question pervades Sartre's philosophical writings, his drama and his fiction, and even his criticism, which is savagely moral rather than aesthetic: Genet is a "saint" because of his negation of conventional morality; Giacometti is a great sculptor, for his wiry, fragile figures show man stripped of all "artificial" attributes.

This radical dualism between consciousness and object, lucidity and density, or, in Sartre's terminology, the *Pour-soi* and the *En-soi,* tends, by implication, toward a rejection of the social possibility, as Merleau-Ponty pointed out in his famous critique of Sartre, *Les Adventures de la Dialectique.* In accepting only *man* and *things* Sartre overlooks the *entremonde,* the both-and, that in-between-world of symbolism, value, and history—all that "man" finds and has found to be true. It is as if the individual consciousness alone counts, and both history and the social order are something extraneous. And of course, this sensibility takes the individual consciousness as something that, "naturally," does not incorporate into itself history (its memory) or the social order (its roles). That is to say, any memory, and any social role, is unnatural. Sartre defines integrity as *permanently* revolutionary, revolutionary against any of its conceivable concrete circumstances. That is why he is the greatest and deepest of the *philosophes,* and probably the last.

This hatred of the physical and limiting, of the concrete and irreducible, represents at its deepest reaches—to shift into another idiom—a rejection of the doctrine of the Incarnation, which in one of its meanings expresses the possibility that the concrete and the limiting—the flesh—may enter into union with spirit. To enter into the world at all, the spirit must become flesh—concrete and embodied. We know no naked essences. This union constitutes, in Donne's phrase, "that subtle knot" which makes us man. The Incarnation is the epitome of the very both-and which Sartre has it in mind to split apart. But it is Sartre's power, even perhaps his greatness, that he can move us with his dream of radical freedom, and make us, for a moment, desire to untie that knot.

No one can doubt in reflecting upon Burke's penetration of these matters that he illuminated the heart of portentous issues, that he played, indeed, a prophetic role. If his revolutionary opponents conceived of the self as an entity separate from, and hidden behind, false appearances, their modern intellectual descendants have professed what, to coin a phrase, we might call a conspiracy theory of reality. Not the appearances of society, they have maintained, but the secret and hypothetical economic or sexual basis is the "reality." Our naive experience of the world, we hear, is deceptive; the truth is behind the appearances, waiting to emerge under the proper auspices, and when the proper key is turned. Marx, for example, conceives of society as it has heretofore existed as a constricting thing, inimical to spontaneity and freedom—the derivation of these terms in Marxist thought should now be familiar—and he argues that all historical societies at best have helped to move toward, at worst

ego and superego formation; that is, with the establishing of identity and of principles. The father's own identity, in turn, is the result of his own ancestry. Groups in which the family structure is weak, or the father's sense of identity uncertain, or in which the father is actually likely to desert the family—as in the case of the American Negro at the present time—tend to be characterized by identity "crises" and deep uncertainty about goals and values. As Burke argues repeatedly in the *Reflections,* imaginative awareness of the links between himself and his past prevents the individual from feeling that his existence is arbitrary, or, in the fashionable term, absurd.

Another link, in Burke's thought, is the link to one's contemporaries: to the family, first of all, but extending beyond that to the neighborhood and the region, and thence to the nation and the civilization. Burke characteristically moves outward, from the immediate to the more remote, insisting upon the importance of the group closest to the individual: "To be attached to the subdivision, to love the little platoon we belong to in society, is the first principle (the germ, as it were) of public affections. It is the first *link* [my italics] in the series by which we proceed towards a love to our country, and to mankind." Concerned to protect the various groups to which the individual is most immediately linked, and which help to constitute his identity, Burke characteristically refuses to begin in the abstract, unhistorical way with Mankind or the Brotherhood of Man. Here again Burke anticipated some of the best in modern social thought, and in particular that which may be said to derive from Georg Simmel's *The Web of Group Affiliation.* Simmel argues that a person's identity is formed by the "pattern" of his group affiliation, and that individuality is maintained by variety among the patterns. The more distinctive groups there are—clubs, professional associations, church congregations, and so on—and the more independent they are, the more various will be the patterns of affiliation, and the wider, therefore, will be the possibilities of individuality. Other social scientists—I particularly have in mind the work of Almond and Verba—have pointed out that independent groups, by fostering commitments on levels below the political and the ideological help to defanaticize the political order. They produce a kind of tolerance through complexity of commitment.

Still another link, for Burke, was the link to place. A man's identity is very much involved with his attachment to place, his sense of himself as associated with a geographic locality. The length of time he has lived there has much to do with the strength of such local feeling, as do the distinctive characteristics of the place itself. Burke was attached to the "irregularities" of things, and instinctively rejected a uniformitarian idea of "reason." But the link to place also has much to do with ownership; the man who owns his house is likely to have a deeper imaginative involvement with the neighborhood than one who does not. And here we may observe that Burke, drawing upon Locke, perhaps, but also on his own common sense, put a very high valuation on the protection of property. He did not make that grotesque but familiar distinction between property rights and human rights, but viewed property as a human right. It is not, after all, a vegetable or a mineral right.

In proportion as such links as these were dissolved, Burke thought, man's identity would be dissolved as well. The links prevented him from floating away psychologically as a kind of angry abstraction, or, to put it another way, from resembling, psychically, those odd modern sculptures, composed of coat hangers, tin cans, and stove bolts. And we may indeed suppose that much of the distinctive pain of modern existence does proceed from the assault that has been carried forward against such links. They sometimes have been weakened or broken, of course, by historical developments of a nonideological character—by industrialization, by urbanization, by the widening possibilities of geographical and social mobility. But the point to be made here is that the bad effects of these developments have been intensified, rather than moderated, by the ideology Burke fought. A moral assault as well has been conducted on these natural links, a moral assault that would seem to have as its intention the isolation of the individual, the reduction of him to a "free" self. Think of the deeply antidomestic implications of progressive pressure for sexual freedom and for relaxed divorce laws and for more abortions. Or the implications of the advocacy, by R. H. Tawney, on moral grounds, of a 100 percent death tax.

I would like to turn now to the matter which plays a very important role in Burke's political thought; it is, like the links I have been talking about, a psychological point primarily, but also, like them, it issues in a political principle. For Burke's politics, like any genuinely conservative politics, places a high valuation on *habit.* "Prejudice," he says in the *Reflections,* "renders a man's virtues his habit, and not a series of unconnected acts. Through just prejudice, his duty becomes a part of his nature." This high valuation of habit proceeds from an awareness of the complexity of social life, and from the elementary observation—though Burke was the first to make it; in a sense *he* was the discoverer of the unconscious—that habit performs complex tasks with greater ease and efficiency than does the conscious reason. The daily tasks that we perform most easily (we say, usually, that we perform them "naturally"), from tying our shoes to handling the day's social encounters, we perform habitually. If we were forced to think them through analytically, our activities would come rapidly to a halt. There is a sense, indeed, in which it is really habit, paradoxically enough, that renders one free, since freedom actually is experienced only as a quality of an activity. One is free to do this or that; one is not "free" in an abstract way apart from activity.

Castiglione spoke of the courtier's quality of *sprezzatura,* by which he meant his ability to perform his role with ease; through long practice, that is, he could perform it *with ease*—"naturally." And in a similar way Lord Chesterfield advised his son to practice entering a drawing room properly, so that he could do it with ease. A skillful musician is "freer" to play his instrument than a novice. And these examples may be taken as synecdochic of our other activities.

It will be seen, therefore, that considerable advantage will reside in circumstances that permit social roles themselves to be rooted in habit, though no conceivable circumstance of course could render them entirely habitual. And the sort of society advocated throughout Burke's works operates to strengthen the element of habit in social role. Wealth, property, and power are not to pass with great rapidity from one hand to another. He opposed mobility rapid enough to endanger social habit. "I do not hesitate to say," he wrote in the *Reflections,* "that the road to eminence and power from obscure condition ought not to be made too easy, nor a thing too much of course. If rare merit be the rarest of all things, it ought to pass through some sort of probation." In the society thus adumbrated, a man might be a soldier, a merchant, a landholder, or a nobleman, and would expect to remain one. His sense of himself would be that his identity was to a considerable degree "given" rather than willed. But in a more fluid condition of society this is much less the case. Individuals become to a much greater degree free to create themselves, become, in Don Quixote's marvelous phrase, the children of their deeds rather than the children of their actual parents. But to the extent that careers are open to talents, to the extent, that is, that one's social role is the result of one's own talent and will, one's identity must be experienced as *arbitrary.* One might just as well have willed something else. And when identity thus partakes of the quality of the willed and the arbitrary, it is experienced as a kind of mask, or even as a lie. One's roles seem absurd, perhaps even hateful. The self comes to stand in an ironic or antagonistic relationship to all its social manifestations. Perhaps this is one reason why the literature of the Enlightenment, responding at once to actual conditions of increasing social mobility, but also to the ideological assumption that mobility is simply *good,* has as one of its central themes the critique of roles and appearances. Even such ostensibly conservative writers as Swift and Goldsmith shock conventional views by examining society through the wrong end of a telescope or from the perspective of a Chinaman.

Nevertheless, as Burke saw, there is an intimate connection between habit and ease, and this applies as much to society at large as to the individual. The vast majority of its activities, from delivering the mail to running a legislature, go forward smoothly so long as they follow habitual procedures. It is the habits of society—its customs, institutions, and prejudices—that embody the results of its historical experience and enable it to function and preserve its coherence in the present. It was one of Burke's great accomplishments as a political philosopher to show that Hobbes and Locke erred in assigning to reason rather than to habit the function of maintaining the stability of a society. Habit, to be sure, is not an appropriate instrument for dealing with *novel* experience; but on that very account, as Burke saw, a society is better off if it can absorb novelty in small and manageable amounts.

At the beginning of this essay, I spoke of the moral division of the West. We may observe here that that division is less exacerbated, even though present, in England and America than in France, say, or Italy. A study entitled *The Civil Culture* which was published recently by Gabriel Almond and Sidney Verba, makes a Burkean point about this. Ideological division is less comprehensive in those two countries precisely because they have not had revolutions, and have attempted, so to speak, to solve their problems *one at a time.* In consequence, such solutions have had less tendency to become features of a comprehensive program. Novelty was absorbed gradually. Almond and Verba, moreover, agree with Burke in viewing revolutionary ideology as the mortal enemy of stable representative government, which depends, they argue, on a number of quite subtle "informal" factors—upon a general atmosphere of trust among the citizens, upon a tradition of political legitimacy, and upon a tacit agreement to "play by the rules." Paradoxically, they argue, representative institutions thrive only in an atmosphere of *limited* political commitment on the part of most people. A political commitment cannot become so powerful that it refuses to subordinate itself to the assumptions about trust, legitimacy, and playing by the rules. Most persuasively, Almond and Verba define the attitude appropriate to the citizen in what they call a "civic culture": He simultaneously does *not* participate in politics and assumes that *he could if he wanted to.* The civic culture thus balances activity and passivity by a norm Almond and Verba call "the potentially active citizen." We may notice, moreover, the contrast between this attitude and the one recommended by civics texts and democratic ideologists, who urge participation and activism.

It is only recently, it seems to me, that scholars and social scientists have recovered anything like Burke's imagination of the delicacy and complexity of our social arrangements. I have in mind the works of Talcott Parsons, Leonard Broom, Robert Merton, and Almond and Verba, among others, as well as the resurgence of interest in those aspects of such older writers as Bagehot and Simmel which bear on the question of the sources of social stability.* In society, as Burke put it,

*Merton and Broom, for example, have provided the theoretical framework for a sociology of anger which would be highly relevant to American society at the present time and which in a variety of ways confirms Burke's insights. Our common sense assumption is that non-neurotic anger proceeds from a "grievance" and would disappear if the griev-

"there are often some obscure and almost latent causes, things which appear at first of little moment, on which a very great part of its prosperity or adversity may most essentially depend." And further, that "it is with infinite caution that any man ought to venture upon pulling down an edifice which has answered in any tolerable degree for ages the common purposes of society."

The emphasis in Burke's writing upon man in his historical existence and his denigration of "abstract" speculation have led many to suppose that his thought is pragmatic in character, and informed by no permanent principles. John Morley, for example, who wrote a good short book on Burke during the nineteenth century, was of this opinion. But this view is quite mistaken and ignores the special way in which Burke made use of history.

Burke considered that an "eternal law" is discoverable in history. Men, he says, "attain to the moral reason in their collective experience, they realize and embody it in their stable social relations and organization." For Burke, that is to say, the moral law is eternal and universal, though men cannot, because of their limited reason, apprehend it directly. The moral law does, however, acquire concrete existence and so may be apprehended, historically—in man's stable (and the word is crucial) social arrangements. The stability of those arrangements demonstrates that the moral law is being obeyed. Thus there exists for Burke two sources of our knowledge of the "eternal law"—Christian revelation and our historical experience. From this perspective, novel theories of government and human nature, though they may be the product of brilliant thinkers, can scarcely compare in validity either with revelation or with institutions that have been the creation of many generations. Such novel theories are presumptuous in attempting to set themselves up as

---

ance were "corrected." In his classic study *Suicide,* however, Emile Durkheim showed that feelings of grievance and deprivation are relative to goals—that, paradoxically, such feelings intensify as possibility is enhanced. Robert Merton moved a step further in the relativization of grievance in his development of "reference group theory." The individual feels deprived, he shows, relative to those with whom he is accustomed to compare himself. The feeling of deprivation flows from the comparison, for it is the comparison which gives the meaning to the objective circumstance (see Merton's great essay "Notes Toward a Theory of Reference Group Behavior" in *Social Theory and Social Structure*). Leonard Broom has added a further dimension to our understanding of social anger by, in effect, internalizing Merton's conception of relative deprivation. Broom applies the theory of relative deprivation to the question of social status. Pointing out that an individual's status is not a monolithic thing, but is made up of manifold components—wealth, education, ethnicity, occupation, neighborhood, and so forth—Broom shows that comparisons can be made between one component and another. An individual might be "high" in one—say education—and "low" in another—perhaps ethnicity. Comparing one with the other, he would feel *relatively* deprived as regards his low component. Consistency among the components of an individual's status produces a better social "fit"; conversely, status inconsistency is generative of social anger. It is worth noticing that rapid mobility—as on the campus today—almost inevitably generates status inconsistency (see Broom's "Social Differentiation and Stratification" in *Sociology Today,* eds. Merton, Broom, and Cottrell).

rivals of "eternal law," and their inadequacy is proved by the catastrophes that result when they are used as principles of government.

When the statesman acts in conformity with the eternal law, Burke thinks, *tranquillity* is fostered in society. Running through his work is a vocabulary indicative of a set of fundamental polarities. On the one hand are the qualities to be desired in society: stability, public tranquillity, peace, quiet, order, harmony, regularity, unity, decorum. Opposed to these are the symptoms of social disease: discord, contradiction, confusion, violence, excess, the need for coercion. The task of the statesman is to promote "tranquillity."

The attitudes and doctrines that informed the French Revolution, Burke thinks, make tranquillity impossible. Asserting against an actual society rights derived from a mythical state of nature, and celebrating a freedom equally mythical—"man is born free"—the theorists wielded a weapon to which any society would be vulnerable. Against such demands, he said, "no agreement is binding; these admit no temperament and no compromise; anything withheld is so much fraud and injustice." On the other hand, the rights Burke was defending were rights he had known as historical facts. It was those rights that he put in the path of a permanent shattering of tranquillity, a permanent revolution.

Of course, the belief that tranquillity is man's social goal has by no means been a matter of universal agreement. There are those, and Burke knew them well, who delight in agitation; there are literary and intellectual *voyeurs* of revolution; there are temperaments for which, as Burke said, it "is a war or a revolution or it is nothing." There are those who, finally, agree with Goethe that the achievement of tranquillity represents the defeat of the human spirit. Faust, that symbol of much, at least, in the modern temper, is never to say to the moment, *"Verweile doch, du bist so schön"* ("Stay, thou art so fair."). Only a perpetual dissatisfaction, for the Faustian spirit, is truly human. Faust represents the deep antiontologicality which is, as we have seen, one feature of the modern mind—its hatred of what *is,* of the given, its impatience with what it regards as "irrational" differences of nationality, social class, race, or sex (modernity is coeducational, as, indeed, was Faust). And of course it is differences that define particular existence—this, and not that. Yet in opposition to this temper, there is another and older sense of things, an alternative to the restless spirit of transformation, and which most certainly is willing to say to the moment, to the world, "Stay, thou art so fair." Do not change: *Be.* In his splendid brief study of Piero della Francesca, Bernard Berenson speaks of a quality to be found in many of the greatest portraits that date from before the nineteenth century. A kind of silence surrounds those figures, he says; they do not gesture or grimace at us from the canvas. A portrait by Piero or Botticelli, Velasquez or Murillo, Reynolds or Gainsborough, seems to say that the existence of its subject in no way appeals to *our* presence before the canvas. Those dukes and cardinals and princesses and statesmen take their existence as a matter of course. They are *there*, self-contained; their being is concrete, actual, accepted. And it may be that sense of being which really is in harmony with the deepest intuitions of the West about the proper mode of the human, for it is that sense which comes to us from the oldest and most continuous of our moral traditions—from Plato and Aristotle, Cicero, Aquinas, Hooker, Elyot, Samuel Johnson, Burke; and so, in politics, it is to Burke that we logically turn as we seek to reconstitute that tradition in the teeth of another revolution.

RICHARD M. WEAVER

The Southern Tradition at Bay

All studies of American civilization must recognize the strong polarity existing since early times between North and South. The government of the United States was founded on abstract propositions. The facts of varying topography, climate, and race made regional development inevitable; the regions arriving at their own interpretations of the propositions produced, on the political level, sectionalism. These circumstances have posed a problem for writers who sought to characterize the United States, and the problem has been solved in the only way possible: that is, by taking the mentality and the institutions of the majority section as best entitled to the name American. I expect to speak of the South therefore as a minority within the nation, whose claim to attention lies not in its success in impressing its ideals upon the nation or the world, but in something I shall insist is higher—an ethical claim which can be described only in terms of the mandate of civilization. In its battle for survival the South has lost ground, but it has kept from extinction some things whose value is emphasized by the disintegration of the modern world.

This work concerns itself with a tradition, which means a recognizable pattern of belief and behavior transmitted from one generation to the next. Traditions must have, of course, a sufficient coherence to be distinguishable as integers; yet in characterizing a tradition as "Southern" one encounters the same difficulties as in characterizing another "American." Within each there will be dissidence and minority reports. It is plain that

From Richard M. Weaver, *The Southern Tradition at Bay*, George Core and M. E. Bradford, eds. (New Rochelle, N.Y.: Arlington House, 1968), pp. 29–44. Reprinted by permission of M. E. Bradford.

there were things done in the South which were not "Southern," and things done in the North that were not "Northern," as we are compelled to understand these terms. Really we are faced with a problem in logic, and it is enough, I think, to be aware of the fallacies of composition and division. The first is an assumption that what is true of a part, or even of a number of parts—the proportion being incapable of determination—is necessarily true of the whole. The second is an assumption that what is true of the whole is also true of every single part. To say that Southerners have differed in point of view from Yankees does not speak for every single Southerner, but it does express a substantial truth.*

However much it may offend our sense of fairness, it is a demonstrable fact that the group in power speaks for the country, that the element which controls the government, the education, the means of publication is the nation in so far as its collective action goes. There is truth in the saying that the state is that part of the population which knows what it wants, or better, has a moral ambition. In assaying the Southern tradition, therefore, I have taken the spirit which dominated, and I shall no more apologize for speaking of it than others have for speaking of the New England mind or the American character. It is not the province of this work to discuss early Southern abolition societies or the spread of French infidelity in Southern educational centers save to the extent that they called forth, or served to illuminate by contrast, that unified and preponderating mind which produced the Confederate South.

If asked to tell why in these days Southern history is entitled to thoughtful consideration, I should list first of all the fact that the South, alone among the sections, has persisted in regarding science as a false messiah. This by itself indicates that the Southern tradition has a center of resistance to the most powerful force of corruption in our age. While the Western world has gone after false gods, it has clung, often at the cost of scorn and insult, to its lares of the field. More concretely, it has not, in the same measure as "progressive" sections of the country, become engrossed in means to the exclusion of ends.

The precarious state of our civilization has grown with our control over nature, though we were promised an opposite result. We have assembled a vast warehouse of machinery which would, it was hoped, if not minister directly to the civilizing spirit, at least free other forces for that ministration. Yet this spirit shows signs of failing—the signs were in evidence before the World Wars—and everywhere crassness, moral ob-

---

*It is useless to argue against generalization; a world without generalization would be a world without knowledge. The chaotic and fragmentary thinking of the modern age is due largely to an apprehensiveness, inspired by empirical methods, over images, wholes, general truths, so that we are intimidated from reaching the conclusions we must live by. The exception neither proves nor disproves the rule; in the original sense of the maxim it tests the rule: *exceptio probat regulam.*

tuseness, and degradation are on the increase. We have been led to believe that man's chief task is the conquest of nature, including of course space and time. Mere advances in mechanical power, and especially superior mobility, have been greeted as steps in an automatic progress. The thought was plausible enough to find wide acceptance, so that now it is a dogma with which the clever can exploit the unthinking; perhaps indeed its great attraction lay in the emancipation from thinking. Science was hypostatized; a great machine appeared to have been set in motion which needed only operation to produce a civilization beyond present conception. It is easy, while occupied with technics and under the influence of robotlike labor, to forget that the most difficult task is to train and govern men for their own good.

The painful truth is now beginning to emerge that a flourishing technology may make civilization more rather than less difficult of attainment. It leads to mobilization of external forces; it creates enormous concentrations of irresponsible power; through an inexorable standardization it destroys refinement and individuality.* Other things it does too, and now with the greatest of all wars behind us, which we fought with the least enthusiasm and settled amid the greatest moral confusion, it behooves us to examine some alternatives.

We must see first of all that the kingdom of civilization is within. We must confess that the highest sources of value in life are the ethical and aesthetic conceptions with which our imagination invests the world. We must admit that man is to be judged by the quality of his actions rather than by the extent of his dominion. Civilization is a discipline, an achievement in self-culture and self-control, and the only civilizing agent is a spirit manifesting itself through reason, imagination, and religious inspiration, and giving a sort of mintage to acts which would otherwise be without meaning.

A civilized tradition implies a center, from which control is exerted, and it is through this control that we give quality to actions. Civilized man carries a sense of restraint into his behavior both toward nature and his fellow beings. The first of these is piety, the second ethics.

Piety comes to us as a warning voice that we must think as mortals, that it is not for us either to know all or to control all. It is a recognition of our own limitations and a cheerful acceptance of the contingency of nature, which gives us the protective virtue of humility. The attitude of science, on the other extreme, has become impious to the fullest degree. It has encouraged a warfare between man and nature, a fanatical warfare, in which without clearly defined war aims, we seek the total overthrow of an opponent. But nature is not an opponent, as ancient systems of belief

---

*Of great consequence is the fact that scientific advance has led to a breakdown of communication between the generations, and thereby has helped to destroy tradition.

could have instructed us; it is the matrix of our being, and as such scientists we are parricides. Piety is a realization that beyond a certain point victories over nature are pyrrhic. The thought is implicit in the legend of Prometheus, and I have no doubt that the deep suspicion with which medieval theologians viewed early explorations of the physical world was intuition.* They sensed, apparently, the peril in these conquests, a *hubris* leading to vainglory, egotism, impatience, a feeling that man can dispense with all restraints. Every legend of man's fall is a caution against presuming to know everything, and an indirect exhortation to piety; and the disappearance of belief in original sin has done more than anything else to prepare the way for sophistical theories of human nature and society. Man has lost piety toward nature in proportion as he has left her and shut himself up in cities with rationalism for his philosophy.

And here enters one of the alarming facts of our cultural condition. It is the "spoiled child" psychology which appears in all urban populations. This malady, described by Ortega y Gasset in *The Revolt of the Masses,* afflicts any people who have lived so long in an artificial environment that they have lost a sense of the difficulty of things. Their institutionalized world is a product of toil and discipline; of this they are no longer aware. Like the children of rich parents, they have been pampered by the labor and self-denial of those who went before; they begin to think that luxuries, though unearned, are rightfully theirs. They fret when their wishes are not gratified; they turn to cursing and abusing; they look for scapegoats. If the world does not conform to our heart's desire, some *person* is guilty! So runs their tune. Liberals of the type who think for *The Nation* and *The New Republic* are in a constant state of vexation over the unmalleability of the world.

The agrarian South, close to the soil and disciplined in expectation, has never behaved as the spoiled child. It has suffered more afflictions than Job but has continued to call God and nature good. It accepts the unchangeable and hopes that it is providential. As a result, the backwoods Southern farmer does not feel as sorry for himself as the better heeled, better padded, and more expensively tutored Northern city cousin. This acceptance of nature, with an awareness of the persistence of tragedy, is the first element of spirituality, and a first lesson for the poor bewildered modern who, amid the wreckage of systems, confesses inability to understand the world.

---

*Now comes David Lilienthal, chairman of the Tennessee Valley Authority, saying that "Research must have a 'soul.' Intelligence is not enough without a spiritual and humane purpose. Research that is only 'enormously developed intelligence' . . . can lead only to one catastrophe after another, one war after another, each more horrible and mechanically perfect than its predecessor, to the exploitation and devastation of natural resources, and finally to the most terrible catastrophe of all, a nonmoral rather than a moral world."

If asked whether the South has any genuine claim to be considered aristocratic, I would say yes, and this is it. The South has kept something of the attitude of the soldier: Aware of the battle, he has only contempt for the tender, querulous, agitated creature of modern artifice, sighing for the comforts he is "entitled to," and protesting that the world cannot really be like this. I am sure that Lee, so reserved in expression, so wise in thought, had this in mind when he called self-denial the greatest lesson to be learned. If part of our happiness comes through transformation of the outward world, another part comes through the pruning of desire, and we return to the original proposition that civilization is a matter of inner conditioning and adaptation.

As piety respects the mystery of nature, so ethics, the restraining sentiment which we carry into the world of our fellow beings, respects the reality of personality. It is well if our code of ethics has a religious origin, so that its power to impress derives from some myth or some noble parable. Its purpose, in any case, is to lead everyone to a relatively selfless point of view, and to make him realize the plurality of personalities in the world. Above all, it must insist upon the rightness of right and keep in abeyance the crude standard of what will pay. A Southern writer, thinking to reflect upon the Yankee Benjamin Franklin, asserted that honesty is not a policy at all, but a principle. The gibe was perhaps unmerited, but there is peril in promising temporal rewards for the things we must do out of profound ethical belief.

It will seem to many anomalous that a slaveholding society like the South should be presented as ethically superior. Yet the endeavor to grade men by their moral and intellectual worth may suggest a more sensitive conscience than proscription of individual differences. I do not claim that the South did this successfully, but the great intellectual effort which went into the defense of slavery indicates an ethical awareness and established some conclusions not yet entirely refuted. More important than this, however, was the astonishing resistance to the insidious doctrines of relativism and empiricism which the Southerner carried about with him. It was manifest in his religion, it showed in his deportment, and it became conspicuous in his conduct of war. . . . Many Northerners had similar conceptions, but I believe fair-minded students of America will admit that in the North conditions were arising which made maintenance of these difficult. They were precisely the conditions which had drawn from Burke the cry: "The age of chivalry is gone—that of sophisters, economists, and calculators has succeeded." It is a remark whose truth has increased with the years. The North was in the first stages of commercialism, and no way has been found to reconcile this with ancient ideals of honor.

Personality can develop only in a humane environment, and nowhere in America has this distillation of life flourished as in the South. Its love

of heroes, its affection for eccentric leaders, its interest in personal anecdote, in the colorful and the dramatic, discounted elsewhere as charming
weaknesses, are signs that it reveres the spiritual part of man. It has
instinctively disliked, though it has by now partially succumbed to, the
dehumanizing influence of governments and factories. Individualism and
personality are making a stand—perhaps a Custer's last stand—in the
South.

Civilization is measured by its power to create and enforce distinctions. Consequently there must be some source of discrimination, from
which we bring ideas of order to bear on a fortuitous world. Knowledge
and virtue constitute this source, and these two things, it must be said to
the vexation of the sentimental optimists, are in their nature aristocracies.
Participation in them is open to all. This much of the doctrine of equality
is sound, but the participation will never occur in equal manner or degree, so that however we allow men to start in the world, we may be sure
that as long as standards of quality exist, there will be a sorting out.
Indeed, we are entitled to say categorically that unless such standards are
operative, civilization does not exist, or that it has fallen into decay. That
no man was ever born free and no two men ever born equal is a more
sensible saying than its contrary. To the extent that the South has preserved social structure and avoided the creation of masses, it has maintained the only kind of world in which values can long survive.

A society in the true sense must have exclusive minorities of the wise
and good who will bear responsibility and enjoy prestige. Otherwise
either it will be leaderless, or its leadership will rest on forces of darkness;
for there is little difference between the tribal chieftain who wins his place
by brute force and the demagogue of the mass state who wins his by
appeal to mass appetite. The man of a civilized tradition, therefore, will
find nothing strange in the idea of hierarchy. Out of the natural reverence
for intellect and virtue there arises an impulse to segregation, which
broadly results in coarser natures, that is, those of duller mental and
moral sensibility, being lodged at the bottom and those of more refined
at the top. Schemes to control this process, or to expedite it, such as
Plato's system of education, testify to our sense of its wisdom. The terms
"society" and "mass" are really antonyms. One implies an intelligible
order, with the best elements where decisions are to be made, whatever
the mechanism of selection may be. "Mass" is shapeless, impotent, really
unintelligible. Because it depends upon an ordering of qualities and
places, civilization is in fact a protest against this featureless condition.

The notion that all ideas of rank are inimical to liberty is found only
among those who have not analyzed the relationship between freedom
and organization. It is the process of leveling which distorts reality and
leaves us with a situation that is, literally, impossible to conceive. The
most assured way to undermine civilization is to surrender to criteria of

uniformity and objectivity, losing sight of the fact that the objective cannot be prescriptive and failing to make those distinctions which have their
basis in human ambition. True, it requires a degree of tough-mindedness
to accept the fact of civilization, just as it requires sternness to execute
moral laws, for both are discriminatory; and many forces which would
destroy it have been abetted by men of good will, and have come creeping
in among us, appealing to blind appetite, to special interest, and capitaliz-
ing on a partial awareness of what is at stake. We cannot do better in this
connection than ponder the wonderful speech of Ulysses in *Troilus and
Cressida*. Just as the deep mind of Goethe grasped the true significance
of the French Revolution while the jejune and the half-educated were
being misled, so the marvelous understanding of Shakespeare saw in an
instant the consequences of a classless society:

> O, when degree is shak'd,
> Which is the ladder to all high designs,
> The enterprise is sick! How could communities,
> Degrees in school and brotherhoods in cities,
> Peaceful commerce from dividable shores,
> The primogenitive and due of birth,
> Prerogative of age, crowns, sceptres, laurels,
> But by degree stand in authentic place?
> Take but degree away, untune that string,
> And hark, what discord follows! each thing meets
> In mere oppugnancy: the bounded waters
> Should lift their bosoms higher than the shores,
> And make a sop of all this solid globe;
> Strength should be lord of imbecility,
> And the rude son should strike his father dead:
> Force should be right; or rather, right and wrong,
> Between whose endless jar justice resides,
> Should lose their names, and so should justice too.
> Then everything includes itself in power,
> Power into will, will into appetite;
> And appetite, an universal wolf,
> So doubly seconded with will and power,
> Must make perforce an universal prey,
> And last eat up itself.

This is Shakespeare on nihilism. Milton too, it would seem, though a
fierce republican and a foe of absolute authority, believed that

> orders and degrees
> Jar not with liberty, but well consist.

It was a denial of such propositions that shocked Southern political
thinkers. They could not understand how anyone, looking at the face of
society and cherishing values, which must always appear tyrannous in the

divisions they enforce among men, could preach equality and ridicule the veneration of age and eminence. Such views tended to break down the organization of the world and to substitute a lawless competition of unequals.

Those who seek to evade this dilemma by declaring that ability alone should count, a natural plea in our age of specialization, are often disingenuous, for they narrow down "ability" to mean some special skill, aptitude, or ingenuity at an isolated task. But in the political community ability must take account of the whole man, his special competences plus his personality and his moral disposition, even his history. It is well that people are not ranked for measurable efficiency as engines are for horsepower, but rather for the total idea we have of them. Thus again we face the topic of the whole man and the evil of reducing him to an abstraction to insure his political qualification.

Southern political theory was a *rationale* of society; the Northern theory it was designed to confute was largely a set of aspirations unrealizable even logically.* It was a political romanticism, not then subject to severe testing because the Northern world was fluid and expanding. Every old and settled society comes to terms with the physical world and the psychic world, and it forms a judgment that efforts to change either beyond a certain point will cost more than they will yield. The South was in the position of Europe or even Asia; it felt that it had discerned some necessary limitations of existence; the North felt that the South was compounding with ancient evils. Hence the epithets were "fool" and "villain." The North had Tom Paine and his postulates assuming the virtuous inclinations of man; the South had Burke and his doctrine of human fallibility and of the organic nature of society. A difference so wide is not easily composed in any country, and in the United States there were aggravations.

It is a wonder that the South did not draw more freely from Burke, who understood clearly the power of sentiment in civilized communities. A culture defines itself by crystallizing around what I should call "unsentimental sentiments." These are feelings which determine a common attitude toward large phases of experience; they impel us, on critical occasions of life, to sense more than we would sense and do more than we would do if we were only economic man. There is no demonstrable connection between them and our physical survival, and therefore from the standpoint of materialism or nihilism they are excessive in the same way as any sentimental display. They originate in our world view, in our ultimate vision of what is proper for men as higher beings; and they are kept from being sentimental in fact by a metaphysic or a theology which

*It could be pointed out here that political machines have been the working arrangement behind what was ostensibly "democracy."

assigns them a function understandable through imagination. The propriety of any given sentiment will rest on our profoundest view of life; our attitude toward the dead, toward traditional institutions, toward the symbols of community life—all come from a metaphysical dream of the world which we have created, or have been taught. It is the loss of this view, and the determination of matters in a narrow context of material interest—let us recall the horror with which the direct, practical judgments of a successful moneymaker are greeted in a family of inherited refinement—which mark the subsidence of our power to support civilization against the will of outward being continually pressing upon us. Burke saw the French Revolution as an assault upon just such conceptions:

> All of the pleasing illusions, which made power gentle, and obedience liberal, which harmonized the different shades of life, and which, by a bland assimilation, incorporated into politics the sentiments which beautify and soften private society, are to be dissolved by this new conquering empire of light and reason. All of the decent drapery of life is to be rudely torn off. All the superadded ideas, furnished from the wardrobe of a moral imagination, which the heart owns and the imagination ratifies, as necessary to cover the defects of our naked and shivering nature, and to raise it to dignity in our own estimation, are to be exploded as ridiculous, absurd, and antiquated fashion.

Speaking for a century which had valued men for their "correct sentiments," Burke contended thus for the spiritual character of society against sansculottism. And looking at our own "second American Revolution," we find the South charging the North with lack of sentiment. A Northern professor resident in the South has written that Southerners apply the term "Yankee" as the Greeks did "barbarian." The kinship of ideas cannot be overlooked. The Greek knew that the barbarian could not participate in his luminous world of myth and actuality. The sentiments of a culture may indeed be "delicate arabesques of convention," the appreciation of which demands a state of grace. Their value will lie in their nonutility, in their remoteness from practical concerns, which keeps us from immersion in the material world. So the Southerners who belonged to the tradition thought they saw in the leveling spirit of the North, in its criteria of utility, in its plebian distrust of forms, in its spirit of irreverence—and all of these must be mentioned with apologies to Northern people whom they do not characterize—a kind of barbarian destructiveness, not willed perhaps, but certain in its effect.

There is a point of view from which the sentiments and formalities of civilization will appear absurd, and many Americans, especially those close to the frontier, have fancied a virtue in taking it. But a frontier is by definition not civilization, and the unbought grace of life thrives in a different environment. The destruction of sentiment leaves us not animals, who have their own nobility, but ruined men. Considerable importance must therefore be attached to the Southern fondness for pleasing illusions.

The Southern mind has been sufficiently conscious to reorganize subversive influences, by which I mean anything tending to undermine that moral or "sentimental" order constituting civilization. We can explain thus its reaction to French rationalism, and in a more limited field to German "higher criticism."

The instance of Jefferson has led to a supposition that French radicalism found hospitality in the South. To the extent that it was linked with the cause of American independence, this was true; but when that cause had been won, and the South began to consider its necessities and the more permanent arrangements of peace, libertarian and equalitarian doctrines languished. It has consistently exhibited a distrust of social programs initiated on the basis of hypothesis. One could go further and say that the South has a deep suspicion of all theory, perhaps of intellect. It has always been on the side of blood and soil, of instinct, of vitalism. Something in its climate, in its social life predisposes it to feel that "gray is all theory, and green is life's golden tree."

To say that the South had a *rationale* of society is not to say that it favored what has come to be known as "rational planning." On the contrary, it has held that society, though of intelligible structure, is a product of organic growth, and that a tested *modus vivendi* is to be preferred to the most attractive experiment. George Fitzhugh expressed the belief in an epigram when he wrote, "Philosophy will blow up any government that is founded on it." And today, when the South pleads to be allowed "to work out its own problems in its own way," it more often than not has no plans for working them out. Its "way" is not to work them out, but to let some mechanism of adjustment achieve a balance. It is this which has clashed with the North's impulse to toil, "to help the world go around," to have a rational accounting of everything. Undoubtedly it has relation to the attitude of piety, which would respect the course of things and frowns on a busy human interference with what nature seems to have planned or providence ordained.

The German mentality was only a little less suspect than the French, and "German neologism," as it was termed, was viewed as the most dangerous solvent of religion. Learned investigations into the historicity of a religion are not, as time has proved, a means of encouraging reverence for that religion. A religion may be indifferent both to history and to reality of the plebeian sort, which is the reality of correspondence to the visible world. Its origin may embrace things fabulous, and its doctrines may incorporate paradoxes. It would be easy to show, indeed, that the power of Christianity over long periods and in varying intellectual climates lies in its candid acceptance of the paradoxes of existence. This means that its appeal will be to the moral imagination and its endorsement through our experience of life. Literalism is the materialism of religion, and this materialism too, except in the crudest exhibitions of Fundamentalism, the South has shunned.

At the same time it looked with disfavor upon New England's voyages into seas of Transcendentalism and Unitarianism. And if it is asked which course has best conserved religion as an active principle in life, we must admit that here again the South chose right. It viewed these as England viewed continental skepticism, and the fact that modern decadence, political, social, and moral, began in continental Europe, indicates where the instinct of survival lay. Despite sins which are as scarlet, the South has remained a Christian country in that it has persisted in describing the relationship of man to the universe in religious symbols.

Naturally the South did not see these trends as we can see them today, but I think that Southern churchmen of the educated group came close to seeing them. These men were intensely conservative; therefore they had a point of view. In times of profound revolutionary change, it is not the liberals, the "progressives," the social democrats who discern what is at issue, as I shall invoke Leon Trotsky to witness. It is the men of the old order who see most clearly the implications of the new. The failure of values, the dissolution of traditional bonds, the fragmentation of life, which were but as signs then, were nevertheless pointed out. No full diagnosis of the disorder was made, and probably there was none capable of making it. A growing sense for the last fifty years that civilization is at a crossroads, deepened by collapses of astounding violence and consequence, has inspired a greater study of the condition of man.

WILLMOORE KENDALL

Equality and the American Political Tradition

"Every Frenchman," Charles de Gaulle has written somewhere, "wants a special privilege or two; that is how he expresses his passion for Equality." "Every American," I suppose an equally cynical observer here in the United States might say, "wants a right or two that he is by no means willing to concede to everybody else; that is how the American expresses *his* passion for Equality." The tacit premise in each case—that of the Frenchman who seeks special privileges, that of the American who denies to others rights that he claims for himself—must go something like this:

From Willmoore Kendall, *Willmoore Kendall Contra Mundum*, edited by Nellie D. Kendall(New Rochelle, N.Y.: Arlington House, 1971). Copyright © 1971 by Arlington House. Reprinted by permission of Nellie Kendall.

The Frenchman, the American, has an official "commitment" to equality that he "handles" by paying it lip service but refusing to live up to it; or, if you like, Both the Frenchman and the American publicly profess equality as a political ideal, but violate that ideal in the detail of their day-to-day living. Now, in the case of the Frenchman, at least, the official commitment, or public profession, is clear enough; the French Revolution did indeed do its mischief under the slogan "Liberty, Equality, Fraternity," and, throughout French history, the slogan has been conspicuously displayed in French public places, vociferously iterated in French political discourse. If the Frenchman doesn't live up to the slogan, including its middle term, "Equality," he is indeed the man of divided counsels, the schizoid of the de Gaulle epigram; we are entitled to think poorly of him. But what about the American? Is the epigram correct in suggesting that the American who wants the exercise of a couple of rights that he "brazenly" denies to others also has a public commitment to equality? Is he also refusing to live up to a political ideal to which he nevertheless pays lip service, and to which his forefathers have paid lip service before him? Is he also schizoid? I think the prevailing scholarly answer to these questions is, Yes, he has the same official commitment to equality as the Frenchman and, no less than the Frenchman, knows perfectly well that he does. Ask for proof that this is true, and quick as a flash you will be told about the findings of the team that produced Gunnar Myrdal's *American Dilemma.* The team, in order to get on with their study of race relations in the United States (but, of course, especially in the South), wanted to know not merely, How do Americans actually behave in race relations? They wanted to know also, How do Americans think—or say they think— they ought to behave? To this end they put to their respondents in effect the question, What political deals do you as an American believe in? And wherever they turned, even in the benighted South, they were told (quite usefully, it happens, for the purpose in hand), We believe in Liberty and Equality; the American political Creed is Liberty and Equality. Nor, since Myrdal published his book, do I recall any piece of writing in which that finding has been called into question. The American, we are constantly told, does have a public commitment to equality that—purely aside from the fact that he ought to anyway—he ought to live up to because it *is* his public commitment. And if he doesn't live up to it, he is in the same boat with the Frenchman; we are entitled to think poorly of him. (As, if we are Liberal, we certainly will.)

The Myrdal finding has, for the rest, a certain surface plausibility. The Declaration of Independence, we are reminded, does, indeed, say, as plain as the nose on your face, "All men are created equal," and does indeed sound as if it meant something should be done about it. We Americans, we are reminded, did indeed fight *our* Revolution under the Declaration, so that equality, here as in France, is indeed a slogan over which our hearts go—or ought to go—pit-a-pat. Never mind that you don't see it about quite as much as in France. Never mind, even, that the major egalitarian movement of our time in America, the Civil Rights movement, pins to its banners the slogan "Freedom," *not* "Equality." Never mind, either, that the word order in the Myrdal finding is suspiciously French—"Liberty, Equality," not, as in the Declaration of Independence, "Equality, Liberty." Never mind anything. Both the Declaration of Independence and Gunnar Myrdal say we are committed to equality as a political goal, so committed we are.

Now, as will have been guessed already, I have—or have begun to have—some doubts about all that, and I propose to ventilate those doubts in this article. Craving the reader's forbearance, however, I am going to come at them in a rather roundabout way and begin my argument with a thesis, or statement, that may seem rather far afield, namely, a thesis or statement about the United States Supreme Court.

There is shaping up amongst us—amongst Us the people of the United States—a series of *problems* relating to the *powers* of the Supreme Court. (I was tempted to write, "An *issue* concerning the powers of the Supreme Court," but I am glad I didn't, since I believe the best hope for all of us is that the problems I speak of shan't ever turn into an issue, properly speaking, with lines sharply drawn, positions deeply entrenched, compromise or temporizing solutions irrevocably renounced; the problems I write of have *not* yet become an issue, and I celebrate the fact.) I repeat: There are problems shaping up amongst us about the powers of the Supreme Court, and these problems are sufficiently urgent to enable us to say: Every educated American ought to know what those problems are, how far they have already developed as problems, and what we can conclude, in a brief article like this one, as to their meaning as problems. It is, let me say, a complicated business, which I as a specialist can only try to make as simple as possible; and it will perhaps help if I begin by making about them a few observations that, taken one by one, can be kept reasonably free of complexities and technicalities.

First, the problems that are now shaping up about the powers of the Supreme Court are, as bones of contention, *new* problems. Which is to say, we must not confuse them with, for example, the problem about the powers of the Supreme Court that arose under the New Deal. Then the issue—and it *was* an issue—had to do with the traditional power of the Supreme Court to take in its hand an enactment of the Congress, scrutinize it, and, if the learned justices saw fit, declare it null and void, or unconstitutional. The problems now shaping up, we must be clear, have nothing to do with that issue; there is, at the moment, no clash between the Supreme Court and Congress, at least not overtly. And, to put it the other way around, the age of the New Deal, the age of the late Franklin Delano Roosevelt, knew nothing of the problems, the problems relating to the powers of the Supreme Court, that are now shaping up; and we must, I repeat, be clear about that, lest the problems slip through our fingers.

Second, the problems I speak of are not—not yet, anyhow—of such character as to make of the Supreme Court itself an issue (though Liberals sometimes try to state the problems in a way that *would* make it an issue). Nothing has happened up to now that is likely to put Conservatives into the business of trying to abolish the Supreme Court, or of trying to revise its role in the American constitutional system. It is not, in short, that we have entered upon a period when the Conservatives are anti-Supreme Court, the Liberals pro-Supreme Court, and may the best man win. To put it that way is to misunderstand what the fight is really over.

Third, the problems—the problems that are "up," or at least shaping up, as contrasted with the potential problems, the ones that may begin to shape up later—have to do (this much, happily, *is* simple) with a single clause in the Fourteenth Amendment to the Constitution of the United States, namely, the clause concerning the equal protection of the laws—and that clause's equally famous sister, the "due process clause," which frequently comes up also, but comes up merely as the more convenient formula, as the lawyers see it, for achieving the objectives of the equal protection clause. Or, to make it just a little more complicated, the problems have to do with the relation of those two clauses to the Tenth Amendment to the Constitution of the United States. And here, I *must* go into a little history—about the Tenth Amendment, the Fourteenth Amendment, *and,* most particularly, the *idea* of equality (which is the key word in the whole business) in the American political tradition.

The roots of the American political tradition—so we are told, anyhow, by the official custodians of our national lore—lie in two great documents, the Declaration of Independence and the Philadelphia Constitution. The two documents were, as you know, written within a few brief—brief, but of course, crowded—years of one another, and by representatives of one and the same people, that is, of We (or, watching our grammar, Us) the people of the United States; and, that being the case, we have always liked to tell ourselves, We the people of the United States, that the two documents say more or less the same sort of thing—as, having been written so close together by *our* representatives, why shouldn't they? And yet—it gives me no pleasure to point it out—and yet, the most casual look at the two documents reveals that on one important point they do not say the same thing at all, or, if you like, that on one important point one of the two documents is eloquent and emphatic, the other, if I may put it so, tight-lipped and uncommunicative. Concretely, the Declaration of Independence puts forth, as one of the truths we the people hold as "self-evident," the proposition: All men are created equal.

It puts that proposition forward, indeed, as the very *first* of the truths we hold, and seems, therefore, to put it forward as *the* truth, along with the truth about certain natural rights, that is to be planted at the very heart of the American political experience. Not, I hasten to add, that anyone appears to have been very clear as to what it *meant* to declare all men created equal; no doubt the words, even at the moment they were uttered, meant different things to different persons, even to different persons among those immediately concerned. To some the words no doubt meant merely that all men were created equal in the eyes of God. To some they no doubt meant merely that all men were created with an equal claim to justice under the existing law. For some they no doubt expressed the hope, though merely the hope, that the republic about to be formed would be that land, the first land of all lands ever and anywhere, in which men would *become* equal, that is, achieve the equality of which humble and disadvantaged men have often dreamt dreams that other men have called Utopian. To some the words no doubt meant merely the hope that America would be a land in which men would be anyhow more equal than elsewhere—a land in which *in*equalities among men would be less glaring, less intimately related to what we fashionably call the accident of birth, less likely to be handed down to, say, the third and fourth generations. To some the words no doubt meant the hope that the new republic would be one in which men—well, white men, and male men only, not female men, for no one had yet thought of going in for that sort of thing—would cast equal votes in at least some elections for public office. To some they *may* have meant—that is all I can say because I find no evidence of it—the hope that America would be a land in which government, political authority, would take steps to *make* men equal—we cannot exclude the possibility, and must mention it because that is what the words have come, in the fullness of time, to mean to some amongst us, some even of the most learned amongst us.

But whatever the words may have meant to whomever, there are two things we may assert with some finality: first, that the Framers of the Philadelphia Constitution, by contrast with the Declaration, did not so much as mention the topic of equality in the new instrument of government—not even in the Preamble, where, remember, they pause to list the purposes (a more perfect union, the blessings of liberty, justice, etc.) for which We the people ordain and establish the Constitution, and where, if nowhere else, one might have expected them to recall that first proposition of the Declaration under which and for which, remember, they had just fought a great war; and second, that Publius, when he came to write the *Federalist*—which, we are told, is also one of the documents in which the American political tradition is rooted—has a way, if I may put it so, of clamming up whenever (as does sometimes happen) the topic of equality heaves into sight. And perhaps we can add, third, that when Madison, during the First Session of Congress, penned the Bill of Rights, he also failed to mention equality, and this despite the fact that the model he certainly had before him—the Virginia Declaration of Rights—begins with at least a courtly *bow* to equality. Let us, if you like, be cautious, and not make too much of all this; the fact stands that the only place you can go, among our so-called basic documents, to find equality placed high among the "values" of Us, the people of the United States, is the Declaration of Independence. Nor is it, I think, quite good enough to say: The Constitution, the Federalist, the Bill of Rights *naturally* did not have to say anything about equality; it was already there, as part of our political Credo, in the Declaration. Our Founding Fathers were *not,* I insist, all *that* reluctant to say things a second time. We can, rather, hardly avoid the conclusion that the Constitution, the Federalist, and the Bill of Rights conspicuously *avoid* any commitment on the point of equality—beyond, of course, the tacit commitment to the equal right of all men, under the existing laws, to equal and just treatment in the courts of law. But note that I say "under the *existing* laws." There is in the three post-Declaration documents no suggestion, as maybe there is maybe there isn't in the Declaration of Independence, that the existing laws ought to be made over, so to speak, in the *image* of equality. That idea, if it was ever there at all, promptly disappears after the Declaration of Independence, and does not appear again, in the American political tradition, until, to say the least, a much later date—perhaps, but only perhaps, in the Fourteenth Amendment (which was, as we know, adopted soon after the Civil War); I think not until certain Supreme Court cases that are the source of the problems I spoke of at the beginning, and that, I repeat, I believe, or fear, to be shaping up.

Now: what about the Fourteenth Amendment? Did it bring the promise of equality—that *promise* of equality for the citizens of our Republic that some people see in the Declaration of Independence—did the Fourteenth Amendment bring the promise of equality back within the central meaning of our political experience? Certainly it restored the *word* "equal" to our political vocabulary; certainly it guarantees to all, and apparently in as plain language as anyone could ask for, the "equal" protection of the laws. But here, as so often happens in our constitutional law, the plain language, upon examination, proves not to be plain at all, and for a reason I have already anticipated, namely: The equal protection clause of the Fourteenth Amendment does not tell us, will never tell us no matter how hard we squeeze it, which of *two* things it actually means, and we must be very clear as to what those two things are. It might mean *first,* as the reader is already prepared to hear me say, that all are to have the equal protection of the *existing* laws, which *existing* laws may involve any amount you like of *in*equality, of *un*equal treatment, of *un*equal rights and privileges. Or it might mean *second* that, if I may put it so (I think no one ever has before), all are entitled to laws that in fact *give* equal protection to each. Now, if it means the first of these things, then all it calls for is the impartial enforcement of existing laws—existing laws, we must add, however unjust or inequitable those laws may be. If it means the second, it can of course become a standard—nay, *the* standard—by which existing laws may be tested and—where they fail to meet the test—set aside. In the first case, the laws would continue, after the Fourteenth Amendment as before, to be made—equal or unequal, equitable or inequitable, just or unjust—exclusively by the Congress and by the state legislatures, according to *their* lights. A man might, armed with the Fourteenth Amendment, go into the courts and demand the protection to which the existing laws, as made by Congress and the State legislatures, entitle him. But he could *never* go into the courts and say: "I demand that this law be set aside, be declared unconstitutional, because it is the kind of law that in and of itself gives unequal protection to different citizens." In the second case—that is, if the Fourteenth Amendment means that all are entitled to laws that in fact *give* equal protection to each—Congress and the State legislatures no longer have the last word about the existing laws; if those laws fail to meet the test of equal protection, then the courts are entitled to strike them down, and to keep on striking them down until we have laws that, in the courts' view, do give equal protection. In the first case—that is, if the Fourteenth Amendment merely guarantees the equal protection of the existing laws—the promise of equality in the Declaration of Independence remains just where it was before the Fourteenth Amendment was adopted, which is to say, pretty much nowhere among our public commitments. In the second case—that is, if the Fourteenth Amendment guarantees laws that will in fact provide equal protection— the equal protection clause becomes, as of the moment of its adoption, a summons to a legal revolution—and, necessarily, a legal revolution that must ultimately be presided over by the Supreme Court. So I can now repeat my question in a new and, I think, more manageable form: Does the Fourteenth Amendment call for the equal protection of existing laws? Or does it call for revising existing laws until they confer equal protection? And if I have dwelt long and teacherishly over the point, it is for a very good reason, namely: Until one grasps these two possible meanings of the Fourteenth Amendment, one cannot hope to understand the problems that are shaping up in the United States about the Supreme Court—about, most particularly, the prayer decisions, and about so-called reapportionment.

Now, perhaps my one claim to uniqueness among students of the Fourteenth Amendment is that I do not believe the issue as to which of the two meanings is the "correct" one will ever be settled by appeal to the document itself. A pretty good case, to be sure, can be made out for each, but also neither case is such that it is likely to satisfy the proponents of the other. When the Supreme Court points to the plain language of the Fourteenth Amendment and says, The Mississippi ruling that keeps James Meredith from enrolling at Ole Miss denies James Meredith the equal protection of the laws, and is therefore unconstitutional because it violates the Fourteenth Amendment, it does have on its side—well, the plain language of the Fourteenth Amendment, which appears to guarantee to James Meredith *the* equal protection of the laws. And when Governor Ross Barnett answers that the Supreme Court is misinterpreting the Fourteenth Amendment, he also has some things to point to. He can, for instance, point to the fact—an incontestable fact by the way—that the very session of Congress that enacted the Fourteenth Amendment established a segregated school in the District of Columbia—which is to say: If the Fourteenth Amendment has the meaning the Supreme Court says it has, so that it prohibits segregated schools, the authors of the Amendment didn't know that that was what it meant, which is surprising to say the least. Governor Barnett can also point to the speeches made by the state legislators in the process of ratifying the Fourteenth Amendment. Here, also, we find no evidence that the men who added the Fourteenth Amendment to our constitutional law contemplated a legal revolution presided over by the Supreme Court. And Governor Barnett can, finally, point to the fact—again an incontestable fact—that the Supreme Court itself, for decades and decades after the Fourteenth Amendment went into effect, leaned almost entirely toward the view that it guaranteed only the equal protection of existing laws—which is to say, Governor Barnett has behind him the Supreme Court's own long-pull tradition. But don't—because I state his points vigorously—understand me to be saying that Governor Barnett wins the argument. *My* point is that the argument, when conducted in those terms—and who ever heard of it being conducted in any other terms?—is inconclusive, and always will be. We shall never—never, never—be able to answer the question, What is the *true, intended* meaning of the Fourteenth Amendment? to everybody's satisfaction.

Let me round out that picture—that picture of the background of the problems that are shaping up—by bringing into it the Tenth Amendment as well—the Tenth Amendment, and the implicit principle of the Philadelphia Constitution that the Tenth Amendment merely restates. The Philadelphia Constitution, which, as we all know, was formed by the *representatives* of the original thirteen states—the Philadelphia Constitution assigned certain powers and functions of government to a newly created *federal* government (the conduct of foreign affairs, for example, the national defense, the regulation of interstate commerce, etc.); but by clear implication it left all other powers and functions of government precisely where they had been before the Philadelphia Constitution was adopted, that is, with the states themselves. One of these powers, pretty clearly, one certainly reserved to the states, was the control of the suffrage, the making of decisions as to who in the United States may vote. Another such power, again pretty clearly, was the control of education—that is, the making of decisions about our public schools: what kind of education they are to provide, what persons shall attend what schools, etc. Still another such power, another of those powers reserved to the states, was the whole business of making decisions about the relation between church and state—or, as I like to put it, between religion and politics: whether to have an established religion, whether to bring religion into the public schools or keep it out of the public schools, etc. Yet another such power, a power clearly reserved to the states, was the control of districting—the drawing of the lines that form the districts in which Congressmen, and State Senators, and State representatives, are elected—the power to decide, therefore, (to use the fashionable jargon) whether our legislatures, national and state, are to be "rural-dominated," or "urban-dominated," or so devised as to give both country-folk and city-folk a fair shake. Let's tick them off again—the four powers we have mentioned that were clearly reserved to the states, since they are part and parcel of our business here: the control of the suffrage, the control of education, the handling of problems of Church and State, and the control of legislative districts. At least these four powers, according to the Philadelphia Constitution, were to be *monopolies* of the states and their governments; at least these four things the state governments were to go ahead and run just as they would have had there been no federal government; at least these four things the new federal government was to keep its hand *off* of; at least these four things, therefore, the Supreme Court was to keep *its* hands off of, because the Supreme Court is an agency of the federal government, and what the federal government cannot touch the Supreme Court presumably cannot touch. That, if I may put it so, was the original *deal* between the states and the federal government; nothing, I hasten to add, sacred about it, nothing that couldn't be revised as time went on, but still, the original deal, as written into the Philadelphia Constitution, and as clearly understood on all sides.

Now, the Tenth Amendment, which as I have intimated we have *got* to bring into our picture, merely hammers down that original deal: Some powers and functions, it says in effect, are entrusted to the federal government; all remaining powers, including, of course, those four we have mentioned, are reserved to the states, that is, to the state governments, and to the people of the states, who presumably control the state governments just as We the people of the United States control the federal government. It says in effect: The deal's a deal: For some purposes we are going to be a nation, and have uniform laws and regulations all over the country; for other purposes we are going to remain separate states— thirteen of them, or fifteen of them, or forty-four or forty-eight or fifty— and have different laws and regulations within these separate states. The deal's a deal, the Tenth Amendment says in effect, and can only be revised by the same solemn process by which it, the deal, came into effect. The deal's a deal, and can only be revised by Us, the people of the United States—which means, under the Philadelphia Constitution: The deal can be revised only by constitutional amendment, or, failing that, by congressional action under the "necessary and proper" clause. Powers can indeed, it says in effect, be moved across the line—powers now exercised by the states can indeed be assigned to the federal government—but only by a solemn act of Us the people of the United States acting through those instruments of government that are most intimately ours.

Now, put all that, all I have just said about the Tenth Amendment, put all that together with what I said above about the Fourteenth Amendment—put the two together and you will see where we have to come out: If the equal protection clause of the Fourteenth Amendment means merely that all are entitled to the impartial application of existing laws, then the original deal between states and federal government is still on; since there has been no constitutional amendment revising the deal, then the suffrage, education, religion, legislative districting all remain on the side of the line that belongs to the states. But if the equal protection and due process clauses of the Fourteenth Amendment mean that the laws must be revised and reinterpreted so as to in fact *give* equal protection to all, then the deal is off. If the two clauses mean that the laws must *give* equal protection to all, then any state enactment, or policy, or practice, that discriminates in favor of some persons and so against other persons, becomes the business of the Supreme Court—and so the business of the federal government. The Tenth Amendment line—between powers entrusted to the federal government and powers reserved to the states— loses all of its meaning as a line. Or, to put the matter in its most dramatic terms: If the Fourteenth Amendment means that the laws must give equal protection to all, then the Fourteenth Amendment *repeals* the Tenth Amendment. For the Tenth Amendment either gives equal protection or doesn't give equal protection, and if it does not give equal protection, then, according to the Fourteenth Amendment, it is, to that extent, void. And that consequence may properly be recognized, under our constitutional system, by the United States Supreme Court. And we are at last in position to talk business about the problems I speak of as shaping up as really major problems—in particular, civil liberties, desegregation, and over-representation—and to fix attention on and explain what is making them major problems, namely, that the American Conservatives are resisting Supreme Court innovations under all three headings. The problems are, I am saying, major problems because the Conservatives are dragging their feet in all three areas, and because the Liberals are unwilling to acquiesce in their doing so.

The Conservatives *do* drag their feet—let the Liberals take note that I concede the point. When a Conservative reads in his newspaper that nearly 90 percent of the Southern schools are still segregated, and that the rate at which Southern schools are being desegregated is tapering off, he does not—unlike the Liberal—feel moved to condemnation of the White Southerners for their allegedly wicked ways. When the Conservative learns, once again, that hundreds of thousands of Southern Negroes are denied the vote, he feels no stirring in his heart to go teach those Southerners a lesson about democracy. When the Conservative finds himself up against proof that the kids in the public schools of Middletown, Connecticut—which is 90 percent Catholic—recite "Hail Marys" in the classrooms and even in the corridors, he does *not* feel that liberty has died in America—any more than he feels that liberty has died in America when he learns that the public schools of the State of California are conducted just as they would be if California were populated exclusively by atheists and agnostics. And when the Liberal hammers the Conservative over the head with the awful fact that the good folk of New Haven and Hartford—again I speak of Connecticut, because I have lived there most of the time for many years—do not have the voice in the state legislature to which their numbers might seem to entitle them—when the Liberal hammers the Conservative over the head with that awful fact, I say, he feels no temptation to order a couple of divisions of the U.S. Army to Connecticut, to restore its republican form of government. I repeat: I concede the point that the Conservatives drag their feet on what are fashionably called civil liberties, equal representation, desegregation. I shall, indeed, go further and concede another point, namely, the Conservative will not feel differently about these matters, *basically* at least will not feel differently about them, when he learns that a federal court has ordered the public schools of Middletown to *stop* reciting "Hail Marys," and that the court order is being *defied.* Not, of course, that he likes a situation where court orders are being defied; he does not. But he sees more things to be involved than just a court order. And he values some of those things equally with the sanctity of court orders.

Finally—though this is a point I make rather than concede—Conservatives are likely to continue to drag their feet on these matters for a long time off in the future. The Liberal may not like that. He may think it shocking. He may—I often think he does—hate the Conservative for it. But he had best get it through his head that those are the facts of life, and he had better, for the sake of his ulcers, get ready to live with them for quite a while. For if he doesn't, he simply doesn't understand American politics in their present phase, and, worse still, doesn't understand the *main* fact about even himself, namely, he is no Joshua. Joshua commanded the sun and the stars to stand still and they obeyed him. But when that would-be Joshua the American Liberal commands the sun and stars to stand still, they do not obey tomorrow or the next day. The Liberal's struggle for what he calls civil liberties, if he ever wins it, is going to be won in only one way, which is by *persuasion*—that is, by persuading the Conservatives, who are I believe the overwhelming majority of Us the people of the United States, over to his point of view. Not by court orders. Not by ordering federal troops to Little Rock, or Oxford, or Birmingham. But by *convincing* the Conservatives. And that, let me assure him, is going to take some doing.

Why is it going to take some doing? Well, let me, by way of summary, go back over the political science of the matter as I have laid it out.

All the current hullaballoo about civil liberties, about desegregation, about redistricting on a one-man-one-vote basis, is, I am saying, the result of one thing, namely, the Supreme Court decided, a few years ago, to revise its own traditional interpretation of the Fourteenth Amendment. From now on, it said in effect, the Fourteenth Amendment is going to require not equal protection under existing laws, but the revision of existing laws so that they will give equal protection. And the effect of that change of mind and heart on the part of the Supreme Court was, quite simply, this: It put the Supreme Court into the business of upsetting the deal—the deal between the federal government and the states—written into the Philadelphia Constitution and the Tenth Amendment. The Conservative, however—and my hope for this article is that it will help to make him better understood—the Conservative was brought up to believe that that deal can be altered only by Us the people acting through the amendment process of the Philadelphia Constitution, or, in a pinch, by a consensus of Us the people acting through Congress under the necessary and proper clause. He *still* regards the suffrage, the relations between Church and State, the drawing of lines for legislative districts, education—he *still* regards these things as the business exclusively of the states, as not, therefore, the business of the federal government, and not, therefore, the business of the Supreme Court. He still regards the equal protection and due process clauses of the Fourteenth Amendment as guarantees merely of impartial enforcement of existing laws. He still does not want to help silence "Hail Marys" in the State of Connecticut, because he still does not want Connecticut to be interfering in the affairs of *his* state. That is the Conservative state of mind—the American political tradition—with regard to the issues involved in recent Supreme Court innovations. And I repeat to the Liberals: Do not underestimate the Conservative politically. There is a lot of him, must be a lot of him because he is pretty certainly the overwhelming majority of the American people. And what I referred to as the problems that are shaping up I can now nail down as follows. About the future—the future of civil liberties, of desegregation, etc.—there are as I see it two possibilities: either the Liberals—and I make no distinction, for this purpose, between the Liberals and the Supreme Court—either the Liberals pull in their horns and decide to do it the hard way, that is, by persuading Us the American people over to their point of view; or, second, the Liberals will continue their present strategy, which is to attempt—from a mere minority position in American politics—to impose the new interpretation by sheer fiat of the Supreme Court. Either first, I say, the Liberals and the Supreme Court pull in their horns and let us get back to deciding these matters by public debate, or, second, we face a future of more Oxfords, more prayer decisions, more interference by the Supreme Court with the electoral and districting practices of the states—with more hard feelings, more use of federal troops against American citizens, more attempts to bring about social revolution by court order. Either the one or the other. And I, as a Conservative, hope for the first—the Supreme Court pulling in its horns—but fear, because of the fanaticism of the contemporary Liberal, the second.

HARRY V. JAFFA

Equality as a Conservative Principle

> So whatever you wish that men would do to you, do so to them; for this is the law and the prophets.
>
> —JESUS

> As I would not be a *slave,* so I would not be a *master.* This expresses my idea of democracy. Whatever differs from this, to the extent of the difference, is no democracy.
>
> —ABRAHAM LINCOLN

That Conservatism should search for its meaning implies of course that Conservatism does not have the meaning for which it is searching. This might appear paradoxical, since a Conservative is supposed to have

From Harry V. Jaffa, *How to Think About the American Revolution* (Durham, N.C.: Carolina Academic Press, 1978), pp. 13–23, 32–48. Reprinted by permission of Carolina Academic Press. This essay was originally presented at a panel, "Conservatism's Search for Meaning," sponsored by the American Political Science Assocation.

something definite to conserve. Unfriendly critics sometimes suggest that what we Conservatives conserve, or wish to conserve, is money. But since many of us, like Socrates, live in thousandfold poverty, this is manifestly untrue. Yet our plight might be said to resemble that of a man with a great hoard of gold or diamonds. Suppose such a man suddenly awoke to find that his treasure was no longer precious, and that it held no more meaning for the rest of the world than sand or pebbles. How strange the world would look to that man! How strange that man would look to the world, vainly clinging to his pile of rubbish.

In today's political vocabulary, Conservatism is contrasted with Liberalism and Radicalism. In this strange world, however, I cannot imagine Liberalism or Radicalism searching for meaning. Liberalism and Radicalism are confident of their meaning, and the world is confident of their confidence. Yet once upon a time, a Liberal was thought to be more diffident. He was someone who recognized the fallibility of human reason and its susceptibility to the power of the passions. He tended therefore to be tolerant of human differences. A liberal regime was one in which such differences were in a sense institutionalized. James Madison's extended republic embracing a multiplicity of factions, in which no faction might become a majority or impose its will upon a majority, is the classic instance in the modern world of such a regime. But the New Liberal is committed to policies which tend not to recognize the propriety of differences. Consider the rigidity of such slogans as "one man, one vote," "racial balance," "affirmative action," "guaranteed income," "war on poverty," "generation of peace." All these imply a degree of certainty as to what is beneficial, which makes those who doubt appear to be obscurantists or obstructionists, standing in the way of welfare either out of stupidity or out of a vested interest in ill fare.

The only significant differences I can see between today's Liberals and today's Radicals concern means rather than ends. How often during the "troubles" of the late 1960s did we hear the Liberals deplore the Radicals' violence, telling them that they should "work within the system"? How often did we hear these same Liberals praise the Radicals for their "idealism," asking only that they learn patience? But the Radicals made a great deal more sense. If their ideals were so praiseworthy, then a system which obstructed their fulfillment was blameworthy. And why work within a blameworthy system for praiseworthy ends?

Liberalism and Radicalism both reject the wisdom of the past, as enshrined in the institutions of the past, or in the morality of the past. They deny legitimacy to laws, governments, or ways of life which accept the ancient evils of mankind, such as poverty, inequality, and war, as necessary—and therefore as permanent—attributes of the human condition. Political excellence can no longer be measured by the degree to which it ameliorates such evils. The only acceptable goal is their abolition. Liberalism and Radicalism look forward to a state of things in which the means of life, and of the good life, are available to all. They must be available in such a way that the full development of each individual—which is how the good life is defined—is not merely compatible with, but is necessary to, the full development of all. Competition between individuals, classes, races, and nations must come to an end. Competition itself is seen as the root of the evils mankind must escape. The good society must be characterized only by cooperation and harmony. The Old Liberalism saw life as a race, in which justice demanded for everyone only a fair or equal chance in the competition. But the New Liberalism sees the race itself as wrong. In every race there can be but one winner, and there must be many losers. Thus the Old Liberalism preserved the inequality of the Few over and against the Many. It demanded the removal of artificial or merely conventional inequalities. But it recognized and demanded the fullest scope for natural inequalities. But the New Liberalism denies natural no less than conventional inequalities. In the Heaven of the New Liberalism, as in that of the Old Theology, all will be rewarded equally. The achievement of the good society is itself the only victory. But this victory is not to be one of man over man, but of mankind over the scourges of mankind. No one in it will taste the bitterness of defeat. No one need say, "I am a loser, but I have no right to complain. I had a fair chance." The joys of victory will belong to all. Unlike the treasures of the past, the goods of the future will be possessed by all. They will not be diminished or divided by being common. On the contrary, they will for that very reason increase and intensify. No one will be a miser—or a Conservative.

I have intimated that what is today called Conservatism—the New Conservatism—may in fact be the Old Liberalism. Indeed, it may be the Old Radicalism as well. Leo Strauss used to delight in pointing out that the most conservative or even reactionary organization in the United States was called the Daughters of the American Revolution. Certainly, if American Conservatism has any core of consistency and purpose, it is derived from the American Founding. The uncertainty as to the meaning of American Conservatism is, as we shall see, an uncertainty as to the meaning of the American Founding. But this uncertainty does not arise from any doubt as to the status of the Revolution. So far as I know, there has never been any Benedict Arnold Society of American Patriotism. Nor do American Conservatives meet, either openly or secretly, to toast "the King (or Queen) across the water." The status of feudalism and monarchy are for American Conservatives exactly what they are for American Liberals or Radicals. Perhaps the best description of the *ancien regime* from the American point of view is still that of Mark Twain in *A Connecticut Yankee in King Arthur's Court.*

American Conservatism is then rooted in a Founding which is, in turn, rooted in revolution. Moreover, the American Revolution represented the most radical break with tradition—with the tradition of Europe's feudal past—that the world had seen. It is true that the American revolutionaries saw some precedent for their actions in the Whig Revolution of 1689. But that revolution at least maintained the fiction of a continued and continuous legality. The British Constitution that resulted from the earlier revolution may have had some republican elements. But the American constitutions—state and federal—that resulted from the later revolution had *no* monarchical or aristocratic elements. They were not merely radically republican, but were radically republican in a democratic sense.[1] The sovereignty of the people has never been challenged within the American regime, by Conservatives any more than by Liberals or Radicals.

The regime of the Founders was wholly devoted to what they understood as civil and religious liberty and was in that sense a liberal regime. But the Founders understood themselves to be revolutionaries, and to celebrate the American Founding is therefore to celebrate revolution. However mild or moderate the American Revolution may now appear, as compared with subsequent revolutions in France, Russia, China, Cuba, or elsewhere, it nonetheless embodied the greatest attempt at innovation that human history had recorded. It remains the most radical attempt to establish a regime of liberty that the world has yet seen.

What were the principles of the American Revolution? What are the roots of the American Founding? One would think that after nearly two hundred years this question could be easily answered. Never did men take more pains to justify what they were doing at every step of the way than did the patriots of the Revolution. Never was the fashioning of a plan of government better documented than that hammered out in Philadelphia in the summer of 1787. Never was such a plan more fully debated before adoption than that which came before the several ratifying conventions. Never was an actual regime, as distinct from a hypothetical one, so enshrined in theoretical reasoning as was the constitution of 1787 in the *Federalist Papers.* And yet the matter is unresolved.

Our perplexity that this should be so is less surprising when we reflect that the course of American history for more than "four score and seven years" was one of deep-seated controversy, culminating in one of the bitterest wars of modern times. Until the resort to arms, these conflicts almost always took the form of debates as to the meaning of the Founding. And the Founding documents, and their principal glosses, were invariably cited on both sides in these debates. In more respects than one, American history and Jewish history resembled each other. Mid-century British liberals, like their American counterparts, were also divided. In 1861 Lord Acton wrote an essay entitled "Political Causes of the American Revolution,"[2] in which he expressed no doubt that the Confederacy was fighting for the same principles of independence for which Washington had fought. But Lord Acton's countryman, John Stuart Mill, in another essay written shortly afterwards,[3] was just as sure that Lincoln's government was fighting to preserve these same principles. That the contestants appealed to the same political dogmas—even as they read the same Bible and prayed to the same God—only intensified the struggle. As sectarians of the same faith, they fought each other as only those fight who see their enemies as heretics.

American Conservatism today is still divided, not surprisingly, along lines which have divided Americans since before the Civil War. Sir Winston Churchill once said that the American Civil War was the last great war fought between gentlemen. Certainly Churchill had in mind the patriotism and the gallantry of men like Lee, Jackson, and Davis on the Confederate side, and Lincoln, Grant, and Sherman on the side of the Union. But I think he also had in mind the dignity of the principles that both sides held, and the tragedy inherent in the possibility that these same principles should seem to speak differently to men of equal integrity and devotion.

But gentlemanship, like patriotism, is not enough. Not Jefferson Davis or, for that matter, John C. Calhoun—surely one of the most intelligent men who ever lived—saw as deeply into the meaning of the American principles as Abraham Lincoln. And so—to borrow a phrase from the late Willmoore Kendall—let us have no foolishness about both sides being equally right. That the South lost the war on the battlefield does not in the least mean that it lost the argument. From Alexander Stephens to Willmoore Kendall, its champions have lost none of their fervor. So far are they from admitting defeat, that, on the contrary, they repeatedly proclaim victory.

In a recent book entitled *The Basic Symbols of the American Political Tradition,** Kendall, together with George Carey, takes the position that the arch-heretic, the man who "derailed" our tradition, was Abraham Lincoln. According to Kendall and Carey, all the Liberal and Radical demands, which would today transform constitutional into totalitarian government, are imperatives of Equality. And the power of this idea, or the power which the Radicals and Liberals have derived from it, stems from a misinterpretation or misapplication of the Declaration of Independence. According to Kendall and Carey, the Declaration is not the central document of our Founding, nor is it the true source of the symbols of the Founding. Nor does the expression of the doctrine of Equality in the Declaration mean what Abraham Lincoln said it meant, nor what the Liberals and Radicals of today wish it to mean. Nothing in our pre-

*Baton Rouge: Louisiana State University Press. 1970. Pp. xi, 163.

Revolutionary past, or in the constitution-building period of the Revolutionary generation, justified making Equality the end or goal to be secured by the American regime. Equality as an end became the official principle of the regime only by a retrospective interpretation of "four score and seven years," an interpretation enshrined by Abraham Lincoln at Gettysburg. The Gettysburg Address, say Kendall and Carey, was a rhetorical trick. It made the victory of the Union armies the occasion for an official transformation of our constitutional, Conservative revolutionary past, into a sanction for a Radical-Liberal revolutionary future.

Now we maintain that the truth about these matters is almost the exact opposite of what Kendall and Carey say it is. We believe that the Declaration of Independence is the central document of our political tradition, not because of any trick played by Abraham Lincoln, but because it is the most eloquent, as well as the most succinct, statement of the political teaching of all the great documents of the period. The sentiments of the Declaration are not unique to it. Jefferson was the draftsman of a representative assembly, and his gift lay in finding memorable phrases that articulated the thoughts that everyone wished expressed. The doctrine of Equality, which is indeed the key to all the thoughts in the Declaration, is also to be found in at least seven of the bills of rights accompanying the original state constitutions.[4] It is implied if not expressed in the Declaration of the First Continental Congress (1774) and in the Declaration of the Causes and Necessity of Taking Up Arms (1775). Kendall and Carey believe that the idea of Equality dropped out of sight when the constitution of 1787 came to be written, and that the constitutional morality of the *Federalist Papers* has nothing to do with it. They are dead wrong on both counts. The idea of Equality, as expressed in the Declaration, is the key to the morality of "the laws of nature and of nature's God." It is this natural law which the Constitution—and the regime of which the Constitution is a feature—is designed to implement. The abandonment of the idea of Equality is perforce an abandonment of that morality and that constitutionalism. It is perforce an abandonment of the "ought" for the "is." It would be an abandonment of that higher law tradition which is the heart of that civility—and that Conservatism— which judges men and nations by permanent standards. As we propose to demonstrate, the commitment to Equality in the American political tradition is synonymous with the commitment to those permanent standards. Whoever rejects the one, of necessity rejects the other, and in that rejection opens the way to the relativism and historicism that is the theoretical ground of modern totalitarian regimes.

Basic Symbols is replete with references to the "enormous impact on American scholarship and thinking"[5] of Lincoln's alleged "derailment" of the American political tradition. Yet Kendall and Carey do not provide a single example of that "derailed" scholarship. The central role of Equality in American life and thought was asserted long ago by Alexis de Tocqueville in his *Democracy in America,* written in the 1830s. Lincoln grew up in the Jacksonian America that Tocqueville had observed, and it is hardly surprising that he responded powerfully to what was already the most powerful force in the world in which he moved. That the Gettysburg Address somehow transformed the *ethos* of American life—and of American scholarship—would have required a demonstration that Kendall and Carey nowhere attempt. It would have required an analysis of Lincoln's reasoning on Equality, in its theoretical and practical bearings, pointing out how and why this was a new way of understanding Equality and how this new way had affected others. That is to say, it would have required evidence that Equality was now understood differently because of Lincoln and that the way Equality was now understood was not because of an inheritance from pre-Lincolnian egalitarianism, or from that inheritance modified by any of the other countless writers on the subject.

In fact, the only work which has ever attempted a full analysis of the theoretical and practical meaning of Equality in Lincoln's political thought is my *Crisis of the House Divided.* [6] In it I pointed out that American historical scholarship, insofar as it had perceived the impact of Equality upon Lincoln's policies in the 1850s, had thoroughly rejected it. Indeed, in the field of Lincoln scholarship, as distinct from popular writing, *Crisis of the House Divided* was, as far as I know, the first book in the twentieth century to take a distinctly favorable view of Lincoln's policies in the 1850s. Since its publication in 1959, Don E. Fehrenbacher's *Prelude to Greatness: Lincoln in the 1850's* (1962), has made a powerful addition to this point of view.

The seven hundred years' providential march of Equality, of which Tocqueville wrote,[7] has certainly continued, as Tocqueville predicted it would. Many of its effects have been bad, as he also predicted. Tocqueville was much influenced in his view of Jacksonian America by the American Whigs he met—by the party of Adams, Clay, and Webster. He never met a young follower of these men named Abraham Lincoln. Yet Lincoln's articulation of the Whig critique of a demagogic egalitarianism, expressed particularly in his Lyceum (1838)[8] and Temperance (1842)[9] speeches, contains remarkable parallels to Tocqueville. Certainly Lincoln and Tocqueville saw the threat to the nation from slavery and racial difference in very similar ways. To impute an indiscriminate egalitarianism to Lincoln, as Kendall and Carey do, is as absurd as to impute it to Tocqueville.

Vaguely imputing Lincolnian effects to American scholarship, *Basic Symbols* nowhere comes to grips with the character of Lincoln's thought. Nor does it ever allude to the articulation of that thought in *Crisis of the House Divided.* This is all the more remarkable, in that Kendall not only had read *Crisis,* but had published a lengthy review of it in *National*

Review, [10] which he reprinted in *The Conservative Affirmation.* [11] Had he thought ill of it, we could understand his passing over it later. But in fact he praised it extravagantly. We believe it to be the most generous review ever written about a book with which the reviewer so thoroughly disagreed. We feel obliged to quote it at some length now, not because of the praise, but because of the disagreement. We do so, moreover, because it seems to us to explain a missing link in *Basic Symbols'* polemic against Lincoln. *Basic Symbols* is silent not only about the actual reasoning in Lincoln's thought about Equality, but also about the great subject that occasioned nearly everything Lincoln said and wrote about Equality: slavery. So far as I can recall, the word "slavery" never occurs in *Basic Symbols.* Yet *Basic Symbols* wrestles with Equality on every page—like Jacob wrestling with the Angel of the Lord, we are tempted to say. To do so, without once mentioning slavery, would be like a critique of Hamlet that never mentions the ghost. Fortunately, Kendall does mention slavery in his review of *Crisis of the House Divided* and enables us thereby to form a juster view of what he says about Equality in *Basic Symbols.*

Kendall states, quite correctly, that "The central problem of *Crisis of the House Divided* is the status in the American political tradition of the 'all men are created equal' clause of the Declaration of Independence."[12] He adds that

. . . Jaffa's Lincoln (and Jaffa) sees it as the indispensable presupposition of the entire American political experience; either you accept it as *the* standard which that experience necessarily takes as its point of departure, or you deny the meaning of the entire American experience. As for the status of Abraham Lincoln *vis-à-vis* the Signers and Framers, Jaffa's Lincoln sees the great task of the nineteenth century as that of affirming the cherished accomplishment of the Fathers by *transcending* it. Concretely, this means to construe the equality clause as having an allegedly unavoidable meaning with which it was always pregnant, but which the Fathers apprehended only dimly.[13]

According to Kendall, the question which is "tacit, but present on every page of the book,"[14] is the question

whether the Civil War was, from the standpoint of natural right and the cause of self-government, the "unnecessary war" of the historians of the past fifty or sixty years, or a war that *had* to be fought in the interest of freedom for all mankind.

Jaffa's answer to the question is that the war did indeed have to be fought—once the South had gone beyond slaveholding . . . to assert the "positive goodness" of slavery, and so to deny the validity of the equality-clause standard as the basic axiom of our political system. . . . And, *within the limits* to which he for sound reasons of strategy confines himself, Jaffa's case for that answer seems to this reviewer as nearly as possible irrefragable.

His readers will, therefore, be well-advised to keep a sharp lookout *for those limits,* lest Jaffa launch them, and with them the nation, upon a political future the very thought of which is hair-raising: a future made up of an endless series of Abraham Lincolns, each persuaded that he is superior in wisdom and virtue to the Fathers, each prepared to insist that those who oppose this or that new application of the equality standard are denying the possibility of self-government, each ultimately willing to plunge America into Civil War rather than concede his point. . . .

In his concluding paragraph, Kendall declared:

The idea of natural right is not so easily reducible to the equality clause, and there are better ways of demonstrating the possibility of self-government than imposing one's own views concerning natural right upon others. . . .[15]

According to Kendall and Carey, the supreme "symbol" of the American political tradition is the virtuous people, or the representatives of the virtuous people, deliberating under God. We have no quarrel with this formulation, as far as it goes. We prefer, on the whole, to speak of the principles of the tradition, rather than its symbols. We propose to prove by the American political tradition, that a people become a people only by virtue of the principle of Equality. Here we would point out that it was this same American people, deliberating according to the laws laid down in the Constitution, laws to which all equally had consented, that elected Abraham Lincoln President of the United States. No violence was used in this election, unless it was in the South, where there were no electors for Lincoln. No one has ever been entitled to take office according to the canons of consensus laid down by Kendall and Carey, if it was not Lincoln. Did he not appeal to the "basic symbols" precisely in their sense when he spoke these fateful lines on March 4, 1861?

Why should there not be a patient confidence in the ultimate justice of the people? Is there any better, or equal hope, in the world? . . . If the Almighty Ruler of nations, with his eternal truth and justice, be on your side of the North, or on yours of the South, that truth, and that justice, will surely prevail, by the judgment of this great tribunal, the American people.[16]

Was not the decision of the seceding states, to break up the government, rather than submit to Lincoln's election, a defiance of the virtuous people, deliberating according to the rules of the Constitution, and under God? Was not that election a decision by a constitutional majority, in which all rights of constitutional minorities had been carefully preserved? Had not Lincoln sworn an oath, before God and the people, to "take Care that the Laws be faithfully executed" and to "preserve, protect, and defend the Constitution"? How can Kendall—how can anyone—call Lincoln's fidelity to that oath, incorporating as it does all that is sacred to the American political tradition, "imposing one's own view concerning natural right upon others"?[17]

Kendall thought that Jaffa would "launch [his readers] and with them the nation upon a political future the very thought of which is hair-raising. . . ."[18] This future would be made up

of an endless series of Abraham Lincolns, each persuaded that he is superior in wisdom and virtue to the Fathers, each prepared to insist that those who oppose this or that new application of the equality standard are denying the possibility of self-government, each ultimately willing to plunge America into Civil War rather than concede his point. . . .[19]

My readers will by now perceive that this is good Confederate caricature suitable for declamation—after playing "Dixie"—at a meeting decorated by the Stars and Bars. The warning strikes me as somewhat extravagant, given the number of my readers and the magnitude of the intellectual demands that Kendall says my book puts upon them. Kendall's premise seems to be that Lincoln—or anyone—who opposed American slavery thereby favored each and every "application of the equality standard." But this standard, we are also told, leads to "the cooperative commonwealth of men who will be so equal that no one will be able to tell them apart."[20] In short, it will lead to the modern totalitarian slave state. Kendall's case against Lincoln then comes down to this: Lincoln's opposition to slavery leads to slavery.

Now, even if this were not self-contradictory, we would have the right to ask, why is the slavery to which Lincoln leads us worse than that which he helped to end? But of course, we are faced here with a play on words, or a confusion of two meanings of Equality. Lincoln never sought, or believed in, an equality of *condition*. What he did believe in was an equality of *rights*. Over and over again, he denied that he thought that men were equal in wisdom, virtue, or ability, or that they should all have the same rewards. Lincoln said in 1858:

Certainly the negro is not our equal in color—perhaps not in many other respects; still, in the right to put into his mouth the bread that his own hands have earned, he is the equal of every other man. . . . In pointing out that more has been given [to] you, you cannot be justified in taking away the little which has been given [to] him. All I ask for the negro is that if you do not like him, let him alone. If God gave him little . . . that little let him enjoy.[21]

Surely no simpler nor more eloquent appeal ever was made to the principles of natural justice. Equality here meant nothing more than the equal right of all men to be treated justly. In his message to Congress of July 4, 1861, Lincoln defined the cause of the Union. It was, he said, to maintain in the world

that form, and substance of government, whose leading object is, to elevate the condition of men—to lift artificial weights from all shoulders, to clear the paths of laudable pursuit for all, to afford all, an unfettered start, and a fair chance, in the race of life.[22]

Kendall and Carey refer repeatedly to Lincoln having "curious" no-tions of what Equality meant which, they say, "even his worshippers cannot deny."[23] But, curiously enough, they give no explanation what-ever of this assertion. One of the speeches which they list as supporting this contention is the one from which we have just quoted. Is giving everyone an *unfettered* start and a fair chance what is "curious"? Is not this the idea behind the Statue of Liberty? Is it curious that we should be proud to call ourselves the land, not of the slave, but of the free? Have we not been the Promised Land for countless millions who have fled from persecution and oppression in the Egypt of the Old World? Was it not always an anomaly for the Promised Land itself to have slavery? And is not Abraham Lincoln himself the very most "basic symbol" within the American political tradition of personal self-reliance, of bootstrap in-dividualism? In this connection we cannot refrain from telling one of our favorite Lincoln stories. A visitor came into his office in the White House one day to find him blacking his boots. "Why, Mr. President," the aston-ished man exclaimed, "do you black your own boots?" "Whose boots do you think I black?" growled Lincoln.

We observed that Kendall and Carey never, to our knowledge, men-tion slavery in *Basic Symbols*. But the following passage seems to elevate Inequality to the status we had thought belonged to its opposite.

Is the American political tradition [they ask] the tradition of the textbooks, which indeed situates the "all men are created equal" clause at the center of our political experience, *or is it the tradition of American life as it is actually lived and thus a tradition of inequality?*[24]

Here Kendall and Carey confuse the "is" with the "ought" of a political tradition. "Life as it is actually lived" should refer not only to what people *do,* but also to the ethical norms or imperatives by which they understand the meaning of what they do. Kendall and Carey refer repeatedly to the American people as being a Christian people. Would they identify Chris-tians solely by their observance of the golden rule, *i.e.,* only by their lives as they are "actually [*i.e.,* selfishly] lived"?

Kendall, we noted, thinks that Lincoln (and Jaffa) points us toward a state of society in which men are "so equal that no one will be able to tell them apart." Yet were not all slaves equally denied the privileges of freedom, without regard to age, sex, virtue, or intelligence? Did they not all receive the same "wages," regardless of how much or how little they worked? Kendall and Carey speak—inaccurately—of the Declaration of Independence as referring to a Christian people. Christianity is a re-vealed religion. But in its references to "self-evident" truths and to "Na-ture" and "Nature's God," the Declaration certainly has reference to natural, not to revealed theology. Still, the moral commands of the Decalogue are held by many Christians to be knowable by unassisted human reason as well as by Biblical revelation. And American slavery was as much an institutionalized denial of the moral claims of the Ten Commandments as Hitler's concentration camps or the Gulag Archipelago. Since slaves were legally chattels, they could make no legal contracts, including marriage. How could children honor their fathers and mothers, when the fathers and mothers were not lawfully married, when they had no lawful power over their children, and when they could not acquire any of the property which is at the foundation of family life? How could the prohibition against adultery be regarded, when there was no lawful distinction between fornication and adultery? How could chastity be a virtue for those who had no lawful power over their own bodies? How could prohibitions against covetousness and theft be addressed to those who could possess no property and all the fruits of whose labor were taken from them? How could slaves regard the injunction against bearing false witness, when their testimony could never be given in court against white men? And did not the example of Moses, who had killed a slave master, justify any one in striking down another who obstructed his path to freedom?

American slavery treated all men of a certain class as having their worth determined by their membership in that class. This is equally the root of contemporary totalitarianism. To be elevated, or regarded as worthy, because one is white, proletarian, or Aryan, or to be degraded and scorned as a Negro, a capitalist, or a Jew, does not involve any ultimate distinction of principle. Kendall's denunciation of the "cooperative commonwealth" of those whose identities are lost in "equality" is utterly stultified by his refusal to condemn American slavery and by his condemnation of Lincoln for condemning it.

The "real" American political tradition, say Kendall and Carey, is not one of Equality. Except in the form of a rhetorical question, they do not positively assert that it is one of Inequality. Putting together their various formulations, *the* "basic symbols" of our tradition are—or is—the representative assembly (or assemblies) of the virtuous people deliberating under God. (There is the same difficulty with singular and plural here, as in the case of The United States.) We have no quarrel with the emphasis they place upon deliberation, or upon the need for morality and religion among the institutions of a *free* people. We think there is a fundamental misunderstanding implied in their case for legislative supremacy among the three branches of government. We think they confuse the supremacy of legislation, conceived as an act of the sovereign people in its constitution-making role, and legislation as an exercise of the ordinary powers of government provided by the Constitution. But this difference arises from the far more fundamental difference we have, concerning what it is that makes discrete individuals into a sovereign people, and hence what it is that authorizes any people to institute government, "laying its foundation on such principles and organizing its powers in such form, as to them shall seem most likely to effect their Safety and Happiness." Kendall and Carey assume the existence of the people, and never ask what it is, from the viewpoint of the Founding Fathers, that entitled the American people to consider themselves as sovereign. But the answer to that question, as we propose to demonstrate, is Equality.

The Declaration of Independence, of course, affirms it to be a self-evident truth, "that all men are created equal." Within short intervals during the Revolution, the people of the several states adopted new constitutions. Most of these contained preambles, bills or declarations of rights, which gave the "foundation of principles" upon which they were to erect the "forms" of government they thought most likely to effect their safety and happiness. For example, Virginia stated "That all men are by nature equally free and independent"; Pennsylvania, "That all men are born equally free and independent"; Vermont, "That all men are born equally free and independent"; Massachusetts, that "All men are born free and equal"; New Hampshire, that "All men are born equally free and independent"; Delaware, "That all government of right originates from the people [and] is founded in compact only. . . ."[25] Maryland also said "that all government of right originates from the people, [and] is founded in compact only. . . ."[26]

Now we contend that all these statements of principle, where they are not verbally identical, all mean one and the same thing. It will be observed that Virginia, Pennsylvania, Vermont, and New Hampshire say "equally free and independent." Massachusetts says "free and equal." Clearly, "equal" and "independent" mean the same thing. Also, "born" and "by nature" mean the same thing. Delaware and Maryland vary this language slightly by saying that rightful government is "founded in compact only." This expression, we shall see, means simply that government is the result of an agreement by men who were originally, or by nature, or born, equally free and independent. Jefferson's "created equal" is simply the most succinct formulation of this commonly understood doctrine.

Willmoore Kendall devoted the last years of his life to an extraordinary effort to read John Locke out of the American political tradition. That there was a compact theory much older than the American, he knew. That Socrates had appealed to one, he knew from the *Crito* of Plato. But he didn't trust the Old Pagan, as "The People versus Socrates Revisited" showed. With a great swoop, he lighted finally upon the Mayflower Compact. Here he found at last, if not a compact theory, at least a compact. No matter, if the Pilgrims didn't have a theory, Kendall would supply it to them! The important thing was that there was not a word in the

Mayflower Compact about Equality, and there was something—not much, but something—about "advancing the Christian faith." So Kendall labeled his second chapter in *Basic Symbols* "In the Beginning: The May-flower Compact," and tried to prove that the Founding Fathers—who were now, in fact, the Founding Great-great-great-great-Grandsons—had always meant substantially what the men of the Mayflower Compact had meant. That is to say, they had meant what they would or could or should have meant if they too had been born before John Locke. But all this effort was in vain. While we would never contend that there are *no* non-Lockean elements in the Founding, or that the Founding Fathers always interpreted the Lockean elements in a Lockean manner, Locke is nonetheless there. The primary appeals to principles in the Revolution are Lockean. The principle of limited, constitutional government, by which the Fathers rejected despotism and by which they constructed their own governments, were fundamentally Lockean. Without understanding this, no other aspects of the Revolution, or of the American political tradition, are intelligible.

The spirit of Locke's political teaching is conveyed well by the open-ing sentence of his *First Treatise*: "Slavery is so vile and miserable an estate of man, and so directly opposite to the generous temper and courage of our nation, that it is hardly to be conceived that an Englishman, much less a gentleman, should plead for it."[27] The major part of the treatise is devoted to a refutation of Sir Robert Filmer's *Patriarcha* (1680), a work which attempts to found absolute monarchy upon a title derived from Adam. Locke demonstrates the absurdity of such a title, not to mention the difficulty of finding its rightful possessor! But consider the language of the Continental Congress, in the Declaration of the Causes and Neces-sity of Taking Up Arms, July 6, 1775:

If it was possible for men, who exercise their reason to believe, that the divine Author of our existence intended a part of the human race to hold an absolute property in, and an unbounded power over others . . . the inhabitants of these colonies might at least require from the parliament of Great Britain some evi-dence, that this dreadful authority over them, has been granted to that body.[28]

Did ever a great revolution in human affairs ever begin with such sar-casm? Can one not hear the very accents of Locke's *First Treatise* as he rakes old Filmer over the coals? One thinks, for example, of Sir Robert's derivation of kingly power from paternal power, citing the Biblical injunc-tion to honor one's father. To this Locke retorted with evident glee that the Bible speaks of honoring one's father *and mother* and asks why Sir Robert does not find queenly as well as kingly authority in such injunc-tions. But the Continental Congress, in rejecting the proposition that any part of the *human race* (not merely Englishmen vis-à-vis Englishmen) might hold a right of property in any other part, clearly condemned in principle *all* slavery. And this they might do, only if, in their right to nondespotic rule, *all men are equal.*

In his attack on Filmer, Locke characterizes his "system" in this "little compass." "[I]t is," says Locke, "no more but this":

That all government is absolute monarchy.[29]

"And the ground he builds on is this":

That no man is born free.[30]

Robert A. Goldwin observes that "Locke's own political teaching may be stated in opposite terms but with similar brevity. . . ."[31] Goldwin's first Lockean proposition is this:

All government is limited in its powers and exists only by the consent of the governed.[32]

And, says Goldwin, the ground Locke builds on is this:

All men are born free.[33]

The argument for absolute monarchy—or despotism, for they are the same—is grounded in Locke in the proposition that no man is born free. The argument for limited government (or constitutional government, for they are the same) is grounded in Locke in the proposition that all men are born free. But we shall see that in Locke—and *in the nature of things*—the proposition that all men are born free is itself an inference from the proposition that all men are born equal. The equality of all men by nature and the freedom of all men by nature differ as the concavity of a curved line differs from its convexity. The two are distinguishable, but inseparable.

Let us now turn to the famous passage in *The Second Treatise,* in which Locke considers "what state all men are naturally in."[34] It is, he says,

a state of perfect freedom to order their actions and dispose of their possessions and persons as they think fit, within the bounds of the law of nature, without asking leave or depending upon the will of any other man.[35]

But it is also, he continues,

[a] state . . . of equality, wherein all the power and jurisdiction is reciprocal, no one having more than another; there being nothing more evident than [meaning thereby that it is self-evident] that creatures of the same species and rank . . . should also be equal one amongst another without subordination and subjection. . . .[36]

We would rephrase Locke's argument as follows: There is no difference between man and man as there is between man and, for example, dog, such that one is recognizable as the other's natural superior. And if men are not *naturally* subordinate, one to another—as all the brute creation are *naturally* subordinate to man—then they are *naturally* not in a state of government, or civil society. They are, instead, *naturally* free and independent, or *born* free and independent. But they are born free and independent, *because* they are born—or created—equal.

There can be no question—and Kendall and Carey do not question—that the just powers of government in the American political tradition are derived from the consent of the governed. Kendall and Carey treat consent however as if it were an ultimate and not a derived principle. But that is not the way Locke or the Founders treated it. They derived it from man's natural freedom and equality. It is the recognition of Equality which not only gives rise to consent, but also which provides consent with a positive content of meaning. Kendall and Carey, by allowing consent to stand alone, as if it were an ultimate principle, have no basis for saying what it is to which men might reasonably consent. In 1854, Lincoln quoted his notable antagonist thus:

> Judge Douglas frequently, with bitter irony and sarcasm, paraphrases our argument by saying: "The white people of Nebraska are good enough to govern themselves, *but they are not good enough to govern a few miserable negroes!!*"
> Well, I doubt not that the people of Nebraska are, and will continue to be as good as the average of people elsewhere. I do not say the contrary. What I do say is, that no man is good enough to govern another man, *without that other's consent.* [37]

Kendall and Carey, like Douglas, do not see that the people's right to give their consent is itself derived from the equality of *all* men and therefore limits and directs what it is to which they may rightfully consent. Their view leads to the conclusion that whatever any particular people may be persuaded by demagogues to agree or consent to, becomes "right." Calling the people "virtuous" and saying that they deliberate "under God" may become a mere cloak for vice and hypocrisy, as our examination of the ethics of slavery showed.

That men are by nature free and equal is the ground simultaneously of political obligation—of consent as the immediate source of the just powers of government—and of a doctrine of limited government and of an ethical code. Because man is by nature a rational being, he may not rule other rational beings as if they were mere brutes. Because man is not all-wise or all-powerful, because his reason is swayed by his passions, he may not be a judge in his own cause, and he may *not* therefore rule other men despotically. Men do not need the consent of brute creation to rule over it. Nor does God need the consent of men rightfully to exercise his Providential rule over them. Man is the in-between being, between beast and God, "a little lower than the angels." Consent is that ground of obligation which corresponds with this "in-betweenness." It is the contemplation of this universe, articulated as it is into the intelligible hierarchy of beast, man, and God, which not only brings consent as a principle into view, but also enlightens it, and brings it thereby into harmony with "the Laws of Nature and of Nature's God." To repeat, the proposition that all men are created equal implies an understanding of man, in the light of the universe, in the light of the distinction between the human and the subhuman on the one hand, and of the human and the superhuman on the other. As we have already observed, it does *not,* for this reason, ignore the very important differences between man and man. On the contrary, it is for the sake of those differences that it denies any man the right to rule others, *as if* those others were beasts. And there are no standing rules, and impartial judges, to govern the differences between slaves and their owners and masters. For the rule of a master to be a matter of right, the master would have to differ from the servant, as God is supposed to differ from man. Whatever one's beliefs as to the *existence* of Divinity, it is evident—or self-evident—that no man possesses that power or wisdom which we suppose that God—if He exists—possesses. While not supposing for a moment that the Founders did not believe in the actual existence of God, their assumptions about Equality—which include assumptions about the subhuman and the superhuman—are independent of the validity of any particular religious beliefs. In the decisive respect, their assumptions are not assumptions at all, but observations of a world in which the difference between men and beasts provides a clear and distinct idea of what the Divine nature, in its politically relevant aspects, must be.

Kendall and Carey suppose that the constitutional morality of *The Federalist* has nothing whatever to do with Equality. That they are wrong becomes clear the moment one understands that the proposition that all men are created equal is not about man alone, but about man, God, and Nature; and that Nature implies the difference between the human and the subhuman, as well as that between the human and the superhuman. Consider the famous passage of Madison's in the fifty-first *Federalist:*

If men were angels, no government would be necessary. If angels were to govern men, neither external nor internal controls on government would be necessary. In framing a government which is to be administered by men over men, the great difficulty lies in this: you must first enable the government to control the governed; and in the next place oblige it to control itself.[38]

Here the very nature of the problem that constitutionalism is meant to solve is determined by the meaning of Equality.

But does not constitutionalism imply an ethics as well as a politics? Do we not recognize that the equality of all men by nature, leading as it does to civil society, is the justification for the *inequalities* of civil society? Do we not thereby see that officials are but men and must live under the laws that they make and administer? (Abraham Lincoln: "The master not only governs the slave without his consent; but he governs him by a set of rules altogether different from those which he prescribes for himself."[39]) Do we not recognize that *our* consent makes *their* acts lawful, and that in obeying them, we are not deferring to our superiors in nature, but only to the principle of authority that is in ourselves? Is it not this that makes obedience not demeaning (not slavish), but dignified, and sometimes even noble? But still further, does not Equality, which makes *our* consent necessary to the laws *we* obey, oblige us to recognize the *same* rights in *other* men? Does it not also tell us that we may not consider other men mere means to our ends—as we may consider the brute creation—or as we may be considered by a Divine Providence whose power and wisdom so far transcends our own? (Are we not taught by Revelation that God does *not* consider us as mere means, but that this is not necessary to His being, but represents the miracle of His grace?) Do not all the totalitarian slave states of our time rest upon theoretical propositions in which race or class differences delude some men to consider themselves superhuman? And does not this delusion lie at the root of their bestiality? Is it not this that makes them think that, for the sake of the classless society, or the thousand year Reich, everything is permitted to them? Surely Abraham Lincoln was right when he said that the doctrine of human equality was "the father of all moral principle [amongst] us."[40]

There is a tendency among Conservatives to identify Equality with some species of socialism or—in Kendall's words—with "the cooperative commonwealth of men who will be so equal that no one will be able to tell them apart." But the doctrine of Equality, in particular in its Lockean sense, is essential to the defense of the institution of private property in the modern world. For the doctrine of Equality holds that what men are by nature, that is, prior to civil society, determines what purposes civil society may rightfully serve. It is this that determines what rights are inalienable, and what rights may—or must—reasonably be surrendered to society. It was axiomatic for the Founders that the rights of conscience were never surrendered to civil society, and that therefore civil society might never rightfully enact laws in matters that were wholly and exclusively matters of conscience. It took more than a generation after the Revolution to uproot all the colonial laws which, directly or indirectly, "established" religion, by giving one or another religious belief the assistance of law. Moreover, the determined way in which men like Jefferson and Madison acted to get rid, not only of religious establishment in all its forms, but also of such vestiges of feudal law as primogeniture and entail, proves how little regard they had for that colonial past Kendall tried to make the ground of the American political tradition.

Primogeniture and entail were anachronisms on the American scene. They were essentially limitations upon the right of a man to control his own property and to dispose of it at his pleasure. They were props of aristocracy, inimical to the spirit both of democracy and of capitalism. They were, so to speak, elements of a "Tory socialism." But Locke had taught that men were by nature property-acquiring animals. He had taught that both life and liberty became valuable and were themselves natural rights, above all because they culminated in the possession and enjoyment of property. No one in America who heard the Declaration of Independence read out for the first time had any doubt that pursuing happiness meant primarily, as Virginia had already put it, "acquiring and possessing property." It was because the Parliament of Great Britain had appeared to assert a right to tax the colonists without their consent by making laws and statutes "in all cases whatsoever," that they had revolted. But men like George Washington—as vigorous a land speculator as ever lived—were driven into rebellion in part by their inability to get the government at Westminster to grant patents and titles to the land they had surveyed in such places as the Ohio valley. Government, in their view, existed to facilitate the acquisition and enjoyment of private property. Such property might be taxed—with their consent—so that the government might be able to protect that same property. But it might not tax them to render nugatory, in any manner or sense, their efforts *in* acquiring and possessing property. The principle of Equality, far from enfranchising any leveling action of government, is the ground for the recognition of those human differences which arise *naturally,* but in *civil society,* when human industry and acquisitiveness are emancipated. We saw that Madison reflected the doctrine of Equality, when he attributed the need for constitutional government, and constitutional morality, to the difference between men and angels. But he reflected it no less when, in the tenth *Federalist,* he put as the *"first* object of government," the protection "of different and *unequal* faculties of acquiring property. . . ."[41] In his *Second Treatise,* Locke had put the origin of property in human labor. It was the natural right—the equal right—which each man had to his own body, and therefore to the labor of that body, that was the ultimate foundation of the right to private property in civil society. How can Kendall and Carey not have seen, as Lincoln saw, that the denial of Equality was the denial of the principle upon which private property, as well as every other personal freedom, rested? Nothing illustrates better Lincoln's egalitarianism, and his attitude toward property, than the following message, which he sent to a meeting of the Workingmen's Association in New York, during the Civil War:

Let not him who is houseless [wrote Lincoln] pull down the house of another; but let him labor diligently and build one for himself, thus by example assuring that his own [house] shall be safe from violence when built.[42]

Surely here is the wisdom of Solomon and of a just and generous Conservatism.

We turn finally to two myths propagated by Kendall and Carey which, it seems to us, have been stumbling blocks for American Conservatives—particularly for those who have forgotten their American history. According to *Basic Symbols* it was Lincoln who somehow invented a *"constitutional status"* for the Declaration and, by his enumeration of "four score and seven years" in the Gettysburg Address, spuriously caused the occasion for Independence to become that of our birth *"as a nation."* What was established on July 4, 1776, they say, was not a nation, but only "a baker's dozen of new sovereignties."[43] In short, what the thirteen colonies did that day was not merely to declare themselves independent of Great Britain, but to declare themselves independent of each other. Here is Lincoln, taking up that claim, in his message to Congress, July 4, 1861:

Therein [that is, by the Declaration of Independence] the "United Colonies" were declared to be "Free and Independent States"; but, even then, the object plainly was not to declare their independence of *one another,* or of the *Union;* but directly the contrary, as their mutual pledge, and their mutual action, before, at the time, and afterwards, abundantly show.[44]

How can Kendall and Carey revive this old Confederate propaganda without even alluding to the "abundant" evidence with which Lincoln had refuted it?

However indeterminate the character of American federalism may have been at that early date, there can be no question but that the thirteen former colonies, now states, remained united, and always, before the rest of the world, assumed the character of a single person. Passing over the pledge of unity in the Declaration itself, and the further pledge in the Articles of Confederation that the Union shall be perpetual, we would direct attention to Article VI of the Constitution. It declares that "All Debts contracted and Engagements entered into, before the Adoption of this Constitution, shall be as valid against the United States under this Constitution, as under the Confederation." Thus the United States "before the Adoption of this Constitution," the United States "under the Confederation," and the United States "under this Constitution," are all *the same United States.* According to Article VI, the one from which the many were formed—according to *e pluribus unum,* the motto of the United States—did not result from the Constitution. But if the Constitution did not cause the Union, then the Union (that is the Union of the People of the United States) must have caused the Constitution. But if the Union as a sovereign entity had an origin before 1787, when else can it have been except on July 4, 1776? If the Declaration gave birth to the Union which gave birth to the Constitution, it must itself have *constitutional status.*[45] And so it always has had in the statutes of the United States. Lincoln was of course perfectly correct in what he said at Gettysburg, and elsewhere, upon this topic.

But is it proper to refer to the Union which came into being in 1776 as a *nation?* Certainly neither Union nor nation were fully formed—any more than any other infant—at birth. But Thomas Jefferson, writing to James Madison, on August 30, 1823, referred without hesitation to a meeting that had taken place in the previous month, as "an anniversary assemblage of the nation on its birthday."[46] I would venture to doubt whether anyone can find any expression by any American statesman during the first fifty years following independence that contradicts the opinion that July 4, 1776, was the birthday of *the nation.* These were the formative years of Lincoln's life. He grew up, strange to say, believing what Jefferson said about our being a nation, just as he grew up believing Jefferson when he wrote "that all men are created equal."

We come now to Kendall and Carey's contention that Equality, which had admittedly (and unfortunately) loomed so large in the Declaration, had somehow disappeared when the Constitution, and the federal bill of rights, came to be written. Our readers will readily perceive that this alleged omission *is* an omission, only if the Declaration itself lacked *constitutional status.* But we have just proved that it *does* have that *status.* The Declaration authorized each of the thirteen states separately, and all of them collectively, to "institute new Government" such as to them "shall seem most likely to effect their Safety and Happiness." The statement of principles in the Declaration of Independence properly accompanied a revolutionary change in political allegiance. It also properly accompanied a dissolution of one social compact and the formation of another (or others). There was a good deal of contemporaneous discussion as to whether the dissolving of the political allegiance of the colonists to the British crown also constituted a dissolution of the social compact among themselves. According to James Madison, "The question was brought before Congress at its first session by Doctor Ramsay, who contested the election of William Smith; who, though born in South Carolina, had been absent at the date of independence. The decision was, that his birth in the Colony made him a member of society in its new as well as its original state."[47] We can easily imagine some Tories, who were driven out of the country, contesting this decision! In any event, there was no such revolutionary change as occurred in 1776, in the interval between 1776 and 1787. The absence of a new declaration of principles in 1787, far from indicating that the Framers had forgotten the old one, is a sign that they remembered it perfectly. Had they changed their minds about those principles in any way, a new one might have been indicated. But they had not changed their minds, and the country that ratified the Constitution understood perfectly that the principles of 1776, as expressed not only in the national Declaration of Independence, but also in all the state declarations accompanying the state constitutions, governed the new Constitution as well.

The principles of the Declaration are not, however, merely presupposed in the Constitution. They are present in the very first words of the Constitution as those words were understood by those who drafted and adopted it. "We the People of the United States," implies the existence of a *compact* in precisely the sense in which Delaware and Maryland used that term in their declarations of rights. In the debates on nullification, in the early 1830s, speakers on all sides of that difficult question, prefaced their remarks by saying that compact was the basis of all free government. In one of his last writings, an essay on "Sovereignty," Madison affirmed as a matter of course "that all power in just and free governments is derived from compact."[48] By compact, he said, he meant "the theory which contemplates a certain number of individuals as meeting and agreeing to form one political society, in order that the rights, the safety, and the interest of each may be under the safeguard of the whole."[49] "The first supposition" of such an agreement, said Madison, "is that each individual being previously independent of the others, the compact which is to make them one society must result from the free consent of *every* individual."[50] If then the people of the United States, who ordained the Constitution of the United States, are a free people, they must have been formed into civil society by the free consent of *every* individual. But that would not be possible unless every individual, then and since, forming part of the people of the United States, like all mankind, in the original and originating sense, had been by the laws of nature and of nature's God, "created equal."

NOTES

1. On the difference between the Whiggery of the English and American Revolutions, see H. V. Jaffa, *Equality and Liberty: Theory and Practice in American Politics,* (New York: Oxford University Press, 1965), Chapter 6, hereinafter cited as *Equality and Liberty.*
2. *The Rambler,* n.s. 5 (May 1861).
3. "The Contest in America," *Fraser's Magazine,* February–May 1862.
4. See text accompanying notes 25–26 *infra.*
5. Willmoore Kendall and George W. Carey, *Basic Symbols of the American Political Tradition* (Baton Rouge: Louisiana State University Press, 1970), p. 156.
6. H. V. Jaffa, *Crisis of the House Divided: An Interpretation of the Issues in the Lincoln–Douglas Debates* (Garden City, N.Y.: Doubleday, 1959); reissued in paper with a new Introduction, (Seattle: University of Washington Press, 1973), hereinafter cited as *Crisis.*
7. A. de Tocqueville, *Democracy in America,* vol. 2 (New York: Alfred A. Knopf, 1945), pp. 34–35, 99–103, 215–21, 226–27, 304–305.
8. R. Basler, ed., *The Collected Works of Abraham Lincoln,* 9 vols. (New Brunswick, N.J.: Rutgers University Press, 1953), vol. 1, pp. 108–15, hereinafter cited as *Lincoln.*
9. Ibid., pp. 271–79.
10. Kendall, Book Review, *National Review* 7 (159), 461, hereinafter cited as Book Review.
11. Willmoore Kendall, *The Conservative Affirmation* (Chicago: Henry Regnery, 1963) pp. 249–52.
12. Book Review, p. 461.
13. Ibid.

14. Ibid.
15. Ibid., pp. 461–62.
16. *Lincoln,* vol. 4, p. 270.
17. Book Review, pp. 461–62.
18. Ibid., p. 462.
19. Ibid.
20. Ibid.
21. *Lincoln,* vol 2, p. 520.
22. *Lincoln,* vol. 4, p. 438.
23. Ibid., pp. 14, 156.
24. Ibid., pp. 14–15 (emphasis added).
25. R. L. Perry, ed., *Sources of Our Liberties* (New York: McGraw-Hill, 1964), pp. 311–82.
26. Ibid., p. 346.
27. John Locke, *Two Treatises of Government,* sec. 7, edited by Thomas I. Cook (New York: Hafner, 1947), hereafter cited as *Two Treatises.*
28. Henry Steele Commager, ed., *Documents of American History* (New York: Appleton, Century-Crofts, 1963), p. 92, hereinafter cited as *Documents.*
29. *Two Treatises,* p. 8.
30. Ibid.
31. Robert A. Goldwin, "John Locke," in Leo Strauss and Joseph Cropsey, eds., *History of Political Philosophy* (Chicago: University of Chicago Press, 1972; 2nd ed.), p. 451.
32. Ibid.
33. Ibid.
34. *Two Treatises,* p. 121.
35. Ibid.
36. Ibid.
37. *Lincoln,* vol. 2, p. 266.
38. *The Federalist,* Modern Library ed. (New York: Random House, 1937), p. 337, hereinafter cited as *The Federalist.*
39. *Lincoln,* vol. 2, p. 266.
40. Ibid., p. 499.
41. *The Federalist,* p. 55 (emphasis added).
42. *Lincoln,* vol. 7, pp. 259–60.
43. Ibid., pp. 88, 90.
44. *Lincoln,* vol. 4, p. 433 (footnotes omitted).
45. *Documents,* p. 100 (editor's note).
46. R. Ginsberg, ed., *A Casebook on the Declaration of Independence* (New York: Crowell, 1967), p. 32.
47. 4 *Letters and Other Writings of James Madison,* vol. 4, ed. by R. Worthington (1884), p. 392.
48. Ibid., p. 391.
49. Ibid.
50. Ibid., p. 392.

PART II

The Status of Freedom

THE SECOND PART of this book explores the status of freedom, freedom being the banner of another important section of the conservative movement. Even as the quest for "tradition" dominated the intellectual efforts of most of the contributors to Part One, so the investigation of the nature and value of freedom preoccupies these thinkers.

Albert Jay Nock is at this point introduced on account of the arrant lengths to which he takes his opposition to the state and because the lengths to which he takes his position achieve an intellectual clarity in antistatism that is also valuable sentimentally. He is little known nowadays; in fact he was never widely known, although he is one of those few who are survived by a cult. There is indeed a Nockian Society, whose members pass along to each other the parerga of the master. Some of those who admire him do so exclusively on account of his prose style, which was one of the best ever, though there are those who think of it as rather too lacy, and who decry his Americanizations as self-conscious, something like the Duke of Windsor saying ain't.

Mr. Nock was the editor of the original *Freeman* magazine, which is not easily situated in the spectrum of American politics as currently drawn. It lasted four years, from 1920 to 1924, and made a singular impression on the literary set. Mr. Nock affected to take no interest in the political direction of the *Freeman*, pledging himself only to publish what was good, never mind the point of view of the writer. Throughout his life, he recalled in his intellectual autobiography, *Memoirs of a Superfluous Man*, he was a poor judge of character. "A person might be a survivor of the saints or he might be the devil's rag-baby, for all I should know. . . . [But] if a captain of industry made me his personnel-manager he would find me worth a ducal salary." The talent was however not enough to keep the journal afloat, and Mr. Nock walked away from the *Freeman* toward a position of elitist individualism. He cherished the memory of Henry George the single taxer, whom he considered the most original social thinker of modern times. He maintained that if 10,000 critically situated people in America would only read the *Social Statics* of Herbert Spencer, the world would forever after be relieved of the blight of statism. He wrote a strangely unknown tract called *Our Enemy, The State,* of which the essay here published is an autobiographically adapted précis. His literary passions were always preeminent, and to the scholarly community Mr. Nock is known as the translator and exegete of Rabelais, as well as the author of *A Journey into Rabelais' France,* a charming, brilliant little volume in the tradition, assuming there were such a tradition, of Henry Adams' *Mont-St.-Michel and Chartres.*

In his essay "Anarchist's Progress," Nock uses the idiom of the total individualist, well known in the conservative American tradition, who rejects almost completely the claims of the state. For the sake of intellectual clarity, it is sometimes valuable to extend an argument to its extreme. Nock is all-American in the use of the tall tale. "His general sense of political duty"—he is referring to the town drunkard of a youthful experience, whom he contrasts with the public official—"I must say, still seems to me as intelligent and competent as that of any man I have met in the many, many years that have gone by since then, and his mode of expressing it still seems about as effective as any I could suggest." On he goes into dogmatical antistatism, carried so far as to conclude that what's wrong even with the church and family is "mostly due to the historical connection of these two institutions with the State." He makes the provocative point that crime is the monopoly of the state. He undertakes to explain the institution of the state as a device by which money is taken from one set of pockets in order to be put into another set of pockets (he was a lifelong friend of Charles Beard).

But then, concerning political action, even for the sainted sake of anarchy, he was indisputably conservative. Among the final essays in the book is another by Nock, which is striking in its beauty and in its programmatic resignation. It is adumbrated in this essay. Far from hoisting the black banner of the anarchist and sounding the tocsin of revolt, he passes action by: "I was never much for evangelization; I am not sure enough that my opinions are right, and even if they were, a secondhand opinion is a poor possession." He makes, in effect, a conservative's concession to the existing order. He would not tear down that order even if he had the power to do so, he says, because it is, after all, the product of the American mind. And off he goes, into the mists of privacy, from which, one supposes—one hopes—he will someday be rescued, if not because of what he has to say about the state, although that is indisputably illuminating, then because of his wit and style and the quiet, authoritative scholarship that conferred such unobtrusive distinction on all of his writings.

Nock expressed the anarchist paradoxes (taxation is theft, conscription is slavery, etc.) as well as any American ever has. But he left the paradoxes in the air, a kind of skywriting to be read and admired, gradually dispersing all the while; contemporary libertarian economists and philosophers, however, have eagerly turned from contemplation to action. Or rather, they have taken up the kind of theorizing that prepares the ground and sets the limits of action. In the past two decades there has been a major effort to reconsider the origins of the state, to breathe life back into social contract theory and firmly establish the limits of state power. It suffices to mention three major works attacking the same problem from different angles: Gordon Tullock and James Buchanan's *The Calculus of Consent* (1962); Robert Nozick's *Anarchy, State, and Utopia* (1974); and Richard Epstein's *Takings* (1985). From starting points as different as public choice theory, natural rights philosophy, and the legal doctrine of eminent domain, each has reconstructed the idea of limited government in accord with the postulates of individual liberty.

But perhaps the most influential popular defense of personal liberty and limited government remains Milton Friedman's *Capitalism and Freedom.* With the possible exception of Paul Samuelson, Friedman is perhaps the best known living American economist. During his long career at the University of Chicago—he is now a scholar at the Hoover Institution—he refined the doctrines of monetarism in a series of stunning articles and books, applied those doctrines to the history of the business cycle in America (in his important *A Monetary History of the United States,* written with Anna Schwartz), and preached the good news of slow, steady monetary growth to millions through his column in *Newsweek.* The essay included here presents the philosophical heart of *Capitalism and Freedom*—the primacy of liberty (the reader should note that Friedman refers to his position as "liberal," in the classical or nineteenth century sense of the term) and the dependence of political upon economic freedom.

The late Frank Meyer came to conservatism through the agony of Communism (he is the author of the memorable *The Moulding of Communists*). He was thought by some to have emerged overtouched by ideological rigidity. In fact, close students of his journalism (he wrote regularly for *National Review,* of which he was a senior editor) have remarked the diligence with which he pursued the fusionists' dream of a conservatism that is both assertive in its commitment to individual freedom and yet aware of the mitigating roles of tradition and culture. It was his particular enterprise to try to consummate that fusion. "The New Conservatism and the State" is a section from his *In Defense of Freedom,* presenting his rejoinder to Russell Kirk's (and other traditionalists') attempts to subordinate liberty to virtue or community. What is especially piquant about the argument is his attempt to trump the traditionalists with Aristotle (one of their own favorites), who affirmed that virtue must be freely chosen if it is to be real. This leaves out of account Aristotle's teaching that moral virtue is a habit, and the reader will have to decide for himself whether Meyer's attempt to fuse libertarianism and traditionalism is successful. Some critics, notably Murray Rothbard (see his "Frank S. Meyer: The Fusionist as Libertarian Manqué," reprinted in George Carey, ed., *Virtue and Freedom: The Conservative-Libertarian Debate*), have maintained that the effort is in fact compromised (or redeemed, in Rothbard's view) by its libertarian, i.e., nonfusionist, premises.

What Harry V. Jaffa's essay "On the Nature of Civil and Religious Liberty" does, and does superbly, is make the case for the nonavailability of the theoretical right to freedom for those who desire to use it in order to destroy—freedom. His is the answer to the assertion of the libertarian totalists (and the not-so-totalists—see Milton Friedman's essay) that everyone has equally the right to speak, indeed that it is impudent to ask, even, what it is that they wish to say. In a demonstration of transporting lucidity, he undertakes to show that American freedom under the Constitution was by inference promulgated on the understanding that the use of it would not be available as a matter of right to those who seriously threaten (as opposed to merely intend) the abolition of the rights of others; and that therefore the cant phrase about the duty of tolerant men to tolerate intolerance is just that, cant: specious, frivolous. Conservatives who have struggled to formulate a plausible opposition to the extension of freedom to those who desire to use it in order to eliminate freedom, have here an exemplary handling of the apparent dilemma. Mr. Jaffa, by the way, is no mean phrase-maker. He is the author of the most recent version of "Rum, Romanism, and Rebellion." It was he who composed, in behalf of Senator Barry Goldwater, the resonant phrase, "Extremism in the defense of liberty is no vice; moderation in the pursuit of justice is no virtue," thus depriving Mr. Goldwater, in the opinion of the embittered, of the freedom to be elected President of the United States.

Even as the first three essays in this section can be read as critiques of the Burkean traditionalism of Part One, so Mr. Jaffa's argument can be understood as a response to the fundamental claims of libertarianism. As against Friedman and Meyer, in particular, he holds that liberty cannot be the ultimate principle of political life except insofar as it becomes a principle of justice, therefore of equality, as grounded in the laws of nature and of nature's God. Those laws precede human choice, indeed are the condition of all human choice as distinguished from whim or passionate impulse, and require the erection of a polity that deserves the loyalty of its citizens, even unto the sacrifice of liberty—and life. It is clear that on the value of freedom, too, the debate within conservatism is joined at a very high and spirited level.

Anarchist's Progress

When I was seven years old, playing in front of our house on the outskirts of Brooklyn one morning, a policeman stopped and chatted with me for a few moments. He was a kindly man, of a Scandinavian blonde type with pleasant blue eyes, and I took to him at once. He sealed our acquaintance permanently by telling me a story that I thought was immensely funny; I laughed over it at intervals all day. I do not remember what it was, but it had to do with the antics of a drove of geese in our neighborhood. He impressed me as the most entertaining and delightful person that I had seen in a long time, and I spoke of him to my parents with great pride.

At this time I did not know what policemen were. No doubt I had seen them, but not to notice them. Now, naturally, after meeting this highly prepossessing specimen, I wished to find out all I could about them, so I took the matter up with our old colored cook. I learned from her that my fine new friend represented something that was called the law, that the law was very good and great, and that everyone should obey and respect it. This was reasonable; if it were so, then my admirable friend just fitted his place, and was even more highly to be thought of, if possible. I asked where the law came from, and it was explained to me that men all over the country got together on what was called election day, and chose certain persons to make the law and others to see that it was carried out; and that the sum-total of all this mechanism was called our government. This again was as it should be; the men I knew, such as my father, my uncle George, and Messrs. So-and-so among the neighbors (running them over rapidly in my mind), could do this sort of thing handsomely, and there was probably a good deal in the idea. But what was it all for? Why did we have law and government, anyway? Then I learned that there were persons called criminals; some of them stole, some hurt or killed people or set fire to houses, and it was the duty of men like my friend the policeman to protect us from them. If he saw any he would catch them and lock them up, and they would be punished according to the law.

A year or so later we moved to another house in the same neighborhood, only a short distance away. On the corner of the block—rather a long block—behind our house stood a large one-story wooden building, very dirty and shabby, called the Wigwam. While getting the lie of my new surroundings, I considered this structure and remarked with disfavor the kind of people who seemed to be making themselves at home there. Some one told me it was a "political headquarters," but I did not know what that meant, and therefore did not connect it with my recent researches into law and government. I had little curiosity about the Wigwam. My parents never forbade my going there, but my mother once casually told me that it was a pretty good place to keep away from, and I agreed with her.

Two months later I heard some one say that election day was shortly coming on, and I sparked up at once; this, then, was the day when the lawmakers were to be chosen. There had been great doings at the Wigwam lately; in the evenings, too, I had seen noisy processions of drunken loafers passing our house, carrying transparencies, and tin torches that sent up clouds of kerosene-smoke. When I had asked what these meant, I was answered in one word, "politics," uttered in a disparaging tone, but this signified nothing to me. The fact is that my attention had been attracted by a steam calliope that went along with one of the first of these processions, and I took it to mean that there was a circus going on; and when I found that there was no circus, I was disappointed and did not care what else might be taking place.

On hearing of election day, however, the light broke in on me. I was really witnessing the august performances that I had heard of from our cook. All these processions of yelling hoodlums who sweat and stank in the parboiling humidity of the Indian-summer evenings—all the squalid goings-on in the Wigwam—all these, it seemed, were part and parcel of an election. I noticed that the men whom I knew in the neighbourhood were not prominent in this election; my uncle George voted, I remember, and when he dropped in at our house that evening, I overheard him say that going to the polls was a filthy business. I could not make it out. Nothing could be clearer than that the leading spirits in the whole affair were most dreadful swine; and I wondered by what kind of magic they could bring forth anything so majestic, good, and venerable as the law. But I kept my questionings to myself for some reason, though, as a rule, I was quite a hand for pestering older people about matters that seemed anomalous. Finally, I gave it up as hopeless, and thought no more about the subject for three years.

An incident of that election night, however, stuck in my memory. Some devoted brother, very far gone in whisky, fell by the wayside in a vacant lot just back of our house, on his way to the Wigwam to await the returns. He lay there all night, mostly in a comatose state. At intervals of something like half an hour he roused himself up in the darkness, apparently aware that he was not doing his duty by the occasion, and tried to sing the chorus of "Marching Through Georgia," but he could never get quite through three measures of the first bar before relapsing into somnolence. It was very funny; he always began so bravely and earnestly, and always petered out so lamentably. I often think of him. His general sense of political duty, I must say, still seems to me as intelligent and as competent as that of any man I have met in the many, many years that have gone by since then, and his mode of expressing it still seems about as effective as any I could suggest.

When I was just past my tenth birthday, we left Brooklyn and went to live in a pleasant town of 10,000 population. An orphaned cousin made her home with us, a pretty girl who soon began to cut a fair swath among the young men of the town. One of these was an extraordinary person, difficult to describe. My father, a great tease, at once detected his resemblance to a chimpanzee, and bored my cousin abominably by always speaking of him as Chim. The young man was not a popular idol by any means, yet no one thought badly of him. He was accepted everywhere as a source of legitimate diversion, and in the graduated, popular scale of local speech was invariably designated as a fool—a born fool, for which there was no help. When I heard he was a lawyer, I was so astonished that I actually went into the chicken-court one day to hear him plead some trifling case, out of sheer curiosity to see him in action; and I must say I got my money's worth. Presently the word went around that he was going to run for Congress, and stood a good chance of being elected; and what amazed me above all was that no one seemed to see anything out of the way about it.

My tottering faith in law and government got a hard jolt from this. Here was a man, a very good fellow indeed—he had nothing in common with the crew who herded around the Wigwam—who was regarded by the unanimous judgment of the community, without doubt, peradventure, or exception, as having barely sense enough to come in when it rained; and this was the man whom his party was sending to Washington as contentedly as if he were some Draco or Solon. At this point my sense of humor forged to the front and took permanent charge of the situation, which was fortunate for me, since otherwise my education would have been aborted, and I would perhaps, like so many who have missed this great blessing, have gone in with the reformers and uplifters; and such a close shave as this, in the words of Rabelais, is a terrible thing to think upon. How many reformers there have been in my day, how nobly and absurdly busy they were, and how dismally unhumorous! I can dimly remember Pingree and Altgeld in the Middle West, and Godkin, Strong, and Seth Low in New York. During the nineties, the goodly fellowship of the prophets buzzed about the whole country like flies around a tar-barrel—and, Lord! where be they now?

It will easily be seen, I think, that the only unusual thing about all this was that my mind was perfectly unprepossessed and blank throughout. My experiences were surely not uncommon, and my reasonings and inferences were no more than any child, who was more than half-witted, could have made without trouble. But my mind had never been perverted or sophisticated; it was left to itself. I never went to school, so I was never indoctrinated with pseudopatriotic fustian of any kind, and the plain, natural truth of such matters as I have been describing, therefore, found its way to my mind without encountering any artificial obstacle.

This freedom continued, happily, until my mind had matured and toughened. When I went to college I had the great good luck to hit on probably the only one in the country (there certainly is none now) where all such subjects were so remote and unconsidered that one would not know they existed. I had Greek, Latin, and mathematics, and nothing else, but I had these until the cows came home; then I had them all over again (or so it seemed) to make sure nothing was left out; then I was given a bachelor's degree in the liberal arts, and turned adrift. The idea was that if one wished to go in for some special branch of learning, one should do it afterward, on the foundation laid at college. The college's business was to lay the foundation, and the authorities saw to it that we were kept plentifully busy with the job. Therefore, all such subjects as political history, political science, and political economy were closed to me throughout my youth and early manhood; and when the time came that I wished to look into them, I did it on my own, without the interference of instructors, as any person who has gone through a course of training similar to mine at college is quite competent to do.

That time, however, came much later, and meanwhile I thought little about law and government, as I had other fish to fry; I was living more or less out of the world, occupied with literary studies. Occasionally some incident happened that set my mind perhaps a little farther along in the old sequences, but not often. Once, I remember, I ran across the case of a boy who had been sentenced to prison, a poor, scared little brat, who had intended something no worse than mischief, and it turned out to be a crime. The judge said he disliked to sentence the lad; it seemed the wrong thing to do; but the law left him no option. I was struck by this. The judge, then, was doing something as an official that he would not dream of doing as a man, and he could do it without any sense of responsibility, or discomfort, simply because he was acting as an official and not as a man. On this principle of action, it seemed to me that one could commit almost any kind of crime without getting into trouble with one's conscience. Clearly, a great crime had been committed against this boy; yet nobody who had had a hand in it—the judge, the jury, the prosecutor, the complaining witness, the policemen and jailers—felt any responsibility about it, because they were not acting as men, but as officials. Clearly, too, the public did not regard them as criminals, but rather as upright and conscientious men.

The idea came to me then, vaguely but unmistakably, that if the primary intention of government was not to abolish crime but merely to monopolize crime, no better device could be found for doing it than the inculcation of precisely this frame of mind in the officials and in the public; for the effect of this was to exempt both from any allegiance to those sanctions of humanity or decency which anyone of either class, acting as an individual, would have felt himself bound to respect—nay, would have wished to respect. This idea was vague at the moment, as I say, and I did not work it out for some years, but I think I never quite lost track of it from that time.

Presently I got acquainted in a casual way with some office-holders, becoming quite friendly with one in particular, who held a high elective office. One day he happened to ask me how I would reply to a letter that bothered him; it was a query about the fitness of a certain man for an appointive job. His recommendation would have weight; he liked the man, and really wanted to recommend him—moreover, he was under great political pressure to recommend him—but he did not think the man was qualified. Well, then, I suggested offhand, why not put it just that way?—it seemed all fair and straightforward. "Ah yes," he said, "but if I wrote such a letter as that, you see, I wouldn't be reelected." This took me aback a bit, and I demurred somewhat. "That's all very well," he kept insisting, "but I wouldn't be reelected." Thinking to give the discussion a semihumorous turn, I told him that the public, after all, had rights in the matter; he was their hired servant, and if he were not reelected, it would mean merely that the public did not want him to work for them any more, which was quite within their competence. Moreover, if they threw him out on any such issue as this, he ought to take it as a compliment; indeed, if he were reelected, would it not tend to show in some measure that he and the people did not fully understand each other? He did not like my tone of levity, and dismissed the subject with the remark that I knew nothing of practical politics, which was no doubt true.

Perhaps a year after this I had my first view of a legislative body in action. I visited the capital of a certain country, and listened attentively to the legislative proceedings. What I wished to observe, first of all, was the kind of business that was mostly under discussion; and next, I wished to get as good a general idea as I could of the kind of men who were entrusted with this business. I had a friend on the spot, formerly a newspaper reporter who had been in the press gallery for years; he guided me over the government buildings, taking me everywhere and showing me everything I asked to see.

As we walked through some corridors in the basement of the Capitol, I remarked the resonance of the stonework. "Yes," he said thoughtfully, "these walls, in their time, have echoed to the uncertain footsteps of many a drunken statesman." His words were made good in a few moments when we heard a spirited commotion ahead, which we found to proceed from a good-sized room, perhaps a committee room, opening off the corridor. The door being open, we stopped, and looked in on a strange sight.

In the centre of the room, a florid, square-built, portly man was dancing an extraordinary kind of break-down, or *kazák* dance. He leaped straight up to an incredible height, spun around like a teetotum, stamped his feet, then suddenly squatted and hopped through several measures in a squatting position, his hands on his knees, and then leaped up in the air and spun around again. He blew like a turkey cock, and occasionally uttered hoarse cries; his protruding and fiery eyes were suffused with blood, and the veins stood out on his neck and forehead like the strings of a bass-viol. He was drunk.

About a dozen others, also very drunk, stood around him in crouching postures, some clapping their hands and some slapping their knees, keeping time to the dance. One of them caught sight of us in the doorway, came up, and began to talk to me in a maundering fashion about his constituents. He was a loathsome human being; I have seldom seen one so repulsive. I could make nothing of what he said; he was almost inarticulate, and in pronouncing certain syllables he would slaver and spit, so that I was more occupied with keeping out of his range than with listening to him. He kept trying to buttonhole me, and I kept moving backward; he had backed me thirty feet down the corridor when my friend came along and disengaged me, and as we resumed our way, my friend observed for my consolation that "you pretty well need a mackintosh when X talks to you, even when he is sober."

This man, I learned, was interested in the looting of certain valuable public lands; nobody had heard of his ever being interested in any other legislative measures. The florid man who was dancing was interested in nothing but a high tariff on certain manufactures; he shortly became a Cabinet officer. Throughout my stay I was struck by seeing how much of the real business of legislation was in this category—how much, that is, had to do with putting unearned money in the pockets of beneficiaries— and what fitful and perfunctory attention the legislators gave to any other kind of business. I was even more impressed by the prevalent air of cynicism, by the frankness with which everyone seemed to acquiesce in the view of Voltaire, that government is merely a device for taking money out of one person's pocket and putting it into another's.

These experiences, commonplace as they were, prepared me to pause over and question certain sayings of famous men, when subsequently I ran across them, which otherwise I would perhaps have passed by without thinking about them. When I came upon the saying of Lincoln, that the way of the politician is "a long step removed from common honesty," it set a problem for me. I wondered just why this should be generally true, if it were true. When I read the remark of Mr. Jefferson, that "whenever a man has cast a longing eye on office, a rottenness begins in his conduct," I remembered the judge who had sentenced the boy, and my officeholding acquaintance who was so worried about reelection. I tried to reexamine their position, as far as possible putting myself in their place, and made a great effort to understand it favorably. My first view of a parliamentary body came back to me vividly when I read the despondent observation of John Bright, that he had sometimes known the British Parliament to do a good thing, but never just because it was a good thing. In the meantime I had observed many legislatures, and their principal occupations and preoccupations seemed to me precisely like those of the first one I ever saw, and while their personnel was not by any means composed throughout of noisy and disgusting scoundrels (neither, I hasten to say, was the first one), it was so unimaginably inept that it would really have to be seen to be believed. I cannot think of a more powerful stimulus to one's intellectual curiosity, for instance, than to sit in the galleries of the last Congress, contemplate its general run of membership, and then recall these sayings of Lincoln, Mr. Jefferson, and John Bright.*

It struck me as strange that these phenomena seemed never to stir any intellectual curiosity in anybody. As far as I know, there is no record of its ever having occurred to Lincoln that the fact he had remarked was striking enough to need accounting for, nor yet to Mr. Jefferson, whose intellectual curiosity was almost boundless, nor yet to John Bright. As for the people around me, their attitudes seemed strangest of all. They all disparaged politics. Their common saying, "Oh, that's politics," always pointed to something that in any other sphere of action they would call shabby and disreputable. But they never asked themselves why it was that in this one sphere of action alone they took shabby and disreputable

---

*As indicating the impression made on a more sophisticated mind, I may mention an amusing incident that happened to me in London two years ago. Having an engagement with a member of the House of Commons, I filled out a card and gave it to an attendant. By mistake I had written my name where the member's should be, and his where mine should be. The attendant handed the card back, saying, "I'm afraid this will 'ardly do, sir. I see you've been making yourself a member. It doesn't go quite as easy as that, sir—though from some of what you see around 'ere, I wouldn't say as 'ow you mightn't think so."

conduct as a matter of course. It was all the more strange because these same people still somehow assumed that politics existed for the promotion of the highest social purposes. They assumed that the State's primary purpose was to promote through appropriate institutions the general welfare of its members. This assumption, whatever it amounted to, furnished the rationale of their patriotism, and they held to it with a tenacity that on slight provocation became vindictive and fanatical. Yet all of them were aware, and if pressed, could not help acknowledging, that more than 90 percent of the State's energy was employed directly against the general welfare. Thus one might say that they seemed to have one set of credenda for weekdays and another for Sundays, and never to ask themselves what actual reasons they had for holding either.

I did not know how to take this, nor do I now. Let me draw a rough parallel. Suppose vast numbers of people to be contemplating a machine that they had been told was a plow, and very valuable—indeed, that they could not get on without it—some even saying that its design came down in some way from on high. They have great feelings of pride and jealousy about this machine, and will give up their lives for it if they are told it is in danger. Yet they all see that it will not plow well, no matter what hands are put to manage it, and in fact does hardly any plowing at all; sometimes only, with enormous difficulty and continual tinkering and adjustment can it be got to scratch a sort of furrow, very poor and short, hardly practicable, and ludicrously disproportionate to the cost and pains of cutting it. On the other hand, the machine harrows perfectly, almost automatically. It looks like a harrow, has the history of a harrow, and even when the most enlightened effort is expended on it to make it act like a plow, it persists, except for an occasional 6 or 8 percent of efficiency, in acting like a harrow.

Surely such a spectacle would make an intelligent being raise some enquiry about the nature and original intention of that machine. Was it really a plow? Was it ever meant to plow with? Was it not designed and constructed for harrowing? Yet none of the anomalies that I had been observing ever raised any enquiry about the nature and original intention of the State. They were merely acquiesced in. At most, they were put down feebly to the imperfections of human nature which render mismanagement and perversion of every good institution to some extent inevitable; and this is absurd, for these anomalies do not appear in the conduct of any other human institution. It is no matter of opinion, but of open and notorious fact, that they do not. There are anomalies in the church and in the family that are significantly analogous; they will bear investigation, and are getting it, but the analogies are by no means complete, and are mostly due to the historical connection of these two institutions with the State.

Everyone knows that the State claims and exercises the monopoly of crime that I spoke of a moment ago, and that it makes this monopoly as strict as it can. It forbids private murder, but itself organizes murder on a colossal scale. It punishes private theft, but itself lays unscrupulous hands on anything it wants, whether the property of citizen or of alien. There is, for example, no human right, natural or Constitutional, that we have not seen nullified by the United States Government. Of all the crimes that are committed for gain or revenge, there is not one that we have not seen it commit—murder, mayhem, arson, robbery, fraud, criminal collusion and connivance. On the other hand, we have all remarked the enormous relative difficulty of getting the State to effect any measure for the general welfare. Compare the difficulty of securing conviction in cases of notorious malfeasance, and in cases of petty private crime. Compare the smooth and easy going of the Teapot Dome transactions with the obstructionist behavior of the State toward a national child-labor law. Suppose one should try to get the State to put the same safeguards (no stronger) around service-income that with no pressure at all it puts around capital-income; what chance would one have? It must not be understood that I bring these matters forward to complain of them. I am not concerned with complaints or reforms, but only with the exhibition of anomalies that seem to me to need accounting for.

In the course of some desultory reading I noticed that the historian Parkman, at the outset of his volume on the conspiracy of Pontiac, dwells with some puzzlement, apparently, upon the fact that the Indians had not formed a State. Mr. Jefferson, also, who knew the Indians well, remarked the same fact—that they lived in a rather highly organized society, but had never formed a State. Bicknell, the historian of Rhode Island, has some interesting passages that bear upon the same point, hinting that the collisions between the Indians and the whites may have been largely due to a misunderstanding about the nature of land-tenure, that the Indians, knowing nothing of the British system of land-tenure, understood their land-sales and land-grants as merely an admission of the whites to the same communal use of land that they themselves enjoyed. I noticed, too, that Marx devotes a good deal of space in *Das Kapital* to proving that economic exploitation cannot take place in any society until the exploited class has been expropriated from the land. These observations attracted my attention as possibly throwing a strong side light upon the nature of the State and the primary purpose of government, and I made note of them accordingly.

At this time I was a good deal in Europe. I was in England and Germany during the Tangier incident, studying the circumstances and conditions that led up to the late war. My facilities for this were exceptional, and I used them diligently. Here I saw the State behaving just as I had seen it behave at home. Moreover, remembering the political theories of the eighteenth century, and the expectations put upon them, I was struck with the fact that the republican, constitutional-monarchical and autocratic States behaved exactly alike. This has never been sufficiently remarked. There was no practical distinction to be drawn among England, France, Germany, and Russia; in all these countries the State acted with unvarying consistency and unfailing regularity against the interests of the immense, the overwhelming majority of its people. So flagrant and flagitious, indeed, was the action of the State in all these countries, that its administrative officials, especially its diplomats, would immediately, in any other sphere of action, be put down as a professional-criminal class, just as would the corresponding officials in my own country, as I had already remarked. It is a noteworthy fact, indeed, concerning all that has happened since then, that if in any given circumstances one went on the assumption that they were a professional-criminal class, one could predict with accuracy what they would do and what would happen, while on any other assumption one could predict almost nothing. The accuracy of my own predictions during the war and throughout the Peace Conference was due to nothing but their being based on this assumption.

The Liberal party was in power in England in 1911, and my attention became attracted to its tenets. I had already seen something of Liberalism in America as a kind of glorified mugwumpery. The Cleveland Administration had long before proved what everybody already knew, that there was no essential difference between the Republican and Democratic parties; an election meant merely that one was in office and wished to stay in, and the other was out and wished to get in. I saw precisely the same relation prevailing between the two major parties in England, and I was to see later the same relation sustained by the Labour Administration of Mr. Ramsay MacDonald. All these political permutations resulted only in what John Adams admirably called "a change of impostors." But I was chiefly interested in the basic theory of Liberalism. This seemed to be that the State is no worse than a degenerate or perverted institution, beneficent in its original intention, and susceptible of restoration by the simple expedient of "putting good men in office."

I had already seen this experiment tried on several scales of magnitude, and observed that it came to nothing commensurate with the expectations put upon it or the enormous difficulty of arranging it. Later I was to see it tried on an unprecedented scale, for almost all the Governments engaged in the war were Liberal, notably the English and our own. Its disastrous results in the case of the Wilson Administration are too well known to need comment; though I do not wish to escape the responsibility of saying that of all forms of political impostorship, Liberalism always seemed to me the most vicious, because the most pretentious and specious. The general upshot of my observations, however, was to show me that whether in the hands of Liberal or Conservative, Republican or Democrat, and whether under nominal constitutionalism, republicanism or autocracy, the mechanism of the State would work freely and naturally in but one direction, namely, against the general welfare of the people.

So I set about finding out what I could about the origin of the State, to see whether its mechanism was ever really meant to work in any other direction, and here I came upon a very odd fact. All the current popular assumptions about the origin of the State rest upon sheer guesswork; none of them upon actual investigation. The treatises and textbooks that came into my hands were also based, finally, upon guesswork. Some authorities guessed that the State was originally formed by this-or-that mode of social agreement, others by a kind of muddling empiricism, others by the will of God, and so on. Apparently none of these, however, had taken the plain course of going back upon the record as far as possible to ascertain how it actually had been formed, and for what purpose. It seemed that enough information must be available; the formation of the State in America, for example, was a matter of relatively recent history, and one must be able to find out a great deal about it. Consequently I began to look around to see whether anyone had ever anywhere made any such investigation, and if so, what it amounted to.

I then discovered that the matter had, indeed, been investigated by scientific methods, and that all the scholars of the Continent knew about it, not as something new and startling, but as a sheer commonplace. The State did not originate in any form of social agreement, or with any disinterested view of promoting order and justice. Far otherwise. The State originated in conquest and confiscation, as a device for maintaining the stratification of society permanently into two classes—an owning and exploiting class, relatively small, and a propertyless dependent class. Such measures of order and justice as it established were incidental and ancillary to this purpose; it was not interested in any that did not serve this purpose, and it resisted the establishment of any that were contrary to it. No State known to history originated in any other manner, or for any other purpose than to enable the continuous economic exploitation of one class by another.*

This at once cleared up all the anomalies which I had found so troublesome. One could see immediately, for instance, why the hunting tribes and primitive peasants never formed a State. Primitive peasants never made enough of an economic accumulation to be worth stealing; they lived from hand to mouth. The hunting tribes of North America never formed a State, because the hunter was not exploitable. There was no way to make another man hunt for you; he would go off in the woods and forget to come back; and if he were expropriated from certain hunting-

---

*There is a considerable literature on this subject, largely untranslated. As a beginning, the reader may be conveniently referred to Mr. Charles A. Beard's *Rise of American Civilization* and his work on the Constitution of the United States. After these he should study closely— for it is hard reading—a small volume called *The State* by Professor Franz Oppenheimer, of the University of Frankfurt. It has been well translated and is easily available.

grounds, he would merely move on beyond them, the territory being so large and the population so sparse. Similarly, since the State's own primary intention was essentially criminal, one could see why it cares only to monopolize crime and not to suppress it; this explained the anomalous behavior of officials, and showed why it is that in their public capacity, whatever their private character, they appear necessarily as a professional-criminal class, and it further accounted for the fact that the State never moves disinterestedly for the general welfare, except grudgingly and under great pressure.

Again, one could perceive at once the basic misapprehension which forever nullifies the labors of Liberalism and Reform. It was once quite seriously suggested to me by some neighbors that I should go to Congress. I asked them why they wished me to do that, and they replied with some complimentary phrases about the satisfaction of having someone of a somewhat different type "amongst those damned rascals down there." "Yes, but," I said, "don't you see that it would be only a matter of a month or so—a very short time, anyway—before I should be a damned rascal, too?" No, they did not see this; they were rather taken aback; would I explain? "Suppose," I said, "that you put in a Sunday-school superintendent or a Y.M.C.A. secretary to run an assignation-house on Broadway. He might trim off some of the coarser fringes of the job, such as the badger game and the panel game, and put things in what Mayor Gaynor used to call a state of 'outward order and decency,' but he *must* run an assignation-house, or he would promptly hear from the owners." This was a new view to them, and they went away thoughtful.

Finally, one could perceive the reason for the matter that most puzzled me when I first observed a legislature in action, namely, the almost exclusive concern of legislative bodies with such measures as tend to take money out of one set of pockets and put it into another—the preoccupation with converting labor-made property into law-made property, and redistributing its ownership. The moment one becomes aware that just this, over and above a purely legal distribution of the ownership of natural resources, is what the State came into being for, and what it yet exists for, one immediately sees that the legislative bodies are acting altogether in character, and otherwise one cannot possibly give oneself an intelligent account of their behavior.*

Speaking for a moment in the technical terms of economics, there are two general means whereby human beings can satisfy their needs and

---

*When the Republican convention which nominated Mr. Harding was almost over, one of the party leaders met a man who was managing a kind of dark-horse, or one-horse, candidate, and said to him, "You can pack up that candidate of yours, and take him home now. I can't tell you who the next President will be; it will be one of three men, and I don't just yet know which. But I can tell you who the next Secretary of the Interior will be, and that is the important question, because there are still a few little things lying around loose that the boys want." I had this from a United States Senator, a Republican, who told it to me merely as a good story.

desires. One is by work—*i.e.,* by applying labor and capital to natural resources for the production of wealth, or to facilitating the exchange of labor-products. This is called the economic means. The other is by robbery—*i.e.,* the appropriation of the labor-products of others without compensation. This is called the political means. The State, considered functionally, may be described as *the organization of the political means,* enabling a comparatively small class of beneficiaries to satisfy their needs and desires through various delegations of the taxing power, which have no vestige of support in natural right, such as private landownership, tariffs, franchises, and the like.

It is a primary instinct of human nature to satisfy one's needs and desires with the least possible exertion; everyone tends by instinctive preference to use the political means rather than the economic means, if he can do so. The great desideratum in a tariff, for instance, is its license to rob the domestic consumer of the difference between the price of an article in a competitive and a noncompetitive market. Every manufacturer would like this privilege of robbery if he could get it, and he takes steps to get it if he can, thus illustrating the powerful instinctive tendency to climb out of the exploited class, which lives by the economic means (exploited, because the cost of this privilege must finally come out of production, there being nowhere else for it to come from), and into the class which lives, wholly or partially, by the political means.

This instinct—and this alone—is what gives the State its almost impregnable strength. The moment one discerns this, one understands the almost universal disposition to glorify and magnify the State, and to insist upon the pretence that it is something which it is not—something, in fact, the direct opposite of what it is. One understands the complacent acceptance of one set of standards for the State's conduct, and another for private organizations, of one set for officials, and another for private persons. One understands at once the attitude of the press, the Church and educational institutions, their careful inculcations of a specious patriotism, their nervous and vindictive proscriptions of opinion, doubt or even of question. One sees why purely fictitious theories of the State and its activities are strongly, often fiercely and violently, insisted on; why the simple fundamentals of the very simple science of economics are shirked or veiled, and why, finally, those who really know what kind of thing they are promulgating, are loath to say so.

The outbreak of the war in 1914 found me entertaining the convictions that I have here outlined. In the succeeding decade nothing has taken place to attenuate them, but quite the contrary. Having set out only to tell the story of how I came by them, and not to expound them or indulge in any polemic for them, I may now bring this narrative to an end, with a word about their practical outcome.

It has sometimes been remarked as strange that I never joined in any agitation, or took the part of a propagandist for any movement against the State, especially at a time when I had an unexampled opportunity to do so. To do anything of the sort successfully, one must have more faith in such processes than I have, and one must also have a certain dogmatic turn of temperament, which I do not possess. To be quite candid, I was never much for evangelization; I am not sure enough that my opinions are right, and even if they were, a secondhand opinion is a poor possession. Reason and experience, I repeat, are all that determine our true beliefs. So I never greatly cared that people should think my way, or tried much to get them to do so. I should be glad if they *thought*—if their general turn, that is, were a little more for disinterested thinking, and a little less for impetuous action motivated by mere unconsidered prepossession—and what little I could ever do to promote disinterested thinking has, I believe, been done.

According to my observations (for which I claim nothing but that they are all I have to go by) inaction is better than wrong action or premature right action, and effective right action can only follow right thinking. "If a great change is to take place," said Edmund Burke, in his last words on the French Revolution, "the minds of men *will be fitted to it.*" Otherwise the thing does not turn out well, and the processes by which men's minds are fitted seem to me untraceable and imponderable, the only certainty about them being that the share of any one person, or any one movement, in determining them is extremely small. Various social superstitions, such as magic, the divine right of kings, the Calvinist teleology, and so on, have stood out against many a vigorous frontal attack, and thrived on it, and when they finally disappeared, it was not under attack. People simply stopped thinking in those terms; no one knew just when or why, and no one even was much aware that they had stopped. So I think it very possible that while we are saying, "Lo, here!" and "Lo, there!" with our eye on this or that revolution, usurpation, seizure of power, or what not, the superstitions that surround the State are quietly disappearing in the same way.

My opinion of my own government and those who administer it can probably be inferred from what I have written. Mr. Jefferson said that if a centralization of power were ever effected at Washington, the United States would have the most corrupt government on earth. Comparisons are difficult, but I believe it has one that is thoroughly corrupt, flagitious, tyrannical, oppressive. Yet if it were in my power to pull down its whole structure overnight and set up another of my own devising—to abolish the State out of hand, and replace it by an organization of the economic means—I would not do it, for the minds of Americans are far from fitted to any such great change as this, and the effect would be only to lay open the way for the worse enormities of usurpation—possibly, who knows? with myself as the usurper! After the French Revolution, Napoleon!

Great and salutary social transformations, such as in the end do not cost more than they come to, are not effected by political shifts, by movements, by programs and platforms, least of all by violent revolutions, but by sound and disinterested thinking. The believers in action are numerous, their gospel is widely preached, they have many followers. Perhaps among those who will see what I have here written, there are two or three who will agree with me that the believers in action do not need us—indeed, that if we joined them, we should be rather a dead weight for them to carry. We need not deny that their work is educative, or pinch pennies when we count up its cost in the inevitable reactions against it. We need only remark that our place and function in it are not apparent, and then proceed on our own way, first with the more obscure and extremely difficult work of clearing and illuminating our own minds, and second, with what occasional help we may offer to others whose faith, like our own, is set more on the regenerative power of thought than on the uncertain achievements of premature action.

MILTON FRIEDMAN

Capitalism and Freedom

In a much quoted passage in his inaugural address, President Kennedy said, "Ask not what your country can do for you—ask what you can do for your country." It is a striking sign of the temper of our times that the controversy about this passage centered on its origin and not on its content. Neither half of the statement expresses a relation between the citizen and his government that is worthy of the ideals of free men in a free society. The paternalistic "what your country can do for you" implies that government is the patron, the citizen the ward, a view that is at odds with the free man's belief in his own responsibility for his own destiny. The organismic "what you can do for your country" implies that government is the master or the deity, the citizen, the servant or the votary. To the free man, the country is the collection of individuals who compose it, not something over and above them. He is proud of a common heritage and loyal to common traditions. But he regards government as a

From Milton Friedman, *Capitalism and Freedom* (Chicago: University of Chicago Press, 1962), pp. 1–21. Reprinted by permission of University of Chicago Press.

means, an instrumentality, neither a grantor of favors and gifts, nor a master or god to be blindly worshipped and served. He recognizes no national goal except as it is the consensus of the goals that the citizens severally serve. He recognizes no national purpose except as it is the consensus of the purposes for which the citizens severally strive.

The free man will ask neither what his country can do for him nor what he can do for his country. He will ask rather, "What can I and my compatriots do through government" to help us discharge our individual responsibilities, to achieve our several goals and purposes, and above all, to protect our freedom? And he will accompany this question with another: How can we keep the government we create from becoming a Frankenstein that will destroy the very freedom we establish it to protect? Freedom is a rare and delicate plant. Our minds tell us, and history confirms, that the great threat to freedom is the concentration of power. Government is necessary to preserve our freedom, it is an instrument through which we can exercise our freedom; yet by concentrating power in political hands, it is also a threat to freedom. Even though the men who wield this power initially be of good will and even though they be not corrupted by the power they exercise, the power will both attract and form men of a different stamp.

How can we benefit from the promise of government while avoiding the threat to freedom? Two broad principles embodied in our Constitution give an answer that has preserved our freedom so far, though they have been violated repeatedly in practice while proclaimed as precept.

First, the scope of government must be limited. Its major function must be to protect our freedom both from the enemies outside our gates and from our fellow-citizens: to preserve law and order, to enforce private contracts, to foster competitive markets. Beyond this major function, government may enable us at times to accomplish jointly what we would find it more difficult or expensive to accomplish severally. However, any such use of government is fraught with danger. We should not and cannot avoid using government in this way. But there should be a clear and large balance of advantages before we do. By relying primarily on voluntary cooperation and private enterprise, in both economic and other activities, we can insure that the private sector is a check on the powers of the governmental sector and an effective protection of freedom of speech, of religion, and of thought.

The second broad principle is that government power must be dispersed. If government is to exercise power, better in the county than in the state, better in the state than in Washington. If I do not like what my local community does, be it in sewage disposal, or zoning, or schools, I can move to another local community, and though few may take this step, the mere possibility acts as a check. If I do not like what my state does, I can move to another. If I do not like what Washington imposes, I have few alternatives in this world of jealous nations.

The very difficulty of avoiding the enactments of the federal government is of course the great attraction of centralization to many of its proponents. It will enable them more effectively, they believe, to legislate programs that—as they see it—are in the interest of the public, whether it be the transfer of income from the rich to the poor or from private to governmental purposes. They are in a sense right. But this coin has two sides. The power to do good is also the power to do harm; those who control the power today may not tomorrow; and, more important, what one man regards as good, another may regard as harm. The great tragedy of the drive to centralization, as of the drive to extend the scope of government in general, is that it is mostly led by men of goodwill who will be the first to rue its consequences.

The preservation of freedom is the protective reason for limiting and decentralizing governmental power. But there is also a constructive reason. The great advances of civilization, whether in architecture or painting, in science or literature, in industry or agriculture, have never come from centralized government. Columbus did not set out to seek a new route to China in response to a majority directive of a parliament, though he was partly financed by an absolute monarch. Newton and Leibnitz, Einstein and Bohr, Shakespeare, Milton, and Pasternak, Whitney, McCormick, Edison, and Ford, Jane Addams, Florence Nightingale, and Albert Schweitzer—no one of these opened new frontiers in human knowledge and understanding, in literature, in technical possibilities, or in the relief of human misery in response to governmental directives. Their achievements were the product of individual genius, of strongly held minority views, of a social climate permitting variety and diversity.

Government can never duplicate the variety and diversity of individual action. At any moment in time, by imposing uniform standards in housing, or nutrition, or clothing, government could undoubtedly improve the level of living of many individuals; by imposing uniform standards in schooling, road construction, or sanitation, central government could undoubtedly improve the level of performance in many local areas and perhaps even on the average of all communities. But in the process, government would replace progress by stagnation, it would substitute uniform mediocrity for the variety essential for that experimentation which can bring tomorrow's laggards above today's mean. . . .

It is widely believed that politics and economics are separate and largely unconnected, that individual freedom is a political problem and material welfare an economic problem, and that any kind of political arrangements can be combined with any kind of economic arrangements. The chief contemporary manifestation of this idea is the advocacy of "democratic Socialism" by many who condemn out of hand the restrictions on individual freedom imposed by "totalitarian Socialism" in Russia, and who are persuaded that it is possible for a country to adopt

the essential features of Russian economic arrangements and yet to ensure individual freedom through political arrangements. The thesis of
this chapter is that such a view is a delusion, that there is an intimate
connection between economics and politics, that only certain combinations of political and economic arrangements are possible, and that in
particular, a society which is socialist cannot also be democratic, in the
sense of guaranteeing individual freedom.

Economic arrangements play a dual role in the promotion of a free
society. On the one hand, freedom in economic arrangements is itself a
component of freedom broadly understood, so economic freedom is an
end in itself. In the second place, economic freedom is also an indispensable means toward the achievement of political freedom.

The first of these roles of economic freedom needs special emphasis
because intellectuals in particular have a strong bias against regarding
this aspect of freedom as important. They tend to express contempt for
what they regard as material aspects of life, and to regard their own
pursuit of allegedly higher values as on a different plane of significance
and as deserving of special attention. For most citizens of the country,
however, if not for the intellectual, the direct importance of economic
freedom is at least comparable in significance to the indirect importance
of economic freedom as a means to political freedom.

The citizen of Great Britain, who after World War II was not permitted to spend his vacation in the United States because of exchange control, was being deprived of an essential freedom no less than the citizen
of the United States, who was denied the opportunity to spend his vacation in Russia because of his political views. The one was ostensibly an
economic limitation on freedom and the other a political limitation, yet
there is no essential difference between the two.

The citizen of the United States who is compelled by law to devote
something like 10 percent of his income to the purchase of a particular
kind of retirement contract, administered by the government, is being
deprived of a corresponding part of his personal freedom. How strongly
this deprivation may be felt and its closeness to the deprivation of religious freedom, which all would regard as "civil" or "political" rather than
"economic," were dramatized by an episode involving a group of farmers
of the Amish sect. On grounds of principle, this group regarded compulsory federal old age programs as an infringement of their personal individual freedom and refused to pay taxes or accept benefits. As a result,
some of their livestock were sold by auction in order to satisfy claims for
social security levies. True, the number of citizens who regard compulsory old age insurance as a deprivation of freedom may be few, but the
believer in freedom has never counted noses.

A citizen of the United States who under the laws of various states is
not free to follow the occupation of his own choosing unless he can get
a license for it, is likewise being deprived of an essential part of his

freedom. So is the man who would like to exchange some of his goods with, say, a Swiss for a watch but is prevented from doing so by a quota. So also is the Californian who was thrown into jail for selling Alka Seltzer at a price below that set by the manufacturer under so-called fair trade laws. So also is the farmer who cannot grow the amount of wheat he wants. And so on. Clearly, economic freedom, in and of itself, is an extremely important part of total freedom.

Viewed as a means to the end of political freedom, economic arrangements are important because of their effect on the concentration or dispersion of power. The kind of economic organization that provides economic freedom directly, namely, competitive capitalism, also promotes political freedom because it separates economic power from political power and in this way enables the one to offset the other.

Historical evidence speaks with a single voice on the relation between political freedom and a free market. I know of no example in time or place of a society that has been marked by a large measure of political freedom, and that has not also used something comparable to a free market to organize the bulk of economic activity.

Because we live in a largely free society, we tend to forget how limited is the span of time and the part of the globe for which there has ever been anything like political freedom; the typical state of mankind is tyranny, servitude, and misery. The nineteenth century and early twentieth century in the Western world stand out as striking exceptions to the general trend of historical development. Political freedom in this instance clearly came along with the free market and the development of capitalist institutions. So also did political freedom in the golden age of Greece and in the early days of the Roman era.

History suggests only that Capitalism is a necessary condition for political freedom. Clearly it is not a sufficient condition. Fascist Italy and Fascist Spain, Germany at various times in the last seventy years, Japan before World Wars I and II, tsarist Russia in the decades before World War I—are all societies that cannot conceivably be described as politically free. Yet, in each, private enterprise was the dominant form of economic organization. It is therefore clearly possible to have economic arrangements that are fundamentally capitalist and political arrangements that are not free.

Even in those societies, the citizenry had a good deal more freedom than citizens of a modern totalitarian state like Russia or Nazi Germany, in which economic totalitarianism is combined with political totalitarianism. Even in Russia under the tsars, it was possible for some citizens, under some circumstances, to change their jobs without getting permission from political authority because Capitalism and the existence of private property provided some check to the centralized power of the state.

The relation between political and economic freedom is complex and by no means unilateral. In the early nineteenth century, Bentham and the Philosophical Radicals were inclined to regard political freedom as a means to economic freedom. They believed that the masses were being hampered by the restrictions that were being imposed upon them, and that if political reform gave the bulk of the people the vote, they would do what was good for them, which was to vote for laissez-faire. In retrospect, one cannot say that they were wrong. There was a large measure of political reform that was accompanied by economic reform in the direction of a great deal of laissez-faire. An enormous increase in the well-being of the masses followed this change in economic arrangements.

The triumph of Benthamite liberalism in nineteenth-century England was followed by a reaction toward increasing intervention by government in economic affairs. This tendency to collectivism was greatly accelerated, both in England and elsewhere, by the two World Wars. Welfare rather than freedom became the dominant note in democratic countries. Recognizing the implicit threat to individualism, the intellectual descendants of the Philosophical Radicals—Dicey, Mises, Hayek, and Simons, to mention only a few—feared that a continued movement toward centralized control of economic activity would prove *The Road to Serfdom,* as Hayek entitled his penetrating analysis of the process. Their emphasis was on economic freedom as a means toward political freedom.

Events since the end of World War II display still a different relation between economic and political freedom. Collectivist economic planning has indeed interfered with individual freedom. At least in some countries, however, the result has not been the suppression of freedom, but the reversal of economic policy. England again provides the most striking example. The turning point was perhaps the "control of engagements" order which, despite great misgivings, the Labour party found it necessary to impose in order to carry out its economic policy. Fully enforced and carried through, the law would have involved centralized allocation of individuals to occupations. This conflicted so sharply with personal liberty that it was enforced in a negligible number of cases, and then repealed after the law had been in effect for only a short period. Its repeal ushered in a decided shift in economic policy, marked by reduced reliance on centralized "plans" and "programs," by the dismantling of many controls, and by increased emphasis on the private market. A similar shift in policy occurred in most other democratic countries.

The proximate explanation of these shifts in policy is the limited success of central planning or its outright failure to achieve stated objectives. However, this failure is itself to be attributed, at least in some measure, to the political implications of central planning and to an unwillingness to follow out its logic when doing so requires trampling roughshod on treasured private rights. It may well be that the shift is only a temporary interruption in the collectivist trend of this century. Even so, it illustrates the close relation between political freedom and economic arrangements.

Historical evidence by itself can never be convincing. Perhaps it was sheer coincidence that the expansion of freedom occurred at the same time as the development of capitalist and market institutions. Why should there be a connection? What are the logical links between economic and political freedom? In discussing these questions we shall consider first the market as a direct component of freedom, and then the indirect relation between market arrangements and political freedom. A by-product will be an outline of the ideal economic arrangements for a free society.

As liberals, we take freedom of the individual, or perhaps the family, as our ultimate goal in judging social arrangements. Freedom as a value in this sense has to do with the interrelations among people; it has no meaning whatsoever to a Robinson Crusoe on an isolated island (without his Man Friday). Robinson Crusoe on his island is subject to "constraint," he has limited "power," and he has only a limited number of alternatives, but there is no problem of freedom in the sense that is relevant to our discussion. Similarly, in a society freedom has nothing to say about what an individual does with his freedom; it is not an all-embracing ethic. Indeed, a major aim of the liberal is to leave the ethical problem for the individual to wrestle with. The "really" important ethical problems are those that face an individual in a free society—what he should do with his freedom. There are thus two sets of values that a liberal will emphasize— the values that are relevant to relations among people, which is the context in which he assigns first priority to freedom, and the values that are relevant to the individual in the exercise of his freedom, which is the realm of individual ethics and philosophy.

The liberal conceives of men as imperfect beings. He regards the problem of social organization to be as much a negative problem of preventing "bad" people from doing harm as of enabling "good" people to do good; and, of course, "bad" and "good" people may be the same people, depending on who is judging them.

The basic problem of social organization is how to coordinate the economic activities of large numbers of people. Even in relatively backward societies, extensive division of labor and specialization of function is required to make effective use of available resources. In advanced societies, the scale on which coordination is needed, to take full advantage of the opportunities offered by modern science and technology, is enormously greater. Literally millions of people are involved in providing one another with their daily bread, let alone with their yearly automobiles. The challenge to the believer in liberty is to reconcile this widespread interdependence with individual freedom.

Fundamentally, there are only two ways of coordinating the economic activities of millions. One is central direction involving the use of coercion—the technique of the army and of the modern totalitarian state. The other is voluntary cooperation of individuals—the technique of the marketplace.

The possibility of coordination through voluntary cooperation rests on the elementary—yet frequently denied—proposition that both parties to an economic transaction benefit from it, *provided the transaction is bilaterally voluntary and informed.*

Exchange can therefore bring about coordination without coercion. A working model of a society organized through voluntary exchange is a *free private enterprise exchange economy*—what we have been calling competitive capitalism.

In its simplest form, such a society consists of a number of independent households—a collection of Robinson Crusoes, as it were. Each household uses the resources it controls to produce goods and services that it exchanges for goods and services produced by other households, on terms mutually acceptable to the two parties to the bargain. It is thereby enabled to satisfy its wants indirectly by producing goods and services for others, rather than directly by producing goods for its own immediate use. The incentive for adopting this indirect route is, of course, the increased product made possible by division of labor and specialization of function. Since the household always has the alternative of producing directly for itself, it need not enter into any exchange unless it benefits from it. Hence, no exchange will take place unless both parties do benefit from it. Cooperation is thereby achieved without coercion.

Specialization of function and division of labor would not go far if the ultimate productive unit were the household. In a modern society, we have gone much farther. We have introduced enterprises which are intermediaries between individuals in their capacities as suppliers of service and as purchasers of goods. And similarly, specialization of function and division of labor could not go very far if we had to continue to rely on the barter of product for product. In consequence, money has been introduced as a means of facilitating exchange and of enabling the acts of purchase and of sale to be separated into two parts.

Despite the important role of enterprises and of money in our actual economy, and despite the numerous and complex problems they raise, the central characteristic of the market technique of achieving coordination is fully displayed in the simple exchange economy that contains neither enterprises nor money. As in that simple model, so in the complex enterprise and money-exchange economy, cooperation is strictly individual and voluntary *provided (a)* that enterprises are private, so that the ultimate contracting parties are individuals, and *(b)* that individuals are effectively free to enter or not to enter into any particular exchange, so that every transaction is strictly voluntary.

It is far easier to state these provisos in general terms than to spell them out in detail, or to specify precisely the institutional arrangements most conducive to their maintenance. Indeed, much of technical economic literature is concerned with precisely these questions. The basic requisite is the maintenance of law and order to prevent physical coercion of one individual by another and to enforce contracts voluntarily entered into, thus giving substance to "private." Aside from this, perhaps the most difficult problems arise from monopoly—which inhibits effective freedom by denying individuals alternatives to the particular exchange—and from "neighborhood effects"—effects on third parties for which it is not feasible to charge or recompense them. . . .

So long as effective freedom of exchange is maintained, the central feature of the market organization of economic activity is that it prevents one person from interfering with another in respect of most of his activities. The consumer is protected from coercion by the seller because of the presence of other sellers with whom he can deal. The seller is protected from coercion by the consumer because of other consumers to whom he can sell. The employee is protected from coercion by the employer because of other employers for whom he can work, and so on. And the market does this impersonally and without centralized authority.

Indeed, a major source of objection to a free economy is precisely that it does this task so well. It gives people what they want instead of what a particular group thinks they ought to want. Underlying most arguments against the free market is a lack of belief in freedom itself.

The existence of a free market does not of course eliminate the need for government. On the contrary, government is essential both as a forum for determining the "rules of the game" and as an umpire to interpret and enforce the rules decided on. What the market does is to reduce greatly the range of issues that must be decided through political means, and thereby to minimize the extent to which government need participate directly in the game. The characteristic feature of action through political channels is that it tends to require or enforce substantial conformity. The great advantage of the market, on the other hand, is that it permits wide diversity. It is, in political terms, a system of proportional representation. Each man can vote, as it were, for the color of tie he wants and get it; he does not have to see what color the majority wants and then, if he is in the minority, submit.

It is this feature of the market that we refer to when we say that the market provides economic freedom. But this characteristic also has implications that go far beyond the narrowly economic. Political freedom means the absence of coercion of a man by his fellowmen. The fundamental threat to freedom is power to coerce, be it in the hands of a monarch, a dictator, an oligarchy, or a momentary majority. The preservation of freedom requires the elimination of such concentration of power to the fullest possible extent and the dispersal and distribution of whatever power cannot be eliminated—a system of checks and balances. By removing the organization of economic activity from the control of political authority, the market eliminates this source of coercive power. It enables economic strength to be a check to political power rather than a reinforcement.

Economic power can be widely dispersed. There is no law of conservation which forces the growth of new centers of economic strength to be at the expense of existing centers. Political power, on the other hand, is more difficult to decentralize. There can be numerous small independent governments. But it is far more difficult to maintain numerous equipotent small centers of political power in a single large government than it is to have numerous centers of economic strength in a single large economy. There can be many millionaires in one large economy. But can there be more than one really outstanding leader, one person on whom the energies and enthusiasms of his countrymen are centered? If the central government gains power, it is likely to be at the expense of local governments. There seems to be something like a fixed total of political power to be distributed. Consequently, if economic power is joined to political power, concentration seems almost inevitable. On the other hand, if economic power is kept in separate hands from political power, it can serve as a check and a counter to political power.

The force of this abstract argument can perhaps best be demonstrated by example. Let us consider first, a hypothetical example that may help to bring out the principles involved, and then some actual examples from recent experience that illustrate the way in which the market works to preserve political freedom.

One feature of a free society is surely the freedom of individuals to advocate and propagandize openly for a radical change in the structure of the society—so long as the advocacy is restricted to persuasion and does not include force or other forms of coercion. It is a mark of the political freedom of a capitalist society that men can openly advocate and work for Socialism. Equally, political freedom in a socialist society would require that men be free to advocate the introduction of Capitalism. How could the freedom to advocate Capitalism be preserved and protected in a socialist society?

In order for men to advocate anything, they must in the first place be able to earn a living. This already raises a problem in a socialist society, since all jobs are under the direct control of political authorities. It would take an act of self-denial whose difficulty is underlined by experience in the United States after World War II with the problem of "security" among Federal employees, for a socialist government to permit its employees to advocate policies directly contrary to official doctrine.

But let us suppose this act of self-denial to be achieved. For advocacy of Capitalism to mean anything, the proponents must be able to finance their cause—to hold public meetings, publish pamphlets, buy radio time, issue newspapers and magazines, and so on. How could they raise the funds? There might and probably would be men in the socialist society with large incomes, perhaps even large capital sums in the form of government bonds and the like, but these would of necessity be high public officials. It is possible to conceive of a minor socialist official retaining his job although openly advocating Capitalism. It strains credulity to imagine the socialist top brass financing such "subversive" activities.

The only recourse for funds would be to raise small amounts from a large number of minor officials. But this is no real answer. To tap these sources, many people would already have to be persuaded, and our whole problem is how to initiate and finance a campaign to do so. Radical movements in capitalist societies have never been financed this way. They have typically been supported by a few wealthy individuals who have become persuaded—by a Frederick Vanderbilt Field, or an Anita McCormick Blaine, or a Corliss Lamont, to mention a few names recently prominent, or by a Friedrich Engels, to go farther back. This is a role of inequality of wealth in preserving political freedom that is seldom noted—the role of the patron.

In a capitalist society, it is only necessary to convince a few wealthy people to get funds to launch any idea, however strange, and there are many such persons, many independent foci of support. And, indeed, it is not even necessary to persuade people or financial institutions with available funds of the soundness of the ideas to be propagated. It is only necessary to persuade them that the propagation can be financially successful, that the newspaper or magazine or book or other venture will be profitable. The competitive publisher, for example, cannot afford to publish only writing with which he personally agrees; his touchstone must be the likelihood that the market will be large enough to yield a satisfactory return on his investment.

In this way, the market breaks the vicious circle and makes it possible ultimately to finance such ventures by small amounts from many people without first persuading them. There are no such possibilities in the socialist society; there is only the all-powerful state.

Let us stretch our imagination and suppose that a socialist government is aware of this problem and is composed of people anxious to preserve freedom. Could it provide the funds? Perhaps, but it is difficult to see how. It could establish a bureau for subsidizing subversive propaganda. But how could it choose whom to support? If it gave to all who asked, it would shortly find itself out of funds, for Socialism cannot repeal the elementary economic law that a sufficiently high price will call forth a large supply. Make the advocacy of radical causes sufficiently remunerative, and the supply of advocates will be unlimited.

Moreover, freedom to advocate unpopular causes does not require that such advocacy be without cost. On the contrary, no society could be stable if advocacy of radical change were costless, much less subsidized. It is entirely appropriate that men make sacrifices to advocate causes in which they deeply believe. Indeed, it is important to preserve freedom only for people who are willing to practice self-denial, for otherwise freedom degenerates into license and irresponsibility. What is essential is that the cost of advocating unpopular causes be tolerable and not prohibitive.

But we are not yet through. In a free market society, it is enough to have the funds. The suppliers of paper are as willing to sell it to the *Daily Worker* as to the *Wall Street Journal.* In a socialist society, it would not be enough to have the funds. The hypothetical supporter of Capitalism would have to persuade a government factory making paper to sell to him, the government printing press to print his pamphlets, a government post office to distribute them among the people, a government agency to rent him a hall in which to talk, and so on.

Perhaps there is some way in which one could overcome these difficulties and preserve freedom in a socialist society. One cannot say it is utterly impossible. What is clear, however, is that there are very real difficulties in establishing institutions that will effectively preserve the possibility of dissent. So far as I know, none of the people who have been in favor of Socialism and also in favor of freedom have really faced up to this issue, or made even a respectable start at developing the institutional arrangements that would permit freedom under Socialism. By contrast, it is clear how a free market capitalist society fosters freedom.

A striking practical example of these abstract principles is the experience of Winston Churchill. From 1933 to the outbreak of World War II, Churchill was not permitted to talk over the British radio, which was, of course, a government monopoly administered by the British Broadcasting Corporation. Here was a leading citizen of his country, a Member of Parliament, a former cabinet minister, a man who was desperately trying by every device possible to persuade his countrymen to take steps to ward off the menace of Hitler's Germany. He was not permitted to talk over the radio to the British people because the BBC was a government monopoly and his position was too "controversial."

Another striking example, reported in the January 26, 1959, issue of *Time,* has to do with the Blacklist Fadeout. Says the *Time* story,

> The Oscar-awarding ritual is Hollywood's biggest pitch for dignity, but two years ago dignity suffered. When one Robert Rich was announced as top writer for the *The Brave One,* he never stepped forward. Robert Rich was a pseudonym, masking one of about 150 writers . . . blacklisted by the industry since 1947 as suspected Communists or fellow travelers. The case was particularly embarrassing because the Motion Picture Academy had barred any Communist or Fifth Amendment pleader from Oscar competition. Last week both the Communist rule and the mystery of Rich's identity were suddenly rescripted.
>
> Rich turned out to be Dalton (*Johnny Got His Gun*) Trumbo, one of the original

"Hollywood Ten" writers who refused to testify at the 1947 hearings on Communism in the movie industry. Said producer Frank King, who had stoutly insisted that Robert Rich was "a young guy in Spain with a beard": "We have an obligation to our stockholders to buy the best script we can. Trumbo brought us *The Brave One* and we bought it." . . .

In effect it was the formal end of the Hollywood blacklist. For barred writers, the informal end came long ago. At least 15% of current Hollywood films are reportedly written by blacklist members. Said Producer King, "There are more ghosts in Hollywood than in Forest Lawn. Every company in town has used the work of blacklisted people. We're just the first to confirm what everybody knows."

One may believe, as I do, that Communism would destroy all of our freedoms, one may be opposed to it as firmly and as strongly as possible, and yet, at the same time, also believe that in a free society it is intolerable for a man to be prevented from making voluntary arrangements with others that are mutually attractive because he believes in or is trying to promote Communism. His freedom includes his freedom to promote Communism. Freedom also, of course, includes the freedom of others not to deal with him under those circumstances. The Hollywood blacklist was an unfree act that destroys freedom because it was a collusive arrangement that used coercive means to prevent voluntary exchanges. It didn't work precisely because the market made it costly for people to preserve the blacklist. The commercial emphasis, the fact that people who are running enterprises have an incentive to make as much money as they can, protected the freedom of the individuals who were blacklisted by providing them with an alternative form of employment, and by giving people an incentive to employ them.

If Hollywood and the movie industry had been government enterprises or if in England it had been a question of employment by the British Broadcasting Corporation it is difficult to believe that the Hollywood Ten or their equivalent would have found employment. Equally, it is difficult to believe that under those circumstances, strong proponents of individualism and private enterprise—or indeed strong proponents of any view other than the status quo—would be able to get employment.

Another example of the role of the market in preserving political freedom was revealed in our experience with McCarthyism. Entirely aside from the substantive issues involved and the merits of the charges made, what protection did individuals, and in particular government employees, have against irresponsible accusations and probings into matters that it went against their conscience to reveal? Their appeal to the Fifth Amendment would have been a hollow mockery without an alternative to government employment.

Their fundamental protection was the existence of a private-market economy in which they could earn a living. Here again, the protection was not absolute. Many potential private employers were, rightly or wrongly, averse to hiring those pilloried. It may well be that there was far less justification for the costs imposed on many of the people involved than for the costs generally imposed on people who advocate unpopular causes. But the important point is that the costs were limited and not prohibitive, as they would have been if government employment had been the only possibility.

It is of interest to note that a disproportionately large fraction of the people involved apparently went into the most competitive sectors of the economy—small business, trade, farming—where the market approaches most closely the ideal free market. No one who buys bread knows whether the wheat from which it is made was grown by a Communist or a Republican, by a constitutionalist or a Fascist, or, for that matter, by a Negro or a white. This illustrates how an impersonal market separates economic activities from political views and protects men from being discriminated against in their economic activities for reasons that are irrelevant to their productivity—whether these reasons are associated with their views or their color.

As this example suggests, the groups in our society that have the most at stake in the preservation and strengthening of competitive capitalism are those minority groups which can most easily become the object of the distrust and enmity of the majority—the Negroes, the Jews, the foreign-born, to mention only the most obvious. Yet, paradoxically enough, the enemies of the free market—the Socialists and Communists—have been recruited in disproportionate measure from these groups. Instead of recognizing that the existence of the market has protected them from the attitudes of their fellow countrymen, they mistakenly attribute the residual discrimination to the market.

FRANK S. MEYER

The New Conservatism and the State

There is this much truth to John Stuart Mill's doctrine that truth will always prevail in the free marketplace of ideas, and this much only: Given a society free of the power of a totalizing state, truth will survive alongside all the errors and will outlive each of them. Nor, given the human condition, can we expect more. Freedom, which is of the human essence, implies the possibility of producing error as well as finding truth. To achieve a good society requires men unremittingly devoted to the pursuit

From Frank S. Meyer, *In Defense of Freedom: A Conservative Credo* (Chicago: Henry Regnery, 1962), pp. 127–37, 164–67. Reprinted by permission of Henry Regnery Company.

of good and truth, but it requires also that no one have the power to impose beliefs by force upon other men—and this whether those beliefs be false or true.

It is clear why this is so if the beliefs are false; it is more difficult to see why this is still so if they are true. Why cannot state power, if held by governors imbued with true principle, be used to force virtue upon men? Why should error not be forcibly destroyed? The answer lies, as I hope what I have written has demonstrated, in the nature of man and of virtue. The only "virtue" that can be enforced would be a virtue that consisted in conforming one's behavior to external dictation. Truly to be able to choose good and truth requires a freedom which, unfortunately, also makes it possible for men to choose evil and error. In a word, good and truth cannot be enforced, because by their essential nature they cannot be made real in men unless they are freely chosen.

At the political level, therefore (that is, at the level which has to do with power in the social order), the essential requisite for a good society is such a division of power that no single center will be able to enforce beliefs upon men by force, or to inhibit and destroy other beliefs by force. This principle can be reduced to a simpler maxim: The state must be limited to its proper function of preserving order. But this will only be possible when the person is considered as the central moral entity, and society as but a set of relations between persons, not as an organism morally superior to persons. For if society be given a moral status superior to persons, then it follows both implicitly and logically that society has the right to create an arm to enforce its moral rights. That arm can only be the unlimited Leviathan state. If ultimate moral righteousness rests in society, it is justified in enforcing its righteousness, and the state which is its arm cannot be limited by any rights inherent in individual persons.

Therefore, resistance to the growing collectivist tyranny of the century requires a theory of society and of the state that has as its first principle the vindication of the person. It is at this point—in its attitude toward the person and society—that the New Conservatism fails most signally to offer resistance to collectivist liberalism.

It is not that the New Conservatives have the urge to plan and engineer the social order; they have no stake, ideological or material, in the hegemony of the bureaucratic elite; their detestation of the values and the goals of collectivist liberalism is strong and certain; their criticism of the effects of liberal collectivism on the life of our time is penetrating and effective. No one has written with more eloquence and feeling of the horrors of a gradually collectivizing society than Russell Kirk or Robert A. Nisbet. Kirk's chapter, "The Problem of Social Boredom," in *A Program for Conservatives,* [1] Nisbet's chapter, "The Loss of Commu-

nity," in *The Quest for Community*, [2] delineate the process of dehumanization of the individual human being today with admirable precision and
with deep concern for the oppression of personality in a collectivizing
society.

Yet both of them, like the other New Conservatives, are blind to the
effective cause of the conditions they describe with such justified loath-
ing. The weight of the collective, of "society," upon the individual person, limiting his access to the transcendental sources of his being, to
the foundations of value outside history and outside society—this is the
prime cause of the human *malaise* which the New Conservatives describe
so well. The "social boredom," the "alienation," which Kirk and Nisbet
lament, is not the result of a "loss of community," but the result of an
excess of state-enforced community. For "community" (except as it is
freely created by free individual persons), community conceived as a
principle of social order prior and superior to the individual person,
can justify any oppression of individual persons so long as it is carried
out in the name of "community," of society or of its agent, the state.

This is the principle of collectivism, and it remains the principle of
collectivism even though the New Conservatives who speak of "community" would prefer a congeries of communities based upon locality, occupation, belief, caste, class, traditional ties, to the totalizing and equalizing
national or international community which is the goal of the collectivists.
This is to their credit. Better a multitude of enforced collectivities, so that
the individual human being may wrest for himself an area of autonomy
out of simultaneous partial loyalty to several of them, or out of precarious
existence in the interstices between them, than a single all-embracing
Leviathan community which will totally subordinate him. But what the
New Conservatives will not see is that there are no solid grounds on
which the kind of "community" they propose as the end toward which
social existence should be ordered can be defended against the kind of
"community" the collectivists propose.

Their defense may be based on taste, on preference for one kind of
superindividual organism rather than another; but then there is no fundamental reason why their position should prevail over that of the collectivists. Or they could claim that the network of multitudinous
"communities" which they prefer is less of a threat to the freedom of the
individual person. But this argument in favor of their kind of community
over the collectivists' depends upon a primary judgment that individual
persons are the entities in terms of which the goodness or badness of the
social order should be judged. This defense, however, the New Conservatives reject. Putting the individual person at the center of political
thought is to them the greatest of political and social evils. Caught within
the pattern of concepts inherited from classical political theory, they

cannot free themselves from the doctrine that men find their true being only as organic parts of a social entity, from which and in terms of which their lives take value. Hence the New Conservatives cannot effectively combat the essential political error of collectivist liberalism: its elevation of corporate society, and the state which stands as the enforcing agency of corporate society, to the level of final political ends.

The evils around us, they see, but the underlying causes of those evils they cannot understand. Russell Kirk, for example, using so apparently innocent an example as the Federal Government's school-lunch program, can show how the liberal-collectivist bureaucracy—putatively executing "the will of the people," and on the most seemingly benevolent of motives—penetrates into hitherto local and private concerns of individual citizens. But in the next breath he will castigate the central axiom upon which a political theory that could resist such usurpations must be based.

Critical though he is of the growth of centralized state power, he insists, following Burke, that "society is an immortal being . . . a *spiritual* entity."[3] And, as always when the set of interrelations between individual human beings that is social existence is raised to the level of a being endowed with corporate personality, the one error is followed logically and inevitably by another and even more dangerous one. The apotheosis of society leads directly to a theoretical concept of the state which would foreclose effective opposition to the totalizing state of contemporary society. Once it is believed that society is a being, society has rights. And by the very magnitude of its stature as compared with that of any individual person, those rights overshadow and take unlimited precedence over the rights of individual persons. A being of such grandeur that it is a veritable god, containing and expressing terrestrial existence, must have the right and the power to defend itself and to execute its will. From the deification of society arises the deification of the state, which is society in its active aspect. Believing that "society is a spiritual entity," it becomes impossible for the New Conservatives to see the state as physical power in the hands of a specific group of human beings. It becomes impossible to understand that the state, though a necessity of human existence, has an unlimited potential for evil the moment its power increases beyond the strict necessities of its function.

These disciples of Edmund Burke, however, believe with him that the state is a divine organ without whose positive action men cannot achieve virtue, that "He Who gave our nature to be perfected by our virtue, willed also the necessary means of its perfection.—He willed therefore the state—He willed its connexion with the source and original archetype of all perfection."[4]

So Russell Kirk:

Government is . . . a device of Divine wisdom to supply human wants. . . . The government may justly perform all those labors which surpass the reach of individual abilities. . . .[5]

It is true Mr. Kirk includes among the desirable ends of state activity, "to secure every man in his natural liberty," and this is excellent. But he adds "and to advance the culture of society," thus, by proposing for the state unnatural and swollen power, negating the end of liberty. Throughout his writing he makes it clear that, though he dislikes many of the activities of the contemporary state, he will not accept in principle its limitation to its essential functions. Insisting with Burke that society has a divine being and that from it the state derives a *mystique* independent of its limited function as an instrument of persons, he polemicizes against any political theory based upon the primacy of the individual person.

No doubt a state controlled by men imbued with Mr. Kirk's principles would enforce and encourage social and cultural conditions highly superior to those enforced and encouraged by contemporary collectivism, whether welfarist, Socialist or Communist. Such men might even voluntarily limit the use of the power available to them through the state—though this is questionable, considering the tendency of power to corrupt and the historical record of the best of men when in command of power. But what is important on the level of political theory is not what uses men wish to make of power, but whether power theoretically unlimited (as it is bound to be if society and the state are considered as beings superior to individual persons) can possibly conduce to a good social order.

What the New Conservatives are saying is that the state is the proper organ for the enforcement of virtue. When this concept is combined with the antecedent concept of society as a primary moral being, the individual person's control over his destiny, his freedom to search for and to choose virtue, is absorbed into the destiny of society. Its virtue must be his virtue—which is no more nor less than the central tenet of totalitarianism.

Walter Berns, who (though he refuses to call himself a New Conservative) expresses these concepts with great ability and force, insists that "government should seek to . . . promote the virtue of citizens,"[6] and calls upon the classical tradition of political theory to support his argument that virtue, not freedom, is the primary principle of the state. Once again the conditions of classical society, of the society of the *polis*, are taken as the norm of human existence. The basic philosophical position of the great classical political theorists, which reflected the limitations of their vision, is elevated as the prime law of moral-political existence; their highest insights, which broke through those limitations and glimpsed the concept of the person as the center of moral existence, are forgotten. The

Aristotle who wrote ". . . in order to be good one must be in a certain state when one does the several acts, i.e., one must do them as a result of choice and for the sake of the acts themselves"[7] is forgotten, while the Aristotle who expressed the fundamental Greek outlook, that man is primarily not an autonomous person but a *polis* animal, is taken as an oracle.

Certainly the concern of the New Conservatives with the achievement of virtue is a just concern. Ultimately this is the most important of problems. All that I am contending is that it is not a *political* problem, that it is not the concern of the state, that virtue cannot be enforced or brought about by political means. Political thought and political action must be concerned with establishing and maintaining the conditions of freedom. True, freedom, though it is the end of political theory and political action, is not the end of men's existence. It is a condition, a decisive and integral condition, but still only a *condition* of that end, which is virtue. The New Conservatives are right when they insist that a consideration of men in society must come to grips with the problem of virtue. They are only wrong in demanding that that problem be solved by the exercise of political power. But here their error is a serious one, for it is an error which they share with the collectivists who care not at all for virtue or for freedom.*

By their insistence on the use of political power for the inculcation of virtue, by their refusal to take a principled position in defense of a state limited to establishing the conditions of freedom, they disqualify themselves as effective opponents of liberal collectivism. The New Conservatives are left neither the champions of Leviathan that the collectivist liberals are, nor the enemies of Leviathan that the principled conservatives are, but mere critical observers of Leviathan undiminished. . . .

---

*It is advisedly that I have omitted from this discussion what is the most important of the associations related to the inculcation of virtue: the association for the worship of God, the church. Questions are involved here that go much deeper than the political or the social; and I am not personally able, at this point in my life, to speak with certainty on these questions.

That no civilization can come into being or develop without being informed by one kind or another of relationship between the men who make it up and God, I am certain; that Christianity, which informs Western civilization, is the highest and deepest relationship to the Divine that men can attain, I am also certain; but I am not able to say that any single institutional church is the bearer of God's spirit on earth. And this makes it impossible for me to discuss the church in the terms of this book. At the very least, it is of the category of those institutions which fulfill a function that is necessary, but which can be fulfilled in a number of different ways. If, however, it should be true that a single church is the direct expression of God's love for men, then that church would be, like the state and the family, necessary in its essential form to human existence.

In either case, the association of human beings for the worship of God, the church, is, of all human associations, the most important and the most directly related to the inculcation of virtue. But still it is individual persons, in that association, who, with the sustenance of God's grace, themselves as persons are virtuous or not, inculcate virtue or fail to do so.

The priority of the person and the derivative character of suprapersonal entities, analyzed in this discussion of the economic system and the educational system, apply with equal force to all sets of relationships between men. Those relationships may be of the kind best described as institutions, or as associations, or as communities. They may be in their essential form necessary to human existence, like the state and the family. They may fulfill a function which is necessary, but which can be fulfilled in many different ways, like the economic system or the educational system. Or they may be totally voluntary, like a professional association, or a charitable guild, or a chess club. But all of them are instrumentalities only. Depending upon their structure, they can make the movement of human beings toward virtue easier or more difficult—but that is all. The institution, the association, the community, is neither virtuous nor unvirtuous, and cannot itself inculcate virtue. Only individual persons can do this.

Individual persons cannot, of course, be virtuous or guide others to virtue by their own unaided powers. There is a moral and intellectual order, based upon the constitution of being, grasped and interpreted by generation upon generation, upon which men must draw. But the knowledge, the understanding, the belief, which that intellectual and moral order represents, has meaning only for sentient human beings, not for any suprahuman collectivity—institution, association, or community. Truth has meaning only for persons; beauty illumines the consciousness only of persons; virtue can be pursued only by persons.

A social order is a good social order to the degree that men live as free persons, under conditions in which virtue can be freely realized, advanced and perpetuated. Freedom has its risks, because it may not be virtue but vice that men advance; but all existence has its risks. Unless men are free to be vicious they cannot be virtuous. No community can make them virtuous. Nor can any community force upon them conditions antagonistic to virtue if the state does not, with its power, give coercive strength to community, and so long as the state, fulfilling its limited but necessary functions, protects individual persons from force and fraud by other persons and associations of persons.

The person is the locus of virtue. No other men, no associations of other men, can deprive him of the freedom to pursue virtue and inculcate virtue in others, if the state is maintained in its limited function, giving no sanction to the imposition of coercion by men upon men and protecting each man from coercion by his fellows.

NOTES

1. Chicago: Henry Regnery Co., 1954.
2. New York: Oxford University Press, 1953.

3. *The Conservative Mind* (Chicago: Henry Regnery Co., 1953), p. 18, emphasis in original.
4. Burke, *Works* [Bohn edition], Vol. II, p. 370.
5. *Beyond the Dreams of Avarice* (Chicago: Henry Regnery, 1956), pp. 146–47.
6. *Freedom, Virtue and The First Amendment* (Baton Rouge: Louisiana State University Press, 1957), p. 256.
7. *Nicomachean Ethics*, VI, 12 (1144ua).

HARRY V. JAFFA

On the Nature of Civil and Religious Liberty

There is general agreement among Americans that the central political issue of our time is the worldwide conflict between Communist totalitarianism and political freedom, that freedom whose principles are affirmed in such documents as the Declaration of Independence and the Gettysburg Address. All decent Americans repudiate Communism and recognize their obligation to do what lies in their power to prevent its ascendancy or triumph. Yet in the field of civil liberties there is profound confusion as to what, in crucial cases, decent, freedom-loving citizens may do. With respect to freedom of speech and the closely related freedoms of assembly, association, and the right of petition, the question continually arises: Can we deny these freedoms or rights to Communists, or their agents or coadjutors, without ourselves ceasing, by that denial and to the extent of the denial, to constitute a free society? And, conversely, is it not true that if we do allow Communists the full advantage of these civil liberties we may allow them so to weaken and confuse our resistance that Communism may thereby be enabled to succeed? In short, may it not be true that the indispensable means for denying success to Communism are at the same time the necessary instruments for the self-immolation of freedom? That we may be confronted with such a dilemma has certainly puzzled the will of many conscientious lovers of freedom amongst us. Perhaps even more serious is the sharp conflict which has developed from time to time between those who have grasped one or another horn of the supposed dilemma.

This difficulty is not a new one in the experience of this republic under its present constitution. We should remember that if Thomas Jefferson opposed the Alien and Sedition Acts, George Washington favored them. The Civil War, however, presented the problem in its most acute form. It would perhaps not be inapt to sum up the experience of the years 1861

From *The Conservative Papers*, edited by Ralph de Toledano and Karl Hess (New York: Doubleday Anchor, 1964), pp. 250–68. Copyright © 1964 by Ralph de Toledano and Karl Hess. Reprinted by permission of Doubleday & Company.

to 1865 by saying that no American statesman ever violated the ordinary maxims of civil liberties more than did Abraham Lincoln, and few seem to have been more careful of them than Jefferson Davis. Yet the cause for the sake of which the one slighted these maxims was human freedom, while the other, claiming to defend the forms of constitutional government, found in those forms a ground for defending and preserving human slavery. In his message to Congress on July 4, 1861, President Lincoln propounded the universal problem within the particular crisis in these words:

And this issue embraces more than the fate of these United States. . . . It forces us to ask: "Is there, in all republics, this inherent and fatal weakness? Must a Government, of necessity, be too *strong* for the liberties of its own people, or too *weak* to maintain its own existence?"

That the liberties Lincoln had in mind were the civil liberties referred to above is shown by his defense, in a major section of that address, of his suspensions of the writ of habeas corpus. All civil liberties depend absolutely upon the privilege of this writ, since no one can exercise his freedom of speech or of association, for example, if he can be detained or imprisoned at the pleasure of any official. It is well then to consider that since the Constitution (Article I, Section 9) provides that the privilege of the writ of habeas corpus may be suspended "when in cases of rebellion or invasion the public safety may require it," the Constitution must contemplate the lawful abridgment under certain circumstances of the freedoms of the First Amendment. It must do so unless the First Amendment is supposed to have canceled that part of the original Constitution which allows the suspension. No one seriously maintains this, however, because every good thing the people of the United States seek to accomplish in and through their government depends upon the ability of that government to preserve itself. And certainly nothing that led to the adoption of the First Amendment in any way affected the reasons for believing that "in cases of rebellion and invasion" the government might not be able to survive without suspending the writ.

When Lincoln defended his suspensions of the writ of habeas corpus in his Fourth of July message, he was mainly concerned to justify its suspension by the *Executive.* The provision of the Constitution in question is in the article that sets forth the powers (and the limitations upon the powers) of *Congress.* Lincoln's explanation of why the power to suspend cannot be confined to Congress is a masterly example of constitutional construction:

Now, it is insisted that Congress, and not the Executive, is vested with this power. But the Constitution itself is silent as to which or who is to exercise the power; and as the provision was plainly made for a dangerous emergency, it cannot be believed the framers of the instrument intended that in every case the danger should run its course until Congress could be called together; the very assembling of which might be prevented, as was intended in this case, by the rebellion.

Earlier in the same message, however, Lincoln had taken much broader ground. Provisions of the Constitution, taken literally, can be in conflict, sometimes in direct contradiction, with each other. As we have seen, the command of the First Amendment that "Congress shall make no law . . . abridging the freedom of speech," is in a certain sense incompatible with the proposition that Congress may, in time of rebellion or invasion, suspend the writ of habeas corpus. And so Lincoln, while denying that he had violated the Constitution, maintained nonetheless that, if he had done so he would have been justified. For the Constitution also commanded him to "take care that the laws be faithfully executed," and he had sworn an oath so to execute them. All the laws were being resisted, and failing of execution, in nearly one third of the states, and the whole government faced dissolution if its authority could not be restored. But, he asked, if the Constitution denied him the power to suspend the writ of habeas corpus, should he prefer the total destruction of all the laws, and the government, to the very limited violation of this one law? Lincoln summed the matter up in his usual succinct way:

Are all the laws *but one* to go unexecuted, and the Government itself go to pieces, lest that one be violated?

It is the thesis of this paper that civil liberties are, as their name implies, liberties of men in civil society. As such, they are to be correlated with the duties of men in civil society, and they are therefore subject to that interpretation which is consistent with the duty of men to preserve the polity which incorporates their rights. But the preservation of a civil society does not and cannot mean merely its physical preservation or territorial integrity; nor can it mean merely its freedom from foreign domination or, for that matter, from domestic usurpation. For Lincoln, the preservation of the Union meant all of these things, but it meant above all the preservation of a body whose soul remained *dedicated* to the principles of the Declaration of Independence. The classic example of a dilemma in interpreting the Constitution, and one whose resolution may well serve as a guide for resolving the difficulty with which this paper began, is that afforded by the Fifth Amendment in the decades immediately preceding the Civil War. Among other things, the amendment charges Congress that "No person shall be . . . deprived of life, liberty, or property, without due process of law." The pro-slavery Southerners maintained—and Chief Justice Taney in the Dred Scott decision upheld the assertion—that a congressional prohibition of slavery in any United States territory (as in the Missouri Compromise legislation of 1820) had the effect of freeing slaves that a man had lawfully brought with him into a territory. This, it was held, constituted an arbitrary deprivation of property. The antislavery Northerners, on the other hand, pointed to the fact that Negroes were recognized many times by the Constitution as persons (e.g., Article I, Section 2, par. 3; ibid., Section 9, par. 1; and Article IV, Section 2, par. 3). They further insisted that by the terms of the same amendment, no Negro, being a person, might be held in slavery in a territory. The specific and immediate cause of the Civil War was precisely this difference over whether the Fifth Amendment made it the duty of Congress to prohibit or to protect slavery in the territories. Every candid student of this question must come to see, I believe, that the language of the Constitution admits with nearly perfect impartiality of either interpretation. In the so-called fugitive-slave clause of the Constitution—the word "slave" or "slavery" never occurs before the Thirteenth Amendment—a sanction undoubtedly is given to state laws which, in turn, treat certain "persons" as if they were not persons, that is, as if they were chattels. In short, the word "person" is treated in the Constitution in such ways that some persons may be either subjects of rights of their own, or mere objects of the rights of others. How to resolve this confusion in the text of the Constitution could not be decided by reference to the Constitution alone. As in many great matters, the meaning of the Constitution had and has to be sought outside the Constitution itself. The great debates that preceded the Civil War, above all the Lincoln-Douglas debates, turned on the question of the authority and meaning of the principles propounded in the Declaration of Independence, as the guide for interpreting the Constitution. For there could be no doubt that if the Declaration was authoritative, and if Negroes were included in the proposition that "all men are created equal," then the free-soil interpretation of the Fifth Amendment had to prevail, Chief Justice Taney to the contrary notwithstanding.* It is too little realized that the final word in the greatest of all American controversies is pronounced in the magisterial opening of the Gettysburg Address. Stephen A. Douglas had said, and the proslavery Southerners agreed, that we existed as a nation only in virtue of the Constitution, and the Constitution not only tolerated but gave legal guarantees to the institution of human slavery. When Lincoln pronounced "Fourscore and seven years," he forever fixed the year 1776 as the year of the nation's nativity. In so doing he did not downgrade the Constitution; he merely affirmed in the most solemn manner what he held to be the essential cause of the dignity of the Constitution: that it was an instrument for better securing those human rights affirmed in the Declaration, that the Union which was to become "more perfect" took as its

---

*On this whole subject, see my *Crisis of the House Divided: An Interpretation of the Issues in the Lincoln-Douglas Debates* (New York: Doubleday, 1959), esp. Chapter XIV, "The Universal Meaning of the Declaration of Independence."

standard of perfection, its ends or principles, the "laws of Nature and of Nature's God" invoked in the earlier document.

The Union was created by its dedication to the equality of man. Slavery, Lincoln held, might be tolerated as a necessity, but only so long as it was understood to be a necessary evil. Douglas sought a middle position, a national "don't care" policy which would allow the settlers in the territories to decide as they wished in the matter of slavery. This, Lincoln said with scorn, attempted to treat as a matter of indifference something to which no human being could be indifferent. It was, he said, as vain as the search for a man who should be neither a living man nor a dead one. Lincoln preferred the candid proslavery argument, where the issue could be squarely joined. And he argued with unbreakable logic that if the slaveowner's interpretation of the Fifth Amendment were correct, and if the Negroes' humanity were either denied or treated as of no account, then the moral basis of the authority of the whole Constitution had to be called into question, and the American Revolution itself could be regarded as an expression of mere force without right.

Free government rests upon the consent or opinion of the governed. Law is an expression of opinion, and the opinion upon which the law rests is more fundamental than the law itself. "In this and like communities," Lincoln said in the first of his joint debates with Douglas, "public sentiment is everything. With public sentiment, nothing can fail; without it, nothing can succeed. Consequently, he who molds public sentiment, goes deeper than he who enacts statutes or pronounces decisions. He makes statutes and decisions possible or impossible to be executed." The Constitution was the creation of a people committed in the Declaration to the idea of human dignity. Although the people is sovereign, its sovereignty may not be exercised in a manner inconsistent with the moral ground of its own authority.

"All men are created equal" is called a self-evident truth. What does this mean? Not that all men are equal in intelligence, virtue, strength, or beauty. They are equal in certain "rights," and the meaning of these rights can perhaps be most easily expressed today in this negative way: There is no difference between man and man, such as there is between man and animals of other species, which makes any man, that is, any normal adult human being, the natural ruler of any man. Man is by nature the master of dog, horse, cow, or monkey. He is equally the master of the dangerous wild animals he cannot domesticate, because he can kill or capture them as a result of his natural superiority, and not because of mere accident. The rights which men evidently have over other animals, they do not, it is equally evident, have over each other. Men are not angels—who, it may be supposed, would require no government—nor are there angels to govern men. Government, which does not arise directly from *nature,* is then grounded upon *consent.* To repeat, government does not arise *directly* from nature, but it does arise *indirectly,* to the extent that consent, to be the ground of legitimate authority, must itself be based upon a recognition of the essential difference between man and the brutes. If the consent of the governed were given to a regime which treated the rulers as if they were gods or angels, differing essentially in their nature from the ruled, the regime would also be illegitimate. Deception and force are equally incapable of giving rise to legitimate authority. Legitimacy cannot then be claimed for any regime in which the rulers treat the ruled as if they are animals of another species, as if the governed can be used as mere instruments for the advantage of the rulers. Such a regime is illegitimate, we repeat, even if the ruled, for whatever reason, believe that their own highest good consists in gratifying the rulers. The governed, in a civilized regime must, by the principles of our Declaration, be treated as beings with ends of intrinsic worth, which ends the government serves. Cattle may be killed, their flesh eaten, and their skins used to clothe human bodies, because of the indefeasible, objective natural difference between the soul of a man and the soul of a brute.

The Declaration, as we have seen, speaks of the specific nature of man and, inferentially, of its difference from other species, as self-evident. By this it is meant that we cannot demonstrate the essential likeness of men to each other and their difference from other animals. This is because all understanding of the world, all demonstration about the world, proceeds *from* the experience by which we grasp the terms of such propositions as "This is a man, this is a dog, this is a tree, etc." A self-evident truth is not one which everyone necessarily admits to be true; it is one the evidence for which is contained in the terms of the proposition, and which is admitted to be true by everyone *who already grasps the meaning of the terms.* Very young children, lunatics, and savages, are for various reasons deficient in those operations of the mind which issue in the abstractions, man, dog, horse, tree, etc. Hence, until their deficiencies are somehow overcome, they cannot be responsible members of civil society.

The men who founded our system of government were not moral or political relativists, as those terms are understood today. In affirming that all men are created equal, they expressed their conviction that human freedom depends upon the recognition of an order that man himself does not create. Man is not free to disregard the hierarchy of souls in nature. The equality of man flows from and corresponds to the inequality of the human and the subhuman, as it corresponds also to the inequality of the human and the superhuman. For man is part of the order of nature, and his dignity derives from the whole of which he is a part. This whole, being the cause of the dignity of the part which is man, is possessed of a dignity greater than man, for every cause is greater than the effects of which it is the cause. But the whole is not known to us as we and brute creation—

the parts—are known. It is a mystery, but a mystery to which man alone in the universe is open. This fact is the ground of freedom of thought, which in turn is the ground of all other freedoms, including civil liberties. Freedom of thought is not freedom to deny that two and two is four. Someone who denies this may be more pitied than censured, but we do not see in his denial a consummation of his freedom. To repeat, all our liberties rest upon the objective fact of the specific difference of the human soul from subhuman souls, and the highest virtue of this difference is the human capacity to confront the mystery of the universe. This is what we mean when we say that the Declaration of Independence affirms the principle of the dignity of man. To call this principle an ideology—which means a mere rationalization of vulgar self-interest—is to demean and debase it. To call it a mere "ideal" is perhaps even worse. An ideal is distinguished from what is real, and the Declaration speaks not of something unreal, but of something real in the highest degree, namely, *truth*. Moreover, there are many ideals, but there is but one truth. To be guided by the laws of Nature and of Nature's God means to be guided not by multiple fantasies but by the unitary ground of actual existence. Present-day skepticism as to the laws of nature mentioned in the Declaration, does not supply us with an alternative ground for justifying civil liberty. Absolute skepticism is a self-devouring monster. Theoretically, it means doubting the ability to doubt. Practically, it teaches that if there is nothing that need be believed as true, neither is there anything that need be disbelieved. Unlimited skepticism quickly transforms itself into unlimited dogmatism. Political freedom exists only upon that wise and tolerant middle ground where men do not treat other men as brutes because they know that they themselves are not gods. But this restraint, this proud humility, is the attribute of those, and only those, who see in the order of nature the ground of the moral and political order.

Let us now turn to the problem with which we began. Does a free society prove false to itself if it denies civil liberties to Communists, Nazis, or anyone else who would use these liberties, if he could, as a means of destroying the free society? The answer, I believe, is now plain that it does not. In saying this I do not counsel, or even justify, any particular measure for dealing with persons of such description. What is right in any case depends upon the facts of that case, and I am here dealing only with principles, not their application. However, those who think that every denial of civil liberties is equally derogatory of the character of a free society, without reference to the character of the persons being denied, make this fundamental error: They confuse means with ends. Free speech is a priceless and indispensable attribute of a free society because it is a necessary means for deliberating upon public policy. But this deliberation does not extend to everything; above all, it does not extend to the question of whether the community shall exchange its freedom for slavery. Certain ends are fixed, and their fixity is the condition of mutability in other respects. The government may deliberate how to secure the rights to life and to liberty of all; it may never deliberate *whether* they shall be secured. Certain proposals can never be entertained by a civilized community. The essence of all such proposals would be to kill or enslave someone or some group in the community and distribute their property among the rest. Obviously, in any community in which such a proposal were seriously entertained, even for a moment, those who are proposed for proscription might rightfully consider themselves in a state of war with the rest, and feel justified in using every means to preserve themselves. But the right *not to be proscribed* is inherent in every part of the community, severally, and in the whole community, collectively. Hence *no one* ever has the right to introduce or advocate such a thing. Thus speech calling for the proscription of individuals or classes is inherently wrong, and there is an inherent right in every community to treat it as criminal, wholly apart from any consequences which can be foreseen at the moment.

Just as majority rule is a device for deciding matters of common interest where unanimity is impossible, but can never be rightfully used to destroy the minority, so free speech is a device for deliberating upon the common interest, but can never be rightfully employed to propose the destruction of either a majority or minority. Yet this is precisely what both Nazis and Communists do. Both are creeds calling for the proscription of individuals and groups innocent of any crime. The Nazis believe that one so-called race, the Aryan master race, is so superior to all others that it has the right to treat other men as if they were animals of another species. They do not hesitate to exterminate masses of human beings as if they were plague-bearing rats, or to use their skin as parchment, as if they were cattle. And Communists differ morally from Nazis only in proposing a so-called class, the proletariat, instead of a race, as the sole subject of moral right. For Nazis, morality is an intraracial, for Communists an intraclass phenomenon. Neither believe that faith is to be kept or, indeed, that there are any binding moral rules which extend beyond the barriers of race or class. The Nazis would, and have, proscribed every racial strain beyond the pale of their elite; and the Communists do the same with every class which they do not associate with the dictatorship of the proletariat. An American Communist is one who, if he knows the meaning, and accepts the discipline, of the Party, would use power arbitrarily to deprive his fellow citizens of their property and liberty and, if they resisted, their lives.

Communists and Nazis, I maintain, have no right to the use of free speech in a free society. However, whether it is wise or expedient to deny them its use is another matter. I believe that the United States is a sufficiently civilized and a sufficiently stable community to bear the advocacy of almost anything, whether it be National Socialism, Communism, or Cannibalism. I would take my stand with Jefferson, who in his first inaugural address said, "If there be any among us who would wish to dissolve this Union or to change its republican form, let them stand undisturbed as monuments of the safety with which error of opinion may be tolerated where reason is left free to combat it." But Jefferson only tolerated error; he did not in any way concede a right of the enemies of republican government to change it into a contrary form. As the context of this celebrated passage will show, it was only the impotence of the enemies of republican government which, in Jefferson's view, made it expedient, and right only because expedient, to tolerate them. And thus it was not inconsistent, as some critics have charged, for Jefferson to have instituted prosecutions by state officials for sedition, as he did, if experience revealed that the enemies of republican government were not as impotent as he had supposed. I would accordingly contend that, while it is seldom either expedient or wise to suppress the peaceful advocacy even of inhuman doctrines in a community like ours, it is not for that reason unjust. But in communities very unlike ours—for example, in a new African nation, constantly threatened by relapse into primitive barbarism on the one hand, and by the barbarism of Communism on the other—the advocacy of many inhuman and indecent things would constantly have to be prohibited.

John Stuart Mill is the most famous of those who have or seem to have demanded absolute freedom of thought and expression. Yet, in the first chapter of his essay *On Liberty,* in the very next paragraph after he proposes his great libertarian principle, he adds a qualification which his present-day followers often overlook or disregard. "It is, perhaps, hardly necessary to say," says Mill, quite mistaken as to the necessity, "that this doctrine is meant to apply only to human beings in the maturity of their faculties." The principle of liberty does not apply either to children or to those of less than legal age. Mill is very clear that he presupposes moral characters already formed, and not only able to distinguish right from wrong but disposed toward the right by a decent upbringing. Still further, Mill excludes from the application of his principle "those backward states of society in which the race itself may be considered in its nonage." Barbarians, like children, must be guided for their own good. "Despotism," he says, in a classic passage, "is a legitimate mode of government in dealing with barbarians, provided the end be their improvement, and the means justified by actually effecting that end. Liberty, as a principle, has no application to any state of things anterior to the time when mankind have become capable of being improved by free and equal discussion." I would ask those who today consider themselves followers of John Stuart Mill, what principle would exclude from the enjoyment of civil liberties the subjects of Akbar or Charlemagne, but admit the followers of Hitler or Stalin? Mill's great error was not that of believing moral qualifications were not necessary as a basis for the exercise of liberty. His error lay in his failure to discern that barbarism lurked as a potentiality of modern society no less than that of the Dark Ages. He perceived accurately the depth to which the spirit of modern science had penetrated the Western world, and he was right in believing that scientific progress in that world, and even beyond that world, was essentially irreversible. But he was utterly mistaken, in common with nearly all the thinkers of his time, in believing that the effect of the scientific spirit was to make men more temperate and just. The ability to be guided to improvement by conviction and persuasion, he said, had been "long since reached in all nations with whom we need here concern ourselves." He did not think it possible that a highly civilized modern nation could be persuaded to abandon the principle of persuasion. But we, who have seen Weimar Germany, the freest marketplace of ideas the world has ever known, give itself up to the Nazis, know differently. And we have also seen modern science flourish both in Hitler's Germany and Stalin's Russia. We know today that there is no necessary correlation between modern physics, chemistry, biology, and mathematics, not to mention the many branches of engineering, and a gentle and tolerant temper. Whatever the intention of the founders of modern science, there is nothing in its method which precludes its appropriation by men who are, in every other respect, barbarians.

There is no passage in the literature dealing with civil liberties more celebrated than the dissenting opinion of Mr. Justice Holmes in the Abrams case of 1919. The superlibertarians of our time quote it endlessly, and recite it as a litany, so much so that one wonders if many of them have not utterly forgotten the Declaration of Independence, with which it is, in many respects, in flagrant contradiction. We will present extensive selections.

Persecution for the expression of opinions seems to me perfectly logical. If you have no doubt of your premises or your power and want a certain result with all your heart you naturally express your wishes in law and sweep away all opposition. To allow opposition by speech seems to indicate that you think the speech is impotent . . . or that you do not care wholeheartedly for the result, or that you doubt either your power or your premises. But when men have realized that time has upset many fighting faiths, they may come to believe even more than they believe the very foundations of their own conduct that the ultimate good desired is better reached by free trade in ideas—that the best test of truth is the power of the thought to get itself accepted in the competition of the market, and that truth is the only ground upon which their wishes safely can be carried out. That, at any rate, is the theory of our Constitution. . . .

I think that we should be eternally vigilant against attempts to check the expression of opinions that we loathe and believe to be fraught with death, unless they so imminently threaten immediate interference with the lawful and pressing purposes of the law that an immediate check is required to save the country.

I wholly disagree with the argument of the Government that the First Amendment left the common law as to seditious libel in force. History seems to me against the notion.

I should like first to notice Holmes' last point. No one today doubts that the First Amendment did leave the common law of seditious libel in force in the states in 1791. Since the publication of Leonard W. Levy's *Legacy of Suppression: Freedom of Speech and Press in Early American History* (Harvard University Press, 1960) all controversy on that subject seems to be at an end. Some doubt remains as to whether the First Amendment, which explicitly laid a prohibition only on *Congress,* allowed the *federal* courts to enforce the common law of seditious libel. But that the *states* remained free to enforce it, and did enforce it, is not in dispute. In his draft of the Kentucky Resolutions of 1798, in the third section, Jefferson cited the language of the Tenth Amendment, and then observed that

no power over freedom of religion, freedom of speech, or freedom of the press being delegated to the United States by the Constitution, *nor prohibited by it to the States,* all lawful powers respecting the same did of right remain, and were reserved to the States or the people: that thus was manifested their determination to retain to themselves the right of judging how far licentiousness of speech and of the press may be abridged without lessening their useful freedom. . . . [italics added].

Nothing can be clearer than that, according to Jefferson, the First Amendment laid a prohibition *only* on the federal government. So far was Jefferson from any theoretical views that would prevent the people or their governments from abridging freedom of speech and press, that he insisted that the right of judging when and to what degree they ought to be abridged was a right reserved to them by the Tenth Amendment.

In the same section Jefferson went on to speak of religious freedom in a way that distinguished it profoundly from other civil liberties. In the Constitution, he said, the people "guarded against all abridgment by the United States of the freedom of religious opinions and exercises, and retain to themselves *the right of protecting* the same [italics added]. . . ." According to Jefferson the Constitution left to the states and the people the right to judge how far freedom of speech and press might be *abridged,* but left to the same authority the right only of *protecting* freedom of religious opinions. For Jefferson this distinction between religious opinion and other opinions was fundamental. In the *Notes on Virginia,* Query XVII, he says that the legitimate powers of government extend only to those natural rights which we have submitted to government and "The rights of conscience we never submitted, we could not submit." It is in this context that he pronounces the famous dictum, that "Reason and free inquiry are the only effectual agents against error," adding immediately, "Give a loose to them, they will support the true religion by bringing every false one to their tribunal." In the Virginia Statute for Religious Freedom, again referring to religious truth and error, he wrote "that truth is great and will prevail if left to herself . . . errors ceasing to be dangerous when it is permitted freely to contradict them." Dumas Malone, in the latest volume of his Jefferson biography (*Jefferson and the Ordeal of Liberty.* Boston: Little, Brown and Company, 1962) searches the writings of his hero in vain for even a single statement in which Jefferson defends unconditionally any freedom of opinion other than religious opinion. He finally concludes, quoting the "reason and free inquiry" passage, that for Jefferson "freedom of thought was an absolute, and *it may be assumed* that he applied [such maxims] not merely to religious opinion but to all opinion [italics added]." But Malone is wrong. It is no accident that he is forced to make such an assumption. The evidence does not exist because Jefferson did not say what he did not believe.

Freedom of thought was indeed an absolute for Jefferson. "The error seems not sufficiently eradicated, that the operations of the mind, as well as the acts of the body, are subject to the coercion of the laws," he also wrote in Query XVII. "The legitimate powers of government extend to such acts only as are injurious to others. But it does me no injury for my neighbor to say there are twenty gods, or no God. It neither picks my pocket nor breaks my leg." With the purely theoretical question of whether there is no God or twenty, Jefferson says government has no rightful business. But on the practical aspect of the question of whether the mind has a right to entertain such questions, and whether men must be left free by government to entertain them, there was no place in Jefferson's thinking for any neutrality. The error that the mind is not inherently free to speculate, is an error which, Jefferson says, seems not to be "sufficiently eradicated." To deny the power and right of the soul to confront the universe is a denial of human nature. Marxism, for example, by teaching that all opinions on the relation of man to God and to nature are nothing but ideology, that is, devices whereby the mind justifies and thereby cooperates in particular ways of relieving the demands of the body, treats the distinction between body and mind as essentially insignificant. It is no accident that every government professing Marxism therefore attempts to coerce the operations of the mind as well as those of the body. One cannot be equally tolerant then, and certainly Jefferson was not, of opinions destructive, and of opinions not destructive, of the regime of liberty itself. The sphere comprehended by what Jefferson called religious opinions, was essentially the sphere of theory. In his pungent phrase, it was the sphere in which a man's opinion, one way or another, neither picked Jefferson's pocket nor broke his leg. But political opinions, as they bore on the security of the government which preserved men's absolute liberty of theoretical opinion, were not matters of similar indifference. These Jefferson did not entrust to the mere hazard of any "market" of ideas. In his second inaugural address he wrote:

No inference is here intended, that the laws, provided by the State against false and defamatory publications, should not be enforced; he who has time, renders a service to public morals and public tranquillity, in reforming these abuses by the salutary coercions of the law. . . .

Mr. Justice Holmes has written that persecution is perfectly logical if you do not doubt your premises or your power. But there are different kinds of "persecution." Jefferson was sick of the long, melancholy record of human government by superstition and terror. To be blunt, he had no doubt of the premises from which he deduced their illegitimacy, and he recorded his confidence when he proclaimed these premises to be self-evident truths. It was to end persecution that he and his partisans drew the sword of what was indeed a fighting faith. To persecute persecutors, or to be intolerant of intolerance is then not the contradiction that dilettantes of political philosophy sometimes affect.

As the crisis of the Civil War approached, many frenzied efforts were made to placate Southern opinion. In 1860, in the wake of John Brown's raid, Senator Douglas of Illinois proposed a sedition law to punish abolitionist propaganda as an incitement to crime. In the Cooper Union speech, Lincoln argued against any such legislation. But he never even suggested that it would be wrong to pass such a law because it violated freedom of speech or of the press. "If slavery is right," said Lincoln, "all words, acts, laws, and constitutions against it, are themselves wrong, and should be silenced, and swept away. . . . All they ask, we could readily grant, if we thought slavery right; all we ask, they could as readily grant, if they thought it wrong. Their thinking it right, and our thinking it wrong, is the precise fact upon which depends the whole controversy." Freedom of speech was logically subordinate to personal freedom, because a man who was a slave could not demand the right to speak. Lincoln argued over and over, with a logic which no one can now deny, that there was no principle by which the enslavement of Negroes could be justified, which could not also justify the enslavement of white men. The sheet-anchor of our liberties was not the Constitution but the principle of the Declaration of Independence, which alone gave life and meaning to the Constitution. To say that the Constitution protects the right to deny that all men are created equal, is as much as to say that it protects the right to deny any obligations to obey its law.

Lincoln and Jefferson both believed that a free government is the slowest and most reluctant to restrict the liberties even of its most dangerous and fanatical enemies. It is the one which least needs to protect itself by such distasteful means, because it is the one which commands the loyalty of the mass of the citizens by the benefits they feel in their daily lives. Still, it is necessary that our loyalty be enlightened, and to that end we must ever possess ourselves of the true standard by which to measure our blessings. If we fail to see the sanity and nobility of the charter of our own freedom, we will fail to recognize the barbarism of totalitarian doctrines. And it is much better if we repudiate the foul and perverted reasonings that would justify the bestiality of a Hitler or a Stalin, and all their regimes have spawned, by the force of opinion among us. For the more we accomplish by opinion, the less we will have to do by law.

PART III

The Critique of Rationalism

THE ARGUMENTS in the first two parts of this book converge on the larger question of the capabilities of reason. What can we know and how far can reason guide us in political and social life? The question is not, alas, academic; the century is polluted by the attempts of men, some well-meaning, some tyrannical, to manufacture a new kind of man and a new kind of society according to the specifications of a rationalist blueprint. Whether called Mass Man, Communist Man, or Mao Man, he is, in Michael Oakeshott's expressive phrase, an "individual manquè"—a simulacrum of a free and rational human being. Notice, please, it is not reason that conservatives disparage, but rationalism—the abuse of reason, the deformity that results when reason ceases to recognize its own limitations.

The difficulty is that, while agreeing on the need for a critique of rationalism, conservatives disagree on the capabilities of reason. The very distinction between the two terms is, for some, highly questionable: The proper functioning of reason, they say, ought to be called "rationalism"; its abuse ought rather to be called "irrationalism." While the semantic point is well taken, it is also true that the usage is now common among conservatives, and for that reason is (provisionally) adopted here. "Rationalism" as a pejorative term owes its currency above all to the classic work of Michael Oakeshott, *Rationalism in Politics,* with which the student of conservatism should be familiar (the title essay and "On Being Conservative," in particular). It nevertheless seemed sensible to exclude those essays in favor of a similar, briefer treatment by Friedrich A. Hayek, whose *The Road to Serfdom* (1944), an apodictic demonstration of Socialism's incompatibility with liberty, was a great stimulus to the first stirrings of American conservatism.

Rationalism in politics means, in Oakeshott's challenging phrase, making politics as the crow flies, i.e., ideologically. Hayek, a student of the great Austrian economist Ludwig von Mises and for many years a professor of economics at the University of Chicago, shows that this mode of thought is characteristic of one major stream of Continental (primarily French) social criticism, which he labels "scientism" to distinguish it from the other principal stream, which issues into social science properly understood (recall Jeffrey Hart's essay). The one tradition insists on science's ability to order society according to a rational plan; the other counsels the dependence of reason on nonrational circumstances, its inability to survey and command the whole of society, its limited room to maneuver in the interstices of society. Placing Burke, Hume, and Tocqueville squarely in the latter camp, Hayek shows why traditionalism is closer to the free market analysis of libertarianism than is commonly thought. With great authority he points to the free market as the paradigm of a social order emerging spontaneously from the interplay of decentralized choices—from the workings of a mysterious process that can be comprehended only as a historical whole, as what the traditionalists would call (indeed, what Hayek calls): tradition.

Eric Voegelin pursues the same insight in a different direction, back to the philosophical origins of the notion that human reason can, godlike, wholly reorder the conditions of human existence. To locate the first appearance of this doctrine—which he identifies as "gnosticism," after the Christian heresy—he looks past the eighteenth century philosophers on whom Hayek concentrates and arrives at Joachim of Flora in the fourteenth century. The characterization of gnosticism is drawn from his short book *The New Science of Politics,* which along with *The Ecumenic Age* is the best introduction to his difficult body of thought. His masterwork is *Order and History,* a five-volume exploration (*The Ecumenic Age* is one of these) of the irruptions of the transcendent into man's historical existence.

In contrast to both Hayek and Voegelin, Leo Strauss presents a profound critique of rationalism that culminates in the renewed authority of reason to guide moral and political life. Not the reason of Hegel or Rousseau or Hobbes, however, but the practical wisdom, the prudence, of statesmen—especially as explicated and defended by Aristotle. The stupendous essay by Strauss here reproduced is the epilogue of a book called *Essays on the Scientific Study of Politics,* edited by the late Herbert J. Storing. (The contributors are all, or most of them, former students of Professor Strauss, always assuming that there is such a thing as a former student of Leo Strauss.) Besides providing a trenchant (and exhilarating) account of classical political science, his essay delivers blow after devastating blow to the positivist social science that dominates today's academy.

A disabling feature of modern social science is its exaggerated devotion to the quantitative methods of the physical sciences. No doubt this happened on account of the high prestige of the physical sciences during the nineteenth century, which prestige remains high at the present time. Yet this imitativeness, in one sense, has not been thoroughgoing enough.

Even in the physical sciences, empiricism does not stand alone; it is employed to test theory. But the hypothesis comes first, then the experiment validates or denies it. Without the prior hypothesis the testing process would have no direction.

The incompletely digested empiricism of much social science has had pernicious effects of varying degrees of seriousness. There is the prevalent triviality of much of it. Lacking criteria of relevance, the social scientist bemuses himself with marginal or microscopic subjects. The empirical method itself can establish priorities leading to extensive work on, say, voting behavior—where empirical measurement is easy—while directing attention away from other more important areas. Often the empiricist has an unacknowledged theory that directs his operations in a clandestine way and issues in self-confirming pseudoscientific conclusions about, say, the authoritarian personality; or, as Strauss points out, the method can have pernicious political implications precisely because of what it ignores. A laborious comparative study of coercion and freedom in the United States and the Soviet Union would issue in the conclusion that there is more coercion and less freedom in the U.S.S.R. But the implication would be that the difference between the two societies was merely quantitative; the entire question of goals, of the informing vision of society, would be ignored.

Strauss (like Voegelin) was born in Germany but came to America in the late thirties, eventually settling down at the University of Chicago, where he taught political philosophy. He was unquestionably one of the most influential teachers of his age (two of his students and at least four writers who were influenced by his teachings are represented in this volume). The great themes of his lifework were, first, Athens and Jerusalem, reason and revelation, which he saw as locked in a creative tension that could not be resolved (by reason) but that constituted and animated Western civilization; and second, the radical division between ancients and moderns within the history of political philosophy. His questions were Socratic, centering on the status of natural right—of the right and wrong that exist by nature, independent of human will. It is the serious contemplation of this question that distinguishes him from the critics of rationalism who presuppose, dogmatically, that reason is impotent to guide political life because it is enthralled to the spirit of its age. He argued (particularly in *Natural Right and History*) that reason could be emancipated from history and positivist science. Strauss proceeded by the careful analysis of the text, trying to understand the author as he had understood himself, and by the deceptively simple practice of taking the text seriously, presided over a renaissance of political philosophy even within the walls of the American academy.

FRIEDRICH A. HAYEK

Freedom, Reason, and Tradition

> Nothing is more fertile in prodigies than the art
> of being free; but there is nothing more arduous than
> the apprenticeship of liberty. . . . Liberty is gener-
> ally established with difficulty in the midst of storms;
> it is perfected by civil discords; and its benefit cannot
> be appreciated until it is already old.
>
> —ALEXIS DE TOCQUEVILLE

1. Though freedom is not a state of nature but an artifact of civilization, it did not arise from design. The institutions of freedom, like everything freedom has created, were not established because people foresaw the benefits they would bring. But once its advantages were recognized, men began to perfect and extend the reign of freedom and, for that purpose, to inquire how a free society worked. This development of a theory of liberty took place mainly in the eighteenth century. It began in two countries, England and France. The first of these knew liberty; the second did not.

As a result, we have had to the present day two different traditions in the theory of liberty:[1] one empirical and unsystematic, the other speculative and rationalistic[2]—the first based on an interpretation of traditions and institutions which had spontaneously grown up and were but imperfectly understood, the second aiming at the construction of a utopia, which has often been tried but never successfully. Nevertheless, it has been the rationalist, plausible, and apparently logical argument of the French tradition, with its flattering assumptions about the unlimited powers of human reason, that has progressively gained influence, while the less articulate and less explicit tradition of English freedom has been on the decline.

This distinction is obscured by the facts that what we have called the French tradition of liberty arose largely from an attempt to interpret British institutions and that the conceptions which other countries formed of British institutions were based mainly on their description by French writers. The two traditions became finally confused when they merged in the liberal movement of the nineteenth century and when even

From Friedrich A. Hayek, *The Constitution of Liberty* (Chicago: University of Chicago Press, 1960), pp. 54–70. Reprinted by permission of University of Chicago Press.

leading British liberals drew as much on the French as on the British tradition.[3] It was, in the end, the victory of the Benthamite Philosophical Radicals over the Whigs in England that concealed the fundamental difference which in more recent years has reappeared as the conflict between liberal democracy and "social" or totalitarian democracy.[4]

This difference was better understood a hundred years ago than it is today. In the year of the European revolutions in which the two traditions merged, the contrast between "Anglican" and "Gallican" liberty was still clearly described by an eminent German-American political philosopher. "Gallican Liberty," wrote Francis Lieber in 1848, "is sought in the *government,* and according to an Anglican point of view, it is looked for in a wrong place, where it cannot be found. Necessary consequences of the Gallican view are, that the French look for the highest degree of political civilization in *organization,* that is, in the highest degree of interference by public power. The question whether this interference be despotism or liberty is decided solely by the fact *who* interferes, and for the benefit of which class the interference takes place, while according to the Anglican view this interference would always be either absolutism or aristocracy, and the present dictatorship of the *ouvriers* would appear to us an uncompromising aristocracy of the *ouvriers.* "[5]

Since this was written, the French tradition has everywhere progressively displaced the English. To disentangle the two traditions it is necessary to look at the relatively pure forms in which they appeared in the eighteenth century. What we have called the "British tradition" was made explicit mainly by a group of Scottish moral philosophers led by David Hume, Adam Smith, and Adam Ferguson,[6] seconded by their English contemporaries, Josiah Tucker, Edmund Burke, and William Paley, and drawing largely on a tradition rooted in the jurisprudence of the common law.[7] Opposed to them was the tradition of the French Enlightenment, deeply imbued with Cartesian rationalism; the Encyclopedists and Rousseau, the Physiocrats and Condorcet, are their best-known representatives. Of course, the division does not fully coincide with national boundaries. Frenchmen like Montesquieu and, later, Benjamin Constant and, above all, Alexis de Tocqueville are probably nearer to what we have called the British than to the French tradition.[8] And, in Thomas Hobbes, Britain has provided at least one of the founders of the rationalist tradition, not to speak of the whole generation of enthusiasts for the French Revolution, like Godwin, Priestley, Price, and Paine, who (like Jefferson after his stay in France[9]) belong entirely to it.

2. Though these two groups are now commonly lumped together as the ancestors of modern liberalism, there is hardly a greater contrast imaginable than that between their respective conceptions of the evolution and functioning of a social order and the role played in it by liberty.

The difference is directly traceable to the predominance of an essentially empiricist view of the world in England and a rationalist approach in France. The main contrast in the practical conclusions to which these approaches led has recently been well put, as follows: "One finds the essence of freedom in spontaneity and the absence of coercion, the other believes it to be realized only in the pursuit and attainment of an absolute collective purpose";[10] and "one stands for organic, slow, half-conscious growth, the other for doctrinaire deliberateness; one for trial and error procedure, the other for an enforced solely valid pattern."[11] It is the second view, as J. S. Talmon has shown in an important book from which this description is taken, that has become the origin of totalitarian democracy.

The sweeping success of the political doctrines that stem from the French tradition is probably due to their great appeal to human pride and ambition. But we must not forget that the political conclusions of the two schools derive from different conceptions of how society works. In this respect the British philosophers laid the foundations of a profound and essentially valid theory, while the rationalist school was simply and completely wrong.

Those British philosophers have given us an interpretation of the growth of civilization that is still the indispensable foundation of the argument for liberty. They find the origin of institutions, not in contrivance or design, but in the survival of the successful. Their view is expressed in terms of "how nations stumble upon establishments which are indeed the result of human action but not the execution of human design."[12] It stresses that what we call political order is much less the product of our ordering intelligence than is commonly imagined. As their immediate successors saw it, what Adam Smith and his contemporaries did was "to resolve almost all that has been ascribed to positive institution into the spontaneous and irresistible development of certain obvious principles—and to show with how little contrivance or political wisdom the most complicated and apparently artificial schemes of policy might have been erected."[13]

This "antirationalistic insight into historical happenings that Adam Smith shares with Hume, Adam Ferguson, and others"[14] enabled them for the first time to comprehend how institutions and morals, language and law, have evolved by a process of cumulative growth and that it is only with and within this framework that human reason has grown and can successfully operate. Their argument is directed throughout against the Cartesian conception of an independently and antecedently existing human reason that invented these institutions and against the conception that civil society was formed by some wise original legislator or an original "social contract."[15] The latter idea of intelligent men coming together for deliberation about how to make the world anew is perhaps the most characteristic outcome of those design theories. It found its perfect expression when the leading theorist of the French Revolution, Abbé Sieyès, exhorted the revolutionary assembly "to act like men just emerging from the state of nature and coming together for the purpose of signing a social contract."[16]

The ancients understood the conditions of liberty better than that. Cicero quotes Cato as saying that the Roman constitution was superior to that of other states because it "was based upon the genius, not of one man, but of many; it was founded, not in one generation, but in a long period of several centuries and many ages of men. For, said he, there never has lived a man possessed of so great a genius that nothing could escape him, nor could the combined powers of all men living at one time possibly make all the necessary provisions for the future without the aid of actual experience and the test of time."[17] Neither republican Rome nor Athens—the two free nations of the ancient world—could thus serve as an example for the rationalists. For Descartes, the fountainhead of the rationalist tradition, it was indeed Sparta that provided the model; for her greatness "was due not to the preeminence of each of its laws in particular . . . but to the circumstance that, originated by a single individual, they all tended to a single end."[18] And it was Sparta which became the ideal of liberty for Rousseau as well as for Robespierre and Saint-Just and for most of the later advocates of "social" or totalitarian democracy.[19]

Like the ancient, the modern British conceptions of liberty grew against the background of a comprehension, first achieved by the lawyers, of how institutions had developed. "There are many things specially in laws and governments," wrote Chief Justice Hale in the seventeenth century in a critique of Hobbes, "that mediately, remotely, and consequentially are reasonable to be approved, though the reason of the party does not presently or immediately and distinctly see its reasonableness. . . . Long experience makes more discoveries touching conveniences or inconveniences of laws than is possible for the wisest council of men at first to foresee. And that those amendments and supplements that through the various experiences of wise and knowing men have been applied to any law must needs be better suited to the convenience of laws, than the best invention of the most pregnant wits not aided by such a series and tract of experience. . . . This adds to the difficulty of a present fathoming of the reason of laws, because they are the production of long and iterated experience which, though it be commonly called the mistress of fools, yet certainly it is the wisest expedient among mankind, and discovers those defects and supplies which no wit of man could either at once foresee or aptly remedy. . . . It is not necessary that the reasons of the institution should be evident unto us. It is sufficient that they are instituted laws that give a certainty to us, and it is reasonable to observe them though the particular reason of the institution appear not."[20]

3. From these conceptions gradually grew a body of social theory that showed how, in the relations among men, complex and orderly and, in a very definite sense, purposive institutions might grow up which owed little to design, which were not invented but arose from the separate actions of many men who did not know what they were doing. This demonstration that something greater than man's individual mind may grow from men's fumbling efforts represented in some ways an even greater challenge to all design theories than even the later theory of biological evolution. For the first time it was shown that an evident order which was not the product of a designing human intelligence need not therefore be ascribed to the design of a higher, supernatural intelligence, but that there was a third possibility—the emergence of order as the result of adaptive evolution.[21]

Since the emphasis we shall have to place on the role that selection plays in this process of social evolution today is likely to create the impression that we are borrowing the idea from biology, it is worth stressing that it was, in fact, the other way round. There can be little doubt that it was from the theories of social evolution that Darwin and his contemporaries derived the suggestion for their theories.[22] Indeed, one of those Scottish philosophers who first developed these ideas anticipated Darwin even in the biological field,[23] and the later application of these conceptions by the various "historical schools" in law and language rendered the idea that similarity of structure might be accounted for by a common origin[24] a commonplace in the study of social phenomena long before it was applied to biology. It is unfortunate that at a later date the social sciences, instead of building on these beginnings in their own field, re-imported some of these ideas from biology and with them brought in such conceptions as "natural selection," "struggle for existence," and "survival of the fittest," which are not appropriate in their field; for in social evolution, the decisive factor is not the selection of the physical and inheritable properties of the individuals but the selection by imitation of successful institutions and habits. Though this operates also through the success of individuals and groups, what emerges is not an inheritable attribute of individuals, but ideas and skills—in short, the whole cultural inheritance which is passed on by learning and imitation.

4. A detailed comparison of the two traditions would require a separate book; here we can merely single out a few of the crucial points on which they differ.

While the rationalist tradition assumes that man was originally endowed with both the intellectual and the moral attributes that enabled him to fashion civilization deliberately, the evolutionists made it clear that civilization was the accumulated hard-earned result of trial and error, that it was the sum of experience, in part handed from generation to generation as explicit knowledge, but to a larger extent embodied in tools and institutions which had proved themselves superior—institutions whose significance we might discover by analysis but which will also serve men's ends without men's understanding them. The Scottish theorists were very much aware how delicate this artificial structure of civilization was which rested on man's more primitive and ferocious instincts being tamed and checked by institutions that he neither had designed nor could control. They were very far from holding such naive views, later unjustly laid at the door of their liberalism, as the "natural goodness of man," the existence of a "natural harmony of interests," or the beneficent effects of "natural liberty" (even though they did sometimes use the last phrase). They knew that it required the artifices of institutions and traditions to reconcile the conflicts of interest. Their problem was how "that universal mover in human nature, self love, may receive such direction in this case (as in all others) as to promote the public interest by those efforts it shall make towards pursuing its own."[25] It was not "natural liberty" in any literal sense, but the institutions evolved to secure "life, liberty, and property," which made those individual efforts beneficial.[26] Not Locke, nor Hume, nor Smith, nor Burke, could ever have argued, as Bentham did, that "every law is an evil for every law is an infraction of liberty."[27] Their argument was never a complete laissez-faire argument, which, as the very words show, is also part of the French rationalist tradition and in its literal sense was never defended by any of the English classical economists.[28] They knew better than most of their later critics that it was not some sort of magic but the evolution of "well-constructed institutions," where the "rules and principles of contending interests and compromised advantages"[29] would be reconciled, that had successfully channeled individual efforts to socially beneficial aims. In fact, their argument was never antistate as such, or anarchistic, which is the logical outcome of the rationalistic laissez-faire doctrine; it was an argument that accounted both for the proper functions of the state and for the limits of state action.

The difference is particularly conspicuous in the respective assumptions of the two schools concerning individual human nature. The rationalistic design theories were necessarily based on the assumption of the individual man's propensity for rational action and his natural intelligence and goodness. The evolutionary theory, on the contrary, showed how certain institutional arrangements would induce man to use his intelligence to the best effect and how institutions could be framed so that bad people could do least harm.[30] The antirationalist tradition is here closer to the Christian tradition of the fallibility and sinfulness of man, while the perfectionism of the rationalist is in irreconcilable conflict with it. Even such a celebrated figment as the "economic man" was not an original part of the British evolutionary tradition. It would be only a slight exaggeration to say that, in the view of those British philosophers, man was by nature lazy and indolent, improvident and wasteful, and that it was only by the force of circumstances that he could be made to behave economically or would learn carefully to adjust his means to his ends. The *homo oeconomicus* was explicitly introduced, with much else that belongs to the rationalist rather than to the evolutionary tradition, only by the younger Mill.[31]

5. The greatest difference between the two views, however, is in their respective ideas about the role of traditions and the value of all the other products of unconscious growth proceeding throughout the ages.[32] It would hardly be unjust to say that the rationalistic approach is here opposed to almost all that is the distinct product of liberty and that gives liberty its value. Those who believe that all useful institutions are deliberate contrivances and who cannot conceive of anything serving a human purpose that has not been consciously designed are almost of necessity enemies of freedom. For them freedom means chaos.

To the empiricist evolutionary tradition, on the other hand, the value of freedom consists mainly in the opportunity it provides for the growth of the undesigned, and the beneficial functioning of a free society rests largely on the existence of such freely grown institutions. There probably never has existed a genuine belief in freedom, and there has certainly been no successful attempt to operate a free society, without a genuine reverence for grown institutions, for customs and habits and "all those securities of liberty which arise from regulation of long prescription and ancient ways."[33] Paradoxical as it may appear, it is probably true that a successful free society will always in a large measure be a tradition-bound society.[34]

This esteem for tradition and custom, of grown institutions, and of rules whose origins and rationale we do not know does not, of course, mean—as Thomas Jefferson believed with a characteristic rationalist misconception—that we "ascribe to men of preceding age a wisdom more than human, and . . . suppose what they did beyond amendment."[35] Far from assuming that those who created the institutions were wiser than we are, the evolutionary view is based on the insight that the result of the experimentation of many generations may embody more experience than any one man possesses.

6. We have already considered the various institutions and habits, tools and methods of doing things, which have emerged from this process and constitute our inherited civilization. But we have yet to look at those rules of conduct which have grown as part of it, which are both a product and a condition of freedom. Of these conventions and customs of human intercourse, the moral rules are the most important but by no means the

only significant ones. We understand one another and get along with one another, are able to act successfully on our plans, because, most of the time, members of our civilization conform to unconscious patterns of conduct, show a regularity in their actions that is not the result of commands or coercion, often not even of any conscious adherence to known rules, but of firmly established habits and traditions. The general observance of these conventions is a necessary condition of the orderliness of the world in which we live, of our being able to find our way in it, though we do not know their significance and may not even be consciously aware of their existence. In some instances it would be necessary, for the smooth running of society, to secure a similar uniformity by coercion, if such conventions or rules were not observed often enough. Coercion, then, may sometimes be avoidable only because a high degree of voluntary conformity exists, which means that voluntary conformity may be a condition of a beneficial working of freedom. It is indeed a truth, which all the great apostles of freedom outside the rationalistic school have never tired of emphasizing, that freedom has never worked without deeply ingrained moral beliefs and that coercion can be reduced to a minimum only where individuals can be expected as a rule to conform voluntarily to certain principles.[36]

There is an advantage in obedience to such rules not being coerced, not only because coercion as such is bad, but because it is, in fact, often desirable that rules should be observed only in most instances and that the individual should be able to transgress them when it seems to him worthwhile to incur the odium which this will cause. It is also important that the strength of the social pressure and of the force of habit which insures their observance is variable. (It is this flexibility of voluntary rules which in the field of morals makes gradual evolution and spontaneous growth possible, which allows further experience to lead to modifications and improvements.) Such an evolution is possible only with rules which are neither coercive nor deliberately imposed—rules which, though observing them is regarded as merit and though they will be observed by the majority, can be broken by individuals who feel that they have strong enough reasons to brave the censure of their fellows. Unlike any deliberately imposed coercive rules, which can be changed only discontinuously and for all at the same time, rules of this kind allow for gradual and experimental change. The existence of individuals and groups simultaneously observing partially different rules provides the opportunity for the selection of the more effective ones.

It is this submission to undesigned rules and conventions whose significance and importance we largely do not understand, this reverence for the traditional, that the rationalistic type of mind finds so uncongenial, though it is indispensable for the working of a free society. It has its foundation in the insight which David Hume stressed and which is of decisive importance for the antirationalist, evolutionary tradition—namely, that "the rules of morality are not the conclusions of our reason."[37] Like all other values, our morals are not a product but a presupposition of reason, part of the ends which the instrument of our intellect has been developed to serve. At any one stage of our evolution, the system of values into which we are born supplies the ends which our reason must serve. This givenness of the value framework implies that, although we must always strive to improve our institutions, we can never aim to remake them as a whole and that, in our efforts to improve them, we must take for granted much that we do not understand. We must always work inside a framework of both values and institutions which is not of our own making. In particular, we can never synthetically construct a new body of moral rules or make our obedience to the known rules dependent on our comprehension of the implications of this obedience in a given instance.

7. The rationalistic attitude to these problems is best seen in its views on what it calls superstition.[38] I do not wish to underestimate the merit of the persistent and relentless fight of the eighteenth and nineteenth centuries against beliefs which are demonstrably false.[39] But we must remember that the extension of the concept of superstition to all beliefs which are not demonstrably true lacks the same justification and may often be harmful. That we ought not to believe anything which has been shown to be false does not mean that we ought to believe only what has been demonstrated to be true. There are good reasons why any person who wants to live and act successfully in society must accept many common beliefs, though the value of these reasons may have little to do with their demonstrable truth.[40] Such beliefs will also be based on some past experience but not on experience for which anyone can produce the evidence. The scientist, when asked to accept a generalization in his field, is of course entitled to ask for the evidence on which it is based. Many of the beliefs which in the past expressed the accumulated experience of the race have been disproved in this manner. This does not mean, however, that we can reach the stage where we can dispense with all beliefs for which such scientific evidence is lacking. Experience comes to man in many more forms than are commonly recognized by the professional experimenter or the seeker after explicit knowledge. We would destroy the foundations of much successful action if we disdained to rely on ways of doing things evolved by the process of trial and error simply because the reason for their adoption has not been handed down to us. The appropriateness of our conduct is not necessarily dependent on our knowing why it is so. Such understanding is one way of making our conduct appropriate, but not the only one. A sterilized world of beliefs, purged of all elements whose value could not be positively demonstrated,

would probably be not less lethal than would an equivalent state in the biological sphere.

While this applies to all our values, it is most important in the case of moral rules of conduct. Next to language, they are perhaps the most important instance of an undesigned growth, of a set of rules which govern our lives but of which we can say neither why they are what they are nor what they do to us. We do not know what the consequences of observing them are for us as individuals and as a group. And it is against the demand for submission to such rules that the rationalistic spirit is in constant revolt. It insists on applying to them Descartes' principle which was "to reject as absolutely false all opinions in regard to which I could suppose the least ground for doubt."[41] The desire of the rationalist has always been for the deliberately constructed, synthetic system of morals, for the system in which, as Edmund Burke has described it, "the practice of all moral duties, and the foundations of society, rested upon their reasons made clear and demonstrative to every individual."[42] The rationalists of the eighteenth century, indeed, explicitly argued that, since they knew human nature, they "could easily find the morals which suited it."[43] They did not understand that what they called "human nature" is very largely the result of those moral conceptions which every individual learns with language and thinking.

8. An interesting symptom of the growing influence of this rationalist conception is the increasing substitution, in all languages known to me, of the word "social" for the word "moral" or simply "good." It is instructive to consider briefly the significance of this.[44] When people speak of a "social conscience" as against mere "conscience," they are presumably referring to an awareness of the particular effects of our actions on other people, to an endeavor to be guided in conduct not merely by traditional rules but by explicit consideration of the particular consequences of the action in question. They are in effect saying that our action should be guided by a full understanding of the functioning of the social process and that it should be our aim, through conscious assessment of the concrete facts of the situation, to produce a foreseeable result which they describe as the "social good."

The curious thing is that this appeal to the "social" really involves a demand that individual intelligence, rather than rules evolved by society, should guide individual action—that men should dispense with the use of what could truly be called "social" (in the sense of being a product of the impersonal process of society) and should rely on their individual judgment of the particular case. The preference for "social considerations" over the adherence to moral rules is, therefore, ultimately the result of a contempt for what really is a social phenomenon and of a belief in the superior powers of individual human reason.

The answer to these rationalistic demands is, of course, that they require knowledge which exceeds the capacity of the individual human mind and that, in the attempt to comply with them, most men would become less useful members of society than they are while they pursue their own aims within the limits set by the rules of law and morals.

The rationalist argument here overlooks the point that, quite generally, the reliance on abstract rules is a device we have learned to use because our reason is insufficient to master the full detail of complex reality.[45] This is as true when we deliberately formulate an abstract rule for our individual guidance as when we submit to the common rules of action which have been evolved by a social process.

We all know that, in the pursuit of our individual aims, we are not likely to be successful unless we lay down for ourselves some general rules to which we will adhere without reexamining their justification in every particular instance. In ordering our day, in doing disagreeable but necessary tasks at once, in refraining from certain stimulants, or in suppressing certain impulses, we frequently find it necessary to make such practices an unconscious habit, because we know that without this the rational grounds which make such behavior desirable would not be sufficiently effective to balance temporary desires and to make us do what we should wish to do from a long-term point of view. Though it sounds paradoxical to say that in order to make ourselves act rationally we often find it necessary to be guided by habit rather than reflection, or to say that to prevent ourselves from making the wrong decision we must deliberately reduce the range of choice before us, we all know that this is often necessary in practice if we are to achieve our long-range aims.

The same considerations apply even more where our conduct will directly affect not ourselves but others and where our primary concern, therefore, is to adjust our actions to the actions and expectations of others so that we avoid doing them unnecessary harm. Here it is unlikely that any individual would succeed in rationally constructing rules which would be more effective for their purpose than those which have been gradually evolved; and, even if he did, they could not really serve their purpose unless they were observed by all. We have thus no choice but to submit to rules whose rationale we often do not know, and to do so whether or not we can see that anything important depends on their being observed in the particular instance. The rules of morals are instrumental in the sense that they assist mainly in the achievement of other human values; however, since we only rarely can know what depends on their being followed in the particular instance, to observe them must be regarded as a value in itself, a sort of intermediate end which we must pursue without questioning its justification in the particular case.

9. These considerations, of course, do not prove that all the sets of moral beliefs which have grown up in a society will be beneficial. Just as a group may owe its rise to the morals which its members obey, and their values in consequence be ultimately imitated by the whole nation which the successful group has come to lead, so may a group or nation destroy itself by the moral beliefs to which it adheres. Only the eventual results can show whether the ideals which guide a group are beneficial or destructive. The fact that a society has come to regard the teaching of certain men as the embodiment of goodness is no proof that it might not be the society's undoing if their precepts were generally followed. It may well be that a nation may destroy itself by following the teaching of what it regards as its best men, perhaps saintly figures unquestionably guided by the most unselfish ideals. There would be little danger of this in a society whose members were still free to choose their way of practical life, because in such a society such tendencies would be self-corrective; only the groups guided by "impractical" ideals would decline, and others, less moral by current standards, would take their place. But this will happen only in a free society in which such ideals are not enforced on all. Where all are made to serve the same ideals and where dissenters are not allowed to follow different ones, the rules can be proved inexpedient only by the decline of the whole nation guided by them.

The important question that arises here is whether the agreement of a majority on a moral rule is sufficient justification for enforcing it on a dissenting minority or whether this power ought not also to be limited by more general rules—in other words, whether ordinary legislation should be limited by general principles just as the moral rules of individual conduct preclude certain kinds of action, however good may be their purpose. There is as much need of moral rules in political as in individual action, and the consequences of successive collective decisions as well as those of individual decisions will be beneficial only if they are all in conformity with common principles.

Such moral rules for collective action are developed only with difficulty and very slowly. But this should be taken as an indication of their preciousness. The most important among the few principles of this kind that we have developed is individual freedom, which it is most appropriate to regard as a moral principle of political action. Like all moral principles, it demands that it be accepted as a value in itself, as a principle that must be respected without our asking whether the consequences in the particular instance will be beneficial. We shall not achieve the results we want if we do not accept it as a creed or presumption so strong that no considerations of expediency can be allowed to limit it.

The argument for liberty, in the last resort, is indeed an argument for principles and against expediency in collective action,[46] which, as we shall see, is equivalent to saying that only the judge and not the administrator may order coercion. When one of the intellectual leaders of nineteenth-century liberalism, Benjamin Constant, described liberalism as the *système de principes*, [47] he pointed to the heart of the matter. Not only is liberty a system under which all government action is guided by principles, but it is an ideal that will not be preserved unless it is itself accepted as an overriding principle governing all particular acts of legislation. Where no such fundamental rule is stubbornly adhered to as an ultimate ideal about which there must be no compromise for the sake of material advantages—as an ideal which, even though it may have to be temporarily infringed during a passing emergency, must form the basis of all permanent arrangements—freedom is almost certain to be destroyed by piecemeal encroachments. For in each particular instance it will be possible to promise concrete and tangible advantages as the result of a curtailment of freedom, while the benefits sacrificed will in their nature always be unknown and uncertain. If freedom were not treated as the supreme principle, the fact that the promises which a free society has to offer can always be only chances and not certainties, only opportunities and not definite gifts to particular individuals, would inevitably prove a fatal weakness and lead to its slow erosion.

10. The reader will probably wonder by now what role there remains to be played by reason in the ordering of social affairs, if a policy of liberty demands so much refraining from deliberate control, so much acceptance of the undirected and spontaneously grown. The first answer is that, if it has become necessary to seek appropriate limits to the uses of reason here, to find these limits is itself a most important and difficult exercise of reason. Moreover, if our stress here has been necessarily on those limits, we have certainly not meant to imply thereby that reason has no important positive task. (Reason undoubtedly is man's most precious possession.) Our argument is intended to show merely that it is not all-powerful and that the belief that it can become its own master and control its own development may yet destroy it. What we have attempted is a defense of reason against its abuse by those who do not understand the conditions of its effective functioning and continuous growth. It is an appeal to men to see that we must use our reason intelligently and that, in order to do so, we must preserve that indispensable matrix of the uncontrolled and nonrational which is the only environment wherein reason can grow and operate effectively.

The antirationalistic position here taken must not be confounded with irrationalism or any appeal to mysticism. [48] What is advocated here is not an abdication of reason but a rational examination of the field where reason is appropriately put in control. Part of this argument is that such an intelligent use of reason does not mean the use of deliberate reason in the maximum possible number of occasions. In opposition to the naive rationalism which treats our present reason as an absolute, we must continue the efforts which David Hume commenced when he "turned against the enlightenment its own weapons" and undertook "to whittle down the claims of reason by the use of rational analysis."[49]

The first condition for such an intelligent use of reason in the ordering of human affairs is that we learn to understand what role it does in fact play and can play in the working of any society based on the cooperation of many separate minds. This means that, before we can try to remold society intelligently, we must understand its functioning; we must realize that, even when we believe that we understand it, we may be mistaken. What we must learn to understand is that human civilization has a life of its own, that all our efforts to improve things must operate within a working whole which we cannot entirely control, and the operation of whose forces we can hope merely to facilitate and assist so far as we understand them. Our attitude ought to be similar to that of the physician toward a living organism: Like him, we have to deal with a self-maintaining whole which is kept going by forces which we cannot replace and which we must therefore use in all we try to achieve. What can be done to improve it must be done by working with these forces rather than against them. In all our endeavors at improvement we must always work inside this given whole, aim at piecemeal, rather than total, construction,[50] and use at each stage the historical material at hand and improve details step by step rather than attempt to redesign the whole.

None of these conclusions are arguments against the use of reason, but only arguments against such uses as require any exclusive and coercive powers of government; not arguments against experimentation, but arguments against all exclusive, monopolistic power to experiment in a particular field—power which brooks no alternative and which lays a claim to the possession of superior wisdom—and against the consequent preclusion of solutions better than the ones to which those in power have committed themselves.

NOTES

The quotation at the head of the chapter is taken from Alexis de Tocqueville, *Democracy in America* (New York: Knopf, 1945), trans. Henry Reeve, ed. Philips Bradley, Vol. I, chap. xiv, pp. 246 f.; cf. also Vol. II, chap. ii, p. 96: "The advantages that freedom brings are shown only by the lapse of time, and it is always easy to mistake the cause in which they originate." An earlier and slightly longer version of this chapter has appeared in *Ethics*, Vol. LXVIII (1958).

1. Tocqueville remarks somewhere: "Du dix-huitième siècle et de la révolution, étaient sortis deux fleuves: le premier conduisant les hommes aux institutions libres, tandis que le second les menant au pouvoir absolu." Cf. the observation by Sir Thomas E. May, *Democracy in Europe* (London, 1877), II, 334: "The history of the one [France], in modern times, is the history of Democracy, not of liberty: the history of the other [England] is the history of liberty, not of Democracy." See also G. de Ruggiero, *The*

History of European Liberalism, trans. R. G. Collingwood (Oxford: Oxford University Press, 1927), esp. pp. 12, 71, and 81. On the absence of a truly liberal tradition in France see E. Faguet, *Le Libéralisme* (Paris, 1902), esp. p. 307.

2. "Rationalism" and "rationalistic" will be used here throughout in the sense defined by B. Groethuysen, in "Rationalism," *E.S.S.,* XIII, 113, as a tendency "to regulate individual and social life in accordance with principles of reason and to eliminate as far as possible or to relegate to the background everything irrational." Cf. also M. Oakeshott, "Rationalism in Politics," *Cambridge Journal,* Vol. I (1947).

3. See E. Halévy, *The Growth of Philosophic Radicalism* (London: Macmillan, 1928), p. 17.

4. Cf. J. L. Talmon, *The Origins of Totalitarian Democracy* (London: Praeger, 1952). Though Talmon does not identify "social" with "totalitarian" democracy, I cannot but agree with H. Kelsen ("The Foundations of Democracy," *Ethics,* LXVI, Part 2 [1955], 95 n.) that "the antagonism which Talmon describes as tension between liberal and totalitarian democracy is in truth the antagonism between liberalism and socialism and not between two types of democracy."

5. Francis Lieber, "Anglican and Gallican Liberty," originally published in a South Carolina newspaper in 1849 and reprinted in *Miscellaneous Writings* (Philadelphia, 1881), p. 282. See also p. 385: "The fact that Gallican liberty expects everything from *organization* while Anglican liberty inclines to *development,* explains why we see in France so little improvement and expansion of institutions; but when improvement is attempted, a total abolition of the preceding state of things—a beginning *ab ovo*—a rediscussion of the first elementary principles."

6. An adequate account of this philosophy of growth which provided the intellectual foundations for a policy of freedom has yet to be written and cannot be attempted here. For a fuller appreciation of the Scottish-English school and its differences from the French rationalist tradition see D. Forbes, "Scientific Whiggism: Adam Smith and John Millar," *Cambridge Journal,* Vol. VII (1954), and my own lecture, *Individualism, True and False* (Dublin, 1945), reprinted in *Individualism and Economic Order* (London and Chicago, 1948) (the latter particularly for the role played by B. Mandeville in this tradition which I am passing over here). For further reference see the earlier version of this article in *Ethics,* Vol. LXVIII (1958).

7. See especially the work of Sir Matthew Hale referred to in n. 20, below.

8. Montesquieu, Constant, and Tocqueville were often regarded as Anglomaniacs by their compatriots. Constant was partly educated in Scotland, and Tocqueville could say of himself that "So many of my thoughts and feelings are shared by the English that England has turned into a second native land of the mind for me" (A. de Tocqueville, *Journeys to England and Ireland,* ed. J. P. Mayer [New Haven: Yale University Press, 1958], p. 13). A fuller list of eminent French thinkers who belonged more to the evolutionary "British" than to the rationalistic "French" tradition would have to include the young Turgot and E. B. de Condillac.

9. On Jefferson's shift from the "British" to the "French" tradition as a result of his stay in France see the important work by O. Vossler, *Die amerikanischen Revolutionsideale in ihrem Verhältnis zu den europäischen* (Munich, 1929).

10. Talmon, *op. cit.,* p. 2.

11. *Ibid.,* p. 71. Cf. also L. Mumford, *Faith for Living* (New York, 1940), pp. 64–66, where a contrast is drawn between "ideal liberalism" and "pragmatic liberalism," and W. M. McGovern and D. S. Collier, *Radicals and Conservatives* (Chicago, 1958), where "conservative liberals" and "radical liberals" are distinguished.

12. A. Ferguson, *An Essay on the History of Civil Society* (Edinburgh, 1767), p. 187.

13. [Francis Jeffrey], "Craig's Life of Millar," *Edinburgh Review,* IX (1807), 84. F. W. Maitland much later spoke similarly somewhere of "the stumbling forward in our empirical fashion, blundering into wisdom."

14. Forbes, *op. cit.,* p. 645. The importance of the Scottish moral philosophers as forebears of cultural anthropology has been handsomely acknowledged by E. E. Evans-Pritchard, *Social Anthropology* (London, 1951), pp. 23–25.

15. L. von Mises, *Socialism* (new ed.; New Haven: Yale University Press, 1951), p. 43, writes with reference to the social contract: "Rationalism could find no other possible explanation after it had disposed of the old belief which traced social institutions back to divine sources or at least to the enlightenment which came to man through divine inspiration. Because it led to present conditions, people regarded the development of social life as absolutely purposeful and rational; how then could this development have come about except through conscious choice in recognition of the fact that it was purposeful and rational?"

16. Quoted by Talmon, *op. cit.,* p. 73.

17. M. Tullius Cicero, *De re publica* ii. 1, 2; cf. also ii. 21. 37. Neratius, a later Roman jurist quoted in the *Corpus iuris civilis,* even went so far as to exhort lawyers: "Rationes eorum quae constituuntur inquiri non oportet, alioquin multer quae certa sunt subvertuntur" ("We must avoid inquiring about the rationale of our institutions, since otherwise many that are certain would be overturned"). Although in this respect the Greeks were somewhat more rationalistic, a similar conception of the growth of law is by no means absent. See, e.g., the Attic orator Antiphon, *On the Choreutes* par 2. (*Minor Attic Orators,* ed. K. J. Maidment [Loeb Classical Library (Cambridge, Mass: Harvard University Press, 1941)], I, 247), where he speaks of laws having "the distinction of being the oldest in this country, . . . and that is the surest token of good laws, as time and experience show mankind what is imperfect."

18. R. Descartes, *A Discourse on Method* (Everyman ed.), Part II, p. 11.

19. Cf. Talmon, *op. cit.,* p. 142. On the influence of the Spartan ideal on Greek philosophy and especially on Plato and Aristotle see F. Ollier, *Le Mirage spartiate* (Paris, 1933), and K. R. Popper, *The Open Society and Its Enemies* (London, 1945).

20. "Sir Matthew Hale's Criticism on Hobbes Dialogue on the Common Law," reprinted as an appendix to W. S. Holdsworth, *A History of English Law,* Vol. V (London, 1924), 504–505 (the spelling has been modernized). Holdsworth rightly points out the similarity of some of these arguments to those of Edmund Burke. They are, of course, in effect an attempt to elaborate ideas of Sir Edward Coke (whom Hobbes had criticized), especially his famous conception of the "artificial reason" which (*Seventh Report,* ed. I. H. Thomas and I. F. Fraser [London, 1826], IX, 6) he explains as follows: "Our days upon earth are but a shadow in respect of the old ancient days and times past, wherein the laws have been by the wisdom of the most excellent men, in many succession of ages, by long and continued experience (the trial of light and truth) fined and refined, which no one man (being of so short a time), albeit he had the wisdom of all the men in the world, in any one age could ever have affected or attained unto." Cf. also the legal proverb: "Per varios usus experientia legem fecit."

21. The best discussion of the character of this process of social growth known to me is still C. Menger, *Untersuchungen,* Book III and Appendix VIII, esp. pp. 163–65, 203–204n., and 208. Cf. also the discussion in A. Macbeath, *Experiments in Living* (London, 1952), p. 120, of "the principle laid down by Frazer [*Psyche's Task,* p. 4] and endorsed by Malinowski and other anthropologists, that no institution will continue to survive unless it performs some useful function" and the remark added in a footnote: "But the function which it serves at a given time may not be that for the sake of which it was originally established"; and the following passage, in which Lord Acton indicates how he would have continued his brief sketches of freedom in antiquity and Christianity (*Hist. of Freedom,* p. 58): "I should have wished . . . to relate by whom and in what connection, the true law of the formation of free States was recognised, and how that discovery, closely akin to those which, under the names of development, evolution, and

continuity, have given a new and deeper method to other sciences, solved the ancient problem between stability and change, and determined the authority of tradition on the progress of thought; how that theory, which Sir James Mackintosh expressed by saying that Constitutions are not made, but grow; the theory that custom and the national qualities of the governed, and not the will of the government, are the makers of the law."

22. I am not referring here to Darwin's acknowledged indebtedness to the population theories of Malthus (and, through him, of R. Cantillon) but to the general atmosphere of an evolutionary philosophy which governed thought on social matters in the nineteenth century. Though this influence has occasionally been recognized (see, e.g., H. F. Osborn, *From the Greeks to Darwin* [New York, 1894], p. 87), it has never been systematically studied. I believe that such a study would show that most of the conceptual apparatus which Darwin employed lay ready at hand for him to use. One of the men through whom Scottish evolutionary thought reached Darwin was probably the Scottish geologist James Hutton.

23. See A. O. Lovejoy, "Monboddo and Rousseau" (1933), reprinted in *Essays in the History of Ideas* (Baltimore: Johns Hopkins University Press, 1948).

24. It is perhaps significant that the first clearly to see this in the field of linguistics, Sir William Jones, was a lawyer by training and a prominent Whig by persuasion. Cf. his celebrated statement in the "Third Anniversary Discourse" delivered February 2, 1786, in *Asiatick Researches*, I, 422, and reprinted in his *Works* (London, 1807), III, 34: "The *Sanscrit* language, whatever be its antiquity, is of a wonderful structure; more perfect than the Greek, more copious than the *Latin*, and more exquisitely refined than either, yet bearing to both of them a stronger affinity, both in the roots of verbs and in the forms of grammar, than could possibly have been produced by accident: so strong indeed, that no philologer could examine them all three, without believing them to have sprung from some common source, which, perhaps, no longer exists." The connection between speculation about language and that about political institutions is best shown by one of the most complete, though somewhat late, statements of the Whig doctrine by Dugald Stewart, *Lectures on Political Economy* (delivered 1809–10), printed in *The Collected Works of Dugald Stewart* (Edinburgh, 1856), IX, 422–24, and quoted at length in a note to the earlier version of this chapter in *Ethics*, Vol. LXVIII (1958). It is of special importance because of Stewart's influence on the last group of Whigs, the *Edinburgh Review* circle. Is it an accident that in Germany her greatest philosopher of freedom, Wilhelm von Humboldt, was also one of her greatest theorists of language?

25. Josiah Tucker, *The Elements of Commerce* (1755) in *Josiah Tucker: A Selection*, ed. R. L. Schuyler (New York: Columbia University Press, 1931), p. 92.

26. That for Adam Smith in particular it was certainly not "natural liberty" in any literal sense on which the beneficial working of the economic system depended, but liberty under the law, is clearly expressed in *Wealth of Nations*, Book IV, chapter v, II, 42–43: "That security which the laws in Great Britain give to every man that he shall enjoy the fruits of his own labour, is alone sufficient to make any country flourish, notwithstanding these and twenty other absurd regulations of commerce: and this security was perfected by the revolution, much about the same time that the bounty was established. The natural effort of every individual to better his own condition, when suffered to exert itself with freedom and security, is so powerful a principle, that it is alone, and without any assistance, not only capable of carrying on the society to wealth and prosperity, but of surmounting a hundred impertinent obstructions with which the folly of human laws too often incumbers its operations." Cf. C. A. Cooke, "Adam Smith and Jurisprudence," *Law Quarterly Review*, LI (1935), 328: "The theory of political economy that emerges in the 'Wealth of Nations' can be seen to be a consistent theory of law and legislation . . . the famous passage about the invisible hand rises up as the essence

of Adam Smith's view of law"; and also the interesting discussion in J. Cropsey, *Polity and Economy* (The Hague, 1957). It is of some interest that Smith's general argument about the "invisible hand," "which leads man to promote an end which was no part of his intention," already appears in Montesquieu, *Spirit of the Laws,* I, 25, where he says that "thus each individual advances the public good, while he only thinks of promoting his own interest."

27. J. Bentham, *Theory of Legislation,* 5th ed. (London, 1887), p. 48.

28. See D. H. MacGregor, *Economic Thought and Policy* (Oxford: Oxford University Press, 1949), pp. 54–89, and Lionel Robbins, *The Theory of Economic Policy* (London, 1952), pp. 42–46.

29. E. Burke, *Thoughts and Details on Scarcity,* in *Works,* VII, 398.

30. Cf., e.g., the contrast between D. Hume, *Essays,* Book I, vi, p. 117: "Political writers have established it as a maxim, that, in contriving any system of government, and fixing the several checks and controuls of the constitution, every man ought to be supposed a *knave,* and to have no other end, in all his actions, than private interest" (the reference is presumably to Machiavelli, *Discorsi,* I, 3: "The lawgiver must assume for his purposes that all men are bad"), and R. Price, *Two Tracts on Civil Liberty* (London, 1778), p. 11: "Every man's will, if perfectly free from restraint, would carry him invariably to rectitude and virtue." See also my *Individualism and Economic Order* (London and Chicago, 1948), pp. 11–12.

31. See J. S. Mill, *Essays on Some Unsettled Questions of Political Economy* (London, 1844), Essay V.

32. Ernest Renan, in an important essay on the principles and tendencies of the liberal school, first published in 1858 and later included in his *Essais de morale et de critique* (now in *Œuvres complètes,* ed. H. Psichari, II [Paris, 1947], 45 f.) observes: "Le libéralisme, ayant la prétention de se fonder uniquement sur les principes de la raison, croit d'ordinaire n'avoir pas besoin de traditions. Là est son erreur. . . . L'erreur de l'école libérale est d'avoir trop cru qu'il est facile de créer la liberté par la réflexion, et de n'avoir pas vue qu'un établissement n'est solide que quand il a des racines historiques. . . . Elle ne vit pas que tous ses efforts ne pouvait sortir qu'une bonne administration, mais jamais la liberté, puisque la liberté résulte d'un droit antérieur et supérieur à celui de l'État, et non d'une déclaration improvisée ou d'un raisonnement philosophique plus ou moins bien déduit." Cf. also the observation by R. B. McCallum in the Introduction to his edition of J. S. Mill, *On Liberty* (Oxford, 1946), p. 15: "While Mill admits the great power of custom, and within limits its uses, he is prepared to criticise all those rules which depend upon it and are not defended by reason. He remarks, 'People are accustomed to believe, and have been encouraged in the belief by some who aspire to the character of philosophers, that their feelings on subjects of this nature, are better than reasons and render reasons unnecessary.' This is the position which Mill, as a utilitarian rationalist, was bound never to accept. It was the 'sympathy-antipathy' principle which Bentham considered was the basis of all systems of other than the rationalist approach. Mill's primary contention as a political thinker is that all these unreasoning assumptions should be weighed and considered by the reflective and balanced judgment of thinking men."

33. Joseph Butler, *Works,* ed. W. E. Gladstone (Oxford, 1896), II, 329.

34. Even Professor H. Butterfield, who understands this better than most people, finds it "one of the paradoxes of history" that "the name of England has come to be so closely associated with liberty on the one hand and tradition on the other hand" (*Liberty in the Modern World* [Toronto, 1952], p. 21).

35. T. Jefferson, *Works,* ed. P. L. Ford, XII (New York, 1905), 111.

36. See, e.g., E. Burke, *A Letter to a Member of the National Assembly,* in *Works,* VI, 64: "Men are qualified for civil liberty, in exact proportion to their disposition to put moral chains

upon their appetites; in proportion as their love of justice is above their rapacity; in proportion as their soundness and sobriety of understanding is above their vanity and presumption; in proportion as they are more disposed to listen to the council of the wise and good, in preference to the flattery of knaves." Also James Madison in the debates during the Virginia Ratifying Convention, June 20, 1788 (in *The Debates in the Several State Conventions, on the Adoption of the Federal Constitution, etc.*, ed. J. Elliot [Philadelphia, 1863], III, 537): "To suppose that any form of government will secure liberty or happiness without any virtue in the people, is a chimerical idea." And Tocqueville, *Democracy*, I, 12: "Liberty cannot be established without morality, nor morality without faith"; also II, 235: "No free communities ever existed without morals."

37. Hume, *Treatise*, Book III, Part I, sec. 1 (II, 235), the paragraph headed "Moral Distinctions Not Deriv'd from Reason": "The rules of morality, therefore, are not conclusions of our reason." The same idea is already implied in the scholastic maxim, "Ratio est instrumentum non est judex." Concerning Hume's evolutionary view of morals, I am glad to be able to quote a statement I should have been reluctant to make, for fear of reading more into Hume than is there, but which comes from an author who, I believe, does not look at Hume's work from my particular angle. In *The Structure of Freedom* (Stanford, Calif.: Stanford University Press, 1958), p. 33, C. Bay writes: "Standards of morality and justice are what Hume calls 'artifacts'; they are neither divinely ordained, nor an integral part of original human nature, nor revealed by pure reason. They are an outcome of the practical experience of mankind, and the sole consideration in the slow test of time is the utility each moral rule can demonstrate toward promoting human welfare. Hume may be called a precursor of Darwin in the sphere of ethics. In effect, he proclaimed a doctrine of the survival of the fittest among human conventions—fittest not in terms of good teeth but in terms of maximum social utility."

38. Cf. H. B. Acton, "Prejudice," *Revue internationale de philosophie*, Vol. XXI (1952), with the interesting demonstration of the similarity of the views of Hume and Burke; also the same author's address, "Tradition and Some Other Forms of Order," *Proc. Arist. Soc.*, 1952–53, especially the remark at the beginning that "liberals and collectivists join together against tradition when there is some 'superstition' to be attacked." See also Lionel Robbins, *The Theory of Economic Policy* (London, 1952), p. 196n.

39. Perhaps even this is putting it too strongly. A hypothesis may well be demonstrably false and still, if some new conclusions follow from it which prove to be true, be better than no hypothesis at all. Such tentative, though partly erroneous, answers to important questions may be of the greatest significance for practical purposes, though the scientist dislikes them because they are apt to impede progress.

40. Cf. Edward Sapir, *Selected Writings in Language, Culture, and Personality*, ed. D. G. Mandelbaum (Berkeley: University of California Press, 1949), p. 558: "It is sometimes necessary to become conscious of the forms of social behavior in order to bring about a more serviceable adaptation to changed conditions, but I believe it can be laid down as a principle of far-reaching application that in the normal business of life it is useless and even mischievous for the individual to carry the conscious analysis of his cultural patterns around with him. That should be left to the student whose business it is to understand these patterns. A healthy unconsciousness of the forms of socialized behavior to which we are subject is as necessary to society as is the mind's ignorance, or better unawareness, of the workings of the viscera to the health of the body." See also p. 26.

41. Descartes, *op. cit.*, Part IV, p. 26.

42. E. Burke, *A Vindication of Natural Society*, Preface, in *Works*, I, 7.

43. P. H. T. Baron d'Holbach, *Système social* (London, 1773), I, 55, quoted in Talmon, *op. cit.*, p. 273. Similarly naïve statements are not difficult to find in the writings of contemporary psychologists. B. F. Skinner, e.g., in *Walden Two* (New York, 1948), p. 85, makes

the hero of his utopia argue: "Why not experiment? The questions are simple enough. What's the best behavior for the individual so far as the group is concerned? And how can the individual be induced to behave in that way? Why not explore these questions in a scientific spirit?

"We could do just that in Walden Two? We had already worked out a code of conduct—subject, of course, to experimental modification. The code would keep things running smoothly if everybody lived up to it. Our job was to see that everybody did."

44. Cf. my article "Was ist und was heisst 'sozial'?" in *Masse und Demokratie*, ed. A. Hunold (Zurich, 1957), and the attempted defense of the concept in H. Jahrreiss, *Freiheit und Sozialstaat* ("Kölner Universitätsreden," No. 17 [Krefeld, 1957]), now reprinted in the same author's *Mensch und Staat* (Cologne and Berlin, 1957).

45. Cf. Tocqueville's emphasis on the fact that "general ideas are no proof of the strength, but rather of the insufficiency of the human intellect" (*Democracy*, II, 13).

46. It is often questioned today whether consistency is a virtue in social action. The desire for consistency is even sometimes represented as a rationalistic prejudice, and the judging of each case on its individual merits as the truly experimental or empiricist procedure. The truth is the exact opposite. The desire for consistency springs from the recognition of the inadequacy of our reason explicitly to comprehend all the implications of the individual case, while the supposedly pragmatic procedure is based on the claim that we can properly evaluate all the implications without reliance on those principles which tell us which particular facts we ought to take into account.

47. B. Constant, "De l'arbitraire," in *Œuvres politiques de Benjamin Constant*, ed. C. Louandre (Paris, 1874), pp. 91–92.

48. It must be admitted that after the tradition discussed was handed on by Burke to the French reactionaries and German romanticists, it was turned from an antirationalist position into an irrationalist faith and that much of it survived almost only in this form. But this abuse, for which Burke is partly responsible, should not be allowed to discredit what is valuable in the tradition, nor should it cause us to forget "how thorough a Whig [Burke] was to the last," as F. W. Maitland (*Collected Papers*, I [Cambridge: Cambridge University Press, 1911], p. 67) has rightly emphasized.

49. S. S. Wolin, "Hume and Conservatism," *American Political Science Review*, XLVIII (1954), 1001; cf. also E. C. Mossner, *Life of David Hume* (London, 1954), p. 125: "In the Age of Reason, Hume set himself apart as a systematic anti-rationalist."

50. Cf. K. R. Popper, *The Open Society and Its Enemies* (London, 1945), *passim*.

ERIC VOEGELIN

Gnosticism—The Nature of Modernity

The clash between the various types of truth in the Roman Empire ended with the victory of Christianity. The fateful result of this victory was the dedivinization of the temporal sphere of power. To anticipate, the advent

From Eric Voegelin, *The New Science of Politics* (Chicago: University of Chicago Press, 1952), pp. 107–32. Copyright © 1952 by University of Chicago. Reprinted by permission of University of Chicago Press.

of modernity would bring about a redivinization of man and society. It is important at this point to define our terms, especially since both the concept of modernity and the periodization of history depend upon the meaning of redivinization. Therefore, by dedivinization we mean the process by which the culture of polytheism died from experiential atrophy, and human existence in society became reordered, through the grace of the world-transcendent God, by the experience of man's destination as eternal life in beatific vision. By redivinization, however, we do not mean a revival of polytheistic culture in the Greco-Roman sense. The characterization of modern political mass movements as neo-pagan, which has a certain vogue, is misleading because it sacrifices the historically unique nature of modern movements to a superficial resemblance. Modern redivinization has its origins rather in Christianity itself, deriving from components that were suppressed as heretical by the universal church.

Within Christianity itself, then, there has existed a tension between the central tradition which viewed man's destiny as transcendent and eternal and a suppressed tradition which looked forward in time to the establishment of a Kingdom of God in the world. Historically, the tension derives from the origin of Christianity as a Jewish messianic movement. The experience of the early Christian communities oscillated between the eschatological expectation of the Parousia that would bring the Kingdom of God and the understanding of the church as the apocalypse of Christ in history. Since the Parousia did not occur, the church actually evolved from the eschatology of the Kingdom of God in history toward the eschatology of transhistorical, supernatural perfection. In this evolution the specific essence of Christianity separated from its historical origin.[1] This separation began within the life of Jesus itself,[2] and it was on principle completed with the Pentecostal descent of the Spirit. Nevertheless, the expectation of an imminent coming of the Kingdom was stirred to white heat again and again by the suffering of the persecutions, and the most grandiose expression of eschatological pathos, the Revelation of St. John, was included in the canon in spite of misgivings about its compatibility with the idea of the church. The inclusion had fateful consequences, for with the Revelation was accepted the revolutionary annunciation of the millennium in which Christ would reign with his saints on this earth.[3] Not only did the inclusion sanction the permanent influence within Christianity of the broad mass of Jewish apocalyptic literature but it also raised the immediate question how chiliasm could be reconciled with the idea and existence of the church. If Christianity consisted in the burning desire for deliverance from the world, if Christians lived in expectation of the end of unredeemed history, if their destiny could be fulfilled only by the Realm in the sense of chapter 20 of Revelation, the church was reduced to an ephemeral community of men waiting for the great event and hoping that it would occur in their lifetime. On the theoretical level the problem could be solved only by the tour de force of interpretation which Saint Augustine performed in the *Civitas Dei*. There he roundly dismissed the literal belief in the millennium as "ridiculous fables" and then boldly declared the Realm of the thousand years to be the reign of Christ in His church in the present saeculum that would continue until the Last Judgment and the advent of the eternal Realm in the beyond.[4]

The Augustinian conception of the church, without substantial change, remained historically effective to the end of the Middle Ages. The revolutionary expectation of a Second Coming that would transfigure the structure of history on earth was ruled out as "ridiculous." The Logos had become flesh in Christ; the grace of redemption had been bestowed on man; there would be no divinization of society beyond the pneumatic presence of Christ in His church. Jewish chiliasm was excluded along with polytheism, just as Jewish monotheism had been excluded along with pagan, metaphysical monotheism. This left the church as the universal spiritual organization of saints and sinners who professed faith in Christ, as the representative of the *Civitas Dei* in history, as the flash of eternity into time. And correspondingly it rendered the power organization of society merely temporal—a manifestation of that part of human nature that will pass away with the transfiguration of time into eternity. The one Christian society was articulated into its spiritual and temporal orders. In its temporal articulation it accepted the *conditio humana* without chiliastic fancies, while it heightened natural existence by the representation of spiritual destiny through the church. . . .

Western Christian society thus was articulated into the spiritual and temporal orders, with pope and emperor as the supreme representatives in both the existential and the transcendental sense. From this society with its established system of symbols emerge the specifically modern problems of representation, with the resurgence of the eschatology of the realm. Such resurgence had a long social and intellectual prehistory, but the desire for a redivinization of society produced a definite symbolism of its own only toward the end of the twelfth century. Our analysis here will start from the first clear and comprehensive expression of the idea in the work of Joachim of Flora.

Joachim broke with the Augustinian conception of a Christian society when he applied the symbol of the Trinity to the course of history. In his speculation, the history of mankind had three periods corresponding to the three persons of the Trinity. The first period of the world was the age of the Father; with the appearance of Christ began the age of the Son. But the age of the Son will not be the last one; it will be followed by a third age of the Spirit. The three ages were characterized by intelligible increases in spiritual fulfillment. The first age unfolded the life of the layman; the second age brought the active and contemplative life of the priest; the third age, would bring the perfect spiritual life of the monk. Moreover, the ages had comparable internal structures and a calculable length. From the comparison of structures it appeared that each age opened with a trinity of leading figures, that is, with two precursors, followed by the leader of the age himself; and from the calculation of length it followed that the age of the Son would reach its end in 1260. The leader of the first age was Abraham; the leader of the second age was Christ; and Joachim predicted that by 1260 there would appear the *Dux e Bablyone*, the leader of the third age.[5]

In his trinitarian eschatology Joachim created the aggregate of symbols which govern the self-interpretation of modern political society to this day.

The first of these symbols is the conception of history as a sequence of three ages, of which the third age is intelligibly the final Third Realm. As variations of this symbol are recognizable the humanistic and encyclopedist periodization of history into ancient, medieval, and modern history: Turgot's and Comte's theory of a sequence of theological, metaphysical, and scientific phases; Hegel's dialectic of the three stages of freedom and self-reflective spiritual fulfillment; the Marxian dialectic of the three stages of primitive Communism, class society, and final Communism; and, finally, the National Socialist symbol of the Third Realm— though this is a special case requiring further attention.

The second symbol is that of the leader.[6] It had its immediate effectiveness in the movement of the Franciscan spirituals who saw in Saint Francis the fulfillment of Joachim's prophecy, and its effectiveness was reinforced by Dante's speculation on the *Dux* of the new spiritual age. It then can be traced in the paracletic figures, the *homines spirituales* and *homines novi*, of the late Middle Ages, the Renaissance, and Reformation; it can be discerned as a component in Machiavelli's *principe;* and in the period of secularization it appears in the supermen of Condorcet, Comte, and Marx, until it dominates the contemporary scene through the paracletic leaders of the new realms.

The third symbol, sometimes blending into the second, is that of the prophet of the new age. In order to lend validity and conviction to the idea of a final Third Realm, the course of history as an intelligible, meaningful whole must be assumed accessible to human knowledge, either through a direct revelation or through speculative gnosis. Hence, the Gnostic prophet—or, in the later stages of secularization, the Gnostic intellectual—becomes an appurtenance of civilization. Joachim himself was the first instance of the species.

The fourth symbol is that of the brotherhood of autonomous persons. The third age of Joachim, by virtue of its new descent of the spirit, will transform men into members of the new realm without sacramental mediation of grace. In the third age the church will cease to exist because the charismatic gifts that are necessary for the perfect life will reach men without the administration of sacraments. While Joachim himself conceived the new age concretely as an order of monks, the idea of a community of the spiritually perfect who can live together without institutional authority was formulated on principle. The idea was capable of infinite variations. It can be traced in various degrees of purity in medieval and Renaissance sects, as well as in the Puritan churches of the saints; in its secularized form it has become a formidable component in the contemporary democratic creed; and it is the dynamic core in the Marxian mysticism of the realm of freedom and the withering-away of the state.

The National Socialist Third Realm is a special case. To be sure, Hitler's millennial prophecy authentically derives from Joachitic speculation, mediated in Germany through the Anabaptist wing of the Reformation and through the Johannine Christianity of Fichte, Hegel, and Schelling. Nevertheless, the concrete application of the trinitarian schema to the first German Reich that ended in 1806, the Bismarck Reich that ended in 1918, and the *Dritte Reich* of the National Socialist movement sounds flat and provincial if compared with the world-historical speculation of the German idealists, of Comte, or of Marx. This nationalist, accidental touch is due to the fact that the symbol of the *Dritte Reich* did not stem from the speculative effort of a philosopher of rank but rather from dubious literary transfers. The National Socialist propagandists picked it up from Moeller van den Bruck's tract of that name.[7] And Moeller, who had no National Socialist intentions, had found it as a convenient symbol in the course of his work on the German edition of Dostoevski. The Russian idea of the Third Rome is characterized by the same blend of an eschatology of the spiritual realm with its realization by a political society. This other branch of political redivinization must now be considered.

Only in the West was the Augustinian conception of the church historically effective to the point where it resulted in the clear double representation of society in the spiritual and the temporal powers. The fact that the temporal ruler was situated at a considerable geographical distance from Rome certainly facilitated this evolution. In the East developed the Byzantine form of Caesaropapism, in direct continuity with the position of the emperor in pagan Rome. Constantinople was the Second Rome, as we see from the declaration of Justinian concerning the *consuetudo Romae:* "By Rome, however, must be understood not only the old one but also our royal city."[8] After the fall of Constantinople to the Turks, the idea of Moscow as the successor to the Orthodox empire gained ground in Russian clerical circles. Let me quote the famous passages from a letter of Filofei of Pskov to Ivan the Great:

The church of the first Rome fell because of the godless heresy of Apollinaris. The gates of the second Rome at Constantinople were smashed by the Ishmael- ites. Today the holy apostolic church of the third Rome in thy Empire shines in the glory of Christian faith throughout the world. Know you, O pious Tsar, that all empires of the orthodox Christians have converged into thine own. You are the sole autocrat of the universe, the only tsar of all Christians. . . . Accord- ing to the prophetic books all Christian empires have an end and will converge into one empire, that of our gossudar, that is, into the Empire of Russia. Two Romes have fallen, but the third will last, and there will not be a fourth one.[9]

It took about a century to institutionalize the idea. Ivan IV was the first Rurikide to have himself crowned, in 1547, as czar of the Orthodox;[10] and in 1589 the patriarch of Constantinople was compelled to institute the first autocephalous patriarch of Moscow, now with the official recognition of Moscow as the Third Rome.[11]

The dates of the rise and institutionalization of this idea are impor- tant. The reign of Ivan the Great coincides with the consolidation of the Western national states (England, France, and Spain), and the reigns of Ivan IV and of Theodore I coincide with the Western Reformation. Pre- cisely at the time when the Western imperial articulation ultimately disin- tegrated, when Western society rearticulated itself into the nations and the plurality of churches, Russia entered on her career as the heir of Rome. From her very beginnings Russia was not a nation in the Western sense but a civilizational area, dominated ethnically by the Great Russians and formed into a political society by the symbolism of Roman continua- tion.

That Russian society was in a class by itself was gradually recognized by the West. In 1488 Maximilian I still tried to integrate Russia into the Western political system by offering a royal crown to Ivan the Great. The Grand Duke of Moscow refused the honor on the grounds that his author- ity stemmed from his ancestors, that it had the blessing of God, and, hence, that there was no need of confirmation from the Western em- peror.[12] A century later, in 1576, at the time of the Western wars with the Turks, Maximilian II went a step further by offering Ivan IV recognition as the emperor of the Greek East in return for assistance.[13] Again the Russian ruler was not interested even in an imperial crown, for, at that time, Ivan was already engaged in building the Russian Empire through the liquidation of the feudal nobility and its replacement by the *oprichnina,* the new service nobility.[14] Through this bloody operation Ivan the Terri- ble stamped on Russia the indelible social articulation which has deter- mined her inner political history to this day. Transcendentally Russia was distinguished from all Western nations as the imperial representative of Christian truth, and through her social rearticulation, from which the czar emerged as the existential representative, she was radically cut off from the development of representative institutions like those of the Western national states. Napoleon, finally, recognized the Russian problem when, in 1802, he said that there were only two nations in the world: Russia and the Occident.[15]

Russia developed a type of representation which was *sui generis* in both the transcendental and the existential respects. The Westernization since Peter the Great did not change the type fundamentally because it had practically no effect with regard to social articulation. One can speak, indeed, of a personal Westernization in the ranks of the high nobility, in the wake of the Napoleonic Wars, in the generation of Chaadaev, Gagarin, and Pecherin; but the individual servants of the czar did not transform themselves into an estate of the nobility, into an articulate *baronagium*. Perhaps the necessity of cooperative class action as the condition of a political Westernization of Russia was not even seen; and certainly, if the possibility for an evolution in this direction ever existed, it was finished with the Dekabrist revolt of 1825. Immediately afterward, with Khomyakov, began the Slavophilic, anti-Western philosophy of history which the apocalypse of the Third Rome reconceived, with broad effectiveness in the intelligentsia of the middle nobility, as the messianic, eschatological mission of Russia for mankind. In Dostoevski this superimposition of messianism crystallized in the curiously ambivalent vision of an autocratic, orthodox Russia that somehow would conquer the world and in this conquest blossom out into the free society of all Christians in the true faith.[16] It is this ambivalent vision which, in its secularized form, inspires a Russian dictatorship of the proletariat that in its conquest of the world will blossom out into the Marxian realm of freedom. The tentative Western articulation of Russian society under the liberal czars became an episode of the past with the revolution of 1917. The people as a whole have become again the servants of the czar in the old Muscovite sense, with the cadres of the Communist party as its service nobility; the *oprichnina* which Ivan the Terrible had established on the basis of an agricultural economy was reestablished with a vengeance on the basis of an industrial economy.[17]

From the exposition of Joachitic symbols, from the cursory survey of their later variants, and from their blending with the political apocalypse of the Third Rome, it will have become clear that the new eschatology decisively affects the structure of modern politics. It has produced a well-circumscribed symbolism by means of which Western political societies interpret the meaning of their existence, and the adherents of one or the other of the variants determine the articulation of society domestically as well as on the world scene. Up to this point, however, the symbolism has been accepted on the level of self-interpretation and described as a historical phenomenon. It must now be submitted to critical analysis of its principal aspects, and the foundation for this analysis must be laid through a formulation of the theoretically relevant issue.

The Joachitic eschatology is, by its subject matter, a speculation on the meaning of history. In order to define its special character, it must be set off against the Christian philosophy of history that was traditional at the time, that is, against Augustinian speculation. Into the traditional speculation had entered the Jewish-Christian idea of an end of history in the sense of an intelligible state of perfection. History no longer moved in cycles, as it did with Plato and Aristotle, but acquired direction and destination. Beyond Jewish messianism in the strict sense the specifically Christian conception of history had advanced toward the understanding of the end as a transcendental fulfillment. In his elaboration of this theoretical insight Saint Augustine distinguished between a profane sphere of history, in which empires rise and fall, and a sacred history, which culminates in the appearance of Christ and the establishment of the church. He, furthermore, imbedded sacred history in a transcendental history of the *Civitas Dei* which includes the events in the angelic sphere as well as the transcendental eternal sabbath. Only transcendental history, including the earthly pilgrimage of the church, has direction toward its eschatological fulfillment. Profane history, on the other hand, has no such direction; it is a waiting for the end; its present mode of being is that of a *saeculum senescens,* of an age that grows old.[18]

By the time of Joachim, Western civilization was growing strongly; and an age that began to feel its muscles would not easily bear the Augustinian defeatism with regard to the mundane sphere of existence. The Joachitic speculation was an attempt to endow the immanent course of history with a meaning that was not provided in the Augustinian conception. And for this purpose Joachim used what he had at hand, that is, the meaning of transcendental history. In this first Western attempt at an immanentization of meaning the connection with Christianity was not lost. The new age of Joachim would bring an increase of fulfillment within history, but the increase would not be due to an immanent eruption; it would come through a new transcendental irruption of the spirit. The idea of a radically immanent fulfillment grew rather slowly, in a long process that roughly may be called "from humanism to enlightenment"; only in the eighteenth century, with the idea of progress, had the increase of meaning in history become a completely intramundane phenomenon, without transcendental irruptions. This second phase of immanentization shall be called "secularization."

From the Joachitic immanentization a theoretical problem arises which occurs neither in classic antiquity nor in orthodox Christianity, that is, the problem of an eidos of history.[19] In Hellenic speculation, to be sure, we also have a problem of essence in politics; the polis has an eidos both for Plato and for Aristotle. But the actualization of this essence is governed by the rhythm of growth and decay, and the rhythmical embodiment and disembodiment of essence in political reality is the mystery of existence; it is not an additional eidos. The soteriological truth of Christianity, then, breaks with the rhythm of existence; beyond temporal successes and reverses lies the supernatural destiny of man, the perfection through grace in the beyond. Man and mankind now have fulfillment, but it lies beyond nature. Again there is no eidos of history, because the eschatological supernature is not a nature in the philosophical, immanent sense. The problem of an eidos in history, therefore, arises only when Christian transcendental fulfillment becomes immanentized. Such an immanentist hypostasis of the eschaton, however, is a theoretical fallacy. Things are not things, nor do they have essences, by arbitrary declaration. The course of history as a whole is no object of experience; history has no eidos, because the course of history extends into the unknown future. The meaning of history, thus, is an illusion, and this illusionary eidos is created by treating a symbol of faith as if it were a proposition concerning an object of immanent experience.

The fallacious character of an eidos of history has been shown on principle—but the analysis can and must be carried one step further into certain details. The Christian symbolism of supernatural destination has in itself a theoretical structure, and this structure is continued into the variants of immanentization. The pilgrim's progress, the sanctification of life, is a movement toward a telos, a goal; and this goal, the beatific vision, is a state of perfection. Hence, in the Christian symbolism one can distinguish the movement as its teleological component, from a state of highest value as the axiological component.[20] The two components reappear in the variants of immanentization; and they can accordingly be classified as variants which either accentuate the teleological or the axiological component or combine them both in their symbolism. In the first case, when the accent lies strongly on movement, without clarity about final perfection, the result will be the progressivist interpretation of history. The aim need not be clarified because progressivist thinkers, men like Diderot or d'Alembert, assume a selection of desirable factors as the standard and interpret progress as qualitative and quantitative increase of the present good—the "bigger and better" of our simplifying slogan. This is a conservative attitude, and it may become reactionary unless the original standard be adjusted to the changing historical situation. In the second case, when the accent lies strongly on the state of perfection, without clarity about the means that are required for its realization, the result will be utopianism. It may assume the form of an axiological dream world, as in the utopia of More, when the thinker is still aware that the dream is unrealizable and knows why it is; or, with increasing theoretical illiteracy, it may assume the form of various social idealisms, such as the abolition of war, of unequal distribution of property, of fear and want. And, finally, immanentization may extend to the complete Christian symbol. The result will then be the active mysticism which envisions a state of perfection to be achieved through a revolutionary transfiguration of the nature of man, as, for instance, in Marxism.

Our analysis can now be resumed on the level of principle. The attempt at constructing an eidos of history will lead into the fallacious immanentization of the Christian eschaton. The understanding of the attempt as fallacious, however, raises baffling questions with regard to the type of man who will indulge in it. The fallacy looks rather elemental. Can it be assumed that the thinkers who indulged in it were not intelligent enough to penetrate it? Or that they penetrated it but propagated it nevertheless for some obscure evil reason? . . . Obviously one cannot explain seven centuries of intellectual history by stupidity and dishonesty. A drive must rather be assumed in the souls of these men which blinded them to the fallacy.

The nature of this drive cannot be discovered by submitting the structure of the fallacy to an even closer analysis. The attention must rather concentrate on what the thinkers achieved by their fallacious construction. On this point there is no doubt. They achieved a certainty about the meaning of history, and about their own place in it, which otherwise they would not have had. Certainties, we know, are demanded for the purpose of overcoming the anxiety of uncertainty; and the next question then would be: What specific uncertainty was so disturbing that it had to be overcome by the dubious means of fallacious immanentization? One does not have to look far afield for an answer. Uncertainty is the very essence of Christianity. The feeling of security in a "world full of gods" is lost with the gods themselves; when the world is dedivinized, communication with the world-transcendent God is reduced to the tenuous bond of faith, in the sense of Hebrew 11:1, as the substance of things hoped for and the proof of things unseen. Ontologically, the substance of things hoped for is nowhere to be found but in faith itself; and, epistemologically, there is no proof for things unseen but again this very faith.[21] The bond is tenuous, indeed, and it may snap easily. The life of the soul in openness toward God, the waiting, the periods of aridity and dullness, guilt and despondency, contrition and repentance, forsakenness and hope against hope, the silent stirrings of love and grace, trembling on the verge of a certainty which if gained is lost—this entire mode may prove too heavy a burden. . . . The danger of a breakdown of faith to a socially relevant degree will increase as Christianity becomes a worldly success: that is, it will grow when Christianity penetrates a civilizational area thoroughly, supported by institutional pressure, and when, at the same time, it undergoes an internal process of spiritualization, of a more complete realization of its essence. The more people are drawn or pressured into the Christian orbit, the greater will be the number among them who do not have the spiritual stamina for the heroic adventure of the soul that is Christianity. In addition, the likeliness of a fall from faith will increase

when education, literacy, and intellectual debate bring the full seriousness of Christianity to the understanding of ever more individuals. Both
of these processes characterized the high Middle Ages. Historical detail
is not our present concern here; it will be sufficient to refer summarily
to the growing town societies with their intense spiritual culture as the
primary centers from which the danger radiated into Western society at
large.

If the predicament of a fall from faith in the Christian sense occurs as
a mass phenomenon, the consequences will depend on the content of the
prevailing culture. A man cannot fall back on himself in an absolute sense,
because, if he tried, he would find very soon that he has fallen into the
abyss of his despair and nothingness; he will have to fall back on a less
differentiated culture of spiritual experience. Under the civilizational
conditions of the twelfth century it was impossible to fall back into Greco-
Roman polytheism, because it had disappeared as the living culture of a
society; and the stunted remnants could hardly be revived as a substitute
for Christianity, because they had lost their spell precisely for those men
who had tasted of Christianity. The fall could be interrupted only by
experiential alternatives, sufficiently close to the experience of faith that
only a discerning eye would see the difference, but receding far enough
from it to remedy the uncertainty of faith in the strict sense. Such alternative experiences were at hand in the gnosis which had accompanied
Christianity from its very beginnings.[22]

The economy of this essay does not allow a description of the gnosis
of antiquity or of the history of its transmission into the Western Middle
Ages; it is enough to say that at the time gnosis was a living religious
culture on which men could fall back. The attempt at immanentizing the
meaning of existence is fundamentally an attempt at bringing our knowledge of transcendence into a firmer grip than the *cognitio fidei,* the cognition of faith, will afford; and Gnostic experiences offer this firmer grip in
so far as they are an expansion of the soul to the point where God is
drawn into the existence of man. This expansion will engage the various
human faculties; and, hence, it is possible to distinguish a range of Gnostic varieties according to the faculty which predominates in the operation
of getting this grip on God. Gnosis may be primarily intellectual and
assume the form of speculative penetration of the mystery of creation and
existence, as, for instance, in the contemplative gnosis of Hegel or Schelling. Or it may be primarily emotional and assume the form of an indwell-
ing of divine substance in the human soul, as, for instance, in paracletic
sectarian leaders. Or it may be primarily volitional and assume the form
of activist redemption of man and society, as in the instance of revolutionary activists like Comte, Marx, or Hitler. These Gnostic experiences, in
the amplitude of their variety, are the core of the redivinization of society,
for the men who fall into these experiences divinize themselves by sub-

stituting more massive modes of participation in divinity for faith in the Christian sense.[23]

A clear understanding of these experiences as the active core of immanentist eschatology is necessary, because otherwise the inner logic of the Western political development from medieval immanentism through humanism, enlightenment, progressivism, liberalism, positivism, into Marxism will be obscured. The intellectual symbols developed by the various types of immanentists will frequently be in conflict with one another, and the various types of Gnostics will oppose one another. One can easily imagine how indignant a humanistic liberal will be when he is told that his particular type of immanentism is one step on the road to Marxism. It will not be superfluous, therefore, to recall the principle that the substance of history is to be found on the level of experiences, not on the level of ideas. Secularism could be defined as a radicalization of the earlier forms of paracletic immanentism, because the experiential divinization of man is more radical in the secularist case. Feuerbach and Marx, for instance, interpreted the transcendent God as the projection of what is best in man into a hypostatic beyond; for them the great turning point of history, therefore, would come when man draws his projection back into himself, when he becomes conscious that he himself is God, when as a consequence man is transfigured into superman.[24] This Marxian transfiguration does, indeed, carry to its extreme a less radical medieval experience which draws the spirit of God into man, while leaving God himself in his transcendence. The superman marks the end of a road on which we find such figures as the "godded man" of English Reformation mystics.[25] These considerations, moreover, will explain and justify the earlier warning against characterizing modern political movements as neopagan. Gnostic experiences determine a structure of political reality that is *sui generis*. A line of gradual transformation connects medieval with contemporary gnosticism. And the transformation is so gradual, indeed, that it would be difficult to decide whether contemporary phenomena should be classified as Christian because they are intelligibly an outgrowth of Christian heresies of the Middle Ages or whether medieval phenomena should be classified as anti-Christian because they are intelligibly the origin of modern anti-Christianism. The best course will be to drop such questions and to recognize the essence of modernity as the growth of gnosticism.

Gnosis was an accompaniment of Christianity from its very beginnings; its traces are to be found in Saint Paul and Saint John.[26] Gnostic heresy was the great opponent of Christianity in the early centuries; and Irenaeus surveyed and criticized its manifold variants in his *Adversus Haereses* (*ca.* 180)—a standard treatise on the subject that still will be consulted with profit by the student who wants to understand modern political ideas and movements. Moreover, besides the Christian gnosis there also existed a Jewish, a pagan, and an Islamic gnosis; and quite possibly the common origin of all these branches of gnosis will have to be sought in the basic experiential type that prevailed in pre-Christian Syriac civilization. Nowhere, however, has gnosis assumed the form of speculation on the meaning of immanent history as it did in the high Middle Ages. Gnosis does not by inner necessity lead to the fallacious construction of history which characterizes modernity since Joachim. Hence, in the drive for certainty there must be contained a further component which bends gnosis specifically toward historical speculation. This further component is the civilizational expansiveness of Western society in the high Middle Ages. It is a coming-of-age in search of its meaning, a conscious growth that will not put up with the traditional view that civilization was declining, senescent. And, in fact, the self-endowment of Western civilization with meaning closely followed the actual expansion and differentiation. The spiritual growth of the West through the orders since Cluny expressed itself, in Joachim's speculation, in the idea of a Third Realm of the monks; the early philosophical and literary humanism expressed itself in Dante's and Petrarch's idea of an Apollinian Imperium, a Third Realm of intellectual life that succeeds the imperial spiritual and temporal orders;[27] and in the Age of Reason Condorcet conceived the idea of a unified civilization of mankind in which everybody would be a French intellectual.[28] The social carriers of the movements, in their turn, changed with the differentiation and articulation of Western society. In the early phases of modernity they were the townspeople and peasants in opposition to feudal society; in the later phases they were the progressive bourgeoisie, the socialist workers, and the Fascist lower middle class. And, finally, with the prodigious advancement of science since the seventeenth century, the new instrument of cognition would become, one is inclined to say inevitably, the symbolic vehicle of Gnostic truth. In the Gnostic speculation of scientism this particular variant reached its extreme when the positivist perfector of science replaced the era of Christ by the era of Comte. Scientism has remained to this day one of the strongest Gnostic movements in Western society; and the immanentist pride in science is so strong that even the special sciences have each left a distinguishable sediment in the variants of salvation through physics, economics, sociology, biology, and psychology.

This analysis of the components in modern Gnostic speculation does not claim to be exhaustive, but it has been carried far enough to enable us to recognize the experiences which determine the political articulation of Western society under the symbolism of the Third Realm. . . . Following the Aristotelian procedure, the analysis started from the self-interpretation of society by means of the Joachitic symbols of the twelfth century. Now that their meaning has been clarified through theoretical understanding, a date can be assigned to the beginning of this civilizational course. A suitable date for its formal beginning would be the activation of ancient gnosticism through Scotus Eriugena in the ninth century, because his works, as well as those of Dionysius Areopagita which he translated, were a continuous influence in the underground Gnostic sects before they came to the surface in the twelfth and thirteenth centuries.

This is a long course of a thousand years, long enough to have aroused reflections on its decline and end. These reflections on Western society as a civilizational course that comes into view as a whole because it is moving intelligibly toward an end have raised one of the thorniest questions to plague the student of Western politics. On the one hand, as you know, there begins in the eighteenth century a continuous stream of literature on the decline of Western civilization; and, whatever misgivings one may entertain on this or that special argument, one cannot deny that the theorists of decline on the whole have a case. On the other hand, the same period is also characterized by an exuberantly expansive vitality in the sciences, in technology, in the material control of environment, in the increase of population, of the standard of living, of health and comfort, of mass education, of social consciousness and responsibility; and again, whatever misgivings one may entertain with regard to this or that item on the list, one cannot deny that the progressivists have a case, too. This conflict of interpretations leaves in its wake the adumbrated thorny question, that is, the question how a civilization can advance and decline at the same time. A consideration of this question suggests itself, because it seems possible that the analysis of modern gnosticism will furnish at least a partial solution of the problem.

Gnostic speculation overcame the uncertainty of faith by receding from transcendence and endowing man and his intramundane range of action with the meaning of eschatological fulfillment. As this immanentization progressed experientially, civilizational activity became a mystical work of self-salvation. The spiritual strength of the soul which in Christianity was devoted to the sanctification of life could now be diverted into the more appealing, more tangible, and, above all, so much easier creation of the terrestrial paradise. Civilizational action became a *divertissement,* in the sense of Pascal, but a *divertissement* which demonically absorbed into itself the eternal destiny of man and functioned as a substitute for the life of the spirit. Nietzsche most tersely expressed the nature of this demonic diversion when he raised the question why anyone should live in the embarrassing condition of being in need of the love and grace of God. "Love yourself through grace—was his solution—then you are no longer in need of your God, and you can act the whole drama of Fall and Redemption to its end in yourself."[29] And how can this miracle be achieved, this miracle of self-salvation, and how this redemption by extending grace to yourself? The great historical answer was given by the successive types of Gnostic action that have made modern civilization what it is. The miracle was worked successively through the literary and artistic achievement which secured the immortality of fame for the humanistic intellectual, through the discipline and economic success which certified salvation to the Puritan saint, through the civilizational contributions of the liberals and progressives, and, finally, through the revolutionary action that will establish the Communist or some other Gnostic millennium. Gnosticism, thus, most effectively released human forces for the building of a civilization because on their fervent application to intramundane activity was put the premium of salvation. The historical result was stupendous. The resources of man that came to light under such pressure were in themselves a revelation, and their application to civilizational work produced the truly magnificent spectacle of Western progressive society. However fatuous the surface arguments may be, the widespread belief that modern civilization is Civilization in a preeminent sense is experientially justified; the endowment with the meaning of salvation has made the rise of the West, indeed, an apocalypse of civilization.

On this apocalyptic spectacle, however, falls a shadow; for the brilliant expansion is accompanied by a danger that grows apace with progress. The nature of this danger became apparent in the form which the idea of immanent salvation assumed in the gnosticism of Comte. The founder of positivism institutionalized the premium on civilizational contributions in so far as he guaranteed immortality through preservation of the contributor and his deeds in the memory of mankind. There were provided honorific degrees of such immortality, and the highest honor would be the reception of the meritorious contributor into the calendar of positivistic saints. But what should in this order of things become of men who would rather follow God than the new Augustus Comte? Such miscreants who were not inclined to make their social contributions according to Comtean standards would simply be committed to the hell of social oblivion. The idea deserves attention. Here is a Gnostic paraclete setting himself up as the world-immanent Last Judgment of mankind, deciding on immortality or annihilation for every human being. The material civilization of the West, to be sure, is still advancing; but on this rising plane of civilization the progressive symbolism of contributions, commemoration, and oblivion draws the contours of those "holes of oblivion" into which the divine redeemers of the Gnostic empires drop their victims with a bullet in the neck. This end of progress was not contemplated in the halcyon days of Gnostic exuberance. Milton released Adam and Eve with "a paradise within them, happier far" than the Paradise lost; when they went forth, "the world was all before them," and they were cheered "with meditation on the happy end" of salvation through Christ. But when historically man goes forth, with the Gnostic "Paradise within him," and when he penetrates into the world before him, there is little cheer in meditation on the not so happy end.

The death of the spirit is the price of progress. Nietzsche revealed this mystery of the Western apocalypse when he announced that God was dead and that He had been murdered.[30] This Gnostic murder is constantly committed by the men who sacrifice God to civilization. The more fervently all human energies are thrown into the great enterprise of salvation through world-immanent action, the farther the human beings who engage in this enterprise move away from the life of the spirit. And since the life of the spirit is the source of order in man and society, the very success of a Gnostic civilization is the cause of its decline.

A civilization can, indeed, advance and decline at the same time—but not forever. There is a limit toward which this ambiguous process moves; the limit is reached when an activist sect which represents the Gnostic truth organizes the civilization into an empire under its rule. Totalitarianism, defined as the existential rule of Gnostic activists, is the end form of progressive civilization.

NOTES

1. On the transition from eschatological to apocalyptic Christianity see Alois Dempf, *Sacrum Imperium* (Munich and Berlin, 1929), pp. 71 ff.
2. Albert Schweitzer, *Geschichte der Leben Jesu Forschung* (Tübingen, 1920), pp. 406 ff.; and Maurice Goguel, *Jésus,* 2d ed. (Paris, 1950), the chapter on "La Crise galiléenne."
3. On the tension in early Christianity, the reception of Revelation, and its subsequent role in Western revolutionary eschatology see Jakob Taubes, *Abendländische Eschatologie* (Bern, 1947), esp. pp. 69 ff.
4. Augustinus, *Civitas Dei,* xx, 7, 8, and 9.
5. On Joachim of Flora see Herbert Grundmann, *Studien über Joachim von Floris* (Leipzig, 1927); Dempf, *op. cit.,* pp. 269 ff.; Ernesto Buonaiuti, *Gioacchino da Fiore* (Rome, 1931); the same author's "Introduction" to Joachim's *Tractatus super quatuor evangelia* (Rome, 1930); and the chapters on Joachim in Jakob Taubes' *Abendländische Eschatologie* and Karl Löwith's *Meaning in History* (Chicago, 1949).
6. For further transformations of Joachitism see Appendix I, "Modern Transfigurations of Joachism," in Löwith, *op. cit.*
7. Moeller van den Bruck, *Das Dritte Reich* (Hamburg, 1923). See also the chapter on "Das Dritte Reich und die Jungen Völker" in Moeller van den Bruck, *Die politischen Kräfte* (Breslau, 1933). The symbol gained acceptance slowly. The second edition of the *Dritte Reich* appeared only in 1930, five years after the author's death through suicide; see the "Introduction" by Mary Agnes Hamilton to the English edition, *Germany's Third Empire* (London, 1934).
8. *Codex Justinianus* i. xvii. 1. 10. We are quoting the legal formalization of the idea. On the nuances of meaning with regard to the foundation and organization of Constantinople, in 330, see Andrew Alföldi, *The Conversion of Constantine and Pagan Rome,* translated by Harold Mattingly (Oxford, 1948), Chapter ix: "The Old Rome and the New." The tension between the two Romes may be gathered from Canon 3 of the Council of Constantinople in 381: "The Bishop of Constantinople to have the primacy of honor next after the Bishop of Rome, because that Constantinople is New Rome" (Henry Bettenson, *Documents of the Christian Church* [New York, 1947], p. 115).

9. On the Third Rome see Hildegard Schaeder, *Moskau—Das Dritte Rom: Studien zur Geschichte der politischen Theorien in der slavischen Welt* (Hamburg, 1929); Joseph Olšr, *Gli ultimi Rurikidi e le base ideologiche della sovranità dello stato Russo* ("Orientalia Christiana," Vol. XII [Rome, 1946]); Hugo Rahner, *Vom Ersten bis zum Dritten Rom* (Innsbruck, 1950); Paul Miliukov, *Outlines of Russian Culture,* Part I; *Religion and the Church* (Philadelphia, 1945), pp. 15 ff.

10. George Vernadsky, *Political and Diplomatic History of Russia* (Boston, 1936), p. 158.

11. *Ibid.,* p. 180.

12. *Ibid.,* p. 149.

13. Rahner, *op. cit.,* p. 15.

14. Vernadsky, *op. cit.,* pp. 169 ff.

15. Napoleon, *Vues politiques* (Rio de Janeiro, *s.a.*), p. 340.

16. For this view of Dostoevski see Dmitri Merezhkovski, *Die religiöse Revolution* (printed as Introduction to Dostoevski's *Politische Schriften* [Munich, 1920]), and Bernhard Schultze, *Russische Denker* (Wien, 1950), pp. 125 ff.

17. Alexander von Schelting, *Russland und Europa* (Bern, 1948), pp. 123 ff. and 261 ff.

18. For an account of the Augustinian conception of history see Löwith, *op. cit.*

19. On the eidos of history see Hans Urs von Balthasar, *Theologie der Geschichte* (Einsiedeln, 1950), and Löwith, *op. cit.,* passim.

20. For the distinction of the two components (which was introduced by Troeltsch) and the ensuing theological debate see Hans Urs von Balthasar, *Prometheus* (Heidelberg, 1947), pp. 12 ff.

21. Our reflections on the uncertainty of faith must be understood as a psychology of experience. For the theology of the definition of faith in Hebrew 11:1, which is presupposed in our analysis, see Thomas Aquinas *Summa theologica* ii/ii. Q. 4, Art. 1.

22. The exploration of gnosis is so rapidly advancing that only a study of the principal works of the last generation will mediate an understanding of its dimensions. Of special value are Eugène de Faye, *Gnostiques et gnosticisme,* 2d ed.; (Paris, 1925); Hans Jonas, *Gnosis und spätantiker Geist* (Göttingen, 1934); Simone Pétrement, *Le Dualisme chez Platon, les Gnostiques et les Manichéens* (Paris, 1947); and Hans Söderberg, *La Religion des Cathares* (Uppsala, 1949).

23. For a general suggestion concerning the range of Gnostic phenomena in the modern world see Balthasar, *Prometheus,* p. 6.

24. On the superman of Feuerbach and Marx see Henri de Lubac, *Le Drame de l'humanisme athée,* 3d ed. (Paris, 1945), pp. 15 ff.; Löwith, *op. cit.,* especially the quotation on p. 36 concerning the "new men"; and Eric Voegelin, "The Formation of the Marxian Revolutionary Idea," *Review of Politics,* Vol. XII (1950).

25. The "godded man" is a term of Henry Nicholas (see Rufus M. Jones, *Studies in Mystical Religion* [London, 1936], p. 434).

26. On gnosis in early Christianity see Rudolf Bultmann, *Das Urchristentum im Rahmen der antiken Religionen* (Zurich, 1949).

27. On the Apollinian Imperium as a Third Realm see Karl Burdach, *Reformation, Renaissance, Humanismus,* 2d ed. (Berlin and Leipzig, 1926), pp. 133 ff.; and the same author's *Rienzo und die geistige Wandlung seiner Zeit* (Berlin, 1913–28), Vol. II/I; *Vom Mittelalter zur Reformation,* p. 542.

28. Condorcet, *Esquisse* (1795), pp. 310–18.

29. Nietzsche, *Morgenröthe,* § 79.

30. On the "murder of God" passages in Nietzsche, prehistory of the idea, and literary debate see Lubac, *op. cit.,* pp. 40 ff. For the most comprehensive exposition of the idea in Nietzsche's work see Karl Jaspers, *Nietzsche: Einführung in das Verständnis seines Philosophierens* (Berlin and Leipzig, 1936), under the references in the register.

LEO STRAUSS

The New Political Science

... [The] new approach to political things emerged shortly before World War I; it became preponderant and at the same time reached its mature or final form before, during, and after World War II. It need not be a product or a symptom of the crisis of the modern Western World—of a world which could boast of being distinguished by ever broadening freedom and humanitarianism; it is surely contemporary with that crisis. ...

To state that issue means to bring out the fundamental difference between the new political science and the old. To avoid ambiguities, irrelevancies, and beatings around the bush, it is best to contrast the new political science directly with the "original" of the old, that is, with Aristotelian political science.

For Aristotle, political science is identical with political philosophy because science is identical with philosophy. Science or philosophy consists of two kinds, theoretical and practical or political; theoretical science is subdivided into mathematics, physics (natural science), and metaphysics; practical science is subdivided into ethics, economics (management of the household), and political science in the narrower sense; logic does not belong to philosophy or science proper but is, as it were, the prelude to philosophy or science. The distinction between philosophy and science or the separation of science from philosophy was a consequence of the revolution which occurred in the seventeenth century. This revolution was primarily not the victory of Science over Metaphysics but what one may call the victory of the new philosophy or science over Aristotelian philosophy or science. Yet the new philosophy or science was not equally successful in all its parts. Its most successful part was physics (and mathematics). Prior to the victory of the new physics, there was not the science of physics simply: There was Aristotelian physics, Platonic physics, Epicurean physics, Stoic physics; to speak colloquially, there was no metaphysically neutral physics. The victory of the new physics led to the emergence of a physics which seemed to be as metaphysically neutral as, say, mathematics, medicine, or the art of shoemaking. The emergence of a metaphysically neutral physics made it possible for "science" to become independent of "philosophy," and in fact an authority for the latter. It

From *Essays on the Scientific Study of Politics,* edited by H. J. Storing (New York: Holt, Rinehart, & Winston, 1962), Epilogue, pp. 307–27. Copyright © 1962 by Holt, Rinehart & Winston, Inc. Reprinted by permission of Holt, Rinehart & Winston.

paved the way for an economic science that is independent of ethics, for sociology as the study of nonpolitical associations as not inferior in dignity to the political association, and, last but not least, for the separation of political science from political philosophy as well as the separation of economics and sociology from political science. Secondly, the Aristotelian distinction between theoretical and practical sciences implies that human action has principles of its own which are known independently of theoretical science (physics and metaphysics) and therefore that the practical sciences do not depend on the theoretical sciences or are not derivative from them. The principles of action are the natural ends of man toward which man is by nature inclined and of which he has by nature some awareness. This awareness is the necessary condition for his seeking and finding appropriate means for his ends, or for his becoming practically wise or prudent. Practical science, in contradistinction to practical wisdom itself, sets forth coherently the principles of action and the general rules of prudence ("proverbial wisdom"). Practical science raises questions that within practical or political experience, or at any rate on the basis of such experience, reveal themselves to be the most important questions and that are not stated, let alone answered, with sufficient clarity by practical wisdom itself. The sphere governed by prudence is then in principle self-sufficient or closed. Yet prudence is always endangered by false doctrines about the whole, of which man is a part, by false theoretical opinions. Prudence is therefore always in need of defense against such opinions, and that defense is necessarily theoretical. The theory defending prudence is misunderstood, however, if it is taken to be the basis of prudence. This complication—the fact that the sphere of prudence is, as it were, only de jure but not de facto wholly independent of theoretical science—makes understandable, although it does not by itself justify, the view underlying the new political science according to which no awareness inherent in practice, and in general no natural awareness, is genuine knowledge, or in other words only "scientific" knowledge is genuine knowledge. This view implies that there cannot be practical sciences proper, or that the distinction between practical and theoretical sciences must be replaced by the distinction between theoretical and applied sciences—applied sciences being sciences based on theoretical sciences that precede the applied sciences in time and in order. It implies above all that the sciences dealing with human affairs are essentially dependent on the theoretical sciences—especially on psychology, which in the Aristotelian scheme is the highest theme of physics, not to say that it constitutes the transition from physics to metaphysics—or become themselves theoretical sciences to be supplemented by such applied sciences as the policy sciences or the sciences of social engineering. The new political science is then no longer based on political experience but on what is called scientific psychology. Thirdly, according to the

Aristotelian view, the awareness of the principles of action shows itself primarily to a higher degree in public or authoritative speech, particularly in law and legislation, rather than in merely private speech. Hence Aristotelian political science views political things in the perspective of the citizen. Since there is of necessity a variety of citizen perspectives, the political scientist or political philosopher must become the umpire, the impartial judge; his perspective encompasses the partisan perspectives because he possesses a more comprehensive and a clearer grasp of man's natural ends and their natural order than do the partisans. The new political science, on the other hand, looks at political things from without, in the perspective of the neutral observer, in the same perspective in which one would look at triangles or fish, although or because it may wish to become "manipulative"; it views human beings as an engineer would view materials for building bridges. It follows that the language of Aristotelian political science is identical with the language of political man; it hardly uses a term that did not originate in the market place and is not in common use there; but the new political science cannot begin to speak without having elaborated an extensive technical vocabulary. Fourthly, Aristotelian political science necessarily evaluates political things; the knowledge in which it culminates has the character of categorical advice and of exhortation. The new political science, on the other hand, conceives of the principles of action as "values" which are merely "subjective"; the knowledge it conveys has the character of prediction and only secondarily that of hypothetical advice. Fifthly, according to the Aristotelian view, man is a being *sui generis,* with a dignity of its own; man is the rational and political animal. Man is the only being that can be concerned with self-respect; man can respect himself because he can despise himself; he is "the beast with red cheeks," the only being possessing a sense of shame. His dignity is then based on his awareness of what he ought to be or how he should live. Since there is a necessary connection between morality (how a man should live) and law, there is a necessary connection between the dignity of man and the dignity of the public order: The political is *sui generis* and cannot be understood as derivative from the subpolitical. The presupposition of all this is that man is radically distinguished from nonman, from brutes as well as from gods, and this presupposition is ratified by common sense, by the citizen's understanding of things; when the citizen demands or rejects, say, "freedom from want for all," he does not mean freedom from want for tigers, rats, or lice. This presupposition points to a more fundamental presupposition according to which the whole consists of essentially different parts. The new political science, on the other hand, is based on the fundamental premise that there are no essential or irreducible differences; there are only differences of degree; in particular there is only a difference of degree between men and brutes or between men and robots. In other words, according to the new political science, or the universal science of which the new political science is a part, to understand a thing means to understand it in terms of its genesis or its conditions and hence, humanly speaking, to understand the higher in terms of the lower: the human in terms of the subhuman, the rational in terms of the subrational, the political in terms of the subpolitical. In particular the new political science cannot admit that the common good is something that is.

Prior to the emergence of the new political science, political science had already moved very far from Aristotelian political science in the general direction of the new political science. Nevertheless it was accused of paying too much attention to the law or to the Ought, and of paying too little attention to the Is or to the actual behavior of men. For instance it seemed to be exclusively concerned with the legal arrangements regarding universal suffrage and its justification and not to consider at all how the universal right to vote is exercised; yet democracy as it is is characterized by the manner in which that right is exercised. We may grant that not so long ago there was a political science which was narrowly legalistic—which, for example, took the written constitution of the U.S.S.R. very seriously—but we must add immediately that that error had been corrected, as it were in advance, by an older political science, the political science of Montesquieu, of Machiavelli, or of Aristotle himself. Besides, the new political science, in its justified protest against a merely legalistic political science, is in danger of disregarding the important things known to those legalists; "voting behavior" as it is now studied would be impossible if there were not in the first place the universal right to vote, and this right, even if not exercised by a large minority for very long periods, must be taken into consideration in any long-range prediction since it may be exercised by all in future elections taking place in unprecedented and therefore particularly interesting circumstances. That right is an essential ingredient of democratic "behavior," for it partly explains "behavior" in democracies (for example, the prevention by force or fraud of certain people from voting). The new political science does not simply deny these things, but it literally relegates them to the background, to "the habit background"; in so doing it puts the cart before the horse. Similar considerations apply, for instance, to the alleged discovery by the new political science of the importance of "propaganda"; that discovery is in fact only a partial rediscovery of the need for vulgar rhetoric, a need that had become somewhat obscured from a few generations which were comforted by faith in universal enlightenment as the inevitable by-product of the diffusion of science, which in its turn was thought to be the inevitable by-product of science. Generally speaking, one may wonder whether the new political science has brought to light anything of political importance which intelligent political practitioners with a deep knowledge of history, nay, intelligent and educated journalists, to say nothing of the old political science at its best, did not know at least as well beforehand. The main substantive reason, however, for the revolt against the old political science would seem to be the consideration that our political situation is entirely unprecedented and that it is unreasonable to expect earlier political thought to be of any help in coping with our situation; the unprecedented political situation calls for an unprecedented political science, perhaps for a judicious mating of dialectical materialism and psychoanalysis to be consummated on a bed supplied by logical positivism. Just as classical physics had to be superseded by nuclear physics so that the atomic age could come in via the atomic bomb, the old political science has to be superseded by a sort of nuclear political science so that we may be enabled to cope with the extreme dangers threatening atomic man; the equivalent in political science of the nuclei are probably the most minute events in the smallest groups of human beings, if not in the life of infants; the small groups in question are certainly not of the kind exemplified by the small group that Lenin gathered around himself in Switzerland during World War I. In making this comparison we are not oblivious of the fact that the nuclear physicists show a greater respect for classical physics than the nuclear political scientists show for classical politics. Nor do we forget that, while the nuclei proper are simply prior to macrophysical phenomena, the "political" nuclei, which are meant to supply explanations for the political things proper, are already molded, nay constituted by the political order or the regime within which they occur: An American small group is not a Russian small group. We may grant that our political situation has nothing in common with any earlier political situation except that it is a political situation. The human race is still divided into a number of the kind of societies that we have come to call states and that are separated from one another by unmistakable and sometimes formidable frontiers. Those states still differ from one another not only in all conceivable other respects but above all in their regimes and hence in the things to which the preponderant part of each society is dedicated or in the spirit which more or less effectively pervades each society. These societies have very different images of the future so that for all of them to live together, in contradistinction to uneasily coexisting, is altogether impossible. Each of them receiving its character from its regime is still in need of specific measures for preserving itself and its regime and hence is uncertain of its future. Acting willy-nilly through their governments (which may be governments in exile), these societies still move as if on an uncharted sea and surely without the benefit of tracks toward a future that is veiled from everyone and which is pregnant with surprises. Their governments still try to determine the future of their societies with the help partly of knowledge, partly of guesses, the recourse to guesses still being partly necessitated by the secrecy in which their most important opponents shroud their most important plans or projects. The new political science which is so eager to predict is, as it admits, as unable to predict the outcome of the unprecedented conflict peculiar to our age as the crudest soothsayer of the most benighted tribe. In former times people thought that the outcome of serious conflicts is unpredictable because one cannot know how long this or that outstanding leader in war or counsel will live, or how the opposed armies will act in the test of battle or similar things. We have been brought to believe that chance can be controlled or does not seriously affect the fate of societies. Yet the science that is said to have rendered possible the control of chance has itself become the refuge of chance: Man's fate depends now more than ever on science or technology, hence on discoveries or inventions, hence on events whose precise occurrence is by their very nature not predictable. A simply unprecedented political situation would be a situation of no political interest, that is, not a political situation. Now if the essential character of all political situations was grasped by the old political science, there seems to be no reason why it must be superseded by a new political science. In case the new political science should tend to understand political things in non-political terms, the old political science, wise to many ages, would even be superior to the new political science in helping us to find our bearings in our unprecedented situation in spite or rather because of the fact that only the new political science can boast of being the child of the atomic age.

But one will never understand the new political science if one does not start from that reason advanced on its behalf which has nothing whatever to do with any true or alleged blindness of the old political science to any political things as such. That reason is a general notion of science. According to that notion, only scientific knowledge is genuine knowledge. From this it follows immediately that all awareness of political things that is not scientific is cognitively worthless. Serious criticism of the old political science is a waste of time; for we know in advance that it could only have been a pseudo science, although perhaps including a few remarkably shrewd hunches. This is not to deny that the adherents of the new political science sometimes engage in apparent criticism of the old, but that criticism is characterized by a constitutional inability to understand the criticized doctrines on their own terms. What science is, is supposed to be known from the practice of the other sciences, of sciences that are admittedly in existence and not mere desiderata, and the clearest examples of such sciences are the natural sciences. What science is, is supposed to be known, above all, from the science of science, that is, logic. The basis of the new political science then is logic, that is, a particular kind of logic; the logic in question is not, for instance, Aristotelian or Kantian or Hegelian logic. This means, however, that the new political science rests on what for the political scientist as such is a mere assumption that he is not competent to judge on its own terms, namely, as a logical theory, for that theory is controversial among the people who must be supposed to be competent in such matters, the professors of philosophy. The political scientist is competent, however, to judge it by its fruits; he is competent to judge whether his understanding of political things as political things is helped or hindered by the new political science that derives from the logic in question. He is perfectly justified in regarding as an imposition the demand that he comply with "logical positivism" or else plead guilty to being a "metaphysician." He is perfectly justified in regarding this epithet as not "objective," because it is terrifying and unintelligible like the war cries of savages.

What strikes a sympathetic chord in every political scientist is less the demand that he proceed "scientifically"—for mathematics also proceeds scientifically and political science surely is not a mathematical discipline—than the demand that he proceed "empirically." This is a demand of common sense. No one in his senses ever dreamed that he could know anything, say, of American government as such or of the present political situation as such except by looking at American government or at the present political situation. The incarnation of the empirical spirit is the man from Missouri, who has to be shown. For he knows that he, as well as everyone else who is of sound mind and whose sight is not defective, can see things and people as they are with his eyes, and that he is capable of knowing how his neighbors feel; he takes it for granted that he lives with other human beings of all descriptions in the same world and that because they are all human beings, they all understand one another somehow; he knows that if this were not so, political life would be altogether impossible. If someone offered him speculations based on extrasensory perception, he would turn his back more or less politely. The old political science would not quarrel in these respects with the man from Missouri. It did not claim to know better or differently than he such things as that the Democratic and Republican parties are now, and have been for some time, the preponderant parties in this country, and that there are presidential elections every fourth year. By admitting that facts of this kind are known independently of political science, it admitted that empirical knowledge is not necessarily scientific knowledge or that a statement can be true and known to be true without being scientific, and, above all, that political science stands or falls by the truth of the prescientific awareness of political things. Yet one may raise the question of how one can be certain of the truth of empirical statements that are prescientific. If we call an elaborate answer to this question an epistemology, we may say that an empiricist, in contradistinction to an empirical, statement is based on the explicit assumption of a specific epistemology. Yet every epistemology presupposes the truth of empirical statements. Our perceiving things and people is more manifest and more reliable than any "theory of knowledge"—any explanation of how our perceiving things and people is possible—can be; the truth of any "theory of knowledge" depends on its ability to give an adequate account of this fundamental reliance. If a logical positivist tries to give an account of a "thing" or a formula for a "thing" in terms of mere sense data and their composition, he is looking, and bids us to look, at the previously grasped "thing"; the previously grasped "thing" is the standard by which we judge his formula. If an epistemology, for example solipsism, manifestly fails to give an account of how empirical statements as meant can be true, it fails to carry conviction. To be aware of the necessity of the fundamental reliance that underlies or pervades all empirical statements means to recognize the fundamental riddle, not to have solved it. But no man needs to be ashamed to admit that he does not possess a solution to the fundamental riddle. Surely no man ought to let himself be bullied into the acceptance of an alleged solution—for the denial of the existence of a riddle is a kind of solution of the riddle—by the threat that if he fails to do so he is a "metaphysician." To sustain our weaker brethren against that threat, one might tell them that the belief accepted by the empiricists, according to which science is in principle susceptible of infinite progress, is itself tantamount to the belief that being is irretrievably mysterious.

Let us try to restate the issue by returning first to our man from Missouri. A simple observation seems to be sufficient to show that the man from Missouri is "naive": He does not see things with his eyes; what he sees with his eyes are only colors, shapes, and the like; he would perceive "things," in contradistinction to "sense data," only if he possessed "extrasensory perception"; his claim—the claim of common sense—implies that there is "extrasensory perception." What is true of "things," is true of "patterns," at any rate of those patterns which students of politics from time to time claim to "perceive." We must leave the man from Missouri scratching his head; by being silent, he remains in his way a philosopher. But others do not leave it at scratching their heads. Transforming themselves from devotees of *emperia* into empiricists, they contend that what is perceived or "given" is only sense data; the "thing" emerges by virtue of unconscious or conscious "construction"; the "things" which to common sense present themselves as "given" are in truth constructs. Common sense understanding is understanding by means of unconscious construction; scientific understanding is understanding by means of conscious construction. Somewhat more precisely, common sense understanding is understanding in terms of "things possessing qualities"; scientific understanding is understanding in terms of "functional relations between different series of events." Unconscious constructs are ill-made, for their making is affected by all sorts of purely "subjective" influences; only conscious constructs can be well-made, perfectly lucid, in every respect the same for everyone, or "objective." Still, one says with greater right that we perceive things than that we perceive human beings as human beings, for at least some of the properties which we ascribe to things are sensually perceived, whereas the soul's actions, passions, or states can never become sense data. Now, that understanding of things and human beings which is rejected by empiricism is the understanding by which political life, political understanding, political experience stand or fall. Hence, the new political science, based as it is on empiricism, must reject the results of political understanding and political experience as such, and since the political things are given to us in political understanding and political experience, the new political science cannot be helpful for the deeper understanding of political things: it must reduce the political things to nonpolitical data. The new political science comes into being through an attempted break with common sense. But that break cannot be consistently carried out, as can be seen in a general way from the following consideration. Empiricism cannot be established empiricistically: it is not known through sense data that the only possible objects of perception are sense data. If one tries therefore to establish empiricism empirically, one must make use of that understanding of things which empiricism renders doubtful: the relation of eyes to colors or shapes is established through the same kind of perception through which we perceive things as things rather than sense data or constructs. In other words, sense data as sense data become known only through an act of abstraction or disregard which presupposes the legitimacy of our primary awareness of things as things and of people as people. Hence, the only way of overcoming the naïveté of the man from Missouri is in the first place to admit that that naïveté cannot be avoided in any way or that there is no possible human thought which is not in the last analysis dependent on the legitimacy of that naïveté and the awareness or the knowledge going with it.

We must not disregard the most massive or the crudest reason to which empiricism owes much of its attractiveness. Some adherents of the new political science would argue as follows: One cannot indeed reasonably deny that prescientific thought about political things contains genuine knowledge; but the trouble is that within prescientific political thought, genuine knowledge of political things is inseparable from prejudices or superstitions; hence one cannot get rid of the spurious elements in prescientific political thought except by breaking altogether with prescientific thought or by acting on the assumption that prescientific thought does not have the character of knowledge at all. Common sense contains genuine knowledge of broomsticks; but the trouble is that this knowledge has in common sense the same status as the alleged knowledge concerning witches; by trusting common sense one is in danger of bringing back the whole kingdom of darkness with Thomas Aquinas at its head. The old political science was not unaware of the imperfections of political opinion, but it did not believe that the remedy lies in the total rejection of common sense understanding as such. It was critical in the original sense, that is, discerning, regarding political opinion. It was aware that the errors regarding witches were found out without the benefit of empiricism. It was aware that judgments or maxims which were justified by the uncontested experience of decades, and even of centuries, or millennia, may have to be revised because of unforeseen changes; it knew, in the words of Burke, "that the generality of people are fifty years, at least, behind hand in their politics." Accordingly, the old political science was concerned with political improvement by political means as distinguished from social engineering; it knew that those political means include revolutions and also wars, since there may be foreign regimes (Hitler Germany is the orthodox example) that are dangerous to the free survival of this country, regimes that would be expected to transform themselves gradually into good neighbors only by the criminally foolish.

Acceptance of the distinctive premises of the new political science leads to the consequences which have been sufficiently illustrated. . . . In the first place, the new political science is constantly compelled to borrow from common sense knowledge, thus unwittingly testifying to the truth that there is genuine prescientific knowledge of political things which is the basis of all scientific knowledge of them. Secondly, the logic on which the new political science is based may provide sufficient criteria of exactness; it does not provide objective criteria of relevance. Criteria of relevance are inherent in the prescientific understanding of political things; intelligent and informed citizens distinguish soundly between important and unimportant political matters. Political men are concerned with what is to be done politically here and now in accordance with principles of preference of which they are aware, although not necessarily in an adequate manner; it is those principles of preference which supply the criteria of relevance in regard to political things. Ordinarily a political man must at least pretend to "look up" to something that at least the preponderant part of his society looks up to. That which at least everyone who counts politically is supposed to look up to, that which is politically the highest, gives a society its character; it constitutes and justifies the regime of the society in question. The "highest" is that through which a society is "a whole," a distinct whole with a character of its own, just as for common sense "the world" is a whole by being overarched by heaven of which one cannot be aware except by "looking up." There is obviously, and for cause, a variety of regimes and hence of what is regarded as the politically highest, that is, of the purposes to which the various regimes are dedicated. The qualitatively different regimes, or kinds of regimes, and the qualitatively different purposes constituting and legitimating them, then, by revealing themselves as the most important political things, supply the key to the understanding of all political things and the basis for the reasoned distinction between important and unimportant political things. The regimes and their principles pervade the societies throughout, in the sense that there are no recesses of privacy which are simply impervious to that pervasion as is indicated by such expressions, coined by the new political science, as "the democratic personality." Nevertheless, there are political things that are not affected by the difference of regimes. In a society which cannot survive without an irrigation system, every regime will have to preserve that system intact. Every regime must try to preserve itself against subversion by means of force. There are both technical things and politically neutral things (things that are common to all regimes) that are necessarily the concern of political deliberation without ever being as such politically controversial. The preceding remarks are a very rough sketch of the view of political things that was characteristic of the old political science. According to that view, what is most important for political science is identical with what is most important politically. To illustrate this by a present-day example, for the old-fashioned political scientists today, the most important concern is the Cold War or the qualitative difference, which amounts to a conflict, between liberal democracy and Communism.

The break with the common sense understanding of political things compels the new political science to abandon the criteria of relevance that are inherent in political understanding. Hence, the new political science lacks orientation regarding political things; it has no protection whatever, except by surreptitious recourse to common sense, against losing itself in the study of irrelevancies. It is confronted by a chaotic mass of data into which it must bring an order alien to those data, an order originating in the demands of political science as a science anxious to comply with the demands of logical positivism. The universals in the light of which the old political science viewed the political phenomena (the various regimes and their purposes) must be replaced by a different kind of universals. The first step toward the finding of the new kind of universals may be said to take this form: What is equally present in all regimes (the politically neutral) must be the key to the different regimes (the political proper, the essentially controversial); what is equally present in all regimes is, say, coercion and freedom; the scientific analysis of a given regime will then indicate exactly—in terms of percentages—the amount of coercion and the amount of freedom peculiar to it. That is to say, as political scientists we must express the political phenomena par excellence, the essential differences or the heterogeneity of regimes, in terms of the homogeneous elements which pervade all regimes. What is important for us as political scientists is not the politically important. Yet we cannot forever remain blind to the fact that what claims to be a purely scientific or theoretical enterprise has grave political consequences—consequences which are so little accidental that they appeal for their own sake to the new political scientists: Everyone knows what follows from the demonstration, which presupposes the begging of all important questions, that there is only a difference of degree between liberal democracy and Communism in regard to coercion and freedom. The Is necessarily leads to an Ought, all sincere protestations to the contrary notwithstanding. The second step toward the finding of the new kind of universals consists in the following reasoning: All political societies, whatever their regimes, surely are groups of some kind; hence, the key to the understanding of political things must be a theory of groups in general. Groups must have some cohesion and groups change; we are then in need of a universal theory which tells us why or how groups cohere and why or how they change. Seeking for those whys or hows, we shall discover n factors and m modes of their interaction. The result of this reduction of the political to the sociological—a reduction that, it is claimed, will make our understanding of political things more "realistic"—is in fact a formalism unrivaled in any scholasticism of the past. All peculiarities of political societies, and still more of the political societies with which we are concerned as citizens, become unrecognizable if restated in terms of the vague generalities which hold of every conceivable group; at the end of the dreary and boring process we understand what we are interested in not more but less than we understood it at the beginning. What in political language are called the rulers and the ruled (to say nothing of oppressors and oppressed) become through this process nothing but different parts of a social system, of a mechanism, each part acting on the other and being acted upon by it; there may be a stronger part but there cannot be a ruling part; the relation of parts of a mechanism supersedes the political relation. We need not dwell on the next, but not necessarily last, step of the reasoning which we are trying to sketch, namely, the requirement that the researches regarding groups must be underpinned, nay, guided by "a general theory of personality" or the like; we know nothing of the political wisdom or the folly of a statesman's actions until we know everything about the degree of affection which he received from each of his parents, if any. The last step might be thought to be the use by the new political science of observations regarding rats: Can we not observe human beings as we observe rats, are decisions which rats make not much simpler than the decisions which humans frequently make, and is not the simpler always the key to the more complex? We do not doubt that we can observe, if we try hard enough, the overt behavior of humans as we observe the overt behavior of rats. But we ought not to forget that in the case of rats we are limited to observing overt behavior because they do not talk, and they do not talk because they have nothing to say or because they have no inwardness. Yet to return from these depths to the surface, an important example of the formalism in question is supplied by the well-known theory regarding the principles of legitimacy which substitutes formal characteristics (traditional, rational, charismatic) for the substantive principles which are precisely the purposes to which the various regimes are dedicated and by which they are legitimated. The universals for which the new political science seeks are "laws of human behavior"; those laws are to be discovered by means of "empirical" research. There is an amazing disproportion between the apparent breadth of the goal (say, a general theory of social change) and the true pettiness of the researches undertaken to achieve that goal (say, a change in a hospital when one head nurse is replaced by another). This is no accident. Since we lack objective criteria of relevance, we have no reason to be more interested in a world-shaking revolution that affects directly or indirectly all men than in the most trifling "social changes." Moreover, if the laws sought are to be "laws of human behavior" they cannot be restricted to human behavior as it is affected by this or that regime. But human behavior as studied by "empirical" research always occurs within a peculiar regime. More precisely, the most cherished techniques of "empirical" research in the social sciences can be applied only to human beings living now in countries in which the governments tolerate research of this kind. The new political science is therefore constantly tempted (and as a rule it does not resist that temptation) to absolutize the relative or peculiar, that is, to be parochial. We have read statements about "the revolutionary" or "the conservative" which did not even claim to have any basis other than observations made in the United States at the present moment; if those statements had any relation to facts at all, they might have some degree of truth regarding revolutionaries or conservatives in certain parts of the United States today, but they reveal themselves immediately as patently wrong if taken as they were meant—as descriptions of the revolutionary or the conservative as such; the error in question was due to the parochialism inevitably fostered by the new political science.

At the risk of some repetition, we must say a few words about the language of the new political science. The break with the political understanding of political things necessitates the making of a language different from the language used by political men. The new political science rejects the latter language as ambiguous and imprecise and claims that its own language is unambiguous and precise. Yet this claim is not warranted. The language of the new political science is not less vague but more vague than the language used in political life. Political life would be altogether impossible if its language were unqualifiedly vague; that language is capable of the utmost unambiguity and precision, as in a declaration of war or in an order given to a firing squad. If available distinctions like that between war, peace, and armistice prove to be insufficient, political life finds, without the benefit of political science, the right new expression (Cold War as distinguished from Hot or Shooting War) that designates the new phenomenon with unfailing precision. The alleged vagueness of political language is primarily due to the fact that it corresponds to the complexity of political life, or that it is nourished by long experience with political things in a great variety of circumstances. By simply condemning prescientific language, instead of deviating from usage in particular cases because of the proven inadequacy of usage in the cases in question, one simply condemns oneself to unredeemable vagueness. No thoughtful citizen would dream of equating politics with something as vague and empty as "power" or "power relations." The thinking men who are regarded as the classic interpreters of power, Thucydides and Machiavelli, did not need these expressions; these expressions as now used originate, not in political life, but in the academic reaction to the understanding of political life in terms of law alone; these expressions signify nothing but that academic reaction. Political language does not claim to be perfectly clear and distinct; it does not claim to be based on a full understanding of the things which it designates unambiguously enough; it is suggestive: It leaves those things in the penumbra in which they come to sight. The purge effected by "scientific" definitions of those things has the character of sterilization. The language of the new political science claims to be perfectly clear and distinct and, at the same time, entirely provisional; its terms are meant to imply hypotheses about political life. But this claim to undogmatic openness is a mere ceremonial gesture. When one speaks of "conscience" one does not claim to have fathomed the phenomenon indicated by that term. But when the new political scientist speaks of the "Superego," he is certain that anything meant by "conscience" which is not covered by the "Superego" is a superstition. As a consequence he cannot distinguish between a bad conscience which may induce a man to devote the rest of his life to compensating another man to the best of his powers for an irreparable damage and "guilt feelings" which one ought to get rid of as fast and as cheaply as possible. Similarly he is certain to have understood the trust which induces people to vote for a candidate to high office by speaking of the "father image"; he does not have to inquire whether and to what extent the candidate in question deserves that trust—a trust different from the trust which children have in their father. The allegedly provisional or hypothetical terms are never questioned in the process of research, for their implications channel the research in such directions that the "data" which might reveal the inadequacy of the hypotheses never turn up. We conclude that to the extent to which the new political science is not formalistic, it is vulgarian. This vulgarianism shows itself particularly in the "value-free" manner in which it uses and thus debases terms that originally were meant only for indicating things of a noble character—terms like "culture," "personality," "values," "charismatic," and "civilization."

The most important example of the dogmatism to which we have alluded is supplied by the treatment of religion in the new political or social science. The new science uses sociological or psychological theories regarding religion which exclude, without considering, the possibility that religion rests ultimately on God's revealing Himself to man; hence those theories are mere hypotheses which can never be confirmed. Those theories are in fact the hidden basis of the new science. The new science rests on a dogmatic atheism which presents itself as merely methodological or hypothetical. For a few years, logical positivism tried with much noise and little thought to dispose of religion by asserting that religious assertions are "meaningless statements." This trick seems to have been abandoned without noise. Some adherents of the new political science might rejoin with some liveliness that their posture toward religion is imposed on them by intellectual honesty: Not being able to believe, they cannot accept belief as the basis of their science. We gladly grant that, other things being equal, a frank atheist is a better man than an alleged theist who conceives of God as a symbol. But we must add that intellectual honesty is not enough. Intellectual honesty is not love of truth. Intellectual honesty, a kind of self-denial, has taken the place of love of truth because truth has come to be believed to be repulsive and one cannot love the repulsive. Yet just as our opponents refuse respect to unreasoned belief, we on our part, with at least equal right, must refuse respect to unreasoned unbelief; honesty with oneself regarding one's unbelief is in itself not more than unreasoned unbelief probably accompanied by a vague confidence that the issue of unbelief versus belief has long since been settled once and for all. It is hardly necessary to add that the dogmatic exclusion of religious awareness proper renders questionable all long-range predictions concerning the future of societies.

The reduction of the political to the subpolitical is the reduction of primarily given wholes to elements which are relatively simple, that is, sufficiently simple for the research purpose at hand yet necessarily susceptible of being analyzed into still simpler elements *in infinitum*. It implies that there cannot be genuine wholes. Hence it implies that there cannot be a common good. According to the old political science, there is necessarily a common good, and the common good in its fullness is the good society and what is required for the good society. The consistent denial of the common good is as impossible as every other consistent manifestation of the break with common sense. The empiricists who reject the notion of wholes are compelled to speak sooner or later of such things as "the open society," which is their definition of the good society. The alternative (if it is an alternative) is to deny the possibility of a substantive public interest but to admit the possibility of substantive group interests; yet it is not difficult to see that what is granted to the goose, "the group," cannot be consistently denied to the gander, "the country." In accordance with this, the new political science surreptitiously reintroduces the common good in the form of "the rules of the game" with which all conflicting groups are supposed to comply because those rules, reasonably fair to every group, can reasonably be admitted by every group. The "group politics" approach is a relic of Marxism, which more reasonably denied that there can be a common good in a society consisting of classes that are locked in a life and death struggle, overt or hidden, and therefore found the common good in a classless and hence stateless society comprising the whole human race. The consistent denial of the common good requires a radical "individualism." In fact, the new political science appears to teach that there cannot be a substantive public interest because there is not, and cannot be, a single objective approved by all members of society: murderers show by their action that not even the prohibition against murder is, strictly speaking, to the public interest. We are not so sure whether the murderer wishes that murder cease to be a punishable action or rather that he himself get away with murder. Be this as it may, this denial of the common good is based on the premise that even if an objective is to the interest of the overwhelming majority, it is not to the interest of all; no minority however small, no individual however perverse must be left out. More precisely, even if an objective is to the interest of all but not believed by all to be to the interest of all, it is not to the public interest; everyone is by nature the sole judge of what is to his interest; his judgment regarding his interest is not subject to anybody else's examination on the issue whether his judgment is sound. This premise is not the discovery or invention of the new political science; it was stated with the greatest vigor by Hobbes, who opposed it to the opposite premise which had been the basis of the old political science proper. But Hobbes still saw that his premise entails the war of everybody against everybody and hence drew the conclusion that everyone must cease to be the sole judge of what is to his interest if there is to be human life; the individual's reason must give way to the public reason. The new political science denies in a way that there is a public reason; government may be a broker, if a broker possessing "the monopoly of violence," but it surely is not the public reason. The true public reason is the new political science, which judges in a universally valid, or objective, manner what is to the interest of each, for it shows to everyone what means he must choose to attain his attainable ends, whatever those ends may be. It has been shown earlier in this volume what becomes of the new political science, or of the only kind of rationality which the new political science still admits, if its Hobbesian premise is not conveniently forgotten: The new form of public reason goes the way of the old.

The denial of the common good presents itself today as a direct consequence of the distinction between facts and values according to which only factual judgments, not value judgments, can be true or objective. The new political science leaves the justification of values or of preferences to "political philosophy" or, more precisely, to ideology on the ground that any justification of preferences would have to derive values from facts and such derivation is not legitimately possible. Preferences are not strictly speaking opinions and hence cannot be true or false, whereas ideologies are opinions and, for the reason given, false opinions. Whereas acting man has necessarily chosen values, the new political scientist as pure spectator is not committed to any value; in particular, he is neutral in the conflict between liberal democracy and its enemies. The traditional value systems antedate the awareness of the difference between facts and values; they claimed to be derived from facts—from Divine Revelation or from similar sources, in general from superior or perfect beings which as such unite in themselves fact and value; the discovery of the difference between facts and values amounts therefore to a refutation of the traditional value systems as originally meant. It is at least doubtful whether those value systems can be divorced from what present themselves as their factual bases. At any rate, it follows from the difference between facts and values that men can live without ideology: They can adopt, posit, or proclaim values without making the illegitimate attempt to derive their values from facts or without relying on false or at least unevident assertions regarding what is. One thus arrives at the notion of the rational society or of the nonideological regime: a society that is based on the understanding of the character of values. Since this understanding implies that before the tribunal of reason all values are equal, the rational society will be egalitarian or democratic and permissive or liberal: The rational doctrine regarding the difference between facts and values rationally justifies the preference for liberal democracy—contrary to what is intended by that distinction itself. In other words, whereas the new political science ought to deny the proposition that there can be no society without an ideology, it asserts that proposition.

One is thus led to wonder whether the distinction between facts and values, or the assertion that no Ought can be derived from an Is, is well founded. Let us assume that a man's "values" (that is, what he values) are fully determined by his heredity and environment, that is, by his Is, or that there is a one-to-one relation between value a and Is A. In this case the Ought would be determined by the Is or derivative from it. But the very issue as commonly understood presupposes that this assumption is wrong; man possesses a certain latitude; he can choose not only from among various ways of overt behavior (like jumping or not jumping into a river to escape death at the hands of a stronger enemy who may or may not be able to swim) but from among various values; this latitude, this possibility has the character of a fact. A man lacking this latitude—for example, a man for whom every stimulus is a value or who cannot help giving in to every desire—is a defective man, a man with whom something is wrong. The fact that someone desires something does not yet make that something his value; he may successfully fight his desire or if his desire overpowers him he may blame himself for this as for a failure on his part;

only choice, in contradistinction to mere desire, makes something a man's value. The distinction between desire and choice is a distinction among facts. Choice does not mean here the choice of means to pre-given ends; choice here means the choice of ends, the positing of ends or, rather, of values. Man is then understood as a being which differs from all other known beings because it posits values; this positing is taken to be a fact. In accordance with this, the new political science denies that man has natural ends—ends toward which he is by nature inclined; it denies more specifically the premise of modern natural right, according to which self-preservation is the most important natural end; man can choose death in preference to life, not only in a given situation, out of despair, but simply: He can posit death as his value. The view that the pertinent Is is our positing of values, in contradistinction to the yielding to mere desires, necessarily leads to Oughts of a radically different character from the so-called Oughts corresponding to mere desires. We conclude that the "relativism" accepted by the new political science according to which values are nothing but objects of desire is based on an insufficient analysis of the Is, that is, of the pertinent Is; and, furthermore, that one's opinion regarding the character of the Is settles one's opinion regarding the character of the Ought. We must leave it open here whether a more adequate analysis of the pertinent Is, that is, of the nature of man, does not lead to a more adequate determination of the Ought or beyond a merely formal characterization of the Ought. At any rate, if a man is of the opinion that as a matter of fact all desires are of equal dignity since we know of no factual consideration which would entitle us to assign different dignities to different desires, he cannot but be of the opinion—unless he is prepared to become guilty of gross arbitrariness— that all desires ought to be treated as equal within the limits of the possible, and this opinion is what is meant by permissive egalitarianism.

There is then more than a mysterious preestablished harmony between the new political science and a particular version of liberal democracy. The alleged value-free analysis of political phenomena is controlled by an unavowed commitment built into the new political science to that version of liberal democracy. That version of liberal democracy is not discussed openly and impartially, with full consideration of all relevant pros and cons. We call this characteristic of the new political science its democratism. The new political science looks for laws of human behavior to be discovered by means of data supplied through certain techniques of research which are believed to guarantee the maximum of objectivity; it therefore puts a premium on the study of things which occur frequently now in democratic societies: Neither those in their graves nor those behind the Curtains can respond to questionnaires or to interviews. Democracy is then the tacit presupposition of the data; it does not have to become a theme; it can easily be forgotten: The wood is forgotten for the trees; the laws of human behavior are in fact laws of the behavior of human beings more or less molded by democracy; man is tacitly identified with democratic man. The new political science puts a premium on observations which can be made with the utmost frequency, and therefore by people of the meanest capacities. Thus it frequently culminates in observations made by people who are not intelligent about people who are not intelligent. While the new political science becomes ever less able to see democracy or to hold a mirror to democracy, it ever more reflects the most dangerous proclivities of democracy. It even strengthens those proclivities. By teaching in effect the equality of literally all desires, it teaches in effect that there is nothing that a man ought to be ashamed of; by destroying the possibility of self-contempt, it destroys, with the best of intentions, the possibility of self-respect. By teaching the equality of all values, by denying that there are things which are intrinsically high and others which are intrinsically low as well as by denying that there is an essential difference between men and brutes, it unwittingly contributes to the victory of the gutter. Yet this same new political science came into being through the revolt against what one may call the democratic orthodoxy of the immediate past. It had learned certain lessons which were hard for that orthodoxy to swallow regarding the irrationality of the masses and the necessity of elites; if it had been wise it would have learned those lessons from the galaxy of antidemocratic thinkers of the remote past. It believed that it had learned in other words that, contrary to the belief of the orthodox democrats, no compelling case can be made for liberalism (for example, for the unqualified freedom of such speech as does not constitute a clear and present danger) nor for democracy (free elections based on universal suffrage). But it succeeded in reconciling those doubts with the unfaltering commitment to liberal democracy by the simple device of declaring that no value judgments, including those supporting liberal democracy, are rational, and hence that an iron-clad argument in favor of liberal democracy ought in reason not even to be expected. The very complex pros and cons regarding liberal democracy have thus become entirely obliterated by the poorest formalism. The crisis of liberal democracy has become concealed by a ritual which calls itself methodology or logic. This almost willful blindness to the crisis of liberal democracy is part of that crisis. No wonder then that the new political science has nothing to say against those who unhesitatingly prefer surrender, that is, the abandonment of liberal democracy, to war.

Only a great fool would call the new political science diabolic: It has no attributes peculiar to fallen angels. It is not even Machiavellian, for Machiavelli's teaching was graceful, subtle, and colorful. Nor is it Neronian. Nevertheless one may say of it that it fiddles while Rome burns. It is excused by two facts: It does not know that it fiddles, and it does not know that Rome burns.

PART IV

Political Economy and the Welfare State

Having canvassed the principal theoretical questions in modern American conservatism, we now turn to its achievements on a more practical level, beginning with its approaches to the economic and political legacy of the New Deal. That legacy consists above all in the Welfare State (drastically expanded, to be sure, by the Great Society and enriched by the largesse of the Nixon administration) and the Keynesian economic policies designed if not to pay for it, then at least to stretch out the payments on it until the fabled long run when, according to Keynes's famous wisecrack, we are all dead.

The conservative critique of Keynesian economics was not long in coming. Henry Hazlitt, one of the most lucid writers on economics in our time, was making cogent sorties against it thirty years ago (e.g., *The Failure of the New Economics* [1959]). His books, including the classic primer *Economics in One Lesson,* restored the polemical edge to classical economics that had manifestly been lacking in the dark days of the Great Depression. In the meantime, academic economists were leading a counterrevolution of their own, converging from different directions on the same prize: Ludwig von Mises, Israel Kirzner, and Friedrich A. Hayek proceeding from the methodological individualism of Austrian economics; Milton Friedman from the correlations of the money supply and the business cycle; and James Buchanan and other public choice theorists from the keen observation that while welfare economists had a lot to say about "market failure," they had yet to notice the parallel phenomenon of "government failure": The same problems of collective action present in the marketplace were (absent an entirely separate account of human nature for political as opposed to economic man) present in the actions of government that were supposed to cure the market's imperfections. The reader might be forgiven for thinking that the prize on which these economists were converging was the Nobel Prize, inasmuch as three of them (Hayek, Friedman, Buchanan) have won it, and the rest deserve it.

In the past decade, however, the attack on Keynesian fiscal policy has come most prominently from a new direction—the supply side. Most of the elements that went into the making of supply-side economics were not new—they were staples of classical and neoclassical analysis; but the amalgamation of them in the late 1970s created a new and dynamic phenomenon. Arthur Laffer (of the famous Curve), Jude Wanniski, George Gilder, and others, with the adroit political assistance of Congressman Jack Kemp and President Ronald Reagan, captured the public imagination with the prospect of lowering marginal tax rates to encourage economic growth. Paul Craig Roberts, the author of the original Kemp-Roth tax cut bill in 1976 and Assistant Secretary of the Treasury for economic policy in the first year of the Reagan administration, contributes a brilliant essay outlining the chief tenets of the supply-side school as they bear on the deficiencies of the Keynesian paradigm.

It is a peculiarity of supply-side analysis that it does not challenge the Welfare State as such; in fact, its apostles often present it as the only way of *paying* for the Welfare State without wrecking the economy. This is a useful reminder that opposition to the Welfare State and to the New Deal is not a universal article of faith among conservatives. Indeed, among many neoconservatives and some traditionalists, the idea of the Welfare State is regarded as eminently conservative, in the precise sense of the word. The Welfare State was, on the whole, a prudent adaptation of American government to the social realities of the twentieth century, they argue: a way to conserve the blessings of liberty in the face of challenges from the radical Left and Right, to temper the materialism of our civilization, to promote a sense of common good among the citizenry. George Will, the shrewd columnist and television commentator (formerly the Washington editor of *National Review*) argues for a conservative version of the Welfare State in his book *Statecraft as Soulcraft: What Government Does,* from which the present essay is taken. This chapter may particularly be compared to Milton Friedman's and Frank Meyers' doctrines in Part Two, and stands as an example of the anxiety over America's modernity that inspires many neo-conservative interpretations of American politics.

But granting for the moment that the Welfare State ought to be a conservative concern, a second question arises at once: Will it work? Can it help those who ought to be helped without generating a dependency effect, without encouraging the very evil that it intends to cure or at least palliate? Charles Murray's breathtaking answer is No. Murray's book, *Losing Ground,* from which this essay is adapted, was an instant event. It presented soberly, compassionately the record of the Great Society's programs, conceived in benevolence but dedicated, in practice, to the breakup of the black family, the creation of a vast urban underclass battening on the welfare system, the generation of misery and exploitation in amounts dwarfing the ills that they had set out to cure. On poverty, education, employment, welfare, all the fronts on which President Johnson unleashed the federal bureaucracy, Murray demonstrates not the simple but the tragic failures—for the cost in human well-being and shattered self-respect was high—of the Great Society. The essay presented here combines his reflections on the ideology of the new programs with his compelling proof of "the constraints on helping." As a former believer and participant in this great attempt at social regeneration, he illuminates the subject as no one else has.

PAUL CRAIG ROBERTS

The Breakdown of the Keynesian Model

There is much talk these days about "the crisis in Keynesian economics." That some such crisis exists is evident from the bewilderment and impotence our economic policy makers are displaying in their confrontation with economic reality. But what exactly is the nature of this crisis? What went wrong and what can put it right?

The answer, I would suggest, is almost embarrassingly simple. Today in the United States, public economic policy is formulated in bland disregard of the human incentives upon which the economy relies. Instead it is based on the Keynesian assumption that the gross national product (GNP) and employment are determined only by the level of aggregate demand or total spending in the economy. Unemployment and low rates of economic growth are seen as evidence of insufficient spending. The standard remedy is for government to increase total spending by incurring a deficit in its budget. GNP, it is believed, will then rise by some multiple of the increase in spending. Keynesian economics focuses on estimating the "spending gap" and the "multiplier" so that the necessary deficit can be calculated.

This view of economic policy is enshrined in the large-scale econometric forecasting models upon which both Congress and the Executive Branch rely for simulations of economic policy alternatives. It is a view that is extraordinary in its emphasis on spending. True, it is obvious that if people did not buy, no one would produce for market. It also seems obvious that the more people buy, the more will be produced and, therefore, that the use of government fiscal policy to increase total demand will increase total production or GNP. All this is so obvious to Keynesians that they believe any fiscal policy that produces an increase in government spending, even a spending increase matched by a tax increase, will produce an increase in GNP.

The concept of the "balanced-budget multiplier" illustrates the primacy that Keynesians give to spending as the determinant of production. According to this concept, government can increase total spending and, thereby, GNP by raising taxes and spending the revenues. The reasoning is as follows. People do not pay the higher taxes only by reducing their spending (consumption); they also reduce their savings. Therefore, when

From Paul Craig Roberts, "The Breakdown of the Keynesian Model," *The Public Interest*, no. 52 (Summer 1978), pp. 20–33. Copyright © 1978 by National Affairs, Inc. Reprinted by permission of *The Public Interest* and the author.

taxes are raised, the decrease in private spending is less than the increase in government spending. Conversely, a cut in tax rates, matched by a decrease in government spending, would result in a reduction in total spending (i.e., saving would increase), a fall in GNP, and a rise in unemployment.

For years after the 1964 Presidential election, college students were asked a standard question on economic exams: What would happen if Barry Goldwater's prescription for a tax cut, matched by a spending cut, were implemented? They missed the answer if they did not reply that there would be a reduction in aggregate demand and, therefore, a fall in GNP and employment. Alas, for too many policy makers that is still the answer.

Since the "balanced-budget multiplier" implies that the greater the increase in taxes and in government spending, the greater the increase in GNP, it is a wonder no one ever asked what happens to production as tax rates rise. This question confronts economic policy with the incentive effects it has disregarded. It should be obvious even to Keynesians that when marginal tax rates are high, people will prefer additional leisure to additional current income, and additional current consumption to additional future income. As work effort and investment decline, production will fall, regardless of how great an increase there might be in aggregate demand. Such a recognition of disincentives implies a recognition of incentives, and Keynesians are gradually having to rethink the answer to their standard question about Barry Goldwater. Once one recognizes that people produce and invest for income, and that income depends on tax rates, one has reached the realization that *fiscal policy causes changes not just in demand but also in supply.*

The Economics of Supply

The economics of spending has thoroughly neglected the economics of supply. On the supply side there are two important relative prices governing production. One price determines the choice between additional current income and leisure; the other determines the choice between additional future income (investment) and current consumption. Both prices are affected by the marginal tax rates. The higher the tax rates on earnings, the lower the cost of leisure and current consumption, in terms of foregone after-tax income.

As an illustration, consider the decision to produce. There are two uses of time—work and leisure. Each use has a price relative to the other. The price of additional leisure is the amount of income foregone by not working, and it is influenced by the tax rates. The higher the tax rates, the smaller the amount of after-tax income foregone by enjoying additional leisure. In other words, the higher the tax rates, the lower the relative price of leisure. When the marginal tax rate reaches 100 percent, the relative price of additional leisure becomes zero. At that point, additional leisure becomes a free good, because nothing has to be sacrificed in order to acquire it.

We often hear that a person works the first five months of the year for the government, and then starts working for himself. But that is not the way it goes. The first part of the year, he works for himself; he only begins working for the government when his income reaches taxable levels. The more he earns, the more he works for the government, until rising marginal rates discourage him from further work.

Take the case of a physician who encounters the 50 percent rate after six, eight, or ten months of work. He is faced with working another six, four, or two months for only 50 percent of his earnings. Such a low after-tax return on their efforts encourages doctors to share practices, to reduce their working hours, and to take longer vacations. The high tax rates thus shrink the tax base by discouraging them from earning additional amounts of taxable income. They also drive up the cost of medical care by reducing the supply of medical services. A tax-rate reduction would raise the relative price of leisure and result in more taxable income earned and also in a greater supply of medical services.

The effect of tax rates on the decision to earn additional taxable income is not limited to physicians or to the top tax bracket; it operates across the spectrum of tax brackets. Studies by Martin Feldstein show that the tax rates on the average worker practically eliminate the gap between his after-tax take-home pay and the level of untaxed unemployment compensation he could be receiving if he did not work. In this case, a marginal tax rate of 30 percent (including state and Federal income taxes and Social Security taxes) reduces the relative price of leisure so much that, by making unemployment competitive with work, it has raised the measured rate of unemployment by 1.25 percent and shrunk GNP and the tax base by the lost production of 1 million workers.

It is useful to give another example to illustrate that it is not just the top marginal rate that causes losses to GNP, employment, and tax revenues by discouraging people from earning additional taxable income. Blue-collar workers do not yet encounter the top marginal tax rate (although if inflation continues to push up money incomes, and the tax-rate structure remains unadjusted for inflation, it will not be many years before they do). Nevertheless, the marginal tax rates that many blue-collar workers already face are high enough to discourage them from earning additional taxable income. Take the case of a carpenter facing only a 25 percent marginal tax rate. For every additional $100 he earns before income tax, he gets to keep $75. Suppose that his house needs painting and that he can hire a painter for $80 a day and hire himself out for $100 a day. However, since his after-tax earnings are only $75, he saves $5 by painting his own house, so it pays him to choose not to earn the additional $100. In this case, the tax base shrinks by $180—of which $100 is the foregone earnings of the carpenter, and $80 is the lost earnings of the painter who is not hired. (Also, the productive efficiency associated with the division of labor vanishes.)

Suppose, instead, that the marginal tax rate on additional earnings by the carpenter were reduced to 15 percent. In this case, his after-tax earnings would be $85, and it would pay him to hire the painter. The reduction in the marginal tax rate would thus expand the tax base upon which revenues are collected by $180.

Studies by Gary Becker have made it clear that capital and labor are employed by households to produce utility through nonmarket activities (e.g., a carpenter painting his own house). Utility produced in this way is not purchased with income subject to taxation. Therefore, the amount of household-owned capital and labor supplied in the market will be influenced by marginal tax rates. The lower the after-tax income earned by supplying additional labor and capital in the market, the less the utility that the additional income can provide, and the more likely it is that households can increase their utility by allocating their productive resources to non-market activities. A clear implication of the new household economics is that *the amount of labor and capital supplied in the market is influenced by the marginal tax rates.*

Now consider how relative prices affect the choice concerning the use of income. There are two uses of income, consumption and saving (investment), and each has a price in terms of the other. The price of additional current consumption is the amount of future income foregone by enjoying additional current consumption. The higher the tax rates, the smaller the amount of after-tax future income foregone by enjoying additional current consumption. In other words, the higher the tax rates, the lower the relative price of current consumption.

Take the case of an Englishman facing the 98 percent marginal tax rate on investment income. He has the choice of saving $50,000 at a 17 percent rate of return, which would bring him $8,500 per year before taxes, or purchasing a Rolls Royce. Since the after-tax value of that $8,500 additional income is only $170 per year, the price of additional consumption is very low: He can enjoy having a fine motor car by giving up only $170 per year of additional income. This is why so many Rolls Royces are seen in England today. They are mistaken for signs of prosperity, whereas in fact they are signs of high tax rates on investment income.

A tax-rate reduction would raise the price of current consumption relative to future income, and thus result in more savings, making possible a growth in real investment. A rate reduction not only increases disposable income and total spending, *it also changes the composition of total spending toward more investment.* Thus, labor productivity, employment, and real GNP are raised above the levels that would result from the same amount of total spending more heavily weighted toward current consumption.

Tax Cuts and Rebates

The econometric models upon which the government relies for simulations of policy alternatives do not take into account these supply-side effects on GNP of these relative price changes. Consider the alternatives faced by the Keynesian policy maker who wants "to get the economy moving again." His goal is to increase aggregate demand or total spending. How can he do this? He has the choice between the balanced-budget multiplier (i.e., increasing both taxes and government spending) or a deficit. He will discard the balanced-budget multiplier, because it is relatively weak and deficits are more politically acceptable than legislating higher tax rates. Having settled on a deficit, he has to choose how to produce it. He can hold tax revenues constant and increase government spending, or he can hold government spending constant and cut tax revenues. In the latter case, he has a choice between rebates and permanent reductions in tax rates. Wanting the most stimulus for his deficit dollar, he will ask for econometric simulations of his three policy alternatives: a tax rebate, a tax rate reduction, or an increase in government spending programs.

The simulations, all based on Keynesian assumptions, will show that a revenue reduction of a given amount, whether in the form of a rebate of personal income taxes or a reduction in personal-income-tax rates, will raise disposable income—and thereby spending and GNP—by the same amount. The policy maker may prefer the rebate for reasons of "flexibility." The spending stimulus may not be required in the following year, and, if it is, he has the option of providing it either by another rebate or by an increase in government spending programs. But on the basis of the econometric simulation, he will be indifferent as to the choice between rebates and rate reductions. As for his third option, an increase in government spending programs, the simulation may report that, dollar for dollar, an increase in government purchases (as contrasted with transfers) will have a more powerful impact on GNP because the government spends all of the money, whereas if it is returned to consumers they will save part of it. Based on the econometric simulation of his alternatives, he will conclude that there is no compelling economic reason in favor of any of the three, and he will make his choice on a political basis.

But the econometric models have misled the policy maker. Unlike a reduction in personal-income-tax rates, a rebate affects no individual choice at the margin. It does not change the relative prices governing the choices between additional current income and leisure or between additional future income and current consumption. It does not raise the relative prices of leisure and current consumption. Therefore, a rebate directly stimulates neither work nor investment. For any given revenue reduction, a rebate cannot cause as great an increase in GNP as a rate reduction, because it does not affect the choices that would cause people to allocate more time and more income to increasing production for the market.

An increase in government spending fares no better by comparison, and may fare even worse. It too fails to raise the after-tax rewards for work and investment. Furthermore, it increases the percentage of total resources used in the government sector. If the government sector uses resources less efficiently than the private sector, as seems to be the case, the result is a decline in the efficiency with which resources are used— which means GNP would be less than it otherwise would be. Yet the econometric simulations of the policy maker's alternatives will pick up none of the incentive and disincentive effects of these relative price changes. Instead, they focus on the effects of these alternatives on disposable income and on spending.

There are a number of adverse consequences of this extraordinary preoccupation with spending. One is that *the models exaggerate the net tax-revenue losses that result from cutting tax rates.* The only "feedback effect" on the tax base and tax revenues that they provide for is the expansion of GNP in response to an increase in demand. They do not provide for the expansion in GNP that results from higher after-tax rewards for work and investment. The supply-side "feedback effects" are ignored. Similarly, revenue gains from tax-rate increases will be overestimated, because the disincentive effects are left out.

A second consequence follows from the popular misidentification of a tax rebate as a tax cut, and from a similar tendency on the part of most policy makers to see rebates and rate cuts as variations of the same policy instrument. If Milton Friedman is correct that personal consumption is a function of *permanent* income, a temporary rebate has little impact even on spending. Thus, on the basis of experience with rebates, tax cuts *per se* might come to be seen as relatively ineffectual, leaving the field open to proponents of government spending programs.

A third consequence is that the true effects of large tax increases (such as the proposed energy taxes, or the $227 billion increase in the Social Security tax over the next decade) will not be accurately calculated. Policy makers see these tax increases as withdrawals from disposable income and spending, and their only concern is "to put money back" into spending so that aggregate demand does not fall. However, these tax increases change the *relative* prices and incentives of leisure and work, consumption and investment. They produce resource reallocations that have adverse implications for employment and the rate of economic growth. Yet the econometric models, as now constructed, flash no warning lights.

Consider what Arthur Laffer, in the *Wall Street Journal,* has called the "tax wedge." The Social Security tax increase provides a good example of this phenomenon. It is a tax on employment, and, as economists should know, a tax on employment will reduce employment. The employer's decision to hire is based on the gross cost to him of an employee. The employee's decision to work is based on his after-tax pay. We know that the higher the price, the less the quantity demanded, and the lower the price, the less the quantity supplied. The Social Security tax both raises the price to the demander and lowers it to the supplier. By increasing the Social Security tax, policy makers reduced both job opportunities and the inclination to work.* They raised the cost of labor relative to capital for the employer, and they narrowed the gap between unemployment compensation and after-tax take-home pay for a wider range of workers. Since the revenues available for paying Social Security benefits depend on both the tax rates and the number of people paying into the system, the increase in rates will be offset to some degree by a decrease in the number of people paying into the system. It is hard to see how the Social Security system can be saved by decreasing employment, or how increasing the demand for unemployment compensation is likely to free general revenues for Social Security benefits.

"Crowding Out" Investment

There are at least two other important points on which economic policy is misinformed by the neglect of incentives and of choices made at the margin. One is the impact on GNP of reductions in the corporate-income-tax rate, and the other is the controversy over whether government fiscal policy "crowds out" private investment.

Simulations run by the Congressional Budget Office and the House Budget Committee on two of the three large-scale commercial econometric models show *declines* in GNP as a result of reductions in corporate-tax rates. In one of the models, corporate investment did not depend on after-tax profits in a very strong way, but was very sensitive to changes in interest rates. Since interest rates rise as the Treasury increases its borrowing to finance the deficit resulting from the tax cut, investment falls, and *the model predicted a decline in GNP as the result of a tax-rate reduction that increased the profitability of investment.* †

The other model predicted that a corporate-tax-rate reduction would slightly raise real GNP after a lag of a couple of quarters, but it predicted

---

*Theoretically, the effect on work effort depends on the present value of the Social Security benefits and taxes. If the increased tax means increased future benefits, the employee's work decision will take into account his increased future income, as well as his reduced current income. However, the recent changes in the Social Security law raised taxes and reduced benefits as a proportion of pay before retirement. As the *Wall Street Journal* put it, "the extra money will go to pay people now or soon to be on the retirement rolls, not to finance your own high living in the 21st century" (February 6, 1978).

†According to staff in the Office of Management and Budget, there have recently been changes in the model, but one can still get the perverse result because a reduction in the tax rate directly and substantially reduces multiunit housing starts.

a lower nominal GNP for two years. Nominal GNP declined because the corporate-tax-rate reduction reduced the user cost of capital, the price markup, and thereby the inflation rate, thus lowering the nominal price level.

To the extent that Keynesians think about the "crowding out" of private investment by fiscal policy, it is in terms of upward pressure on interest rates as a result of government borrowing to finance budget deficits. They do not realize that *investment is crowded out by taxation, regardless of whether the budget is in balance.* To understand how, consider the following example. Suppose that a 10-percent rate of return must be earned if an investment is to be undertaken. In the event that government imposes a 50-percent tax rate on investment income, investments earning 10 percent will no longer be undertaken. Only investments earning 20 percent before tax will return 10 percent after tax. Taxation crowds out investment by reducing the number of profitable investments. When tax rates are reduced, after-tax rates of return rise, and the number of profitable investments increases.

So "crowding out" cannot be correctly analyzed merely in terms of events in the financial markets: "Crowding out" occurs in terms of real output. It is the preempting of production capacity by government outlays, regardless of whether these outlays are financed by taxing, borrowing, or money creation.

Responding to Incentives

A concern with the supply-side effects of fiscal policy is incompatible with the concept of economic policy that currently reigns in the Congress and in the Executive Branch. Members of the House Budget Committee asked Alice Rivlin, director of the Congressional Budget Office, and Bert Lance, then director of the Office of Management and Budget, about the neglect of the incentive effects of tax-rate changes on supply and also about the econometric predictions that GNP would fall in response to a reduction in corporate tax rates.

Dr. Rivlin said that she and her staff had been "particularly troubled" by model findings that GNP declines if corporate tax rates are reduced. However, she went on to say:

Studies have generally found that tax-rate changes are less important than changes in the cost of capital and changes in levels of national output in influencing the level of investment. It follows that an investment tax credit or liberalized depreciation will increase investment more than a corporate-tax-rate reduction of equivalent revenue loss. While we do not believe that corporate-tax-rate cuts reduce investment, it would not be surprising to find that tax cuts had only a minor expansionary effect.

The OMB staff reply to this question was ambiguous.

Both CBO and OMB realized that the question about incentive effects most fundamentally challenged their concept of economic policy. The comments of Rivlin, Lance, and the OMB staff all unequivocally acknowledged that the econometric models upon which they rely for guidance in the choice of economic policy alternatives do not include any relative price effects of changes in personal-income-tax rates. However, since they believe that the performance of the economy is a function of spending levels, not of production incentives, they expressed no concern over this neglect. They said that economic theory and empirical studies leave it unclear whether the neglected supply-side effects are important; regardless of how the issue is resolved, they questioned the practical importance of supply incentives for short-run policy analysis.

There are two parts to this argument. One is that it is unclear whether lowering personal-income-tax rates will increase or reduce work effort. The other is that it is unclear whether any incentive effects on work effort and investment would show up as quantitatively important in a short-run policy framework. The first proposition questions the existence of the incentive effects; the second questions whether they would be effective in time to deal with an immediate problem of economic stabilization.

It is easy to dispose of the latter point. The long-run consists of a series of short-runs. If policies that are effective over a longer period are neglected because they do not have an immediate impact, and if policies that are damaging over the longer period are adopted because they initially have beneficial results, then policy makers will inevitably come to experience, sometime in the future, a period when they will have no solution for the crisis they have provoked. In the United States, that future might be now.

As for the first point, Rivlin acknowledged that a personal-income-tax-rate reduction raises the relative price of leisure, and that work effort will increase as people substitute income for leisure. This is known in economics as the "substitution effect," and it works to increase supply. However, Rivlin also said:

It is also theoretically arguable that when a tax cut provides people with more after-tax income, many of them will *reduce* effort through what is called the income effect. For most people, leisure has some positive value, and it may even be a "luxury" good; these people could respond to a tax reduction by reducing their working hours, benefiting from more leisure time and still maintaining their after-tax income. For other people who like their work, there may be little or no labor supply response to the income *or* the substitution effect. In much of the United States economy, work weeks are fixed, leaving little possibility for individuals to make marginal adjustments in hours of work.

In other words, CBO believes that the "income effect" works to decrease supply.

Rivlin then went on to say that it was an empirical question whether the "income effect" offset the "substitution effect," referred to a narrow range of studies that left the question unresolved, and concluded: "In the range of policy options that we have been dealing with, I think the assumption that changes in marginal tax rates have no quantitatively significant effect on labor supply is quite plausible."

But the concept of a targeted or desired level of income unaffected by the cost of acquiring such income is foreign to the price-theoretical perspective of economic science. Rivlin's idea that people respond to a cut in income-tax rates by maintaining their existing income levels while enjoying more leisure implies that, if their tax rates went up, they would work harder in order to maintain their desired income level. Lester Thurow has actually employed this reasoning to argue for a wealth tax. According to Thurow, a wealth tax is a costless way to raise revenues because the "income effect" runs counter to and dominates the "substitution effect." He assumes that people have a targeted level of wealth, irrespective of the cost of acquiring it. Therefore, he says, a tax on wealth will cause people to work harder in order to maintain, after tax, their desired wealth level.

Note the perverse ways in which people respond to incentives and disincentives according to the Rivlin-Thurow line of argument: When tax rates go down and the relative price of leisure rises, people demand more leisure; when tax rates go up and the relative price of leisure falls, people demand less leisure. In economics, any time the "income effect" works counter to the "substitution effect," we have the relatively rare case of what is called an "inferior good" (i.e., people purchase less of it as their income rises). Since income is command over all goods, Rivlin's argument implies that *all* goods are inferior goods: A tax cut will cause people to purchase only more leisure, not more income (i.e., goods). What kind of people are these? Well, the only kind of people who fit this kind of economic analysis are people who respond to a monetary incentive in perverse ways.

Perhaps Rivlin merely meant to say that lower tax rates would allow people to have a *little* more income for a *little* less work. Even so, as long as she maintains that the "income effect" works counter to the "substitution effect," her argument carries the implication that goods in general are inferior.

A Perverse Logic

Whatever the weight one assigns this point, there is a more fundamental defect in her argument. Notice the stunning inconsistency: People respond to a tax-rate reduction "by reducing their working hours . . . and still maintaining their after-tax income." But it is impossible for people *in the aggregate* to reduce their work effort and maintain the same level of *aggregate* real income! If people respond to tax cuts by working less, real

GNP would fall, and it would be impossible to increase real disposable income, spending, and demand in the aggregate. Rivlin's argument is directed against the effectiveness of incentives in raising aggregate output, but if she were correct, it would mean that Keynesian fiscal policy also is ineffective!

The fatal error in the Rivlin-Thurow argument can be put this way: It derives from trying to aggregate a series of partial equilibrium analyses (individual responses to a change in relative prices) and, in the aggregate, ignoring the *general* equilibrium effects.

There are various ways a noneconomist can grasp this point. Assume that the government cuts taxes and maintains a balanced budget by reducing spending. In this case, the higher income accorded the taxpayers whose rates are reduced must be matched by a negative impact on the incomes of recipients of government spending. Some or all of these may be the same people. Assume, for example, that both the tax burden and government spending are evenly distributed. In this case the "income effect" (the substitution of leisure for work) "nets out" for each individual. Since the aggregate income effect is zero, it cannot offset the "substitution effect" (the substitution of work for leisure).

If taxes are cut and government spending is unchanged (resulting in a budget deficit), the nominal disposable income of taxpayers as a group will rise relative to the nominal disposable income of the recipients of government spending as a group. The former will be able to bid real resources away from the latter. The real income gains of the former will be matched by the real income losses of the latter. Since the bidding will raise prices, the real income loss might be suffered by individuals who hold money. Regardless of who loses and who gains, the individual income effects "net out," leaving only the "substitution effects," which unambiguously increase work effort.

There can be no aggregate "income effect" unless the impact of incentives is to raise real aggregate income. Economic theory makes it perfectly clear that a tax-rate reduction will increase work effort and total output.

In the final analysis, Rivlin's argument is not that the supply-side incentive effects are unimportant, but the equally false argument that their impact is perverse—that is, only a tax-rate *increase* can produce a rise in real national income! She may not actually believe any such thing, of course—but that is where her reasoning leads her.

From Economics to Politics

An economist might see the flaw in the Rivlin-Thurow argument, but it is not obvious to politicians. Take something simple, like Rivlin's assertion that a fixed work-week precludes adjustment of the labor supply to tax-rate changes. To an economist her assertion is obviously false, but to the politician it sounds reasonable enough. He will not realize that the "adjustments" will be reflected in absenteeism rates, turnover rates, the average duration of unemployment, labor negotiations for shorter work-weeks and more paid vacation rather than higher wages, and in the quality and intensity of work. Nor will he think of the entrepreneur who, because of high tax rates, loses his incentive to innovate—to make the economy itself (all of us) more productive.

Besides, one has to have an idealistic view of government to believe that politicians even want to know. The Keynesian concept of the economy is that of an unstable private sector that must be stabilized by fiscal and monetary policies of the government. This view has served as a ramp for the expansion of the interests of government. It has also served the interests of economists by transforming them from ivory-tower denizens to public-spirited social activists, a transformation which has much increased their power and enlivened their life-styles. Unemployment can always be said to be too high. And the rate of economic growth can always be found to be below "potential." This means that there is always a "scientific" economic reason for expanding government spending programs that enlarge the constituencies of the Congress and of the Federal bureaucracy. From the standpoint of the private interests of policy makers, Keynesian economic policy will always be judged a success.

To write about all of the problems of econometrics and economic policy would require a book, not an article, but one other important problem must be mentioned in closing. Professor Robert Lucas has demonstrated that the standard econometric models assume that the structure of the economy remains invariant under wide variations in policy paths. What this means is that the models assume that people do not learn. But people do learn, and their expectations change as they experience various policies: They may not repeat the same behavior in response to the same policy at different times. Therefore, the policy simulation may always misinform the policy makers. This is not an optimistic note on which to end an article about public policy in a country that believes we need a great deal of it. But our faith in public policy has exceeded our knowledge, and we will find out that, in this area, there is no such thing as free faith.

GEORGE F. WILL

A Conservative Welfare State

> Protection is not a principle, but an expedient.
>
> —BENJAMIN DISRAELI

In 1964, a conservative citizen, speaking with the zeal of a convert, which he was, gave a nationally televised speech in support of Barry Goldwater's candidacy. The citizen denounced "people who view the tax as a means of achieving changes in our social structure."[1] In 1981, in another speech, the same fellow said approximately the same thing:

The taxing power of government must be used to provide revenues for legitimate government purposes. It must not be used to regulate the economy or bring about social change.[2]

Now, the consistency of Ronald Reagan's views is one of the wonders of American political life. But another wonder is that anyone, especially the fortieth President, would talk like that. No previous President has stressed as much as Ronald Reagan has the possibility and importance of changing society by changing the tax code. Clearly, Reagan came to Washington convinced that certain tax changes are the key to his economic program, which is, in turn, the key to his comprehensive plan for revitalizing American society and improving Americans' spirits. He obviously believes that public policies should reward and thereby nurture the attributes essential to strength (industriousness, thrift, deferral of gratification) and should discourage the attributes inimical to economic vitality (idleness, dissipation, self-indulgence). And he would not deny that laws establishing, protecting, and regulating the institution of property are examples of kinds of laws that have the effect, intended or not, of shaping the spirit of society. Tax deductions and tax exemptions are not alternatives to social programs. They are social programs. And unlike many such, they often achieve their intended effects. They alter behavior on a large scale for the advancement of chosen goals.

In the 1976 campaign for the Republican presidential nomination, Reagan repeatedly said: "I've always thought that the best thing government can do is nothing." But surely the truth, regarding every significant

From George F. Will, *Statecraft as Soulcraft: What Government Does* (New York: Simon & Schuster, 1982), pp. 122–139. Copyright © 1983 by G.F.W., a Maryland corporation. Reprinted by permission of Simon & Schuster.

aspect of social life, is that the one thing government cannot do is "nothing." This is true in two senses. First, a decision not to alter the status quo is a decision to do something. It is a decision to continue the public policies—the complex weave of laws and customs—that underlie any significant sphere of social action. Second, it is peculiar to speak as though laissez-faire policies amounted to government's "doing nothing." Conservatives rightly cultivate a saving sense of the complexity of the social organism, a sense that protects society from the overbearing political pretense that government can superintend all relationships. But a "free-market" economic system is a system; it is a public product, a creation of government. Any important structure of freedom is a structure, a complicated institutional and cultural context that government must nurture and sustain.

Obviously "free speech" is not free in the sense that it is free of prerequisites; it is not free of a complicated institutional frame. Free speech, as much as a highway system, is something government must establish and maintain. The government of a country without the rare and fragile traditions of civility, without education and communication capabilities, could proclaim freedom of speech and resolutely stand back. But the result would not be free speech. It would be mayhem, and the triumph of incivility. Similarly, a capitalistic economic system, with all the institutions, laws, regulations, dispositions, habits, and skills that make it work, is not part of the constitution of the universe. It does not spring up from the social soil unbidden, like prairie grass. It requires an educational system, banking and currency systems, highly developed laws of commerce, and much more.

Many conservatives are fond of the epigram that the phrase "political economy" represents the marriage of two words that should be divorced on the grounds of incompatibility. But clear-minded persons can more reasonably object to the phrase on the ground that the adjective "political" is a superfluous modifier because any economic arrangement is, by definition, a political arrangement. Try to define "the political" in a way that severs it from ideas central to economic life—ownership, contracts, corporations, trade unions, the right to strike, antitrust principles. Of course, before the Depression nationalized concern with "the economy," the use of the definite article would have seemed odd. Few people then thought about the nation's aggregate economic output. Even just sixty years ago, economic statistics were so rudimentary that the central government did not know how many people were employed, or wanted to be, or what the Gross National Product was. It had no need to know, in the sense that it acknowledged no clear responsibility for policies that required a sophisticated national information base. But since late October 1929, the public has felt bound up with a single economic dynamic, and this feeling has found consistent expression in a political fact: The

President is held accountable for the aggregate economic performance.

Conservatives are understandably impatient with the familiar liberal formulation about "giving human rights priority over property rights." But conservatives, in their eagerness to put government in its place (which they think is down, and far away), argue just as fatuously that "only people produce wealth; government does not." Government produces the infrastructure of society—legal, physical, educational, from highways through skills—that is a precondition for the production of wealth. The unlovely locution "human capital" reflects the impulse to reduce all social categories to economic ones, but it also reflects a recognition that investment must be made in people before they can be socially competent. And it is obvious, once you think about it, that government is, and must be, a major investor. Very stern adherents of laissez-faire doctrine object not just to the practice of redistributing income, but even to the phrase "distribution of income." They think it implies that income is not purely "earned" but is in part just "received" as a result of social processes rather than pure individual effort. But the social processes are undeniable. So, when John D. Rockefeller told Congress, in all sincerity, that "the good Lord gave me my money," he not only defined regulation as impiety, he denied government's role in the generation of wealth.

Ideological capitalists are like many proponents of abortion in that they are guilty of the neutrality fallacy. Proabortion activists worked successfully to impose, by Federal judicial power, the policy of abortion on demand, to impose it in fifty states that did not want such a policy. Those persons should not now argue that their undertaking, unlike that of opponents reacting to them, is "value-free," and does not involve "imposing" values on the community. It is comparably untenable for those who favor a purer capitalism to argue that they, unlike all advocates of different systems, are acting "neutrally" by keeping, or taking, "economics" out of politics, or vice versa.

A famous economist, who has a Nobel Prize and (what is almost as much fun) a regular column in *Newsweek*, recently became so exasperated with me (for some deviation from laissez-faire orthodoxy) that he wrote a stiff note. He said that he likes what I write—except when I write about economics. I am too exquisitely polite to have replied that I like what he writes—except when he writes about politics, and he rarely writes about anything else.

When Napoleon tersely summarized his social doctrine in four words—"Careers open to talents"—he was not formulating an employment policy; he was not talking economics. If we are to be properly conscious of our politics, if our politics is to be properly conscious of itself, we must be wide awake to this fact: Choosing an economic system, or choosing substantially to revise significant economic policies, is a political, which means moral, undertaking. It is the authoritative assignment of values, the encouragement of some behavior and values and the discouragement of others.

If conservatism is to engage itself with the way we live now, it must address government's graver purposes with an affirmative doctrine of the welfare state. The idea of such an affirmation may, but should not, seem paradoxical. Two conservatives (Disraeli and Bismarck) pioneered the welfare state, and did so for impeccably conservative reasons: to reconcile the masses to the vicissitudes and hazards of a dynamic and hierarchical industrial economy. They acted on the principle of "economy of exertion," using government power judiciously to prevent less discriminating, more disruptive uses of power. Today, the conservative affirmation of the welfare state should be grounded on, and conservative purposes for the welfare state should be derived from, three additional considerations. They are considerations of prudence, intellectual integrity, and equity. A welfare state is certainly important to, and probably indispensable to, social cohesion, and hence to national strength. A welfare state is implied by conservative rhetoric. A welfare state can be an embodiment of a wholesome ethic of common provision.

The doctrine underlying the political economy of the American welfare state was enunciated in 1877, by Chief Justice Waite, in *Munn* v. *Illinois.* The court upheld an Illinois statute regulating rates in grain elevators, holding that private property

becomes clothed with a public interest when used in a manner to make it of public consequence, and affect the community at large. When, therefore, one devotes his property to a use in which the public has an interest, he, in effect, grants to the public an interest in that use, and must submit to be controlled by the public for the common good, to the extent of the interest he has thus created.[3]

That opinion proclaimed an idea whose time did not come as social policy for several generations. But it has now come and is not apt to depart. For conservatives to doubt the strength and durability of this consensus is intellectually idle and politically feckless. This consensus cannot, of course, be allowed to erase the distinction between public and private spheres. That distinction is indispensable not only to the preservation of a tolerable degree of liberty, but to the preservation of public-spiritedness as well. It is essential to the habit of subordinating some private interests to the public interest. But conservatives must come to terms with the public's assumption that private economic decisions often are permeated with a public interest and hence are legitimate subjects of political debate and intervention.

Recent years have done damage to the idea that the dangers and discords of life elsewhere cannot get a visa to visit here. Conservatives know that even in the misnamed "democratic age," democracy has been a rarity, and the "democratic age" is barely two hundred years old—a historical blink. The age was born at approximately the same time as the steam engine, with the age of cheap energy that made rapid economic growth relatively easy. The growth may have made democracy possible because it dampened the most testing social tensions.

The widespread belief that economic growth would democratize prosperity—that a rising tide would raise all boats—reduced the demand for redistributionist politics, in which political decisions would determine the allocation of opportunity and wealth. But when the social question is not just how to bake a larger economic pie, but how to carve the pie, then the stakes of politics become bigger, and politics becomes more bitter. Like it or not, that is a permanent question on the national agenda. It is so because an economic order represents a political choice, and is a government product. We are all in it together, as citizens.

American conservatism needs a Burke, a Disraeli—a self-conscious practitioner who can articulate the principles implicit in the statecraft he practices. Regarding the welfare state, conservatives practice politics more realistically than they preach. In 1953 the conservative party had a President for the first time in a generation, and that party had majorities in both Houses of Congress for the last time in more than a generation. Yet there was no attempt to undo what Franklin Roosevelt had done. Neither, however, was there an attempt to formulate a philosophically conservative rationale and program for the modern state.

A conservative doctrine of the welfare state is required if conservatives are even to be included in the contemporary political conversation. Conservatives need ways to make the welfare state more compatible with conservative governmental values, and to make it more affirmative of conservative social values. Granted, a welfare state can aggravate the centrifugal tendencies of modern society. By enlarging the political allocation of wealth and opportunity, it can raise the stakes, and the temperature, of politics, making the state much more a focus of contention than a force of cohesion. But by expressing a limited but clear ethic of common provision, a welfare state can be, on balance, unifying. It can nationalize concern for moderate and cooperative policies to promote the economic growth that alone can pay for general entitlements. A structure of public entitlements can do what private property alone cannot do: give everyone a stake in the stability and success of the social system.

What most conservatives know by intuition, and many liberals now know by experience, is this. Government is not efficient at providing goods and services. It is good at writing checks, and at providing incentives and disincentives that cause self-interested persons—that is, almost everybody—to behave in various ways. So a welfare state run on conservative principles will provide the poor with cash to buy necessities from the private sector, thereby reducing the need for an enormous social-service bureaucracy. And a conservative welfare state will provide incentives—such as deductions from taxes for medical-insurance premiums —to cause the private sector to weave much of the net of security that people demand in every developed, industrial society.

In addition to these conservative principles of government, there are social goals for a conservative welfare state. The first is to strengthen what Burke called the "little platoons" that are, even more meaningfully than individuals, the molecular units of society. Conservatives should be leading the fight for a welfare system that supports rather than disintegrates families. The more we learn about the radiating consequences of disintegrated families, the more clearly we can see the social costs—from unemployment to crowded prisons—of neglecting that most important "little platoon." In addition, a conservative welfare state will use government to combat the tendency of the modern bureaucratic state to standardize and suffocate diversity. To give just one example, a conservative welfare state would give to individuals tax credits—a tax subsidy—to offset tuition payments to private schools. This incentive to private education, especially at the secondary level, would stimulate competition against one of the nation's most powerful lobbies and its strongest near-monopoly, public education. This is not to disparage public education. On the contrary, public policy should encourage a leavening diversity from private sources, and should encourage bracing competition from private schools, precisely because education is the most important public business, and because public schools always will and should have by far the greater number of students.

My purpose here is only to sample the range of possible uses of assertive government to achieve conservative goals. For nearly half a century conservatism was, or felt itself to be, in the political wilderness. Although there were some conservative Presidents and some conservative legislating majorities in Congress during this period, conservatism generally was a doctrine in, and of, opposition. During this period it became cranky and recriminatory. Therefore, a question posed by the coming to power of self-conscious conservatism is this: Can there be conservatism with a kindly face?

Another question is: Can conservatives come to terms with a social reality more complex than their slogans? Conservatives rightly stress equality of opportunity rather than equality of outcomes. Conservatives are, therefore, fond of the metaphor of a footrace: All citizens should be roughly equal at the starting line of the race of life. But much that we have learned and continue to learn—and we are learning a lot—about early-childhood development suggests that "equality of opportunity" is a much more complicated matter than most conservatives can comfortably acknowledge. Prenatal care (which the "right to life" movement should regard as something of a "right"), infant stimulation, childhood nutrition and especially home environment—all these and other influences affect the competence of a young "runner" as he or she approaches the academic hurdles that so heavily influence social outcomes in America. There is, of course, vast scope for intelligent disagreement as to what can and should be done to make "equality of opportunity" more than an airy abstraction. But surely it is indisputable that "equality of opportunity" can be enhanced by various forms of state action.

The most important reason conservatives should give for their vision of the welfare state is the most important reason for doing anything, politically. It is justice. Saint Thomas Aquinas said that justice, which is giving individuals their due "with constant and perpetual will,"[4] is a "habit" *(habitus)*. Justice depends, therefore, on a certain disposition. It depends on—in a sense, it is—a state of mind. A society that is organized socially and justified philosophically the way ours is must take special care to supply itself with the rhetoric, institutions, and policies which encourage that state of mind. Neither the spirit of the age nor the premises received from the past (which have produced that spirit) will do the work. The political philosophy of modernity, taking its bearings from the strongest passions, does not emphasize, and so does not nurture, the habit of regarding our fellow citizens as united in a great common enterprise.

Our arrangements may have been ably explicated by those who arranged them. *Federalist* 51 is, with the possible exception of *Federalist* 10, the most important short essay on the American government and psyche. Remember:

This policy of supplying by opposite and rival interests, the defect of better motives . . .[5]

It is almost as though the Founders thought they had devised a system so clever that it would work well even if no one had good motives—even if there was no public-spiritedness. But unfortunately, just as there are social roots of political behavior, there are social consequences of political behavior—and political expectations. A nation that announces, at its outset, that it can dispense with "better motives" than self-interest in politics does not encourage self-restraint, self-denial, and moderation in any sphere of life. Drawing upon Montesquieu, many Founders thought that commerce—the submersion of passion and interest in pursuit of private gain—was more reliable than public virtue as a basis of political stability. But real conservatives have said it well and often: Democracy subverts itself if it subverts the habits of self-restraint, self-denial, and public-spiritedness. That danger defines the drama of democracy in a commercial nation, one devoted to inflaming and satisfying appetites.

Now, just as myth can be conducive to reasonableness in societies, self-interestedness can be conducive to the public interest. The obvious virtue of laissez-faire economics is the voluntary performance of many socially useful functions. Its vision of a relatively frictionless mechanism of social adjustment is at once rationalistic and romantic. It is hard to say which is more American, romanticism or capitalism. Perhaps it is wrong, in America, to distinguish them.

The question is not does capitalism (or socialism; or a mixed economy) work? Of course it does. So did the Pony Express. The question is what do you mean by "work"? There is more to judging economic arrangements than how far, smoothly, and fast they expand the Gross National Product. De Tocqueville spoke of "a theory of manufactures more powerful than customs and laws,"[6] and such capitalism has proved to be. It is difficult for statesmen, or anyone else, to measure what De Tocqueville called "the slow and quiet action of society upon itself,"[7] because the action is so slow and quiet. But that action must be watched.

Societies, like individuals, can be, to a considerable extent, defined by their admirations. A society which orients politics to acquisition is apt to be a society in which admiration accrues to the most successful acquirers. Furthermore, a prerequisite of capitalism in the early stages of accumulation is the suppression of spontaneous desire. Democracy and capitalism are compatible only as long as the habits of political and economic self-restraint (deferral of gratification; industriousness; thrift) reinforce one another. The question is what happens when the ethics of a commercial civilization—the relentless manufacturing of appetites, and the incitement to gratify them on credit—undermines self-restraint in political and economic behavior? The essence of childishness is an inability to imagine an incompatibility between one's appetites and the world. Growing up involves, above all, a conscious effort to conform one's appetites to a crowded world. By so thoroughly taking our political, hence our moral, bearings from the low but strong and steady passions, are we in danger of lingering in perpetual childishness? A society that seeks a steady expansion of desires and a simultaneous satisfaction of them may be, at least in the short run, a great place for advertising account executives and manufacturers of small appliances. But over time, it must be unstable domestically and vulnerable internationally.

Having decided at the outset that all men are, self-evidently, created equal, Americans have spent two centuries pondering equality. There has never been any doubt that certain inequalities are constitutive of sound social policies; they are prerequisites for desirable social ends. A society determined to have rapid economic growth through predominantly private market mechanisms must provide the requisite rewards for the persons most proficient at generating wealth. That means inequality. A just society is not one in which the allocation of wealth, opportunity, authority and status is equal. Rather, it is one in which inequalities are reasonably related to reasonable social goals. Therefore justice, as well as elementary utilitarian considerations, requires a hierarchy of achievement. Furthermore, equality, when defined in terms of rights derivative from passions, is not conducive to community. And questions as to how much equality of material condition society needs or morality demands or the economy can stand are less interesting than this question: How equal a distribution of ideas and sentiments is needed for social cohesion and all that derives from it? Such cohesion depends on a revived sense of citizenship. That sense depends on rehabilitating from the ravages of modern thought and practice the status of the political vocation and of government. The place to begin is with the task of putting economic argument in its place. That place, as Jefferson and Hamilton understood, is within the political argument, and subordinate to political choices. Only then shall we have a politics that nurtures the spiritual in a nation that is predisposed by its modernity toward preoccupation with the material.

NOTES

Epigraph: Benjamin Disraeli, in a speech to the House of Commons, April 25, 1843.

1. Ronald Reagan, October 27, 1964.
2. Reagan, Address to a Joint Session of Congress, February 15, 1981.
3. Chief Justice Morrison R. Waite, *Munn* v. *Illinois,* 94 U.S. 113–126 (1876), p. 126.
4. Thomas Aquinas, *The Summa Theologica of St. Thomas Aquinas,* trans. by The Fathers of the English Dominican Province (New York: Benzinger, 1914), II, no. II, question 58, art. I.
5. James Madison, *The Federalist,* Jacob E. Cooke, ed. (Middletown, Conn.: Wesleyan University Press, 1961), No. 51, p. 349.
6. De Tocqueville, p. 159.
7. Ibid., vol. I, p. 416.

CHARLES MURRAY

The Constraints on Helping

Poverty

Even as the War on Poverty was beginning, its premises of self-help and open opportunities were lagging behind a new intellectual consensus that would shape policy very shortly.

To understand its power, one first must understand that poverty did

From Charles Murray, *Losing Ground: American Social Policy 1950–1980* (New York: Basic Books, 1984), pp. 26–29, 179–185, 199–202, 205–218. Reprinted by permission of Basic Books.

not simply climb upward on our national list of problems; it abruptly reappeared from nowhere. In the prologue to this book, 1950 was described as a year in which poverty was not part of the discourse about domestic policy—indeed, as a year in which the very word "poverty" was seldom used. The silence was not peculiar to 1950. From the outset of the Second World War until 1962, little in the popular press, in political rhetoric, or in the published work of American scholars focused on poverty in America.[1]

When poverty did get into the news before 1964, the treatment of it tended to reflect surprise that it existed at all. In November 1960, three weeks after the presidential election and the day after Thanksgiving (a deliberate juxtaposition), Edward R. Murrow broadcast a *CBS Reports* called "Harvest of Shame." It showed that tens of thousands of migrant workers were miserably paid, housed, educated, and nourished—problems that middle-class America apparently associated only with the 1930s and *The Grapes of Wrath*.

The viewing public and numerous editorial writers were shocked—a fact in itself illustrative of the obliviousness toward poverty. The more instructive reaction, however, was Murrow's own. A few months later, the day after he was sworn in as director of the United States Information Agency, one of his first acts was to try to persuade the BBC to cancel a scheduled broadcast of "Harvest of Shame." That Edward R. Murrow, the embodiment of journalistic independence, would try to stop a news show on grounds that it would be taken out of context suggests how aberrant the poverty in "Harvest of Shame" was taken to be.

In the intellectual community, phenomena such as poverty among migrant workers were seen as peripheral. Norman Podhoretz, recalling the leftist intellectual circles in which he moved during the 1950s, points out that the essential *economic* success of the American system was taken as a given even by those who were most bitterly critical of the social system. He continues:

That there were still "pockets" of unemployment and poverty, and that there was still a great spread in the distribution of income and wealth, everyone realized. But the significance of such familiar conditions paled by comparison with a situation that now seemed to defy the rule that there could be nothing new under the sun: the apparent convergence of the entire population into a single class.[2]

Podhoretz's observation held true through the 1960 presidential campaign. Poverty was, in the terms of that campaign, something that happened mostly in Appalachia—not only in the Kennedy campaign rhetoric, but in the minds of those Democrats who considered themselves true liberals. When Arthur Schlesinger decided to proselytize among members of the liberal establishment on behalf of John Kennedy in 1960, he made his case on issues that he knew to be the ones that were exercising his friends and colleagues in the liberal wing of the party. He chose as his theme that Kennedy was the man for an era in which the struggle for material subsistence had essentially been solved.[3]

Against this backdrop, the emergence of the structural view of the poverty problem was unexpected and rapid. As of the beginning of 1962, no one was talking about poverty; by the end of 1963 it was the hottest domestic policy topic other than civil rights. But it was not just "poverty" that was being talked about. "Structural poverty" was now at issue.

"Structural poverty" refers to poverty that is embedded within the nature of the system (or demographics) and will not be eradicated by economic growth. Its elimination, according to the proponents of this view of poverty, requires radical surgery. "The most visible structuralists," writes James Patterson, "were not social workers or government bureaucrats looking for ways to improve the situation of individuals, but social scientists and left-wing writers who took a broad and reformist view of the functional relationship between inequality and the social system."[4]

One such writer was Michael Harrington, who in 1962 published a book that was the most visible single reason for the sudden popularity of poverty. The book was *The Other America.* Its thesis was that a huge population of poor people—50 million by his count—was living in our midst, ignored. They consisted of the aged, the unskilled, the women heading households with small children, and others who were bound to be bypassed no matter how much economic growth occurred, because of the way that the system distributed income.[5]

The importance of Harrington's book was not in its details but in its central message: America was not the single-class, affluent society that a complacent intellectual establishment had assumed, but a deeply riven society in which the poor had been left to suffer unnoticed. Kennedy read *The Other America* and Dwight MacDonald's evangelizing review of it in *The New Yorker* and ordered the beginning of the staff work that Lyndon Johnson would later seize upon for his crusade.[6]

It was a time when books became banners for causes—*Silent Spring* was published at about the same time, and *Unsafe at Any Speed* followed a few years later—and it is always difficult in such cases to determine how much was cause and how much effect. Certainly others had been forwarding a structuralist view of poverty both within and without the Kennedy administration.[7] But even if the poor were bound to have been rediscovered in the early 1960s, Harrington was their pamphleteer, *The Other America* their *Common Sense.*

Once the argument had been made, it became very unfashionable for an intellectual in good standing to argue with it. A few, such as Irving Kristol, made note of Harrington's factual inaccuracies and his reliance on dubious evidence.[8] Later, even some of Harrington's sympathetic colleagues would dispute the centerpiece arguments about intergenerational poverty.[9] But much of what Harrington had to say seemed indisputable. The population did include large numbers of poor people, and they didn't seem to be moving up the way that they were supposed to do. To quibble was to sound like the Chamber of Commerce.

If poverty was not an aberration, not a matter of "pockets" but structurally built into the American system, then it was necessarily true that the initial antipoverty bills represented a half-hearted and wrong-headed approach to the problem. Poverty was not going to be eradicated by a Job Corps or a few loans to small businessmen. Sweeping changes in the income distribution system were needed—a cool analytic conclusion to some, but more often a conviction held with "a passionate sense of urgency," as Jeremy Larner and Irving Howe put it. "[I]n a nation as rich as the United States," they declaimed, "it is an utter moral scandal that even the slightest remnant of poverty should remain."[10]

In a technical sense, the structuralists made a case only for the proposition that much, not all, of American poverty derived from structural characteristics. Their message was an antidote to the folk wisdom that anyone with enough gumption could make a good living. But the "passionate sense of urgency" got in the way of balance. What emerged in the mid-1960s was an almost unbroken intellectual consensus that the individualist explanation of poverty was altogether outmoded and reactionary. Poverty was not a consequence of indolence or vice. It was not the just deserts of people who didn't try hard enough. It was produced by conditions that had nothing to do with individual virtue or effort. *Poverty was not the fault of the individual but of the system. . . .*

The Homogenization of the Poor

Historically, the United States has been a nation of people who were either poor or the children of poor parents. Only in the last half of the twentieth century has a large proportion of the middle class become so far removed from poverty that the lack of money became horrifying in itself.[11]

Few of the American poor defined their lives in terms of their poverty. Neither did society. The "poor" were a varied lot with complex status distinctions to be drawn. There were the genteel poor who had lost their money but not their manners. There were the poor people who were called "trash"—not just without money, but also uncouth and generally unpleasant company. There were the immigrant poor who, at the same time they were climbing out of poverty, maintained elaborate status structures even in the most crowded tenements. And there were the farmers. Forty-two percent of the population lived on farms in 1900, and most of them were cash-poor. But, from the time of Jefferson down through the years, the farmers were widely seen as (or saw themselves to be) the backbone of the nation and on a considerably higher moral plane than the effete rich.

Status distinctions among the poor began with the assumption that people are responsible for their actions and, specifically, responsible for taking care of themselves and their families as best they could. Missouri farmers and New York immigrants might have had wildly different status distinctions in other respects, but in both communities, and everywhere that poor people lived together, the first distinction was made on this basis. A person might work hard and be poor; that was the way of the world. Poverty had nothing to do with dignity. A person might be out of a job once in a while because of hard times. That too was the way of the world, and a temporary situation. But a person who was chronically unable to hold onto a job, who neglected children and spouse, was a bum and a no-good, consigned to the lowest circle of status.

Once it was assumed that the system is to blame when a person is chronically out of work and that the system is even to blame when a person neglects spouse and family, then the moral distinctions were eroded. The first casualty inevitably was the moral approbation associated with self-sufficiency. In the 1950s, the reason for "getting people off welfare" was to keep them from being a drag on the good people—meaning the self-sufficient people—and to rescue them from a degrading status. It was not necessary to explain *why* it was better to be self-sufficient; it was a precondition for being a member of society in good standing. In the late 1960s, with the attack on middle-class norms and the rise of the welfare rights movement, this was no longer good enough. Self-sufficiency was no longer taken to be an intrinsic *obligation* of healthy adults.

Among the people who held this view, the next casualty of the assumption that "the system is to blame" was the distinction between the deserving poor and the undeserving poor. Blame is the flip side of praise. To praise the poor who are self-sufficient is to assign to them responsibility for their upstandingness. But if one family is responsible for its success, the next family bears at least a measure of responsibility for its failure. It was much less complicated simply to treat "the poor" as a homogeneous group of victims.

It must be remembered that the shift in opinion was localized. A survey in 1967 showed that 42 percent of Americans still thought poverty reflected "lack of effort," another 39 percent thought that lack of effort had at least something to do with it, and only 19 percent blamed poverty on "circumstances beyond control."[12] But what the mass of Americans thought did not shape the reform period. In academic and policy-making circles, the conversion was nearly unanimous. The very term "deserving poor" was laughed out of use—witness the reaction of political columnists and cartoonists to the use of "truly needy" by the Reagan administration.

Only the poor were homogenized. In the day-to-day life of the rest of society, the elite, like the broad middle class, continued as always to differentiate the clever from the dull, the upright from the outlaw, the industrious from the indolent. But when it came to the poor, all must be victims. They were not permitted to be superior to one another.

The Policy Implications of Homogenization

If the poor were all victims, then policy had to be changed. First of all, welfare had to be cleansed of its stigma. Welfare historically had been a blot on the recipient's reputation; to be on welfare was to be inferior to one's neighbors who were not on welfare. But if it was not the welfare recipient's fault that welfare was needed, the stigma was wrong and unfair.

The portrayal and administration of the welfare system changed dramatically to fit the new wisdom. The key administrative changes for AFDC (Aid to Families with Dependent Children) were . . . directives against investigations of eligibility and court decisions easing restrictions on eligibility. In addition, OEO (Office for Economic Opportunity) took a more direct stand against stigma. As early as 1965, it was sending emissaries to spread the word that it was morally permissible to be on welfare. Community Action grants provided the wherewithal for booklets, speeches, and one-on-one evangelizing by staff workers. Welfare was to be considered a right, not charity.

The government's efforts were reinforced by the National Welfare Rights Organization, founded in 1966 and led by George Wiley. By 1967, the NWRO was large enough to hold its first annual convention in Washington. The innovative aspect of the welfare rights movement was not that poor people were organizing. Poor people had been marching on Washington since the town was built. But the age-old slogan was missing. No longer, as always before, did the protesters proclaim that "We don't want charity, we want jobs." In the last half of the 1960s the NWRO demonstrators were not demonstrating so much for jobs as for the right to long-term, unfettered, generous charity.[13]

Piven and Cloward cite evidence that the efforts of the community organizers were successful in reducing the stigma.[14] Such results are plausible. One of the major sources of the stigma attached to welfare was the middle class. For poor people who aspired to be like them in respectability, the appearance of in-the-flesh representatives of the middle class saying that welfare was their due must have had a telling effect. One may visualize, for example, the situation of parents in a slum who have taught their offspring to believe it is shameful to accept welfare. Then the children come home reporting that the supervisors on the Summer Job program, or the Organizers of the Community Development project, or the lawyers down at the Legal Services storefront office are saying that such notions are all wrong. Welfare is a right. The parents are dupes. The irony is that parents who have taught their children that welfare is shameful tend to be the kind of people who also teach their children to treat lawyers and supervisors and organizers as role models. How do the parents now convincingly reply, "I don't care what those people [the very people you are supposed to admire] said, it's still wrong . . ."?

Getting rid of the stigma of welfare was a deliberate goal. But another effect was not; it just happened as a logical consequence of denying that people are responsible for their condition: Because the system is to blame, all people on welfare are equally deserving of being given a hand. No one could disqualify himself on moral grounds from eligibility for public assistance—whether or not he was ready to help himself. There was no longer a mechanism for stamping someone unworthy. On the contrary, many of the social-service programs required as a condition of eligibility that the participants be failures. It could not be otherwise. Programs to rehabilitate drug addicts have to be restricted to drug addicts; programs to employ the hard-core unemployed must be restricted to the hard-core unemployed; and so on.

Theoretically, the social service and educational programs could have gotten around this selectivity by providing other programs aimed at those who were especially "worthy"—those who were giving their all and needed just a little more help to escape from poverty for good. But the mindset was too strong. "Elite" was fast becoming a dirty word in the mid-1960s among whites; "elitism" would soon be a form of bigotry to rank with racism and, later, sexism and ageism. Blacks were especially sensitized. Long ago, W.E.B. Du Bois had urged special emphasis on "the talented tenth" among blacks, and the approach had since become identified with a compliance with middle-class values (at best), Tom-ism (more likely), and general lack of militance at a time when power to the people was in vogue.

The unwillingness to acknowledge moral inequality was a hallmark of Great Society social programs and persisted throughout the 1970s. It was not just that the squeaky hinges (the failures) got the oil. Administrators of programs made Kafkaesque rules to avoid revealing that some poor people are brighter or of better character or more industrious than others.

One case in point, the "magnet schools," may be used to illustrate the general phenomenon. The purpose of the magnet schools was to lure white middle-class students back into urban school systems by setting up inner-city schools that were open to enrollment from throughout the city and were provided with special resources in a specific area—science, or the arts, or simply a strenuous college-prep program. The theory was that the magnet schools would not only reduce white flight among those who saw an opportunity in the magnet school; they would also break the back of the stereotypes that contributed to white flight from urban schools in general. It was one of the more plausible of the educational innovations of the time.

Some of the vocational schools and elementary schools achieved positive results.[15] But administrators of the high schools with an academic program soon ran up against a dilemma. Inner-city public education was so bad that only a few black students had adequate preparation to enter and successfully complete the curriculum in the magnet school. What should be done? One solution would have been to proceed as planned. The gifted black students who were in the program, even if they were fewer than had been hoped, would have a high-quality education they would not have gotten otherwise, and the white students (and their parents) would see what black students could do, given the opportunity. But few of the magnet schools took this course.

The common solution was rather to impose a racial quota to ensure that "enough" black students got into the magnet school. The results were as one would predict: To fill the quota, black students with inadequate skills were admitted. Then the school had either to flunk the students who could not keep up (unthinkable) or to soften the standards. But softening the standards destroyed the attractions of the magnet school for the white parents it was supposed to entice. And the stereotypes that the magnet schools were to dispel were reinforced. The white students went away with incontrovertible evidence from personal experience that even the brightest black students (for that is what they were *supposed* to be) were not competitive with white students.

The magnet schools story has numerous analogues among other programs of the time. Social programs were initiated with the professed purpose of creating successes from failures. But to create a success, an indispensable element is praise for accomplishment. And if praise for the ones who succeed is to be detailed, emphatic, and credible, it soon becomes necessary to distribute blame as well. Praise is meaningless without the assumption that the people who succeeded are in some practical way *better* than the people who failed, and this the administrators of the programs and the ideologues of the new wisdom were unwilling to confront head-on. To see some as better was perceived as denying that the failures were victims.

The Role of the Means-Tested Programs

Arguably the most insidious single change affecting status relationships within the poor community had nothing to do with the Great Society's social-action programs but with the introduction of "means-tested" welfare benefits.

One of the insights of game theory is the psychological importance of natural boundaries—those things that make it easier to quit smoking than to cut down and that lead bargainers to compromise on a round number or to "split the difference." With poor people, the boundary was accepting *no charity at all* from anyone outside the family. Many readers will be able to verify the power of this demarcation line from their earliest lessons about the family tradition: "We may not have had much money, but we never took a penny of charity," was one common formula; or "We have always paid our own way" or "We have always pulled our own weight." The idioms and the tradition were pervasive.

Means-tested programs effectively ended such useful boasts. One may approve or disapprove of Food Stamps and Medicaid and housing assistance, but one result was unavoidable. Virtually all low-income persons became welfare recipients (remember that by 1980 Food Stamps alone counted more than 21 million recipients). Pride in independence was compromised, and with it a certain degree of pressure on the younger generation to make good on the family tradition.

More importantly, the working people who made little money lost the one thing that enabled them to claim social status. For the first time in American history, it became socially acceptable within poor communities to be unemployed, because working families too were receiving welfare. Over a period of years, such changes in the rules of the economic game caused status conventions to flip completely in some communities. Why, at bottom, should working confer social status? Originally, there were two reasons. One was that nonworking people were a threat to the wealth and well-being of the rest of the community. The second was that nonworking people were visibly outcasts; they lived worse than anyone else. Once these highly functional sources of the status are removed, the vaunted "work ethic" becomes highly vulnerable. The notion that there is an intrinsic good in working even if one does not have to may have impressive philosophical credentials, but, on its face, it is not very plausible—at least not to a young person whose values are still being formed. To someone who is not yet persuaded of the satisfactions of making one's own way, there is something laughable about a person who doggedly keeps working at a lousy job for no tangible reason at all. And when working no longer provides either income or status, the last reason for working has truly vanished. The man who keeps working is, in fact, a chump. . . .[16]

Robbing Peter to Pay Paul: Transfers from Poor to Poor

When we think of transfers, we usually think in terms of economic transfers from richer to poorer. In reality, social policy can obligate one citizen to turn over a variety of "goods" as a donation on behalf of some other person; access to parking spaces reserved for the handicapped is a simple example.

Sometimes these noneconomic transfers, like the economic ones, are arranged so that the better-off give up something to the worse-off, and the argument about whether the transfer is appropriate follows the lines of the issues I have just raised. But in a surprising number of instances the transfers are mandated by the better-off, while the price must be paid by donors who are just as poor as the recipient.

Now suppose that the same hypothetical "I" considers the case of two students in an inner-city high school. Both come from poor families. Both have suffered equal deprivations and social injustices. They have the same intelligence and human potential. For whatever reasons—let us assume pure accident—the two students behave differently in school. One student (the good student) studies hard and pays attention in class. The other student (the mischievous student) does not study and instead creates disturbances, albeit good-natured disturbances, in the classroom.

I observe a situation in which the teacher expels the mischievous student from the classroom more or less at will. The result is that he becomes further alienated from school, drops out, and eventually ends up on welfare or worse. I know that the cause of this sequence of events (his behavior in class) was no worse than the behavior of millions of middle-class students who suffer nothing like the same penalty. They too are kicked out of class when they act up, but for a variety of reasons they stay in school and eventually do well. Further yet, I know that the behavior of the teacher toward the student is biased and unfairly harsh because the student is an inner-city black and the teacher is a suburban white who neither understands nor sympathizes with such students.

On all counts, then, I observe that the mischievous student expelled from the classroom is a victim who deserves a system that does not unfairly penalize him. I therefore protect him against the bias and arbitrariness of the teacher. The teacher cannot expel the student from class unless the student's behavior meets certain criteria far beyond the ordinary talking and laughing out of turn that used to get him in trouble.

The result, let us say, is that the student continues to act as before, but remains in the classroom. Other students also respond to the reality of the greater latitude they now have. The amount of teaching is reduced, and so is the ability of students to concentrate on their work even if they want to.

I know, however, that some benefits are obtained. The mischievous student who formerly dropped out of school does not. He obtains his diploma, and with it some advantages in the form of greater education (he learned something, although not much, while he stayed in school) and a credential to use when applying for a job.

This benefit has been obtained at a price. The price is not money—let us say it costs no more to run the school under the new policy than under the old. No transfers have been exacted from the white middle class. The transfer instead is wholly from the good student to the mischievous one. For I find that the quality of education obtained by the good student deteriorated badly, both because the teacher had less time and energy for teaching and because the classroom environment was no longer suitable for studying. One poor and disadvantaged student has been compelled (he had no choice in the matter) to give up part of his education so that the other student could stay in the classroom.

What is my rationale for enforcing this transfer? In what sense did the good student have an excess of educational opportunity that he could legitimately be asked to sacrifice?

The example has deliberately been constructed so that neither student was intrinsically more deserving than the other. The only difference between the two was behavioral, with one student behaving in a more desirable way than the other student. Even under these unrealistically neutral conditions, it is hard to avoid the conclusion that the transfer was unjustifiable. Now, let us make the example more realistic.

A student who reaches adolescence in an inner-city school with high motivation to study and learn does not do so by accident. The motivation is likely to reflect merit—on the student's part, on the parents' part, or on a combination of the two. In the good student's behavior I am observing not just a "desirable" response but a praiseworthy one.

Further, if we make the example realistic, the good student does not transfer simply an abstract deterioration in the quality of education, from a potentially fine education to a merely adequate one. The more likely loss is a much greater one, from an adequate education that might have prepared the good student to take advantage of opportunities for higher education to an inadequate education that leaves the good student, no matter how well motivated, without essential tools to pursue basic routes to advancement.

Once again, let me consider my rationale without giving myself an easy out. I may not assume that classroom instruction is not really affected by disruption; it is. I may not assume that counselors will be able shortly to change the behavior of the mischievous student. I may not assume that the school will provide separate tracks for the attentive student; the same philosophy that led to greater student rights also led to restrictions and even prohibitions on separate tracks for the better students. Most of all, I may not assume that the good student is superhuman. He may be admirable, but he is not necessarily able to get himself a good education no matter what obstacles I put in his way.

Such transfers from poor to poor are at the heart of the inequities of social policy. Saying that we meant well does not quite cover our transgressions. Even during the period of the most active reform we could not help being aware, if only at the back of our minds, of certain moral problems. When poor delinquents arrested for felonies were left on probation, as the elite wisdom prescribed they should be, the persons put most at risk were poor people who lived in their neighborhoods. They, not the elite, gave up the greater part of the good called "safety" so that the disadvantaged delinquent youth should not experience the injustice of punishment. When job-training programs were set up to function at the level of the least competent, it was the most competent trainees who had to sacrifice their opportunities to reach their potentials. When social policy reinforced the ethic that certain jobs are too demeaning to ask people to do, it was those who preferred such jobs to welfare whose basis for self-respect was stripped from them.

More generally, social policy after the mid-1960s demanded an extraordinary range of transfers from the most capable poor to the least capable, from the most law-abiding to the least law-abiding, and from the most responsible to the least responsible. In return, we gave little to these most deserving persons except easier access to welfare for themselves—the one thing they found hardest to put to "good use."

We blinked at these realities at the time. The homogenizing process . . . helped us to blink; the poor were all poor, all more or less in the same situation, we said. All *would* be deserving, we preferred to assume, if they had not been so exploited by society, by the system. But at bottom it is difficult to imagine under what logic we thought these transfers appropriate.

The Net Happiness Challenge

The peculiarity of a transfer, as opposed to the other uses of tax monies, is that the direct benefit goes only to the recipient. If I pay for garbage collection, I, the payer, get a benefit. My garbage disappears. I may argue about whether the garbage collection service is efficiently operated and whether I am getting value for money, but I do not argue about whether, somehow, my garbage must be made to disappear, and so must my neighbor's garbage. If I pay for Food Stamps with my tax dollars, the government is making quite a different request of me and undertaking a much different responsibility. The government judges that my income is large enough that a portion of it should be given to someone whose income, the government has decided, is too small. And when, for example, the Food Stamps are buying milk for a malnourished child, I am pleased that they should do so. But I may legitimately ask two things of the government that exercises such authority. First, I may ask that the government be *right*—right in deciding that, in some cosmic scheme of things, my resources are "large enough" and the recipient's are "too small." Second, I may ask that the transfer be successful, and therein lies a problem. . . .

A Thought Experiment

To illustrate the general problem we are about to approach, let me pose a problem in the form that Einstein used to call a "thought experiment." Whereas Einstein used the device to imagine such things as the view from the head of a column of light, we will use it for the more pedestrian purpose of imagining the view from the office of a middle-echelon bureaucrat. Our task: to think through how to structure a specific government social-action program so that it might reasonably be expected to accomplish net good.

The experiment calls for us to put ourselves in the role of a government planner who must implement a new piece of legislation: The Comprehensive Anti-Smoking Act. The act has several provisions common to the genre. It establishes a federal agency to coordinate the federal government's activities related to the goal of less smoking. A large antismoking advertising campaign is planned. Federal matching funds are provided for school systems that teach courses on the perils of smoking.

In addition to these initiatives, the legislation provides for direct, concrete incentives for people to quit smoking. A billion dollars will be appropriated annually for the indefinite future, to be used for cash rewards to persons who quit. We are in charge of designing this effort, with complete freedom to specify whatever rules we wish, provided they are consistent with constitutional rights. After five years an evaluation will be conducted to determine whether the number of cigarettes consumed and the number of smokers have been reduced by the program.

The challenge in this experiment is to use the $1 billion in a way that (in our own best estimate) will meet this test. My proposition is that we cannot do so: that any program we design will either (1) have no effect on smoking or (2) actually *increase* smoking. I maintain that we are helpless to use the billion dollars to achieve our goal.

DESIGNING THE PROGRAM

The heart of the problem is designing a reward that will induce smokers to quit—and will not induce others to begin smoking, continue smoking, or increase their smoking to become eligible to receive the reward. Let us work through one scenario to illustrate the nature of the conundrum.

Three sets of choices will decisively affect the success or failure of the program: choices about

1. the size of the reward,
2. conditions for receiving the reward, and
3. eligibility to participate in the program.

What is a first approximation of a program that has a good chance of working?

Choosing the Size of the Reward. We know from the outset that the reward cannot be small. No one will quit smoking for pocket change, other than those who were going to quit anyway. On the other hand, the theoretical power of a cash reward is plausible—almost anyone would become and remain a nonsmoker in return for $1 million. We settle on the sum of $10,000 as a reward that is an extremely powerful inducement to large numbers of persons.[17]

Conditions for Receiving the Reward. We seek a middle ground between conditions that maximize the likelihood that a person has permanently quit smoking and conditions that make the reward so difficult to win that few will bother. Thus, for example, we reject plans that would spread the reward over several years. Eventually we decide to require that a person must remain smoke-free for one year. We make the award a one-time prize, so that people have no incentive to recommence smoking to qualify for another $10,000. A repayment scheme is added: People who begin smoking again will have to give up their award.

Eligibility to Participate. The intent of the program is to appeal to the heavy smoker whose health is most at risk. On the other hand, it would defeat our purpose to limit eligibility too severely—to persons, for example, who have smoked three packs a day for twenty years—because in so doing we would disqualify many people in the vulnerable group of moderate smokers who are likely to become heavy, lifelong smokers unless something is done. The compromise solution we reach is to require that a person have smoked at least one pack a day for five years.

Now let us consider the results.

AFTER ONE YEAR

We think ahead a year, and are pleased. The $10,000 reward has substantial effects on the people who are eligible for the program on day one—that is, persons who have smoked at least a pack a day for five years at the time the experiment begins. The effect is not unfailing; not everyone quits smoking to get the reward; and we must assume that not everyone who stops for a year is able to avoid a relapse. Some cheating occurs despite our precautions. But some people quit smoking permanently as a direct result of the program.

We recognize, of course, that we achieve the effect inefficiently. Thousands of persons in the target population quit smoking every year even in the absence of a monetary reward. Under the program, they collect money for doing what they would have done anyway. But the problem posed in our thought experiment says nothing about being efficient; the problem is only to create a program that reduces net smoking.

AFTER TWO YEARS

We think ahead two years, and are disturbed. For now comes time to examine the effects of the program on people who have been smoking a pack a day but for a period of less than five years when the program begins.

Everyone who would have quit after four years and eleven months continues to smoke for another month. These cigarettes represent an increase in smoking that must be subtracted from the gross reduction in smoking created by the program. *Almost* everyone who would otherwise have quit during any point in the fifth year continues to smoke until the five-year requirement has been met. Or, to put it more generally: We find that for all persons who have been smoking less than the required period of time, the program provides a payment to continue. For the person who has been smoking for exactly four years, the payment is $10,000 in return for smoking for one more year. Given that the smoking habit has its own attractions, the payment is exceedingly effective. In fact, we notice an unfortunate imbalance: For the person who has already smoked for five years (our target population), the inducement of $10,000 to quit must fight against the attractions of smoking and is not always adequate to achieve the desired result. For the smoker who has not reached this limit, the inducement to continue smoking is reinforced by those very attractions. Thus the effective power of $10,000 to induce continued smoking for one year in the one population is much greater than its power to induce cessation of smoking for one year in the other.

To this point, we have been concerned only with those who were already smoking at the pack-a-day level. Now we consider the effects of the program on smokers who had been smoking less than that amount. We find that a significant number of smokers increase their consumption to a pack a day, for the same reason. (Everyone who smokes nineteen cigarettes a day increases to twenty, almost everyone who smokes eighteen cigarettes a day increases to twenty, and so on.) This effect is strongest among those persons who think they "should" quit but who doubt their ability to quit without help. For them—through a process of plausible but destructive logic—it seems that the best way to do what they think they want to do (to quit smoking) is to smoke more.

Among those who are nonsmokers, the effects are entirely negative.

A considerable number of teenagers who were wavering between starting or not starting to smoke decide in favor of smoking—they can enjoy smoking now, and then give it up when they qualify for the reward.

AFTER FIVE YEARS

When we think ahead five years, we note a final logical by-product of the program. Quitting the habit after five years of smoking a pack a day is generally more difficult than quitting sooner and after lesser levels of smoking. Many people who try to stop when the fifth year is ended find that the $10,000 is no longer a sufficient inducement, though it may have seemed to them a few years earlier that it would be. The rules of the program have made heavy smokers out of people who would have remained light smokers and thereby have induced a certain number of people not only to smoke more and longer until they became eligible for the $10,000 but to become impervious to the effects of the reward once they do become eligible.

What is the net outcome? If 90 percent of the population had been smoking for five years when the program began, we might still argue that the program would show a net reduction in smoking. But only about 15 percent of the adult population smokes a pack a day or more.[18] Let us estimate that a third of this number have been smoking at that rate for more than five years. If so, our plan has the potential for reducing smoking among 5 percent of the adult population and the potential for increasing smoking among 95 percent of the adult population. It is exceedingly difficult to attach numbers to the considerations we have just reviewed without coming to the conclusion that the program as specified would have the net effect of increasing both the number of cigarettes consumed and the number of smokers.

BACK TO SQUARE ONE

When we reconsider the three parameters and try to select a combination that meets the challenge, the nature of their interdependence becomes clear. Suppose, for example, that we require a smoking history of at least ten years, and thereby, as intended, reduce the number of persons who are drawn into smoking just because of the reward. But such a step makes no difference in the calculations of those who have already been smoking more than five years (they are, in effect, operating under the logic of a five-year eligibility rule). Among those who have smoked less than five years, the change in the eligibility requirement has two counterproductive effects. First, persons who have smoked less than five years constitute a large proportion of smokers that the program should be reaching—younger, with more to gain from quitting. By extending the requirement to ten years, the program has been made irrelevant to many of them. For those who do think that far ahead, the effects will tend to be harmful, inducing a sense that there will be time to quit—and profit to be made—at a later point in their lives. Thus lengthening the eligibility period to ten years does not help; it makes matters worse.

As we ponder ways out of this bind, it becomes clear that the most dramatic reductions in smoking occur among persons who quit the soonest—a person who quits smoking at age sixty-five saves only a few years' worth of smoking, whereas a person who quits at twenty saves decades. Why not focus our efforts among the very young? Even granting the tendency of the award to encourage smoking so as to qualify, perhaps this will be more than counterbalanced by the very long periods of "savings" that will result from each success. So we target the program at youth (perhaps by installing an age-eligibility criterion—the specific method makes no difference). But the results are even more disastrous. The qualification criteria must be loose, because only a tiny fraction of the teenaged smokers we want to reach have had time to smoke very long. The result, when combined with a significant reward for quitting, is that the inducement effect is overpowering. Even teenagers who have no desire to smoke at all find it worth inculcating the habit for a year (or whatever our time limit is reduced to). Once started, only a proportion of those who smoked *only* because the program existed and who fully intended to quit are actually able to quit. The age effect backfires: While it is true that inducing a youngster to quit (who otherwise would not have quit) saves decades of smoking, it is equally true that inducing a youngster to start costs decades of smoking, and we produce far more of the latter than the former.

TWO WAYS OUT

We give up on a continuing program. Instead, we propose that the program be made a one-time, never-to-be-repeated offer: Announce the program, give everyone who is *already* eligible a chance to enroll, but give no one a reason to start smoking or to increase their smoking in order to become eligible. State loudly and unequivocally that the program will never be repeated. We will at least achieve the success of the first year.

Theoretically, this scheme might (but only might) reduce net smoking.[19] In practice, it is guaranteed that the program will be continued. A successful one-time effort will be refunded immediately and on a larger scale. Congress rarely cancels even a failed social program, let alone a successful one. . . .

Ultimately, the logic of the situation drives us to the one configuration of awards that surely will reduce net smoking: We offer a dollar amount to everyone who does not smoke, but make them pay it back if they ever start. Since this will cost far more than a billion dollars a year, we seek permission to increase the budget, pointing out that, while it may be expensive, our way out will in fact reduce smoking, whereas the alternatives will not. But some unfriendly critic points out that all we need do is levy a fine on everyone who begins smoking (or who continues to smoke) that is equal to the reward we propose to offer for not starting. The effects on smoking will be essentially the same (a $10,000 penalty ought to have about as much effect as a $10,000 reward for persons at most income levels), and the government will get a lot of revenue to boot. This proposal is of course also rejected, on grounds that it is unfair to the poor.

As one experiments with different combinations of rules, it becomes apparent that the traps we encounter in the first approximations are generalizable. Any change in the parameters intended to reduce one problem raises a new one. Why should this be? Is it intrinsic to the process? Or is it a peculiarity of an example I carefully chose?

Laws of Social Programs

At first glance, the smoking example seems most apt for a certain type of social program, the one that seeks to change behavior from X to Y—what might be called "remedial" social programs. It seems less analogous, if not altogether irrelevant, to programs such as AFDC that simply provide an allowance without (through the allowance itself) trying to stimulate change. But in fact it applies to transfer programs of all types. In all cases, the transfer is legitimized by the recipient's being in a certain condition (whether smoking or poverty) that the government would prefer the recipient not be in. The burden of the smoking example is not that we failed to reduce smoking—to achieve the desired behavioral change—but that we increased the number of people who end up in the undesired condition. This charge applies to transfers in general.

The reasons why are not idiosyncratic. Let me suggest some characteristics we observed in the thought experiment that occur so widely and for such embedded reasons that they suggest laws. That is, no matter how ingenious the design of a social transfer program may be, we cannot—in a free society—design programs that escape their influence. Together, they account for much of the impasse we observe in the antismoking example and point to some important principles for designing social programs that work.

1. THE LAW OF IMPERFECT SELECTION. Any objective rule that defines eligibility for a social transfer program will irrationally exclude some persons.

It can always be demonstrated that some persons who are excluded from the Food Stamps program are in greater need than some persons who receive Food Stamps. It can always be demonstrated that someone who is technically ineligible for Medicaid really "ought" to be receiving it, given the intent of the legislation.

These inequities, which are observed everywhere, are not the fault of inept writers of eligibility rules, but an inescapable outcome of the task of rule-writing. Eligibility rules must convert the concept of "true need" into objectified elements. The rules constructed from these bits and pieces are necessarily subject to what Herbert Costner has called "epistemic error"—the inevitable gap between quantified measures and the concept they are intended to capture.[20] We have no way of defining "truly needy" precisely—not those who truly need to stop smoking, nor those truly in need of college scholarships or subsidized loans or disability insurance. Any criterion we specify will inevitably include a range of people, some of whom are unequivocally the people we intended to help, others of whom are less so, and still others of whom meet the letter of the eligibility requirement but are much less needy than some persons who do not.

Social welfare policy in earlier times tended to deal with this problem by erring in the direction of exclusion—better to deny help to some truly needy persons than to let a few slackers slip through. Such attitudes depended, however, on the assumption that the greater good was being served. Moral precepts had to be upheld. Whenever a person was inappropriately given help, it was bad for the recipient (undermining his character) and a bad example to the community at large.

When that assumption is weakened or dispensed with altogether, it follows naturally that the Law of Imperfect Selection leads to programs with constantly broadening target populations. If persons are not to blame for their plight, no real harm is done by giving them help they do not fully "need." No moral cost is incurred by permitting some undeserving into the program. A moral cost *is* incurred by excluding a deserving person. No one has a scalpel sharp enough to excise only the undeserving. Therefore it is not just a matter of political expedience to add a new layer to the eligible population rather than to subtract one (though that is often a factor in the actual decision-making process). It is also the morally correct thing to do, given the premises of the argument.

2. THE LAW OF UNINTENDED REWARDS. Any social transfer increases the net value of being in the condition that prompted the transfer.

A deficiency is observed—too little money, too little food, too little academic achievement—and a social transfer program tries to fill the gap—with a welfare payment, Food Stamps, a compensatory education program. An unwanted behavior is observed—drug addiction, crime, unemployability—and the program tries to change that behavior to some other, better behavior—through a drug rehabilitation program, psychotherapy, vocational training. In each case, the program, however unintentionally, *must* be constructed in such a way that it increases the net value of being in the condition that it seeks to change—either by increasing the rewards or by reducing the penalties.

For some people in some circumstances, it is absurd to think in terms of "net value," because they so clearly have no choice at all about the fix they are in or because the net value is still less desirable than virtually any alternative. Paraplegics receiving Medicaid cannot easily be seen as "rewarded" for becoming paraplegics by the existence of free medical care. Poor children in Head Start cannot be seen as rewarded for being poor. Persons who are in the unwanted condition *completely involuntarily* are not affected by the existence of the reward.

But the number of such pure examples is very small. Let us return to the case of the middle-aged worker who loses his job, wants desperately to work, but can find nothing. He receives Unemployment Insurance, hating every penny of it. He would seem to be "completely involuntarily" in his situation and his search for a job unaffected by the existence of Unemployment Insurance. In fact, however, his behavior (unless he is peculiarly irrational) *is* affected by the existence of the Unemployment Insurance. For example, the cushion provided by Unemployment Insurance may lead him to refuse to take a job that requires him to move to another town, whereas he would take the job and uproot his home if he were more desperate. Most people (including me) are glad that his behavior is so affected, that he does not have to leave the home and friends of a lifetime, that he can wait for a job opening nearby. But he is not "completely involuntarily" unemployed in such a case, and the reason he is not is that the Unemployment Insurance has made the condition of unemployment more tolerable.

Our paraplegic anchors one end of the continuum labeled "Degree of Voluntarism in the Conditions that Social Policy Seeks to Change or Make Less Painful," and our unemployed worker is only slightly to one side of him—but he is to one side, not in the same place. The apparent unattractiveness of most of the conditions that social policy seeks to change must not obscure the continuum involved. No one chooses to be a paraplegic, and perhaps no one chooses to be a heroin addict. But the distinction remains: Very few heroin addicts developed their addiction by being tied down and forcibly injected with heroin. They may not have chosen to become addicts, but they *did* choose initially to take heroin.

Let us consider the implications in terms of the archetypical social program for helping the chronic unemployed escape their condition, the job-training program.

Imagine that a program is begun that has the most basic and benign inducement of all, the chance to learn a marketable skill. It is open to everybody. By opening it to all, we have circumvented (for the time being) the Law of Unintended Rewards. All may obtain the training, no matter what their job history, so no unintended reward is being given for the condition of chronic unemployment.

On assessing the results, we observe that the ones who enter the program, stick with it, and learn a skill include very few of the hardcore unemployed whom we most wanted to help. The typical "success" stories from our training program are persons with a history of steady employment who wanted to upgrade their earning power. This is admirable. But what about the hardcore unemployed? A considerable number entered the program, but almost all of them dropped out or failed to get jobs once they left. Only a small proportion used the training opportunity as we had hoped. The problem of the hardcore unemployed remains essentially unchanged.

We may continue to circumvent the Law of Unintended Rewards. All we need do is continue the job-training program unchanged. It will still be there, still available to all who want to enroll, but we will do nothing to entice participation. Our theory (should we adopt this stance) is that, as time goes on, we will continue to help at least a few of the hardcore unemployed who are in effect skimmed from the top of the pool. We may even hope that the number skimmed from the top will be larger than the number who enter the pool, so that, given enough time, the population of hardcore unemployed will diminish. But this strategy is a gradualist one and relies on the assumption that other conditions in society are not creating more hardcore unemployed than the program is skimming off.

The alternative is to do something to get more of the hardcore unemployed into the program, and to improve the content so that more of them profit from the training. And once this alternative is taken, the program planner is caught in the trap of unintended rewards. Because we cannot "draft" people into the program or otherwise coerce their participation, our only alternative is to make it more attractive by changing the rules a bit.

Suppose, for example, we find that the reason many did not profit from the earlier program was that they got fired from (or quit) their new jobs within a few days of getting them, and that the reason they did so had to do with the job-readiness problem. The ex-trainee was late getting to work, the boss complained, the ex-trainee reacted angrily and was fired. We observe this to be a common pattern. We know the problem is not that the ex-trainee is lazy or unmotivated, but that he has never been socialized into the discipline of the workplace. He needs more time, more help, more patience than other workers until he develops the needed work habits. Suppose that we try to compensate—for example, by placing our trainees with employers who are being subsidized to hire such persons. The employer accepts lower productivity and other problems in return for a payment to do so (such plans have been tried frequently, with mixed results). Given identical work at identical pay, the ex-trainee is being rewarded for his "credential" of hardcore unemployment. He can get away with behavior that an ordinary worker cannot get away with.

May we still assume that the program is making progress in preparing its trainees for the real-world marketplace? Will the hardcore unemployed modify their unreliable behavior? What will be the effect on morale and self-esteem among those trainees who were succeeding in the program before the change of rules? It is tempting to conclude that the program has already ceased to function effectively for anyone anymore, that the change in rules has done more harm than good. But my proposition is for the moment a more restricted one: The reward for unproductive behavior (both past and present) now exists.

What of the case of a drug addict who is chronically unemployed because (let us assume) of the addiction? It might seem that the unintended reward in such a case is innocuous; it consists of measures to relieve the addict of his addiction, measures for which the nonaddict will have no need or use. If we were dealing with an involuntary disability—our paraplegic again—the argument would be valid. But in the case of drug addiction (or any other behavior that has its rewards), a painless cure generally increases the attractiveness of the behavior. Imagine, for example, a pill that instantly and painlessly relieved dependence on heroin, and the subsequent effects on heroin use.

Thus we are faced with the problem we observed in the thought experiment. The program that seeks to change behavior must offer an inducement that unavoidably either adds to the attraction of, or reduces the penalties of engaging in, the behavior in question.

We are now ready to tackle the question of when a social program can reasonably be expected to accomplish net good and when it can reasonably be expected to produce net harm. Again let us think in terms of a continuum. All social programs, I have argued, provide an unintended reward for being in the condition that the program is trying to change or make more tolerable. But some of these unintended rewards are so small that they are of little practical importance. Why then can we not simply bring a bit of care to the design of such programs, making sure that the unintended reward is *always* small? The reason we are not free to do so lies in the third law of social programs:

3. THE LAW OF NET HARM. The less likely it is that the unwanted behavior will change voluntarily, the more likely it is that a program to induce change will cause net harm.

A social program that seeks to change behavior must do two things. It must induce participation by the persons who are to benefit, as described under the Law of Unintended Rewards. Then it must actually produce the desired change in behavior. It must succeed, and success depends crucially on one factor above all others: the price that the participant is willing to pay.

The more that the individual is willing to accept whatever needs to be done in order to achieve the desired state of affairs, the broader the discretion of the program designers. Thus, expensive health resorts can withhold food from their guests, hospitals can demand that their interns work inhuman schedules, and elite volunteer units in the armed forces can ask their trainees to take risks in training exercises that seem (to the rest of us) suicidal. Such programs need offer no inducement at all except the "thing in itself" that is the *raison d'être* of the program—a shapelier body, a career as a physician, membership in the elite military unit. Similarly, the drug addict who is prepared to sign over to a program a great deal of control over his own behavior may very well be successful— witness the sometimes impressive success rates of private treatment clinics.

The smaller the price that the participant is willing to pay, the greater the constraints on program design. It makes no difference to an official running a training program for the hardcore unemployed that (for example) the Marine Corps can instill exemplary work habits in recruits who come to the Corps no more "job-ready" than the recruits to the job-training program. If the training program tried for one day to use the techniques that the Marine Corps uses, it would lose its participants. Boot camp was not part of the bargain the job trainees struck with the government when they signed on. Instead, the training program must not only induce persons to join the program (which may be fairly easy). It must also induce them to stay in the program, induce them to cooperate with its curriculum, and induce them, finally, to adopt major changes in outlook, habits, and assumptions. The program content must be almost entirely carrot.

There is nothing morally reprehensible in approaches that are constrained to use only positive inducements. The objections are practical.

First, it is guaranteed that success rates will be very low. The technology of changing human behavior depends heavily on the use of negative reinforcement in conjunction with positive reinforcement. The more deeply engrained the behavior to be changed and the more attractions it holds for the person whose behavior is involved, the more important it is that the program have both a full tool kit available to it *and* the participant's willingness to go along with whatever is required. The Marine Corps has both these assets. Social programs to deal with the hardcore unemployed, teenaged mothers, delinquents, and addicts seldom do.

Second, as inducements become large—as they must, if the program is dealing with the most intractable problems—the more attractive they become to people who were not in need of help in the first place. We do not yet know how large they must finally become. We do know from experience, however, that quite generous experimental programs have provided extensive counseling, training, guaranteed jobs, and other supports—and failed.[21] We can only guess at what would be enough—perhaps a matter of years of full-time residential training, followed by guaranteed jobs at double or triple the minimum wage; we do not know. Whatever they are, however, consider their effects on the people not in the program. At this point, it appears that any program that would succeed in helping large numbers of the hardcore unemployed will make hardcore unemployment a highly desirable state to be in.

The conditions that combine to produce net harm are somewhat different in the theoretical and the practical cases, but they come to the same thing. Theoretically, any program that mounts an intervention with sufficient rewards to sustain participation and an effective result will generate so much of the unwanted behavior (in order to become eligible for the program's rewards) that the net effect will be to increase the incidence of the unwanted behavior. In practice, the programs that deal with the most intractable behavior problems have included a package of rewards large enough to induce participation, but not large enough to produce the desired result.

My conclusion is that social programs in a democratic society tend to produce net harm in dealing with the most difficult problems. They will inherently tend to have enough of an inducement to produce bad behavior and not enough of a solution to stimulate good behavior; and the more difficult the problem, the more likely it is that this relationship will prevail. The lesson is not that we can do no good at all, but that we must pick our shots.

NOTES

1. In the card catalog of the Library of Congress, for example, under the heading of "poverty," these are the numbers of titles about American poverty by publication date:

1940–49	1
1950–59	1
1960–63	2
1964–69	89
1970–79	137

In all, one finds only four titles under "poverty" with a publication date during the twenty-four years from 1940 to 1963. Obviously, the holdings under the heading of "poverty" do not begin to exhaust the actual materials on the subject, but the proportions illustrate the relative interest in the topic over time.

2. Norman Podhoretz, *Breaking Ranks: A Political Memoir* (New York: Harper & Row, 1979), 75.
3. Arthur Schlesinger, *Kennedy or Nixon: Does It Make Any Difference?* quoted in Podhoretz, *Breaking Ranks,* 101–102.
4. James T. Patterson, *America's Struggle Against Poverty 1900–1980* (Cambridge, Mass.: Harvard University Press, 1981), 94.
5. Michael Harrington, *The Other America* (New York: Macmillan, 1962).
6. Patterson, *America's Struggle,* 99.
7. John K. Galbraith, in *The Affluent Society* (Boston: Houghton Mifflin, 1958), had expressed a structuralist view of American poverty, but the message had been submerged in the attention given to his arguments about affluence and public goods. During the early 1960s officials within the Department of Health, Education, and Welfare, especially those around Wilbur Cohen, assistant secretary for legislation, were working on plans that foreshadowed the later reforms (Cohen himself became secretary of HEW under Johnson). See Patterson, *America's Struggle,* chapters 6–9, for an historical account of the rediscovery of poverty and the triumph of the structuralist approach during the 1960–65 period.
8. Podhoretz, who was in a transition from one end of the political spectrum to another, provides in *Breaking Ranks* an entertaining account of the period when *The Other America* was gaining attention.
9. See, for example, Stephen Thernstrom, "Is There Really a New Poor?" *Dissent* 15 (January/February 1968): 59–64.
10. Jeremy Larner and Irving Howe, eds., *Poverty: Views From the Left* (New York: William Morrow, 1968). The authors were writing these words in 1965, at the outset of the War on Poverty.
11. Most farmers were cash poor until this century. As many as 40 percent of wage earners were poor by the standards of the day in 1900, using the figures of John Ryan, *A Living Wage* (New York: Arno, 1971, copyright 1906). Robert Hunter, *Poverty* (New York: Macmillan, 1907) uses a rock-bottom poverty level based on a standard of living "that a man would demand for his horses or slaves" and arrives at an estimate of 20 percent poor in the northern industrial states. By the contemporary standard (the official poverty line), it seems likely that a large majority of the population was living in poverty. See the discussion in Patterson, *America's Struggle,* 6–13.
12. Figures cited in Patterson, *America's Struggle,* 172.
13. Frances Fox Piven and Richard A. Cloward, *Regulating the Poor: The Functions of Public Welfare* (New York: Vintage Books, 1971) is an excellent source of data on this issue.
14. Ibid., 287–305.
15. I am indebted for information on the magnet school experience to Dr. Norman Gold, senior research associate at the National Institute of Education, who was a leading participant in the development and evaluation of the early magnet school experiments. For the published record, see Eugene C. Royster, D. Catherine Baltzell, and Fran Cheryl Simmons, *Study of the Emergency School Aid Act Magnet School Program: Final Report* (Washington, D.C.: National Institute of Education, 1979); and Robert A. Dentler, D. Catherine Baltzell, and Kent J. Chabotar, *Quality Integrated Magnet Schools and Their Cost* (Washington, D.C.: National Institute of Education, 1983).
16. Piven and Cloward, in *Regulating the Poor,* make a similar point: "When large numbers of people come to subsist on the dole, many of them spurning what little low-wage work may exist, those of the poor and near-poor who continue to work are inevitably

affected. From their perspective, the ready availability of relief payments (often at levels only slightly below prevailing wages) undermines their chief claim to social status: namely, that although poor they nevertheless earn their livelihood. If most of them react with anger, others react by asking, 'Why work?' " (p. 343). Parenthetically, it is interesting how many of Piven's and Cloward's points, made in support of a left-radical critique of social policy, coincide with those in critiques from the other end of the political spectrum.

17. Other types of rewards (a trip to Jamaica, or a full college scholarship for one's first-born, for example) do not seem to change the nature of the calculation, nor does the payment schedule associated with the reward.

18. *Statistical Abstract of the United States* 1981 (Washington, D.C.: Bureau of the Census, 1982), table 202.

19. Even a one-time program would not work unless the government could convince people that it meant what it said. Some people, aware of the inertial tendencies of government programs, are sure to assume that the reward will be available again in the future and behave accordingly.

20. Herbert Costner, "Theory, Deduction, and Rules of Correspondence," in Hubert M. Blalock, Jr., ed., *Causal Models in the Social Sciences* (Chicago: Aldine Atherton, 1971), 299–319.

21. Probably the most extreme available example is the $82 million "Supported Work" program conducted by the Manpower Demonstration Research Corporation. Its findings are summarized in Board of Directors, Manpower Demonstration Research Corporation, *Summary and Findings of the National Supported Work Demonstration* (Cambridge, Mass.: Ballinger, 1980). The hardcore unemployed who volunteered for the program were provided with intensive orientation *and* nonjob supports *and* a subsidized job (generally for twelve months). The evaluation claimed modest success (in terms of the cost-benefit ratio over the long term) for two of the groups, AFDC mothers and ex-addicts; it did not claim success for the other two groups (ex-offenders and youth). These results had to be based, unfortunately, on those persons who could still be found after the program. Despite intensive efforts by the evaluators to track down members of the samples, continuous follow-up information after eighteen months could be obtained for only 48 percent of the AFDC sample, 16 percent of the ex-addict sample, 28 percent of the ex-offender sample, and 35 percent of the youth sample (computed from table 3–1, 47). This raises the serious problem of what is called "sample attrition bias"; for example, it is highly unlikely that the 16 percent of the ex-addicts who could be found were representative of the sample as a whole in their job behavior. The report does not address this issue. The more salient point is that, even taking the conclusions at face value, the program, providing an unprecedented level of support, did not make a substantial dent in the behavior of the hardcore unemployed. We do not yet know what level of intervention would do the job. Even at the levels of support provided by the Supported Work program, the unintended reward is quite tangible and large. See Ken Auletta, *The Underclass* (New York: Random House, 1982), for an absorbing narrative account of the people and the program.

PART V

Contemporary Challenges
and the Social Order

No LIST of modern social problems would fail to include the reform-weary American political system; judicial activism; affirmative action and race relations; abortion and the assault on traditional morality. The idea of this section is to tune in on the thinking of highly competent people who have mused on these problems. There may be no paradigmatic "conservative" position on any one of them. But rigorous thought, an active imagination, and an anti-ideological disposition are the common denominators. And each of the authors quoted here, in his own way, demonstrates an aspect of the conservative intelligence examining a particular problem, whether narrow or broad.

Edward C. Banfield wrote his classic essay "In Defense of the American Party System" almost twenty years ago, before the various and still ongoing efforts to "reform" it really got going, beginning in the early 1970s. The more the presidential nominating process has been changed to try to "democratize," i.e., ideologize, our politics, the more bombastic and incoherent American public life has become, confirming his thesis that it was the unplanned, undogmatic, prudential character of the traditional party system, capable of accommodating a multiplicity of interests, that helped to keep our politics moderate and stable. (If the reader wishes to see Banfield's opinion of the post-1972 reforms, he should consult "Party 'Reform' in Retrospect," reprinted in his recent collection, *Here the People Rule.*)

As a professor at the University of Chicago, the University of Pennsylvania, and Harvard University (where he is the George D. Markham Professor of Government Emeritus), Banfield has been one of the most influential, and controversial, political scientists in America, drawing on sociology, economics, and the other social sciences (as in his iconoclastic *The Unheavenly City*) to prove, in a manner reminiscent of Hayek, the limitations of reason in modern society. He warns especially of the *unintended* consequences of reforms, of the radiating effects of political change on the entire social system.

Many of the most pressing social questions confronting the nation are the by-products of activist decisions by the Supreme Court. The exclusionary rule, affirmative action, pornography, abortion, busing for racial integration, prayer in schools—all have been catapulted onto the national agenda by some act or acts of judicial imperialism. At one time it was thought that the regular arrogation of power to the judiciary would stop with the Warren Court, but it has continued. And every year new books on jurisprudence appear, justifying the Court's activism and goading it on to ever-greater adventurism. Part of the problem, in the law schools, is that courses in constitutional law no longer study the Constitution—by reading *The Federalist,* the seminal speeches in the Federal Convention, Story's *Commentaries,* etc.—but only the case law arising under it, a method guaranteed to teach students that the Constitution is what the judges say it is. The philosophical source of this delusion is the jurisprudence of Justice Oliver Wendell Holmes, Jr.

Holmes made his academic reputation by studying the common law, but as Walter Berns shows in his brilliant essay, Holmes established his judicial reputation by treating the Constitution as if *it* were common law—not a permanent charter of limited government, but a mass of ill-digested precedents that judges were free to adapt to their own purposes. In Holmes's view, which owed much to Darwin, the law must evolve in accord with the changing circumstances of society: The judges are to fit the Constitution to our "felt necessities," not our tastes and opinions to the Constitution.

Although Holmes's reputation is that of an advocate of judicial restraint—indeed, Chief Justice Rehnquist in his celebrated article, "On the Notion of a Living Constitution," endorses Holmes's philosophy—the truth is that by making the Constitution follow the Zeitgeist rather than the other way around, Holmes provides the theoretical groundwork for judicial activism as well as for the positivist version of judicial restraint (i.e., deference to legislative majorities without any higher law limitations).

Conservative jurisprudence today is thus in danger of being co-opted by the premises of activism. It is this danger that makes Walter Berns's devastating critique of Holmes so vital. (*N.b.,* for the same reason the essay may be compared to Harry Jaffa's indictment of Southern traditionalism in Part One.) A resident scholar at the American Enterprise Institute and a prominent interpreter of the Supreme Court, Berns has written an essay that shatters the Holmes legend.

The trend of recent Supreme Court decisions on affirmative action has been toward expanding already existing programs, many of which amount to exemptions from the equal protection of the laws, into a standing system of mandatory racial entitlements. The line is that the quotas are only temporary and will be dismantled when the victory over racial injustice is won. Thomas Sowell, an insightful economist and social commentator, demonstrates in his book *Civil Rights: Rhetoric or Reality?* why that promise is an illusion and why the justifications for most affirmative action programs are wrong-headed. In this excerpt, he explains the logical and statistical fallacies used to disguise the ideological passions (what he calls the "civil rights vision") animating the contemporary civil rights movement, implicitly distinguishing the principle of equal opportunity as the heart of a genuine civil rights policy. His appreciation of the variety and complexity of modern social relations is a bracing corrective to the lifeless abstractions of social engineers.

In the final essay in this section, Joseph Sobran confronts the assault on the family and on moral precepts in general. He asks, how is it possible for the Supreme Court, in a divided opinion, to have unleashed abortion on demand upon American society? That is to say, how could the abortion mills have sprung not only into life but into public respectability (at least putative respectability)? With the astuteness that he brings to all his social commentary, Sobran, a senior editor of *National Review,* observes:

The arguments for abortion have shifted suspiciously. . . . Once it was a necessary evil whose malign effects would be *minimized* by legalization. Then we weren't supposed to pass judgment: It was a "religious" issue concerning which legislation was, under secular government, inappropriate. Today we are urged to recognize it as a positive good, a "basic right." Not only must we tolerate it, we must pay for it with public funds. It has become a "right of conscience," and never mind the consciences of taxpayers who don't want to pay for it.

The enormity of legalized abortion, he argues, is part of a much larger phenomenon, what he calls the "abortion culture," comprising legalized pornography, sex education in the schools, established irreligion in the public square. Sobran calculates that the vectors of the abortion culture, dominating the universities and elite opinion, point squarely toward socialism; and by the argument from paradox, at which technique he is a master, he illustrates how the new culture is gradually displacing the old in America. Anecdote and example follow one another in quick succession, the juxtapositions piling up until the point is clear, vivid, unforgettable. This essay first appeared in the *Human Life Review* and is reprinted in Sobran's book, *Single Issues.* As a statement of the outrage that energized the New Right and launched social conservatives into American politics by the millions beginning in the late 1960s, it is invaluable; but it is insightful, too, on the potential sources of social regeneration in America. For it is to revelation *and* reason, to the harmony of the revealed truths of religion and the self-evident truths of the Declaration of Independence, that Sobran appeals for moral sustenance.

EDWARD C. BANFIELD

In Defense of the American Party System

The American party system has been criticized on four main grounds: (1) the parties do not offer the electorate a choice in terms of fundamental principles; their platforms are very similar and mean next to nothing; (2) they cannot discipline those whom they elect, and therefore they cannot carry their platforms into effect; (3) they are held together and motivated less by political principle than by desire for personal, often material, gain, and by sectional and ethnic loyalties; consequently party politics is personal and parochial; and (4) their structure is such that they cannot correctly represent the opinion of the electorate; in much of the country there is in effect only one party, and everywhere large contributors and special interests exercise undue influence within the party.[1]

These criticisms may be summarized by saying that the structure and operation of the parties do not accord with the theory of democracy or, more precisely, with that theory of it which says that everyone should have a vote, that every vote should be given exactly the same weight, and that the majority should rule.

"It is a serious matter," says Maurice Duverger, a French political scientist who considers American party organizations "archaic" and "undemocratic," "that the greatest nation in the world, which is assuming responsibilities on a worldwide scale, should be based on a party system entirely directed towards very narrow local horizons."[2] He and other critics of the American party system do not, however, base their criticism on the performance of the American government. They are concerned about procedures, not results. They ask whether the structure and operation of the parties is consistent with the logic of democracy, not whether the party system produces—and maintains—a good society, meaning, among other things, one in which desirable human types flourish, the rights of individuals are respected, and matters affecting the common good are decided, as nearly as possible, by reasonable discussion.[3]

If they were to evaluate the party system on the basis of results, they would have to conclude that on the whole it is a good one. It has played an important part (no one can say how important, of course, for innumerable causal forces have been at work along with it) in the production of

From *Political Parties, U.S.A.*, ed. Robert A. Goldwin (Chicago: Rand McNally, 1961), 21–39. Copyright 1961 by Kenyon College Public Affairs Conference Center. Reprinted by permission.

a society which, despite all its faults, is as near to being a good one as any and nearer by far than most; it has provided governments which, by the standards appropriate to apply to governments, have been humane and, in some crises, bold and enterprising; it has done relatively little to impede economic growth and in some ways has facilitated it; except for the Civil War, when it was, as Henry Jones Ford said, "the last bond of union to give way,"[4] it has tended to check violence, moderate conflict, and narrow the cleavages within the society; it has never produced, or very seriously threatened to produce, either mob rule or tyranny, and it has shown a marvelous ability to adapt to changing circumstances.

Not only has the American party system produced good results, it has produced better ones than have been produced almost anywhere else by other systems. Anyone who reflects on recent history must be struck by the following paradox: Those party systems that have been more democratic in structure and procedure have proved least able to maintain democracy; those that have been most undemocratic in structure and procedure—conspicuously those of the United States and Britain—have proved to be the bulwarks of democracy and of civilization.

This paper explores this paradox. It maintains that there is an inherent antagonism between "democracy of procedure" and "production of, and maintenance of, a good society," that some defects of procedure are indispensable conditions of success from the standpoint of results, and that what the critics call the "archaic" character of the American party system is a very small price to pay for government that can be relied upon to balance satisfactorily the several conflicting ends that must be served.

Difficulties in Planning Change

Before entering into these matters, it may be well to remind the reader how difficult is the problem of planning social change.

Social relationships constitute systems: They are mutually related in such a manner that a change in one tends to produce changes in all of the others. If we change the party system in one respect, even a seemingly trivial one, we are likely to set in motion a succession of changes which will not come to an end until the whole system has been changed. The party system, moreover, is an element of a larger political system and of a social system. A small change in the structure or operation of parties may have important consequences for, say, the family, religion, or the business firm.

The changes that we intend when making a reform, if they occur at all, are always accompanied by others that we do not intend. These others may occur at points in the system far removed from the one where the change was initiated and be apparently unrelated to it. Commonly changes produced indirectly and unintentionally turn out to be much more important than the ones that were sought. This is a fact that is seldom fully taken into account. Those who support a particular reform are often indifferent to its consequences for values that they either do not share or consider subordinate. Even those who feel obliged to take a wide range of values into account do not usually try very hard to anticipate the indirect consequences of reforms—often for a very good reason: The complexity of the social system makes the attempt implausible. Usually we take it on faith that the consequences we get by intention justify the risk we take of incurring others that we do not intend or want. Since these others are seldom recognized as consequences of our action at all (they either go unnoticed or seem to have "just happened"), the basis of our faith is not called into question.

No doubt it is a great help to the practical reformer to have tunnel vision. But those who are concerned with the welfare of society as a whole must take the widest perspective possible. They must try to identify all of the consequences that will follow from a reform—the unintended ones no less than the intended, the remote, contingent, and imponderable no less than the immediate, certain, the specifiable. And they must evaluate all of these consequences in the light of a comprehensive system of values.

Those who devise "improvements" to a social system can rarely hope to attain all of their ends; usually they must be prepared to sacrifice some of them to achieve others. This is so because resources are usually limited and also because there are often incompatibilities among ends such that a gain in terms of some necessarily involves a loss in terms of others. The reformer must therefore economize. He must be able to assign priorities to all ends in such a way that he can tell how much of each to sacrifice for how much of others, on various assumptions as to "supply."

The critics of the party system tend to value democratic procedure for its own sake, that is, apart from the results it produces. There is no reason why they should not do so. But they are in error when they do not recognize that other values of equal or greater importance are often in conflict with democratic procedure, and that when they are, some sacrifice of it is essential in order to serve the other values adequately. If they faced up to the necessity of assigning priorities among all of the irrelevant ends, they would not, it is safe to say, put "democratic procedure" first. Probably they, and most Americans, would order the ends as follows:

1. The party system must above all else provide governments having the will and capacity to preserve the society and to protect its members. Any sacrifice in other ends ought to be accepted if it is indispensable to securing this end.

2. The party system must insure periodic opportunity to change the government by free elections. Any sacrifice of other ends (except the one mentioned) ought to be accepted if it is indispensable to securing this one.

3. The party system should promote the welfare of the people. By "welfare" is meant some combination of two kinds of values: "principles," what is thought to be good for the society, described in rather general terms, and "interests," the ends individuals and groups seek to attain for their own good, as distinguished from that of the society. The party system should produce governments that assert the supremacy of principles over interests in some matters; in others it should allow interests to prevail and should facilitate the competitive exercise of influence.

4. The party system should moderate and restrain such conflict as would threaten the good health of the society. Other conflict it should not discourage.

5. The party system should promote and exemplify democracy, meaning reasonable discussion of matters affecting the common good in which every voice is heard.

These ends have been listed in what most Americans would probably consider a descending order of importance. In devising a party system, we ought not to try to serve fully each higher end before serving the one below it at all. The first two ends are exceptions to this rule, however: each of them must be attained even if the others are not served at all. With respect to the remaining three, the problem is to achieve a proper balance—one such that no reallocation from one end to another would add to the sum of value.

Finally, we must realize that we can rarely make important social changes by intention. The most we can do is to make such minor changes as may be consistent with, and more or less implied by, the fixed features of the situation in which we are placed. Even to make minor changes in an institution like a political party requires influence of a kind and amount that no group of reformers is likely to have or to be able to acquire. It is idle to propose reforms that are merely desirable. There must also be some possibility of showing, if only in a rough and conjectural way, that they might be carried into effect.

With respect to the American party system, it seems obvious that the crucial features of the situation are all fixed. The size of our country, the class and cultural heterogeneity of our people, the number and variety of their interests, the constitutionally given fragmentation of formal authority, the wide distribution of power which follows from it, the inveterate taste of Americans for participation in the day-to-day conduct of government when their interests are directly at stake—these are all unalterable features of the situation. Taken together, they mean that the party system can be reformed only within very narrow limits.

A Model Party System

Let us imagine a system free of the alleged defects of ours. In this model system, every citizen is motivated—highly so—by political principles, not subsidiary ones, but ones having to do with the very basis of the society. (In France and Italy, Duverger says approvingly, political warfare "is not concerned with subsidiary principles but with the very foundations of the state and the nature of the regime."[5]) The electoral system, moreover, is such as to give every side on every issue exactly the weight that its numbers in the population warrant; no group or interest is over- or underrepresented. ("One's thoughts turn," Duverger says, "to the possibility of a truly scientific democracy, in which parliament would be made up of a true sample of the citizens reproducing on a reduced scale the exact composition of the nation, made up, that is, according to the very methods that are used as a basis for public opinion surveys like the Gallup polls."[6])

Assuming that the society is divided by the usual number of cleavages (e.g., haves versus have-nots, segregationists versus antisegregationists, isolationists versus internationalists, etc.), the following would result:

1. There would be a great many parties, for no citizen would support a party with which he did not agree fully.

2. The parties would tend to be single-issue ones. If logically unrelated issues (for instance, segregation and isolationism) were linked together in a party program, only those voters would support the party who chanced to be on the same side of all of the linked issues. The number of these voters would decrease as the number of issues so linked increased.

3. Parties would be short-lived. They would come into and pass out of existence with the single issues they were organized to fight.

4. In their election campaigns and propaganda, parties would emphasize their single defining principles. This would tend to widen the cleavages along which the parties were formed.

5. Ideological issues, not practical problems, would constitute the substance of politics.[7]

6. The number of such issues pressing for settlement at any one time (but being incapable of settlement because of their ideological character) would always be more than the system could accommodate.[8]

7. Coalitions of parties would seldom form, and such as did form would be highly unstable. Party leaders would find compromise almost impossible because it would lead to loss of highly principled supporters.

8. Coalitions of parties being unstable, governments would also be unstable and therefore lacking in power and decision.

9. Those selected for positions of political leadership would tend to be ideologues skilled in party dialectics and symbolizing the party and its positions. Practical men, especially those with a talent for compromise and those symbolizing qualities common to the whole society, would be excluded from politics.

10. Matters having no ideological significance (a category that includes most local issues) would either be endowed with a spurious one or else would be left outside the sphere of politics altogether.[9]

These points should suffice to show that a system with a perfectly democratic structure would not produce results acceptable in terms of the criteria already listed.

Now let us introduce into the model system one of the alleged defects which the critics find most objectionable in the American party system. Let us suppose that at least half of the electorate is prevailed upon to exchange its vote in matters of fundamental principle for advantages that have nothing to do with principle, especially private profit, sectional gain, and nationality "recognition."

One effect of this would be to reduce greatly the intensity of ideological conflict and to make political life more stable and conservative. This, in fact, seems to be what happened when American parties first came into being. John Adams tells in his diary how in 1794 "ten thousand people in the streets of Philadelphia, day after day, threatened to drag Washington out of his house and effect a revolution in the government, or compel it to declare war in favor of the French Revolution and against England."[10] After parties had been organized, however, patronage took the place of ideological fervor. "The clubs of the social revolutionists which had sprung up in the cities, blazing with incendiary ideas caught from the French Revolution," Henry Jones Ford says, "were converted into party workers, and their behavior was moderated by considerations of party interest."[11]

Another effect would be to encourage the formation of a few (probably two) stable parties. These might begin as alliances among the profit minded, the sectional minded, and the nationality minded, but to attract support from principled voters the parties would have to seem to stand for something—indeed, for anything and everything. Since no faction of them could hope to win an election by itself, principled voters would attach themselves to those parties that they found least objectionable. The parties would develop corporate identities and mystiques; principled voters would then subordinate their differences out of "loyalty" to the party and in response to its demands for "regularity." Competition for middle-of-the-road support would cause the parties to offer very similar programs. This competition might lead to there being only two parties, but this result would probably be insured by introducing another supposed defect into the system: a principle of representation (single-member districts and plurality voting) which, by letting the winner take all, would force small parties to join large ones in order to have some chance of winning.

In one way or another, the "defects" of the system would tend to produce these consequences—consequences which have in fact been produced in the United States:

1. A strong and stable government would be possible. The country would be governed by the party that won the election, or (given the particular complexities of the American system) by two closely similar parties engaged in give-and-take and, therefore, in a sense constituting one party under two names.

2. There would be a high degree of continuity between administrations elected from different parties. Elections would not shake the nation to its foundations because the competing parties would be fundamentally in agreement. Agreement would be so built in by countless compromises within the parties (each of which would be under the necessity of attracting middle-of-the-road support) that a change of party would seldom entail complete reversal of policy in an important matter.

3. There would exist many substructures of power that would be largely or wholly impervious to the influence of political principle or ideology. "Machines"—party organizations of the profit minded, the sectional minded, and the nationality minded—would not be inclined to offer pie in the sky or to stir the emotions of the masses because they could count upon getting their votes in other ways. These essentially apolitical centers of power would therefore exert a stabilizing and conservative influence throughout the political system. By making businesslike deals with the leaders of the "machines," the president could sometimes buy freedom to do as he thought best in matters of principle.

4. The diversity of the principles and the multiplicity of the interests within the party would be another source of strength to the leader elected from it. He could afford to offend some elements of the party on any particular question because there would be enough other elements unaffected (or even gratified) to assure his position. The more fragmented his party, the less attention he would have to pay to any one fragment of it.

5. The assertion of interests (as distinguished from principles) would be encouraged. The profit minded, the sectional minded, and the nationality minded would in effect give up representation on matters of principle in order to get it on matters involving their interests. Thus two different systems of representation would work simultaneously. The party leader would act as a trustee, disregarding interests in favor of principles. ("Congress represents locality, the President represents the nation," Ford wrote in 1898.[12]) Meanwhile legislators dependent on machines and, in general, on profit minded, sectional minded, and nationality minded voters would act as agents of interests. The trustee of principles (the president) and the agents of interests (congressmen) would of necessity bargain with each other; by allowing the agents of interests some successes—but only in this way—the trustee of principles could win their support in the matters he considered most important. Thus, there would be achieved that balancing of interests and of interests

against principles (the most important principles usually being vindicated) that a good party system should produce.

6. The formation of deep cleavages would nevertheless be discouraged. The competition of the parties for the middle-of-the-road vote; their tendency to select practical men of wide popular appeal, rather than ideologues, for positions of leadership; and the definition of the politicians' task as being that of finding the terms on which people who disagree will work together, rather than that of sharpening ideological points—these would all be unifying tendencies.

Some critics of the American party system have attributed its alleged defects to the absence of class consciousness in our society. No doubt there is some truth in this. But causality may run the other way also. We may be lacking in class consciousness because our politicians are prevented by the nature of the party system from popularizing the rhetoric of the class struggle; the party system actually induces the voter to forgo the allurements of principle and ideology by offering him things he values more: for example, personal profit, sectional advantage, and nationality "recognition."[13]

In those countries where the voter expresses at the polls his ideology rather than his interests, he may do so not from choice but because the party system leaves him no alternative. In such countries, class warfare may be the principal subject matter of politics simply because matters of greater importance to the voters are not at stake.

Experience in the underdeveloped areas seems to bear out the claim that certain "defects" in a party system may be essential to good government. The transplanted "defects" of the American party system are among the factors that have made the Philippines the most democratic country in Southeast Asia. According to Professor Lucian W. Pye:

The image of leadership that evolved in the Philippines was clearly that of the politician who looked after the particular interests of voters. Elsewhere the pattern of the Western impact under colonialism gave emphasis to the role of the rational administrator who apparently operated according to the principles of efficiency and who was not supposed to be influenced by political pressures within the society. Consequently, when the politicians emerged in these societies, they tended to become the champions of nationalistic ideologies and even the enemies of the rational administrators.[14]

In the Philippines, as at home, our party system has had the defects of its virtues—and the virtues of its defects. On the one hand, Pye says, the Philippines have never had an efficient administrative machinery, and the demand for higher standards of personal integrity among their public officials is reminiscent of the muckraking era of American politics; on the other hand, "the Philippine electorate seems to recognize that the most fundamental question in politics is who is going to control the government, and thus, while the parties have not had to expend much effort in trying to distinguish themselves ideologically from each other, the expenditures of money on political campaigns in the Philippines are probably the highest in proportion to per capita income of any country in the world."[15]

Making Parties "Responsible"

Some think that the American party system can be reformed without changing its nature essentially. Several years ago, a Committee on Parties of the American Political Science Association proposed making certain "readjustments" in the structure and operation of the party system to eliminate its "defects." These readjustments, the committee said, would give the electorate "a proper range of choice between alternatives" in the form of programs to which the parties would be committed and which they would have sufficient internal cohesion to carry into effect. Thus, the two-party system would be made more "responsible."[16]

What this means is not at all clear. *Responsibility* here seems to be a synonym for accountability, that is, the condition of being subject to being called to account and made to take corrective action in response to criticism. In the case of a party, this can mean nothing except going before an electorate, and in this sense all parties are by definition responsible. *Responsibility* can have no other meaning in this context; as William Graham Sumner remarked, "a party is an abstraction; it cannot be held responsible or punished; if it is deprived of power it fades into thin air and the men who composed it, especially those who did the mischief and needed discipline, quickly reappear in the new majority."[17]

Leaving aside both the question of what "responsibility" means when applied to a party and the more important one of whether as a matter of practical politics such "readjustments" could be made, let us consider how the political system would probably be affected by the changes proposed.

The hope that the two-party system might be made to offer a choice between distinct alternatives is illusory for at least two reasons. One is that a party which does not move to the middle of the road to compete for votes condemns itself to defeat and eventually, if it does not change its ways, to destruction. But even if this were not the case, the parties could not present the electorate with what reformers think of as "a valid choice." The reason is that the issues in our national life are such that there does not exist any one grand principle by which the electorate could be divided into two camps such that every voter in each camp would be on the "same" side of all issues. The idea of "left" and "right" is as close as we come to having such a grand principle, and it has little or no application to many issues.[18] The logic of "left" and "right" does not, for example, imply opposite or even different positions on (for example) foreign policy, civil liberties, or farm subsidies. Without a grand principle which will make unities—opposed unities—of the party programs, the electorate cannot be offered "a valid choice." A choice between two market baskets, each of which contains an assortment of unrelated items, some of which are liked and some of which are disliked, is not a "valid" choice in the same sense that a choice between two market baskets, each of which contains items that "belong together" is a "valid" one. In the American party system, most items are logically unrelated. This being so, "valid" choice would become possible only if the number of parties was increased to allow each party to stand for items that *were* logically related, if one issue became important to the exclusion of all the others, or if, by the elaboration of myth and ideology, pseudo-logical relations were established among items.

The hope that the parties might commit themselves to carry out their programs is also illusory. A party could do this only if its leaders were able to tell the president and the party members in Congress what to do, and could discipline them if they failed to do it. Therefore, unless, like the Russians, we were to have two sets of national leaders, one in governmental office and another much more important one in party office, it would be necessary for our elected leaders—in effect, the president, since only he and the vice-president are elected by the whole nation—to control the congressmen and senators of their party. This would be possible only if the president could deny reelection to members of Congress who did not support the party program. Thus, instead of merely bringing forward and electing candidates, as they do now, "responsible" parties would have to govern the country. We would have a parliamentary system with the president in a position somewhat like that of the British prime minister, except (a very important difference) that, not being a part of the legislature, he could not use it as a vehicle through which to exert his leadership.[19] The legislature would in fact have no function at all.

This great shift of power to the president would remedy another "defect" in the party system: its receptivity to the demands of interest groups.[20] With the president in full control of Congress, logrolling would cease or virtually cease. It would do so because no one could any longer make the president pay a price for assistance in getting legislation passed; the traders who now sell their bits and pieces of power to the highest bidders would have to lower their prices and would probably go out of business. With their opportunities for exercising influence vastly reduced, interest groups would be less enterprising both in their efforts to anticipate the effects of governmental action and in bringing their views to the attention of the policymakers.

The making of policy would thus pass largely into the hands of technical experts within the majority party, the White House, and the executive departments. These would be mindful of principles and impatient of interests. They would endeavor to make "coherent" policies, meaning, presumably, policies not based on compromise.[21] In all important matters, however, "the public interest" would prove an insufficient guide; the experts, when confronted with the necessity of choosing between alternatives that were equally in the public interest—that is, when no authoritative, ultimate criterion of choice existed for them to apply—would by the very necessities of the case have to balance the competing values as best they could, which means that they would have to fall back upon their personal tastes or professional biases.[22] Thus they would do badly (but in the name of "impartial administration") what is now done reasonably well by the political process.

The destruction of political traders and of local centers of power would mean also that the president's power would derive from somewhat different sources than at present. Instead of relying upon logrolling and patronage to get the votes he would need in Congress, he would have to rely upon direct appeals by the electorate. To some extent he might manipulate the electorate by charm and personality; TV and the arts of Madison Avenue would become more important in politics. But in order to get elected he would have to depend also, and to a greater extent, upon appeals to political principle or ideology. Whereas the political trader maintains his control by giving and withholding favors to individuals (a circumstance which makes his control both dependable in its operation and cheap), the president would have to maintain *his* by the uncertain and costly expedient of offering to whole classes of people—the farmer, the aged, the home owner, and so on—advantages that they would have only at each other's expense. If charm and the promise of "something for everybody" did not yield the amount of power he required to govern the country, the president might find it necessary to exploit whatever antagonisms within the society might be made to yield more power. Class and ethnic differences might in this event serve somewhat the same function as logrolling and patronage do now. Mayor LaGuardia, for example, depended for power upon direct, personal appeal to the voters rather than upon organization. His charm and his support of "liberal" programs are well remembered. But it should not be forgotten that he depended also upon exploitation of ethnic loyalties and antipathies. According to Robert Moses,

It must be admitted that in exploiting racial and religious prejudices LaGuardia could run circles around the bosses he despised and derided. When it came to raking ashes of Old World hates, warming ancient grudges, waving the bloody shirt, tuning the ear to ancestral voices, he could easily outdemagogue the demagogues. And for what purpose? To redress old wrongs abroad? To combat foreign levy or malice domestic? To produce peace on the Danube, the Nile, the Jordan? Not on your tintype. Fiorello LaGuardia knew better. He knew that the aim of the rabble rousers is simply to shoo into office for entirely extraneous, illogical and even silly reasons the municipal officials who clean city streets, teach in schools, protect, house and keep healthy, strong and happy millions of people crowded together here.[23]

That a president might rely more upon appeals to political principle does not at all mean that better judgments or results would follow. For the discussion of principles would probably not be *serious;* it would be for the purpose of securing popular interest and consent, not of finding a wise or right course of action. As long ago as 1886, Sir Henry Sumner Maine observed that democracy was tending toward government by salesmanship. Party and corruption had in the past always been relied upon to bring men under civil discipline, he said, but now a third expedient had been discovered:

This is generalization, the trick of rapidly framing, and confidently uttering, general propositions of political subjects. . . . General formulas, which can be seen on examination to have been arrived at by attending only to particulars few, trivial or irrelevant, are turned out in as much profusion as if they dropped from an intellectual machine; and debates in the House of Commons may be constantly read, which consisted wholly in the exchange of weak generalities and strong personalities. On a pure Democracy this class of general formulas has a prodigious effect. Crowds of men can be got to assent to general statements, clothed in striking language, but unverified and perhaps incapable of verification; and thus there is formed a sort of sham and pretence of concurrent opinion. There has been a loose acquiescence in a vague proposition, and then the People, whose voice is the voice of God, is assumed to have spoken.[24]

Efforts to create "levity of assent," as Maine called it, will become more important in our politics to the extent that other means of bringing men under civil discipline are given up or lost.

The Danger of Meddling

A political system is an accident. It is an accumulation of habits, customs, prejudices, and principles that have survived a long process of trial and error and of ceaseless response to changing circumstance. If the system works well on the whole, it is a lucky accident—the luckiest, indeed, that can befall a society, for all of the institutions of the society, and thus its entire character and that of the human types formed within it, depend ultimately upon the government and the political order.

To meddle with the structure and operation of a successful political system is therefore the greatest foolishness that men are capable of. Because the system is intricate beyond comprehension, the chance of improving it in the ways intended is slight, whereas the danger of disturbing its working and of setting off a succession of unwanted effects that will extend throughout the whole society is great.

Democracy must always meddle, however. An immanent logic impels it to self-reform, and if other forces do not prevent, it must sooner or later reform itself out of existence.[25]

The logic of this is as follows. The ideal of democracy legitimates only such power as arises out of reasonable discussion about the common good in which all participate. Power that comes into being in any other way (e.g., by corruption, logrolling, appeals to sentiment or prejudice, the exercise of charm or charisma, "hasty generalization," terror, etc.) is radically undemocratic, and people inspired by the democratic ideal will therefore endeavor to eliminate it by destroying, or reforming whatever practices or institutions give rise to it.

No society, however, can be governed *solely* by reasonable discussion about the common good; even in a society of angels there might be disagreement about what the common good requires in the concrete case.[26] In most societies, far more power is needed to maintain civil discipline and protect the society from its enemies than can be got simply by reasonable discussion about the common good. Therefore the logical culmination of democratic reform, viz., the elimination of all undemo-cratic sources of power, would render government—and therefore the preservation of the society—impossible. Democratic reform can never reach this point, of course, because, before reaching it, democracy itself would be destroyed and the impetus to further reform removed.

So far as it does succeed, however, the tendency of democratic reform is to reduce the power available for government. Such loss of power as occurs from the elimination of undemocratic sources of it will seldom be offset by increases in power of the kind that arises from reasonable discussion about the common good. Since there is a point beyond which no increase in democratic power is possible (the capacity of a society to engage in reasonable discussion about the common good being limited), reform, if carried far enough, must finally reduce the quantity of power.

There is, then, a danger that reform will chip away the foundations of power upon which the society rests. But this is not the only danger. A greater one, probably, is that in making some forms of undemocratic power less plentiful, reform may make others more plentiful, and by so doing set off changes that will ramify throughout the political system, changing its character completely. If, for example, politicians cannot get power by the methods of the machine (corruption, favor giving, and patronage), they may get it by other methods, such as charm, salesman-ship, and "hasty generalization." The new methods may be better than the old by most standards (they cannot, of course, be better by the standard of democracy, according to which *all* power not arising from reasonable discussion about the common good is absolutely illegitimate); but even if they are better, the new methods may not serve as well as the old, or may not serve at all, in maintaining an effective political system and a good society.

Reform is, of course, far from being the only force at work. Compared to the other forces, some of which tend to produce competing changes and others of which tend to check all change, reform may be of slight effect. This is certainly true in general of such reform as is sought through formal organizations by people called *reformers*. It is much less true of reform in the broader sense of the general view and disposition of "the great body of right-thinking people." This kind of reform is likely to be of pervasive importance in the long run, although its effects are seldom what anyone intended.

Jefferson may have been right in saying that democracy cannot exist without a wide diffusion of knowledge throughout the society. But it may be right also to say that it cannot exist *with* it. For as we become a better and more democratic society, our very goodness and democracy may lead us to destroy goodness and democracy in the effort to increase and perfect them.

NOTES

1. These criticisms are made, for example, by the French political scientist, Maurice Duverger, in *Political Parties* (New York: Wiley, 1954). For similar criticisms by Americans, see especially Committee on Political Parties of the American Political Science Association, *Toward a More Responsible Two-Party System* (New York: Rinehart, 1950), and E. E. Schattschneider, *Party Government* (New York: Farrar & Rinehart, 1942). Criticisms of American parties are summarized and analyzed in Austin Ranney, *The Doctrine of Responsible Party Government* (Urbana: University of Illinois Press, 1954). Defenses of the American party system include A. Lawrence Lowell, *Essays on Government* (Boston: Houghton Mifflin, 1889), chapters I, II; Arthur N. Holcombe, *The Political Parties of Today* (New York: Harper, 1925); and *Our More Perfect Union* (Cambridge: Harvard University Press, 1950); Pendleton Herring, *The Politics of Democracy* (New York: Norton, 1940); and Herbert Agar, *The Price of Union* (Boston: Houghton Mifflin, 1950).
2. Duverger, *Political Parties*, 53.
3. The report of the Committee on Parties of the American Political Science Association, cited before, discusses the "effectiveness" of parties entirely in terms of procedure. Duverger does the same.
4. Henry Jones Ford, *The Rise and Growth of American Politics* (New York: Macmillan, 1900), 303.
5. Duverger, *Political Parties*, 419.
6. Ibid., 158.
7. In France, according to Siegfried, "every argument becomes a matter of principle; the practical results are relegated to second place." André Siegfried, "Stable Instability in France," *Foreign Affairs*, XXXIV (April 1956): 395.
8. According to Siegfried: "The difficulty is that too many questions of fundamental importance on which the various parties have cause to disagree have come up for discussion at one time." Ibid., 399.
9. In France, Luethy says, "politics," which deals with ideological matters, and the "state," i.e., the bureaucracy, which deals with practical ones, function "in watertight compartments" with the consequence that French democracy is an amalgam of absolutist administration on the one hand and of anarchy, tumultuous or latent, on the other.

Herbert Luethy, *France Against Herself* (New York: Meridian Books, 1957), 61. On this see also Siegfried, "Stable Instability," 399.

10. Quoted by Henry Jones Ford, *American Politics,* 125.

11. Ibid., 144.

12. Ibid., 187. For a recent brilliant account of how the two systems of representation work, see Willmoore Kendall, "The Two Majorities," *Midwest Journal of Political Science* IV, no. 4 (November 1960), 317–45.

13. "In coordinating the various elements of the population for political purposes," Ford says, "party organization tends at the same time to fuse them into one mass of citizenship, pervaded by a common order of ideas and sentiments, and actuated by the same class of motives. This is probably the secret of the powerful solvent influence which American civilization exerts upon the enormous deposits of alien population thrown upon this country by the torrent of emigration. Racial and religious antipathies, which present the most threatening problems to countries governed upon parliamentary principles, melt with amazing rapidity in the warm flow of a party spirit which is constantly demanding, and is able to reward the subordination of local and particular interests to national purposes." (*American Politics,* 306–307.)

14. Lucian W. Pye, "The Politics of Southeast Asia," in G. Almond and J. Coleman, eds., *The Politics of the Developing Areas* (Princeton, N.J.: Princeton University Press, 1969), 97.

15. Ibid., 123, 126.

16. See the Committee Report, *Two Party System,* 1, 85.

17. William Graham Sumner, *The Challenge of Facts* (New Haven, Conn.: Yale University Press, 1914), 271–72.

18. One can imagine a set of symbols connected with a diffuse ideology dividing the society into two camps, and to a certain extent this exists. But it is hard to see in what sense this would present the electorate with "a valid choice." In other words, the existence of a body of nonsense which is treated as if it were a grand principle ought not to be regarded by reasonable critics of the party system as equivalent to the grand principle itself.

19. The prime minister is the leader of his party outside as well as inside Parliament. Party leaders who are not also members of Parliament take no part in the running of the government, as the late Professor Harold Laski discovered when, as a leader of the Labour party, he presumed to give advice to Prime Minister Attlee. The party leaders discipline their followers by threatening to deprive them of renomination; accordingly most members of the House are "backbenchers" who participate in its affairs only as audience, and the function of the House as a whole is to criticize and advise the leaders of the majority party.

20. Cf. Report of the Committee on Parties, *Two Party System,* 19–20.

21. Ibid., 19.

22. This argument is developed in E. C. Banfield, *Political Influence* (Glencoe, Ill.: Free Press, 1961), Chapter 12.

23. Robert Moses, *LaGuardia: A Salute and a Memoir* (New York: Simon & Schuster, 1957), 37–38.

24. Sir Henry Sumner Maine, *Popular Government* (New York: Henry Holt, 1886), 106–108.

25. For data and analysis pertinent to the discussion that follows, see James Q. Wilson, *The Amateur Democrat* (Chicago: University of Chicago Press, 1962).

26. See Yves R. Simon, *The Philosophy of Democratic Government* (Chicago: University of Chicago Press, 1951), Chapter 1.

WALTER BERNS

Oliver Wendell Holmes, Jr., and the Question of Judicial Activism

It is not customary to regard judges as statesmen, but the unique powers of the Supreme Court of the United States make it easier for an American judge to gain this distinction. In a very real sense the task of expounding the Constitution converts the Supreme Court justice into a lawgiver, because to expound the meaning of the powers granted, the limits imposed, and the relations established by this document is to give the nation the law by which it lives. Nor is this merely law in the narrow sense of the term. On the contrary, in the course of its regular work the Court has the opportunity to give the nation the principles by which it governs itself, which is to say, the principles by which it lives. An English friend of Oliver Wendell Holmes understood this when he said that the "Supreme Court of the United States is not merely a tribunal where the controversies of men are resolved; it is also a legislature in which the life of the nation is given form and color."[1]

It is sometimes said that the Court follows the election returns, and there is some truth to this; but in a larger sense the relationship is reversed, and what the Court says to the nation is likely to be of more importance than what the nation says to the Court. The Court speaks mainly through its decisions, and legal decisions embody principles. In the case of constitutional decisions these are principles that are supposed to guide the conduct of public affairs. The Court also speaks in its opinions, and these opinions can affect public affairs by affecting public sentiment. "With public sentiment, nothing can fail; without it nothing can succeed," Abraham Lincoln said; and the democratic statesman must heed the sentiment expressed by the public in an election. But Lincoln knew that the public did not generate a sentiment on public questions independent of the words and deeds of political leaders, so he went on to add that "he who moulds public sentiment, goes deeper than he who enacts statutes or pronounces decisions [because he] makes statutes and decisions possible or impossible to be executed."[2] Opinions in important constitutional cases may play as significant a role in the molding of public sentiment as do the decisions making the law. Professor Edmond Cahn

From Walter Berns, "Oliver Wendell Holmes, Jr." in Morton Frisch and Richard Stevens, eds., *American Political Thought* (Itasca, Ill.: F. E. Peacock Publishers, 1983). Reprinted by permission of F. E. Peacock Publishers.

had this in mind when he said of one member of the current Court, Justice Hugo Black, that he is not only "one of the few authentically great judges in the history of the American bench," but also a member of a "certain select company of heroes [Thomas Jefferson, James Madison, John Marshall and Abraham Lincoln] who, at various crises in the destiny of our land, have created, nurtured, and preserved the essence of the American ideal."[3] Perhaps some students of the contemporary political situation would regard this praise of Black as extravagant, doubting that any jurist, however great, can justly be put in the exalted company of those who found and preserve great nations. But Lincoln's greatness consisted as much in his words as in his deeds, and anyone who knows, with Lincoln, that, generally speaking, laws depend on opinion, or sentiment, and that opinion is formed by words, knows the role of rhetoric in statesmanship. A seat on the bench, even the supreme bench, is not the equivalent of a presidential platform at Gettysburg when the president is Lincoln, but a great jurist's words do not fall on deaf ears; they are heard and studied by men outside the courtroom, by journalists and teachers, as well as by legislators, who themselves speak to the public and thereby sometimes teach it.

Oliver Wendell Holmes was a master of words and is commonly reckoned to be one of the greatest of our Supreme Court justices. He was born in 1841 and had already achieved a fair measure of fame by the time he took his place on the Supreme Court in 1902. The son of a famous father, he graduated from Harvard with the class of 1861 and served with distinction in the 20th Regiment, Massachusetts Volunteers, during the Civil War, being three times wounded. He returned to Harvard for his legal education, established his reputation as a legal scholar with the publication in 1881 of *The Common Law* and his reputation as a judge by his long service—almost twenty years—on the Supreme Judicial Court of Massachusetts. President Theodore Roosevelt appointed him to the Supreme Court of the United States in 1902, from which he retired in 1932 at the age of ninety-one, after almost thirty years' service. It was here that he acquired his reputation as one of America's greatest statesmen.

Men noted for their sobriety have praised him in the most extravagant of terms.

No judge of the Supreme Court has done more to establish it in the consciousness of the people. Mr. Justice Holmes is built into the structure of our national life and has written himself into the slender volume of the literature of all times.[4]

So wrote Felix Frankfurter, himself a celebrated jurist and professor of law. Benjamin Cardozo, who took Holmes's place on the Supreme Court on his retirement, said this of him: "He is today for all students of the law and for all students of human society the philosopher and the seer, the greatest of our age in the domain of jurisprudence, and one of the greatest of the ages."[5] "He has been a great judge because he has never ceased to be a philosopher," said Harold Laski.[6]

It is significant that unlike others who have gained fame as judges, Holmes is so frequently praised for his theoretical understanding as well as for his practical work on the Court. John Marshall was a great American judge, and to the extent that he is remembered at all in other places, it is solely for his services to his own country. Holmes, unlike Marshall and the others, occupied a place in a larger world. An American patriot surely—to the end of his life he recounted episodes from his wartime experiences at Ball's Bluff and Antietam—nevertheless he sometimes expressed a preference for England, or at least for certain qualities of English life and society.[7] Most judges would draw their friends from the political world; Holmes drew his from the world of ideas: Harold Laski, William James, Leslie Stephen, Sir Frederick Pollock, Henry and Brooks Adams. Marshall lived in American law, Holmes in Law; Marshall was concerned with men, and perforce, American men, Holmes reflected on Man. Brandeis studied the condition of workers in the textile industry and was a reformer; Holmes reflected on the place of man in the universe and was disdainful of reformers and, indeed, of the very possibility of reform. In short, Holmes was—or was said to be—a philosopher, and his work on the Supreme Court reflects this detachment from the affairs of the world around him. He was, as a more recent and more critical commentator so aptly puts it, "The Judge as Spectator."[8] According to Felix Frankfurter, this detachment was the source of the special quality he brought to his work on the Court.

Though he did not bring to the Court the training of a lawyer accustomed to great affairs, his work is yet in the school of statesmanship. Where others are guided through experience of life, he is led by the divination of the philosopher and the imagination of the poet. He is, indeed, philosopher become king.[9]

Despite such praise of Holmes, and the reputation of the men who bestowed it, it is the thesis of this chapter that no man who ever sat on the Supreme Court was less inclined and so poorly equipped to be a statesman or to teach, as a philosopher is supposed to teach, what a people needs to know in order to govern itself well.

The American government was constituted in order to secure the rights that all men, by nature, possess equally, and to do this with, and only with, the consent of the governed. So declares the Declaration of Independence. The two criteria of good government are complementary but, unfortunately, not necessarily compatible, as we know from our own history where it has so frequently been impossible to get the consent of the governed to policies designed to secure the rights of all. We sometimes forget that so many of our political failures as a nation have been due precisely to the fact that we are a democracy, a regime in which political power is held by the people.

The possibility of democratic misrule was not overlooked by the authors of the Constitution. Indeed, it is a principal theme of *The Federalist* that while the people will rule by right, they will misrule by inclination unless directed by instruction or, more emphatically, checked by carefully contrived institutions. One such institution is judicial review, by means of which the courts enforce the limits placed directly on governments and indirectly on the people. They will rule, but the courts—and primarily the Supreme Court—exist to prevent their ruling in such a manner as to deprive anyone of his "life, liberty, or property, without due process of law," or to deny "the equal protection of the laws," or to refer to another area in which the Court was active during Holmes' tenure, to abridge the freedom of speech. Thus, it has fallen to the courts to frame the remedies required to secure the rights.

To do this the courts must, of course, first define the rights, and as Sir William Blackstone makes clear in his *Commentaries on the Laws of England,* [10] however easy it might be to define a natural right, the rights to be secured by civil society, while derived from or based on natural rights, must be modified, or, strictly speaking, civilized. This is especially true of the right to acquire and use property.

Allowing for the variety of ways in which it manifested itself in litigation, the issue with which the Supreme Court was chiefly concerned during Holmes's tenure was the extent to which the Constitution permitted the national and state governments to regulate the business affairs of a modern industrial nation. Both were forbidden to deprive any person of liberty and property without due process of law, but it was no simple matter to expound the meaning of these deceptively simple words. The doctrine underlying one view of them, usually designated laissez-faire, derived ultimately from the political theory of John Locke and the political-economic theory of Adam Smith, according to which—to state it succinctly—the wealth of nations increases to the extent to which the avarice of men is not inhibited by moral and, what is more to the point here, legal restraints. Men were therefore to be let alone to pursue their own interests and the good of all would be served. But as it turned out, the self-interest of those who owned property—especially the new commercial or industrial property—would lead them to exploit children, to pay low wages, to require long hours of labor and pledges not to join labor unions; it would lead them to set high rates for their services and high prices for their goods. It was this behavior by the capitalists that was followed by the demands for regulation by the socialists or other reformers, and the issue was then drawn.

Holmes was not opposed to capitalism, but he became something of a hero to labor and to those who fostered what many at the time called socialist legislation because his views on the Constitution, and on the manner of its proper interpretation, led him frequently to dissent from decisions favored by capitalists. A famous example is his dissent in the New York Bakery case, *Lochner* v. *New York*.

In a statute typical of those coming out of the reform movement of the time, the state of New York had limited hours of employment in bakeries to sixty hours a week and ten hours a day. A bare majority of the Court invalidated the statute as a violation of the Fourteenth Amendment insofar as it deprived employer and employee alike of their liberty—and more precisely, their liberty to contract with respect to hours of employment.[11] Eight members of the Court acknowledged the priority of the rule of liberty to contract, which meant that in most cases the liberty to enter into contracts, whether for the buying and selling of labor or for the buying and selling of insurance,[12] could not be regulated by Congress or the states. The same eight members of the Court also acknowledged exceptions to this general rule, because they knew that no civil and constitutional right could be absolute. Utah, for example, was permitted to limit hours of employment in mines and smelters to eight hours a day, because of the character of the conditions of such labor, which were understood to be unhealthy and hazardous.[13] The issue to be judged was whether employment in bakeries was hazardous or detrimental to the health of those who contracted to work in them. On this issue the eight justices were divided, 5–3, the majority holding that it was not. Justice John Harlan, who wrote the dissenting opinion for the three, argued, one would have thought persuasively, that the conditions in bakeries led to a high incidence of respiratory diseases, among other things; but his effort did not persuade the five led by Justice Rufus Peckham.

Holmes was alone in his dissent. In what was to become one of his most famous opinions, he objected to the Court's disposition of the case and, as well, to the manner in which it framed the issue. For him the case did not turn on its particular facts; the conditions in bakeries were irrelevant. Indeed, the Constitution was silent on the economic issue:

This case is decided upon an economic theory which a large part of the country does not entertain. If it were a question whether I agreed with that theory, I should desire to study it further and long before making up my mind. But I do not conceive that to be my duty, because I strongly believe that my agreement or disagreement has nothing to do with the right of the majority to embody their opinions in law. . . . [A] constitution is not intended to embody a particular economic theory, whether of paternalism and the organic relation of the citizen to the State or of *laissez faire*. It is made for people of fundamentally differing views. . . .[14]

Here, as in so many cases to follow during his tenure, Holmes's constitutional views happened to correspond to the political views held by reformers and those who later on were to become New Deal Democrats, and he gained their esteem as a result. A few examples will suffice. Three years after the Bakery case he dissented when the Court struck down national legislation providing for the arbitration of labor-management disputes in the railroad industry and outlawing "yellow dog" contracts, that is, contracts by which workers, as a condition of employment, agree not to join a union.[15] In 1918 he voted with the minority to uphold the right of Congress, under its power to regulate commerce among the states, to forbid the interstate shipment of goods produced by child labor. "The question," he insisted, was merely "whether the exercise of its otherwise constitutional power by Congress can be pronounced unconstitutional because of its possible reaction upon the conduct of the States. . . . I should have thought that the most conspicuous decisions of this court had made it clear that the power to regulate commerce . . . could not be cut down or qualified by the fact that it might interfere with the carrying out of the domestic policy of any State. . . ."[16] In 1923 the Court had a case involving a congressional minimum wage law for women employed in the District of Columbia. A divided Court saw it as another deprivation of the liberty to contract and therefore a violation of the Fifth Amendment's due process clause. Speaking for the majority, Justice Sutherland argued that to "sustain the individual freedom of action contemplated by the Constitution, is not to strike down the common good but to exalt it; for surely the good of society as a whole cannot be better served than by the preservation against arbitrary restraint of the liberties of its constituent members."[17] The Chief Justice, William Howard Taft, dissenting for himself and one other member of the Court, insisted that women constituted a special case, thus making the kind of distinction from a general rule that Harlan had made in *Lochner.* Again Holmes, in a separate dissent, would have none of this. The way he read the Constitution there was nothing in it to prevent Congress from setting minimum wages for everyone, men as well as women. Finally, to cite one last example, he wrote a powerful dissent when the Court refused to allow New York to regulate the resale price of theatre tickets.

I think the proper course is to recognize that a state legislature can do whatever it sees fit to do unless it is restrained by some express provision in the Constitution. . . . The truth seems to me to be that, subject to compensation when compensation is due, the legislature may forbid or restrict any business when it has a sufficient force of public opinion behind it.[18]

Whatever form the regulatory legislation took, Holmes was almost sure to vote to uphold it, and to do so in memorable language. ("To quote from Mr. Justice Holmes' opinions," Frankfurter wrote, "is to string pearls.")[19] Nor was he always in dissent. One of his most enduring opinions was written for a unanimous Court in a case upholding an indictment under the Sherman Anti-Trust Act. Just a few years earlier the Court had drawn an arbitrary distinction between manufacturing and commerce, holding the refining of sugar to be the former and therefore not subject to regulation by the national government under its power to regulate interstate commerce.[20] In an opinion that harks back to Marshall's great opinion in *Gibbons* v. *Ogden,* Holmes disposed of the distinction with a figure of speech that focused attention on the enterprise as a whole—here the vast meat packing business—rather than on a particular aspect of it taking place in a stockyard located within one state.

When cattle are sent for sale from a place in one State, with the expectation that they will end their transit, after purchase, in another, and when in effect they do so, with only the interruption necessary to find a purchaser at the stock yards, and when this is a typical, constantly recurring course, the current thus existing is a current of commerce among the States, and the purchase of the cattle is a part and incident of such commerce.[21]

The consequences of this decision were felt not only by the meat packers, who had been accused of conspiring to fix prices in the buying and selling of cattle and meat; the decision also provided the constitutional basis for the exercise of the vast powers needed by a modern industrial state.

In the short run, however, Holmes was usually in the minority in these business regulation cases, and it was not until after he had retired (and Franklin Roosevelt had made a political issue of the Court's handling of them) that the cases in which he had dissented were themselves overruled. Yet his position has never been fully accepted by the Court. He saw the Constitution as granting almost plenary regulatory powers to Congress (and as not denying such powers to the states), and these powers could be used by capitalist and socialist alike. Except that it required compensation for a public taking of property,[22] the Constitution was economically neutral, "made for people of fundamentally differing views."[23] The powers it granted could be used wisely or foolishly—as a judge he did not care how they were used—by those who managed to gain political power. He especially deprecated "the use of the Fourteenth Amendment beyond the absolute compulsion of its words to prevent the making of social experiments that an important part of the community desires . . . even though the experiments may seem futile or even noxious to me and to those whose judgment I most respect."[24] Because the Constitution was almost completely silent on the subject, there was no role the Court could properly play in the governing of this important aspect of the national life. Strangely enough for a man reputed to be a philosopher-king, he exercised no rule in this area and had nothing whatever to teach his "subjects." He thought their efforts to reform foolish, and others may have regarded them as destructive of great constitutional principles, but that was no business of his. From public affairs he was not only remarkably detached, but he was almost wholly indifferent to the efforts of his contemporaries to build a better world. Indeed, he saw "no reason for attributing to man a significance different in kind from that which belongs to a baboon or to a grain of sand."[25]

It is interesting to reflect on what his reputation might have been had his tenure extended into the period after World War II when judicial restraint ceased to be popular among those who constitute the Court's critical audience. In the eyes of this audience it was one thing to allow the dominant forces of the community to express in law their opinions of business corporations, but it was something else to allow the same forces to embody in law their opinions of other human beings, and especially, other classes of human beings. Such laws were frequently discriminatory and, as such, violations of constitutional principles—for example, the constitutional guarantee of the equal protection of the laws. They rarely were to Holmes. Considering his reputation, it is astonishing to read his opinions in cases such as *Bailey* v. *Alabama, Patsone* v. *Pennsylvania,* and above all *Buck* v. *Bell.*

Bailey was a case challenging the notorious system by which state power was utilized to force poor Negroes into a condition of peonage. The system is well described in the *Encyclopaedia of the Social Sciences:*

[A] source of widespread peonage in the south was the custom of making yearly contracts with Negro farm laborers or tenants. Advances were usually made to them so that they could be held for the contracted period and coerced into renewal. . . . In addition statutes provided that to draw advances on "false pretenses" was a criminal offense. The courts interpreted every attempt to leave the plantation as an offense under the statute. The penalty was frequently a fine, which the complaining employer paid, so that the Negro was again in his power.[26]

Bailey signed a one-year contract and received an advance on his wages of one dollar and twenty-five cents a month, or fifteen dollars in all. He quit almost immediately and did not refund the fifteen dollars. The Alabama statute under which he was then convicted made the refusal to perform the labor, or to return the money advanced, *prima facie* evidence of an intent to defraud. In effect, given the facts of what Bailey had done, the jury was required to find fraud, thus to convict of crime, without any evidence of Bailey's purposes or state of mind when he entered into the contract. Chief Justice Hughes, writing for the majority of the Court, said that this arrangement violated the Thirteenth Amendment's provision against involuntary servitude. Holmes, despite his well-known admonition to "think things not words,"[27] dissented, treating the whole matter as if it were a simple breach of contract. If a fine may be imposed for a breach of contract, he argued, then there was no reason why "imprisonment may [not] be imposed in case of failure to pay it."[28] So far as he was willing to look—which was not very far—it was a "perfectly fair and proper contract," and he saw "no reason why the State should not throw its weight on the side of performance."[29] Thus, it was left to the "conservative" Hughes to disclose the enormity only slightly concealed in this system of which the statute itself was only a part, albeit a necessary part, and to declare it a violation of the national Constitution. Holmes, however, true to his principle of deference to legislative authority, which meant here a readiness to accept the legislature's presumption of the intent with which persons such as Bailey entered into these contracts, was unwilling to participate in such an analysis. So far as he was concerned, there was nothing in the Constitution to prevent the dominant forces in Alabama from imposing involuntary servitude on a helpless part of the population, so long as the statute on its face did not declare this to be the intention. This is not the kind of judging that makes heroes in our day, or ought to make heroes in any day, but it was the kind of judging that was all too typical of Holmes.[30]

A Pennsylvania statute made it unlawful for any alien to kill any wild bird or animal and, "to that end," made it unlawful for any alien to own or possess a shotgun or rifle. Patsone, a resident alien, was convicted of owning a shotgun, and was subjected to a fine of $25 and a forfeiture of the gun. In addition to a due process argument, he maintained that the statute, directed as it was solely to aliens, denied him the equal protection of the laws. The case turned on the legitimacy of the classification made by the statute, and this could be determined only in the light of the legislative purpose, assuming that purpose itself to be legitimate. More concretely, assuming that purpose was indeed to preserve the state's wild life (and not to disarm riotous working men), was there any evidence to show that aliens were a greater threat to wild life than were citizens? Holmes, who wrote the majority opinion, argued that the Constitution did not require such evidence. Since a state may classify with reference to the evil it seeks to prevent, the question, according to Holmes, was whether the Court could say that Pennsylvania was unwarranted "in assuming as its premise for the law . . . that aliens were the peculiar source of the evil. . . ." What evidence was the state required to produce in support of this dubious premise? He said it was enough that the Court "had no such knowledge of local conditions" that would allow it to say that the legislature was "manifestly wrong" in its determination.[31] As Yosal Rogat has pointed out, this test of constitutionality is no test at all, especially as applied to the facts of the *Patsone* case. So applied, it "seems to leave no limits at all on the classifications a legislature may make without violating the equal protection clause,"[32] Whence would come the evidence to prove that the "popular speech" of Pennsylvanians was "manifestly wrong" in asserting a tendency on the part of aliens to kill wild life, a tendency not shared by citizens or, for that matter, overcome when the aliens become naturalized? Pennsylvania asserted an interest in preserving wild life, and, Holmes said, since that was a lawful object, "the means adopted for making it effective also might be adopted."[33] Stated otherwise, since the *alleged* end was lawful, the means were lawful, and the Constitution does not require the Court to determine whether the alleged end was the real end, or whether the means adopted were reasonably related to that end.

It was fashionable at that time to praise judicial restraint, because the Court too often acted as if it were a superlegislature with the authority to act as a censor of almost all legislation; but Holmes's answer to the question of the limits of legislative power amounts to judicial abdication. He was not judging; he was refusing to judge; he was willing to accept at face value the legislature's statement of its purpose, and to do this determined the outcome of the case.[34] It would have determined the outcome in *Yick Wo* v. *Hopkins*[35] too, where the statute paraded as a safety measure but was actually a means of discriminating against Chinese laundrymen, if the Court had probed no more deeply than was Holmes's custom. Consider a case coming after he had retired, *Takahashi* v. *Fish and Game Commission*, where the facts were very similar to those in *Patsone*. A California law forbade commercial fishing licenses to aliens who were ineligible for citizenship. Although one of the two dissenters, Justice Reed, made as much as he could out of Holmes's *Patsone* opinion, the Court refused to allow the statute to pass as a conservation measure, striking it down for what it was: an act palpably discriminating against a relatively powerless group of state residents.[36]

But *Bailey* and *Patsone* pale into insignificance when compared with *Buck* v. *Bell*, which could be regarded as one of the most infamous decisions ever handed down by the Court, and probably would be were it not associated with Holmes's great name. His opinion for the majority here displays characteristics that had become familiar by that time: It was brief, epigrammatic, and contemptuous. It was in this spirit that the Constitution was held not to stand in the way of a fascistlike compulsory sterilization program.[37] The program was based on the presumption that feeble-mindedness was simply a recessive unit particle transmitted from generation to generation according to the law discovered by Mendel working with his pea plants. To rid the state of Virginia of mentally defective persons, it was, presumably, only necessary to prevent the carriers of recessive genes from procreating, and this the state proposed to do by performing compulsory surgical operations on the inmates of state institutions. This is "social experimentation" beyond the ordinary—at least in the United States where it has not been customary to permit state officials to tamper with human life—and one would have thought the Court would look long and hard at the legislative facts. For example, even assuming that feeble-mindedness is analogous to a dwarf pea-plant, it would not be asking too much of men whose job it is to preserve constitutional principles to ask the obvious question: How effective will be a program of sterilizing only the known defectives in state institutions? Or, how is it proposed to identify the carriers of recessive genes? That is to say, in a family of four children one of whom is found to be mentally defective (a "dwarf"), it would be necessary to sterilize three: the known defective and the two others who, according to Mendel's law, carry genes 50 percent recessive but who, like the fourth child, appear to be normal. By sterilizing only the likes of Carrie Buck, the known defective, it has been estimated that sixty-eight generations would be required to effect a 10 percent decrease in the number of mentally defective—even assuming the validity of Mendel's thesis. But who are the carriers of cells 50 percent recessive? No one could know. Nevertheless, Virginia was permitted, by a vote of 8–1, to embark on its program. No one questioned the state's presumptions—even though the case had all the earmarks of a friendly suit. (Carrie Buck did not care what was done to her, had no relatives to protect her interests, and her court-appointed attorney was actually a close friend of Bell, the superintendent of the institution.) No one on the Court insisted that the record appeared to be obviously defective, even though while the state called "expert" witnesses to testify on behalf of the statute, there was no record of anyone testifying against it. Justice Butler dissented, but without opinion. Thus Holmes's words were the only ones written in the case. If the grounds for sterilization exist, he said, and he made no effort to find out whether they did, "they justify the result."[38] Not only did he feel nothing outrageous about a state program of compulsory surgical operations, but that there was nothing special about it. "The principle that sustains compulsory vaccination is broad enough to cover cutting the Fallopian tubes. . . ." No smallpox in the one case and no children in the other, but no matter: Carrie Buck was feeble-minded, and her mother was feeble-minded, and her illegitimate child was thought to be at least subnormal. "Three generations of imbeciles are enough," Holmes said disdainfully. As for Carrie Buck's claim that she was denied equal protection because the law applied only to those in state institutions, Holmes dismissed it as the "usual last resort of constitutional arguments. . . ."

The truth is that in *Buck* v. *Bell* Holmes was not merely exercising judicial restraint, or refusing to substitute his judgment as to the wisdom or reasonableness of the statute for the judgment made by the legislature. This was a case that engaged his passions. Whereas he never tired of saying no good would come from the economic regulations or, as he put it more than once, "by tinkering with the institutions of property," he believed in taking "life in hand," eliminating the unfit, and "trying to build a race." That, he said, "would be [his] starting point for an ideal for the law."[39] As Yosal Rogat has said, the high spirits he displayed in his opinion in *Buck* v. *Bell* were "not due to bad taste alone."[40]

These illustrations may serve to remind us that a case can be made for the approach to constitutional interpretation adopted by those colleagues he so frequently opposed. Peckham, for example, may be criticized for the manner in which he judged the facts in the New York Bakery case, but not for a lack of respect for constitutional rights. He may have been wrong concerning the health conditions in bakeries, but he was not wrong to insist that the framing of a remedy to secure a constitutional right requires the Court to exercise an independent judgment concerning the facts alleged in the statutes. In his words, "the mere assertion that the subject relates . . . to the public health [safety, or welfare] does not necessarily render the enactment valid."[41] *Bailey, Patsone,* and *Buck* v. *Bell* are sufficient to prove that.

Surely it is easier to accept the legislature's statement of a statute's purpose and the presumptions underlying it; and it is simpler to say there are no limits to legislative power, because to say there are limits requires the judge to define them. That requires judgment, and it is easier to allow the Constitution to speak for itself. Hence, as Holmes said in *Tyson* v. *Banton,* unless restrained by some express provision in the Constitution, "a state legislature can do whatever it sees fit to do."[42] But the Constitution does not speak for itself, and the provisions in the Constitution are never (or, at least, only very rarely) expressly violated, for the simple reason that a challenged statute does not come to the Court labeled "bill of attainder," "deprivation of liberty without due process," or "denial of equal protection." It comes labeled a health measure, an innocuous fire prevention law, or conservation law. May Congress, for example, enact a law to protect migratory birds? Surely, because the treaty with the Canadians had to be enforced. But are there no limits to the treaty-making power? Holmes found no expressly stated limits, and delighted his admirers by going on to declare that the particular treaty in question was not forbidden either by any "invisible radiation from the general terms of the Tenth Amendment."[43] Memorable words, these. Words almost as famous as "three generations of imbeciles are enough." Words quoted many times during the struggle over the so-called Bricker amendment some thirty years later when an attempt was made to amend the Constitution in order to specify the limits of the treaty power that Holmes refused to specify. And what help did anyone engaged in this struggle receive from Holmes's famous opinion? None at all. He admitted there were limits, but added that "they must be ascertained in a different way."[44] What way, he did not deign even to adumbrate.

What, then, were the Holmesian principles that John Dewey predicted would one day be "accepted commonplaces"?[45] What did this philosopher-king teach his countrymen? In the area of the Court's principal business during his tenure, he taught judicial restraint, and he did so in a manner that exalted the legislative authority by depreciating constitutional authority. It was not that he trusted the legislature, or the people electing it; on the contrary, he had no respect whatever for them. He was simply of the opinion that what others regarded as constitutional questions were in fact merely political questions to be decided with finality in the political process. The majority, or the stronger, were to rule and would receive no instruction from him concerning the manner of their rule because, in this area, the Constitution did not care. His colleagues disagreed, men such as Peckham obviously, for it was they who were responsible for developing the doctrine of liberty of contract that constituted so formidable an obstacle to the political will of the majority or of the stronger; but Harlan and Taft too, for it was they who worked out the exceptions to liberty of contract, exceptions that permitted regulation when employment was unhealthy, or hazardous, or when women were involved, or when the business was "affected with a public interest."[46] To them, even in cases where he voted with them, he left the task of defining the constitutional limits to this law-making power, which is to say, in this area of constitutional law he left to others the task of judging.[47]

Indeed, as Professor Robert K. Faulkner has shown so convincingly, Holmes did not particularly admire judging. In his mind it was less interesting, and as Faulkner puts it, less admirable,[48] than, to use Holmes's own words, "transforming thought." His keenest interest was excited not, he said, "by what are called great questions and great cases, but by little decisions which the common run of selectors would pass by because they did not deal with the Constitution . . . yet which have in them the germ of some wider theory, and therefore of some profound interstitial change in the very tissue of law."[49] Thus, he preferred to trace the common law with Pollock, his English friend, than to discuss a constitutional question with Brandeis, his colleague and friend on the Court. Constitutional questions are very practical questions; they deal with the governing of men. In addition to being legal, they are prudential questions, for their proper answers require a balance to be struck between word and deed, the Constitution and political power, the constitutional principles and the political exigencies. Marshall, as Holmes readily admitted, excelled at this, which is to say, he excelled at judging; and among the qualities that permitted him to excel was his attachment to the Constitution and to the principles of justice it embodied. Holmes lacked this attachment and lacked, as a result, any passionate concern for the civil rights to be defended in constitutional cases.

This is admitted by his friends insofar as property rights were concerned, but they would insist that he was the greatest of all champions of First Amendment rights. It is to this subject that we must now turn.

Holmes certainly did not begin as a libertarian in the modern sense of that term. In 1893 he dissented when a majority of his brethren on the Massachusetts court held it was not a libel for a newspaper to report the arrest on a drunkenness charge of one H.P. Hanson when the man actually arrested had been an A.P.H. Hanson. Unfortunately for the newspaper there was a man named H. P. Hanson who otherwise corresponded to the description published, and he sued. Holmes would have awarded him judgment because, to state it in the terms of the old common law rule Holmes would have adopted, whenever or whatever a man publishes, he publishes at his peril, regardless of his intent. "The only ground, then, on which the matters alleged of and concerning that subject can be found not to be alleged of and concerning the plaintiff, is that the defendant did not intend them to apply to him"[50] and Holmes was unwilling to consider intent, denying that the common law required a showing of malice, and insisting that a man should be held absolutely liable for the natural consequences of his act. Thus, in fashioning a rule, he would have looked to the common law of torts and not to a free government's need of a free and vigorous press. In so doing he took obvious delight in displaying his historical learning, and he did the same thing, but this time while speaking for the Court, when in 1909 the Supreme Court of the United States decided a similar case.[51]

No doubt there is something to be said for a rule of law that protects a man from even innocently published libels, and it did not take *N.Y. Times* v. *Sullivan*[52] to show us the constitutional problems of applying the old rule of absolute tort liability to defamation. It must also be conceded that, at the time these two cases were decided, libel was thought not to involve constitutional questions of free speech and press.[53] Nevertheless, it is significant, but not at all strange, that Holmes did not bother to wonder whether a rule fashioned by Lord Mansfield in 1774 to be applied in a constitutional monarchy was appropriate in 1893 or 1909 to a constitutional democracy. Other judges had done so. James Kent, following the brief submitted by Alexander Hamilton, who was counsel for the defendant newspaper publisher, had long before recognized the need for adapting the old common law of defamation to make it more suitable to republican government,[54] so there was no lack of respectable precedent for what Holmes refused to do. But public law questions, because they involved reflections on what *ought* to be the principles by which a people govern themselves, interested Holmes far less than thought about the law as such, the law independent of its effects on the people subject to it.[55]

It was of course World War I and its aftermath that first required the Supreme Court to expound the meaning of the constitutional rights of free speech and press. With minor exceptions, questions that had been decided finally in the state courts now came to the Supreme Court, and did so for two reasons. In the first place, Congress, essentially for the first time since 1798, began to legislate in a manner involving the First Amendment; and, secondly, because it was held soon after the war that the Fourteenth Amendment contained prohibitions similar to those found in the First Amendment. That is to say, the Constitution was now held to protect speech and press from state abridgment. Holmes played an active role in the deciding of these cases. Indeed, he wrote the opinion for a unanimous Court in the first of them, *Schenck* v. *United States.*[56]

Despite the acclaim he won from libertarians for his famous opinion in that case, it requires no extensive analysis to show that the law he expounded deserves no special place in the hall of libertarian fame. Schenck went to jail, and a week later so did Debs and Frohwerk,[57] and so would every speaker whose words constituted a clear and present danger of bringing about some evil that Congress has a right to prevent. It was, Holmes said, "a question of proximity and degree," which meant a question of how close the words spoken came to effecting the end sought—here the obstruction of the recruitment service. It was assumed without discussion that this was an evil that Congress had a right to prevent. But is the constitutional right to speak freely limited merely to innocuous or ineffective speech, speech that does not threaten what Congress wants to preserve or promote? Holmes ignored this question altogether in *Schenck,* yet an exposition of the constitutional right to free speech surely requires facing it.

Holmes did face it for the first time at the end of that same term when the Court had another Espionage Act case in *Abrams* v. *United States.* This time he was in the minority, and for it he wrote one of the most famous of all dissenting opinions.[58] Here he was not content to allow Congress to define the prohibited end while leaving to the courts only the question of how closely the speech came to effecting that end. Here he attempted to explain to a hostile public why it was important to allow men to express themselves freely, even if what was said was hateful to the dominant opinion. To allow opposition by speech, he suggested at the beginning of his analysis, may be thought to imply one of three things: "that you think the speech impotent . . . or that you do not care wholeheartedly for the result, or that you doubt either your power or your premises."[59] Since he had already referred to Abrams' words as "poor and puny anonymities" and to the leaflet distributed as "silly," a leaflet incapable of causing any injury to any legitimate public interest, it might appear that he adopted the first of these as the ground for his opinion. This would have been wholly in accord with his opinion in *Schenck:* "poor and puny anonymities" present no clear and present danger, and, therefore, Congress may not, because it need not, suppress them. But Holmes did not leave it at this. "To allow opposition by speech" only "seems" to imply one of these three premises, and in what follows Holmes makes clear that his reason for supporting Abrams rests on an entirely different basis, a basis that he found implied in the First Amendment:

But when men have realized that time has upset many fighting faiths, they may come to believe . . . that the ultimate good desired is better reached by free trade in ideas—that the best test of truth is the power of the thought to get itself accepted in the competition of the market, and that truth is the only ground upon which their wishes safely can be carried out. That at any rate is the theory of our Constitution.[60]

Free speech is good because it provides the conditions out of which the truth emerges, and truth is the only ground, or the only safe ground, on which legislation can rest. This is the theory of the First Amendment. This is why it allows opposing speech. It is an experiment, but so is all of life, and so long as it is "part of our system," there can be no suppression of even loathsome opinions "unless they so imminently threaten immediate interference with the lawful and pressing purposes of the law that an immediate check is required to save the country."[61] Except in such rare cases, all opinions must be permitted by the law because, as he said in still another famous dissent, "if there is any principle of the Constitution that more imperatively calls for attachment than any other it is the principle of free thought—not free thought for those who agree with us but freedom for the thought that we hate."[62] We may hate a particular doctrine—the dominant forces of the community may hate it—but we may not suppress it because we need not fear it unless it is the truth, and in that case we ought not to fear it. If it is true, it will win in the free competition of the market, and the Founding Fathers, by commanding Congress to make no law abridging the freedom of speech, commanded us not to fear the truth but rather to live by it. So reads Holmes's exposition in the *Abrams* case.

Such an exposition of why free speech is good may appear to have very respectable antecedents,[63] but it coexists uneasily with some of Holmes's other statements concerning the Constitution as well as with his philosophical position. The Constitution, he said in the Bakery case,[64] "is made for people of fundamentally differing views," and now he interpreted the First Amendment in a manner designed to give the expression of these differing views the protection they need against the dominant opinion. Yet in *Gitlow* v. *New York,* where once again he dissented, this time in favor of the right "of an anarchist (so-called) to talk drool in favor of the proletarian dictatorship,"[65] he wrote a statement that is simply incompatible with his *Abrams* position: "If in the long run the beliefs expressed in proletarian dictatorship are destined to be accepted by the dominant forces of the community, the only meaning of free speech is that they should be given their chance and have their way."[66] This is not an expression of confidence in the power of truth to win in the competition of the market; this is a statement expressing indifference as to which doctrine wins in the competition of the market. It reminds us of one of the seemingly rejected premises in *Abrams,* namely, that "you" allow opposition by speech because "you do not care whole-heartedly for the result." This is to say that the Constitution is politically neutral. But if this is so, if the Constitution is really "made for people of fundamentally differing [political] views"—republican, monarchist, fascist, or communist—then it is emphatically not true that "the only meaning of free speech is that they should be given their chance and have their way." It is not true because if the Constitution does not care which doctrine emerges victorious from the competition of the free market, free speech has no meaning whatever. Why, in such a case, is free speech good? To that question Holmes now had no answer.

He was not here the advocate of judicial restraint, but the purpose for which the judiciary would now intervene was essentially no different from the reason why, in the economic cases, it would refuse to intervene. The Constitution is silent on the large questions of the economic system and on the manner in which the dominant forces in the community use their power to regulate it, whether wisely or foolishly, and the Court may not intervene. The Constitution is equally silent on the larger question of the nature of the polity, or as to whether the doctrine that wins public support is wise or foolish, and here the Court will intervene but only to prevent Congress from doing so. It amounts to the same thing: in expounding the law of the Constitution the Court has nothing to teach those who manage to gain political power. If anything can be said to constitute the opposite of statesmanship, this is surely it. Holmes would not deny it. He readily admitted it when he said, brutally but truly, "that if my fellow citizens want to go to Hell I will help them. It's my job."[67]

Holmes's indifference to constitutional law was expressed implicitly in his speech to the Harvard Law School Association of New York: "I do not think the United States would come to an end if we lost our power to declare an Act of Congress void."[68] It depends on what is meant by the United States. If one means a number of people occupying a certain defined part of the Western Hemisphere, Holmes is probably correct, for then the United States remains the United States whether constituted as it is or as a dictatorship of the proletariat or of a so-called master race. But if one means a republic dedicated to the proposition that all men are created equal in the sense that all men equally possess the rights to life, liberty, and the pursuit of happiness, then Holmes's declaration becomes exceedingly dubious. For this republic now depends, and has depended since at least the days of John Marshall, on the acknowledgment by the people of the United States of three related political propositions: that the majority is capable of misusing the power it enjoys by right, that the Constitution provides the criteria by which the proper use and the misuse of this power are distinguished, and that the Supreme Court is entrusted to enforce these criteria against the majority or whoever it is that manages to exercise political power. It is not simply a case of invalidating legislation that offends constitutional principle; on the majority of occasions when the Court does not invalidate, it nevertheless plays a significant role in maintaining in the public mind an awareness of the distinction between legitimate and illegitimate government and legislation. The Court, precisely because it has the power to invalidate, is, in the words of Professor Charles L. Black, Jr., "the legitimator of the government." In a very real sense, he writes, "the Government of the United States is based on the opinions of the Supreme Court."[69] Holmes's Court could not perform this function because his Court, more than that of any other judge to sit on it, would deny itself the power that Marshall first asserted and that has been an institution of American government ever since. The power to validate and legitimate rests, of course, on the power to invalidate, and "if it ever so much as became known . . . that the Court would not seriously ponder the questions of constitutionality presented to it and declare the challenged statute unconstitutional if it believed it to be so, then its usefulness as a legitimatizing institution would be gone."[70]

Holmes was a man of the law, but the Supreme Court of the United States is not simply, and in one sense not even primarily, a court of law, and this explains his failure as a justice. The Supreme Court is primarily a court of constitutional law in the sense that its power to enforce constitutional principle gives it a role—in one sense the decisive role—in the governing of Americans. But Holmes, who managed to ignore official Washington even while living in it and who took pride in the fact of not reading newspapers, had no interest in government. He said that the law "draws all the juices of life [from] considerations of what is expedient for the community concerned,"[71] but no judge in the history of the Supreme Court made less of an effort to learn what was expedient for the United States, or what the Constitution regarded as expedient for the United States. And contrary to the Holmesian iconographers, no man with anything approaching his length of service on the Court contributed so little in the development of the constitutional law that defines the rights, privileges and immunities of Americans even as it imposes limits on the government.

The cause of his failure in this respect is not hard to find. The Constitution occupied no special place in his thoughts,[72] because the idea of natural principles of justice which the Founders understood to be embodied in the Constitution was wholly alien to his thought. Professor Faulkner has gone so far as to say that what "Marshall had raised, Holmes sought to destroy. The natural constitution behind the written constitution, characteristic of Marshall's jurisprudence and the object of the court's solicitude, was to give way to the will of society and the competitive conditions for its appearance."[73] He was disdainful of the idea of natural rights and of natural law. He saw "no meaning in the rights of man except what the crowd will fight for,"[74] or in the consequences of their breach;[75] or, as he said in still another place, "a right is only the hypostasis of a prophecy."[76] And to say that the "crowd" will fight for something it designates as a right is to say nothing of its existence otherwise: "A dog will fight for his bone."[77] Those who believe otherwise are "naive."[78] Holding such views it is not remarkable that Holmes eschewed the role of judicial statesman.

Rather than attempt to influence the development of American political life guided by the principles of the Constitution, Holmes turned to the study of private law and attempted to find the law of its development in something resembling history.

> The development of our law has gone on for nearly a thousand years, like the development of a plant, each generation taking the inevitable next step, mind, like matter, simply obeying a law of spontaneous growth.[79]

But the growth is not really spontaneous; it is moved by a basic force which is the will of society, and it is the job of the judge to convert that will into law by enforcing it. Whatever he himself may have thought of society's will, as a judge he saw himself as "the supple tool of power."[80] He would attempt to measure the strength, not the justice, of the competing desires of the litigants in a case,[81] and in all doubtful cases rule in favor of the stronger.[82] He regarded this as his duty because it would be compatible with his view of the best government. The best government is not the one established by the Constitution or otherwise modeled on the Declaration of Independence, but one that allows the "dominant power" to rule, regardless of the manner of its rule:

> What proximate test of excellence can be found except correspondence to the actual equilibrium of force in the community—that is, conformity to the wishes of the dominant power? Of course, such conformity may lead to destruction, and it is desirable that the dominant power should be wise. But wise or not, the proximate test of a good government is that the dominant power has its way.[83]

This is an astonishing statement for an American judge to make, and what is perhaps more astonishing is that he gained fame with it, and with others like it. Consider his advice to lawyers: "If you want to know the law and nothing else, you must look at it as a bad man, who cares only for the material consequences which such knowledge enables him to predict. . . ."[84] The truly bad man would be the best lawyer, because he would be the best prophet, and the "prophecies of what the court will do in fact, and nothing more pretentious are what [Holmes meant] by the law."[85] This advice is, of course, of no use whatever to the judge—and Holmes was a judge when he made the statement—and it is also bad advice for the lawyer, who, precisely because he would be a bad man, is unable to weigh the moral considerations that a judge in fact weighs when he makes a decision. A few pages later, for example, Holmes admonishes judges for failing "to recognize their duty of weighing considerations of social advantage" when deciding a case,[86] but a bad man, to the extent that he is bad, will be the instrument least qualified to weigh such considerations. He will be insensitive to them.[87]

Holmes's greatest admirer admitted that he had no experience in public affairs, but insisted that he was able to be a statesman because he was "led by the divination of the philosopher and the imagination of the poet," and that he therefore was able to be the "philosopher become king."[88] It would be truer to say Holmes was a dilettante who dabbled in philosophical works[89] and who was led by his attraction to theory to make theoretical statements about the law. His writings are characterized by a moral skepticism, a brutal cynicism concerning man and political reform, and a lack of attachment to political things. His work gave rise to what is mislabeled legal realism, as well as to the newer "realists," the judicial decision-making school; but it is of no value whatever to anyone who would use the offices of law better to govern, or even merely to govern, the United States. As Faulkner so well says, an "orientation by moral and political ends is absent from Holmes's jurisprudence,"[90] and it is absent because, although he held government office for fifty years, he had no interest in government.

NOTES

1. Harold J. Laski, "Mr. Justice Holmes," *Mr. Justice Holmes,* ed. Felix Frankfurter (New York, Coward-McCann, Inc., 1931), p. 138.
2. Speech at Ottawa, Illinois, August 21, 1858, *Created Equal? The Complete Lincoln-Douglas Debates of 1858,* ed. Paul M. Angle (Chicago: University of Chicago Press, 1958), p. 128.
3. Edmond Cahn, "Justice Black and First Amendment 'Absolutes': A Public Interview," *New York University Law Review,* xxxvii (June 1962), p. 549.
4. Felix Frankfurter, *Mr. Justice Holmes and the Supreme Court,* 2nd ed. (Cambridge: Harvard University Press, 1961), p. 112.
5. Benjamin N. Cardozo, "Mr. Justice Holmes," *Mr. Justice Holmes,* p. 5.
6. Laski, "Mr. Justice Holmes," p. 148.
7. "[Notices of my appointment to the Supreme Court] are so favorable that they make my appointment a popular success but they have the flabbiness of American ignorance. I had to get an appreciation for my book in England before they dared say anything here except in one or two quarters." Holmes to Pollock, Sept. 23, 1902, *Holmes-Pollock Letters,* ed. Mark deWolfe Howe (Cambridge: Harvard University Press, 1941), I, 106.
8. Yosal Rogat, "The Judge as Spectator," *University of Chicago Law Review,* XXXI (Winter 1964), p. 213.
9. Felix Frankfurter, "Mr. Justice Holmes and the Constitution," *Mr. Justice Holmes,* p. 54.
10. Sir William Blackstone, *Commentaries on the Laws of England* 1778 ed., II, 3, 8–9, and *passim.*
11. *Lochner* v. *New York,* 198 U.S. 45 (1905).
12. *Allgeyer* v. *Louisiana,* 165 U.S. 578 (1897).
13. *Holden* v. *Hardy,* 169 U.S. 366 (1898).
14. *Lochner* v. *New York,* at pp. 75–76. Dissenting opinion.
15. *Adair* v. *United States, 208 U.S. 161 (1908).*
16. *Hammer* v. *Dagenhart, 247 U.S. 251, 278 (1918).* Dissenting opinion.

17. *Adkins* v. *Children's Hospital,* 216 U.S. 525, 561 (1923).
18. *Tyson Bros.* v. *Banton,* 273 U.S. 418, 446 (1927). Dissenting opinion.
19. Frankfurter, "Mr. Justice Holmes and the Constitution," p. 85.
20. *United States* v. *E. C. Knight Co.,* 156 U.S. 1 (1895).
21. *Swift and Co.* v. *United States,* 196 U.S. 375, 398–99 (1905).
22. See his opinion for the Court in *Pennsylvania Coal Co.* v. *Mahon,* 260 U.S. 393 (1922).
23. *Lochner* v. *New York,* at p. 76.
24. *Truax* v. *Corrigan,* 257 U.S. 312, 344 (1921).
25. Holmes to Pollock, August 30, 1929, *Holmes-Pollock Letters,* II, 252.
26. *The Encyclopaedia of the Social Sciences,* 1934 ed., Vol. 12, 71.
27. Oliver Wendell Holmes, "Law in Science—Science in Law," *Collected Legal Papers* (New York: Harcourt, Brace, and Co., 1921), p. 238.
28. *Bailey* v. *Alabama,* 219 U.S. 219, 246–47 (1911).
29. *Bailey* v. *Alabama,* at p. 247.
30. His unwillingness to probe beneath the surface of this statute was consistent as well with his account of the development of the common law and especially his discussion of fraud and intent in chapter 4 of his book, *The Common Law,* where he argues that here as elsewhere the law attempts to substitute external standards for "moral standards." He meant by this that the law seeks to avoid the problem of looking into the defendant's state of mind at the time the act was committed by working out an external standard of what would be fraudulent, for example, in the case of the prudent man, and requires every man to avoid that at his peril. See also Yosal Rogat, "Mr. Justice Holmes: A Dissenting Opinion," *Stanford Law Review,* XV (December 1962, March 1963), 276–77.
31. *Patsone* v. *Pennsylvania,* 232 U.S. 138, 144–45 (1914).
32. Rogat, "Mr. Justice Holmes: A Dissenting Opinion," 42.
33. *Patsone* v. *Pennsylvania,* p. 143.
34. See also Holmes's dissent in *Keller* v. *United States,* 213 U.S. 138, 149–51 (1909), where he went so far as to allow Congress to make an irrebuttable presumption respecting the purposes of anyone who hired an alien woman for purposes of prostitution within three years of her entry into the country. His argument ran as follows: Congress may assume that a woman who becomes a prostitute within three years of her entry into the country came as a prostitute or with the intent of becoming one, and such a woman is deportable on the ground that her entry was fraudulent; Congress may also punish anyone who cooperated in such fraudulent entry, or in her unlawful stay in the country; and Congress may presume that anyone who hires her is cooperating in her unlawful stay, and this presumption is not open to rebuttal. In effect, Keller, an American citizen, was presumed to have brought the woman into the country for purposes of prostitution, even though, as Justice Brewer pointed out in his majority opinion, the facts showed incontrovertibly that he had absolutely nothing to do with her entry into the country.
35. *Yick Wo* v. *Hopkins,* 118 U.S. 356 (1886).
36. *Takahashi* v. *Fish and Game Commission,* 334 U.S. 410 (1948).
37. See Walter Berns, "*Buck* v. *Bell*: Due Process of Law?" *Western Political Quarterly,* 17 (December 1953), 762–75.
38. *Buck* v. *Bell,* 274 U.S. 200, 207 (1927).
39. "Ideals and Doubts," *Collected Legal Papers,* p. 306; Holmes to John C. H. Wu, July 21, 1925, in Max Lerner, *The Mind and Faith of Justice Holmes* (New York: Modern Library, 1943), p. 428.
40. Rogat, "Mr. Justice Holmes: A Dissenting Opinion," 28.
41. *Lochner* v. *New York,* p. 57.
42. *Tyson Bros.* v. *Banton,* p. 446, Dissenting opinion.
43. *Missouri* v. *Holland,* 252 U.S. 416, 434 (1920).

44. *Missouri* v. *Holland*, p. 433.
45. John Dewey, "Justice Holmes and the Liberal Mind," *Mr. Justice Holmes*, p. 54.
46. See *Wolfe Co.* v. *Industrial Court*, 262 U.S. 522, 535–36 (1923).
47. "Nowhere in any of the cases we have considered did Holmes help in framing a remedy to secure a constitutional right." Rogat, "Mr. Justice Holmes: A Dissenting Opinion," 305.
48. Robert K. Faulkner, *The Jurisprudence of John Marshall* (Princeton: Princeton University Press, 1968), p. 234.
49. Holmes, "John Marshall," *Collected Legal Papers*, p. 269.
50. *Hanson* v. *Globe Newspaper Co.*, 159 Mass. 293, 301 (1893).
51. *Peck* v. *Tribune Co.*, 214 U.S. 185 (1909).
52. *N.Y. Times* v. *Sullivan*, 376 U.S. 254 (1964).
53. Holmes wrote the majority opinion in *Patterson* v. *Colorado*, 205 U.S. 454 (1907), in which it was held that contempt is a matter of local law (the case involved the libeling of a state judge). He left undecided the question of whether the Fourteenth Amendment incorporated the speech and press provisions of the First. Furthermore, he added, the main purpose of these speech and press provisions was to prevent only previous restraints upon publications and not to prevent subsequent punishment of words that "may be deemed contrary to the public welfare." This, he said citing Blackstone, was the common law of criminal libel. *Patterson* v. *Colorado*, p. 462.
54. *People* v. *Croswell*, 3 John's Cases (N.Y.) 337 (1804).
55. See Kenneth M. Holland, "Roger Taney," in Morton J. Frisch and Richard G. Stevens, eds., *American Political Thought*, 2nd ed. (Itasca, Ill: F. E. Peacock, 1983), p. 181.
56. *Schenck* v. *United States*, 249 U.S. 47 (1919).
57. *Debs* v. *United States*, 249 U.S. 211 (1919); *Frohwerk* v. *United States*, 249 U.S. 204 (1919).
58. "I think that dissent will influence American thinking in a fashion to which only your work in *Lochner* and the *Adair* case have rivalry." Laski to Holmes, April 2, 1920. *Holmes-Laski Letters*, (Cambridge: Harvard University Press), I, 257.
59. *Abrams* v. *United States*, 250 U.S. 616, 630 (1919). Dissenting opinion.
60. *Abrams* v. *United States*, at p. 630.
61. *Abrams* v. *United States*, at p. 630.
62. *United States* v. *Schwimmer*, 279 U.S. 644, 654–55 (1929). Dissenting opinion.
63. "Let [truth] and falsehood grapple; who ever knew truth put to the worse, in a free and open encounter?" John Milton, *Areopagitica* (toward the end). "Liberty, as a principle, has no application to any state of things anterior to the time when mankind have become capable of being improved by free and equal discussion . . . (a period long since reached in all nations with whom we need here concern ourselves). . . ." John Stuart Mill, *On Liberty* (Introductory).
64. See Holland, pp. 171–72.
65. Holmes to Pollock, June 18, 1925, *Holmes-Pollock Letters*, II, 163.
66. *Gitlow* v. *New York*, 268 U.S. 652, 673 (1925). Dissenting opinion.
67. Holmes to Laski, March 4, 1920, *Holmes-Laski Letters*, I, 249.
68. *Collected Legal Papers*, pp. 295–96. He continued: "I do think that the Union would be imperiled if we could not make that declaration as to the laws of the several States."
69. Charles L. Black, Jr., *The People and the Court* (New York: Macmillan, 1960), p. 52.
70. Black, *The People and the Court*, p. 53.
71. Oliver Wendell Holmes, *The Common Law* (Boston: Little, Brown & Co., 1881), p. 35.
72. He never wrote a significant article or delivered a significant speech on the Constitution or on any of its provisions.
73. Faulkner, *The Jurisprudence of John Marshall*, p. 256.
74. Holmes to Laski, July 28, 1916, *Holmes-Laski Letters*, I, 8.
75. Holmes, "The Path of the Law," *Collected Legal Papers*, pp. 168–69.

76. Holmes, "Natural Law," *Collected Legal Papers,* p. 313.
77. Holmes, "Natural Law," *Collected Legal Papers,* p. 314.
78. Ibid., p. 312.
79. Holmes, "The Path of the Law," *Collected Legal Papers,* p. 185.
80. Quoted in Merlo J. Pusey, *Charles Evans Hughes* (New York: Macmillan, 1952), II, 287. The relation between the will of society and the judge is actually somewhat more complicated, but the format of this chapter does not permit its elaboration. The judge in the future may affect "the path of the law," which he may do by availing himself of science, or of a social science, to enable him to know society's will. For an admirable analysis of Holmes's thoughts on this subject, as well as of the emptiness of what it leads to, see Faulkner, *The Jurisprudence of John Marshall,* p. 239 ff.
81. Holmes, "Law in Science—Science in Law," *Collected Legal Papers,* p. 231.
82. Ibid., p. 239.
83. Holmes, "Montesquieu," *Collected Legal Papers,* p. 258.
84. Holmes, "The Path of the Law," *Collected Legal Papers,* p. 171.
85. Ibid., p. 173.
86. Ibid., p. 184.
87. Holmes's bad man would make a good (Holmesian) lawyer because he could best separate law and morals, which, according to Holmes, is a condition of accurate prediction. But consider an example Holmes provides a few pages later. "Three hundred years ago a parson preached a sermon and told a story out of Fox's Book of Martyrs of a man who had assisted at the torture of one of the saints, and afterward died, suffering compensatory inward torment. It happened that Fox was wrong. The man was alive and chanced to hear the sermon, and thereupon he sued the parson. Chief Justice Wray instructed the jury that the defendant was not liable, because the story was told innocently, without malice. He took malice in the moral sense, as importing a malevolent motive." *Collected Legal Papers,* p. 176. If Wray was wrong to do this and therefore wrong about the law, the bad man who tried to predict would have been wrong about the decision. If Wray was correct about the law, it shows that, in this area at least, law and morals cannot be separated. Either way, Holmes is giving bad advice.
88. Frankfurter, "Mr. Justice Holmes and the Constitution," *Mr. Justice Holmes,* p. 54.
89. The Holmes-Laski letters are published in two volumes and 1481 pages, yet there is nothing resembling or approaching a serious discussion of a philosophical problem or even of a philosophical work. References to philosophers abound—both Holmes and Laski regarded themselves and each other as philosophers—but what is said is best described as chit-chat. The reader is invited to test this statement by consulting the index entries under "Hobbes," of which there are some 79. A typical reference by Holmes reads as follows: John M. Zane "thinks Bentham, Austin, and Hobbes little better than asses" (I, 180). There is one reference to statesmanship. It reads as follows in its entirety: I was not greatly impressed by Dean Acheson's support of Brandeis in the *New Republic,* "except for the admirable politeness with which he expressed his difference. He thought B's view more statesmanlike–which is an effective word but needs caution in using it" (I, 473–74). There is no index entry under "Justice."

THOMAS SOWELL

The Civil Rights Vision: From Equal Opportunity to "Affirmative Action"

May 17, 1954 was a momentous day in the history of the United States, and perhaps of the world. Something happened that afternoon that was all too rare in human history. A great nation voluntarily acknowledged and repudiated its own oppression of part of its own people. The Supreme Court decision that day was announced in an atmosphere of high drama, and some observers said that one of the black-robed Justices sat on the great bench with tears in his eyes.

Brown v. *Board of Education* was clearly much more than another legal case to go into the long dusty rows of volumes of court decisions. It represented a vision of man and of the world that touched many hearts across the land and around the world. The anger and rancor it immediately provoked also testified to its importance. In a larger historic context, that such an issue should reach the highest court in the land was itself remarkable. In how many places and in how many eras could an ordinary person from a despised race challenge the duly constituted authorities, force them to publicly defend their decisions, retreat, and finally capitulate?

Brown v. *Board of Education* may have been intended to close the door on an ugly chapter in American history, going back to slavery and including both petty and gross bigotry, blatant discrimination, and violence and terror extending all the way to brutal and sadistic lynchings. Yet it also opened a door to political, constitutional, and human crises. It was not simply a decision but the beginning of a revolution that has not yet run its course, but which has already shown the classic symptoms of a revolution taking a very different path from that envisioned by those who set it in motion.

The civil rights revolution of the past generation has had wide ramifications among a growing variety of groups, and has changed not only the political landscape and social history of the United States, but has also altered the very concept of constitutional law and the role of courts.

Behind the many visible changes has been a change in the way the world is visualized. The civil rights vision is not only a moral vision of the way the world *should* be in the future, but also a cause-and-effect vision

From Thomas Sowell, *Civil Rights: Rhetoric or Reality?* (New York: William Morrow, 1984), pp. 13–16, 37–60. Reprinted by permission of William Morrow and Company.

of the way the world *is* today. This cause-and-effect vision of the way the world works is central to understanding the particular direction of thrust of the civil rights revolution, its achievements, its disappointments, and its sharp changes in meaning that have split its supporters and confounded its critics.

It is far from incidental that the civil rights movement began among black Americans. The basic vision of what was wrong, and of what social effects would follow from what institutional changes, bore the clear imprint of the history of blacks in the United States, though the general principles arrived at were later applied successively to very different groups in American society—to women and the aged, for example, as well as to such disparate racial and ethnic groups as Asians, Hispanics, and American Indians. It is now estimated that 70 percent of the American population is entitled to preferential treatment under "affirmative action." The civil rights vision has even been extended internationally to the plight of the Third World and to racial policies in other nations, such as South Africa.

Ironically, the civil rights revolution began by emphasizing precisely what was unique about the history of black Americans—slavery, Jim Crow laws, and some of the most virulent racism ever seen anywhere. But upon that very uniqueness, *general* principles of morality and causation were established. These principles constitute the civil rights vision of the world. The extent to which that vision corresponds to reality is crucial for understanding both the successes and failures of the civil rights revolution thus far, and for assessing its future prospects and dangers. . . .

One of the most central—and most controversial—premises of the civil rights vision is that statistical disparities in incomes, occupations, education, etc., represent moral inequities, and are caused by "society." Historically, it was easy to show, for example, that segregated white schools had had several times as much money spent per pupil as had segregated black schools and that this translated into large disparities in physical plant, teacher qualifications, and other indices of educational input. Large differences in educational output, such as test scores, seemed readily attributable to these input differences. How well this model applied to other statistical disparities for other groups is another question entirely. Moreover, even for blacks, the causal link has been established by immediate plausibility rather than by systematic verification of an hypothesis.

Another central premise of the civil rights vision is that belief in innate inferiority explains policies and practices of differential treatment, whether expressed in overt hostility or in institutional policies or individual decisions that result in statistical disparities. Moral defenses or causal explanations of these statistical differences in any other terms tend themselves to fall under suspicion or denunciation as racism, sexism, etc.

Again, the question must be raised as to the general validity of these premises, as well as the separate question of their applicability to the special case of blacks.

A third major premise of the civil rights vision is that political activity is the key to improving the lot of those on the short end of differences in income, "representation" in desirable occupations or institutions, or otherwise disadvantaged. Once more, it is possible to cite such things as dramatic increases in the number of black elected officials after passage of the civil rights legislation of the 1960s. But once again, the general validity of the premise for the wide variety of groups covered by civil rights policies must be examined as a separate issue. And once again, even the special case of blacks must be systematically analyzed.

The very meaning of the phrase "civil rights" has changed greatly since the *Brown* decision in 1954, or since the Civil Rights Act of 1964. Initially, civil rights meant, quite simply, that all individuals should be treated the same under the law, regardless of their race, religion, sex or other such social categories. For blacks, especially, this would have represented a dramatic improvement in those states where law and public policy mandated racially separate institutions and highly discriminatory treatment.

Many Americans who supported the initial thrust of civil rights, as represented by the *Brown* v. *Board of Education* decision and the Civil Rights Act of 1964, later felt betrayed as the original concept of equal individual *opportunity* evolved toward the concept of equal group *results.* The idea that statistical differences in results were weighty presumptive evidence of discriminatory processes was not initially an explicit part of civil rights law. But neither was it merely an inexplicable perversion, as many critics seem to think, for it followed logically from the civil rights *vision.*

If the causes of intergroup differences can be dichotomized into discrimination and innate ability, then nonracists and nonsexists must expect equal results from nondiscrimination. Conversely, the persistence of highly disparate results must indicate that discrimination continues to be pervasive among recalcitrant employers, culturally biased tests, hypocritical educational institutions, etc. The early leaders and supporters of the civil rights movement did not advocate such corollaries, and many explicitly repudiated them, especially during the congressional debates that preceded passage of the Civil Rights Act of 1964.[1] But the corollaries were implicit in the vision—and in the long run that proved to be more decisive than the positions taken by the original leaders in the cause of civil rights. In the face of crying injustices, many Americans accepted a vision that promised to further a noble cause, without quibbling over its assumptions or verbal formulations. But visions have a momentum of their own, and those who accept their assumptions have entailed their corollaries, however surprised they may be when these corollaries emerge historically.

From Rights to Quotas

"Equal opportunity" laws and policies require that individuals be judged on their qualifications as individuals, *without regard* to race, sex, age, etc. "Affirmative action" requires that they be judged *with regard* to such group membership, receiving preferential or compensatory treatment in some cases to achieve a more proportional "representation" in various institutions and occupations.

The conflict between equal opportunity and affirmative action developed almost imperceptibly at first, though it later became a heated issue, repeatedly debated by the time the Civil Rights Act of 1964 was being considered by Congress. The term "affirmative action" was first used in a racial discrimination context in President John F. Kennedy's Executive Order No. 10,925 in 1961. But, as initially presented, affirmative action referred to various activities, such as monitoring subordinate decision makers to ensure the fairness of their hiring and promotion decisions, and spreading information about employment or other opportunities so as to encourage previously excluded groups to apply—after which the actual selection could be made *without regard* to group membership. Thus, it was both meaningful and consistent for President Kennedy's Executive Order to say that federal contractors should "take affirmative action to ensure that the applicants are employed, and that employees are treated during employment, without regard to their race, creed, color, or national origin."

Tendencies toward shifting the emphasis from equality of prospective opportunity toward statistical parity of retrospective results were already observed, at both state and federal levels, by the time that the Civil Rights Act of 1964 was under consideration in Congress. Senator Hubert Humphrey, while guiding this bill through the Senate, assured his colleagues that it "does not require an employer to achieve any kind of racial balance in his work force by giving preferential treatment to any individual or group."[2] He pointed out that subsection 703(j) under Title VII of the Civil Rights Act "is added to state this point expressly."[3] That subsection declared that nothing in Title VII required an employer "to grant preferential treatment to any individual or group on account of any imbalance which may exist" with respect to the numbers of employees in such groups "in comparison with the total number or percentage of persons of such race, color, religion, sex, or national origin in any community, State, section or other area."

Virtually all the issues involved in the later controversies over affirmative action, in the specifically numerical sense, were raised in the legislative debates preceding passage of the Civil Rights Act. Under subsection 706(g) of that Act, an employer was held liable only for his own "intentional" discrimination,[4] not for societal patterns reflected in his work force. According to Senator Humphrey, the "express requirement of intent is designed to make it wholly clear that inadvertent or accidental discriminations will not violate the Title or result in the entry of court orders."[5] Vague claims of differential institutional policy impact—"institutional racism"—were not to be countenanced. For example, tests with differential impact on different groups were considered by Humphrey to be "legal unless used for the purpose of discrimination."[6] There was no burden of proof placed upon employers to "validate" such tests.

In general there was to be no burden of proof on employers; rather the Equal Employment Opportunity Commission (EEOC) created by the Act "must prove by a preponderance" that an adverse decision was based on race (or, presumably, other forbidden categories), according to Senator Joseph Clark, another leading advocate of the Civil Rights Act.[7] Senator Clark also declared that the Civil Rights Act "will not require an employer to change existing seniority lists," even though such lists might have differential impact on blacks as the last hired and first fired.[8] Still another supporter, Senator Harrison Williams, declared that an employer with an all-white work force could continue to hire "only the best qualified persons even if they were all white."[9]

In short, Congress declared itself in favor of equal opportunity and opposed to affirmative action. So has the American public. Opinion polls show a majority of blacks opposed to preferential treatment, as is an even larger majority of women.[10] Federal administrative agencies and the courts led the change from the prospective concept of individual equal opportunity to the retrospective concept of parity of group "representation" (or "correction" of "imbalances").

The key development in this process was the creation of the Office of Federal Contract Compliance in the U.S. Department of Labor by President Lyndon Johnson's Executive Order No. 11,246 in 1965. In May 1968, this office issued guidelines containing the fateful expression "goals and timetables" and "representation." But as yet these were still not quotas, for 1968 guidelines spoke of "goals and timetables for the prompt achievement of full and equal employment opportunity." By 1970, however, new guidelines referred to "results-oriented procedures," which hinted more strongly at what was to come. In December 1971, the decisive guidelines were issued, which made it clear that "goals and timetables" were meant to "increase materially the utilization of minorities and women," with "under-utilization" being spelled out as "having fewer minorities or women in a particular job classification than would reasonably be expected by their availability. . . ."[11] Employers were required to confess to "deficiencies in the utilization" of minorities and women whenever this statistical parity could not be found in all job classifications, as a first step toward correcting this situation. The burden of proof—and remedy—was on the employer. "Affirmative action" was now decisively transformed into a numerical concept, whether called "goals" or "quotas."[12]

Though lacking in either legislative authorization or public support for numerical group preferences, administrative agencies of government were able to enforce such policies with the support of the federal courts in general and the U.S. Supreme Court in particular. In the landmark *Weber* case the Supreme Court simply rejected "a literal interpretation" of the words of the Civil Rights Act. Instead, it sought the "spirit" of the Act, its "primary concern" with the economic problems of blacks. According to Justice William Brennan, writing the majority opinion, these words do not bar "temporary, voluntary, affirmative action measures undertaken to eliminate manifest racial imbalance in traditionally segregated job categories."[13] This performance received the sarcastic tribute of Justice Rehnquist that it was *"a tour de force* reminiscent not of jurists such as Hale, Holmes, and Hughes but of escape artists such as Houdini."[14] Rehnquist's dissent inundated the Supreme Court with the legislative history of the Act, and Congress' repeated and emphatic rejection of the whole approach of correcting imbalances or compensating for the past.[15] The spirit of the Act was as contrary to the decision as was the letter.

Equality of Rights and Results

Those who carry the civil rights vision to its ultimate conclusion see no great difference between promoting equality of opportunity and equality of results. If there are not equal results among groups presumed to have equal genetic potential, then some inequality of opportunity must have intervened somewhere, and the question of precisely where is less important than the remedy of restoring the less fortunate to their just position. The fatal flaw in this kind of thinking is that there are many reasons, besides genes and discrimination, why groups differ in their economic performances and rewards. Groups differ by large amounts demographically, culturally, and geographically—and all of these differences have profound effects on incomes and occupations.

Age differences are quite large. Blacks are a decade younger than the Japanese. Jews are a quarter of a century older than Puerto Ricans. Polish Americans are twice as old as American Indians.[16] These represent major differences in the quantity of work experience, in an economy where income differences between age brackets are even greater than black-white income differences.[17] Even if the various racial and ethnic groups were identical in every other respect, their age differences alone would prevent their being equally represented in occupations requiring experience or higher education. Their very different age distributions likewise prevent their being equally represented in colleges, jails, homes for the elderly, the armed forces, sports and numerous other institutions and activities that tend to have more people from one age bracket than from another.

Cultural differences add to the age differences. . . . Half of all Mexican American wives were married in their teens, while only 10 percent of Japanese American wives married that young.[18] Such very different patterns imply not only different values but also very different future opportunities. Those who marry and begin having children earlier face more restricted options for future education and less geographic mobility for seeking their best career opportunities. Even among those young people who go on to colleges and universities, their opportunities to prepare themselves for the better paid professions are severely limited by their previous educational choices and performances, as well as by their selections of fields of study in the colleges and universities. All of these things vary enormously from one group to another.

For example, mathematics preparation and performance differ greatly from one ethnic group to another and between men and women. A study of high school students in northern California showed that four-fifths of Asian youngsters were enrolled in the sequence of mathematics courses that culminate in calculus, while only one-fifth of black youngsters were enrolled in such courses. Moreover, even among those who began this sequence in geometry, the percentage that persisted all the way through to calculus was several times higher among the Asian students.[19] Sex differences in mathematics preparation are comparably large. Among both black and white freshmen at the University of Maryland, the men had had four years of mathematics in high school more than twice as often as the women.[20]

Mathematics is of decisive importance for many more professions than that of mathematician. Whole ranges of fields of study and work are off-limits to those without the necessary mathematical foundation. Physicists, chemists, statisticians, and engineers are only some of the more obvious occupations. In some colleges, one cannot even be an undergraduate economics major without having had calculus, and to go on to graduate school and become a professional economist requires much more mathematics, as well as statistical analysis. Even in fields where mathematics is not an absolute prerequisite, its presence or absence makes a major difference in one's ability to rise in the profession. Mathematics is becoming an important factor in the social sciences and is even beginning to invade some of the humanities. To be mathematically illiterate is to carry an increasing burden into an increasing number of occupations. Even the ability to pass a civil service examination for modest clerical jobs is helped or hindered by one's facility in mathematics.

It is hardly surprising that test scores reflect these group differences in mathematics preparation. Nationwide results on the Scholastic Aptitude Test (SAT) for college applicants show Asians and whites consistently scoring higher on the quantitative test than Hispanics or blacks, and men scoring higher than women.[21] Nor are these differences merely the result of socioeconomic "disadvantage" caused by "society." Black, Mexican American, and American Indian youngsters from families with incomes of $50,000 and up score lower than Asians from families whose incomes are just $6,000 and under.[22] Moreover, Asians as a group score higher than whites as a group on the quantitative portion of the SAT and the Japanese in Japan specialize in mathematics, science, and engineering to a far greater extent than do American students in the United States.[23] Cultural differences are real, and cannot be talked away by using pejorative terms such as "stereotypes" or "racism."

The racial, ethnic, and sex differences in mathematics that begin in high school (or earlier) continue on through to the Ph.D. level, affecting career choices and economic rewards. Hispanic Ph.D.'s outnumber Asian Ph.D.'s in the United States by three-to-one in history, but the Asians outnumber the Hispanics by ten-to-one in chemistry.[24] More than half of all Asian Ph.D.'s are in mathematics, science, or engineering, and more than half the Asians who teach college teach in those fields. By contrast, more than half of all black doctorates are in the field of education, a notoriously undemanding and less remunerative field. So are half the doctorates received by American Indians, not one of whom received a Ph.D. in either mathematics or physics in 1980.[25] Female Ph.D.'s are in quantitatively based fields only half as frequently as male Ph.D.'s.[26]

Important as mathematics is in itself, it is also a symptom of broader and deeper disparities in educational choices and performances in general. Those groups with smaller quantities of education tend also to have lower qualities of education, and these disparities follow them all the way through their educational careers and into the job market. The children of lower income racial and ethnic groups typically score lower on tests all through school and attend lower quality colleges when they go to college at all, as well as majoring in the easier courses in fields with the least economic promise. How much of this is due to the home environment and how much to the deficiencies of the public schools in their neighborhoods is a large question that cannot be answered here. But what is clear is that what is called the "same" education, measured in years of schooling, is not even remotely the same in reality.

The civil rights vision relies heavily on statistical "disparities" in income and employment between members of different groups to support its sweeping claims of rampant discrimination. The U.S. Civil Rights

Commission, for example, considers itself to be "controlling for those factors"[27] when it examines people of the same age with the same number of years of schooling—resolutely ignoring the substance of that schooling.

Age and education do not begin to exhaust the differences between groups. They are simply more readily quantifiable than some other differences. The geographic distributions of groups also vary greatly, with Mexican Americans being concentrated in the southwest, Puerto Ricans in the northeast, half of blacks in the South, and most Asians in California and Hawaii. Differences in income between the states are also larger than black-white income differences, so that these distributional differences affect national income differences. A number of past studies, for example, have shown black and Puerto Rican incomes to be very similar nationally, but blacks generally earn higher incomes than Puerto Ricans in New York and other places where Puerto Ricans are concentrated.[28] Their incomes nationally have shown up in these studies as similar, because there are very few Puerto Ricans living in low-income southern states.

One of the most important causes of differences in income and employment is the way people work—some diligently, carefully, persistently, cooperatively, and without requiring much supervision or warnings about absenteeism, tardiness, or drinking, and others requiring much such concern over such matters. Not only are such things inherently difficult to quantify; any suggestion that such differences even exist is sure to bring forth a storm of condemnation. In short, the civil rights vision has been hermetically sealed off from any such evidence. Both historical and contemporary observations on intergroup differences in work habits, discipline, reliability, sobriety, cleanliness, or cooperative attitude—anywhere in the world—are automatically dismissed as evidence only of the bias or bigotry of the observers. "Stereotypes" is the magic word that makes thinking about such things unnecessary. Yet despite this closed circle of reasoning that surrounds the civil rights vision, there is some evidence that cannot be disposed of in that way.

Self-employed farmers, for example, do not depend for their rewards on the biases of employers or the stereotypes of observers. Yet self-employed farmers of different ethnicity have fared very differently on the same land, even in earlier premechanization times, when the principal input was the farmer's own labor. German farmers, for example, had more prosperous farms than other farmers in colonial America[29]—and were more prosperous than Irish farmers in eighteenth-century Ireland,[30] as well as more prosperous than Brazilian farmers in Brazil,[31] Mexican farmers in Mexico,[32] Russian farmers in Russia,[33] and Chilean farmers in Chile.[34] We may ignore the forbidden testimony from all these countries as to how hard the German farmers worked, how frugally they lived, or how sober they were. Still, the results speak for themselves.

That Jews earn far higher incomes than Hispanics in the United States might be taken as evidence that anti-Hispanic bias is stronger than anti-Semitism—if one followed the logic of the civil rights vision. But this explanation is considerably weakened by the greater prosperity of Jews than Hispanics *in Hispanic countries* throughout Latin America.[35] Again, even if one dismisses out of hand all the observers who see great differences in the way these two groups work, study, or save, major tangible differences in economic performance remain that cannot be explained in terms of the civil rights vision.

One of the commonly used indices of intergroup economic differences is family income. Yet families are of different sizes from group to group, reflecting differences in the incidence of broken homes. Female headed households are several times more common among blacks than among whites, and in both groups these are the lowest income families. Moreover, the proportion of people working differs greatly from group to group. More than three-fifths of all Japanese American families have multiple income earners while only about a third of Puerto Rican families do. Nor is this a purely socioeconomic phenomenon, as distinguished from a cultural phenomenon. Blacks have similar incomes to Puerto Ricans, but the proportion of black families with a woman working is nearly three times that among Puerto Ricans.[36]

None of this disproves the existence of discrimination, nor is that its purpose. What is at issue is whether statistical differences mean discrimination, or whether there are innumerable demographic, cultural, and geographic differences that make this crucial automatic inference highly questionable.

Effects Versus Hopes

Thus far, we have not even considered the actual effects of the incentives and constraints created by affirmative action policies—as distinguished from the rationales, hopes, or claims made for these policies. Because these policies are invoked on behalf of the most disadvantaged groups, and the most disadvantaged classes within these groups, it is especially important to scrutinize the factual record of what has happened to the economic position of such people under both equal opportunity and affirmative policies.

Before crediting either political policy with economic gains, it is worth considering what trends were already under way before they were instituted. Much has been made of the number of blacks in high-level occupations before and after the Civil Rights Act of 1964. What has been almost totally ignored is the historical *trend* of black representation in such occupations before the Act was passed. In the period from 1954 to 1964, for example, the number of blacks in professional, technical, and similar high-level positions more than doubled.[37] In other kinds of occupations, the advance of blacks was even greater during the 1940s—when there was little or no civil rights policy—than during the 1950s when the civil rights revolution was in its heyday.[38]

The rise in the number of blacks in professional and technical occupations in the two years from 1964 to 1966 (after the Civil Rights Act) was in fact *less* than in the one year from 1961 to 1962 (before the Civil Rights Act).[39] If one takes into account the growing black population by looking at percentages instead of absolute numbers, it becomes even clearer that the Civil Rights Act of 1964 represented no acceleration in trends that had been going on for many years. The percentage of employed blacks who were professional and technical workers rose less in the five years following the Civil Rights Act of 1964 than in the five years preceding it. The percentage of employed blacks who were managers and administrators was the same in 1967 as in 1964—and in 1960. Nor did the institution of "goals and timetables" at the end of 1971 mark any acceleration in the long trend of rising black representation in these occupations. True, there was an appreciable increase in the percentage of blacks in professional and technical fields from 1971 to 1972, but almost entirely offset by a reduction in the percentage of blacks who were managers and administrators.[40]

The history of Asians and Hispanics likewise shows long-term upward trends that began years before the Civil Rights Act of 1964 and were not noticeably accelerated by the Act or by later "affirmative action" policies. The income of Mexican Americans rose relative to that of non-Hispanic whites between 1959 and 1969 (after the Civil Rights Act), but no more so than from 1949 to 1959 (before the Act).[41] Chinese and Japanese Americans overtook other Americans in income by 1959—five years before the Civil Rights Act.

Ignoring trends already in progress for years makes before-and-after comparisons completely misleading. Yet that is precisely the approach of supporters of the civil rights vision, who proceed as if "before" was a static situation. Yet the notion that the Civil Rights Act and "affirmative action" have had a dramatic impact on the economic progress of minorities has become part of the folklore of the land, established primarily through repetition and vehemence, rather than evidence.

The evidence of the *political* impact of civil rights changes in the 1960s is far more clear-cut. The number of black elected officials, especially in the South, increased many-fold in a relatively few years, including blacks elected to public office in some places for the first time since the Reconstruction era after the Civil War. Perhaps even more important, white elected officials in the South had to change both their policies and their rhetoric to accommodate the new political reality that blacks could vote.

What is truly surprising—and relatively ignored—is the economic impact of affirmative action on the disadvantaged, for whom it is most insistently invoked. The relative position of disadvantaged individuals within the groups singled out for preferential treatment has generally *declined* under affirmative action. This is particularly clear in data for individuals, as distinguished from families.

Family income data have too many pitfalls to be taken at face value. There are, for example, significant variations in what constitutes a family, both from time to time and from group to group. But since many people insist on using such data, these statistics cannot be passed over in silence. In 1969, *before* the federal imposition of numerical "goals and timetables," Puerto Rican family income was 63 percent of the national average. By 1977, it was down to 50 percent. In 1969, Mexican American family income was 76 percent of the national average. By 1977 it was down to 73 percent. Black family income fell from 62 percent of the national average to 60 percent over the same span.[42]

There are many complex factors behind these numbers. The point here is simply that they do not support the civil rights vision. A finer breakdown of the data for blacks shows the most disadvantaged families—the female-headed, with no husband present—to be not only the poorest and with the slowest increase in money income during the 1970s (a decline in *real* income) but also with money incomes increasing even more slowly than among white, female-headed families. By contrast, black husband-wife families had money incomes that were rising faster than that of their white counterparts.[43] It is part of a more general pattern of the most disadvantaged falling farther behind during the affirmative action era, while the already advantaged forged ahead.

Individual data tell the same story, even more clearly. Those blacks with less education and less job experience—the truly disadvantaged—have been falling farther and farther behind their white counterparts under affirmative action, during the very same years when blacks with more education and more job experience have been advancing economically, both absolutely and relative to their white counterparts. First, the disadvantaged: Black male high school dropouts with less than six years of work experience earned 79 percent of the income of white male high school dropouts with less than six years of work experience in 1967 (before affirmative action quotas) and this *fell* to 69 percent by 1978 (after affirmative action quotas). Over these very same years, the income of black males who had completed college and had more than six years of work experience *rose* from 75 percent of the income of their white counterparts to 98 percent.[44] Some economic trends can be explained in terms of general conditions in the economy, but such diametrically opposite trends during the very same span of years obviously cannot.

There is additional evidence that the advantaged have benefited under affirmative action while the disadvantaged have fallen behind.

Black faculty members with numerous publications and Ph.D.'s from top-rated institutions earned more than white faculty members with the same high qualifications, but black faculty members who lacked a doctorate or publications earned less than whites with the same low qualifications.[45] The pattern of diametrically opposite trends in economic well-being among advantaged and disadvantaged blacks is also shown by the general internal distribution of income among blacks. The top fifth of blacks have absorbed a growing proportion of all income received by blacks, while each of the bottom three fifths has received declining shares.[46] Black college-educated couples with husband and wife working had by 1980 achieved incomes higher than white couples of the same description.[47] Meanwhile, at the other end of the spectrum, the black female-headed household was receiving only 62 percent of the income of white, female-headed households—down from 70 percent in 1970.[48]

None of this is easily reconcilable with the civil rights vision's all-purpose explanation, racism and discrimination. To explain such diametrically opposite trends within the black community on the basis of whites' behavior would require us to believe that racism and discrimination were growing and declining at the same time. It is much more reconcilable with ordinary economic analysis.

Affirmative action hiring pressures make it costly to have no minority employees, but continuing affirmative action pressures at the promotion and discharge phases also make it costly to have minority employees who do not work out well. The net effect is to increase the demand for highly qualified minority employees while decreasing the demand for less qualified minority employees or for those without a sufficient track record to reassure employers.

Those who are most vocal about the need for affirmative action are of course the more articulate minority members—the advantaged who speak in the name of the disadvantaged. Their position on the issue may accord with their own personal experience, as well as their own self-interest. But that cannot dismiss the growing evidence that it is precisely the disadvantaged who suffer from affirmative action.

By the Numbers

AVERAGES VERSUS VARIANCE

One of the remarkable aspects of affirmative action is that, while numbers—and *assumptions* about numbers—abound, proponents of the program are almost never challenged to produce positive numerical evidence for its effectiveness or to support their statistical presuppositions. The mere fact that some group is x percent of the population but only y percent of the employees is taken as weighty presumption of employer discrimination. There are serious statistical problems with this approach, quite aside from substantial group differences in age, education, and cultural values.

Even in a random world of identical things, to say that something happens a certain way *on the average* is not to say that it happens that way *every time.* But affirmative action deals with averages almost as if there were no variance. If Hispanics are 8 percent of the carpenters in a given town, it does not follow that *every* employer of carpenters in that town would have 8 percent Hispanics if there were no discrimination. Even if carpenters were assigned to employers by drawing lots (or by some other random process), there would be *variance* in the proportion of Hispanic carpenters from one employer to another. To convict those employers with fewer Hispanics of discrimination in hiring would be to make statistical variance a federal offense.

To illustrate the point, we can consider some process where racial, sexual, or ideological factors do not enter, such as the flipping of a coin. There is no reason to expect a persistent preponderance of heads over tails (or vice versa) on the *average,* but there is also no reason to expect exactly half heads and half tails every time we flip a coin a few times. That is, *variance* will exist.

To illustrate the effect of statistical variance, a coin was flipped ten times and then this experiment was repeated ten times. Here are the results:

HEADS	3	4	3	4	6	7	2	4	5	3
TAILS	7	6	7	6	4	3	8	6	5	7

At one extreme, there were seven heads and three tails, and at the other extreme eight tails and two heads. Statistics not only have averages, they have variance.

Translate this into employment decisions. Imagine that you are the employer who ends up with eight employees from one group and two from another, even though both groups are the same size and no different in qualifications, and even though you have been unbiased in selecting. Try explaining to EEOC and the courts that you ended up with four times as many employees from one group by random chance! You may be convicted of discrimination, even if you have only been guilty of statistical variance.

Of course some employers are biased, just as some coins are biased because of the way their weight is distributed on the design. This particular coin might have been biased; overall, it came up heads 41 percent of the time and tails 59 percent. But even if the coin was biased toward tails, it still came up heads seven times out of ten in one set of flips. If an employer were similarly biased in *favor* of a particular group, he could still be convicted of discrimination *against* that very group, if they ended up with less than half the "representation" of some other group.

No one needs to assume that this particular coin was unbiased or even that the results were accurately reported. Anyone can collect ten people and have them flip a coin ten times, to see the statistical variance for himself. Frivolous as this might seem, the results have deadly serious implications for the way people are convicted of violating federal laws, regulations, and guidelines. It might be especially instructive if this little experiment were performed by editorial writers for publications that fervently support affirmative action, or by clerks of the Supreme Court.

Even when conclusions are based only on differences that statisticians call "statistically significant," this by no means eliminates the basic problem. What is statistically significant depends upon the probability that such a result would have happened by random chance. A common litmus test used by statisticians is whether the event would occur more than five times out of a hundred by random chance. Applying this common test of statistical significance to affirmative action means that even in the most extreme case imaginable—zero discrimination and zero difference among racial, ethnic, and other groups—the EEOC could still run 10,000 employers' records through a computer and come up with about 500 "discriminators."

The illustration chosen is in fact too favorable to the proponents of affirmative action, because it shows the probability of incorrectly calling an employer a discriminator when there is only *one* group in question that might be discriminated against. Affirmative action has a number of groups whose statistical employment patterns can lead to charges of discrimination. To escape a false charge of discrimination, an employer must avoid being in the fatal 5 percent for *all* the groups in question simultaneously. That becomes progressively harder when there are more groups.

While there is a 95 percent chance for a nondiscriminatory employer to escape when there is only one group, this falls to 86 percent when there are three separate groups and to 73 percent when there are six.[49] That is, even in a world of zero discrimination and zero differences among groups, more than one-fourth of all employers would be called "discriminators" by this common test of statistical significance, when there are six separate groups in question.

What this means is that the courts have sanctioned a procedure which insures that large-scale statistical "discrimination" will exist forever, regardless of what the actual facts may be. They have made statistical variance a federal offense.[50]

Shopping for Discrimination

Often the very same raw data point to different conclusions at different levels of aggregation. For example, statistics have shown that black faculty members earn less than white faculty members, but as these data are broken down by field of specialization, by number of publications, by possession (or nonpossession) of a Ph.D. and by the ranking of the institution that issued it, then the black-white income difference not only shrinks but disappears, and in some fields reverses—with black faculty earning more than white faculty with the same characteristics.[51] For those who accept statistics as proof of discrimination, how much discrimination there is, and in what direction, depends upon how finely these data are broken down.

There is no "objective" or "scientific" way to decide at what level of aggregation to stop breaking the data down into finer categories. Nor have the laws or the courts specified in advance what will and will not be the accepted way to break down the statistics. Any individual or organization contemplating a lawsuit against an employer can arrange that employer's statistics in any number of possible ways and then go shopping among the possibilities for the one that will present the employment pattern in the worst light. This is a very effective strategy in a society in which groups differ enormously in their characteristics and choices, while the prevailing vision makes deviations from a random distribution evidence against the employer.

A discrimination case can depend entirely on what level of statistical breakdown the judge accepts, for different groups will be represented—or "underrepresented"—differently according to how precisely occupations and qualifications are defined. While there were more black than Asian American "social scientists" receiving a Ph.D. in 1980, when social scientists were broken down further, there were nearly three times as many Asian as black *economists.* [52] While male recipients of Ph.D.'s in the social sciences outnumbered female recipients of Ph.D.'s by slightly less than two-to-one in 1980, men outnumbered women by more than four-to-one among doctorates in economics and by ten-to-one among doctorates in econometrics.[53] What is the employer hiring: social scientists, economists or econometricians? He may in fact be looking for an econometrician specializing in international trade—and there may be no statistics available on that. Nor can anyone infer the proportion of women or minority members available in that specialty from their distribution in broader categories, for the distribution changes at every level of aggregation.

The same principle applies in other fields as well. A computer manufacturer who is looking for an engineer is not looking for the same kind of engineer as a company that builds bridges. Nor is there the slightest reason to expect all groups to be distributed the same in these subspecialties as they are among engineers in general. Even within a narrow occupational range such as mathematical specialists, blacks outnumber Asian Americans in gross numbers but Asian Americans outnumber blacks more than two-to-one among statisticians.[54]

When comparing any employer's work force with the available labor pool to determine "underrepresentation," everything depends on how that labor pool is defined—at what level of aggregation. Those who wish to argue for discrimination generally prefer broad, loose, heterogeneous categories. The concept of a "qualified" worker aids that approach. When the barely qualified is treated as being the same as the most highly skilled and experienced, it is the same as staying at a very general level of aggregation. Anything that creates or widens the disparity between what the job requires and how the categories are defined increases the potential for statistical "discrimination."

An employer may be guilty or innocent according to what level of statistical aggregation a judge accepts, after the plaintiffs have shopped around among the many possibilities. But that is only part of the problem. A more fundamental problem is that *the burden of proof is on the accused* to prove his innocence, once suspicious numbers have been found. Shopping around for suspicious numbers is by no means difficult, especially for a federal agency, given statistical variance, multiple groups, multiple occupations, and wide-ranging differences in the characteristics and choices of the groups themselves.

Statistical aggregation is a major factor not only in courts of law but also in the court of public opinion. Many statistics from a very general level of aggregation are repeatedly presented in the media as demonstrating pervasive discrimination. The finer breakdowns are more likely to appear in specialized scholarly journals, read by a relative handful of people. Yet these finer breakdowns of statistics often tell a drastically different story, not only for black-white differences and male-female differences but for other groups as well.

For example, American Indian males earn significantly less than white males, and Asian males earn significantly more. Yet, as one holds a wide range of variables constant, these income differences shrink to the vanishing point. Asian Americans, for example, are distributed geographically in a very different pattern from whites. Asians are concentrated in higher income states, in more urban areas, and have more education. When all of this is held constant, their income advantage vanishes.[55] By the same token, when various demographic and cultural variables—notably proficiency in the English language—are held constant, the income disadvantages of Hispanic and American Indian males also disappear.[56]

It can hardly be expected that discrimination lawsuits and discrimination as a political issue will be correspondingly reduced any time soon. The methods by which it is measured in the courts and in politics insure that it will be a continuing source of controversy.

Poverty and huge intergroup differences in income are serious matters, whether or not discrimination is the cause—and whether or not affirmative action is the cure. Yet any attempt to deal with these very real disadvantages must first cut through the fog generated by a vision more powerful than its evidence—and, in fact, a vision shaping what courts will accept as evidence.

NOTES

1. U.S. Equal Employment Opportunity Commission, *Legislative History of Titles VII and XI of Civil Rights Act of 1964* (Washington, D.C.: U.S. Government Printing Office, no date) pp. 1007–08, 1014, 3005, 3006, 3013, 3160, and *passim.*
2. *Ibid.,* p. 3005.
3. *Ibid.*
4. *Ibid.,* p. 1014.
5. *Ibid.,* p. 3006.
6. *Ibid.,* p. 3160.
7. *Ibid.,* p. 3015.
8. *Ibid.,* p. 3013.
9. Quoted in Nathan Glazer, *Affirmative Discrimination* (New York: Basic Books, 1975), p. 45.
10. For example, *Gallup Opinion Index,* Report 143 (June 1977), p. 23.
11. Nathan Glazer, *Affirmative Discrimination,* p. 49.
12. Much semantic effort has gone into claiming that quotas are rigid requirements while "goals" under "affirmative action" are flexible. Historically, however, quotas have existed in sales, immigration, production, and many other areas, sometimes referring to minima, sometimes to maxima, and with varying degrees of flexibility. The idea that "quota" implies rigidity is a recent redefinition. The objection to quotas is that they are quantitative rather than qualitative criteria, not that they are rigidly rather than flexibly quantitative.
13. *United Steelworkers of America* v. *Weber,* 443 US 193 (1979), p. 207, note 7.
14. *Ibid.,* p. 222.
15. *Ibid.,* pp. 226–52.
16. Thomas Sowell, *Markets and Minorities* (New York: Basic Books, 1981), p. 11.
17. U.S. Bureau of the Census, *Social Indicators,* 1976 (Washington, D.C.: U.S. Government Printing Office, 1977), pp. 454–56.
18. Peter Uhlenberg, "Demographic Correlates of Group Achievement: Contrasting Patterns of Mexican-Americans and Japanese-Americans," *Race, Creed, Color, or National Origin,* ed. Robert K. Yin (Itasca, Illinois: F. E. Peacock Publishers, 1973), p. 91.
19. Lucy W. Sells, "Leverage for Equal Opportunity Through Mastery of Mathematics," *Women and Minorities in Science,* ed. Sheila M. Humphreys (Boulder, Colo.: Westview Press, 1982), pp. 12, 16.
20. *Ibid.,* p. 11.
21. College Entrance Examination Board, *Profiles, College-Bound Seniors, 1981* (New York: College Entrance Examination Board, 1982), pp. 12, 22, 41, 51, 60, 65.
22. *Ibid.,* pp. 27, 36, 46, 55.
23. *Ibid.,* pp. 60, 79; Alexander Randall, "East Meets West," *Science,* November 1981, p. 72.
24. National Research Council, *Science, Engineering, and Humanities Doctorates in the United States* (Washington, D.C.: National Academy of Sciences, 1980), pp. 13, 39.
25. National Research Council, *Summary Report: 1980 Doctorate Recipients from United States Universities* (Washington, D.C.: National Academy Press, 1981), pp. 26, 29.
26. Sue E. Berryman, "Trends in and Causes of Minority and Female Representation Among Science and Mathematics Doctorates," mimeographed, The Rand Corporation, 1983, p. 13.

27. U.S. Commission on Civil Rights, *Unemployment and Underemployment Among Blacks, Hispanics, and Women* (Washington, D.C.: U.S. Commission on Civil Rights, 1982), p. 58.

28. Thomas Sowell, *Ethnic America* (New York: Basic Books, 1981), p. 222.

29. J. C. Furnas, *The Americans* (New York: G. P. Putnam's Sons, 1969), p. 86; Daniel Boorstin, *The Americans* (New York: Random House, 1958), Vol. I, p. 225.

30. Arthur Young, *A Tour in Ireland* (Shannon, Ireland: Irish University Press, 1970), Vol. I, pp. 377–79.

31. Thomas H. Holloway, *Immigrants on the Land* (Chapel Hill, N.C.: University of North Carolina Press, 1980), p. 151.

32. Harry Leonard Sawatzky, *They Sought a Country* (Berkeley: University of California Press, 1971), pp. 129, 244. Apparently Germans prospered in Honduras as well. *Ibid.,* pp. 361, 365.

33. Hattie Plum Williams, *The Czar's Germans* (Lincoln, Nebraska: American Historical Society of Germans from Russia, 1975), pp. 135, 159.

34. Carl Solberg, *Immigration and Nationalism* (Austin: University of Texas Press, 1970), pp. 27, 40.

35. Judith Laikin Elkin, *Jews of the Latin American Republics* (Chapel Hill, N.C.: University of North Carolina Press, 1980), pp. 214–37. See also Robert Weisbrot, *The Jews of Argentina* (Philadelphia: The Jewish Publication Society of America, 1979), pp. 175–184.

36. Thomas Sowell, *Ethnic America,* p. 238.

37. Daniel P. Moynihan, "Employment, Income, and the Ordeal of the Negro Family," *Daedalus,* Fall 1965, p. 752.

38. Daniel O. Price, *Changing Characteristics of the Negro Population* (Washington, D.C.: U.S. Government Printing Office, 1969), pp. 117, 118.

39. *Employment and Training Report of the President, 1981* (Washington, D.C.: U.S. Government Printing Office, 1981), p. 150.

40. *Ibid.,* p. 151.

41. Thomas Sowell, *Ethnic America,* p. 260.

42. Thomas Sowell, *The Economics and Politics of Race* (New York: William Morrow, 1983), p. 187.

43. U.S. Bureau of the Census, *Social Indicators III* (Washington, D.C.: U.S. Government Printing Office, 1980), p. 485.

44. Finis Welch, "Affirmative Action and Its Enforcement," *American Economic Review,* May 1981, p. 132.

45. Thomas Sowell, *Affirmative Action Reconsidered* (Washington, D.C.: American Enterprise Institute, 1975), pp. 16–22.

46. Martin Kilson, "Black Social Classes and Intergenerational Policy," *The Public Interest,* Summer 1981, p. 63.

47. U.S. Bureau of the Census *Current Population Reports,* Series P-20, No. 366 (Washington, D.C.: U.S. Government Printing Office, 1981), pp. 182, 184.

48. U.S. Bureau of the Census, *Current Population Reports,* Series P-60, No. 80, p. 37; *ibid.,* Series P-60, No. 132, pp. 41–42.

49. The probability that a nondiscriminatory employer will escape a false charge of discrimination is 95 percent, when the standard of "statistical significance" is that his employment pattern would not occur more than 5 times out of 100 by random chance. But the probability of escaping the same false charge for three separate groups simultaneously is $(.95)^3$ or about 86 percent. When there are six separate groups, the probability is $(.95)^6$ or about 73 percent. Not all groups are separate; women and the aged, for example, overlap racial and ethnic groups. This complicates the calculation without changing the basic principle.

50. The greater ease of "proving" discrimination statistically, when there are multiple groups, multiple jobs, and substantial demographic, cultural and other differences

between groups, may either take the form of finding more "discriminators" at a given level of statistical significance (5 percent, for example) or using a more stringent standard of statistical significance (1 percent, for example) to produce a more impressive-looking case against a smaller number of "discriminators."

51. Thomas Sowell, *Affirmative Action Reconsidered* pp. 16–22.
52. Commission on Human Resources, National Research Council, *Summary Report: 1980 Doctorate Recipients from United States Universities* (National Academy Press, 1981), p. 27.
53. *Ibid.*, p. 25.
54. U.S. Bureau of the Census, *Current Population Reports*, Series P-23, No. 120 (Washington, D.C.: U.S. Government Printing Office, 1982), p. 5.
55. Barry R. Chiswick, "An Analysis of the Earnings and Employment of Asian-American Men," *Journal of Labor Economics*, April 1983, pp. 197–214.
56. Walter McManus, William Gould and Finis Welch, "Earnings of Hispanic Men: The Role of English Language Performance," *ibid.*, pp. 101–30; Gary D. Sandefur, "Minority Group Status and the Wages of White, Black, and Indian Males," *Social Science Research*, March 1983, pp. 44–68.

JOSEPH SOBRAN

The Abortion Culture

I have often wondered, in moments of idle speculation, how Dwight Eisenhower would feel if he could come back for a day and see his beloved country. He was the first President I clearly remember, and, having been born in 1946, I still feel toward him the kind of child's awe one feels for a grandfather. Not that I don't know what can be said against him. But in my imagination he stands as the embodiment of the America I grew up in. Though I came from a solidly Democratic home and was all for John Kennedy in 1960, I secretly trembled when my young hero took the reins of state from that tremendous old man. Could there really *be* another President?

I imagine myself guiding the revenant Eisenhower down the streets of my home town, and hoping I don't have to explain to him that the Martha Washington Theater, where I used to watch Westerns on Saturday afternoons during his presidency, has become a porno house. If he noticed and asked me about it, his face stern and troubled, I would have to plead for my town by explaining what would trouble him more, that the disgrace was national. He died in 1969, just before the plague really spread (during the Administration of Richard Nixon, as it happened).

Maybe I could whisk him past such public blights and get him into my

From Joseph Sobran, *Single Issues* (New York: Human Life Press, 1983) pp. 112–124. Copyright © 1983, The Human Life Foundation. Reprinted by permission of Human Life Press.

house. But even there he might curiously leaf through a newspaper and see the ads for pornographic movies. He might even turn to the classified ads and find notices of a certain kind of bargain: "ABORTION—$75."

At this point, in my fantasy, I become tongue-tied.

The advent of pornography's liberation was gradual and hard to date. Abortion, however, had its own Pearl Harbor Day. On January 22, 1973, the Supreme Court found abortion virtually on demand to be a constitutional mandate.

But Pearl Harbor Day didn't come out of nowhere. It was preceded by long preparation. You don't attack without armed forces, a power base, a strategy, and some kind of philosophy.

The Supreme Court has its own philosophy, which it has been putting into effect for many years. The offensive began long before 1973. The Court's several incremental decisions in favor of pornography were phases of that offensive, issuing from that same philosophy. In terms of the schools of philosophy, perhaps the nearest approximation we can suggest is positivism.

This doctrine has put the Court at odds with the Declaration of Independence. Consider:

"We hold these truths to be self-evident. . . ." The Court has been dedicated to moral relativism, an attitude more than a philosophy, but an attitude at odds with the notion of any eternal moral truths.

"That all men are created equal . . ." The Court has treated humanity as beginning not with creation, but with birth.

"And that they are endowed by their Creator . . ." The Court has worked hard, within limits imposed not by the Constitution but by political power, to discourage all reference to that Creator, especially in the public schools, where young minds are formed.

"With certain unalienable rights; that among these [is] life . . ." Here is the crux.

The Court has now adopted, in opposition to the Declaration, the great heresy of the twentieth century: that government has not the duty to recognize and protect ("secure") innate human rights, given by God, but the arbitrary power to create and/or destroy positive rights—including the very right to live—at its whim.

The Court, I repeat, is at war with the American tradition, with the whole Western tradition. It would be strange on the face of it if the Court had somehow discovered the real meaning of the Constitution after two hundred years—a real meaning that had escaped that Constitution's authors and the people who had inherited and lived the constitutional tradition over those two centuries.

It surely begins to look very suspicious when that alleged "real" meaning turns out to coincide with the ideology of today's left-wing intellectuals. Yet the Court asks us to accept its word for it that only the

Court speaks for our authentic tradition. It could hardly ask this, or expect our obedience, unless it felt its ideology commanded widespread assent in powerful institutions.

When I reflect that only seven men have foisted such a position on more than 200 million people—not to speak of some 10 million unborn people who have died since 1973, and millions more who will soon die—I can hardly believe my ears when I hear it charged that the antiabortion movement, which seeks essentially to restore the laws of fifty states duly passed by our representatives and struck down abruptly by those seven men, is bent on imposing *its* views on the majority.

No majority ever sanctioned the Court's view. Supporters of legal abortion have consistently refused to put the issue to a democratic test. They prefer to pretend that their ideology is implicit in the Constitution. Those who dispute this are treated not as upholders of a variant opinion but as enemies of constitutional freedoms.

In pornography too, the Court has told us that various antiobscenity laws violate the First Amendment. It has never denied flatly that obscenity is a valid category for legislation, and in fact has admitted that different categories of speech enjoy differing degrees of constitutional protection; but the cumulative effect of its rulings has been much the same.

The *resonance* of the Court's utterances, one might say, has been wholly favorable to sexual explicitness. Many intellectuals of the Left haven't waited for the Court, but have gone ahead and declared "freedom of expression" an absolute, courtesy of the Constitution. The current Court has said little to discourage this bogus extrapolation.

I hardly need say that the real debate isn't about the text of the Constitution. Any text can be rendered ambiguous by captious interpretation. No, the real debate is about our public philosophy, with the Left insisting that its ideology be treated as the true spirit of the Constitution. One effect of the Equal Rights Amendment would be to incorporate a charismatic symbol of leftist ideology into our fundamental law. Whatever the text of ERA may say (and the words themselves appear unexceptionable enough) there can be little doubt that its supporters actually expect the judiciary to make it mean what they want it to mean, with the result that the courts will be empowered to use the flood of litigation that would certainly ensue upon ratification as the occasions for nullifying hundreds of legislative acts. No previous constitutional amendment has ever had such a purely destructive intent. Earlier ones have been meant to serve as bases for legislation; ERA is meant to curtail the scope of representative government.

The First Amendment was meant to limit only the legislative power of the Federal Government. This was true, as every schoolboy once knew, of the whole Bill of Rights: to reserve power to the states and the people. Later Amendments, like the Fourteenth, conferred broader powers on

Congress. But all, in various ways, preserved the principle of legislative supremacy. Even judicial review, as Garry Wills has lately reminded us, was originally defended as an extension of the people's legislative sovereignty, the judiciary upholding fundamental law against particular transgressions by sitting legislatures.

In a tortured sense, ERA might be said to do this. But that is certainly not its spirit. Its concrete aim is to restructure our form of government so as to legitimize the kinds of usurpations the Court has long practiced.

People on both sides of the ideological divide sense that pornography and abortion are deeply related. You can't cheapen (or, if you will, "liberate") sex without cheapening life itself. Sell the one, and you soon buy the other. "Sexual freedom" has come to mean freedom from consequences, from loyalty, from moral responsibility.

By making sex a pastime, the culture of the Left has turned children into party-crashers who deserve expulsion. We even hear hypocritical concern for "unwanted" children, whom it would be cruel not to abort. Nobody is willing to come out for irresponsibility. Instead the Left defines abortion as a responsible act, and interference with it as officious meddling. Proabortion rhetoric, demanding that the abortion decision be left to individual conscience, subtly implies that to get an abortion is to obey rather than defy the sense of right and wrong. Abortion advocates present themselves as the friends, their opponents as the enemies, of conscience.

(The Playboy Philosopher Hugh Hefner has backed abortion for many years. He, for one, saw the connection long ago.)

The whole argument of the Left has been deeply dishonest. At first pornography, sexual license, and abortion were defended in the name of privacy. Now our privacy is affronted at every newsstand.

Free expression was supposed to allow us to be more openly concerned and "caring." We were told it would eliminate the movie violence, for instance, that resulted from repressed and pent-up impulses to physical affection. But today our society is more callous than ever—toward the unborn, toward women. Our movies combine obscenity with a level of violence undreamed of a few years ago. Sadistic pornography has become a big business.

If books and entertainments don't affect people for the worse, it is hard to see how they can hope to change them for the better, and we may as well close our schools and universities. As it happens, the Supreme Court has been busy in this area too. In banning even voluntary prayer in the public schools, it has abridged the free exercise of religion in the name of protecting it. It is only a slight exaggeration to say that the only book the intellectuals of the Left want to ban is the Bible.

Under today's slippery rules, one can easily imagine a teacher leading a class in prayer, only to be charged with violating the First Amendment—while another teacher might show his class a pornographic movie, and claim the *protection* of the First Amendment.

Something like this already happens. Under cultural pressures that go beyond formal laws and the judiciary's explicit prescriptions, all college-level teachers know or sense that it is far safer to attack and deride religion than to defend it. The pious feel cowed; the impious "liberated."

The arguments for abortion have shifted suspiciously too. Once it was a necessary evil whose malign effects would be *minimized* by legalization. Then we weren't supposed to pass judgment; it was a "religious" issue concerning which legislation was, under secular government, inappropriate. Today we are urged to recognize it as a positive good, a "basic right." Not only must we tolerate it, we must pay for it with public funds. It has become a "right of conscience," and never mind the consciences of taxpayers who don't want to pay for it.

The long and the short of this matter is that we now have what I have previously called an established irreligion. The liberal state, according to its Yale enthusiast Bruce Ackerman, is "value-neutral," but has a duty to subsidize the pursuit of random individual values. You may of course practice your religion in the privacy of your home or church, but that mustn't affect your politics or public life. You must respect the rights of unbelievers, even to the extent of behaving as if *you* were an unbeliever.

The Left has mastered this mode of behavior very thoroughly indeed. When doctors like Kenneth Edelin and William Waddill are accused of murdering viable infants by way of consummating abortions, it rallies to their defense without pausing to ask if there is any justice in the charges, let alone considering the clear suffering the victims have undergone. One wonders if there is any conceivable point at which they would recoil and cry, "No! We didn't mean to permit *that!*"

It is worth wondering, too, just what liberal "neutrality" toward religion really means. So far, this "neutrality" has meant putting religion at severe disadvantages. The same forces that insist on government subsidies of abortion rights get livid when you suggest even a modest tax break for parents who send their children to private religious schools.

This posture is at odds with their customary argument that if you can't afford to exercise a right, you are effectively denied its exercise, and government must lend a hand. Liberals lose their liberality when parents want to control and direct their children's education. Ackerman even suggests that the purpose of public education is to counteract oppressive parental influences. To such ends does neutrality, in the "liberal" sense, lead.

This vindictive eagerness to make parents pay twice for private education shows a deep contempt for parents' rights and for religion itself. When was the last time the Left, liberal or radical, protested the persecution of religion behind the Iron Curtain?

If this is "neutrality," then so was the old "separate-but-equal" racial system. What the Left, led by the Supreme Court, has really instituted is not the separation of church and state, but the invidious segregation of religion. Religious convictions are now second-class opinions. If faith can survive Communist persecution, it can survive the milder, subtler discrimination of the secular liberal culture; but it shouldn't have to.

Let us spell out the analogy of this culture to an established church. When the state has an official religion, it may, as in England, tolerate others. But the established church is paid for out of public monies taken compulsorily, as all taxes are, from all citizens. You have to pay for it whether you belong or not. If you want another church in keeping with your own beliefs, you pay for it out of the money the state has left you.

That is how our educational system now works: You pay for the schools from which religion is banned whether your children attend them or not, whether you agree with them or not, whether you think them good influences or not. I recently watched an NBC News exposé of the deterioration of the public schools, and found that classroom violence had been going on under my nose; my fourteen-year-old-son, watching with me, commented, "That's what the public school was like." I had switched him to a Catholic school last fall, not because I suspected what his public school had been like, but because I had decided that he would receive a fuller education in a Catholic school. He, for his part, had assumed until then that the chaos of his daily routine was normal.

But leave aside such specifics of public education's decline. The late sociologist Alvin Gouldner approved, like Ackerman, of public education in principle. In fact he thought it had been very cunning of the "new class" he spoke for to have hoodwinked parents into subsidizing an educational system that quietly subverted their own values. And two radical New York journalists, Alexander Cockburn and James Ridgeway, have lately worried in print about the right-wing attack on the public schools, because, they say, the Left can't survive politically without a public school system to spread leftist attitudes. Such defenses of public education say more than any charges I can level.

At the moment the forces of tradition in America are just beginning to understand how steeply the odds have been fixed against them. Because the religious traditions of this country remain powerful, despite those odds, we haven't had an open and powerful socialist or communist Left here. The closest we have come to the sort of thing France and Italy have was in 1972; but George McGovern's defeat smashed any further chance of that under the two-party system.

Yet there *is* a Left minority in this country, and its main political organ has been the Supreme Court. The mass media and the major universities have helped too to convey the belief that the Court's ideology represents authentic constitutional doctrine. Under this guise the Court has smuggled into law a number of the assumptions and proposals of socialism, with which it clearly has no fundamental quarrel. (The late Justice William O. Douglas, by the way, left a bequest of land to be used by international scholars, with special preference to "scholars" from the Soviet Union, China, Iran, Vietnam, and—of all places—North Korea. Anyone who had predicted this would have been charged with McCarthyism.)

The Courts, the media, and the academics (whose influence, now, reaches down into the schools) form a kind of triangle of cultural power. Each has much to gain by this alliance, reinforcing, as they do, each other's power. (It shouldn't be forgotten that pornography, hard and soft, is the media's great pocketbook issue.)

Taken all together, they very strongly undermine the influence of parents and churches on the beliefs and morals of the young. From this point of view, the student "rebellion" of the sixties wasn't quite what it was called; while the students were rebelling against absent parents, they were actually conforming, with a kind of violent docility, to the secularist and socialist pressures of their immediate college environment. Let it not be forgotten that many of them came from families that had never before had college-educated members but which believed implicitly in "education" as self-improvement, so that the young were peculiarly exposed even by their parents' trust. We should bear in mind too, as we consider these upwardly mobile youth, that, as the historian John Lukacs has remarked, America is the only country where it has been possible to move "up" socially by moving Left politically; a truth attested to by any number of self-congratulatory autobiographies, during the sixties and seventies.

By a fine irony, the more the young conformed to leftist attitudes—by engaging in radical politics and casual sex—the more their liberal elders congratulated them on their "independence." It may be that the wrong youths were getting all the praise. The ones who showed true independence, I would suggest, were those who remained faithful to home values while away from home, quietly resisting all the immediate and clamorous pressures and solicitations of the campus environment. Not least of those pressures was the contempt they endured when they weren't simply ignored. Though they got little credit for it, and no publicity, these students showed a courage we ought to honor.

Unfortunately, even those who didn't flip out in the sixties all too often did unconsciously absorb the two great rules of etiquette imposed and enforced by the culture of the Left: (1) You may never question the goals of socialism, though you should question all things else: (2) You must keep your religion, if any, to yourself. These rules were no less powerful for being uncodified. Unwritten laws are hard to attack precisely because they are hard to identify.

We saw how powerful this second rule was last fall when liberals grew hysterical over Cardinal Medeiros' statement on abortion and, even more, over the Reverend Jerry Falwell and the Moral Majority. To the Left, religion is always a threat, seldom a good—except in the watered-down form of those accommodating clerics who join not only leftist causes (including abortion rights) but the Left's attack on "reactionary" religion. (William Sloane Coffin, between trips to Iran, appeared on the Phil Donahue Show to tell Falwell he was "ignorant.") Such clerics, as James Hitchcock points out, also join the Left in its great silence on the Communist persecution of religion—while calling on the churches to "speak out" against right-wing regimes.

A key strategy—perhaps subliminal—of the cultural Left is to induce the young to adopt "liberalized" sexual attitudes and (the real point) habits that will at once initiate them into the new culture and, especially, burn their bridges back to the old, with its code of family loyalties. The great Russian dissident Igor Shafarevich notes that sexual "liberation" is always one of the devices through which socialist movements rob sex of its sanctity and destroy the fiber of the family.

Once the family is weakened, the dignity of the individual is weakened. People all become interchangeable, with no special perduring commitments to others. Marriage is reduced to a "piece of paper," mere bourgeois convention. In such a moral environment, it is hard to argue against abortion. If people are interchangeable, the powerless among them become disposable. (One begins to hear the case for euthanasia and infanticide; the category of the "unwanted" expands.)

A college setting, like a crazy cult, is the natural place to instill ideologies—"new ideas," as they are approvingly called—into the young. There they are isolated among others like themselves, away from parental supervision. They have no families or children of their own, no stake in property. They are full of energy and ready to explore novelties. Everything seems possible to them. They can hardly believe themselves capable of fatal mistakes; death and tragedy seem a long way off. They are free. They like to take dares; they feel cowardly if they refuse. And they are secretly afraid, terribly susceptible to moral bullying, especially if it claims the mantle of idealism.

They are especially afraid of going back to their parents. After all, this is the age when they are expected to confirm their independence, their self-sufficiency. Making one's own sexual choices is a perennial symbol, as much in Shakespeare as in the cinema (despite their profoundly differing codes), of maturity. How easy it is for the young to be rushed into sex; how hard for them to admit to having made a degrading mistake; that would be to admit that their parents were right about something important. At college it is taboo to admit the truth of *old* ideas.

During the sixties the campuses proved wonderful recruiting grounds for the Left. Sex played an important role, in both positive and unconfessedly negative ways, in making the young feel they had been inducted—irrevocably—into a new social order in which an undifferentiated (some might say promiscuous) love of "mankind" was to supersede old ties.

Beneath all the rhetoric, one of the real meanings of the furor over sex education is whether the new code of the Left, through the medium of professionals whose ideologies assume a "neutral" guise, is going to replace the authority of parents even at the elementary school level. Traditional codes, given the taboo on religion, are sure to be demoted; and, as usual, the real values of the educators will find bolder expression as more authority is taken over from the parents by the state. One way or another, parents' values will be decared "unconstitutional." Both sides sense this—one side with deep apprehension, the other with (to use an old but fitting word) gusto. Parental "tyranny" will give way to state "concern."

At the moment the commonest argument is that parents "fail" to inform their children about sex. No doubt this is often true. Parents also fail to inform their children about religion, but this is still conceded to lie outside the purview of the state.

To the extent that parents do fail, it may be less because they fail to provide biological data than because they fail to give moral, and religious, guidance. And the educators seem reluctant to admit another obvious possibility: that if there is now an increase in sexual mischief (not the term these educators would use) among the young, it is hardly likely to be the result of excessive parental authority. Parents have less authority now than ever before in American history. There were certainly no *more* teen-age pregnancies when the family was strong. Why assume that the solution to any current epidemics is to weaken the family still further?

Isn't it possible, nay, overwhelmingly likely, that the real problem is the new code itself? If the increase in explicitness has only aggravated the perennial weakness of flesh so far, only a fool would dismiss the possibility that the new code, not the family, must be at fault, and that even more of what ails us would hardly cure us.

It seems plain to me, at any rate, that we must face here a merely ideological presumption against the family. There is a parallel in economics. The Left, liberal and radical, has insisted on interfering with the free market—that is, with a system based on voluntary exchange. When the economy falters, the Left's automatic response is not to question its own role, but to demand even more interference. So with the family. The more its status is weakened, the worse the condition of the social fabric; and the more the family is blamed for this. The cure for the ills of statism is always—more statism.

But the deeper question is not whether the family has failed. It is what the family's critics would regard as "success." So far the answer seems to be more access by the young, regardless of their parents' wishes, to contraceptives, penicillin, abortion. In effect, the destruction of the moral influence of parents.

Few would put it this way. But that is only natural. Who favors inflation? There is no organized Inflation Party. But there are plenty of people in strategic positions who have found it expedient to implement policies whose overall result can only be to inflate the currency. And when inflation arrives, those people shake their heads and murmur about the mysterious "causes" of inflation. (It is worth hinting here too that many of them refuse to consider inflation as in any sense a moral problem, unless of course they can pin the blame on their adversaries.)

That, in my view, is also how we get socialism. There is no major socialist party here, any more than there is a small band of financiers plotting in whispers to print paper money until the presses overheat. But there are plenty of people who have been taught to despise the three institutions Shafarevich identifies as the perennial targets of socialism: family, property, and religion. For every person who consciously subscribes to the socialist creed, there are dozens in whom the cultural atmosphere has bred socialist instincts. Many find it hard even to imagine a kind of progress that doesn't consist in state-directed social homogenization.

After all, socialism is the great phenomenon of the twentieth century. It would be remarkable if a system that has held sway over so much of the earth in our time, and has won so many followers even in democratic countries, should leave America unscathed.

I will not enter into the esoteric debates over whether Soviet socialism or German national socialism or Italian corporate socialism or any of the variants in the dozens of people's democratic socialist republics measures up as "true" socialism. To listen to the avowed socialists, you would gather that socialism has been "betrayed" just about every time it has been tried; they are forever insisting that socialism be judged not by its bloody past, but by its radiant future. All one can say is that common sense adjures skepticism toward any dream with such a marked tendency to be betrayed by reality.

Whatever "true" socialism may be, it is pretty clear what *real* socialism is. It is a system that believes that society can be improved by concentrating power in the hands of some elite—racial, intellectual, or ideological—and by destroying institutions that interfere with the state monopoly of power and legitimacy. A socialist is one who thinks he qualifies for membership in such an elite.

This is, to be sure, an unflattering description, but socialism deserves to be defined by its prospective victims, not just by its advocates. True, not all socialists are Lenins; there are degrees of malignity. But the dream itself is malign. For a creed based on alleged insights into the course of history, socialism has been stubbornly resistant to the accumulation of historical evidence. It blames its failures entirely on its enemies, on the things it means to wipe out, on the people it intends to enslave. Like the family and parents.

Reasoning from structure rather than from labels, then, I have no hesitation in calling the general trend of politics, even in America, social-ist. How far the election of a conservative regime will arrest or even reverse this trend, it is too early to say.

That depends largely on how much of a fight the American people put up. I don't expect it to be easy. The resistance will have to be mounted at every level, by people sophisticated in both ideas and power politics.

I do propose one simple measure for every individual who opposes the growth of the supervisory state. Each of us should become familiar with the Constitution, especially the Bill of Rights. It is a surprisingly short and lucid document. Its flavor is not at all what one would assume from hearing ideologues discuss it, in tones suggesting they hold the copyright.

The First Amendment is especially important. Apart from what it says, it was never intended to be the centerpiece of American government. As far as its text is concerned, it limits Federal power, particularly in the area of religion. Clearly it meant, in forbidding a Federal establishment and guaranteeing free worship, to make religion not less but *more* free. By refusing to give one religion a privileged status, the Framers were open-ing the way to multiple religious influences on the state, rather than prohibiting them all. The point was to prevent one church from having an automatic advantage over the others. This should increase, not dimin-ish, the influence of faith on our public life.

The Constitution, in short, is not hostile to religion but friendly to it. Even the Supreme Court has never directly denied this, only evaded it; and Justice Douglas himself once acknowledged ringingly that "we are a religious people whose institutions presuppose a Supreme Being," a clear allusion to the Declaration which he and his peers, on a later occa-sion, were so tragically to flout.

We must especially reject any suggestion that since our government must not declare any religion to represent the whole truth, we as citizens have some sort of secular duty to behave as if all religions were false. Restrictions on the government were not intended to be restrictions on the freedom of the people. On the contrary. Such doctrinaire illogic would also say that since we can't know whether the unborn deserve to live, we must never prevent their being killed. But to say that is to imply that the Bill of Rights is opposed to unalienable rights. And not even the judiciary, the media, and all the academies, yelling in unison at the top of their voices, can make such a position coherent. Let alone true.

PART VI

Foreign Policy
and the Communist Threat

I F THERE IS ONE THING that conservatives agree on, it is that the Soviet Union is an evil empire. Not to understand that is, quite simply, to have lost one's moral bearings, to be condemned to wander the world unable to distinguish between free government and tyranny, unable to tell friend from foe.

Yet the failure to make these elementary moral distinctions is now commonplace in the West, not so much because of cowardice (although it is seldom absent) but because of the increasing relativism of the liberals' worldview. John F. Kennedy, more than thirty-five years ago, was so sure of the malevolence of Fidel Castro that he was willing to authorize (if not in the event to support) an invasion of Cuba designed to liberate it from tyranny. Today, leading Democrats visit Cuba not to liberate it from Communism but to toast Castro and even the dead Che Guevara. "Long live Fidel Castro," Jesse Jackson exclaimed in Havana a few years ago. "Dear Comandante," a group of prominent Democrats wrote fawningly to Nicaragua's Daniel Ortega at about the same time.

How is it that the contemporary liberal retains the basic moral credentials on which to build coherent humanitarian policies? One could not praise Adolf Hitler and toast Himmler and proceed to the altar of civil rights and speak with true resonance. But liberals have long accepted the doctrine that all history hitherto is the history of class struggle—just consult the standard history of the New Deal by Arthur Schlesinger, Jr., for example, which depicts the Great Depression as the crisis of capitalism—except that, in the liberal version, history ends not with the withering away of the state and the classless society, as in Marxism, but with the Welfare State ruled by an unelected but benevolent class of bureaucrats, judges, and liberal intellectuals. In both cases a sort of equality of condition is the putative goal of politics, and all resistance to the onward march of history is defined as perverse, reactionary, obscurantist.

Hoist by their own principles, modern liberals have found it difficult to discern the specific evil of Communism. Indeed, in the late 1960s they virtually collapsed before the New Left's contention that since liberalism had essentially the same ends as Radicalism, it was irrational to continue to plead for liberal means ("work within the system") to Radical ends. Why *not* Revolution? Why *not* the North Vietnamese and Viet Cong rather than the South Vietnamese? Liberalism was at a loss for an answer, and still is. Hence the liberals' peculiar blindness to any threat to American liberty coming from their left.

Whatever difficulties American conservatives have had in avoiding a historicist account of themselves (see Part One and Part Three), they have, to their credit, always recognized the dangers inherent in liberalism's reliance on theories of history, and in particular have been mindful of the affinities between the liberal and the Marxist versions of historical inevitability. Gerhart Niemeyer's essay "The Communist Mind" is a classic epitome of the Marxist worldview, which, he argues, is distinguished by its thoroughgoing reliance on a philosophy of the future. It is this, not its collectivist economics or power politics, that makes the cause of the Soviet Union plausible and even idealistic. Niemeyer is professor of political science emeritus at Notre Dame, an ordained Episcopal priest, and the author of many distinguished studies of Marxism and modern politics. With sure, economical brushstrokes, he depicts the world as it appears to a faithful member of the Communist Party, for whom the End of History justifies any means, any crime, so long as it brings the revolutionary Day of Judgment closer.

James Burnham was a professor of philosophy at New York University at age twenty-five and taught there for twenty years. He went, like others who have contributed to this volume, through socialism and from there to his own brand of conservatism. Although his formal academic qualifications were in philosophy, he became known throughout the academic world as a sociopolitical theorist, and his book *The Managerial Revolution* was treated with the respect given to seminal works. Burnham turned to government service and then back to book writing (*The Struggle for the World, Congress and the American Tradition, Suicide of the West*) and to journalism. He was a senior editor of *National Review* for many years, and was awarded the nation's highest civilian honor, the Medal of Freedom, in 1983. In the first incarnation of this volume (*Did You Ever See a Dream Walking?*) he was (uniquely) invited to submit a selection from his work on the strategic problems posed by the world Communist movement. He replied:

What I suggest here are three excerpts, the first from *The Struggle for the World* and the last two from, respectively, the introduction and the final chapter of *The War We Are In.* This selection (1) combines writing twenty [now forty] years old and a recent writing; (2) includes illustrations of the use of historical reference and analogy in relation to historical analysis. I believe this integral incorporation of history to be of the essence of conservatism and almost always absent from ideologism, especially from liberal ideologism; and it is certainly characteristic of my "method"; (3) includes a summary of the "nature of communism"; (4) gives a retrospective analysis of global developments and an anticipatory analysis of likely future developments.

Burnham was one of the most original strategic thinkers of the past forty years, and the selections here reproduced (unchanged from the first edition) are monuments to his perspicacity. To be sure, his talk of "universal empire" may at first strike the reader as old-fashioned, perhaps even melodramatic. But his point was that it is only in the most capacious historical, strategic, and political contexts that the significance of Berlin, of the Suez Crisis, of the Sino-Soviet split, of Vietnam, can be traced.

Sadly, events have largely confirmed Burnham's predictions of the consequences of American defeat in South Vietnam. The dominoes have fallen, and their reverberations can be felt even today.

In the remaining essays in this section, Norman Podhoretz and Jeane Kirkpatrick examine the moral and strategic causes of this defeat, and trace its consequences for American foreign policy in the succeeding years. Podhoretz, a prominent neoconservative, the long-time editor of *Commentary* magazine, and one of the most incisive political (and literary) critics of his generation, sees the debilitation of United States foreign policy after Vietnam as the result of a crisis of confidence in the policy of containment. First enunciated in the Truman administration, containment in its various modes defined the American response to Communist expansionism for more than thirty years. Under its aegis, NATO and an elaborate system of alliances to safeguard the free world were constructed; the Communist threat to Greece, Turkey, and Iran was lifted; and the independence of Berlin and South Korea was secured. Despite sharp criticism from conservative strategists (e.g., Burnham's *Containment or Liberation?*) and statesmen (e.g., Barry Goldwater) for its refusal to seek a final victory over Communism, containment became the foundation of American foreign policy until the experience of Vietnam. This account of the breakdown in popular and Congressional (especially Democratic) support for containment is drawn from Podhoretz' book *The Present Danger* (1980).

Jeane Kirkpatrick was a political scientist well known for her analysis of mass-elite relations and presidential party politics before she was appointed United States ambassador to the United Nations in 1981. She might be said to have gotten that job not through *The New York Times* but through *Commentary* magazine, which published "Dictatorships and Double Standards"—the famous essay that brought her to the attention of President Ronald Reagan, and that is reprinted below. Recounting further developments in American foreign policy in the aftermath of Vietnam, Mrs. Kirkpatrick investigates the vertiginous collapse of American prestige and power in the Carter administration, paying particular attention to two episodes: the fall of the Shah of Iran and the ouster of Somoza from Nicaragua. In both cases the good intentions of the Carter administration proved to be no match for the grim realities of international politics. In both cases authoritarian governments were replaced not by liberal democracies—as Carter had hoped and assumed—but by totalitarian tyrannies, whether of the theistic or atheistic species.

The problem was that the Carter administration seemed to have become paralyzed by "forces of history." Caught up in the historical flux, America could do nothing to halt the forces of national liberation that were sweeping the Third World, that had swept the United States right out of Vietnam, Carter maintained. And try as he might to co-opt them, they seemed to tilt inevitably against America and the West, no doubt a reaction to the Free World's erstwhile colonialism. Kirkpatrick demonstrates how this view of history led to policies that neglected not only the difference in principle between totalitarian and authoritarian governments, but also the proven ability of at least some authoritarian regimes to evolve in the democratic direction. Thus, in the name of human rights, liberal foreign policy led to great setbacks for the cause of human rights— for the American cause—in Vietnam, Iran, Nicaragua, and elsewhere.

The need to rethink the moral foundations of American foreign policy has nowhere been more cogently expounded than in this memorable essay, a fitting conclusion to our selection of commentaries on the war we are in.

GERHART NIEMEYER

The Communist Mind

The West is still groping to comprehend the nature of the Communist threat. By and large, the effort at understanding our enemy is still lacking in system and purpose. Most writings on Communism presuppose, rather than aspire at, knowledge of what it is that endangers us. Uncritically held assumptions about Communism separate schools of thought from each other. Thus, one school of thought posits that the Communist threat is that of an ambitious great power pursuing an expansive policy in the style of nineteenth-century imperialism. Another presupposes that the threat stems from the existence of the "Communist system," meaning the collectivized economy as such. These are the assumptions underlying our various approaches to the Communist problem. This essay is an attempt to challenge both of the already mentioned presuppositions, even though both point to important elements in the situation. It is submitted that neither the power of Russia nor a foreign collectivist economy endangers our national security and way of life, but that the threat stems from the mentality of the people who are organized in the Communist Party and, through choice, association, and discipline, acquire attitudes of profound and irremediable irrationality. Such people, when in possession of political power, constitute a perennial disturbance to the peace of nations and of the world.

What is it that shapes and orients the Communist mind? Communists feel linked to each other and to the Party by the tenets of belief which go under the name of the Communist ideology. This is a complex structure with many component elements of which the socialist, or collectivist, element has attracted Western attention more than any other. And yet, if one asks whether there is one thing in the ideology that constitutes the key to the Communist mind, it would be the theory of history rather than the doctrine of collectivist economy. Characteristically, the theory of history of Communism is the part that has encountered little objection and less intellectual resistance in the West, even though, for the Communist, it is the doctrine of historical necessity which replaces religion, ethics, and philosophy.

One can reduce the Marxist-Leninist speculation about history to a

---

From Gerhart Niemeyer, *The Communist Mind* (Philadelphia: Intercollegiate Studies Institute, 1963). Reprinted by permission of the author.

simple formula: History is a chain of cause-and-effect successions of certain types of society, each following the preceding one with inexorable necessity. The entire course of history thus is said to obey objective "laws" which can be "scientifically" known. Knowledge of these "laws" enables man not only to understand the past, but to gauge the future, and thus to find the "correct" line of action for the present. Surveying the whole of history from beginning to end, Communism avers that history moves not merely forward but also upward, toward a climax which will constitute the fulfillment of everything that has gone before. Communists believe that history culminates in the fight of the proletariat against capitalism, of which the Communist Party considers itself the cadre organization.

Communists thus look at history in a way which radically differs from that of other people: From the vantage point of the ultimate end, retrospecting the present from the future. The certainty of things to come furnishes the Communist point of view for all problems of the present. Communists claim to know, with "scientific" accuracy, where mankind must eventually arrive. The present and all its aspects assume in this perspective the character of a mere period of transition. To Communists, the future is more real than the present, because it is the ultimate destiny toward which everything present is moving. This way of reversing the normal human perspective of present and future marks a turn from rational to irrational thinking about politics. Something that exists, like man, cannot look upon its own existence from the point of view of a future completion of time, as the Danish philosopher Kierkegaard has reminded us. Existence means to have an open future with a variety of possibilities. To regard the whole of history as if it were already realized, retrospectively, is something not given to man. It is the prerogative of God. Communists, in claiming a foreknowledge that can only be that of a Being above and beyond time, cast themselves in a role not befitting the human situation. This is the deepest source of Communist irrationality. Let us observe that irrationality in some of its applications.

The future is knowable—but only to those trained in its "science," Marxism-Leninism. Marxist analysis has "proved" that a fully human life can be expected not in the present but only in the future that will emerge from the victory of the proletariat over its enemies. The Party has styled itself the "Vanguard" of the proletariat, the organization that is doing unremitting battle against the resisting forces of the present. The Party and its forces are "good," its use of force is justified, its wars are holy, its cause triumphant. Instead of judging in terms of criteria of intrinsic goodness, the Communists judge themselves and others by the yardstick of the "forward movement of history." If anything or anyone is identified with the anticipated future, the verdict is "progressive," meaning "good" because justified by history. Identification with the present or even the past results in a judgment of "reactionary," meaning bad because condemned by history. Motion in time has taken the place of ethics.

The future is already known—that means that, for the Communist in the present, the future is not a matter of open possibilities. Only one kind of road leads from here to the anticipated there. To know this road is the task of political thinking. All Communist thinking therefore turns on the problem of the "correct" choice, the choice of that one road to the future. Compared with all others, the Communist Party claims to know most about this "correct" choice. Being the Vanguard, the element that is furthest advanced in consciousness of the future course of history, the Party is ahead of others in the motion toward the destined goal. It can see what is yet hidden from others. From its insights into things to come, it knows the "true" interests of peoples, classes, and nations, and has the right to overrule the illusory interests which people mistakenly assume to be theirs. The truth unfolds as history moves on. All those who dissent from the Party today will not be able to realize their mistake until the morrow has vindicated its Communist servants.

The Party Line is thus more than expediency. It appears to Communists like the blazing of a trail by a competent guide who alone is familiar with the terrain and aware of the detours that must be taken to arrive at the yet unseen goal. Communists would not necessarily claim that the Party is above mistakes. But they do regard it as in fact infallible, for in comparison with the Party there is nobody who could claim to be more "advanced," nobody with even equally valid insights into the road to be traveled, nobody who could conceivably improve on the Party's judgment. Because the truth that is history becomes accessible through struggle against the forces of reaction, the body which leads in this struggle must, by virtue of its forward position, have superior knowledge. The Party, in Communist eyes, is therefore more than a mere power organization. It is the fountainhead of truth, a truth which, in Lenin's words, is "always concrete." It is a spiritual home. It is the only available framework for meaningful individual action, if the meaning of human action is tied to the promotion of mankind's future destiny. It is the sole structure of order in an otherwise chaotic world. Outside the Party, there is nothing but darkness, reaction, corruption, and hopelessness. Thus even a Communist who has come to doubt the Party's ideology finds it a matter of heartbreaking difficulty to sever himself from the Party and from there to go out into a world where no similar organization links his daily action with universal meaning and a hopeful future.

"The party and the masses" is a chapter by itself. Only the Party can have knowledge of the anticipated future and the road leading there. The masses, caught up in the present and its concerns, cannot sufficiently detach themselves from reactionary influences. The Party, therefore, must "lead and not follow." It must never adjust to people and their interests but rather adjust people to itself and its interests. The proper role for the masses is one of "support" for Party policies. Being unable to appeal to the masses in terms of what the Party alone can know by virtue of Marxism-Leninism, the Party can gain mass support only by playing on the masses' present grievances, discontentments, and needs. One could call this a kind of adjustment of the Party to people and their feelings. But the adjustment is not made in good faith. The Communists are fully and articulately aware that they arouse hopes and make promises which they intend to deny once their strategic objective has been attained thanks to the masses' support. The Party's faithlessness, however, does not trouble the Communist conscience. If the Party deceives and manipulates the masses, it will eventually turn out to have been for the good, as all increases in the Party's power will move history nearer to the anticipated future. The masses, who are incapable of being moved by the "truth," must be led by the Party as children are led by parents.

A similar relationship exists between Party leadership and Party rank and file. The Communist term for this relationship is "democratic centralism." It means in practice that all Party members take part in endless debates and discussions about foregone conclusions. The Communists cannot approach the process of discussion as one of open possibilities, which approach would alone guarantee respect for the minds that converge in give-and-take. Since for the Communists history admits of only one "correct" road, the discussion can also have only one "correct" outcome, and the discussion process is one of attunement to this single choice. Any failure to take "the" correct path is for them necessarily a "deviation," and a deviation is a betrayal of "progress," and thus "reaction." A discussion is for Communists not a process of finding the materials for a forthcoming decision, but rather one of making the members understand the necessity and rationalization of a decision already taken. This is logical only when one pretends to have scientific knowledge of history's "Laws."

The same orientation underlies the typical Communist "toughness." Present shortcomings or setbacks cannot daunt a mind that has made its habitat entirely in the future. The present, from this perspective, must appear nothing but imperfect, hostile, and transitory. From here to the future the road is one of struggle, and the struggle is a "protracted" one, replete with victories and defeats, periods of contention and of lull, battles and campaigns, advances and retreats. The Communist manages to see in present imperfections the expected perfection of the future, as did the Russian lecturer who told Professor Gollwitzer a report on Russia saying that Russians live in beautiful new homes was true, even though at present many Russians do not yet live that way. "To see the future in the present means to think dialectically." (Gollwitzer, *Und Fuehren Wohin Du Nicht Willst*). For a Communist it is one of the basic facts of life that the Party, as long as it exists, must expect to struggle against enemies of superior strength. No campaign, no battle can be considered final except the one that puts its last enemy at its feet. Since the Party has been appointed by History as the instrument to move mankind forward toward the fulfillment of its destiny, the Party's eventual victory is assured. Khrushchev's "We shall bury you!" was meant not as a declaration of intention but as a confident reference to fact, a statement of "knowledge" concerning what will be the end of it all.

The Party's leadership consists of those people who, by virtue of their ideological "correctness," know most about the road that history must take. These people, and the small minority that belongs to the Party, are assumed to be surrounded by hostile influences of vastly superior strength. Organization and strict Party discipline are considered the recipe to the Party's eventual success over even the strongest enemy. Communists trust nobody and believe in nothing, except the Party and its mission. Thus the highest Communist duty is discipline. It is this discipline, permeating the entire personality, which renders Communists so formidable as enemies. The Communists' discipline has its roots in ideological convictions, for the ultimate enforcement consists in the threat of expulsion from the Party. Only those who assume that the Party alone is the enterprise of Progress, and that outside of the Party there is nothing but selfishness and Reaction, will fear expulsion as the Christian fears excommunication. The secret of Communist discipline is the Communists' belief in a world divided between bourgeois reaction and socialist revolution in which the Party leads the forces of progress.

The Communist attitude toward people is based on the assumption that, as there are two ages, the present of capitalism and the future of socialism, there are two ideologies and two kinds of people, the "progressives" and the "reactionaries." The "progressives" are those who help the revolution which is the path toward the future age. All others are reactionary. The Communists' condemnation of all people classified as "reactionaries" follows from their total rejection of present-day society. They compare the present bourgeois and the future socialist society. Of these two, only the future one is considered real human life. It is seen as an age in which all tensions, disharmonies, and shortcomings of human existence will disappear. Man will be fully himself, his thoughts will be one with his actions, his individuality will harmonize with society, his days will no longer be darkened by poverty, oppression, and war. The future alone is the full realization of truth, freedom, and humanity. By contrast, the present age is for Communists totally "false." It is an existence characterized by exploitation, wars, the rule of money, political and economic oppression. Philosophy, religion, and government do not represent truth but merely the interests of the ruling class. Each individual's life is distorted by false institutions and hostile powers. His labor belongs to someone else. His mind is enslaved by false notions. Thus all those who have their interests in the present age rather than in the socialist future are seen as the enemies of truth and humanity. The dividing line between revolutionaries and reactionaries is razor-sharp. For, as Lenin did not tire to point out, there are only two ideologies in the world, bourgeois and socialist, since "mankind has not created a third ideology." Anyone who fails to be socialist, even unwittingly, actually stands on the side of the bourgeoisie. Whether one is "progressive" or not is thus not a matter of intention but "objective" identification—either with the interests of the Party, or else with those of the class enemy.

In Communist eyes, the world is thus bipolarized. This is the characteristic feature of the period of "transition" or "protracted struggle" between Communists and their enemies, a period that constitutes for Communists the framework of their lives and actions. The "period of transition" is filled with the struggle between "two camps." This notion splits everything in two: classes—the bourgeoisie and the proletariat; ideologies—the bourgeois and the socialist ideology; people—the progressives and the reactionaries; nations—the "peace-loving" and the "imperialist" nations; wars—imperialist wars and wars of liberation, and, similarly, laws, philosophies, even methods of science. The criterion of distinction is objective support. He who by his thoughts and actions supports the bourgeoisie does not deserve respect or even existence. He who objectively supports the Party is approved. Since the Party Line, by design, zigs and zags, mere revolutionary conviction alone will not do. One must be able to step fast when the Party changes tactics and to guess right while the change is taking place. What is more, the Communists recognize and accept the support of non-Communist elements. These are officially called "vacillating" elements, who, purely for tactical purposes, constitute a kind of third force between the battle lines. According to the Communists, a third force cannot endure long, for sooner or later it will split, one part coming down on the bourgeois and the other on the Communist side. Until then, these "vacillating" elements can be effectively "neutralized" or even used as allies, albeit with the full knowledge that eventually they must be fought and liquidated as ideological enemies.

There are only two ideologies, the bourgeois and the socialist ideology, but of these the bourgeois is still considered by far stronger. Lenin established the dogma that bourgeois ideological influences would powerfully linger long after the abolition of private property and that they constituted a besetting temptation even to Communist Party members. Hence the proper attitude of Communists toward all people is a basic universal suspicion. The bourgeois ideology is seen lurking under every bed, in every human foible, behind every appearance of slackness or self-interest. Communists characteristically struggle not merely on external battle lines but also against the "enemy within." All people deserve to be distrusted: Trust must be earned by unwavering Party loyalty and can never be securely enjoyed. On the same showing, one can call the Communist attitude toward people one of basic and primary hostility. The Party imagines itself surrounded by enemies on all sides. There may be occasional allies, which are even considered essential to the Party's strategic achievements, but every ally, according to Lenin's admonition, must be "watched as if he were an enemy." In the entire world, only those who have succeeded in fully detaching themselves from the present and its lures can be considered reliable. All others are enemies, if not open, then disguised. The latter, in order to be fought, must first be "unmasked."

Communists have put between themselves and all other people a deliberate and profound alienation, or estrangement. They postulate that all who have not cast their will and thought into the mold of the socialist future cannot live in the same world with Communists. Communists cannot and will not accept the world in which, on their showing, all non-Communists actually live. Thus their design with respect to these other people is to remake them into the Communist image. Communists adopt a totalitarian attitude toward people under their rule because they deny the right of these people to be what they are and want to be, and aim at the forceful creation of an entirely "new man." This is a long educational process, for the duration of which the human material under Communist hands is still considered shaped by bourgeois influences and thus hostile to the Party. The totalitarian plan of re-creating man must therefore be supplemented by the Party's dictatorial power, that is, power "organized for war" (Lenin). The Communist quest for power is thus no ordinary desire to enjoy the distinctions and perquisites of command. It is an enterprise to create the world according to the Communists' idea of what it should have been, and to make men into something which they are not now, never have been, and do not want to be. Communist totalitarianism springs from the arrogation of the role of God.

A Communist, even though he might not be able to quote Marxist scripture and verse for his statements, might sum up his own view of the world as follows: A future socialist society is a certainty. The present bourgeois society must be rejected as totally unworthy and inhuman. Among all men, only a small group, the Communists, possess clear and scientific knowledge of the future while all others are still captive to the prejudices of the present. Between Communists and non-Communists there is thus no community of values. Under these conditions, life, and all politics, must be a continuous struggle. To assume that there could be harmony and unity in the present world would be but a reactionary illusion. Revolutionary realism emphasizes rather than mitigates the conflict. This does not bar stratagems of "coexistence" with the enemy, with the purpose of capturing, through the enemy's own institutions, the loyalties of people still under his influence. No inner reconciliation with the present society and its defending forces, however, can be considered anything else but treason of the Revolution. The good life can come only in the future. The future that is good will emerge from the victorious struggle of the Party against its reactionary enemies. The Party's power, its militant enterprise, its strategies and tactics, its use of force and ruse, its ongoing conquest of loyalties and institutions, are sacred, as the entire revolutionary course of history is sacred. Any resistance to the Party is utterly unjustifiable. One does not measure the Party and its opponents with the same yardstick. The Party alone represents progress and hope; its enemies represent the total evil of the present. Thus, there can be no right to resist the Revolution. Khrushchev, in this sense, told Walter Lippmann that Western opposition to the ongoing Communist world Revolution is impermissible "interference."

A Communist is a man who has the outlook just described. He has steeped himself in it by inclination, choice, and ceaseless indoctrination. The outlook is also bolstered by official Party enforcement. The combination of attraction, semirational persuasion, and enforcement is extremely strong. To see people and situations, the Party, and oneself in the perspectives laid down by dogmatized ideology becomes second nature to a Communist. The grip of the ideology is all the firmer since Communists are not likely to be confronted with any articulate alternative. At one point alone a different set of ideas might make an opposing claim on him: The traditional standards of morality, demanding good will, charity, veracity and faithfulness, pose a conflict with the Communist norm of the class struggle. The struggle-hardened Communist is likely to win this argument with his conscience by persuading himself that since the course of history is known as certain, helping the course of history is the only moral conduct, compared with which traditional morality is nothing but bourgeois sentimentality. Once he commits himself to the belief that history treads an objectively knowable path, all the other arguments of the Party ideology follow with grim but inescapable logic. With regard to this fundamental dogma, the Communist not only finds no alternative view available in the contemporary world, but actually finds himself aided and abetted by Western thought. Positivism, progressivism, historicism have left deep marks on most Western intellectuals. These intellectual patterns are first cousin to the Communist ideology in that they, too, posit a knowable and predictable course of historical causality, the pro-gressive movement of history to higher forms of life, the key role of revolutions, the struggle against the heritage of the past in the name of the future. Opposite views have not yet been sufficiently articulated in the West.

One can say, therefore, that in the West, too, ideologies hold sway and that between the prevailing ideologies in the West and Communism there are certain affinities and similarities. From all other ideologies the Com-munists differ by a trait of character which under different circumstances would be considered admirable: They take their beliefs seriously and expect at all times to act upon them. The Communists are above all ideological activists. This is why they constitute a more deadly threat than others whose thinking may also be irrationally distorted. Any ideology, since it proceeds from irrational premises, is apt to cause profound dis-turbances in the social order. In the Communist case, the character of the disturbance is a militant hostility toward men and existing institutions, a design to subvert, uproot, and destroy everything that exists. This flows from the fact that Communists live in a dream world, of the coming realization of which they are yet "scientifically" convinced. When dreams are carried over into the sober light of the day and become confused with reality, human action loses the quality of sobriety and adopts quixotic features. The substitution of a fictitious future age for the world of actual experience must entail irrationality of action. The irrationality of Com-munists manifests itself in their self-willed alienation from the world in which, after all, they also live.

One must distinguish between substantive and pragmatic rationality, the first concerning basic views of man, society, nature, and life, the second concerning the suitability of means to given ends. The Commu-nists are irrational in a substantive sense. It is their construction of ends, and the realities on which ends are based, which is arbitrarily distorted and contrived. The pragmatic conclusions drawn from these ideological assumptions, however, are quite rational, given the basic postulates. The Communists, in daily life, are concerned almost exclusively with the full range of these pragmatic principles. Their problems are those of the protracted struggle, the Party and its leadership, the strength and weaknesses of the enemy, the assessment of various social forces from the point of view of the strategy and the expediency of this or that policy to be adopted by the Soviet Union. Assuming the need to destroy the present-day world, the Communists have developed the art of destroying social structures to a previously unknown high level. This one must call pragmatic rationality of a sort, just as the "perfect crime" is a variety of pragmatic rationality. What is more, a certain amount of constructive rationality has room within the substantive irrationality of the Communist world view. Even a ruler committed to a dream world can succeed in commanding resources and skills which produce missiles, spaceships, and steel presses. Political madness is capable of creating an illusion of genuine and rational purpose and may even spur the output of great energy applied to ways, means, and instruments.

No amount of technical rationality, though, can remedy a deficiency of substantive rationality. The Communists are and remain in a basic and irremediable conflict with reality. It is, of course, impossible to escape from reality, and the Communists run their head against its walls all the time. On those occasions, they have a choice of trying to suppress resistant reality by sheer power or making concessions in the interest of continuing their struggle. By and large, they have preferred the second course, a course that was initiated by Lenin when he accepted the Peace of Brest Litovsk and, three years later, instituted the NEP. But Lenin also taught them that such concessions must never be made in the spirit of a change of mind. Rather, they are mere temporary retreats. This determination to continue believing in a world of their fancy rather than accepting the lessons taught them by reality bars the Communists forever from the achievement of peace. Not even where they have established total power over men and society have they created anything that could be honored by the name of order. Wherever Communists are organized for power there is hostility, suspicion, insecurity, and disintegration. Nor have they accomplished even within their own Party anything like relations of trust and friendship.

The present age of humanity is deeply disturbed, nations are threatened, institutions and traditions subverted, humanity suppressed, because a movement given to a cult of unreality has organized itself as a political army. There is a widespread misconception that Communists are engendered by conditions of social misery. This is quite contrary to the facts. The truth is that Communists are made by Communists. Tempted by visions of fancy, bribed by a pseudoscientism, they come to believe the reality of dreams, submerge themselves in a world of their own intellectual making, and pretend to be masters of creation. As long as such people are effectively organized for political action, the world can have no peace. Socialism might be conceived as an order of society. The might of Russia may disturb the sleep of other nations' rulers. Neither, however, can be called a fundamental threat to human order and peoples' existence. That threat comes solely from the irrational, alienated, destructive mind that has taken political shape in the Communist Party.

JAMES BURNHAM

Communism: The Struggle for the World

The great captains of military history, varied as they have been in every other respect, have all been noted for their grasp of what military writers call "the key to the situation." At each level of military struggle, from a brief skirmish to the grand strategy of a war or series of wars, they have understood that there is one crucial element which is this key to the situation. The key may be almost anything: a ford across a river, or a hill like Cemetery Ridge at Gettysburg; a swift blow at the enemy reserve, or the smashing of the enemy fleet as at Trafalgar or Salamis; stiff discipline on the flanks as at Cannæ, or a slow strangling blockade for an entire war; a long defensive delay to train an army or win an ally, or a surprise attack on a capital; control of the seas, the destruction of supplies, or the capture of a hero.

The great captain concentrates on the key to the situation. He simplifies, even oversimplifies, knowing that, though the key alone is not enough, without it he will never open the door. He may, if that is his temperament, concern himself also with a thousand details. He never allows details to distract his attention, to divert him from the key. Often he turns the details, which in quantitative bulk total much larger than the key, over to his subordinates. That is why the genius of the great captain is often not apparent to others. He may seem a mere figurehead, indolent, lethargic, letting the real work be done by those around him. They fail to comprehend that the secret of his genius is to know the key, to have it always in mind, and to reserve his supreme exertion for the key, for what decides the issue.

The principles of political struggle are identical with those of military struggle. Success in both political knowledge and political practice depends finally, as in military affairs, upon the grasp of the key to the

From James Burnham, *The Struggle for the World* (New York: John Day, 1947), Chapter 10, pp. 130–35; and James Burnham, *The War We Are In* (New Rochelle, N.Y.: Arlington House, 1967), Chapter 1, pp. 9–23, and Chapter 10, pp.330–43. *The Struggle for the World.* Copyright © 1947 by James Burnham. Reprinted by permission. *The War We Are In.* Copyright © 1967 by James Burnham. Reprinted by permission of Arlington House.

situation. The exact moment for the insurrection, the one issue upon which the election will in reality revolve, the most vulnerable figure in the opposition's leadership, the deeply felt complaint that will rouse the masses, the particular concession that will clinch a coalition, the guarded silence that will permit an exposure to be forgotten, the exact bribe that will open up a new Middle Eastern sphere of influence, the precise hour for a great speech: at each stage and level of the political process there is just one element, or at most a very small number of elements, which determines, which decides.

The great political leader (who is often also a great captain)—Pericles or the elder Cato or Mohammed or Cæsar or Henry of Navarre or Bismarck or Hamilton or Lenin or Innocent III or the younger Pitt—focuses on the key. He feels whether it is a time for expansion or recovery, whether the opposition will be dismayed or stimulated by a vigorous attack, whether internal problems or external affairs are taking political precedence. He knows, in each political phase, what is the central challenge.

During the late twelfth and for most of the thirteenth centuries, the Papacy struggled with the Hohenstaufen Empire, and concluded by destroying the Hohenstaufen. For all of Italy that struggle was in those times the key to the general political situation, no matter how it appeared to those whose political sense was distracted by temporary and episodic details. For the first generation of the fifth century B.C., the political key in the Aegean was the attempt of Persia to conquer the Hellenic world. All of the contests among the Greek states, and all their internal city squabbles, were in reality subordinate to the relation with Persia. For a generation in America, until it was decided by the Civil War, the key was the struggle for a united nation. Everything else in politics, foreign or domestic, was secondary. For Western Civilization as a whole at the turn of the nineteenth century, the key was the contest between England and France. England won, perhaps, because her governing class concentrated on the key, whereas Napoleon, only vaguely glimpsing the key with its shaft of sea power, dissipated his energies.

For a given nation, the political key is located sometimes among internal, sometimes among foreign affairs. For the United States, the key during most of its independent history has been internal: union or slavery or the opening of the West or industrialization or monopoly. For England, quite naturally, it has been more ordinarily, though by no means always, an external relation. It may be the church or the army or the peasant problem, or, for a brief period, a spectacular scandal like the Dreyfus affair or the South Sea Bubble or Teapot Dome.

We have entered a period of history in which world politics take precedence over national and internal politics, and in which world politics literally involve the entire world. During this period, now and until this period ends with the settlement, one way or another, of the problems which determine the nature of the period, all of world politics, and all of what is most important in the internal politics of each nation, are oriented around the struggle for world power between Soviet-based Communism and the United States. This is now the key to the political situation. Everything else is secondary, subordinate.

The key is, much of the time, hidden. The determining struggle is not apparent in the form of individual political issues, as they arise week by week. The deceptive surface is the cause of the political disorientation and futility of so many of the observers and actors, which so particularly infect the citizens and leaders of the United States. They base their ideas and actions on the temporary form of political events, not on the controlling reality.

Yugoslavia disputes with Italy over Trieste. Chiang Kai-shek fights with Chou En-lai over North China. Armenians begin to clamor for an independent Armenia. The new Philippine government confronts a revolt of the Hukbalahaps. Poland argues with Mexico in the Security Council. The French Cabinet calls for an immediate break with Franco. Harry Lundberg and the Communists fight for control of the United States waterfront. The American Labor Party and the Liberal Party jockey for position in New York State. The British Communists apply for admission to the Labour Party. The World Federation of Trade Unions demands an official voice in the United Nations. The International Harvester Company objects to sending tractors to the Balkans. Japanese printers' unions refuse to set up editorials they don't like. Sweden signs a commercial agreement with Moscow. The United States asks for bases in Iceland or the Azores. Bulgaria, Yugoslavia and Albania arm and succor Macedonian partisans. Joseph Clark Baldwin, ousted by the New York Republicans, is endorsed by Vito Marcantonio. Australia objects to the veto power.

The eyes of the public become entangled in the many-colored surface. The exact ethnic complexion of Venezia Giulia is debated with ponderous statistics. Owen Lattimore proves at length that Chiang is not quite democratic and that many peasants support Yenan. Arthur Upham Pope explains that there are reactionary landlords in Iran. Henry Wallace describes the geography of Siberia. *The Nation* catalogues the villainies of Franco. *PM* sturdily denounces the crimes of Greek Royalists. *The New Republic* gives the history of agricultural oppression in the Philippines. The innocent bystanders send in their dollars, join committees, and sign open letters.

The statistics and records and swarms of historical facts are admirable enough to have at hand. But by themselves they are shadows, ashes. If we do not look through them to the living body, the focal fire, we know nothing. If we do not grasp that Trieste and Thrace, and Armenia and

Iran and North China and Sweden and Greece are the border marches between the Communist power and the American power, and that all the statistics and records are filigree work on the historical structure, then we know nothing. We know less than nothing, and we fall into the trap which those who do know deliberately bait with all the statistics and records. It is their purpose to deceive us with the shadows and to prevent us from seeing the body. If we do not know that the American Labor Party has nothing to do with America or with Labor or with any of the issues stated in its program and speeches, but is simply a disguised colony of the Communist power planted within the enemy territory, then, politically, we know nothing. If we do not understand that the World Federation of Trade Unions is merely a device manipulated by the NKVD to further the Communist objective of infiltrating and demoralizing the opponents in the Third World War, then we have not begun to realize what is at issue in the world. The central point is not whether Chiang is a democrat— though that too is an important point—but that he is, in his own fashion, a shield of the United States against the thrust of Communist power out of the Heartland. The debates in the Security Council are not really over the absurd procedural ritual that appears on the surface of the minutes. The ritual is like a stylized formal dance reflecting in art the battle of the Titans.

Walter Lippmann, after a tour of Europe in the spring of 1946, told us in a widely publicized series of articles that the main issue of world politics was the contest between England and the Soviet Union, which was coming to a head in the struggle over Germany. The United States he found to be in the comfortable position of an impartial umpire who could generously intervene to mediate and settle the dispute. Mr. Lippmann was right in insisting on the crucial present role of the fight for Germany. But one look at the political map of Europe, with a side glance at the state of India and the British colonies, should be enough to demonstrate that England could not possibly stand up as principal in a challenge to the Communist power. England in Germany, whatever her intentions, functions as a detachment of the greater power which is the only existing rival in the championship class. If it were really England, and if the pressure of the United States were withdrawn from the European arena, the decision over Germany would long since have been announced.

The determining facts are merely these: Western Civilization has reached the stage in its development that calls for the creation of its Universal Empire. The technological and institutional character of Western Civilization is such that a Universal Empire of Western Civilization would necessarily at the same time be a World Empire. In the world there are only two power centers adequate to make a serious attempt to meet this challenge. The simultaneous existence of these two centers, and only these two, introduces into world political relationships an intolerable disequilibrium. The whole problem is made incomparably sharper and more immediate by the discovery of atomic weapons, and by the race between the two power centers for atomic supremacy, which, independently of all other historical considerations, could likewise be secured only through World Empire.

One of the two power centers is itself a child, a border area, of Western Civilization. For this reason, the United States, crude, awkward, semibarbarian, nevertheless enters this irreconcilable conflict as the representative of Western culture. The other center, though it has already subdued great areas and populations of the West, and though it has adapted for its own use many technological and organizational devices of the West, is alien to the West in origin and fundamental nature. Its victory would, therefore, signify the reduction of all Western society to the status of a subject colony. Once again, the settled peoples of the Plains would bow to the yoke of the erupting Nomads of the Steppes. This time the Nomads have taken care to equip themselves from the arsenal of the intended slaves. The horses and dogs have been transformed into tanks and bombs. And this time the Plains are the entire earth.

Between the two great antagonists there is this other difference, that may decide. The Communist power moves toward the climax self-consciously, deliberately. Its leaders understand what is at stake. They have made their choice. All their energies, their resources, their determination, are fixed on the goal. But the Western power gropes and lurches. Few of its leaders even want to understand. Like an adolescent plunged into his first great moral problem, it wishes, above all, to avoid the responsibility for choice. Genuine moral problems are, however, inescapable, and the refusal to make a choice is also a moral decision. If a child is drowning at our feet, to turn away is to decide, as fully as to save him or to push him under. It is not our individual minds or desires, but the condition of world society, that today poses for the Soviet Union, as representative of Communism, and for the United States, as representative of Western Civilization, the issue of world leadership. No wish or thought of ours can charm this issue away.

This issue will be decided, and in our day. In the course of the decision, both of the present antagonists may, it is true, be destroyed. But one of them must be. . . .

The first sentence of my book, *The Struggle for the World,* which was published early in 1947, reads: "The Third World War began in April 1944." . . .

In a more basic sense, however, what began in the spring of 1944 was not so much a "new" Third World War as a new phase in a continuing war that started in November 1917,* with the Bolshevik conquest of power in Russia, that might indeed be dated most significantly from Lenin's organization of the Bolshevik faction of the Russian Social Democratic Labor Party in 1903: the protracted war of the Communist enterprise for a monopoly of world power. On the coordinates of this longer-term scale, the protracted war is seen as the dominant theme of twentieth-century history, with its major phases fairly well marked, though overlapping: (1) formation and training of the cadres of the revolutionary army (1903–1917); (2) seizure of the initial base, or beachhead (1917); (3) failure of the first direct attack on the advanced Western powers (1917–1923);(4) consolidation and defense of the base (1917–1944);(5) enlargement of the base (1944–1949 explosively, and irregularly in the years following); (6) indirect attack on the Western powers through support of decolonization and of anti-Western nationalism in the underdeveloped regions of Asia, Africa and Latin America (1944–   ); (7) recognition of the United States as the main enemy, and consequent direction of the main effort to the weakening, isolation, and ultimate defeat of the United States (1944–   ). On this same scale the first two "world wars" as well as the post-1956 "Sino-Soviet split" appear as subthemes, disputes *within* one or the other of the two major camps.

The term "Cold War" refers, more or less, to the same set of facts that I have been designating "Third World War." Most people are inclined to interpret either term as an exaggerated metaphor. They feel one doesn't literally mean "war," that the *real* Third World War is something that might happen in the future, when the nuclear bombs start bursting, something that we are trying desperately to avoid while at the same time we prepare for the possibility that it might break out in spite of our best efforts. The Communists do not share this conventional view, though they play up to it through the slogan of "peaceful coexistence." Its practical consequences, therefore, are almost necessarily damaging to the non-Communist side. By conceiving "the war" as a possible event in the future, which we must prepare to deal with if and when it comes, or preferably find ways to avoid altogether, we are led to minimize the importance of the struggle that we are actually engaged in. That clearly demarcated future "war" may never take place, but meanwhile we can be defeated in stages during the course of the actual struggle.

The Cold War (if we prefer that inexact and inadequate name for the war we are in) has its own special features that, taken in their entirety, distinguish it from other wars, though none of them is unique. It is not

*This is the explicit premise of a detailed study by André Fontaine, Foreign Editor of the leading French newspaper, *Le Monde,* the first volume of which was published in France in 1966 with the title: *Histoire de la guerre froide: De la Révolution d'Octobre à la guerre de Corée.*

formally "declared"—a legalism often dispensed with from tribal days to Hitler's. It is a "limited" war, in the sense that the rivals have not been employing their full weaponry and resources. But this restraint is not unusual in other wars. The "phoney war" period of the Second World War is a notable parallel in recent memory. Such periods of muted operations have been common in the protracted conflicts of the past: the Peloponnesian wars; the Punic wars; the prolonged medieval struggle between the Guelph and the Ghibelline factions; the Thirty Years War; the sixteenth–nineteenth centuries' contest among Britain, France, Spain, and Holland for mastery of the seas; prolonged struggles in several epochs of Indian and Chinese history, etc.

If limited in the employment of resources (though the resources that have been brought to bear are in fact greater than in any previous war), the Cold War is not limited in its aim, its geographic scope or the scale of its encounters. The Communist side has from the very beginning been unambiguous about its aim: a World Federation of Soviet Socialist Republics, as it has been expressed in many official programs and manifestoes; a state of affairs in which "the international party shall be the human race," in the words of the hymn of the Revolution; "to bury you," as Khrushchev put it in his peasant rhetoric; a Communist monopoly of world power, as we might summarize it in neutral language, without overspecifying the institutions and internal relationships in which this monopoly might be embodied. If no positive aim has been adopted or stated by the non-Communist side, the most basic war aim of all—namely, survival—is implicit both in the actions taken and in the negative programs, such as "containment" or "competitive coexistence," that are from time to time formulated. In any case, it takes only one side to make a war and to define its stakes.

As for geography, the Cold War is the first in history to involve the entire world; the first two World Wars did not live up to their title. And perhaps the easiest way to grasp the scope and significance of the campaigns of the Cold War—the Third World War, that is—is to consider what has been won and lost as a result of some of them: the Communist conquest, in the immediate post-1944 round, of all the nations of eastern Europe, with 100 million inhabitants; Communist conquest of mainland China, northern Korea and northern Vietnam, Tibet and, in 1960, a first outpost in the Americas; successful defense by the non-Communists (there have been no positive non-Communist victories) of Greece, Malaya, the Philippines, Burma, South Korea, Guatemala, and Indonesia. In very few wars in history, perhaps in none, have there been victories and defeats affecting such vast areas and populations.

One thing that the Cold War has *not* been is "cold." From the very beginning of this present phase, that is, from 1944, there have been fighting and bloodshed. The fighting has extended to every continent—

from Greece to China, Cuba to Zanzibar, Tibet to Venezuela, Indonesia to Hungary, Burundi to Quemoy, Korea and Vietnam to the Congo—and has gone on continuously.

It is hardly surprising that in the conduct of a war there should be shooting and killing. What is perhaps most distinctive about this war we are in is its multidimensional, indeed omnidimensional nature. It is conducted, though with shifting emphases, along every social dimension: economic, political, cultural, racial, psychological, religious as well as military; and the military dimension comprises every sort of guerrilla, terrorist, paramilitary, partisan and irregular combat as well as fighting by conventional forces. The omnidimensional nature of the war follows from the totalitarian and utterly radical nature of Communism. The Communist enterprise is simultaneously a secular religion, a conspiracy, and a new kind of army. According to Communist doctrine, the Communist objective is not merely to take power, but to re-create both man and society, to make a new kind of man in a new kind of society. All that has happened to mankind up until now is "prehistory"; true "history" begins only with the advent of Communism. Existing non-Communist civilization expresses essentially the exploitation and corruption of a class society; it cannot be reformed, but must be overthrown and destroyed, so that the new Communist man can build in its place the new classless Communist society. The Communist enterprise, therefore, in carrying out both its negative and its positive tasks (*i.e.,* destroying class society and building Communism), must concern itself with every social sector and activity, with trade unions as well as armies, churches along with banks, schools and factories as well as governments.

This war we are in is particularly characterized as being omnidimensional, but it perhaps is even more sharply distinctive for the fact that within the omnidimensional deployment psychopolitical operations have been raised to the level of a primary weapons system. It is very difficult for non-Communist military professionals to grasp this fact. According to non-Communist military doctrine and practice, psychopolitical operations ("propaganda") do have a role in modern warfare, but a minor, nonessential role, merely supplementary to the direct fighting by regular forces. But in Communist doctrine, things are often the other way around; the fighting by the regular forces is merely the completing chapter of a struggle that has been conducted for the most part by psychopolitical methods plus, perhaps, paramilitary and other irregular military methods.

To the traditionally trained military mind it seems absurd to say that a psychopolitical weapon can be stronger than a nuclear weapon. Nevertheless, if we think carefully we will realize that in one sense at least this must always be the case, since the nuclear weapon, and any physical weapon, is nothing at all apart from the human will that decides whether or not to trigger it. The fact of the matter is that the psychopolitical operations of the Communist enterprise did successfully neutralize American nuclear arms, both when this country possessed an absolute nuclear monopoly—and thereby a more overwhelming relative military supremacy than any nation has held—and during the much longer period when this country had a decisive nuclear superiority. Indeed, Communist psychopolitical operations continue to block American use of components of its nuclear arsenal that would be dictated by objective strategic considerations.

Stalin conquered Czechoslovakia, as Hitler had done before him, by exclusively psychopolitical means. A long-term global psychopolitical campaign that deceived Western opinion and diverted the Western nations from deterrent intervention was an indispensable element in the Communist conquest of China. Castro's conquest of Cuba was accomplished through an integral blend of psychopolitical and paramilitary measures. The Communists in Moscow, Peking, and New York as well as in Hanoi have openly admitted that they could not hope to defeat the anti-Communist forces in South Vietnam by direct military means, and that their only chance to win would be through the success of psychopolitical operations on the American domestic front. All these are dramatic, big-scale examples, but psychopolitical operations enter as a primary if not the dominant system into every Communist undertaking. . . .

A significant period of the irregular history of the Third World War came to an end and a new period opened in the latter part of 1956. This turning point was marked by two dramatic episodes that took place, in part simultaneously, in the autumn of 1956: the aborted revolt in eastern Europe that swelled up in East Germany and Poland and reached its climax in Hungary; and the aborted Anglo-French invasion of the Suez isthmus (to which the Israeli invasion of the Sinai desert was an incidental appendage). By their outcome these two episodes summarized the net geopolitical results of the preceding period and foreshadowed certain of the trends that were to prevail in the period to follow.

The East European affair proved (1) the Communist regimes had failed to win the allegiance, or even the voluntary adherence, of the peoples of the East European nations, (2) the Communist enterprise was prepared to crush opposition by military force wherever and whenever the opposition was serious and the use of military force feasible, and (3) the Western powers in general and the United States specifically were not prepared to aid an opposition inside the Communist zone by direct or indirect military means, or to furnish any significant quantity of personnel, weapons, supplies, or diplomatic assistance to an opposition struggle. This demonstrated—most importantly, to the Communist leaders—

that there was no substance left in the "policy of liberation" which had figured in the Eisenhower-Dulles rhetoric during the 1952 campaign and had lingered on in some official pronouncements during President Eisenhower's first term. Actually, a policy of liberation had been ruled out in principle, in favor of the policy of containment, as early as the spring of 1950, when President Truman approved National Security Council document NSC-68. But it was the Hungarian revolt that clarified and defined what abandonment (or, at any rate, indefinite postponement) of a perspective of liberation meant in practice.

Moscow, Peking, and the global Communist enterprise knew, by virtue of the Hungarian affair, that they were guaranteed against outside interference within their household. Within the Communist zone they could handle domestic matters in their own fashion, without risking anything worse from outsiders than a routine moralistic scolding. "The imperialists"—so Hungary proved—had swallowed a doctrine cooked up for them by the dialecticians, the doctrine of "the two zones." "The zone of peace" corresponds to the acreage already brought under Communist rule and is off-limits to disturbers; opposition seeking to change or overthrow the government is counterrevolutionary treason, to be crushed by all necessary means. "The zone of war" is the acreage still free from Communist rule. Within the zone of war, opposition—from the Left—that seeks to change or overthrow the government is "progressive"; its actions constitute a "struggle for national liberation," deserving support by "all freedom-loving peoples." This doctrine of the two zones, it may be added, is the essence of "the policy of peaceful coexistence."

The two-zone doctrine applies to the Chinese as to the Soviet sectors of the Communist domain. When the Tibetans revolted against the Chinese Communist protectorate over their country, the United States and its Western allies kept hands strictly off, exactly as in the earlier case of the Hungarians; the reaction was confined as usual to moral indignation. Although the containment principle seems to call for resistance to an attempted extension of the zone of peace, the two-zone doctrine tends to be applied retroactively if the extension is successfully accomplished, with a resultant Communist regime in control of the new area. Even when the extension in the Cuban case reached inside the strategic threshold of the United States' continental base, the influence of the doctrine prevented a serious effort to reclaim the lost island, and led to the floundering, half-hearted catastrophe of the Bay of Pigs. In the confrontation of the autumn of 1962, upon which his strategic reputation rests, President Kennedy limited himself to getting rid of the missiles that posed a direct and intolerable military threat to United States home territory; in return, he accepted Cuban territory under its Communist regime as an integral part of the zone of peace, and therefore off limits for counteraction.

The continuing role of the two-zone doctrine has been evident in the political management of the Vietnam War. Although military necessity has demanded attacks on North Vietnam, these have been kept, for each stage, at the lowest possible intensity—much below what military judgment would ideally call for—and they have been accompanied by repeated formal declarations that the United States does not aim at overthrowing or changing the Communist government of North Vietnam. The Communist regime in North Vietnam lies within the zone of peace, and is therefore inviolable.

The Suez episode was simultaneous with the Hungarian revolt, as if History were emphasizing that it was merely the other face in the toss of a single coin. If we look at a globe or global map we see at once that the Isthmus of Suez is the land bridge between Asia and Africa, and that the water passage through the isthmus—the Suez Canal—is the link between Europe's sea and the Indian Ocean—which might be more descriptively called "the Afro-Asian Ocean." The isthmus is thus one of the earth's key strategic posts; control of the isthmus is one of the primary strategic prizes.

This is of course why Britain and France, realizing that the isthmus was being taken over by an anti-Western Arab revolutionary closely linked to the Soviet power, attempted to regain control for the West by the joint military expedition. The expedition failed, just as the Hungarian revolt failed. It failed, essentially, because President Eisenhower not merely declined to support or even condone it, but actively vetoed it, and compelled Britain and France to withdraw.

The Suez abortion signified:

1. Africa was henceforth open to Asia; the guard had left the bridge. In 1956—to note one sufficiently significant set of symbols—there did not exist a single independent Communist Party south of the Sahara, except for a small Party in South Africa. There were some Communists—mostly whites—but they were attached to one or another of the West European parties. Moreover, there was in 1956 no special bureau in the Soviet Foreign Ministry to handle African affairs; but soon after the Suez episode—in 1958—an African Department was set up, initially under A. V. Budakov. At about the same time, local Communist organizations began to be formed in various of the nations-to-be. Some of these were tied to Soviet or East European principals, others to the Chinese, who exploited the Afro-Asian legitimacy they had acquired by their prominence at the 1955 Bandung conference.

2. European colonialism, largely ousted from Asia and the South Pacific in the period from the end of the Second World War to 1956, was on its way out in Africa. The Suez episode was the opening of the floodgate. The tide of "liberation" swept over the continent with a speed much greater than anyone in any camp had imagined possible, much greater

than that of any comparable phenomenon in prior history. Suez also gave the signal for clearing up several of the Asian remnants of European colonialism (western New Guinea, Goa).

3. The abject failure of Britain and France in the Suez episode, together with the collapse of their African colonial domains which it foretold, confirmed the fact that, whether acting separately or jointly, they were no longer major world powers. And if Britain and France were not, no other European power acting separately or in a limited combination, was. Theoretically it remained possible that a western Europe unified or integrated in some fashion might be able to regain the top global level, but the required degree of integration did not exist and was not in prospect.

4. Both the Soviet Union and the United States acted to abort the Suez invasion, but the initiative was taken by the United States. Throughout, it was the United States that played the major role; the Soviet Union merely tagged along. In this respect the Suez affair was not exceptional. In the liquidation of European colonialism—both in the African phase that lay immediately ahead and in the Asian phase of the preceding period—the United States has invariably played an active, and frequently the leading, role. It may be that historically the epoch of European colonialism had ended in any event, but there is no doubt that the active policy of the United States—most conspicuously in relation to Indonesia, India, and sub-Saharan Africa—speeded the fall of the curtain.

5. Liquidation of European colonialism left a political vacuum in much of Africa, which the native leadership was neither sufficiently large nor adequately trained to fill. Liberation therefore tended to open the road, in varying measure, to chaos, Communism, and neocolonialism.

Throughout this period (and for some years to come) chaos becomes the ally of Communism. It is through political and social chaos that the lingering influences, attitudes, and institutions tying the decolonialized nations to Europe and more generally to Western civilization can be rooted out. With minor and precarious exceptions (Zanzibar, Congo-Brazzaville) the Communists have not yet been in a position to undertake full-scale revolutions in Africa that would result in consolidated Communist regimes. The earlier phase of revolutionary development can take the form of the much easier task of promoting chaos, with the accompanying destruction of Western institutional links and pro-Western individuals.

In many of the new African nations, the economic, political, and military power of the United States has been drawn in to supplement or replace the declining European power in shoring up against chaos and combating the Communist incursions, as well as to advance American economic interest according to the neocolonial mode: *cf.* Congo-Léopoldville, Kenya, Nigeria, Ghana, Ethiopia, as well as Morocco, Tunisia and Algeria in the African north.

Nikita Khrushchev used the phrase "peaceful coexistence" to describe the state of global affairs that was expressed and symbolized in the dual Hungary-Suez episode. The meaning of "peaceful coexistence" must be understood within the system of revolutionary dialectic. So translated, it is seen to be equivalent to "the Cold War," or what I have called "the Third World War." "Peaceful coexistence" *means* the revolutionary struggle of the Communist enterprise against the non-Communist world, conducted as this struggle has *in fact* been conducted since 1944—that is, by all the methods of multidimensional warfare except for general and thus (in our age) nuclear combat. The concept of "peaceful coexistence" includes the two-zone doctrine that I have discussed; it is a violation of peaceful coexistence if the West attempts to stir up opposition within the Communist sphere (the zone of peace); it is a defense of peaceful coexistence when the Communists attempt to stir up opposition right to the point of revolutionary struggle ("war of liberation") within the non-Communist sphere (the zone of war). Such struggle is "for peace" because it is against "the imperialist warmongers and their puppets" and in defense of "the peace-loving masses," and also because it advances the development of the world socialist society in which war will be impossible. The "defense of peace" is identical to the struggle against the non-Communist forces, above all to the struggle against the United States.

The period of "peaceful coexistence" will presumably culminate in "the final struggle," that is, in a general war, when the time is ripe, that will involve nuclear arms. The general war would most probably be initiated by a Communist nuclear strike against the decisive non-Communist targets. This too would be not a contradiction but a fulfillment of peaceful coexistence; the zone of peace would finally be in a position to liquidate the zone of war, and thereby extend the zone of peace to the entire earth; "the international party will be the human race." Meanwhile, however, the warmongers must be prevented from starting all-out war, most particularly a nuclear war, from their side, or from taking any other action—"aggressive" by definition—that would threaten the frontiers or security of the zone of peace.

In short, peaceful coexistence presupposes a "nuclear stalemate"; and there has in fact been a nuclear stalemate, or what has more lately come to be called a "balance of terror," throughout these years. In the Third World War no one has set off a nuclear weapon for combat purposes; that is the fact of the matter. It is clear, moreover, that the main course of events has presupposed the nuclear stalemate: the stabilization of the East European frontier; the draw in Korea; the post-Suez free-for-all in Africa; the acceptance of Communist takeover in China, Tibet, and Cuba; the military conduct of the Vietnam War, etc. Whatever might have happened if some or many nuclear weapons of one kind or another had been used, no one will doubt that they would have greatly altered the way things have gone without them. The nuclear stalemate has been a basic parameter of our epoch.

Most persons think of "nuclear stalemate" as a condition in which the non-Communist nuclear arsenal is counterbalanced by the Communist nuclear arsenal, more specifically, in which United States and Soviet nuclear weapons counterbalance each other—not necessarily because they are equal in quantity, but because each side's nuclear arsenal is capable of visiting "unacceptable" damage on the other side. Such a relationship might induce a nuclear stalemate, but is neither a sufficient nor even a necessary condition. Indeed, "nuclear stalemate" is not fundamentally a quantitative or physical, but a psychological relationship. A nuclear stalemate exists, no matter what the actual weapons situation, when the possessor or possessors of nuclear weapons are not willing to accept the consequences of using them.

In this fundamental sense there seems to have been a nuclear stalemate throughout the Third World War, except perhaps at the time of the Middle Eastern and Quemoy-Matsu crises in 1958, quite independently of the existence, quality, or size of the Communist nuclear arsenal. For most of the period since the Second World War, it has not been Communist nuclear weapons that have counterbalanced United States weapons and thereby created the stalemate. In the early years the Communists did not possess any nuclear weapons; and for many years more the comparatively few they had were not part of a usable weapons system. They have never had a first-rate long-range manned aircraft force for weapons delivery, and their intercontinental missiles did not become operational—and then only slowly—until late 1962 or early 1963. At the time of the superpublicized Cuban confrontation (October 1962) no Soviet ICBMs were yet fully operational.

During these years there have been numerous occasions when the actual use of nuclear weapons or a serious and credible threat to use them was militarily relevant, and would have been highly advantageous to the United States and the West from a military or political standpoint: Soviet takeover of Czechoslovakia, Korea, Hungary, Tibet, Cuba, Vietnam, etc. Nevertheless, the United States has never used nuclear weapons, no matter what the "objective" weapons relationship, nor, except perhaps in 1958, has the United States threatened their use seriously and credibly. The record proves that the stalemate is "subjective." What "deters" United States use of the weapons is not necessarily or fundamentally counterbalancing physical weapons on the other side—which may or may not exist—but a subjective unwillingness to accept the consequences of using its own weapons from whatever motive, rational or irrational; in large part, the record indicates, from feelings of guilt in the American scientists and governmental leaders together with fear about the effect on "world opinion." This guilt and this fear are partly spontaneous in origin, but they have been manipulated, exploited, and heightened through a continuous psywar campaign conducted by the Communists, their fellow travelers, and dupes.

What has counterbalanced the United States nuclear armament thus has not been in reality, for most of these years, and is still not in any decisive sense, a physically opposed Communist nuclear armament. It has been, and still is principally, an actively employed psywar weapons system. The Communist powers do not have to wait for a technological breakthrough to acquire a functioning antiballistic missile system. They have all along possessed a demonstratively effective weapons system that was able to take the advent of missiles in its stride.

True enough, the Communists also have not used nuclear weapons, though they have possessed them for some years. But the motives deterring the Communists and inducing them to accept the stalemate are "dialectically" of a different kind.

There is no sign that the Communists share any of the feelings of guilt about the production, possession, and possible use of nuclear weapons; quite the contrary, by all one can gather, they are very pleased, and they have shown only a minimum of fear of world opinion. However, the Communist leaders have been well aware that the United States' nuclear arsenal has been, first infinitely, and then overwhelmingly, superior to their own. What has presumably deterred them has been, not irrational sentiment, but a perfectly rational calculation of the odds: a realization that they have too much to lose, have in fact everything to lose, by initiating use of nuclear arms. Though in their case too the physical facts do not of themselves determine the strategic response (acceptance of the stalemate), the response made by the Communist leaders is directly correlated with the physical facts, whereas the response of the United States, as we have seen, is altogether independent of the facts.

This dialectical difference in the Communist response suggests a conclusion of some importance. If the physical facts change, if the Communist nuclear arsenal becomes significantly superior to the American arsenal, then we may expect the Communists to alter their response in accordance with these altered physical facts—that is, to use their arsenal instead of sitting on it.

The nuclear stalemate and the two-zone doctrine (together equivalent to "peaceful coexistence") were the premises for a development that has become more and more conspicuous from 1962 on: the loosening of the blocs. In the first phase of the Third World War, two well-defined and cohesive politicostrategic blocs, expressing in their structures the essential nature of the war, formed up on a global scale: the Communists, or

Sino-Soviet bloc, dominated by the Soviet Union; and the Western bloc, dominated by the United States. Somewhat later the attempt was made to constitute a third bloc independent of the first two, known variously as "the Afro-Asian bloc," the "non-aligned nations," or "the Third World." In the last few years the internal cement holding each of the blocs together has been noticeably strained and weakened.

In the case of the Communist bloc there has occurred what is usually referred to as "the Sino-Soviet split," together with the growth of "polycentrism." The loosening of the Western bloc has been most plainly signaled by the unilateral moves taken by Charles de Gaulle, especially by the partial breakdown of the North Atlantic Treaty Organization which has been one consequence of de Gaulle's policy. . . .

In the years from the Cuban missile crisis of 1962 to 1965, Western opinion very nearly convinced itself that "the Cold War was over." The Soviet Union had obviously settled down, and China, if still talking like a revolutionary adolescent, could be handled by "being made part of the community of nations" through diplomatic recognition, UN membership, and expanding trade. If by chance there were big trouble, it would be between the Soviet Union and China, not between either one, or both, and the West. Then came the Chinese nuclear tests and the heated up Vietnam War.

It is only from the past and the present that we can get evidence about the future. Logically it is possible that we are about to begin a decade of global sweetness and light, but nothing that has happened in the past sixty-three years or that is happening today permits us to believe that in actuality things will be so. On the evidence, the probability is overwhelming that the war we are in—Cold War, Third World War, whatever we may prefer to call it—will continue, and that its main theme, though with novel variants, will continue to be the protracted struggle of the Communist enterprise to gain global power. It is more likely, on the evidence, that during the next decade the war we are in will increase rather than decrease in scope and ferocity. Is it not true that today, after all the coexisting and people-to-peopling, the biggest fight since 1945 is taking place? And that after all the polycentralizing, the forces against which we are battling have the united support of all Communists of every nation, party, and faction? Can any rational person suppose that the new Chinese nuclear bombs are a "weapon for peace"? Does Africa look as if it had finished its uhuru pangs and was ready for order and tranquility? Is everybody about to love everybody in the Middle East?

The forms taken by the protracted conflict in the next decade will not be identical to those taken in the last, no doubt. Polycentrism—on both sides—is in some degree a fact; undoubtedly the blocs have loosened. From 1947 until a few years ago the lineup was always simple and obvious: the Communist-plus bloc and the Western-plus bloc, with a shifting, rather amorphous grouping in between. Distinctions and divisions within the two primary blocs have now become more apparent and more significant. On limited issues the lineup can now more frequently breach the normal bloc boundaries (though it should be recalled that this happened more than once in the past, beginning with the Suez affair). Thus, on the Vietnam issue, we find France not only opposed to United States policy— which sort of difference in viewpoint occurs normally within all alliances and blocs—but coming close to practical collaboration with the actively fighting enemies of the United States. From the opposite perspective we find the Soviet Union and China snarling at each other in a fairly substantial political warfare sort of conflict—though in their case, they continue practical collaboration with each other against the United States and its fighting allies.

The internal disputes within the Communist and Western camps as well as in the Third World have been getting increasingly severe, and it is not excluded that these should escalate into armed struggle of one sort or another. There has of course been a good deal of fighting among the nations of the Third World (U.A.R.-Saudi Arabia, India-Pakistan, Algeria-Morocco, Indonesia-Malaysia, Somalia-Kenya, Sudan-Chad, etc.), but as a rule this is quickly absorbed into the overriding global conflict. There seems to have been occasional border skirmishing between the Soviet Union and China, and it is at least possible that larger-scale fighting between the two will take place during the course of the next decade. This would not, however, alter the fundamental character of the war we are in. Historically, the controlling issue would still be the struggle of the Communist enterprise for an effective monopoly of world power.

It is not without precedent that within a dynamic and expanding enterprise there should be internal splits, divisions, and conflicts while at the same time the enterprise as a whole maintains its integrity and continues its growth as against the rival enterprises within its field of operation. Indeed, such processes are so usual as to be part of the law of social formation and growth. This happens within every business organization, social club, church, political party, and fraternal society. Sometimes the internal dispute develops into a struggle for control of the enterprise; sometimes it becomes so irreconcilable that the dissident faction goes over to a rival or opts out altogether.

Let us add that the Sino-Soviet split and the Castrovian eccentricities are not the first disputes within the Communist enterprise. Communists have been disputing among themselves in the most extreme terms since the enterprise started. Several million persons got killed, and 30 million or so sent to concentration camps (where many of them ended up dead also), during the disputes of the late 1920s and the 1930s—a lot more casualties than can be charged against the Sino-Soviet split and polycentrism. But in spite of those millions of casualties, the enterprise as a going concern, an identifiable historical entity, not only maintained its integrity but proved ready to begin a period of astounding growth.

Internal disputes, thus, are not necessarily signs of weakness or decay. They often are, when the enterprise has *already* passed its historical peak, on the way to history's rubbish heap. They can *become* a source of weakness when a rival enterprise is astute enough to exploit the vulnerability that they open up. But frequently they are symptoms of health and vigor—truly "growing pains"—that indicate there is something worth fighting for. Often the internal disputes become sharp and open when the enterprise is in a situation that calls for a strategic turn. In such cases the disputes are correlated with different views about what direction to take.

Stalinist monolithism, after it was successfully consolidated, had elements of great strength, particularly in its ability to concentrate social energies on carefully targeted goals. But a monolithic system is overrigid; it suppresses much creative energy and—unless it really should transform human nature—it inevitably arouses antagonisms that a looser system might disperse harmlessly. Polycentrism—which is considerably more developed in the writings of the experts than in the actualities of the Communist system—can act as a corrective to the excessive global rigidity of the Communist enterprise in the past, adapting it better to, for example, newly posed tasks in Africa, Latin America, and the Middle East; in fact it has already, in some degree, done so.

It was not long after Mohammed's death that Islam was embroiled in fierce and bloody internal disputes. These did not stop the extraordinary explosion of Islam out of the Arabian desert east to Java and westward through North Africa into Spain and France. Within the frame of reference of Islam itself, the disputes, whether judged as struggles for power or for doctrinal purity, were significant enough. But within the frames of reference of Christendom, Hinduism, and paganism, it really didn't matter very much which Islamic wing conquered—which, that is to say, did the burying.

There are—there could not fail to be—differences as well as disputes among Soviet Communism, Chinese Communism, Castrovian Communism, Titoist Communism, Polish and Zanzibarian Communism. The time and circumstances in which Communism took over, the history and culture of the local population, the state of the economy—naturally each of these factors affects the net outcome. But wherever Communism takes over and a Communist regime is consolidated, no matter what the conditions precedent, certain fundamental traits are invariably found. The important means of production and distribution—factories, mines, banks, businesses—are nationalized; a state monopoly of foreign trade is established; agriculture is brought under some sort of collective scheme;

foreign travel is severely restricted, and domestic travel is also limited by job controls, police surveillance, etc.; the private sector of education is eliminated; no organized political opposition is permitted; the press, radio-TV and all other means of communication are made a state or Party monopoly; the state, becoming officially atheist, takes active economic, propagandist, and coercive measures to combat and if possible to eliminate religious belief as well as religious organizations; within the judicial system there is no independent legal corps—prosecution and defense, as well as tribunal, are merely agents of the state; there are no civil liberties or civil rights guaranteed against administrative action; the state intervenes pervasively in all or virtually all phases of social and individual life—is, that is to say, totalitarian; the theoretical order, like the practical order, is based on collective ("class") concepts, not on the individual human being.

If our choice were in truth between the Russian form of Communism and the Chinese form, presented as sole alternatives, it might seem prudent to settle for (let us say) the Russian form. I rather suspect that back of the refusal to face the challenge of the Communist enterprise—a refusal expressed most bluntly in the familiar "Better Red than Dead" slogan—there often does lie the unexpressed conviction that our historical choice is thus restricted, that the only real issue is *which* form of Communism, not whether society will become Communist. But if we adhere in any meaningful sense to Western civilization, we must reject this restriction, since in their substance all forms of Communism are incompatible with the essential ideas, values, traditions, and institutions of Western civilization. As Westerners we must, logically, affirm that we decline to choose or accept the Russian or Chinese or Cuban or any other form or variety of Communism, that we choose an alternative that is not Communism even if the sole actual alternative is death. So long as we are willing to include death among possible alternatives, we shall always be free to choose.

Looked at in this perspective—that is, the perspective of Western metaphysics and civilization—the Sino-Soviet split and Communist polycentrism are brought into clearer focus. They are seen to be conflicts *within* the Communist enterprise—even if they should sharpen to a point that brought war among Communist countries. Skillfully exploited by the non-Communist powers, these conflicts might serve to weaken, perhaps even smash, the Communist enterprise; but without deliberate intervention from outside, they need not have a permanently weakening effect. In any event, they leave the line between the Communist world and the non-Communist world far more significant—indeed, of another order of significance—than any line drawn between differing parts of the Communist world.

Disputes between this and that variant of Communism are not the only type of conflict taking place within the geographical area controlled by Communist regimes. There are also disputes which, in tendency at least, go beyond the limits of Communism, and which thus pose, wherever they develop, the essential issue of Communism *vs.* non-Communism. As conspicuous recent examples, there may be cited the Sinyavsky-Daniel episode in the Soviet Union and the Mihajlov episode in Yugoslavia. The activities, writings, and proposals of the Soviet writers, Andrei Sinyavsky and Yuri Daniel and of Mihajlo Mihajlov, have remained nominally within the general framework of Marxism, but they advocate rights of intellectual dissent, free publication, even political opposition, affirm the primacy of the individual, and are by implication if not explicitly expressing a fundamental criticism of the Communist order. Recognizing this, the Communist regimes, at whatever cost to their liberalized images, are sooner or later compelled to silence and jail them.

There is ample evidence that Sinyavsky, Daniel, and Mihajlov are only conspicuous representatives of deepening movements of dissent among the intellectuals in all the Communist nations, and to some degree among professionals, industrial managers, and technicians. We know, moreover, from the 1956 events in Poland, East Germany, and Hungary, that this sort of restlessness of the intellectuals is frequently the sign of a rising, quite general social discontent, the sources of which in the mass of the population may lie in economic problems, nationalist sentiment, or religious faith that have only an indirect relation to the "demands" articulated by the intellectuals.

It seems likely that in the decade to come these internal tendencies of opposition to the Communist order will expand and intensify. It is quite probable that they will result, during the next few years, in public conflicts; on a small scale they have already done so in 1965 and 1966. In the long run these conflicts which breach the Communist structure are more important to the non-Communist world than the bicentrist or polycentrist struggles of one kind of Communism against another. If our experts and policy-makers devoted one tenth the attention and energy to them that they lavish on polycentrism and Sino-Soviet dialectics, they might discover levers which, properly handled, could bring down the Communist enterprise.

Since the war we are in—the Third World War—has not ended, and is not going to end in the decade to come, it is possible to answer a number of subsidiary questions about what will and will not happen. Will there be (for example) serious disarmament? There will continue to be elaborate, expensive, and well-publicized talk and negotiations about disarmament, as there have been for the past eighteen years. The United States Government will continue to spend tens of millions of dollars on its Disarmament Agency; many officials in this and other countries will make good livings as disarmament specialists. Dozens of private associations will talk, meet, confer, organize and demonstrate for disarmament. But there will not be much disarmament, just as there has not been during the decade past.

How could there be? It is not arms that make conflicts, but conflicts that prompt men to make arms. Since many and profound conflicts remain, so will arms remain, and abundantly. The sufficient comment on the years of disarmament negotiation is the Vietnam War.

The proclaimed disarmament achievements of the past decade were the nuclear test-ban treaty and the agreement against weapons in space vehicles. No doubt the elimination of atmospheric nuclear fallout would be a good thing, though autos, factories, and incinerators produce much more and more lethal atmospheric fallout than anything we have got from nuclear bombs. But the test-ban treaty has not even eliminated atmospheric fallout; France and China have been testing in the atmosphere. And of course the treaty has done nothing at all to reduce nuclear armament. Two additional nations have joined the nuclear club since the treaty was signed; a number more (India, Israel, United Arab Republic, Japan, Brazil, West Germany are among obvious candidates) will probably do so during the next few years. There are more nuclear weapons than ever in existence, and many new sophisticated types have been developed in the post-treaty period.

As for the agreement against weapons in space, it has no enforcement mechanism and is not even a formal treaty. It therefore has only the validity the several powers choose to give it; it will become null whenever any power wishes to nullify it. Meanwhile it exercises little if any inhibiting effect on the development of spatial armament, since this stage of the development would in any case concentrate on the attainment of vehicles (and launching systems) able to mount the arms, toward which goal both major powers are moving as rapidly as they can manage.

The probable net result of disarmament efforts over the next decade is the same as it has been over the last: more arms. The one possibility of an important measure of disarmament would be through acceptance by the United States Government not merely of the words of the disarmament-ideologues—which by and large has already occurred—but of their practical recommendations. Actual disarmament in this case would, it goes without saying, be confined for the most part to the United States and those nations which depend for their arms on the United States.

Will the United Nations, in the next decade, become a genuine "parliament of the nations" and an effective force for global peace, order, liberty, and progress? Again, we can judge the future only by what we can learn from the past. Since the United Nations has not been an effective force in the past, since it has not even tried to act in the important episodes (more exactly, since the major powers have not permitted it to act in the important episodes), why should we expect it to be any different in the near future? Self-evidently, a United Nations organization run mostly, in political matters, by the huge General Assembly, as now, rather than by the Security Council, as in the early years, is less rather than more likely to operate effectively. Self-evidently, a General Assembly made up of 120 miscellaneous nations, half of which are not coherent social entities of any sort, is less likely to operate effectively than an Assembly made up, as when the Charter was signed, of fifty or sixty established nations.

The United Nations will continue, as in the past, to perform certain technical tasks that are globally useful in an age of global technology and business. In political affairs it may occasionally, as in the past, aid the settlement or compromise of minor difficulties and furnish facilities for communication among governments, but when things get serious it will either do nothing or, as not infrequently in the past, provoke and exacerbate troubles. Especially in the case of Africa, the United Nations has already proved its trouble-making potential; and in relation to Africa this is likely to be demonstrated often again in the decade ahead.

Will de Gaulle have succeeded in creating a "Europe of the fatherlands," divorced from the Anglo-Saxons and stretching "from the Atlantic to the Urals," which will become the leader of a Third World holding itself independent from the super-states? The answers are No in general and in detail. De Gaulle's "little Europe," without Russia, does not have resources and power enough to construct a new, fully autonomous bloc—especially while Gaullist insistence on total sovereign independence prevents military and economic integration. If little Europe did stretch out to the Urals, then, in the resultant combination, it could never be France that would be the dominant power. By the nature of the relationship of forces, Russia in that case would be dominant; Europe from the Atlantic to the Urals—excluding the Anglo-Saxon nations, and maintaining restrictions on Germany—would inevitably be a Europe brought within the Soviet Communist bloc. De Gaulle's professed aims are adapted to lofty rhetoric, but in cold matter-of-fact they are not serious, and will fade away when he fades away, as before long he must.

It is equally illusory to suppose that the Third World will pull itself together and go striding forward into order, progress, and power. Some nations of the Third World may do so, and probably will, but the Third World in general will almost surely be in worse rather than better shape as the next decade unrolls. The reasons are not obscure. The population of the underdeveloped and in many cases inherently impoverished nations is rising at historically unprecedented rates, considerably faster than the food supply. Political disorders, resulting from many sorts of internal instability and rivalry, and spurred, often, by both the advanced powers and the United Nations, are increasing rather than quieting down. The interventions and intrigues of the Communist enterprise in the Third World are primarily designed at this stage to bring about confusion, civil dissension, breakdown, and chaos, as part of the strategy of isolating and encircling the "global cities" (western Europe and North America) by the "liberated" (revolutionized) "global countryside" (Asia, Africa, Latin America); the positive task of building a new Communist order in what is now the Third World can be postponed until a later stage.

Indeed, the primary hope for much of the Third World lies in a policy of prudent but vigorous neocolonialism on the part of the Western nations: a policy that would accept the formal independence and autonomy of the Third World nations, but, for the sake of Western military security and mutually beneficial economic development, would furnish military protection, administrative and technical assistance, and productive investment. Thus the Third World will continue to be the arena for the struggle of the great antagonists; the revolutionary attack of the Communist enterprise, usually masked in its early phases as "struggle for liberation," will confront the "neocolonialism"—the term is not without justification—of the West. . . .

The Suez-Hungary episodes of 1956 foreshadowed the major trends of the period that was to follow. In a similar way, the Vietnam War will foreshadow at least some of the major trends in the coming period. I say "will foreshadow" rather than "foreshadows" in order to emphasize that the pattern defined by the episode is not presented statically or in advance. The Suez and Hungarian episodes did not get their particular precognitive significance just because something happened "out there" in history, or because somebody else did something—the Hungarian students and workers rebelling, the French and British armies invading. Their meaning depended also on what we—what the United States, dominant power of the non-Communist world—did about what was happening, on the fact that we stood aside from Hungary and that we actively intervened against Britain and France in Suez.

Just so, it is not merely the fact that something is taking place in Vietnam or that somebody else is doing something there—organized Communist units fighting—that gives the Vietnam episode a symbolic meaning. What we are doing and will do is an essential part of the pattern that will become significant for the future. When that pattern is sufficiently defined, the Vietnam action will be seen, like Suez-Hungary, as a premonitory crisis or turning point. This is plainly figured by the breadth and intensity of both the domestic and the global disputes over United States intervention in Vietnam. These disputes are, in truth, sharper than any others that have taken place over any previous episode of the Cold War. The fact that they are so demonstrates an almost instinctive general awareness of the crucial importance of what is happening in Vietnam.

So far, since shortly after his election as chief of government in his own name and right, Lyndon Johnson, like Harry Truman in relation to the Greek civil war and unlike Dwight Eisenhower in relation to Suez-Hungary, has acted (however equivocal his talk) firmly and forcefully in relation to Vietnam, and a good deal more firmly than the usually prevailing opinion-makers have approved. The basic alternatives ahead in Vietnam can be very simply put. Either the Communists will be beaten badly enough to guarantee that for the next period (there can be no permanent guarantees) there is no chance for a Communist or Communist-dominated government in South Vietnam, or the Communists will get control of South Vietnam. From an anti-Communist standpoint, the ideal outcome would include much more than a de facto guarantee against Communist domination: overthrow of the Communist regime in North Vietnam and perhaps some direct injury to Communist China, such as the destruction of her nuclear installations. But these two are the bare, basic alternatives. It is in terms of these that the world will render its judgment and draw its conclusions. If the first comes about, then the judgment will be victory for the United States, for the anti-Communist Vietnamese and for anti-Communism generally. If the second, the judgment will be victory for Ho Chi Minh, for the Vietcong and for the Communist enterprise as a whole. It is difficult to see how there can be any compromise, any outcome halfway between these two. No matter which side wins, a diplomatic facade can be, and doubtless will be, erected to make the outcome look like a compromise; this is not "the final conflict," and faces must be saved. The fighting may go on a long while inconclusively. But in the last analysis, the Communists either take over South Vietnam or they don't.

If our side wins, our troubles certainly won't be over. But we will have demonstrated that the anti-Communist camp, under American leadership and principally through American men and weapons, can stop the present massive drive of the Communist enterprise to take over Southeast Asia and break through into the Indian subcontinent and the South Seas. We will have demonstrated that the anti-Communist camp, under American leadership and principally through American men and weapons, can handle revolutionary encirclement of the global cities through the global countryside. We will have, not silenced (which is impossible), but refuted the doubters and Softs and cowards and subversives within the anti-Communist camp who have argued that a favorable outcome in Vietnam is beyond American capability. We will have enheartened, and rallied around us, many non-Communist nations who, because of their own comparative weakness, cannot help guiding their own policies by the way the wind is blowing. Already, in fact, by the unexpected firmness we have shown in Vietnam, this effect is evident in the South Pacific region. A number of the small nations there have sent in their own soldiers to fight alongside ours, and have been feeling their way toward some sort of anti-Communist united front. It is certain that the pro-Peking Sukarno regime in Indonesia would not have been overthrown and the Indonesian Communist Party crushed if we had declined the Vietnam challenge. And who could have guessed beforehand that the Burmese leader, General Ne Win, after a years-long record of anti-Western neutralism, would be a friendly visitor to Washington in the late summer of 1966?

If the Communists win in Vietnam, then the sequence of events will be reversed, as nearly everyone really knows. The analysts who spoke of the domino effect were surely right. If the Communist advance cannot be stopped in Vietnam, when American power has been committed to that mission, where then is it to be stopped? "Those who do not like the war in Vietnam," commented the authoritative English weekly, *The Economist* (August 20, 1966), "have a duty to ask themselves where else they think the wave can be stopped. Thailand? But the non-Communist Thais are not going to call for help from a defeated American army, and in any case it is logistically much harder to get help into Thailand than into Vietnam. Burma? Not in the cards. India, then? But the mind swerves away from the difficulty of doing anything to help that fragile country if the guerrillas once get to work in West Bengal or Kerala or wherever. . . . The deal the Americans cannot reasonably be asked to strike is one that threatens to sell the pass to the whole of southern Asia. This is Mr. Johnson's enormous problem. It is also the problem of those who criticize his decision to take America into the war."

The domino effect would not be confined to southern Asia; it would be worldwide. Everywhere, and rightly, confidence in the will and power of the United States would be shaken; everywhere Communists would be emboldened, anti-Communists dismayed. If in spite of the United States the Vietcong could succeed—completing the demonstration begun by Fidel Castro—who need respect or fear the American paper tiger? On a world scale, one may predict with certainty, the revolution would take mighty strides forward.

The response of the United States in case of failure is also predictable. The nation would pull back toward the desperate condition of a Fortress America, riven within by fierce conflicts the preliminary lines of which are already being shaped. The two alternatives are so narrowly poised that, just as we can see such anticipations of a possible Communist defeat in Vietnam as I have cited, so we can see anticipations of a possible Communist victory in the tentative moves already taken toward a Fortress America condition: the widespread call for withdrawal from Vietnam itself, to begin with; the campaign against the President and the Secretaries of State and Defense on the ground that they want the United States to be "world policeman"; the uncritical blanket dissatisfaction with foreign aid and the unanalyzed demand to bring United States troops back from Europe; the switch in strategic defense toward dependence on home-based missiles and submarines. In making his decisions about the Vietnam War, Lyndon Johnson is making also the nation's controlling decisions for the next decade and perhaps the next generation. . . .

NORMAN PODHORETZ

Vietnam and the Crisis of Containment

The period usually called the Cold War began in 1947 when the United States, after several years of acquiescence in the expansion of the Soviet empire, decided to resist any further advance, whether in the form of military invasion by Soviet troops or political subversion by local Communist parties. Up until this point the Russians had enjoyed a free hand. They had been permitted to occupy most of Eastern Europe and to begin installing puppet regimes in one after another of the countries of the region. Now, with Greece and Turkey threatened by the same fate, the United States finally began rousing itself from the semieuphoric and semitorpid state into which it had fallen at the end of World War II. In March 1947, announcing a special program of aid to Greece and Turkey, President Truman, in the doctrine soon to bear his name, declared that "it must be the policy of the United States to support free peoples who are resisting attempted subjugation by armed minorities or by outside pressure."

Within the next few months, the Marshall Plan was launched to aid in the reconstruction of the war-torn economies of Western Europe. Then came a Communist coup in Czechoslovakia, which destroyed the independence of another East European country and the only one with a democratic political system. Partly in response to a similar danger posed

From Norman Podhoretz, *The Present Danger* (New York: Simon & Schuster, 1980), pp. 13–38. Copyright © 1980 by Norman Podhoretz. Reprinted by permission of Simon & Schuster and the author.

to Italy and France by huge local Communist parties subservient to Moscow, and partly to guard against an actual Soviet invasion of Western Europe, the North Atlantic Treaty Organization (NATO) was formed.

The name given to this two-sided politico-military strategy of American resistance to Soviet imperialism was containment, and it remained the guiding principle of American foreign policy until it was replaced two decades later, in 1969, by a new policy and a new presidential doctrine, bearing the name of Richard Nixon.

In one of the Orwellian inversions at which Soviet propaganda has always been so adept, this strategy of resistance, of holding a defensive line against their own imperialistic ambitions, the Russians described and stigmatized (in the words of *The Soviet Diplomatic Dictionary*) as a declaration of war by "the United States and . . . the imperialist military blocs" on "the Soviet Union and other Socialist States after the Second World War."

From that moment to this, any and every lowering of American resistance to Soviet imperialism has been praised by the Russians as a move away from the "Cold War," and any sign of a reawakened concern, let alone of concrete action, has been denounced as a "return to the Cold War."

Thanks to the process of what Fred Iklé has called "semantic infiltration," this Orwellian use of the term "Cold War" has come into currency in the United States and in the West generally. Thus when the Soviet Union sent 75,000 troops into Afghanistan and President Carter responded with expressions of alarm and a relatively mild series of countermeasures, most of them no more than symbolic, a whole rash of articles appeared in the American public prints denouncing the *United States* for this "capricious reversion to the Cold War."[1]

"Here we go again," announced Richard J. Walton, a historian, on the op-ed page of *The New York Times*.[2] "The Cold War, about to expire of old age, is rejuvenated"—not, in Mr. Walton's account, by the Soviet invasion of Afghanistan but by "American politicians" who even before the invasion "were beginning to run against the Russians." Mr. Walton assured us that he was "hardly suggesting that the Russians are beyond reproach," but it was the Americans who were "off to the Cold War" once again.

In similar fashion, Alan Wolfe, writing in *The Nation*,[3] of whose editorial board he is a member, denounced Jimmy Carter for whipping up "Cold War hysteria" in order to win the election. According to Mr. Wolfe, "the invasion fits into an ongoing trend" not, evidently, within the Soviet Union but within the United States: "This is not the first time in the history of the Cold War that the United States has begun to treat Russia as a hostile power, only to have the Russians act like one, thereby confirming American sentiment."

In *Newsweek,*[4] Robert Lasch, the former editor of *The St. Louis Post-Dispatch,* added his voice to the chorus denouncing President Carter for "reviving the Cold War," and doing so, like Truman before him, for no better reason than to "surmount a catastrophic decline in public esteem and win re-election by posing as a tough little rooster, ready to take on the Russians." As for the Soviet invasion of Afghanistan, "it is hardly surprising that the Soviet government, dreading an attack by the West, might decide to nail down the security of its frontiers by taking power in Afghanistan as it previously did in Eastern Europe." We might, Mr. Lasch acknowledged, have been "right to protest it in the United Nations." But there was certainly no need to overreact with hysterics.

Finally, the well-known economist and political commentator Robert Lekachman, while characterizing the Soviet invasion as "blundering," found stronger language with which to describe "the new Cold War fervor" in the United States: Congress, he said, was "enjoying a virulent case of raving patriotism."[5]

Obviously the term "Cold War" is by now so charged with tendentious implications and so loaded with grotesquely unbalanced political judgments that it can no longer serve any serious intellectual purpose. The first thing to do, then, if we really wish to know where we have been, where we are, and where we are going, is to discard it in favor of "containment" when we talk about the role played by the United States in the first act of the great historical drama which opened in 1947.

Although it was in the Truman Doctrine that the policy of containment was officially enunciated, it received its most authoritative expression in an article published in the July 1947 issue of *Foreign Affairs* under the title "The Sources of Soviet Conduct."[6] The author, identified at the time as "Mr. X," was George F. Kennan, the first director of the Policy Planning Staff of the State Department. About thirty years later, in what was perhaps the most dramatic single case of the loss of faith in containment caused by the experience of Vietnam, Kennan for all practical purposes repudiated the position he had taken in this article. Like many others of his generation, the great theorist of containment became what he himself called, with a candor few of the others had the courage or the audacity to match, a "semi-isolationist." But even to Kennan's admirable candor on these momentous issues there were limits. Thus he suggested that it was not so much that he had changed his mind about containment, as that his conception of it had been distorted in practice by an excessive emphasis on the military component of a strategy that he had envisaged as primarily political.

Yet anyone who reads "The Sources of Soviet Conduct" today is unlikely to come away with the impression that Kennan meant to stress the political over the military. His two main points, made not once but several times, are that the Soviet Union is embarked on a long-range strategy to overthrow the societies of the capitalist world and replace them with Communist regimes, and that this aim can only be frustrated by an equally determined strategy of resistance. Thus "the main element of any United States policy toward the Soviet Union must be that of a long-term, patient but firm and vigilant containment of Russian expansive tendencies." Or again: ". . . the Soviet pressure against the free institutions of the Western world is something that can be contained by the adroit and vigilant application of counterforce at a series of constantly shifting geographical and political points, corresponding to the shifts and maneuvers of Soviet policy, but which cannot be charmed or talked out of existence."

No doubt the "counterforce" Kennan had in mind was not exclusively military in nature. But there can be even less doubt that the American interventions into Korea and Vietnam were entirely consistent with his formulations. In fact, when we add to them the statement that the duty of "all good Communists" everywhere in the world "is the support and promotion of Soviet power, as defined in Moscow," we have to conclude that, in principle at least, Kennan's conception of containment imposed a prima facie requirement on the United States to use military force in Korea and Vietnam. For in his view, in each of these cases an effort was being made to expand Soviet power through the expansion of Communist regimes serving Moscow's long-range purposes. That greater practical wisdom or tactical prudence would have counseled nonintervention into Vietnam—on the ground that the chances of success were so slight—says nothing about the principle, or about its applicability to situations where the local conditions might be more favorable to military action. Korea itself was the classic example of such a situation and a test case of the seriousness of containment.

In the years between the enunciation of the policy and the outbreak of the Korean War, the United States had given containment concrete expression in the formation of NATO, and in a variety of actions designed to deter any advance of Soviet power beyond the lines established at the end of World War II and thus far crossed only by the coup in Czechoslovakia (for which, perhaps, the defection of Communist Yugoslavia was regarded as an even trade). At first there had been opposition to the new policy from the Left as well as the Right. On the Left, the argument was that the Soviet Union—in contrast to what the theory of containment supposed—was pursuing a defensive rather than an aggressive policy, and that Stalin wanted only security and peace. On the Right, the theory of Soviet intentions lying behind containment was accepted, but the prescription for American policy was attacked as overly defensive. Whereas the Left advocated disarmament and "understanding," the Right demanded "rollback" and liberation. It was not enough to hold out the hope, as Kennan did, of promoting "tendencies which must eventually find their outlet in either the breakup or the gradual mellowing of Soviet power"; the East European satellites had to be helped to rise up and rebel against their Soviet masters.

Yet neither of these two opposing assaults on containment could make much headway in the early years. The left-wing attack organized itself in Henry Wallace's campaign for the presidency in 1948 and was so badly humiliated at the polls (Wallace receiving not the 10 million votes he had expected but only about a million) that it sank into oblivion as a political force. In the world of ideas, too, the benign interpretation of Soviet intentions suffered a severe pounding at the hands of critics who could point both to Soviet doctrine and to Soviet action in refuting the view that Stalin was interested only in security and peace.

As for the attack from the Right, it turned out to be more rhetorical than real. Thus when—encouraged by a Republican administration in which John Foster Dulles and Richard Nixon, two of the leading critics of containment from the Right, served in high positions—the Hungarians rose up against their Soviet masters, the United States looked on sympathetically but took no action.

The Korean War had also broken out as a result of American encouragement. In that case, however, it was the Communists we encouraged, in the form of an announcement by Secretary of State Dean Acheson seeming to suggest that the defense of South Korea was not a vital American interest. Whether Acheson thus misled the Soviet Union and its North Korean clients by inadvertence, or whether the United States changed its mind at the sight of Communist troops actually invading a non-Communist nation, the American decision to hold the line against any further expansion of Soviet or Communist power was virtually unhesitant. We went to war, and in doing so we demonstrated in unmistakable terms that we were serious about the "application of counterforce at a series of constantly shifting geographical and political points, corresponding to the shifts and maneuvers of Soviet policy"—that is, about containment.

At the same time, the way we fought the war in Korea became a first clear indication that the critics of containment from the Right—for all that they seemed to have one of the two major parties behind them—were to be no more influential in the shaping of American policy than the critics on the Left. In refusing to do more in Korea than repel the North Korean invasion, or, as Truman put it, "to restore peace there and to restore the border,"[7] a policy which his critics on the Right denounced as appeasement and timidity, the United States served notice on the world that it had no intention of going beyond containment to rollback or liberation.

Any lingering doubt as to whether this was the policy of the United States rather than the policy of the Democratic party was removed when the Republicans came into office in 1953 under Eisenhower. Far from adopting a bolder or more aggressive strategy, the new President ended the Korean War on the basis of the status quo ante—in other words, precisely on the terms of containment. And when, three years later, he refrained from going into Hungary, he made it correlatively clear that while the United States would resist the expansion of Soviet power by any and every means up to and including war, it would do nothing—not even provide aid to colonies of the Soviet empire seeking national independence and wishing to throw in their political lot with the democratic world—to shrink the territorial dimensions of Soviet control.

In reality, if not entirely in rhetoric, then, there was a bipartisan consensus behind the policy of containment as outlined by Kennan in "The Sources of Soviet Conduct." But even putting it that way understates the case. The fact is that there was a *national* consensus which went deeper than the realm of electoral politics. Nor did this consensus express itself only in the negative terms of a weakening of the critics of containment from the Left and the Right. There was a positive dimension, caught by Kennan in the peroration of his article with an eloquent flourish that fully matched the magisterial brilliance of the analysis on which it rested:

The thoughtful observer of Russian-American relations will find no cause for complaint in the Kremlin's challenge to American society. He will rather experience a certain gratitude for a Providence which, by providing the American people with this implacable challenge, has made their entire security as a nation dependent on their pulling themselves together and accepting the responsibilities of moral and political leadership that history plainly intended them to bear.

In "pulling themselves together" precisely for these reasons and in this way, the American people experienced a surge of self-confident energy. Instead of the depression which had been expected in the postwar years, there was unprecedented prosperity, and its fruits were being more widely shared than anyone had ever dreamed possible. Millions upon millions of people with low expectations of life found themselves being offered opportunities to improve their lot; in response they worked, they produced, they built, they bred. Even many intellectuals—so recently "alienated" and marginal—joined in what was petulantly derided by the few remaining socialists among them as the "celebration" of America. Yet instead of resulting in a diminution of creativity, this new ethos generated a more exciting literature than the thirties before it or the sixties which would follow. (I think of the emergence in the fifties of such writers who shared in the newly positive attitude toward American society as Saul Bellow, Ralph Ellison, William Styron, Robert Lowell, John Berryman, Lionel Trilling, Reinhold Niebuhr, Hannah Arendt, and George Kennan himself.)

In addition to "pulling themselves together" in this way, the American people also realized Kennan's hope that they would accept "the responsibilities of moral and political leadership that history plainly intended them to bear." They accepted these responsibilities by supporting the Marshall Plan, possibly the most generous program of economic aid the world had ever seen, and by their willingness to pay the price in blood and treasure of policies designed to hold the line against a totalitarian system which had already destroyed any possibility of freedom in large areas of the globe and aimed to extend its barbarous reign over as much of the rest as it could. For this, too, they were rewarded by an upsurge of pride and self-confidence. It was a nation that believed itself capable of assuming leadership in the cause of defending freedom against the threat of totalitarianism. By the end of the decade, when John F. Kennedy succeeded Eisenhower as president, only a small minority of people on the Left doubted that the cause was just or that the will and the means to fight for it were there.

So many Democrats, including the vast majority who served in the upper echelons of the Kennedy administration, have by now repudiated or quietly drifted away from their earlier views that it seems necessary to stress what would otherwise be self-evident about the Kennedy administration: that it was, if anything, more zealous in its commitment to containment than the Eisenhower administration had been. Kennedy ran against his Republican opponent, Nixon, who had of course served as Eisenhower's vice president, on a platform charging that the Republicans had neglected our defenses (allowing a "missile gap" to develop between the United States and the Soviet Union) and that they were, moreover, softer on Communism than he was. (Nixon later came to believe that a major factor in his narrow defeat was Kennedy's success in establishing this point—improbable though it may sound to the ears of a later generation which knew not John—during one of their television debates.)[8]

Once in office, Kennedy and his Secretary of Defense, Robert McNamara, took immediate steps to move away from the Republican strategic doctrine of "massive retaliation"—according to which the United States would respond to any act of Communist aggression with a nuclear strike against the Soviet Union—toward a more flexible posture. As early as 1950, a group of professors from Harvard and MIT (including future members of the Kennedy administration like McGeorge Bundy, Carl Kaysen, Jerome Wiesner, Arthur Schlesinger, Jr., and John Kenneth Galbraith) had warned that the emphasis on nuclear weapons "provided the United States with no effective answer to limited aggression except the wholly disproportionate answer of atomic war. As a result it invited Moscow to use the weapons of guerrilla warfare and internal revolt in marginal areas in the confidence that such local activity would incur only local risks."9 Kennedy himself picked up this theme eight years later, and his call as a senator for a military posture that could respond to such threats as "limited brushfire wars, indirect nonovert aggression, intimidation and subversion, internal revolution,"10 he answered with his policies as president. Among those policies were the attempted invasion of Cuba in the Bay of Pigs and the decision to send American "advisers" and then actual troops in Vietnam.

Although a universally acknowledged disaster, the Bay of Pigs did little to discredit the strategy of containment in general. It was taken as a great tactical blunder and written off as an unfortunate but perhaps necessary stage in the education of a new and inexperienced president.

The decision to go into Vietnam, however, was to have much more radical consequences. In principle, to repeat the point once again, this decision was unremarkable. It followed upon the precedent of Korea in the sense that Vietnam, too, was a country partitioned into Communist and non-Communist areas and where the Communists were trying to take over the non-Communists by force. The difference was that whereas in Korea the North had invaded the South with regular troops, in Vietnam the aggression was taking the form of an apparently internal rebellion by a Communist faction. Very few people in the United States believed that the war in Vietnam was a civil war, but even if they had, it would have made little difference. For whatever the legalistic definition of the case might be, there was no question that an effort was being mounted in Vietnam to extend Communist power beyond an already established line. As such, it represented no less clear a challenge to containment than Korea.

The question, then, was not whether the United States ought to respond; the only question was whether the United States had the means to do so effectively. But given the fact that the new strategic doctrine of the Kennedy administration had been conceived precisely for the purpose of meeting just such a challenge ("indirect nonovert aggression, intimidation and subversion, internal revolution"), it was all but inevitable that Kennedy's answer should be yes. The only dissent from this answer within his administration came from those who argued that military measures would fail unless we also forced the South Vietnamese government to undertake programs of liberal reform. But this argument implicitly called for a greater degree of American intervention than the dispatch of troops alone (and led eventually to the assassination of Diem and the assumption of complete American responsibility for the war).

A case might have been made—and indeed was made, by Hans J.

Morgenthau, among others, outside the administration itself—against American intervention into Vietnam on the ground that the chances of success were too slight and the consequences of failure too great. As Morgenthau saw it, there was nothing wrong with trying to save South Vietnam from Communism, let alone with the strategy of containment in general; what was wrong was the tactical judgment, the attempt to apply a sound policy in an inappropriate and unfavorable situation. Morgenthau added that if we allowed ourselves to get dragged into an interminable war in South Vietnam—which we would be unable to win in any case—it would have the same kind of divisive effects on our society as the Algerian war had had on the French. The interests at stake in Southeast Asia were simply not vital enough to justify the risk.[11]

Sound, and even irrefutable, as this analysis seems in retrospect, it commanded very little assent in official Washington. There the prevailing conviction was that we now had the kinds of counterinsurgency forces required to save South Vietnam from Communism, and there was also what can only be called an itch to test out the new techniques.

But if the only question raised by Vietnam in the early days was the tactical one of whether it was possible for intervention to succeed, more fundamental questions began to be raised as the war dragged on. Whether or not the intervention could succeed, was it necessary or desirable? One of the main assumptions behind containment was that any advance of Communist power amounted to an expansion of Soviet power, but was that necessarily true? Might this not be a case of Chinese expansionism? If so, given the ever widening rift between the Russians and the Chinese, in what sense did American resistance fall under the imperative of containing Soviet expansionism? And if we were now faced with a separate problem of Chinese expansionism, was a mechanical application of the same strategy we had developed to counter the Soviet imperial thrust the best way to deal with it? Or again: might the war in Vietnam actually be an internal Vietnamese affair—a case of covert aggression from the North with local purposes of its own (the unification of the country, and perhaps domination of the whole region, by Hanoi) having little to do with either Soviet or Chinese power? Or finally, might it be an entirely internal *South* Vietnamese affair—a civil war of real significance to no one but the people of that country?

Obviously the rationale for American intervention into Vietnam depended on clear answers to such questions. Yet they were never forthcoming. Or rather, the ground of our policy kept shifting as the years wore on. First we were countering Soviet expansionism, then we were drawing a line in Asia against Chinese expansionism similar to the one we had drawn in Europe against the Russians, then we were fighting to preserve the independence of a friendly country which had been invaded by another, and finally we were preserving the credibility of our commitments to allies in other parts of the world.

In short, to the casualities in blood of the Vietnam War was added another casualty—the loss of clarity which had marked the policy of the United States for twenty years through Democratic and Republican administrations alike.

Nor was this the only wound suffered by containment in Vietnam. There was also a loss of confidence in the ability of the United States to discharge "the responsibilities of moral and political leadership." In saying that "history plainly intended" the United States to bear those responsibilities, Kennan (no American chauvinist, to put it mildly) surely had in mind not some inherent virtue in the American character but the predominance of sheer power with which history, working through two world wars that had finally exhausted the energies of Western Europe, had left the United States. Despite all the talk, friendly or hostile, about American "arrogance" or the "illusion of American omnipotence," this power was not exercised by Americans as though they thought it was absolute. If they really had entertained any such arrogant illusion of omnipotence, they would surely have refused to tolerate Soviet domination of Eastern Europe or the capture of mainland China by the Communists at a time when America enjoyed a nuclear monopoly. But it would on the other side be foolish to deny that before Vietnam, American confidence in American power was very great—not unlimited but great. Anything within reason we wanted to do we believed we had the power to do. This confidence in American power was the second major casualty of the defeat in Vietnam.

As with power, so with "moral and political leadership." If at the beginning domestic criticism of our military intervention into Vietnam was restricted to tactical issues, and if toward the middle the political wisdom of the intervention came into very serious question, by the end the moral character of the United States was being indicted and besmirched. Large numbers of Americans, including even many of the people who had led the intervention in the Kennedy years, were now joining the tiny minority on the Left who had at the time denounced them for stupidity and immorality, and were now saying that going into Vietnam had progressed from a folly to a crime. No greater distance could have been traveled from the original spirit of containment, reaffirmed in such ringing tones in John F. Kennedy's inaugural address ("Let every nation know, whether it wishes us well or ill, that we shall pay any price, bear any burden, meet any hardship, support any friend, oppose any foe, to assure the survival and the success of liberty"), than to this new national mood of self-doubt and self-disgust. The domestic base on which containment had rested was gone.

It was in response to this new political reality that a Republican administration, coming into office under Richard Nixon a little more than twenty years after containment was first enunciated, decided to begin moving away from it and toward a new international role for the United States. In a process not unfamiliar to other countries and other conservative leaders (France under de Gaulle, Israel under Begin), Nixon, who had once denounced containment as "cowardly" and would in the past have been expected to abandon it if at all in favor of a more aggressive stance, moved instead in the other direction—toward withdrawal, retrenchment, disengagement.

As getting into Vietnam had served under Kennedy and Johnson to discredit the old strategy of containment, getting out of Vietnam would now—so Nixon and his National Security Adviser, Henry Kissinger, thought—become the model or paradigm of a new strategy of retreat. American forces were to be withdrawn from Vietnam gradually enough to permit a buildup of South Vietnamese power to the point where the South Vietnamese could assume responsibility for the defense of their own country. The American role would then be limited to supplying the necessary military aid. The same policy, suitably modified according to local circumstances, would be applied to the rest of the world as well. In every major region, the United States would now depend on local surrogates (including Communist China—hence the opening to it—and of course Iran under the Shah) rather than on its own military power to deter or contain any Soviet-sponsored aggression. We would supply arms and other forms of assistance, but from henceforth the deterring and the fighting would be left to others. Thus did the Truman Doctrine give way to the Nixon Doctrine, and containment to strategic retreat.

To be sure, the new policy did not call itself by any such unattractive name as "strategic retreat." It was called "détente" and it was heralded as the beginning of a new era in the relations between the United States and the Soviet Union. In this new era, a "structure of peace" would be built, with cooperation between the two superpowers replacing "confrontation." Negotiations would proceed to limit the proliferation of strategic nuclear weapons, and the Americans and the Russians would also agree to exercise restraint in their dealings with third parties so as to lessen the danger that they might be drawn into direct conflict with each other.

To the critics of "détente" it was clear at the time, as it has become clear to almost everyone in retrospect, that the new strategy rested on the highly questionable assumption that the Soviet Union could be contained by any force other than American power. Nixon and Kissinger believed—or perhaps only hoped against hope—that a combination or "linkage" of surrogate force and positive economic and political incentives would be enough to restrain Soviet adventurism, and where this combination proved insufficient, a serious show of American determination (such as the calling of a nuclear alert during the Yom Kippur War of 1973 in response to a threat of Soviet intervention on the side of Egypt) would make up the lack.

In other words, in their conception of it, "détente" was the highest degree of containment compatible with the post-Vietnam political climate in the United States—a climate in which Congress, supported by the leading centers of opinion within the foreign-policy establishment and the major news media, wanted only to cut back drastically on defense spending and to curtail American commitments abroad to a sparse minimum.

That this was indeed the climate in the Nixon years cannot be seriously questioned. In 1972, for example, the Brookings Institution suggested a $12.5 billion cutback in defense programs (out of a budget of $76.5 billion). Senator Hubert Humphrey endorsed the proposal, while Senator George McGovern declared it inadequate and called for a $30 billion reduction instead. (Later, under the exigencies of his campaign for the presidency, McGovern agreed to settle for a $10 billion reduction.) *The New York Times* also thought that the $12.5 billion cut might be too modest, and devoted a sympathetic editorial[12] to a more radical Brookings plan amounting to what the *Times* characterized as "major surgery." (Brookings considered it more politic to describe its plan as the "elimination of less effective forces and a selective slowdown in modernization.")

The Brookings plan, said the *Times* approvingly,

would eliminate half the strategic bomber and land-based ICBM forces and most air defense. The Navy would lose four of its sixteen carrier task forces and most of its shipbuilding program, the Air Force its chief new tactical air development, the F-15 fighter, and the Army, six active brigades plus some of its swollen support forces.

Nor was this enough:

Bigger savings may be possible in strategic forces by halting deployment of the MIRV multiple warhead missiles, Minuteman III and Poseidon, slowing down development of the ULMS-Trident long-range missile submarine and shifting to a cheaper strategic bomber to replace the projected B-1.

Nor was this enough:

But deep cutbacks in military spending must address themselves to conventional forces, which absorb more than three-fourths of the defense budget.

Nor was even all this enough:

What can be given a close, hard look now . . . is the Pentagon's continuing acquisition of weapons systems, many of them oversophisticated. . . . The Army's 10,000 helicopters, the Navy's unnecessary amphibious forces, and the Air Force's deep-penetration tactical fighters are prime candidates, along with vulnerable $1-billion nuclear carriers, bomber defenses, and support units.

A few weeks later,[13] the *Times* made the philosophy behind these recommendations altogether explicit:

We believe that the Nixon Administration, in its preoccupation with military might, has grievously misjudged America's national security needs in the 1970's. Not only that: the weapons buildup envisaged by this Administration would be wasteful of resources and inherently self-defeating. It would actually detract from American security by heightening suspicions and triggering countermeasures by the Soviet Union.

At a moment when the American defense budget was already beginning to decline in both relative and real terms, while the Soviet Union was forging grimly ahead (this, and not a reciprocal policy of restraint, was the only Soviet countermeasure triggered by our actions), the *Times* concluded:

America's defense budget is exploding, becoming in itself a threat to the security and well-being of the nation.

It was because of this kind of thing that Kissinger evidently came to believe that the United States had suffered a failure of nerve and no longer had the will or the stomach to pursue a serious strategy of containment. He also seems to have believed that the Soviet Union had entered a period of imperial dynamism. His role, like that of Metternich when confronted with the impending collapse of the monarchical system in the face of a rising democratic challenge, was to delay the inevitable for as long as possible. To win time was desirable in itself, and there was in any case a chance that unexpected developments might occur to change the entire picture.

Unfortunately for this conception, the only unexpected developments that actually did occur tended to undermine its viability as a modified strategy of containment. One such development was the failure of what had been the paradigmatic testing ground of the new strategy in Vietnam, where the new idea of containment through surrogate power followed the old idea of containment through American power into an early grave (though the obsequies were not read until four years later, after the fall of the Shah). In the case of Vietnam, not only was the surrogate power unable to hold the line on its own, but in the event, the United States refused even to provide it with the promised aid to defend itself against a military invasion encouraged and supplied with massive quantities of Soviet arms. To make yet another of the many historical ironies generated by this story still more mordant, the "discredited" theory on which we originally went into Vietnam—that the victory of Communism there would be tantamount to an expansion of Soviet power—was vindicated after many detours in the end, as Communist Vietnam allied itself with the Soviet Union against China and then drove on to extend its rule over the whole of Indochina.

The even more "discredited" domino theory was thereby vindicated too—and not merely in Indochina. No sooner had Vietnam fallen than Soviet proxies in the form of Cuban troops appeared in Angola, and again the United States refused to respond. Kissinger and the new president, Gerald Ford, appealed to Congress for aid to the pro-Western faction in Angola, which was being overwhelmed by its Communist rivals with the help of the Cuban troops. But Congress (again supported by the most influential sectors of opinion) said no, and for good measure cut down an effort by the CIA to provide covert assistance to the anti-Communist forces as well. Within the next few years—extending into the new Democratic administration under Jimmy Carter—five more countries (Laos, Ethiopia, Mozambique, Afghanistan, and Cambodia) were taken over by factions supported by and loyal to the Soviet Union, while the United States looked complacently on.

NOTES

1. Letter to the Editor by Howard L. Parsons, *The New York Times,* February 23, 1980.
2. Richard J. Walton: "Reeling Backward," op-ed, *The New York Times,* January 10, 1980.
3. Alan Wolfe: "Cold-War Windfall: Carter's Afghan Security Blanket," *The Nation,* February 2, 1980.
4. Robert Lasch: "Lessons of Korea and Vietnam," *Newsweek,* February 18, 1980.
5. Robert Lekachman: "Scoundrel Time," *The Nation,* February 16, 1980.
6. "Mr. X" [George F. Kennan]: "The Sources of Soviet Conduct," *Foreign Affairs,* July 1947; reprinted in G. F. Kennan: *American Diplomacy 1900–1950* (Chicago: University of Chicago Press, 1951).
7. *Memoirs by Harry S. Truman,* Vol. 2: *Years of Trial and Hope* (Garden City, N.Y.: Doubleday, 1956), p. 341.
8. Richard M. Nixon: *RN: The Memoirs of Richard Nixon,* quoted in Henry Kissinger: *White House Years* (Boston: Little, Brown, 1979), pp. 633–34.
9. Arthur Schlesinger, Jr.: *A Thousand Days* (Boston: Houghton Mifflin, 1965), p. 307.
10. Ibid., pp. 310–11.
11. Hans J. Morgenthau: "Asia: The American Algeria," *Commentary,* July 1961, and "Vietnam—Another Korea?" *Commentary,* May 1962.
12. "Defense Budget-Cutting," editorial, *The New York Times,* June 6, 1972.
13. "Arms and Security," editorial, *The New York Times,* October 13, 1972.

JEANE KIRKPATRICK

Dictatorships and Double Standards

The failure of the Carter administration's foreign policy is now clear to everyone except its architects, and even they must entertain private doubts from time to time about a policy whose crowning achievement was to lay the groundwork for a transfer of the Panama Canal from the United States to a swaggering Latin dictator of Castroite bent. While Carter was President, there occurred a dramatic Soviet military buildup, matched by the stagnation of American armed forces, and a dramatic extension of Soviet influence in the Horn of Africa, Afghanistan, southern Africa, and the Caribbean, matched by a declining American position in all these areas. The United States never tried so hard and failed so utterly to make and keep friends in the Third World.

As if this were not bad enough, in one year, 1979, the United States suffered two other major blows—in Iran and Nicaragua—of large and strategic significance. In each country, the Carter administration not only failed to prevent the undesired outcome, but actively collaborated in the replacement of moderate autocrats friendly to American interests with less friendly autocrats of extremist persuasion. It is too soon to be certain about what kind of regime will ultimately emerge in either Iran or Nicaragua, but accumulating evidence suggests that in both countries things are as likely to get worse as to get better. The Sandinistas in Nicaragua appear to be as skillful in consolidating power as the Ayatollah Khomeini is inept, and leaders of both revolutions display an intolerance and arrogance that do not bode well for the peaceful sharing of power or the establishment of constitutional governments, especially since those leaders have made clear that they have no intention of seeking either.

There were, of course, significant differences in the relations between the United States and each of these countries during the past two or three decades. Oil, size, and proximity to the Soviet Union gave Iran greater economic and strategic import than any Central American "republic," and closer relations were cultivated with the Shah, his counselors, and family than with President Somoza, his advisers, and family. Relations with the Shah were probably also enhanced by our approval of his manifest determination to modernize Iran regardless of the effects of modern-

From Jeane Kirkpatrick, *Dictatorships and Double Standards* (New York: American Enterprise Institute: Simon & Schuster, 1982), pp. 23–52. Copyright © 1982 by the American Enterprise Institute. Reprinted by permission of Simon & Schuster and the author.

ization on traditional social and cultural patterns (including those which enhanced his own authority and legitimacy). And, of course, the Shah was much better-looking and altogether more dashing than Somoza; his private life was much more romantic, more interesting to the media, popular and otherwise. Therefore, Americans were more aware of the Shah than of the equally tenacious Somoza.

But even though Iran was rich, blessed with a product the United States and its allies needed badly, and led by a handsome king, while Nicaragua was poor and rocked along under a long-tenure president of less striking aspect, there were many similarities between the two countries and our relations with them. Both these small nations were led by men who had not been selected by free elections, who recognized no duty to submit themselves to searching tests of popular acceptability. Both did tolerate limited opposition, including opposition newspapers and political parties, but both were also confronted by radical, violent opponents bent on social and political revolution. Both rulers, therefore, sometimes invoked martial law to arrest, imprison, exile, and occasionally, it was alleged, torture their opponents. Both relied for public order on police forces whose personnel were said to be too harsh, too arbitrary, and too powerful. Each had what the American press termed "private armies," which is to say, armies pledging their allegiance to the ruler rather than the "constitution" or the "nation" or some other impersonal entity.

In short, both Somoza and the Shah were, in central ways, traditional rulers of semitraditional societies. Although the Shah very badly wanted to create a technologically modern and powerful nation and Somoza tried hard to introduce modern agricultural methods, neither sought to reform his society in the light of any abstract idea of social justice or political virtue. Neither attempted to alter significantly the distribution of goods, status, or power (though the democratization of education and skills that accompanied modernization in Iran did result in some redistribution of money and power there).

Both Somoza and the Shah enjoyed long tenure, a large personal fortune (much of which was no doubt appropriated from general revenues), and good relations with the United States. The Shah and Somoza were not only anticommunist, they were positively friendly to the United States, sending their sons and others to be educated in our universities, voting with us in the United Nations, and regularly supporting American interests and positions even when these entailed personal and political cost. The embassies of both governments were active in Washington social life, and were frequented by powerful Americans who occupied major roles in this nation's diplomatic, military, and political life. And the Shah and Somoza themselves were both welcome in Washington, and had many American friends.

Though each of the rulers was from time to time criticized by American officials for violating civil and human rights, the fact that the people of Iran and Nicaragua only intermittently enjoyed the rights accorded to citizens in the Western democracies did not prevent successive administrations from granting—with the necessary approval of successive Congresses—both military and economic aid. In the case of both Iran and Nicaragua, tangible and intangible tokens of American support continued until these regimes became the object of a major attack by forces explicitly hostile to the United States.

But once an attack was launched by opponents bent on destruction, everything changed. The rise of violent opposition in Iran and Nicaragua set in motion a succession of events which bore a suggestive resemblance to one another and a suggestive similarity to our behavior in China before the fall of Chiang Kai-shek, in Cuba before the triumph of Castro, in certain crucial periods of the Vietnam War, and more recently, in Angola. In each of these countries, the American effort to impose liberalization and democratization on a government confronted with violent internal opposition not only failed, but actually assisted the coming to power of new regimes in which ordinary people enjoy fewer freedoms and less personal security than under the previous autocracy—regimes, moreover, hostile to American interests and policies.

The pattern is familiar enough: An established autocracy with a record of friendship with the United States is attacked by insurgents, some of whose leaders have long ties to the communist movement, and most of whose arms are of Soviet, Chinese, or Czechoslovak origin. The "Marxist" presence is ignored and/or minimized by American officials and by the elite media on the ground that U.S. support for the dictator gives the rebels little choice but to seek aid "elsewhere." Violence spreads and American officials wonder aloud about the viability of a regime that "lacks the support of its own people." The absence of an opposition party is deplored, and civil rights violations are reviewed. Liberal columnists question the morality of continuing aid to a "rightist dictatorship" and provide assurances concerning the essential moderation of some insurgent leaders who "hope" for some sign that the United States will remember its own revolutionary origins. Requests for help from the beleaguered autocrat go unheeded, and the argument is increasingly voiced that ties should be established with rebel leaders "before it is too late." The President, delaying U.S. aid, appoints a special emissary who confirms the deterioration of the government position and its diminished capacity to control the situation, and recommends various measures for "strengthening" and "liberalizing" the regime, all of which involve diluting its power.

The emissary's recommendations are presented in the context of a growing clamor for American disengagement on grounds that continued involvement confirms our status as an agent of imperialism, racism, and reaction; is inconsistent with support for human rights; alienates us from the "forces of democracy"; and threatens to put the United States once more on the side of history's "losers." This chorus is supplemented daily by interviews with returning missionaries and "reasonable" rebels.

As the situation worsens, the President assures the world that the United States desires only that the "people choose their own form of government"; he blocks delivery of all arms to the government and undertakes negotiations to establish a "broadly based" coalition headed by a "moderate" critic of the regime who, once elevated, will move quickly to seek a "political" settlement to the conflict. Should the incumbent autocrat prove resistant to American demands that he step aside, he will be readily overwhelmed by the military strength of his opponents, whose patrons will have continued to provide sophisticated arms and advisers at the same time the United States cuts off military sales. Should the incumbent be so demoralized as to agree to yield power, he will be replaced by a "moderate" of American selection. Only after the insurgents have refused the proffered political solution and anarchy has spread throughout the nation will it be noticed that the new head of government has no significant following, no experience at governing, and no talent for leadership. By then, military commanders, no longer bound by loyalty to the chief of state, will depose the faltering "moderate" in favor of a fanatic of their own choosing.

In either case, the United States will have been led by its own misunderstanding of the situation to assist actively in deposing an erstwhile friend and ally and installing a government hostile to American interests and policies in the world. At best we will have lost access to friendly territory. At worst the Soviets will have gained a new base. And everywhere our friends will have noted that the United States cannot be counted on in times of difficulty and our enemies will have observed that American support provides no security against the forward march of history.

No particular crisis conforms exactly with the sequence of events described above; there are always variations on the theme. In Iran, for example, the Carter administration—and the President himself—offered the ruler support for a longer time, though by December 1978 the President was acknowledging that he did not know if the Shah would survive, adding that the United States would not get "directly involved." Neither did the United States ever call publicly for the Shah's resignation. However, the President's special emissary, George Ball, "reportedly concluded that the Shah cannot hope to maintain total power and must now bargain with a moderate segment of the opposition" and was "known to have discussed various alternatives that would effectively ease the Shah out of total power" (*Washington Post,* December 15, 1978). There is, furthermore, not much doubt that the United States assisted the Shah's departure and helped arrange the succession of Bakhtiar. In Iran, the Carter administration's commitment to nonintervention proved stronger than strategic considerations or national pride. What the rest of the world regarded as a stinging American defeat, the U.S. government saw as a matter to be settled by Iranians. "We personally prefer that the Shah maintain a major role in the government," the President acknowledged, "but that is a decision for the Iranian people to make."[1]

Events in Nicaragua also departed from the scenario presented above, both because the Cuban and Soviet roles were clearer and because U.S. officials were more intensely and publicly working against Somoza. After the Somoza regime had defeated the first wave of Sandinista violence, the United States ceased aid, imposed sanctions, and took other steps which undermined the status and the credibility of the government in domestic and foreign affairs. Between the murder of ABC correspondent Bill Stewart by a National Guardsman in early June and the Sandinista victory in late July 1979, the U.S. State Department assigned a new ambassador who refused to submit his credentials to Somoza even though Somoza was still chief of state, and called for replacing the government with a "broadly based provisional government that would include representatives of Sandinista guerrillas."[2] Americans were assured by Assistant Secretary of State Viron Vaky that "Nicaraguans and our democratic friends in Latin America have no intention of seeing Nicaragua turned into a second Cuba,"[3] even though the State Department knew that the top Sandinista leaders had close personal ties and were in continuing contact with Havana, and, more specifically, that a Cuban secret-police official, Julian Lopez, was frequently present in the Sandinista headquarters and that Cuban military advisers were present in Sandinista ranks.

In a manner uncharacteristic of the Carter administration, which generally seemed willing to negotiate anything with anyone anywhere, the U.S. government adopted an oddly uncompromising posture in dealing with Somoza. "No end to the crisis is possible," said Vaky, "that does not start with the departure of Somoza from power and the end of his regime. No negotiation, mediation, or compromise can be achieved any longer with a Somoza government. The solution can only begin with a sharp break from the past."[4] Trying hard, we not only banned all American arms sales to the government of Nicaragua but pressured Israel, Guatemala, and others to do likewise—all in the name of ensuring a "democratic" outcome. Finally, as the Sandinista leaders consolidated control over weapons and communications, banned opposition, and took off for Cuba, President Carter warned us against attributing this "evolutionary change" to "Cuban machinations" and assured the world that the United States desired only to "let the people of Nicaragua choose their own form of government."

Yet despite all the variations, the Carter administration brought to the crises in Iran and Nicaragua several common assumptions each of which played a major role in hastening the victory of even more repressive dictatorships than had been in place before. These were, first, the belief that there existed at the moment of crisis a democratic alternative to the incumbent government; second, the belief that the continuation of the status quo was not possible; third, the belief that any change, including the establishment of a government headed by self-styled Marxist revolutionaries, was preferable to the present government. Each of these beliefs was (and is) widely shared in the liberal community generally. Not one of them can withstand close scrutiny.

Although most governments in the world are, as they always have been, autocracies of one kind or another, no idea holds greater sway in the mind of educated Americans than the belief that it is possible to democratize governments, anytime, anywhere, under any circumstances. This notion is belied by an enormous body of evidence based on the experience of dozens of countries which have attempted with more or less (usually less) success to move from autocratic to democratic government. Many of the wisest political scientists of this and previous centuries agree that democratic institutions are especially difficult to establish and maintain—because they make heavy demands on all portions of a population and because they depend on complex social, cultural, and economic conditions.

Two or three decades ago, when Marxism enjoyed its greatest prestige among American intellectuals, it was the economic prerequisites of democracy that were emphasized by social scientists. Democracy, they argued, could function only in relatively rich societies with an advanced economy, a substantial middle class, and a literate population, but it could be expected to emerge more or less automatically whenever these conditions prevailed. Today, this picture seems grossly oversimplified. While it surely helps to have an economy strong enough to provide decent levels of well-being for all, and "open" enough to provide mobility and encourage achievement, a pluralistic society and the right kind of political culture—and time—are even more essential.

In his essay *Representative Government,* John Stuart Mill identified three fundamental conditions which the Carter administration would do well to ponder. These are: "One, that the people should be willing to receive it [representative government]; two, that they should be willing and able to do what is necessary for its preservation; three, that they should be willing and able to fulfill the duties and discharge the functions which it imposes on them."[5]

Fulfilling the duties and discharging the functions of representative government make heavy demands on leaders and citizens, demands for participation and restraint, for consensus and compromise. It is not necessary for all citizens to be avidly interested in politics or well informed about public affairs—although far more widespread interest and mobilization are needed than in autocracies. What *is* necessary is that a substantial number of citizens think of themselves as participants in society's decision-making and not simply as subjects bound by its laws. Moreover, leaders of all major sectors of the society must agree to pursue power only by legal means, must eschew (at least in principle) violence, theft, and fraud, and must accept defeat when necessary. They must also be skilled at finding and creating common ground among diverse points of view and interests, and correlatively willing to compromise on all but the most basic values.

In addition to an appropriate political culture, democratic government requires institutions strong enough to channel and contain conflict. Voluntary, nonofficial institutions are needed to articulate and aggregate diverse interests and opinions present in the society. Otherwise, the formal government institutions will not be able to translate popular demands into public policy.

In the relatively few places where they exist, democratic governments have come into being slowly, after extended prior experience with more limited forms of participation during which leaders have reluctantly grown accustomed to tolerating dissent and opposition, opponents have accepted the notion that they may defeat but not destroy incumbents, and people have become aware of government's effects on their lives and of their own possible effects on government. Decades, if not centuries, are normally required for people to acquire the necessary disciplines and habits. In Britain, the road from the Magna Carta to the Act of Settlement, to the great Reform Bills of 1832, 1867, and 1885, took seven centuries to traverse. American history gives no better grounds for believing that democracy comes easily, quickly, or for the asking. A war of independence, an unsuccessful constitution, a civil war, a long process of gradual enfranchisement, marked our progress toward constitutional democratic government. The French path was still more difficult. Terror, dictatorship, monarchy, instability, and incompetence followed on the revolution that was to usher in a millennium of brotherhood. Only in the twentieth century did the democratic principle finally gain wide acceptance in France, and not until after World War II were the principles of order and democracy, popular sovereignty and authority, finally reconciled in institutions strong enough to contain conflicting currents of public opinion.

Although there is no instance of a revolutionary "socialist" or communist society being democratized, right-wing autocracies do sometimes evolve into democracies—given time, propitious economic, social, and political circumstances, talented leaders, and a strong indigenous demand for representative government. Something of the kind is in progress on the Iberian Peninsula, and the first steps have been taken in Brazil. Something similar could conceivably have also occurred in Iran and Nicaragua if contestation and participation had been more gradually expanded.

But it seems clear that the architects of Carter's foreign policy had little idea of how to go about encouraging the liberalization of an autocracy. In neither Nicaragua nor Iran did they realize that the only likely result of an effort to replace an incumbent autocrat with one of his moderate critics or a "broad-based coalition" would be to sap the foundations of the existing regime without moving the nation any closer to democracy. Yet this outcome was entirely predictable. Authority in traditional autocracies is transmitted through personal relations: from the ruler to his close associates (relatives, household members, personal friends), and from them to people to whom the associates are related by personal ties resembling their own relation to the ruler. The fabric of authority unravels quickly when the power and status of the men at the top are undermined or eliminated. The longer the autocrat has held power and the more pervasive his personal influence, the more dependent a nation's institutions will be on him. Without him, the organized life of the society will collapse, like an arch from which the keystone has been removed. The blend of qualities that bound the Iranian Army to the Shah or the National Guard to Somoza is typical of the relationships—personal, hierarchical, nontransferable—that support a traditional autocracy. The speed with which armies collapse, bureaucracies abdicate, and social structures dissolve once the autocrat is removed frequently surprises American policymakers and journalists accustomed to public institutions based on universalistic norms rather than particularistic relations.

The failure to understand these relations is one source of the failure of U.S. policy in recent administrations. There are others. In Iran and Nicaragua (as previously in Vietnam, Cuba, and China), Washington overestimated the political diversity of the opposition, especially the strength of "moderates" and "democrats" in the opposition movement, underestimated the strength and intransigence of radicals in the movement, and misestimated the nature and extent of American influence on both the government and the opposition.

Confusion concerning the character of the opposition, especially its intransigence and will to power, leads regularly to downplaying the amount of force required to counteract its violence. In neither Iran nor Nicaragua did the United States adequately appreciate the government's problem in maintaining order in a society confronted with an ideologically extreme opposition. Yet the presence of such groups was well known. The State Department's 1977 report on human rights described an Iran confronted with a small number of extreme rightist and leftist terrorists operating within the country. There is evidence that they have received substantial foreign support and training . . . [and] have been responsible for the murder of Iranian government officials and Americans. . . .[6]

The same report characterized Somoza's opponents in the following terms:

A guerrilla organization known as the Sandinista National Liberation Front (FSLN) seeks the violent overthrow of the government, and has received limited support from Cuba. The FSLN carried out an operation in Managua in December 1974, killing four people, taking several officials hostage . . . since then, it continues to challenge civil authority in certain isolated regions.[7]

In 1978, the State Department's report said that Sandinista violence was continuing—after the state of siege had been lifted by the Somoza government.

When U.S. policymakers and large portions of the liberal press interpret insurgency as evidence of widespread popular discontent and a will to democracy, the scene is set for disaster. For if civil strife reflects a popular demand for democracy, it follows that a "liberalized" government will be more acceptable to "public opinion."

Thus, in the hope of strengthening a government, U.S. policymakers are led, mistake after mistake, to impose measures almost certain to weaken its authority. Hurried efforts to force complex and unfamiliar political practices on societies lacking the requisite political culture, tradition, and social structures not only fail to produce desired outcomes; if they are undertaken at a time when the traditional regime is under attack, they actually facilitate the job of the insurgents.

Vietnam presumably taught us that the United States could not serve as the world's policeman; it should also have taught us the dangers of trying to be the world's midwife to democracy when the birth is scheduled to take place under conditions of guerrilla war.

If the Carter administration's actions in Iran and Nicaragua reflect the pervasive and mistaken assumption that one can easily locate and impose democratic alternatives to incumbent autocracies, they also reflect the equally pervasive and equally flawed belief that change per se in such autocracies is inevitable, desirable, and in the American interest. It is this belief which induced the Carter administration to participate actively in the toppling of noncommunist autocracies while remaining passive in the face of communist expansion.

At the time the Carter administration came into office it was widely reported that the President had assembled a team who shared a new approach to foreign policy and a new conception of the national interest. The principal elements of this new approach were said to be two: the conviction that the cold war was over, and the conviction that, this being the case, the United States should give priority to North-South problems and help less developed nations achieve their own destiny.

More is involved in these changes than meets the eye. For, unlikely as it may seem, the foreign policy of the Carter administration was guided by a relatively full-blown philosophy of history which includes, as philosophies of history always do, a theory of social change, or, as it is currently called, a doctrine of modernization. Like most other philosophies of history that have appeared in the West since the eighteenth century, the Carter administration's doctrine predicted progress (in the form of modernization for all societies) and a happy ending (in the form of a world community of developed, autonomous nations).

The administration's approach to foreign affairs was clearly foreshadowed in Zbigniew Brzezinski's 1970 book on the U.S. role in the "technetronic era," *Between Two Ages.* In that book, Brzezinski showed that he had the imagination to look beyond the Cold War to a brave new world of global politics and interdependence. To deal with that new world a new approach was said to be "evolving," which Brzezinski designated "rational humanism." In the new approach, the "preoccupation" with "national supremacy" would give way to "global" perspectives, and international problems would be viewed as "human issues" rather than as "political confrontations." The traditional intellectual framework for dealing with foreign policy would have to be scrapped: "Today, the old framework of international politics . . . with their spheres of influence, military alliances between nation states, the fiction of sovereignty, doctrinal conflicts arising from 19th-century crises—is clearly no longer compatible with reality."[8]

Only the "delayed development" of the Soviet Union, "an archaic religious community that experiences modernity existentially but not quite yet normatively," prevented wider realization of the fact that the end of ideology was already here. For the United States, Brzezinski recommended "a great deal of patience," a more detached attitude toward world revolutionary processes, and a less anxious preoccupation with the Soviet Union. Instead of engaging in ancient diplomatic pastimes, we should make "a broader effort to contain the global tendencies toward chaos," while assisting the processes of change that will move the world toward the "community of developed nations."

The central concern of Brzezinski's book, as of the Carter administration's foreign policy, is with the modernization of the Third World. From the beginning, the administration has manifested a special, intense interest in the problems of the so-called Third World. But instead of viewing international developments in terms of the American national interest, as national interest is historically conceived, the architects of administration policy have viewed them in terms of a contemporary version of the same idea of progress that has traumatized Western imaginations since the Enlightenment.

In its current form, the concept of modernization involves more than industrialization, more than "political development" (whatever that is). It is used instead to designate "the process through which a traditional or pretechnological society passes as it is transformed into a society characterized by machine technology, rational and secular attitudes, and highly differentiated social structures."[9] Condorcet, Comte, Hegel, Marx, and Weber are all present in this view of history as the working-out of the idea of modernity.

The crucial elements of the modernization concept have been clearly explicated by Samuel P. Huntington (who, despite a period at the National Security Council, was assuredly not the architect of the administration's policy). The modernization paradigm, Huntington has observed, postulates an ongoing process of change: complex, because it involves all dimensions of human life in society; systemic, because its elements interact in predictable, necessary ways; global, because all societies will, necessarily, pass through the transition from traditional to modern; lengthy, because time is required to modernize economic and social organization, character, and culture; phased, because each modernizing society must pass through essentially the same stages; homogenizing, because it tends toward the convergence and interdependence of societies; irreversible, because the direction of change is "given" in the relation of the elements of the process; progressive, in the sense that it is desirable and in the long run provides significant benefits to the affiliated people.[10]

Although the modernization paradigm has proved a sometimes useful as well as influential tool in social science, it has become the object of searching critiques that have challenged one after another of its central assumptions. Its shortcomings as an analytical tool pale, however, when compared to its inadequacies as a framework for thinking about foreign policy, where its principal effects are to encourage the view that events are manifestations of deep historical forces which cannot be controlled and that the best any government can do is to serve as a "midwife" to history, helping events to move where they are already headed.

This perspective on contemporary events is optimistic in the sense that it foresees continuing human progress; deterministic in the sense that it perceives events as fixed by processes over which persons and policies can have but little influence; moralistic in the sense that it perceives history and U.S. policy as having moral ends; cosmopolitan in the sense that it attempts to view the world not from the perspective of American interests or intentions but from the perspective of the modernizing nation and the "end" of history. It identifies modernization with both revolution and morality, and U.S. policy with all three.

The idea that "forces" rather than people shape events recurs each time an administration spokesman articulates or explains policy. The President, for example, assured us in February 1979:

The revolution in Iran is a product of deep social, political, religious, and economic factors growing out of the history of Iran itself.[11]

And of Asia he said:

At this moment there is turmoil or change in various countries from one end of the Indian Ocean to the other; some turmoil as in Indochina is the product of age-old enmities, inflamed by rivalries for influence by conflicting forces. Stability in some other countries is being shaken by the process of modernization, the search for national significance, or the desire to fulfill legitimate human hopes and human aspirations.[12]

Harold Saunders, assistant secretary for Near Eastern and South Asian Affairs, commenting on "instability" in Iran and the Horn of Africa, stated:

We, of course, recognize that fundamental changes are taking place across this area of western Asia and northeastern Africa—economic modernization, social change, a revival of religion, resurgent nationalism, demands for broader popular participation in the political process. These changes are generated by forces within each country.[13]

Or here was Anthony Lake, chief of the State Department's Policy Planning staff, on South Africa:

Change will come in South Africa. The welfare of the people there, and American interests, will be profoundly affected by the way in which it comes. The question is whether it will be peaceful or not.[14]

Brzezinski made the point still clearer. Speaking as chief of the National Security Council, he assured us that the struggles for power in Asia and Africa are really only incidents along the route to modernization:

. . . all the developing countries in the arc from northeast Asia to southern Africa continue to search for viable forms of government capable of managing the process of modernization.[15]

No matter that the invasions, coups, civil wars, and political struggles of less violent kinds that one sees all around do not *seem* to be incidents in a global personnel search for someone to manage the modernization process. Neither Brzezinski nor anyone else seemed bothered by the fact that the political participants in that arc from northeast Asia to southern Africa do not *know* that they are "searching for viable forms of government capable of managing the process of modernization." The motives and intentions of real persons are no more relevant to the modernization paradigm than they are to the Marxist view of history. Viewed from this level of abstraction, it is the "forces" rather than the people that count.

So what if the "deep historical forces" at work in such diverse places as Iran, the Horn of Africa, Southeast Asia, Central America, and the United Nations look a lot like Russians or Cubans? Having moved past what the President called our "inordinate fear of Communism," identified by him with the cold war, we should, we are told, now be capable of distinguishing Soviet and Cuban "machinations," which anyway exist mainly in the minds of cold warriors and others guilty of oversimplifying the world, from evolutionary changes, which seem to be the only kind that actually occur.

What can a U.S. President faced with such complicated, inexorable, impersonal processes *do*? The answer, offered again and again by the President and his top officials, was, Not much. Since events are not caused by human decisions, they cannot be stopped or altered by them. Brzezinski, for example, has said: "We recognize that the world is changing under the influence of forces no government can control."[16] And Cyrus Vance has cautioned. "The fact is that we can no more stop change than Canute could still the waters."[17]

The Carter administration's essentially deterministic and apolitical view of contemporary events discouraged an active American response and encouraged passivity. The American inability to influence events in Iran became the President's theme song:

> Those who argue that the U.S. should *or could* intervene directly to thwart [the revolution in Iran] are wrong about the realities of Iran. . . . We have encouraged *to the limited extent of our own ability* the public support for the Bakhtiar government. . . . How long [the Shah] will be out of Iran, we have no way to determine. Future events and his own desires will determine that. . . . It is impossible for anyone to anticipate all future political events. . . . Even if we had been able to anticipate events that were going to take place in Iran or in other countries, obviously our ability to determine those events is very limited. [Emphasis added.][18]

Vance made the same point:

> In Iran our policy throughout the current crisis has been based on the fact that only Iranians can resolve the fundamental political issues which they now confront.[19]

Where once upon a time a President might have sent marines to ensure the protection of American strategic interests, there is no room for force in this world of progress and self-determination. Force, the President told us at Notre Dame, does not work; that is the lesson he extracted from Vietnam. It offers only "superficial" solutions. Concerning Iran, he said:

Certainly we have no desire or ability to intrude massive forces into Iran or any other country to determine the outcome of domestic political issues. This is something that we have no intention of ever doing in another country. We've tried this once in Vietnam. It didn't work, as you well know.[20]

There was nothing unique about Iran. In Nicaragua, the climate and language were different but the "historical forces" and the U.S. response were the same. Military intervention was out of the question. Assistant Secretary of State Viron Vaky described as "unthinkable" the "use of U.S. military power to intervene in the internal affairs of another American republic."[21] Vance provided parallel assurances for Africa, asserting that we would not try to match Cuban and Soviet activities there.

What *is* the function of foreign policy under these conditions? It is to understand the processes of change and then, like Marxists, to align ourselves with history, hoping to contribute a bit of stability along the way. And this, administration spokesmen assure us, is precisely what we are doing. The Carter administration defined the U.S. national interest in the Third World as identical with the putative end of the modernization process. Vance put this with characteristic candor when he explained that U.S. policy vis-à-vis the Third World is "grounded in the conviction that we best serve our interest there by supporting the efforts of developing nations to advance their economic well-being and preserve their political independence." Our "commitment to the promotion of constructive change world-wide" (Brzezinski's words) has been vouchsafed in every conceivable context.

But there is a problem. The conceivable contexts turn out to be mainly those in which noncommunist autocracies are under pressure from revolutionary guerrillas. Since Moscow is the aggressive, expansionist power today, it is more often than not insurgents, encouraged and armed by the Soviet Union, who challenge the status quo. The American commitment to "change" in the abstract ends up by aligning us tacitly with Soviet clients and irresponsible extremists like the Ayatollah Khomeini or, in the end, Yasir Arafat.

Assisting "change" did not lead the Carter administration to undertake the destabilization of a *communist* country. The principles of self-determination and nonintervention are thus both selectively applied. We accepted the status quo in communist nations (in the name of "diversity" and national autonomy), but not in nations ruled by "right wing" dictators or white oligarchies. Concerning China, for example, Brzezinski observed: "We recognize that the PRC and we have different ideologies and economic and political systems. . . . We harbor neither the hope nor the desire that through extensive contacts with China we can remake that nation into the American image. Indeed, we accept our differences."[22] Of Southeast Asia, the President noted in February 1979:

Our interest is to promote peace and the withdrawal of outside forces and not to become embroiled in the conflict among Asian nations. And, in general, our interest is to promote the health and the development of individual societies, not to a pattern cut exactly like ours in the United States but tailored rather to the hopes and the needs and desires of the peoples involved.[23]

But the Carter administration's position shifted sharply when South Africa was discussed. For example, Anthony Lake asserted in late 1978:

We have indicated to South Africa the fact that if it does not make significant progress toward racial equality, its relations with the international community, including the United States, are bound to deteriorate.

Over the years, we have tried through a series of progressive steps to demonstrate that the U.S. cannot and will not be associated with the continued practice of apartheid.[24]

As to Nicaragua, Hodding Carter III said in February 1979:

The unwillingness of the Nicaraguan government to accept the [OAS] group's proposal, the resulting prospects for renewal and polarization, and the human rights situation in Nicaragua . . . unavoidably affect the kind of relationships we can maintain with that government.[25]

And on Latin American autocracies President Carter commented:

My government will not be deterred from protecting human rights, including economic and social rights, in whatever ways we can. We prefer to take actions that are positive, but where nations persist in serious violations of human rights, we will continue to demonstrate that there are costs to the flagrant disregard of international standards.[26]

Something very odd was going on. How did an administration that desired to let people work out their own destinies get involved in determined efforts at reform in South Africa, Zaire, Nicaragua, El Salvador, and elsewhere? How did an administration committed to nonintervention in Cambodia and Vietnam announce that it "will not be deterred" from righting wrongs in South Africa? What should be made of an administration that saw the U.S. interest as identical with economic modernization and political independence and yet heedlessly endangered the political independence of Taiwan, a country whose success in economic modernization and egalitarian distribution of wealth is unequaled in Asia? The contrast is as striking as that between the Carter administration's frenzied speed in recognizing the new dictatorship in Nicaragua and its refusal to recognize the Muzarewa government of Zimbabwe, or its refusal to maintain any presence in Zimbabwe while staffing a U.S. Information Office in Cuba. Not only were there ideology and a double standard at work here, the ideology neither fit nor explained reality, and the double standard involved the Carter administration in the wholesale contradiction of its own principles.

Inconsistencies are a familiar part of politics in most societies. Usually, however, governments behave hypocritically when their principles conflict with the national interest. What made the inconsistencies of the Carter administration noteworthy were, first, the administration's moralism, which rendered it especially vulnerable to charges of hypocrisy; and, second, the administration's predilection for policies that violated the strategic and economic interests of the United States. The Carter administration's conception of national interest bordered on doublethink: it found friendly powers to be guilty representatives of the status quo and viewed the triumph of unfriendly groups as beneficial to America's "true interests."

This logic was quite obviously reinforced by the prejudices and preferences of many Carter administration officials. Traditional autocracies are, in general and in their very nature, deeply offensive to modern American sensibilities. The notion that public affairs should be ordered on the basis of kinship, friendship, and other personal relations rather than on the basis of objective, "rational" standards violates our conception of justice and efficiency. The preference for stability rather than change is also disturbing to Americans, whose whole national experience rests on the principles of change, growth, and progress. The extremes of wealth and poverty characteristic of traditional societies also offend us, the more so since the poor are usually *very* poor and bound to their squalor by a hereditary allocation of role. Moreover, the relative lack of concern of rich, comfortable rulers for the poverty, ignorance, and disease of "their" people is likely to be interpreted by Americans as moral dereliction pure and simple. The truth is that Americans can hardly bear such societies and such rulers. Confronted with them, our vaunted cultural relativism evaporates and we become as censorious as Cotton Mather confronting sin in New England.

But if the politics of traditional and semitraditional autocracy is nearly antithetical to our own—at both the symbolic and the operational level—the rhetoric of progressive revolutionaries sounds much better to us; their symbols are much more acceptable. One reason that some modern Americans prefer "socialist" to traditional autocracies is that the former have embraced modernity and have adopted modern modes and perspectives, including an instrumental, manipulative, functional orientation toward most social, cultural, and personal affairs, a profession of universalistic norms, an emphasis on reason, science, education, and progress, a deemphasis of the sacred, and "rational," bureaucratic organizations. They speak our language.

Because socialism of the Soviet/Chinese/Cuban variety is an ideology rooted in a version of the same values that sparked the Enlightenment and the democratic revolutions of the eighteenth century, because it is modern and not traditional, because it postulates goals that appeal to Christian as well as to secular values (brotherhood of man, elimination of power as a mode of human relations), it is highly congenial to many Americans at the symbolic level. Marxist revolutionaries speak the language of a hopeful future, while traditional autocrats speak the language of an unattractive past. Because left-wing revolutionaries invoke the symbols and values of democracy—emphasizing egalitarianism rather than hierarchy and privilege, liberty rather than order, activity rather than passivity—they are again and again accepted as partisans in the cause of freedom and democracy.

Nowhere is the affinity of liberalism, Christianity, and Marxist socialism more apparent than among liberals who are "duped" time after time into supporting "liberators" who turn out to be totalitarians, and among Left-leaning clerics whose attraction to a secular style of "redemptive community" is stronger than their outrage at the hostility of socialist regimes to religion. In Jimmy Carter—egalitarian, optimist, liberal, Christian—the tendency to be repelled by frankly nondemocratic rulers and hierarchical societies was almost as strong as the tendency to be attracted to the idea of popular revolution, liberation, and progress. Carter was, *par excellence,* the kind of liberal most likely to confound revolution with idealism, change with progress, optimism with virtue.

Where concern about "socialist encirclement," Soviet expansion, and traditional conceptions of the national interest inoculated his predecessors against such easy equations, Carter's doctrine of national interest and modernization encouraged support for all change that takes place in the name of "the people," regardless of its "superficial" Marxist or anti-American content. Any lingering doubt about whether the United States should, in case of conflict, support a "tested friend" such as the Shah or a friendly power such as Zimbabwe against an opponent who despises us is resolved by reference to our "true," our "long-range" interests.

Stephen Rosenfeld of the *Washington Post* described the commitment of the Carter administration to this sort of "progressive liberalism":

The Carter administration came to power, after all, committed precisely to reducing the centrality of strategic competition with Moscow in American foreign policy, and to extending the United States' association with what it was prepared to accept as legitimate wave-of-the-future popular movements around the world—first of all with the victorious movement in Vietnam.
. . . Indochina was supposed to be the state on which Americans could demonstrate their "post-Vietnam" intent to come to terms with the progressive, popular element that Kissinger, the villain, had denied.[27]

In other words, the Carter administration, Rosenfeld tells us, came to power resolved not to assess international developments in the light of "cold war" perspectives but to accept at face value the claim of revolutionary groups to represent "popular" aspirations and "progressive" forces—regardless of the ties of these revolutionaries to the Soviet Union. To this end, overtures were made looking to the "normalization" of relations with Vietnam, Cuba, and the People's Republic of China, and steps were taken to cool relations with South Korea, South Africa, Nicaragua, the Philippines, and others. These moves followed naturally from the conviction that the United States had, as our enemies said, been on the wrong side of history in supporting the status quo and opposing revolution.

One might have thought that this perspective would have been undermined by events in Southeast Asia since the triumph of "progressive" forces there over the "agents of reaction." To quote Rosenfeld again:

In this administration's line, Vietnam has been transformed for much of American public opinion, from a country wronged by the U.S. to one revealing a brutal essence of its own.

This has been a quiet but major trauma to the Carter people (as to all liberals), scarring their self-confidence and their claim on public trust alike.[28]

Presumably, however, the barbarity of the "progressive" governments in Cambodia and Vietnam was less traumatic for the President and his chief advisers than for Rosenfeld, since there was little evidence of changed predispositions at crucial levels of the White House and the State Department. The President continued to behave as before—not like a man who abhors autocrats but like one who abhors only right-wing autocrats.

In fact, high officials in the Carter administration understood better than they seemed to the aggressive, expansionist character of contemporary Soviet behavior in Africa, the Middle East, Southeast Asia, the Indian Ocean, Central America, and the Caribbean. But although the Soviet/Cuban role in Grenada, Nicaragua, and El Salvador (plus the transfer of MiG-23s to Cuba) had already prompted resumption of surveillance of Cuba (which in turn confirmed the presence of a Soviet combat brigade), the President's eagerness not to "heat up" the climate of public opinion remained stronger than his commitment to speak the truth to the American people. His statement on Nicaragua clearly reflected this priority:

It's a mistake for Americans to assume or to claim that every time an evolutionary change takes place in this hemisphere that somehow it's a result of secret, massive Cuban intervention. The fact in Nicaragua is that the Somoza regime lost the confidence of the people. To bring about an orderly transition there, our effort was to let the people of Nicaragua ultimately make the decision on who would be their leader—what form of government they should have.[29]

This statement, which presumably represented the President's best thinking on the matter, is illuminating. Carter's effort to dismiss concern about military events in this specific country as a manifestation of a national proclivity for seeing "Cuban machinations" under every bed constitutes a shocking effort to falsify reality. There was no question in Nicaragua of "evolutionary change" or of attributing such change to Castro's agents. There was only a question about the appropriate U.S. response to a military struggle in a country whose location gives it strategic importance out of proportion to its size or strength.

But that is not all. The rest of the President's statement graphically illustrated the blinding power of ideology on his interpretation of events. When he said that "the Somoza regime lost the confidence of the people," the President implied that the regime had previously rested on the confidence of "the people" but that the situation had now changed. In fact, the Somoza regime had never rested on popular will (but instead on manipulation, force, and habit), and was not being ousted by it. It was instead succumbing to arms and soldiers. However, the assumption that the armed conflict of Sandinistas and Somozistas was the military equivalent of a national referendum enabled the President to imagine that it could be, and should be, settled by the people of Nicaragua. For this pious sentiment even to seem true, the President would have had to be unaware that insurgents were receiving a great many arms from other non-Nicaraguans and that the United States had played a significant role in disarming the Somoza regime.

The President's mistakes and distortions were all fashionable ones. His assumptions were those of people who want badly to be on the progressive side in conflicts between "rightist" autocracy and "leftist" challenges, and prefer the latter, almost regardless of the probable consequences.

To be sure, neither the President nor Vance nor Brzezinski *desired* the proliferation of Soviet-supported regimes. Each asserted his disapproval of Soviet "interference" in the modernization process. But each, nevertheless, remained willing to "destabilize" friendly or neutral autocracies without any assurance that they would not be replaced by reactionary totalitarian theocracies, by totalitarian Soviet client states, or worst of all, by murderous fanatics of the Pol Pot variety.

The foreign policy of the Carter administration failed not for lack of good intentions but for lack of realism about the nature of traditional versus revolutionary autocracies and the relation of each to the American national interest. Only intellectual fashion and the tyranny of Right/Left thinking prevent intelligent men of goodwill from perceiving the *facts* that traditional authoritarian governments are less repressive than revolutionary autocracies, that they are more susceptible of liberalization, and that they are more compatible with U.S. interests. The evidence on all these points is clear enough.

Surely it is now beyond reasonable doubt that the present governments of Vietnam, Cambodia, and Laos are much more repressive than those of the despised previous rulers, that the government of the People's Republic of China is more repressive than that of Taiwan, that North Korea is more repressive than South Korea, and so forth. This is the most important lesson of Vietnam and Cambodia. It is not new, but it is a gruesome reminder of harsh facts.

From time to time a truly bestial ruler can come to power in either type of autocracy—Idi Amin, Papa Doc Duvalier, Joseph Stalin, Pol Pot are examples—but neither type regularly produces such moral monsters (though democracy regularly prevents their accession to power). There are, however, *systemic* differences between traditional and revolutionary autocracies that have a predictable effect on their degree of repressiveness. Generally speaking, traditional autocrats tolerate social inequities, brutality, and poverty, whereas revolutionary autocracies create them.

Traditional autocrats leave in place existing allocations of wealth, power, status, and other resources, which in most traditional societies favor an affluent few and maintain masses in poverty. But they worship traditional gods and observe traditional taboos. They do not disturb the habitual rhythms of work and leisure, habitual places of residence, habitual patterns of family and personal relations. Because the miseries of traditional life are familiar, they are bearable to ordinary people who, growing up in the society, learn to cope, as children born to untouchables in India acquire the skills and attitudes necessary for survival in the miserable roles they are destined to fill. Such societies create no refugees.

Precisely the opposite is true of revolutionary communist regimes. They create refugees by the millions because they claim jurisdiction over the whole life of the society and make demands for change that so violate internalized values and habits that inhabitants flee in the remarkable expectation that their attitudes, values, and goals will "fit" better in a foreign country than in their native land.

The former deputy chairman of Vietnam's National Assembly from 1976 to his defection early in August 1979, Hoang Van Hoan, described the impact of Vietnam's ongoing revolution on that country's more than one million Chinese inhabitants:

They have been expelled from places they have lived in for generations. They have been dispossessed of virtually all possessions—their lands, their houses. They have been driven into areas called new economic zones, but they have not been given any aid.

How can they eke out a living in such conditions reclaiming new land? They gradually die for a number of reasons—diseases, the hard life. They also die of humiliation.[30]

It is not only the Chinese who have suffered in Southeast Asia since the "liberation," and it is not only in Vietnam that the Chinese suffer. By the end of 1978 more than 6 million refugees had fled countries ruled by Marxist governments. In spite of walls, fences, guns, and sharks, the steady stream of people fleeing revolutionary utopias continues.

There is a damning contrast between the number of refugees created by Marxist regimes and those created by other autocracies: More than a million Cubans have left their homeland since Castro's rise (one refugee for every nine inhabitants), as compared to about 35,000 each from Argentina, Brazil, and Chile. In Africa more than five times as many refugees fled Guinea and Guinea-Bissau as left Zimbabwe, suggesting that civil war and racial discrimination are easier for most people to bear than Marxist-style liberation.

Moreover, the history of this century provides no grounds for expecting that radical totalitarian regimes will transform themselves. At the moment there is a far greater likelihood of progressive liberalization and democratization in the governments of Brazil, Argentina, and Chile than in the government of Cuba, in Taiwan than in the People's Republic of China, in South Korea than in North Korea, in Zaire than in Angola, and so forth.

Since many traditional autocracies permit limited contestation and participation, it is not impossible that U.S. policy could effectively encourage this process of liberalization and democratization, provided that the effort is not made at a time when the incumbent government is fighting for its life against violent adversaries, and that proposed reforms are aimed at producing gradual change rather than perfect democracy overnight. To accomplish this, policymakers are needed who understand how actual democracies have come into being. History is a better guide than good intentions.

A realistic policy which aims at protecting our own interest and assisting the capacities for self-determination of less developed nations will need to face the unpleasant fact that, if victorious, violent insurgency headed by Marxist revolutionaries is unlikely to lead to anything but totalitarian tyranny. Armed intellectuals citing Marx and supported by Soviet-bloc arms and advisers will almost surely not turn out to be agrarian reformers, or simple nationalists, or democratic socialists. However incomprehensible it may be to some, Marxist revolutionaries are not contemporary embodiments of the Americans who wrote the Declaration of Independence, and they will not be content with establishing a broad-based coalition in which they have only one voice among many.

It may not always be easy to distinguish between democratic and totalitarian agents of change, but it is also not too difficult. Authentic democratic revolutionaries aim at securing governments based on the consent of the governed and believe that ordinary men are capable of using freedom, of knowing their own interest, of choosing rulers. They do not, like the current leaders in Nicaragua, assume that it will be necessary to postpone elections for three to five years during which time they can "cure" the false consciousness of almost everyone.

If, moreover, revolutionary leaders describe the United States as the scourge of the twentieth century, the enemy of freedom-loving people, the perpetrator of imperialism, racism, colonialism, genocide, war, then they are not authentic democrats or, to put it mildly, friends. Groups which define themselves as enemies should be treated as enemies. The United States is not in fact a racist, colonial power, it does not practice genocide, it does not threaten world peace with expansionist activities. In the last decade especially we have practiced remarkable forbearance everywhere and undertaken the "unilateral restraints on defense spending" recommended by Brzezinski as appropriate for the technetronic era. We have also moved further, faster, in eliminating domestic racism than any multiracial society in the world or in history.

For these reasons and more, a posture of continuous self-abasement and apology vis-à-vis the Third World is neither morally necessary nor politically appropriate. Nor is it necessary or appropriate to support vocal enemies of the United States because they invoke the rhetoric of popular liberation. It is not even necessary or appropriate for our leaders to forswear unilaterally the use of military force to counter military force. Liberal idealism need not be identical with masochism, and need not be incompatible with the defense of freedom and the national interest.

NOTES

1. *Time,* December 18, 1979, p. 33.
2. *The New York Times,* June 28, 1979.
3. Viron Vaky, reported in *The New York Times,* June 27, 1979.
4. The *Washington Post,* June 27, 1979.
5. John Stuart Mill, *Considerations on Representative Government* (Indianapolis, Ind.: Bobbs-Merrill Co., 1958), p. 56.
6. *The New York Times,* July 12, 1979.
7. *Ibid.*
8. Concerning Latin America, Brzezinski observed: "Latin American nationalism, more and more radical as it widens its popular base, will be directed with increasing animosity against the United States unless the United States rapidly shifts its own posture. Accordingly, it would be wise for the United States to make an explicit move to abandon the Monroe Doctrine and to concede that in the new global age geographic or hemispheric contiguity no longer need be politically decisive. Nothing could be healthier for Pan-American relations than for the United States to place them on the same level as its relations with the rest of the world, confining itself to emphasis on cultural-political affinities (as it does with Western Europe) and economic-social obligations (as it does with less-developed countries)." Zbigniew Brzezinski, *Between Two Ages: America's Role in the Technetronic Era* (New York: The Viking Press, 1970), p. 274.
9. James O'Connell, "The Concept of Modernization," in *Comparative Modernization,* Cyril E. Black, ed. (New York: The Free Press, 1976), p. 13.

10. Samuel P. Huntington, "The Change to Change: Modernization, Development and Politics," *Comparative Politics III* (April 1971), pp. 283–322.
11. *Department of State Bulletin,* March 1979, p. 21.
12. *Ibid.,* April 1979, p. 4.
13. *Ibid.,* February 1979, p. 47.
14. *Ibid.,* January 1979, p. 18.
15. *Ibid.,* February 1979, p. 19.
16. *Ibid.,* p. 20.
17. *The New York Times,* August 26, 1979.
18. *Ibid.*
19. *Department of State Bulletin,* March 1979, p. 39.
20. *Ibid.,* February 1979, p. 3.
21. *Ibid.,* March 1979, p. 64.
22. *Ibid.,* February 1979, p. 20.
23. *Ibid.,* April 1979, p. 4.
24. *Ibid.,* January 1979, p. 20.
25. *Ibid.,* May 1979, p. 66.
26. *Ibid.,* September 1979, p. 55.
27. *Washington Post,* August 3, 1979.
28. *Ibid.*
29. *Weekly Compilation of Presidential Documents,* Monday, July 30, 1979, vol. 15, no. 30, pp. 1307–08.
30. *The New York Times,* August 10, 1979.

PART VII

The Spiritual Crisis

THE CHRISTIANITY of T. S. Eliot was an acknowledged thing quite a while ago, after he had attained an irrevocable reputation, but his critics tended to put it down as one of those larger mannerisms that went with his whole way of life as an Anglophile, and anyway, hasn't Christianity become, as Canon Bernard Iddings Bell once remarked, "merely a pastime, preferred by some to golf or canasta"?

But when his *Notes Toward the Definition of Culture* appeared, it became clear to his critics that he had something very concrete in mind in stating his preference for Christianity, that, far from thinking of it as of purely subjective importance, he held religion to be essential to the flowering of any culture. He held, indeed, that where religion is excluded, so is true culture, that such cultures as attempt to endure without religion are undefinable, and that they are most emphatically undesirable. T. S. Eliot was a poet, not an exegete. And it helps in understanding him to think of religion as meaning to him, among other things, the incarnation of the Word—even as, to the historian, spirit is the incarnation in history. Eliot's expressive sense of the horrors of metaphysical desolation, with which, through a single poem, he scarred an entire generation early in his life, suggests also the hunger he felt for the spiritual consolation that finally he took from Christianity.

The essay we have selected from Whittaker Chambers is not altogether typical, because the major part of it is written in the didactic mode with which Chambers was uncomfortable (he did not like schoolmasterish idiom). But in this essay, published posthumously as a part of the collection *Cold Friday*, he felt the need to relate, with A-B-C directness, the phenomenon of Communism to the spiritual desolation of the West; and he did so simply, without ornament, not so much pleading with the reader to understand, for it was a part of his understanding that the reader would not do so, as advising the reader that it was part of the author's witness to say it as he understood it, and that this is the way it was.

Then, suddenly—and completely—the legendary Chambers surfaces, and the magic begins to flow. The keenest human understanding, reflected in the numinous prose, baptized in tragedy. . . . He had received a letter from an old friend, an intelligent and devout Christian, who wrote him: "The Epiphany has fizzled."

I found this a lapidary line: 'The Epiphany has fizzled.' Yet, when the amusing novelty has worn off, it is seen to express chiefly a disconsolate exasperation. It is a kind of continental sadness, like the wail of a locomotive whistle, rushing off (where?) in the night—haunting, yet not true music, a very American sound, just as the locomotive whistle is (or was) perhaps the most American of sounds. . . .

"The one essential condition of human existence," [Chambers quotes Stefan Trofimovitch, a character in Dostoevsky's *The Possessed*, "is that man should always be able to bow down before something infinitely great. If men are deprived of the infinitely great, they will not go on living and will die of despair." It is for this that we crave reality. . . . "I want to know why," [Sherwood Anderson] asked. I want to know why. It is for this we seek a little height, and because of this we do not feel it too high a price to pay if we cannot reach it crawling through a lifetime on our hands and knees, as a wounded man sometimes crawls from a battlefield, if only so as not to die as one more corpse among so many corpses. . . .

And if the old paths no longer lead to a reality that enables men to act with meaning, if the paths no longer seem to lead anywhere—have become a footworn, trackless maze, or, like Russian roads, end after a few miles of ambitious pavement leading nowhere but into bottomless mud and swallowing distance—men will break new paths, though they must break their hearts to do it. They will burst out somewhere, even if such bursting-out takes the form of aberration. For to act in aberration is at least more like living than to die of futility, or even to live in that complacency which is futility's idiot twin. We all know those grand aberrations of our time. We have plenty of names for them. . . . But all the aberrations have one common cause, and point, in the end, in one direction.

Albert Jay Nock's essay, "Isaiah's Job," is surely the best expression of a pessimist's serenity in modern times. The thesis—that it is only The Remnant who understand, but that they most surely do understand, and hear every uncorrupted word that you utter—makes Remnant-serving a most honorable and useful vocation. A close friend of Nock's, the aforementioned Bernard Iddings Bell, once declared that Nock had written this essay whole from a sermon he had heard Bell preach; but never mind, said Bell, the plagiarism doesn't matter, it does matter that the idea was so superbly set down.

And as an epilogue, a personal letter, the final letter, from Whittaker Chambers, dispatched a few weeks before his death.

The Direct Glance

I speak with a certain urgency both because I believe that history is closing in on this people with a speed which, in general they do not realize or prefer not to realize, and because I have a sense that time is closing in on me so that, at this point, I do not know whether or not I shall be given time to complete what I seek to say. I feel, too, a sense of my own inadequacy in many ways. I cannot claim to speak with the authority of many whose learning is greater, whose competency is certified by years of devout effort in special acreages of the mind. I may not claim for the larger meanings of what I shall say: This is truth. I say only: This is my vision of truth; to be checked and rechecked (as I myself continually check and recheck it) against the data of experience. Every book, like every life, is issued ultimately, not to those among whom it appears and lives, but to the judgment of time, which is the sternest umpire. What serious man could wish for his life or his book a judgment less final?

I write as a man who made his way back from a special experience of our time—the experience of Communism. I believe the experience to be the central one, for whichever side prevails the outcome will be shaped decisively by what Communism is and meant to be, and by the conditions that made it possible and made possible the great conflict. *Man's Fate* (or *La Condition Humaine,* to use its French title, which fixes its meaning more clearly) seems to me one of the few books* which have placed a surgical finger upon the problem of man in this century—the problem of the terms on which man can wrest some semblance of his human dignity (some would say save his soul) in a mechanizing world, which is, by force of the same necessity, a revolutionary world. After he had read *Witness,* André Malraux, the author of *Man's Fate,* wrote me: "You are one of those who did not return from Hell with empty hands." I did not answer him. How is one man to say to another: "Great healing spirit"? For it is not sympathy that the mind craves, but understanding of its purposes. I do not know, it is not even for me to say, what value may be set on those

From Whittaker Chambers, *Cold Friday* (New York: Random House, 1964), pp. 67–88. Copyright © 1964 by Esther Chambers. Reprinted by permission of Brandt & Brandt, Literary Agents.

*Some others: Arthur Koestler's *Darkness at Noon* and *The Invisible Writing*; Czeslaw Milosz's *The Captive Mind*; the Abbé Henri de Lubac's *Drama of Atheist Humanism*; Manes Sperber's *The Burned Bramble,* whose French title, *Et le Buisson Devient Cendre (And the Burning Bush Sank to Ash),* again seems to me more meaningful than the English rendering.

scraps and tatters of experience that I brought back with me. They, too, are issued for time to judge. I do not know how they may serve, or whether they have any power to prevail against the many voices in the West today that say, "These are scraps and tatters," and deny them any further meaning.

In *Witness* I sought to make two points which seemed to me more important than the narrative of unhappy events which, time has compelled me to conclude, chiefly interested most readers. The first point had to do with the nature of Communism and the struggle against it. The crux of this matter is the question whether God exists. If God exists, a man cannot be a Communist, which begins with the rejection of God. But if God does not exist, it follows that Communism, or some suitable variant of it, is right.

More follows. A man is obligated, if he seeks to give any effect to his brief life, to tear away all mystery that darkens or distorts, to snap all ties that bind him in the name of an untruth, to push back all limiting frontiers to the end that man's intelligence may be free to realize to the fullest of its untrammeled powers a better life in a better world. I did not spell this out in *Witness*. "Be sure that nothing can be told to any who divined it not before." It is pointless and, indeed, impossible to press anything upon those who are unprepared for it. I set up the proposition and left it to those who could to draw the inference. Precisely, the enlightened community of the West, as could be expected, drew them first. That proposition was, in my opinion, the chief cause of the lightnings that darted at *Witness* and still play about it. They darted not only from the political Left. In time, elements of the Right began to sense that a question had been posed to them. That proposition questioned the whole materialism of the West, and the West is heavily materialist. It is, in fact, this materialism that Communism constantly appeals to and manipulates, not in terms of any easily defined political lines of Left or Right but in terms of a common investment in a materialist view of life, which an important section of the West shares with Communism, and which Communism has simply carried to its utmost logical conclusion in thought and action. This common interest in a common materialism—which nevertheless differs in the West and in Communism in form, degree, qualifications, and reservations—is the grain of truth and sincerity in the West's resentment against Communist "witch hunts." For it feels an affinity and a respect for a materialism which it finds liberating to the mind, while it feels itself unfairly threatened or hurt because reprisals against Communism inevitably touch it as a sympathetic form, though it does not share Communism's political aims. This is a distinction which the non-Communist materialism of the West does not trust the anti-Communists to grasp or respect—the more so since, in action, the line is frequently blurred, so that even when the materialism of the West is assertively anti-Communist it often serves Communist ends.

From this proposition—that the heart problem of Communism is the problem of atheism—followed the second proposition which I set up in *Witness,* also without developing its conclusions. This proposition implied that the struggle of the West with Communism included its own solution. That is to say, in the course of its struggle with Communism, the West would develop or recover those resources (in the main, spiritual and moral) which it held to constitute its superiority to Communism, or in the struggle it would go under. Going under might, I suppose, take one of two forms. The West might simply lose the war in political or physical terms. But I also allowed for the fact that the West might win the war in such terms and still lose it, if the taxing necessities of the conflict brought the West to resemble what it was struggling against, i.e., Communism. A turn in this direction has been perfectly visible in the West for several decades.

The margin of success in the struggle, it seemed to me, lay less in an equality of technology and weapons (so long as weapons paced themselves approximately) than in certain factors within Communism which are little appreciated in the West. These factors were also spiritual and moral even though they expressed indirectly contrary terms, even though Communism expressly denied man's spirit and morality as the West uses the words. These resources I believed to be peculiarly inherent in the Russian Communist Party.

For scale, complexity, and depth, the struggle between Communism and the West is a conflict without any precedent of human record. Other conflicts have unsettled continents. The rise and sweep of the Mongol hordes comes at once to mind and is often cited as a parallel. This was a great surface fire, fed by the dry rot of all the lands it swept, having no plan and purpose beyond plunder and the raw play of ferocious energies, dying out as those purposeless energies died out, and leaving upon history little more than the literal ashes of its passage and a haunting memory of heaps of human bones. It is most like a catastrophe in nature, hurricane or flood, and has, in fact, no parallel at all. Communism first of all asserts a purpose and a plan. Both feed a will to victory that operates on as many multitudinous levels as life is capable of. There is no human creature living in any region so remote that he is not, in some way, affected by that force which each one, sooner or later, faces in what Sir Thomas Browne called "the areopagy and dark tribunal of our hearts." For the distinctive feature of Communism is not that it threatens all continents as no other force has ever done or even that it seeks a radical readjustment of all societies. Its distinctive feature is that it seeks a molecular rearrangement of the human mind. It promotes not only a new world. It promotes a new kind of man. The physical revolutions which it once incited and now imposes, and which largely distract our attention, are secondary to this internal revolution which challenges each man in his mind and spirit. Thus, the phenomenon of Communism is closest in the experience of the West to the rise of Christianity and its gradual transformation of the mind of the ancient world. Hence our puzzlement before the discrepancy between the ends of Communism and its visible personnel, which more or less reflects the bafflement of Pliny in his well-known letter to Trajan about the early Christians. Hence our large-handed contempt for Communists wherever they do not yet hold political power, which almost echoes Lucian's remarks about the Christians in the second century A.D.: "They waste their days, running from Romanism to ism, and imagine that they are achieving great things in treating their friends to children's fairy tales. In the squares, where they all shout the same thing in the same way, they are eaten up with envy. From their dirt, their lousiness, their mendacity, they argue with conviction that they are called to redeem the world."

For the war of Communism with the rest of mankind is first of all a war of ideas. In that war, Communism rejects few means of any kind, or none (its system of ideas justifies this practice). But its first assault is always upon the minds of men; and it is from the conversion of minds that it advances to the conquest of mass bodies and their living space. Each advance enables Communism to expedite conversion by political control since, for those whom it controls, Communism has become the one reality. The West (whatever value the captive may give that word) becomes at most a hope, but a hope that has been defeated (that is why the captives are captive); and it is a hope continuously deferred. Hope deferred not only maketh the heart sick; it stirreth profound suspicions that there is something radically wrong with it. In this case, it stirs a suspicion that exactly to the degree that Communism is felt to be evil and monstrous in its effects, there must be something organically wrong with the West that is unequal to prevailing against a power so conspicuously condign.

This failure to grasp that the basic struggle with Communism is a struggle of ideas has led, in the West, to the failure to grasp the signal fact of the conflict. That fact is that Communism, which in all material ways has been for decades weak to a degree almost unimaginable to the average American, has rallied strength and made its staggering advances precisely at the expense of that West which is in all material ways overwhelmingly superior. With this goes the boundless complacency of the West in supposing that the struggle will be decided in its favor by material means. I cannot remember a time when there was not a lively conviction in the West that the Communist state was about to fall by reason of its own malevolence and inadequacy. This stems from the easily observable fact that Communism is a philosophy of thoroughgoing materialism, brutal in its practical manifestations, because it denies the sanctity of the individual in terms of the self-interest of the community, which, in practice, is the arbitrary will of the shifting consortia that run the state.

Communism is a philosophy of brute materialism. But if we ask: "What is the philosophy of the West?" is there not a certain embarrassment? What *is* the philosophy of the West? In a war for men's minds, what is it that we are offering whose inherent force is so compulsive that it instantly seizes on the imagination of men and incites them to choose it in preference to Communism? In the name of what do we expect them to rise and overthrow Communism which can be done only by an effort of incalculable suffering—and not the suffering of faceless millions (as we so easily think of such things), but the suffering of this father or that mother who love their children whose lives, rather than their own, are the first sacrifice in so one-sided a conflict? Is it Christianity? There are millions of Christians in the Communist Empire whose Western populations are overwhelmingly Christian. Some 40 million must be practicing Catholics. I remember no appeals to the Christians in the name of their common faith with the West. Individual freedom is often mentioned. It is well, perhaps, to remember that freedom, in our understanding of the term, has been restricted largely to the United States and the fringe of Western Europe. In the rest of the world it has no accepted currency, and over large areas of Europe the Second World War and the revolutions that preceded it utterly destroyed the conditions of freedom and raised strong questions in many minds whether or not freedom is practicable in the conditions of our times. *"Der Fahneneid,"* said General Groner to the Kaiser in 1918, suggesting that his swift abdication would be well-viewed, *"ist jetzt nur eine Idee"* (The oath on the colors is now only an idea).

Moreover, these people are not children. They have the acute realism of those who live daily under impending tank treads. The satellite populations can look westward and see that individual freedom is constantly being whittled down in the West in the interest of centralizing government, and they are perfectly competent to infer that this is the result of the play of the same basic forces and factors that have destroyed their own freedom.

We tend to forget—life has been, in general, so good to us, we are so appalled by life under Communism—that thousands of acute intelligences in the East are also peering back at us. We tend to forget what spectacle we present to those eyes which weigh us with the close harshness of men facing awful alternatives. It is not necessary to particularize that spectacle here. But if we think about it a moment, think about it as those others may see it, adding in their sense that our failure fixed their fate on them, is it strange if they do not find the spectacle that the West presents overly reassuring?

When, in History, there appear in swarms such commanding and ferocious types as the Communist, and his bastard brother, the Fascist, our habit of viewing them first of all with aversion, a habit of mind very widespread, especially in the United States, is no longer helpful. The moral judgment may be justified. But is largely pointless. It condemns us to see them continually in terms of effect instead of cause. We limit ourselves to seeing the effects that the Communist, for example, creates. We keep pretty carefully away from the causes that create the Communist. This resolute flight from causes, and resolute dwelling only on effects, leads us into the plight of a man in a maze or a squirrel in a revolving cage. We go round and round; we never come out anywhere. It leads, in thought, to a defeating confusion. In practice, it leads to some pretty extravagant hypocrisy. The spectacle of the West encouraging cultural exchanges with a Communism, which in the next breath it condemns as a barbaric and criminal force, is, to say the least of it, puzzling. It is sometimes argued that with respect to Communism, the West is merely stupid. But stupidity isn't good enough.

Surely it is not too sweeping to say that there is nothing secret about Communism. For decades, its motives, purposes, and specific strategies have been explicitly stated by Communists themselves, and freely disseminated in the West. Even its guiltiest secrets are known in wearisome detail. Seldom in history can the actions of any cause have been subjected to so minute a picking-over in the very course of their occurrence. It makes not the slightest practical difference. On one hand, the disclosures lead to a hue of moral outrage. On the other hand, the West continues to deal with the Communist center as if this were not true. Thus, the West itself engages with respect to Communism in a kind of doublethink which it supposes to be one of Communism's distinctive faculties. This singular behavior is paced by another even more singular. This is the cherishing of a notion, constantly blighted, ever ready to flower anew, that Communism and Communists are about to undergo a change of mind (or "heart") so that henceforth they will no longer act like Communists; they will be like us.

Yet we have seen this manifestation occur on a mass scale more than once. When it does, we enter the realm of illusion. There is a clinical name for it, but it is not stupidity. Stupidity cannot explain; such stupidity has to be explained itself. This persistent flight into fantasy and resistance to reality, accompanied by an emotional play like the boiling of an over-heated engine, suggest much more the energy, now dogged, now frantic, with which certain patients sometimes resist knowing the facts of their condition and its causes because they find the facts too painful to bear. A suspicion stirs that we resist knowing about Communism because we do not wish to know about ourselves, that, in fact, we need scarcely fear Communism if we did not secretly fear ourselves.

This suspicion is fortified by an arresting fact, one which requires no special knowledge to see (it is inescapable), and one, incidentally, that is not often referred to. That fact is that the Communist Empire, born in chaos, backward and weak beyond the imagination of the average man of the West in all the resources that make a modern industrial state power-ful—this desperately weak state has, nevertheless, in the course of four decades, rallied its strength, organized a modern industry almost from scratch, and possessed itself of a third of the earth's land surface and hundreds of millions of new population precisely at the expense of the West which, in all material ways, is enormously superior to it and whose survival it now challenges. Moreover, the fallout of its influence affects millions beyond its official frontiers.

There is a further fact. Communism has achieved this fear at the expense of a West which is not only vastly superior in material, but a West which believes itself to be vastly superior in moral and spiritual resources. It is popular to dismiss Communism as a grubby materialist philosophy imposed by force on slaves whom we expect, sometimes indifferently, sometimes hopefully (we are in one of our hopeful phases) to revolt and overthrow it. But what is the philosophy of the West? In the name of what are we inviting the slaves of the East to revolt? We speak of freedom. Every day that the Communist Empire endures, the word becomes more meaningless for millions.

It is the business of the Communist theoretician, with his eye on the whole sweep of history, to try to assess the relationship of forces in the world at every given moment, to calculate their rate of drift and general direction as a guide to action—in order to take advantage of the con-stantly changing relationships of force to promote a revolution which the Communist holds to be beneficent and, in some degree, fated.

This process in history, and this view of it, Communists call dialectical materialism (or, in that Communist shorthand that we commonly call jargon, Diamat). It is dialectic because it deals with quantities of force in motion, sometimes violent, sometimes gradual. It is called materialism because the Communist mind, like the scientific mind, rejects any super-natural factor in his observation of experience. In short, God is rigorously excluded from the equations of changing force in which the Communist mind tirelessly seeks to grasp, to express, and to act on history at any and every moment.

To try to explain Communism and the Communist while ignoring dialectical materialism is like trying to explain a man's actions while leaving out the chief clue to his mind and his motives and general view-point. Dialectical materialism is the central fact of Communism. Every Communist is a dialectical materialist. Ultimately, he cannot be under-stood in any other terms. This does not mean that all Communists are consistent or successful dialecticians. There are millions of Communists in the world, and they show the same gradations of intelligence and character as millions of anybody else. There are millions of Christians, too, of whom only a comparative handful are theologians (Communists say theoreticians). The mass of Christians is held together by a faith in what suffices to explain to them the meaning of their lives and history, although even highly intelligent communicants may be quite vague about the doctrines of their faith, or even specific articles of it. This is made possible because the center of efficacy of their faith is the Cross, using that symbol in its most inclusive sense. The Cross makes them one in faith even though at thinner fringes of Christendom the efficacy of the Cross is questioned or tends to fade. In much the same way, dialectical material- ism is the effective force of Communism, and even when understanding is weak or lacking, it operates as a faith which explains satisfactorily to millions of Communists the meaning of life and history—reality, as Com- munists say. By this they always mean reality in a state of flux, usually violent. Dialectical materialism is the crux of Communism, and not to understand this means never truly to understand the Communist. It is one reason why the West still does not understand the Communist de- spite the heaps of other highly accurate data about him. Such data remain extraneous, almost irrelevant, because they miss, or bypass, the central fact which makes the Communist a Communist.

This is the fact which absolutely sunders the mind of the Communist from the traditional mind of the West—which makes him in the mass a new breed in history. For our breeds, in this sense, are defined by the view we hold, unconsciously or not, of the world and its meaning, and the meaning of our lives in it. Obviously, a breed of men who hold that everything is in violent flux and change, moving by laws and in a pattern inherent in matter, and having nothing to do with God—obviously, that breed of men is different in kind from the rest of mankind. It is closest, in our time, to the viewpoint of the scientist for whom a simple, solid chair represents a form of energy whose particles, seemingly solid and com- monplace, are in fact in violent motion. This, incidentally, rather than the "progressive" elements in Communism which are usually brought for- ward in such cases, is the instant point of appeal which Communism so often has for the scientists of the West. They feel in Communism the force of a faith based on a material reality which more or less matches their own vision of reality. It is an abstruse view, and the scientists who hold it are lonely men, since the masses of the West cannot possibly understand or sympathize with what the scientists are talking about. The intelligent Communist knows exactly what they are talking about though he may know little or nothing about abstruse physics. Similarly, the scien- tist may know little or nothing about the niceties of dialectical material- ism. Yet each senses that the other's basic view of reality is much the same. The affinity is strong.

In the years when Communism was advancing successfully against the West, there were those who believed that its disruptive power was its power to manipulate a Fifth Column composed of non-Soviet Communists, sympathizers, fellow travellers, dupes, opportunist politicians, hitchhiking with Communism as they would in any other vehicle that seemed to be going part of their way—in short, the kind of debris and dust that almost anything with sufficient gravitational pull attracts and keeps whirling around it. I held that such elements, while dangerous, were not Communism's chief power in the West. I held that power to be something else—the power of Communism to manipulate responsive sections of the West to check, counteract, paralyze, or confuse the rest. Those responsive sections of the West were not Communist, and never had been. Most of the minds that composed them thought of themselves as sincerely anti-Communist. Communism manipulated them, not in terms of Communism, but in terms of the shared historical crisis—peace and social justice being two of the most workable terms. They were free to denounce Communism and Communists (and also anti-Communists) after whatever flourishes their intellectual innocence or arrogance might choose. Communism asked no more. It cared nothing, at this point, about motives. It cared about results.

Unlike Communism, the West held no unified solution for the crisis. In face of the crisis, part of the West reacted with inertia—inertia, in the simple terms of the physics primer, that is, the tendency of a body to remain at rest or in a straight line of motion. But the responsive section offered a solution for the crisis. This solution, whatever differences it assumed from place to place and time to time, whatever disguises political expediency or preference draped or phrased it in, was always the same solution. It was the socialist solution. Derived, as doctrine, from the same source—the historical insights of Karl Marx—the socialist solution differed from the Communist solution chiefly in political methods. One difference consisted in the slower rate of speed at which socialism proposed to apply its solution. Another difference concerned the kind and degree of coercion that socialism would apply to impose its solution. In practice, no socialist government had yet pushed its solution to the point where full coercion must come into play. Therefore, this difference had not yet stood the test of reality. Otherwise, between the end solution that socialism and Communism both hold in view for mankind—the matured planned economy of the future—the difference was so slight that it would be difficult to slip a razor blade between them.

It was no innate charm of socialism that made millions in the West espouse it, just as it was no innate charm of Communism that recruited its millions. It was the force of the historical crisis that made masses of men entertain the socialist solution, which, in fact, sundered the West. It divided the West as a whole against itself. And it divided against itself every nation that might still qualify, in a diminished world, to the rank of great power. In fact, it split almost every great nation into almost equal halves, as major sections more and more tended to show. Hence the intensity of feeling, the swollen pain as around any unhealing fracture.

The divisions in the West passed beyond matters of opinion. The arguments had all been made; the returns were in. The division of the West was organic; it turned upon different breeds of men. The sundering point was a choice between political liberty and economic security. One breed of man held freedom to be the greatest good to the point where regimentation seemed to him the touch of spiritual death, so that he would prefer to die rather than live under the socialist state. The other breed of man held social security, and hence regimentation, to be a simple necessity if he were to live at all in a modern world. The difference had nothing to do with logic of argument. The difference had to do with breeds of men. One or the other principle would determine the future of the West. One would be paramount—one or the other; both could not be. It was increasingly clear that those who held the latter view were in the majority. But when masses of men are so evenly and fiercely divided, the readjustment of reality can scarcely occur without an earthquake, even if the revolution takes a form no more violent than mass balloting. . . .

I received a letter from a close friend of many years standing who is, as I once wrote of him to Rebecca West, "a Conservative by cell-structure." Though he talks about the matter only among intimates, he is an intensely religious man. This religion, too, forms a family climate. He and his family lived actively within their church, decades before church-going became a renewed fashion among us. My friend, though highly literate, is simply devout. In my experience, this combination of high intelligence and devotion is—though the fact may be somewhat dismaying to face— rather unusual.

It was this man who wrote me as follows: "The rector of our church took a reading of the so-called rebirth of religion in the U.S., which he thought had started about 1950. . . . 'The Epiphany has fizzled,' was the way he phrased it. This is sad, but the 'rebirth' was a phoney to begin with." My friend then mentions, as a peculiar token of the failure, the name of a celebrated divine, the author of immensely popular books of a kind of fatuous Couéism, which he turns out in such quantity that he may almost be said to farrow rather than to write them.

I found this a lapidary line: "The Epiphany has fizzled." Yet, when the amusing novelty has worn off, it is seen to express chiefly a disconsolate exasperation. It is a kind of continental sadness, like the wail of a locomotive whistle, rushing off (where?) in the night—haunting, yet not true music, a very American sound, just as the locomotive whistle is (or was) perhaps the most American of sounds. But for any depth of meaning, "The Epiphany has fizzled" isn't good enough.

A decade or so ago the eminent French Catholic theologian, Father

Henri de Lubac, published a book called *The Drama of Atheist Humanism,* a study of rare understanding of certain of the great questioners or lay-sages of our age—Kierkegaard, Feuerbach, Marx, Nietzsche, Dostoevski.

Father de Lubac quotes a letter of Jacques Rivière to the poet Paul Claudel, written in 1907 (when incidentally my generation was about seven years old; and such dates are meaningful for those of us who have survived so long into this frightful age). "I see," Rivière wrote, "that Christianity is dying. . . . We do not know why, above our towns, there still rise those spires which are no longer the prayer of any one of us. We do not know the meaning of those great buildings [*i.e.,* religious institutions—Tr.] which today are surrounded by railroad stations and hospitals, and from which the people themselves have chased the monks. And on the graves, we do not know what is made manifest by those stucco crosses, frosted over with an execrable art."

"And, no doubt," says Father de Lubac, "Claudel's reply to that cry of anguish was a good one: 'Truth is not concerned with how many it persuades.' "

Then Father de Lubac goes on to cite "an almost daily experience" which shows that "certain of the harshest reproaches made against us come both from our worst adversaries and from men of goodwill. The tone, the intention, the inspiration are profoundly different. But the judgments come to much the same thing. An astonishing and significant convergence." There is more. Father de Lubac goes on to another experience, one that bears directly on the so-called rebirth of religion among us and thrusts close to the heart of an instant problem. It is the plight of those seekers who, in deepest sincerity, approach the churches in a need and craving, often desperate, for truth and a haven. They approach, but then they hesitate and stand still. In the end they go no farther.

There follows an eloquent passage. "Among those who thus disappoint us," says Father de Lubac, "some of the clearest-sighted and most spiritual find themselves torn by conflicting feelings. We see them ravished [*seduits*] by the Gospel whose teachings seem to them still full of force and novelty, drawn to the Church in which they sense a more than human reality and the sole institution capable of bringing, together with a remedy for our ills, the solution to the problem of our destiny. But, on the threshold, see what stops them: the spectacle that we make, we, the Christians of today, the Church that we are, that spectacle repels them. . . . It is not that they condemn us violently. It is, rather, that they cannot take us seriously."

This needs no commenting on by me. But I submit that it needs long and careful reflecting on, and that this is inescapable wherever the question of the rebirth of religion, which is raised in general statistically, must be weighed qualitatively. For here is raised a question which lies at the heart of our conflict with Communism. The question is: What is the West's answer to Communism? It is pretty clear, I think, that the more or less anonymous thousands who yearly flee Communism (about whom and whose later fate we rather prefer not to think unless we are compelled to) are fleeing a misery, rather than embracing an alternative idea. Though it works out of necessity in rather different ways, much the same is true of many former Communists whose defections or later testimony makes a week's news. It is the wretchedness of life for them under Communism which impels them; it is Communism's failure in their terms that drives them to the West. This is clearly not the same thing as an answer to Communism. The lack of such an answer defeats our propaganda at the core—and the word "propaganda" used in this sense, is itself suggestive. By an answer I mean a rallying idea, capable of being grasped by, and so overmastering, millions of men of the most diverse kinds because its single force persuades that it brings "together with a remedy for their ills, the solution to the problem of their destiny." In the West, taken as a whole, this idea does not exist. We know this whenever the problem arises, as it does daily, to the people of Asia and Africa, for example—a sense-making notion of what the West stands for, so that they quickly grasp it, and it stirs them to a willingness to die for it, rather than live for any other. Does such an idea exist? Let us not deceive ourselves, but answer truthfully: "It does not exist." "But what about Freedom?" you say. You are saying it to millions who never have been free in your sense, and grasp chiefly that they are free to starve. They will reach quicker for an idea that promises them an end to hunger, even if they suspect that the promise is overblown (for even the most primitive starvelings are, in general, not fools; they are merely not sophisticated in your terms; but they catch on quickly).

So long as such a central rallying idea does not exist, we in the West are likely to go on defending frontiers, even if we are no longer losing provinces. And that regardless of how elaborately the frontiers are manned and weaponed. Maginot Lines are butts to ideas.

On the eve of our time, Stefan Trofimovitch saw our problem clearly enough, even though, as sometimes happens, it took him a pointless lifetime to reach the insight and his last strength to frame it: "The one essential condition of human existence is that man should always be able to bow down before something infinitely great. If men are deprived of the infinitely great, they will not go on living and will die of despair." It is for that we crave reality, for the infinitely great may not be on any less terms. It remains otherwise lies and illusion. It is for that we crave a little height, to reach some notion of the meaning of our reality, and so as not to die of despair. So that we can rise above the paralyzing mood of our time, which we feel as a sense that none of us can really do anything; that things are merely going to happen to us.

If the voice says: "But that is what men have always craved," we will answer: "Yes, always craved." But the problem presents itself in different terms to different generations. Yet the root problem remains always the same. It is: On what terms consistent with their reality men can have God, or whether they must seem for a time even not to have Him. When, also on the eve of our time, another voice cried: "God is dead," the unthinkingly shallow heard in that cry the wildest blasphemy, and the unthinkingly intelligent heard it as a stupid promise of emancipation. But Nietzsche was only reading aloud the transcript of his time. That time comes whenever men remake God so much in their own image that He no longer corresponds to reality. For, of course, God never dies. The generations simply seek how they can have Him in terms of their reality. You cannot offer to the half-starved millions of Asia God as a sole solution to their plight, with the best of them turning away with pity for your stupidity if not with contempt for your dishonesty. But something else is also true: You cannot replace God with Point Four. If you fed the starving millions four square meals a day and studded their primitive lands with automated factories, men would still die of despair.

"I want to know why," one of the most native of our voices [Sherwood Anderson] asked in a line that rises out of all else he did and said because it sums up all the rest. I want to know why. It is for this we seek a little height, and because of this we do not feel it too high a price to pay if we cannot reach it crawling through a lifetime on our hands and knees, as a wounded man sometimes crawls from a battlefield, if only so as not to die as one more corpse among so many corpses. Happy is he who finds any height, however lowly.

That craving for the infinitely great starts with the simplest necessity. It is the necessity to know reality in order, by acting on it directly, to find the measure of men's meaning and stature in that single chance of some seven decades that is allotted them to find it out in. Since, by reason of the irrevocable briefness of that span, life is inherently tragic, the effort to wrest meaning from reality is tragic, too, and means always the necessity to rise above reality at any cost. But it is not the commonplace of tragedy, it is anything that blocks their freedom to enact it meaningfully that kills men with despair. And if the old paths no longer lead to a reality that enables men to act with meaning, if the paths no longer seem to lead anywhere—have become a footworn, trackless maze, or, like Russian roads, end after a few miles of ambitious pavement, leading nowhere but into bottomless mud and swallowing distance—men will break new paths, though they must break their hearts to do it. They will burst out somewhere, even if such bursting-out takes the form of aberration. For to act in aberration is at least more like living than to die of futility, or even to live in that complacency which is futility's idiot twin. We all know those grand aberrations of our time. We have plenty of names for them, political and invective. Communism is one of them. But all the aberrations have one common cause, and point, in the end, in one direction.

Suffering is at the heart of every living faith. That is why man can scarcely call himself a Christian for whom the Crucifixion is not a daily suffering. For it is by the hope that surmounts suffering that true tragedy surmounts pain and has always had the power to sweep men out of the common ugliness of ordeal to that exaltation in which the spirit rises superior to the agony which alone matures it by the act of transcending it. This is what we loosely call greatness. And it is the genius of Christianity to recognize that this capacity for greatness inheres in every man in the nature of his immortal soul, though not every man is called upon to demonstrate it. For it is by the soul that, at the price of suffering, we can break, if we choose, the shackles that an impersonal and rigid Fate otherwise locks upon us. It was the genius of Christianity to whisper to the lowliest man that by the action of his own soul he could burst the iron bonds of Fate with which merely being alive seemed to encase him. Only, it could never be done except at a price, which was suffering. It was because Christianity gave meaning to a suffering endured in all ages, and otherwise senseless, that it swept the minds of men. It still holds them, though the meaning has been blurred as Christianity, in common with the voices of a new age, seeks new escapes from the problem of suffering. But the problem remains and the new escapes circle back to the old one. For in suffering, man motivated by hope and faith affirms that dignity which is lit by charity and truth. This is the meaning of the eternal phrases: Lest one grain perish, and unless a man die, he shall not live—phrases as hackneyed as history and as fresh as the moment in which they rose upon the astonishments of the saints.

Nothing is more characteristic of this age than its obsession with an avoidance of suffering. Nothing dooms it more certainly to that condition which is not childlike but an infantilism which is an incapacity for growth that implies an end. The mind which has rejected the soul, and marched alone, has brought the age to the brink of disaster. Let us say it flatly: What the age needs is less minds than martyrs—less knowledge (knowledge was never so cheap) but that wisdom which begins with the necessity to die, if necessary, for one's faith and thereby liberates that hope which is the virtue of the spirit.

But let us not suppose, like children, that suffering must not take its toll. Suffering implies growth and all growth is an hourly and daily dying. Age is its price as maturity is its crown. Both enjoin their blessings, among which is, supremely, a liberation from the interminable compromise in which all life is lived. Thus, at the end, or with the end in sight, truth alone becomes the compelling need and the quest for truth the only worthwhile occupation, while those engaged in it achieve that good humor of the spirit which most of those achieve who are engaged in any engrossing labor. For they know that constancy rather than energy is the cost of accomplishment in an art so difficult and so long to learn, while tolerance becomes a function of that infinity that opens up to them so near at hand. Truth too is a suffering and may not be had for less. The quest for it is a labor, life's only permanently valid one, and like any labor humbling because only the laborer knows how many mistakes have to be undone or unlearned to make anything, or supposes that he can ever really learn the mystery of his craft.

But I have reached an age, in one sense or another, and a condition where I have no other real interest. The first men who thought at all knew that the sadness of life is inseparable from its beauty—so that wisdom always implies the reaching of a point where a man can smile at both, while minimizing neither. But leave-taking is also the great liberator. The grown man who looks around for the last time has no room in his mind, and no time, for more than reality. And he wants it plain. He has no longer any reason to share it as men do to make it endurable in life, and no reason to care how others share it. This is the ultimate freedom; and what man can count that suffering a cost which has led him to the direct glance that measures what it leaves without fear and without regret?

ALBERT JAY NOCK

Isaiah's Job

One evening last autumn I sat long hours with a European acquaintance while he expounded a politico-economic doctrine which seemed sound as a nut, and in which I could find no defect. At the end he said with great earnestness, "I have a mission to the masses. I feel that I am called to get the ear of the people. I shall devote the rest of my life to spreading my doctrine far and wide among the populace. What do you think?"

An embarrassing question in any case, and doubly so under the circumstances, because my acquaintance is a very learned man, one of the three or four really first-class minds that Europe produced in his generation, and naturally I, as one of the unlearned, was inclined to regard his lightest word with reverence amounting to awe. Still, I reflected, even the greatest mind cannot possibly know everything, and I was pretty sure he had not had my opportunities for observing the masses of mankind, and that therefore I probably knew them better than he did. So I mustered courage to say that he had no such mission and would do well to get the idea out of his head at once; he would find that the masses would not care two pins for his doctrine, and still less for himself, since in such circumstances the popular favorite is generally some Barabbas. I even went so far as to say (he is a Jew) that his idea seemed to show that he was not very well up on his own native literature. He smiled at my jest, and asked what I meant by it; and I referred him to the story of the prophet Isaiah.

It occurred to me then that this story is much worth recalling just now when so many wise men and soothsayers appear to be burdened with a message to the masses. Dr. Townsend has a message, Father Coughlin has one, Mr. Upton Sinclair, Mr. Lippmann, Mr. Chase and the planned-economy brethren, Mr. Tugwell and the New Dealers, Mr. Smith and the Liberty Leaguers—the list is endless. I cannot remember a time when so many energumens were so variously proclaiming the Word to the multitude and telling them what they must do to be saved. This being so, it occurred to me, as I say, that the story of Isaiah might have something in it to steady and compose the human spirit until this tyranny of windiness be overpast. I shall paraphrase the story in our common speech, since it has to be pieced out from various sources; and inasmuch as respectable scholars have thought fit to put out a whole new version of the Bible in the American vernacular, I shall take shelter behind them, if need be, against the charge of dealing irreverently with the Sacred Scriptures.

The prophet's career began at the end of King Uzziah's reign, say about 740 B.C. This reign was uncommonly long, almost half a century, and apparently prosperous. It was one of those prosperous reigns, however, like the reign of Marcus Aurelius at Rome, or the administration of Eubulus at Athens, or of Mr. Coolidge at Washington, where at the end the prosperity suddenly peters out, and things go by the board with a resounding crash. In the year of Uzziah's death, the Lord commissioned the prophet to go out and warn the people of the wrath to come. "Tell them what a worthless lot they are," He said. "Tell them what is wrong, and why, and what is going to happen unless they have a change of heart and straighten up. Don't mince matters. Make it clear that they are positively down to their last chance. Give it to them good and strong, and keep on giving it to them. I suppose perhaps I ought to tell you," He added, "that it won't do any good. The official class and their intelligentsia will turn up their noses at you, and the masses will not even listen.

They will all keep on in their own ways until they carry everything down to destruction, and you will probably be lucky if you get out with your life."

Isaiah had been very willing to take on the job; in fact, he had asked for it; but this prospect put a new face on the situation. It raised the obvious question why, if all that were so, if the enterprise were to be a failure from the start, was there any sense in starting it? "Ah," the Lord said, "you do not get the point. There is a Remnant there that you know nothing about. They are obscure, unorganized, inarticulate, each one rubbing along as best he can. They need to be encouraged and braced up, because when everything has gone completely to the dogs, they are the ones who will come back and build up a new society, and meanwhile your preaching will reassure them and keep them hanging on. Your job is to take care of the Remnant, so be off now and set about it."

Apparently, then, if the Lord's word is good for anything—I do not offer any opinion about that—the only element in Judaean society that was particularly worth bothering about was the Remnant. Isaiah seems finally to have got it through his head that this was the case, that nothing was to be expected from the masses, but that if anything substantial were ever to be done in Judaea, the Remnant would have to do it. This is a very striking and suggestive idea; but before going on to explore it, we need to be quite clear about our terms. What do we mean by the masses, and what by the Remnant?

As the word *masses* is commonly used, it suggests agglomerations of poor and unprivileged people, laboring people, proletarians, and it means nothing like that; it means simply the majority. The mass-man is one who has neither the force of intellect to apprehend the principles issuing in what we know as the humane life, nor the force of character to adhere to those principles steadily and strictly as laws of conduct; and because such people make up the great, the overwhelming majority of mankind, they are called collectively *the masses*. The line of differentiation between the masses and the Remnant is set invariably by quality, not by circumstance. The Remnant are those who by force of intellect are able to apprehend these principles, and by force of character are able, at least measurably, to cleave to them; the masses are those who are unable to do either.

The picture which Isaiah presents of the Judaean masses is most unfavorable. In his view the mass-man, be he high or be he lowly, rich or poor, prince or pauper, gets off very badly. He appears as not only weak-minded and weak-willed, but as by consequence knavish, arrogant, grasping, dissipated, unprincipled, unscrupulous. The mass-woman also gets off badly, as sharing all the mass-man's untoward qualities, and

contributing a few of her own in the way of vanity and laziness, extravagance and foible. The list of luxury-products* that she patronized is
interesting; it calls to mind the women's page of a Sunday newspaper in
1928, or the display set forth in one of our professedly "smart" periodi-
cals. In another place† Isaiah even recalls the affectations that we used
to know by the name of the "flapper gait" and the "debutante slouch."
It may be fair to discount Isaiah's vivacity a little for prophetic fervor;
after all, since his real job was not to convert the masses but to brace and
reassure the Remnant, he probably felt that he might lay it on indiscrimi-
nately and as thick as he liked—in fact, that he was expected to do so. But
even so, the Judaean mass-man must have been a most objectionable
individual, and the mass-woman utterly odious.

If the modern spirit, whatever that may be, is disinclined towards
taking the Lord's word at its face value (as I hear is the case), we may
observe that Isaiah's testimony to the character of the masses has strong
collateral support from respectable Gentile authority. Plato lived into the
administration of Eubulus, when Athens was at the peak of its great
jazz-and-paper era, and he speaks of the Athenian masses with all Isaiah's
fervency, even comparing them to a herd of ravenous wild beasts. Curiously, too, he applies Isaiah's own word *remnant* to the worthier portion
of Athenian society; "there is but a very small *remnant,*" he says, of those
who possess a saving force of intellect and force of character—too small,
precisely as in Judaea, to be of any avail against the ignorant and vicious
preponderance of the masses.

But Isaiah was a preacher and Plato a philosopher; and we tend to
regard preachers and philosophers rather as passive observers of the
drama of life than as active participants. Hence in a matter of this kind
their judgment might be suspected of being a little uncompromising, a
little acrid, or as the French say, *saugrenu.* We may therefore bring forward another witness who was preeminently a man of affairs, and whose
judgment cannot lie under this suspicion. Marcus Aurelius was ruler of
the greatest of empires, and in that capacity he not only had the Roman
mass-man under observation, but he had him on his hands twenty-four
hours a day for eighteen years. What he did not know about him was not
worth knowing, and what he thought of him is abundantly attested
on almost every page of the little book of jottings which he scribbled offhand from day to day, and which he meant for no eye but his own ever
to see.

This view of the masses is the one that we find prevailing at large
among the ancient authorities whose writings have come down to us. In
the eighteenth century, however, certain European philosophers spread

*Isaiah iii. 18–23.
†Chap. iii. 16.

the notion that the mass-man, in his natural state, is not at all the kind of person that earlier authorities made him out to be, but on the contrary, that he is a worthy object of interest. His untowardness is the effect of environment, an effect for which "society" is somehow responsible. If only his environment permitted him to live according to his best lights, he would undoubtedly show himself to be quite a fellow; and the best way to secure a more favorable environment for him would be to let him arrange it for himself. The French Revolution acted powerfully as a springboard for this idea, projecting its influence in all directions throughout Europe.

On this side of the ocean a whole new continent stood ready for a large-scale experiment with this theory. It afforded every conceivable resource whereby the masses might develop a civilization made in their own likeness and after their own image. There was no force of tradition to disturb them in their preponderance, or to check them in a thorough-going disparagement of the Remnant. Immense natural wealth, un-questioned predominance, virtual isolation, freedom from external inter-ference and the fear of it, and, finally, a century and a half of time—such are the advantages which the mass-man has had in bringing forth a civilization which should set the earlier preachers and philosophers at naught in their belief that nothing substantial can be expected from the masses, but only from the Remnant.

His success is unimpressive. On the evidence so far presented one must say, I think, that the mass-man's conception of what life has to offer, and his choice of what to ask from life, seem now to be pretty well what they were in the times of Isaiah and Plato; and so too seem the catas-trophic social conflicts and convulsions in which his views of life and his demands on life involve him. I do not wish to dwell on this, however, but merely to observe that the monstrously inflated importance of the masses has apparently put all thought of a possible mission to the Remnant out of the modern prophet's head. This is obviously quite as it should be, provided that the earlier preachers and philosophers were actually wrong, and that all final hope of the human race is actually centered in the masses. If, on the other hand, it should turn out that the Lord and Isaiah and Plato and Marcus Aurelius were right in their estimate of the relative social value of the masses and the Remnant, the case is somewhat different. Moreover, since with everything in their favor the masses have so far given such an extremely discouraging account of themselves, it would seem that the question at issue between these two bodies of opin-ion might most profitably be reopened.

But without following up this suggestion, I wish only, as I said, to remark the fact that as things now stand Isaiah's job seems rather to go begging. Everyone with a message nowadays is like my venerable European friend, eager to take it to the masses. His first, last, and only thought is of mass-acceptance and mass-approval. His great care is to put his doctrine in such shape as will capture the masses' attention and interest. This attitude toward the masses is so exclusive, so devout, that one is reminded of the troglodytic monster described by Plato, and the assiduous crowd at the entrance to its cave, trying obsequiously to placate it and win its favor, trying to interpret its inarticulate noises, trying to find out what it wants, and eagerly offering it all sorts of things that they think might strike its fancy.

The main trouble with all this is its reaction upon the mission itself. It necessitates an opportunist sophistication of one's doctrine which profoundly alters its character and reduces it to a mere placebo. If, say, you are a preacher, you wish to attract as large a congregation as you can, which means an appeal to the masses, and this in turn means adapting the terms of your message to the order of intellect and character that the masses exhibit. If you are an educator, say with a college on your hands, you wish to get as many students as possible, and you whittle down your requirements accordingly. If a writer, you aim at getting many readers; if a publisher, many purchasers; if a philosopher, many disciples; if a reformer, many converts; if a musician, many auditors; and so on. But as we see on all sides, in the realization of these several desires the prophetic message is so heavily adulterated with trivialities in every instance that its effect on the masses is merely to harden them in their sins; and meanwhile the Remnant, aware of this adulteration and of the desires that prompt it, turn their backs on the prophet and will have nothing to do with him or his message.

Isaiah, on the other hand, worked under no such disabilities. He preached to the masses only in the sense that he preached publicly. Anyone who liked might listen; anyone who liked might pass by. He knew that the Remnant would listen; and knowing also that nothing was to be expected of the masses under any circumstances, he made no specific appeal to them, did not accommodate his message to their measure in any way, and did not care two straws whether they heeded it or not. As a modern publisher might put it, he was not worrying about circulation or about advertising. Hence, with all such obsessions quite out of the way, he was in a position to do his level best, without fear or favor, and answerable only to his august Boss.

If a prophet were not too particular about making money out of his mission or getting a dubious sort of notoriety out of it, the foregoing considerations would lead one to say that serving the Remnant looks like a good job. An assignment that you can really put your back into, and do your best without thinking about results, is a real job; whereas serving the masses is at best only half a job, considering the inexorable conditions that the masses impose upon their servants. They ask you to give them what they want, they insist upon it, and will take nothing else; and following their whims, their irrational changes of fancy, their hot and cold fits, is a tedious business, to say nothing of the fact that what they want at any time makes very little call on one's resources of prophecy. The Remnant, on the other hand, want only the best you have, whatever that may be. Give them that, and they are satisfied and you have nothing more to worry about. The prophet of the American masses must aim consciously at the lowest common denominator of intellect, taste and character among 120 million people; and this is a distressing task. The prophet of the Remnant, on the contrary, is in the enviable position of Papa Haydn in the household of Prince Esterhazy. All Haydn had to do was to keep forking out the very best music he knew how to produce, knowing it would be understood and appreciated by those for whom he produced it, and caring not a button what anyone else thought of it; and that makes a good job.

In a sense, nevertheless, as I have said, it is not a rewarding job. If you can touch the fancy of the masses, and have the sagacity to keep always one jump ahead of their vagaries and vacillations, you can get good returns in money from serving the masses, and good returns also in a mouth-to-ear type of notoriety:

Digito monstrari et dicier, Hic est!

We all know innumerable politicians, journalists, dramatists, novelists and the like, who have done extremely well by themselves in these ways. Taking care of the Remnant, on the contrary, holds little promise of any such rewards. A prophet of the Remnant will not grow purse-proud on the financial returns from his work, nor is it likely that he will get any great renown out of it. Isaiah's case was exceptional to this second rule, and there are others, but not many.

It may be thought, then, that while taking care of the Remnant is no doubt a good job, it is not an especially interesting job, because it is as a rule so poorly paid. I have my doubts about this. There are other compensations to be got out of a job besides money and notoriety, and some of them seem substantial enough to be attractive. Many jobs which do not pay well are yet profoundly interesting, as, for instance, the job of the research-student in the sciences is said to be; and the job of looking after the Remnant seems to me, as I have surveyed it for many years from my seat in the grandstand, to be as interesting as any that can be found in the world.

What chiefly makes it so, I think, is that in any given society the Remnant are always so largely an unknown quantity. You do not know, and will never know, more than two things about them. You can be sure of those—dead sure, as our phrase is—but you will never be able to make even a respectable guess at anything else. You do not know and will never know who the Remnant are, or where they are, or how many of them there are, or what they are doing or will do. Two things you know, and no more: first, that they exist; second, that they will find you. Except for these two certainties, working for the Remnant means working in impenetrable darkness; and this, I should say, is just the condition calculated most effectively to pique the interest of any prophet who is properly gifted with the imagination, insight, and intellectual curiosity necessary to a successful pursuit of his trade.

The fascination and the despair of the historian, as he looks back upon Isaiah's Jewry, upon Plato's Athens, or upon Rome of the Antonines, is the hope of discovering and laying bare the "substratum of right thinking and well-doing" which he knows must have existed somewhere in those societies because no kind of collective life can possibly go on without it. He finds tantalizing intimations of it here and there in many places, as in the Greek Anthology, in the scrapbook of Aulus Gellius, in the poems of Ausonius, and in the brief and touching tribute *Bene merenti* bestowed upon the unknown occupants of Roman tombs. But these are vague and fragmentary; they lead him nowhere in his search for some kind of measure of this substratum, but merely testify to what he already knew a priori, that the substratum did somewhere exist. Where it was, how substantial it was, what its power of self-assertion and resistance was—of all this they tell him nothing.

Similarly, when the historian of two thousand years hence, or two hundred years, looks over the available testimony to the quality of our civilization and tries to get any kind of clear, competent evidence concerning the substratum of right thinking and well-doing which he knows must have been here, he will have a devil of a time finding it. When he has assembled all he can get and has made even a minimum allowance for speciousness, vagueness, and confusion of motive, he will sadly acknowledge that his net result is simply nothing. A Remnant were here, building a substratum, like coral insects—so much he knows—but he will find nothing to put him on the track of who and where and how many they were, and what their work was like.

Concerning all this, too, the prophet of the present knows precisely as much and as little as the historian of the future; and that, I repeat, is what makes his job seem to me so profoundly interesting. One of the most suggestive episodes recounted in the Bible is that of a prophet's attempt—the only attempt of the kind on record, I believe—to count up the Remnant. Elijah had fled from persecution into the desert, where the Lord presently overhauled him and asked what he was doing so far away from his job. He said that he was running away, not because he was a coward, but because all the Remnant had been killed off except himself. He had got away only by the skin of his teeth, and, he being now all the

Remnant there was, if he were killed the True Faith would go flat. The Lord replied that he need not worry about that, for even without him the True Faith could probably manage to squeeze along somehow, if it had to; "and as for your figures on the Remnant," He said, "I don't mind telling you that there are seven thousand of them back there in Israel whom it seems you have not heard of, but you may take My word for it that there they are."

At that time probably the population of Israel could not have run to much more than a million or so; and a Remnant of seven thousand out of a million is a highly encouraging percentage for any prophet. With seven thousand of the boys on his side, there was no great reason for Elijah to feel lonesome; and incidentally that would be something for the modern prophet of the Remnant to think of when he has a touch of the blues. But the main point is that if Elijah the Prophet could not make a closer guess on the number of the Remnant than he made when he missed it by seven thousand, anyone else who tackled the problem would only waste his time.

The other certainty which the prophet of the Remnant may always have is that the Remnant will find him. He may rely on that with absolute assurance. They will find him without his doing anything about it; in fact, if he tries to do anything about it, he is pretty sure to put them off. He does not need to advertise for them, or resort to any schemes of publicity to get their attention. If he is a preacher or a public speaker, for example, he may be quite indifferent to going on show at receptions, getting his picture printed in the newspapers, or furnishing autobiographical material for publication on the side of "human interest." If a writer, he need not make a point of attending any pink teas, autographing books at wholesale, or entering into any specious freemasonry with reviewers. All this and much more of the same order lies in the regular and necessary routine laid down for the prophet of the masses; it is, and must be, part of the great general technique of getting the mass-man's ear—or as our vigorous and excellent publicist, Mr. H. L. Mencken, puts it, the technique of boob-bumping. The prophet of the Remnant is not bound to this technique. He may be quite sure that the Remnant will make their own way to him without any adventitious aids; and not only so, but if they find him employing such aids, as I said, it is ten to one that they will smell a rat in them and will sheer off.

The certainty that the Remnant will find him, however, leaves the prophet as much in the dark as ever, as helpless as ever in the matter of putting any estimate of any kind upon the Remnant, for, as appears in the case of Elijah, he remains ignorant of who they are that have found him, or where they are, or how many. They do not write in and tell him about it, after the manner of those who admire the vedettes of Hollywood, nor yet do they seek him out and attach themselves to his person. They are not that kind. They take his message much as drivers take the directions on a roadside signboard—that is, with very little thought about the signboard, beyond being gratefully glad that it happened to be there, but with very serious thought about the directions.

This impersonal attitude of the Remnant wonderfully enhances the interest of the imaginative prophet's job. Once in a while, just about often enough to keep his intellectual curiosity in good working order, he will quite accidentally come upon some distinct reflection of his own message in an unsuspected quarter; and this enables him to entertain himself in his leisure moments with agreeable speculations about the course his message may have taken in reaching that particular quarter, and about what came of it after it got there. Most interesting of all are those instances, if one could only run them down (but one may always speculate about them), where the recipient himself no longer knows where or when or from whom he got the message; or even where, as sometimes happens, he has forgotten that he got it anywhere, and imagines that it is all a self-sprung idea of his own.

Such instances as these are probably not infrequent, for, without presuming to enroll ourselves among the Remnant, we can all no doubt remember having found ourselves suddenly under the influence of an idea, the source of which we cannot possible identify. "It came to us afterward," as we say; that is, we are aware of it only after it has shot up full-grown in our minds, leaving us quite ignorant of how and when and by what agency it was planted there and left to germinate. It seems highly probable that the prophet's message often takes some such course with the Remnant.

If, for example, you are a writer or a speaker or a preacher, you put forth an idea which lodges in the *Unbewusstsein* of a casual member of the Remnant, and sticks fast there. For some time it is inert; then it begins to fret and fester until presently it invades the man's conscious mind and, as one might say, corrupts it. Meanwhile he has quite forgotten how he came by the idea in the first instance, and even perhaps thinks he has invented it; and in those circumstances the most interesting thing of all is that you never know what the pressure of that idea will make him do.

For these reasons it appears to me that Isaiah's job is not only good but also extremely interesting; and especially so at the present time when nobody is doing it. If I were young and had the notion of embarking in the prophetical line, I would certainly take up this branch of the business; and therefore I have no hesitation about recommending it as a career for anyone in that position. It offers an open field, no competition; our civilization so completely neglects and disallows the Remnant that anyone going in with an eye single to their service might pretty well count on getting all the trade there is.

Even assuming that there is some social salvage to be screened out of the masses, even assuming that the testimony of history to their social value is a little too sweeping, that it depresses hopelessness a little too far, one must yet perceive, I think, that the masses have prophets enough and to spare. Even admitting in the teeth of history that hope of the human race may not be quite exclusively centered in the Remnant, one must perceive that they have social value enough to entitle them to some measure of prophetic encouragement and consolation, and that our civilization allows them none whatever. Every prophetic voice is addressed to the masses, and to them alone; the voice of the pulpit, the voice of education, the voice of politics, of literature, drama, journalism—all these are directed toward the masses exclusively, and they marshal the masses in the way that they are going.

One might suggest, therefore, that aspiring prophetical talent may well turn to another field. *Sat patriae Priamoque datum*—whatever obligation of the kind may be due the masses is already monstrously overpaid. So long as the masses are taking up the tabernacle of Moloch and Chium, their images, and following the star of their god Buncombe, they will have no lack of prophets to point the way that leadeth to the More Abundant Life; and hence a few of those who feel the prophetic afflatus might do better to apply themselves to serving the Remnant. It is a good job, an interesting job, much more interesting than serving the masses; and moreover it is the only job in our whole civilization, as far as I know, that offers a virgin field.

Epilogue: *Il Faut le Supposer Heureux*

*(The following is from the last letter I received
from Whittaker Chambers.—W.F.B.)*

Pipe Creek Farm
Westminster, Md.
April 9, 1961

Dear Bill,

Weariness, Bill—you cannot yet know literally what it means. I wish
no time would come when you do know, but the balance of experience
is against it. One day, long hence, you will know true weariness and will
say: "That was it." My own life of late has been full of such realizations:
"So that was why he did that"; "So that was why she didn't do that"; about
the past acts of people with whom my own age (and hence understanding)
has only just caught up. There's a kind of pathos about it—a rather empty
kind, I'm afraid; the understanding comes too late to do even the tardy
understander much good.

Our kind of weariness. History hit us with a freight train. History has
long been doing this to people, monotonously and usually lethally. But
we (my general breed) tried, as Strachey noted, to put ourselves together
again. Since this meant outwitting dismemberment, as well as resynthe-
sizing a new life-view (grandfather, what big words you use), the sequel
might seem rather remarkable, rather more remarkable than what went
before. But at a price—weariness. People tend to leave Oedipus, shriek-
ing with the blood running down his cheeks—everybody nicely purged
by pity and terror, and so home and to bed. But I was about 23 when I
discovered, rather by chance, that Oedipus went on to Colonus. But each
of us, according to his lights, was arrested in time by the same line—the
one in which Oedipus, looking out from precarious sanctuary after long
flight, sums up: "Because of my great age, and the nobility of my mind,
I feel that all will be well." That is the Oedipus largely overlooked. Of
course, I can say nothing of the nobility of my mind, or even Koestler's
or Camus'; and I realize, too, that Oedipus spoke at a grateful moment
of rescue. One cannot pretend to live at that height. And yet, to reach it

Whittaker Chambers, "Il Faut le Supposer Heureux," *National Review*, XI, No. 4 (July 29,
1961), 47. Reprinted by permission of *National Review*.

even at times is something. One must have got rid of great loads of encumbering nonsense and irrelevance to get there; must have learned to travel quite light—one razor, one change, etc. And I suppose the "well" of the quotation is almost wholly a subjective value. And there remains the price—the weariness I mentioned which none of us complains about, but should take good care not to inflict on other people's lives. I did and I'm sorry about it. We're grateful too.

Something quite different which struck me—what seems to have been your desolation by *Man's Fate* [by André Malraux]. But Hemmelrich goes back (supreme tenderness) to close the door left too hastily open on the bodies of his murdered wife and son. Tchen, about to throw himself and bomb under the automobile, believes that Pei (spared to life because Tchen acts alone) will be able to write more meaningfully by reason of Tchen's act. Kyo takes the cyanide with the sense that the concept of man's dignity enjoins control over his own death. Katow, surrendering even that ultimate, divides his cyanide with those less able to bear man's fate; and walks toward the locomotive through a hall of bodies from which comes something like an unutterable sob—the strangled cry. It may also be phrased: "And the Morning Stars sang together for joy." It may also be phrased: *"Il faut supposer Katow heureux,"* as Camus wrote: *"Il faut supposer Sisyphe heureux."* For each age finds its own language for an eternal meaning.

As always,
Whittaker

Selected Bibliography

THE CONTRIBUTORS

We list here the published books of our contributors that touch, directly or indirectly, on the theme of conservatism.

Edward C. Banfield: *Government Project* (New York: Free Press, 1951); with Martin Meyerson: *Politics, Planning and the Public Interest: The Case of Public Housing in Chicago* (New York: Free Press, 1955); with Laura F. Banfield: *The Moral Basis of a Backward Society* (Glencoe, Ill.: Free Press, 1958): *Political Influence* (New York: Free Press, 1961); with James Q. Wilson: *City Politics* (Cambridge, Mass.: Harvard University Press, 1963); *American Foreign Aid Doctrines* (Washington, D.C.: American Enterprise Institute for Public Policy Research, 1963); *The Unheavenly City: The Nature and Future of Our Urban Enterprise* (Boston: Little Brown, 1970); *The Unheavenly City Revisited* (Boston: Little Brown, 1974); *The Democratic Muse: Visual Arts and the Public Interest* (New York: Basic Books, 1984); *Here the People Rule* (New York: Plenum Press, 1985).

Walter Berns: *Freedom, Virtue, and the First Amendment* (Westport, Conn.: Greenwood Press, 1969); *The First Amendment and the Future of American Democracy* (New York: Basic Books, 1976); *For Capital Punishment* (New York: Basic Books, 1979); *In Defense of Liberal Democracy* (Chicago: Regnery/Gateway, 1984); *Taking the Constitution Seriously* (New York: Simon & Schuster, 1987).

James Burnham: *The Machiavellians, Defenders of Freedom* (New York: John Day, 1943); *The Struggle for the World* (New York: John Day, 1947); *The Coming Defeat of Communism* (New York: John Day, 1950); *Congress and the American Tradition* (Chicago: Henry Regnery, 1959); *The Web of Subversion: Underground Networks in the U.S. Government* (New York: John Day, 1959); *Suicide of the West: An Essay on the Meaning and Destiny of Liberalism* (New York: John Day, 1964); *The Managerial Revolution* (Bloomington, Ind.: Indiana University Press, 1966; orig. ed., 1941); *The War We Are In* (New Rochelle, N.Y.: Arlington House, 1967).

Whittaker Chambers: *Witness* (Chicago: Regnery/Gateway, 1978); *Cold Friday* (New York: Random House, 1964); edited by William F. Buckley, Jr.: *Odyssey of a Friend: Whittaker Chambers' Letters to William F. Buckley, Jr., 1954–1961* (New York: Putnam, 1970).

Milton Friedman: *Essays in Positive Economics* (Chicago: University of Chicago Press, 1953); *Capitalism and Freedom* (Chicago: University of Chicago Press,

1962); with Anna Schwartz: *A Monetary History of the United States, 1867–1960* (Princeton: Princeton University Press, 1963); *The Great Contraction* (Princeton: Princeton University Press, 1965); *There Is No Such Thing as a Free Lunch* (LaSalle, Ill.: Open Court, 1975); with Rose Friedman: *Free to Choose* (New York: Harcourt Brace Jovanovich, 1980); with Rose Friedman: *Tyranny of the Status Quo* (San Diego: Harcourt Brace Jovanovich, 1984).

Jeffrey Hart: *Viscount Bolingbroke, Tory Humanist* (Toronto: University of Toronto Press, 1965); *The American Dissent: A Decade of Modern Conservatism* (Garden City, N.Y.: Doubleday, 1966); *When the Going Was Good: American Life in the Fifties* (New York: Crown Publishers, 1982); *From This Moment On: America in 1940* (New York: Crown Publishers, 1987).

Friedrich A. Hayek: *Freedom and the Economic System* (Chicago: University of Chicago Press, 1939); *The Road to Serfdom* (Chicago: University of Chicago Press, 1944); *Individualism and Economic Order* (Chicago: University of Chicago Press, 1948); *The Counter Revolution of Science: Studies in the Abuse of Reason* (Glencoe, Ill.: Free Press, 1952); *The Political Ideal of the Rule of Law* (Menlo Park, Cal.: Institute for Humane Studies, 1955); *The Constitution of Liberty* (Chicago: University of Chicago Press, 1960); *Studies in Philosophy, Politics, and Economics* (Chicago: University of Chicago Press, 1967); *Law, Legislation and Liberty* (Chicago: University of Chicago Press, 1973–1979, 3 vols.); Vol. 1: *Rules and Order,* 1973; Vol. 2: *The Mirage of Social Justice,* 1977; Vol. 3: *The Political Order of a Free People,* 1979; *New Studies in Philosophy, Politics, Economics, and the History of Ideas* (Chicago: University of Chicago Press, 1978).

Harry V. Jaffa: *Thomism and Aristotelianism* (Chicago: University of Chicago Press, 1952); *Crisis of the House Divided* (Chicago: University of Chicago Press, 1982); with Allan Bloom: *Shakespeare's Politics* (Chicago: University of Chicago Press, 1981); *Equality and Liberty* (New York: Oxford University Press, 1965); *The Conditions of Freedom* (Baltimore: Johns Hopkins University Press, 1975); *How to Think About the American Revolution* (Durham, N.C.: Carolina Academic Press, 1978); editor: *Statesmanship: Essays in Honor of Sir Winston Churchill* (Durham, N.C.: Carolina Academic Press, 1982); *American Conservatism and the American Founding* (Durham, N.C.: Carolina Academic Press, 1984).

Willmoore Kendall: *John Locke and the Doctrine of Majority Rule* (Urbana, Ill.: University of Illinois Press, 1941); *The Conservative Affirmation* (Chicago: Henry Regnery, 1963); edited by Nellie D. Kendall: *Willmoore Kendall Contra Mundum* (New Rochelle, N.Y.: Arlington House, 1971).

Russell Kirk: *John Randolph of Roanoke* (Chicago: University of Chicago Press, 1951); *The Conservative Mind,* 7th revised ed. (Chicago: Regnery Books, 1986); orig. ed., 1953; *A Program for Conservatives* (Chicago: Henry Regnery, 1954); *Academic Freedom* (Chicago: Henry Regnery, 1955); *Beyond the Dreams of Avarice* (Chicago: Henry Regnery, 1956); *Prospects for Conservatives* (Chicago: Gateway Editions, 1956); *The Intelligent Women's Guide to Conservatism*

(New York: Devin-Adair, 1957); *Confessions of A Bohemian Tory* (New York: Fleet Press, 1963); *Edmund Burke: A Genius Reconsidered* (New Rochelle, N.Y.: Arlington House, 1967); *Political Principles of Robert A. Taft* (New York: Fleet Press, 1967); *Enemies of the Permanent Things* (New Rochelle, N.Y.: Arlington House, 1969); *Eliot and His Age* (New York: Random House, 1971); *Roots of American Order* (LaSalle, Ill.: Open Court, 1974); *Decadence and Renewal in the Higher Learning* (South Bend, Ind.: Gateway Editions, 1978); *Portable Conservative Reader* (New York: Penguin Books, 1982); *Watchers at the Strait Gate* (Sauk City, Wis.: Arkham House Publishers, 1984).

Jeane Kirkpatrick: editor: *The Strategy of Deception: A Study of World-Wide Communist Tactics* (New York: Farrar, Straus, 1963); *Dictatorships and Double Standards: Rationalism and Reason in Politics* (New York: Simon & Schuster, 1982); *Legitimacy and Force: The State Papers and Addresses, 1981–1985* (New Brunswick, N.J.: Transaction Books, 1986).

Frank S. Meyer: *The Moulding of Communists* (New York: Harcourt, Brace and Co., 1961); *In Defense of Freedom: A Conservative Credo* (Chicago: Henry Regnery, 1962); editor: *What is Conservatism?* (New York: Holt, 1964); *The Conservative Mainstream* (New Rochelle, N.Y.: Arlington House, 1969).

Charles A. Murray: *Losing Ground: American Social Policy, 1950–1980* (New York: Basic Books, 1984).

Gerhart Niemeyer: *Law Without Force: The Function of Politics in International Law* (Princeton: Princeton University Press, 1941); *An Inquiry into the Soviet Mentality* (New York: F. A. Praeger, 1956); *Communists in Coalition Governments* (Washington, D.C.: American Enterprise Institute, 1963); *Between Nothingness and Paradise* (Baton Rouge: Louisiana State University Press, 1971); *Deceitful Peace: A New Look at the Soviet Threat* (New Rochelle, N.Y.: Arlington House, 1971).

Albert Jay Nock: *Jefferson* (New York: Harcourt, Brace and Co., 1926); *On Doing the Right Thing and Other Essays* (New York: Harper, 1928); Coauthor: *Francis Rabelais: The Man and His Work* (New York: Harper, 1929); *A Journey into Rabelais' France* (New York: Morrow and Co., 1934); *Free Speech and Plain Language* (New York: Morrow and Co., 1937); *Henry George* (New York: Morrow and Co., 1939); *Memoirs of a Superfluous Man* (Chicago: Henry Regnery, 1964); edited by Francis J. Nock: *Selected Letters* (Caldwell, Idaho: Caxton, 1962); *Our Enemy, The State* (Delavan, Wis.: Hallberg, 1983).

Norman Podhoretz: *Doings and Undoings: The Fifties and After in American Writing* (New York: Farrar, Straus, 1964); *Making It* (New York: Random House, 1967); *Breaking Ranks: A Political Memoir* (New York: Harper & Row, 1979); *The Present Danger* (New York: Simon & Schuster, 1980); *Why We Were In Vietnam* (New York: Simon & Schuster, 1982); *The Bloody Crossroads: Where Literature and Politics Meet* (New York: Simon & Schuster, 1986).

Paul Craig Roberts: *Alienation and the Soviet Economy* (Albuquerque, N.M.: University of New Mexico Press, 1971); *Marx's Theory of Exchange* (Palo Alto, Cal.:

Hoover Institution Press, 1973); *The Supply-Side Revolution* (Cambridge, Mass.: Harvard University Press, 1984).

Joseph Sobran: *Single Issues* (New York: Human Life Press, 1983); *The Conservative Manifesto* (New York: Empire Books, 1984).

Thomas Sowell: *Say's Law: An Historical Analysis* (Princeton: Princeton University Press, 1972); *Classical Economics Reconsidered* (Princeton: Princeton University Press, 1974); *Knowledge and Decisions* (New York: Basic Books, 1980); *Ethnic America: A History* (New York: Basic Books, 1981); *Pink and Brown People* (Stanford, Cal.: Hoover Institution Press, 1981); *Markets and Minorities* (New York: Basic Books, 1981); *The Economics and Politics of Race* (New York: William Morrow, 1983); *Civil Rights, Rhetoric or Reality?* (New York: William Morrow, 1984); *Marxism: Philosophy and Economics* (New York: William Morrow, 1985); *A Conflict of Visions* (New York: William Morrow, 1987).

Leo Strauss: *Natural Right and History* (Chicago: University of Chicago Press, 1950); *Persecution and the Art of Writing* (Glencoe, Ill.: Free Press, 1952); *The Political Philosophy of Hobbes* (Chicago: University of Chicago Press, 1953); *Thoughts on Machiavelli* (Glencoe, Ill.: Free Press, 1959); *What Is Political Philosophy?* (New York: Free Press, 1959); *The City and Man* (Chicago: Rand McNally, 1962); *Spinoza's Critique of Religion* (New York: Shocken Books, 1965); *Socrates and Aristophanes* (New York: Basic Books, 1966); *Liberalism: Ancient and Modern* (New York: Basic Books, 1968); *Xenophon's Socratic Discourse: An Interpretation of the Oeconomicus* (New York: Cornell University Press, 1970); *Xenophon's Socrates* (New York: Cornell University Press, 1972); *The Argument and the Action of Plato's Laws* (Chicago: University of Chicago Press, 1975); edited with Joseph Cropsey: *History of Political Philosophy*, 2d ed. (Chicago: University of Chicago Press, 1981); *Studies in Platonic Political Philosophy* (Chicago: University of Chicago Press, 1983).

Eric Voegelin: *The New Science of Politics* (Chicago: University of Chicago Press, 1952); *Order and History* (Baton Rouge: Louisiana State University Press, 1956–87, 5 vols.); Vol. 1: *Israel and Revolution,* 1956; Vol. 2: *The World of the Polis,* 1957; Vol. 3: *Plato and Aristotle,* 1957; Vol. 4: *The Ecumenic Age,* 1974; Vol. 5: *In Search of Order,* 1987; trans. by Gerhart Niemeyer: *Anamnesis* (Notre Dame, Ind.: University of Notre Dame Press, 1978).

Richard M. Weaver: *Ideas Have Consequences* (Chicago: University of Chicago Press, 1984); *The Ethics of Rhetoric* (Chicago: Henry Regnery, 1953); *Visions of Order: The Cultural Crisis of Our Time* (Baton Rouge: Louisiana State University Press, 1964); *Life Without Prejudice, and Other Essays* (Chicago: Henry Regnery, 1966); edited by George Core and M. E. Bradford: *The Southern Tradition at Bay* (New Rochelle, N.Y.: Arlington House, 1968); edited by Richard L. Johannesen, et al.: *Language is Sermonic* (Baton Rouge: Louisiana State University Press, 1985); edited by George M. Curtis III and James J. Thompson, Jr.: *The Southern Essays of Richard M. Weaver* (Indianapolis: Liberty Press, 1987).

George F. Will: *The Pursuit of Happiness and Other Sobering Thoughts* (New York: Harper & Row, 1979); *Statecraft as Soulcraft: What Government Does* (New York: Simon & Schuster, 1982); *The Pursuit of Virtue and Other Tory Notions* (New York: Touchstone Books, 1983); *The Morning After* (New York: The Free Press, 1986).

Further Reading

American conservatism is distinctive, conditioned of course by the special features of American history. But it is also continuous with the orthodox moral and political traditions of Western civilization, and serious students should therefore know something of that tradition. As a prolegomenon to readings in more recent conservative thought, one should read some Plato, particularly the *Republic,* and the best-known Socratic dialogues—*Euthyphro, The Apology of Socrates, Crito*—Aristotle's *Ethics* and *Politics,* Saint Augustine's *City of God,* Virgil's *Aeneid,* and the Old and New Testaments. Highly recommended seminal interpretations are Leo Strauss's *The City and Man* (Chicago: University of Chicago Press, 1964), the essays contained in Leo Strauss and Joseph Cropsey, eds., *History of Political Philosophy,* 2d ed. (Chicago: Rand McNally, 1964), and Eric Voegelin's *Order and History,* 5 vols. (Baton Rouge: Louisiana State University Press, 1956–1987).

Reading in modern political theory is indispensable if only to gain command over some of the terms of the modern controversy. Include Machiavelli's *The Prince* and *Discourses on Livy,* Hobbes's *Leviathan,* Locke's *Second Treatise* and *A Letter Concerning Toleration,* Burke's *Reflections,* Rousseau's *First and Second Discourses* and *Social Contract,* Mill's *On Liberty,* Nietzsche's *Beyond Good and Evil,* Newman's *Apologia Pro Vita Sua.*

A number of narrative histories are helpful, not only to describe the course of Western civilization but to remind us of the art of the statesmen who have shaped and defended it. See particularly the histories written by Thucydides, Macaulay, and Churchill. The latter's *Marlborough* remains probably the greatest political biography of the century. Paul Johnson's works, especially *Modern Times* (New York: Harper & Row, 1983), illustrate the continuing vitality of old-fashioned, capacious, humanizing history, as distinguished from the specialized, often trivialized, monographs of "scientific" historians.

Turning to America, a close acquaintance, please, with the Declaration of Independence, *The Federalist Papers,* and the Constitution. (They are readily available in many editions.) Max Farrand's *The Framing of the*

Constitution (New Haven: Yale University Press, 1913; rev. ed., 1962) remains a readable account of the Philadelphia Convention, but it should be supplemented by Forrest McDonald's splendid study, *Novus Ordo Seclorum: The Intellectual Origins of the Constitution* (Lawrence: University Press of Kansas, 1985). The past two decades have seen a renaissance of scholarship on the American Founding, including Bernard Bailyn's *The Ideological Origins of the American Revolution* (Cambridge, Mass.: Harvard University Press, 1967), Gordon Wood's *The Creation of the American Republic, 1776–1787* (New York: Norton, 1969), Harry V. Jaffa's *American Conservatism and the American Founding* (Durham, N.C.: Carolina Academic Press, 1978), and Walter Berns's *Taking the Constitution Seriously* (New York: Simon & Schuster, 1987). Willmoore Kendall's essays, collected in his *The Conservative Affirmation* (Chicago: Henry Regnery, 1963) and *Willmoore Kendall Contra Mundum* (New Rochelle: Arlington House, 1971), the latter edited by Nellie Kendall, make important contributions to our understanding of the American political and constitutional traditions. The original debate over the Constitution can be studied in Herbert J. Storing's *What the Anti-Federalists Were FOR* (Chicago: University of Chicago Press, 1981) and in the essays collected in Charles R. Kesler's *Saving the Revolution: The Federalist Papers and the American Founding* (New York: The Free Press, 1987).

Abraham Lincoln's political legacy, and the status of equality as a central conservative principle, are assailed in Willmoore Kendall and George W. Carey's *Basic Symbols of the American Political Tradition* (Baton Rouge: Louisiana State University Press, 1970) and M. E. Bradford's valuable *A Better Guide Than Reason* (La Salle, Ill.: Sherwood Sugden, 1979). Both Lincoln and equality are defended in Harry V. Jaffa's *Crisis of the House Divided* (Chicago: University of Chicago Press, 1982; orig. ed., 1959), a masterly analysis of the crucial issues at stake in the Lincoln-Douglas debates, and in his *How to Think About the American Revolution* (Durham, N.C.: Carolina Academic Press, 1978).

The student desiring to survey the general area of conservative thought since the Second World War was handicapped until recently by the fact that most comprehensive attempts to deal with the subject had been polemical. Clinton Rossiter's *Conservatism in America* (New York: Alfred A. Knopf, 1955; rev. ed., 1962) was mildly sympathetic, but a little evasive. Industrious attempts were made to discredit conservatives by linking them with the extremist fringes—present in any broad political movement. The specimen of this approach was *Danger on the Right* (New York: Random House, 1964) by Arnold Forster and Benjamin Epstein. At a more sophisticated level, *The New American Right* (New York: Criterion Books, 1955; revised and updated as *The Radical Right* [Garden City, N.Y.: Doubleday, 1963]), edited by Daniel Bell, sought to discredit the entire American Right through a process of sociologization: The Right is "losing status" and is therefore angry, etc., etc. Allen Guttmann in *The Conservative Tradition in America* (New York: Oxford University Press, 1967) tried to show that while it is thought that there was an important conservative tradition, in fact that tradition is nevertheless entirely liberal; but his view of the American political tradition is drawn entirely from liberal sources, *QED*.

Performing a variation on that theme, Garry Wills, in *Confessions of a Conservative* (New York: Doubleday, 1979), explains that there is an authentic, although unsung, conservative tradition in America, and he is It.

The lack of a conscientious, no-axes-to-grind history of modern conservatism has now been supplied by George H. Nash's *The Conservative Intellectual Movement in America Since 1945* (New York: Basic Books, 1976). This encyclopedic work profiles the leading thinkers of the traditionalist, libertarian, and neoconservative schools, and chronicles their sometimes wavering but finally successful efforts to form a powerful common front against the liberal doctrines prevailing in the academy and in government. William A. Rusher's *The Rise of the Right* (New York: William Morrow, 1984) provides a parallel account of political developments, including the Goldwater campaign and the ascendancy of Ronald Reagan, as seen by the long-time conservative activist and publisher of *National Review*.

For more comprehensive bibliographies of conservatism, consult Nash's book, Louis Filler's *Dictionary of American Conservatism* (New York: Philosophical Library, 1986), and Gregory Wolfe, *Right Minds: A Sourcebook of American Conservative Thought* (Washington, D.C.: Regnery/Gateway, 1987).

Thomas B. Silver carries the history of American conservatism back still further in *Coolidge and the Historians* (Durham, N.C.: Carolina Academic Press, 1982), exposing the distortions and prevarications that masquerade as scholarship in the books of leading liberal historians of the twenties and thirties. This revisionist account is an important first step in reconnecting modern American conservatism with its pre-New Deal roots in the Republican party of Calvin Coolidge and, ultimately, of Lincoln and the Founders. Hadley Arkes looks at contemporary social problems from the perspective of the natural rights principles shared by Coolidge, Lincoln, and the Founders in his astute and witty *First Things* (Princeton: Princeton University Press, 1986) and in *The Philosopher in the City* (Princeton: Princeton University Press, 1981). In the same spirit, Christopher Wolfe invokes the jurisprudence of John Marshall as a rebuke to modern-day judicial activism in his learned *The Rise of Modern Judicial Review: From Constitutional Interpretation to Judge-Made Law* (New York: Basic Books, 1986).

It frequently is said that modern conservatism was born as a response to the French Revolution and its doctrines. Those doctrines constituted—and still do—a profound challenge to the orthodox Western tradition. The student should therefore acquaint himself with the French Revolution and some of the analytical and controversial writing surrounding it. The very abundance of histories of the Revolution may constitute an impediment to knowledge—that abundance plus the ferocious, controversial nature of many of them. For a single responsible and readable history of the Revolution, try M. J. Sydenham's *The French Revolution* (New York: G. P. Putnam's Sons, 1965), or *Paris in the Terror* by Stanley Loomis (Philadelphia: Lippincott, 1964). Burke's *Reflections on the Revolution in France* and Joseph de Maistre's *Works,* edited by Jack Lively (New York: Macmillan, 1965), should be read as important contemporary responses to the Revolution.

Crane Brinton's *The Anatomy of Revolution,* rev. ed. (New York: Vintage Books, 1965) is a classic historical analysis of the structure of revolution. Brinton deals in detail with the French Revolution but shows how the pattern revealed there, and the evolution from reform through the use of force to the use of terror, is exhibited by other revolutions as well. *The Sociological Tradition* by Robert A. Nisbet (New York: Basic Books, 1967), is an important study of such nineteenth-century sociologists as Durkheim, Weber, and de Tocqueville, and has as its central theme the fact that these seminal writers were part of a conservative reaction to the events and doctrines of the French Revolution. In *The Origins of Totalitarian Democracy* (New York: Praeger, 1960), J. L. Talmon demonstrates that modern totalitarianism has its roots in doctrines central to the French Revolution. For the best writing on Burke's moral and political insights, one should consult Peter J. Stanlis' *Edmund Burke and the Natural Law* (Ann Arbor: University of Michigan Press, 1958), Harvey C. Mansfield, Jr.'s *Statesmanship and Party Government* (Chicago: University of Chicago Press, 1965), and two volumes by Francis Canavan, *The Political Reason of Edmund Burke* (Durham, N.C.: Duke University Press, 1960) and *Edmund Burke: Prescription and Providence* (Durham, N.C.: Carolina Academic Press, 1987).

Modern conservatism exhibits at least two main aspects, which are really responses to two challenges. One aspect, the traditionalist, as explained in the Introduction to this volume, arises out of the struggle to preserve traditional Western moral and social principles against the disintegrative assault of liberal doctrine and the disintegrative effect of certain modern social conditions. Both British and American writings have figured prominently here. G. K. Chesterton's *Orthodoxy* (Darby, Penn.: Darby Books, 1980), and C. S. Lewis' *The Abolition of Man* (New York: Macmillan, 1978) and *The Case for Christianity* (New York: Macmillan, 1943) are recommended as profound works in defense of orthodox Christianity. Christopher Dawson's *The Crisis of Western Education* (New York: Sheed & Ward, 1961), Christopher Derrick's *Escape from Scepticism*

(La Salle, Ill.: Sherwood Sugden, 1977), and T. S. Eliot's *Notes Toward the Definition of Culture* (New York: Harcourt Brace, 1949) explore the profound relationship that exists between Christianity and the historic ethos of Western civilization. Russell Kirk has assembled a sprightly collection of traditionalist writings in his *The Portable Conservative Reader* (New York: Penguin Books, 1982). Michael Novak pursues the tie between the Judeo-Christian tradition and economic and political freedom in *The Spirit of Democratic Capitalism* (New York: Simon & Schuster, 1982), as does Irving Kristol, with more attention to the contemporary decay of that relationship, in his *Reflections of a Neo-Conservative* (New York: Basic Books, 1983). Robert A. Nisbet's *Prejudices: A Philosophical Dictionary* (Cambridge, Mass.: Harvard University Press, 1982) is a free-wheeling critique of contemporary liberal pieties and social science dogmas, a collection of Burkean *aperçus* expressed in the style of Voltaire(!).

Not surprisingly, poets have exhibited a special awareness of the roots of meaning in our civilization, and some of them have been particularly effective in raising them into conscious awareness. T. S. Eliot's essays are generally to be recommended, especially his "Tradition and the Individual Talent" (*The Sacred Wood* [New York: Methuen, 1960]), and the essays on humanism in *Selected Essays,* rev. ed. (New York: Harcourt Brace, 1950). Other important poets have written out of analogous traditionalist impulses, for instance, Allen Tate's *Essays of Four Decades* (Chicago: Swallow Press, 1969) and John Crowe Ransom's *The World's Body* (Baton Rouge: Louisiana State University Press, 1968).

The novels of Saul Bellow, Walker Percy, and Peter De Vries exhibit similar insights, though in widely different modes and settings. Hugh Kenner connects literary modernism in all its forms and genres with no less a question than the continuing relevance of the Western experience to the future of the world. This distinguished critic, to whom T. S. Eliot once alluded as perhaps the finest of his generation, wields a style as sinuous and demanding as it is witty; and the student should acquaint himself with his works, particularly *A Homemade World: The American Modernist Writers* (New York: Alfred A. Knopf, 1975) and his magisterial *The Pound Era* (Berkeley: University of California Press, 1971). William F. Buckley, Jr.'s spy novels approach the future of the world from a different direction, chronicling the adventures of his hero Blackford Oakes against the changing background of the Cold War, and showing that political life has room for both moral certitudes and moral dilemmas. In fact, you cannot have one without the other.

In *We Hold These Truths* (New York: Sheed & Ward, 1960), John Courtney Murray provides a readable introduction to the importance of the natural law in the history of American culture and politics and concludes that a revival of this tradition is essential. The revival of serious interest in political philosophy in American academic and intellectual circles is largely due to the teaching and writing of Leo Strauss, whose characteristic approach was a close and critical reading of the original text. His *Natural Right and History* is a profound explication and defense of the tradition of the natural law against the nihilistic claims of positivism and historicism. *Political Philosophy: Six Essays by Leo Strauss* (Indianapolis: Bobbs Merrill, 1975), a collection assembled by his student Hilail Gildin, provides a convenient overview of Strauss's revival of ancient political philosophy and of his interpretation of modern thought. In an entirely different vein, but just as seriously concerned with political theory, is *The New Science of Politics* (Chicago: University of Chicago Press, 1952), in which Eric Voegelin traces the revolutionary and utopian impulses within Western history to the ancient heresy of gnosticism. Michael Oakeshott's *Rationalism in Politics* (New York: Basic Books, 1962) is still another vital commentary on modern political doctrines, closer to Burke and Hume, however, than to Plato and Aristotle.

The neo-conservatives have been for many years in the vanguard of the defense of Western traditions. Of central importance are the multifarious writings of Irving Kristol, especially *Two Cheers for Capitalism* (New York: Basic Books, 1978) and *Reflections of a Neo-Conservative.*

For an example of the neo-conservative approach to social problems, the reader cannot do better than to consult James Q. Wilson's *Thinking About Crime* (2nd edition, New York: Basic Books, 1983).

Midge Decter opposes the ideology of contemporary feminism in *The New Chastity and Other Arguments Against Women's Liberation* (New York: Coward, McCann, and Geoghegan, 1972); to which good cause George Gilder, although not a neo-conservative, contributes in his controversial *Men and Marriage* (Gretna, Louisiana: Pelican Publishers, 1986), which attacks feminism while celebrating womankind. Norman Podhoretz chronicles his own emergence as a neo-conservative in the fascinating *Breaking Ranks: A Political Memoir* (New York: Harper & Row, 1979).

A mention is in order on the unique presence of George Santayana, a writer and thinker not easy to situate, yet profoundly civilized and civilizing. His autobiographical *Persons and Places,* 3 vols. (New York: Charles Scribner's Sons, 1944), is a suitable introduction to this deeply traditional sensibility.

The above writers have been concerned mainly with the recovery and/or preservation of our central moral, religious, and cultural traditions. Others have been primarily concerned to resist the encroachments of the leviathan state on the freedoms of the individual. Much of this resistance has come from the work of economists. Henry Hazlitt has written probably the all-time best seller in the field, the primer, *Economics in One Lesson* (New Rochelle, N.Y.: Arlington House, 1979; orig. ed., 1946). Hazlitt's is the definitive modern short-form presentation of the classical arguments for classical economics, and no matter how abstruse economics can become, the *basic* points are, by the standard of any conservative—basic: basic to the maximization of individual leverage on economic arrangements. The point to remember is that flawless though it is, *Economics in One Lesson* suffers from the inadequacies of a single lesson in anything. Some reading is therefore required in the classics of economics—Adam Smith, David Ricardo, John Stuart Mill, W. Stanley Jevons, Alfred Marshall—as well as in more contemporary works.

Of these, special mention is due to Ludwig von Mises' *Human Action* (New Haven: Yale University Press, 1949) and *Socialism* (Indianapolis: Liberty Fund, 1981); Frank H. Knight's *Risk, Uncertainty, and Profit* (Chicago: University of Chicago Press, 1985); F. A. Hayek's *The Road to Serfdom* (Chicago: University of Chicago Press, 1944) and *The Constitution of Liberty* (Chicago: University of Chicago Press, 1960); Wilhelm Ropke's *A Humane Economy* (Chicago: Henry Regnery, 1960); Milton Friedman's *Capitalism and Freedom* (Chicago: University of Chicago Press, 1962) and *A Monetary History of the United States* (Princeton: Princeton University Press, 1963), the latter written with Anna Schwartz; James Buchanan and Gordon Tullock's *The Calculus of Consent* (Ann Arbor: University of Michigan Press, 1962); George Gilder's *Wealth and Poverty* (New York: Basic Books, 1981); and Richard Epstein's *Takings* (Cambridge: Harvard University Press, 1985). All of these works bridge the gap between economic theory and politics, though no two in quite the same way. As an exercise in pure libertarian political theory, Robert Nozick's *Anarchy, State, and Utopia* (Cambridge, Mass.: Harvard University Press, 1974) is by far the most influential work of the past decade. *The Capitalist Revolution* by Peter L. Berger (New York: Basic Books, 1986) is a stimulating, empirical examination of fifty propositions about prosperity, equality, and liberty that sum up roughly two centuries of economic and social history.

In *Suicide of the West* (Washington: Regnery Books, 1985; orig. ed., 1964), James Burnham examines deeply the conflict between Western civilization and communist doctrine backed by Soviet power, and he probes the crisis in Western morale which has caused the West, rather than the communist world, to emerge as the principal victim of the antagonism. No understanding of modern conservatism is possible without an appreciation of the profundity of the issues involved in this conflict.

For a strategic understanding of the problem, see Burnham's *The Struggle for the World* (New York: John Jay, 1947) and the fascinating, ominous *Kingdoms of the Blind* by Harold W. Rood (Durham, N.C.: Carolina Academic Press, 1980). Richard Pipes connects Soviet strategy with the ideological imperatives of the Soviet regime in *Survival Is Not Enough* (New York: Simon & Schuster, 1984). Part of the problem is that the West faces an opponent that rules an empire and has perforce learned to think as an imperial power, whereas the West has spent the better part of the twentieth century dismantling its empires and inveighing against the very idea of imperial rule. The results for the West—and more often than not for the newly emancipated colonies—have been awful, as Lewis Feuer argues in his revisionist *Imperialism and the Anti-Imperial Mind* (Buffalo: Prometheus Books, 1986). On the general principles of strategy, hardly anyone in recent years has written more cogently and copiously than Edward Luttwak; and the best introduction to his work is *The Grand Strategy of the Roman Empire* (Baltimore: Johns Hopkins University Press, 1976), a splendid example of imperial thinking.

"Know thy enemy" is an indispensable rule of strategy. Some knowledge of communist principles and of the history of the Soviet Union is therefore particularly essential. Robert C. Tucker has assembled the basic writings of Marx, Engels, and Lenin in two useful anthologies, *The Marx-Engels Reader,* 2d ed. (New York: Norton, 1978) and *The Lenin Anthology* (New York: Norton, 1975). The connection between Marxist theory and Stalinist reality is traced at length in Leszek Kolakowski's excellent three-volume *Main Currents of Marxism* (Oxford: Oxford University Press, 1978), and more succinctly in Thomas G. West and Sanderson Schaub, *Marx and the Gulag: Two Essays* (Claremont, Calif.: The Claremont Institute, 1987). Igor Shafarevich's *The Socialist Phenomenon* (New York: Harper & Row, 1980) examines socialism in theory and practice over the ages, linking the Soviet and Marxist cases to a perennial heresy.

To understand the Bolshevik Revolution it helps to know something of the history of Tsarist Russia, the best guide to which is Richard Pipes' *Russia Under the Old Regime* (Cambridge, Mass.: Harvard University Press, 1974). The most satisfactory history of the Revolution remains William Henry Chamberlain's two-volume work, *The Russian Revolution* (New York: Grosset, 1965); and Leonard Schapiro's *The Origins of the Communist Autocracy* (Cambridge, Mass.: Harvard University Press, 1977) covers Lenin's step-by-step consolidation of power. Stalin's purges are explored but not quite explained in Robert Conquest's *The Great Terror* (New York: Macmillan, 1968), and the same author has shed new light on the horrors of Stalin's policy of forced starvation in the Ukraine in *The Harvest of Sorrow: Soviet Collectivization and the Terror Famine* (New York: Oxford University Press, 1986). Of the many accounts of the structure and actual operation of the Soviet government, Merle Fainsod's *How Russia Is Ruled* (Cambridge, Mass.: Harvard University Press, 1963) is the most reliable, but you will have to look hard to find it, inasmuch as it has been supplanted by a new, posthumous edition edited by Jerry F. Hough. The new edition is tame stuff indeed, more or less a repudiation of Fainsod's totalitarian model of the Soviet government in favor of Hough's "interest group" model, as indicated by the new title: *How the Soviet Union Is Governed* (Cambridge: Harvard University Press, 1979).

There have been many deeply moving and illuminating expressions of the individual experience of Communism. From this vast literature, the following are especially recommended: *Speak Memory: An Autobiography Revisited* by Vladimir Nabokov (New York: G. P. Putnam's Sons, 1966); *The Captive Mind* by Czeslaw Milosz (New York: Alfred A. Knopf, 1953); *Doctor Zhivago* by Boris Pasternak (New York: Pantheon Books, 1958); *One Day in the Life of Ivan Denisovich* by Alexander Solzhenitsyn (New York: Praeger, 1963); *Homage to Catalonia* by George Orwell (San Diego: Harcourt Brace, 1969); *The Cypresses Believe in God* by Jose Maria Gironella (New York: Alfred A. Knopf, 1955); *Bread and Wine* by Ignazio Silone, rev. ed. (New York: Atheneum, 1978); *Witness* by Whittaker Chambers (Washington, D.C.: Regnery Books, 1952); *Darkness at Noon* by Arthur Koestler (New York: Bantam Books, 1970); *The Journals of Andre Gide* (New York: Alfred A. Knopf, 1956); *Ward 7* by Valeriy Tarsis (New York: E. P. Dutton, 1965); *Conversations with Stalin* by Milovan Djilas (New York: Harcourt Brace, 1962); *Against All Hope* by Armando Valladares (New York: Alfred A. Knopf, 1986).

The great work of Alexander Solzhenitsyn, *The Gulag Archipelago*, 3 volumes (New York: Harper & Row, 1974–75), is in a class by itself. It is a literary and historical achievement of the first magnitude, a testimony to the inability of even the most highly organized totalitarian regime in the world to crush the human soul.

Index

B&O
IN THE
CIVIL WAR

Illustrations by Lloyd C. Foltz

B & O
in the
CIVIL WAR

___

from the papers of
WM. PRESCOTT SMITH

___

edited by
William E. Bain
author of *Frisco Folks*

SAGE BOOKS
DENVER

Library of Congress Catalog Card Number: 65-25804

Sage Books are published by Alan Swallow

2679 South York Street, Denver 80210

DEDICATION

To my daughter, Betsy Ann, whose company I have shared in many a rail mile of fun trips and who is always as eager as her father to see what lies over the next hill beyond.

Acknowledgments

To the following people and their organizations I wish to express the most sincere thanks for making the puzzle of the life and death of Wm. Prescott Smith live again after some ninety-two years.

Through their time, courtesy, and effort the important role of the Baltimore & Ohio Railroad Company in the Civil War allows these unpublished, forgotten telegrams and messages to be published for all rail fans and those interested in the Civil War.

To Dr. Charles L. Newman, director of the Kent School of Social Work, University of Louisville, Louisville, Kentucky, who made the private collection of three unpublished volumes of "Papers of Wm. Prescott Smith" available to me both during my stay in Louisville and in the privacy of my home here in Kansas, I express extreme gratitude. Also my thanks to the University of Louisville Library for their loan of these papers.

Without the good help of the Library of the Association of American Railroads, Washington, D.C., and the aid of their librarian, Mr. Harry Eddy, this work could not have been completed.

Mr. L. J. McDougle, Assistant Manager of Educational & Group Relations Department, Association of American Railroads, gave his time and effort to answer my many letters to him in regard to Wm. Prescott Smith and spent much effort personally to get this material into a book.

The research done by Miss Peters of the staff of the Enoch Pratt Free Library under the direction of Mrs. Elizabeth C. Litsinger, Head of the Maryland Department of that library, made the life and record of Mr. Smith "spring" once again upon the public scene. These two ladies reviewed old copies of the Baltimore *Sun* and the Baltimore *American* to give me first-hand, eye-witness accounts of this man's important life.

The work and aid of Mrs. Bryce D. Jacobsen, Junior Archivist of the Hall of Records, Annapolis, Maryland, provided many leads for me to follow in further examination of this life and era.

My thanks, too, to Mr. William E. Pyne, Director of Public Relations of the Baltimore & Ohio Railroad Company, who also provided important leads to follow.

The color jacket and the Civil War era sketches were all created especially for this work by Mr. Lloyd C. Foltz, nationally known rail artist and lithographer. Mr. Foltz reviewed all of the messages to and from Wm. Prescott Smith and then after much research into small and large details of engines, cars and dress of the period, proceeded to do the illustrative work.

Mr. John Morris, N.R.H.S. member of Baltimore, Maryland, assisted by Mr. Robert C. Hasek and Richard E. Rose, sought out the grave of Wm. Prescott Smith and his family in Greenmount Cemetery and did the photos for these plates of the grave included in the book. Also to the credit of Mr. Morris goes the additional background research making the author familiar with landmarks today that have changed much since the era of Wm. Prescott Smith.

Typing of the manuscript was done by Mr. Eugene Edwin Nelms, a Wichitan very interested in things of the past. Without his aid this book would have never gotten into print, due to his many volunteer hours of hard work over his typewriter.

Mr. E. G. Hooper, Chairman of N.R.H.S., Inc. of Baltimore, Maryland, gave his valuable aid to the author in checking and advising additional research for the author in his quest for more information on Wm. Prescott Smith.

7

Mr. Robert H. Land, Acting Chief of General Reference & Bibliography Division of the Library of Congress, provided the author with much background on the life of Mr. Smith and his advice to follow leads to other important books and papers added greatly to this work.

Two volumes done by Wm. Prescott Smith himself were carefully reviewed by the author through the courtesy of the A.A.R.: a history and description of the Baltimore & Ohio Railroad, 1853, and the book of *Great Railway Celebrations of 1857* also by Wm. Prescott Smith. Also the book by Fesles Summers, *The Baltimore & Ohio in the Civil War* (1930), and Hungerford's two volumes, *The Story of the Baltimore & Ohio Railroad* (1928), were reviewed by the author during the construction of the work.

Mr. Harry Lee of Wichita, N.R.H.S. member, took many of the photos which were enlarged by Mr. Richard A. Wiley, also of Wichita, for the book.

The map and research for its information were done by N.R.H.S. member T. R. Grosvenor of Wichita.

The color photography was done for the dust jacket by Joachim H. Walther of Wichita, a local commercial photographer. My sincere appreciation to Mrs. Jeanette Adams of Wichita, who took time from her busy schedule to help me with additional typing of this manuscript.

To my wife Gracealee, who "put up" with the author as he delved into things 100 yrs. old in the quest of facts behind the scenes of Wm. Prescott Smith's life.

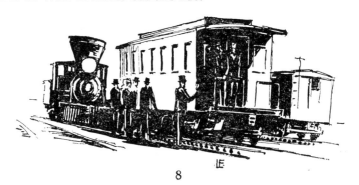

8

Table of Contents

Table of Illustrations

Introduction

Long overdue, the brilliant life and critical position held by one man during the Civil War days and expansion of rail travel and troop movements at last can be told.

This man was Wm. Prescott Smith, master of transportation on the B. & O. from 1860 to July 1, 1866.

This man wisely kept close check on the many hundreds of telegrams and messages crossing his desk, and fortunately in 1917 the old messages were given to the University of Louisville where they remained unpublished until now.

Many of these items will undoubtedly shed much more light on the life and times of that important era and especially on the pioneering of massive movements of men, horses, and supplies over the railroad to Union forces; all guided over the B. & O. by Wm. Prescott Smith.

Contained in the material saved by Mr. Smith are words of sadness, contempt, urgency, and enlightenment, for the "rail fan" and "civil war buff" today.

The life of Wm. Prescott Smith and his early untimely death are well recorded in the obituary notices in Baltimore papers on October 2, 1872, and are being included in this book as written, to keep with the facts of his life and work.

It has been said of this man that, like Abe Lincoln, he came from humble boyhood background, to hold one of the most important positions any man could serve his country from; and fate seemed determined that Wm. Prescott Smith should play out his role in one of the "hot beds" of civil conflict during the war between the states.

Wm. Prescott Smith was a personal friend of President Lincoln and made the journey many times from Baltimore to Washington to confer with Mr. Lincoln. When the President was going to Gettysburg for his immortal address, Wm. Smith prepared the planning to move Mr. Lincoln to and from that battlefield cemetery in safety. From enclosed messages we see that the President's life was in constant danger even as he rode by rail, as mines were placed along trackage hoping to kill or to capture him.

With the very infant American railroad, Wm. P. Smith caused and planned the move of thousands of men to the front lines without losing a single soldier killed in a train wreck or by an accident of careless railroad operation. It was his planning that proved for the nation, both north and south, that outcome of battles and military issues would hinge on ability to be rapidly mobile in troops and supply.

Wm. P. Smith had the best background possible for his important Civil War planning, having been associated with the B. & O. Railroad since 1850, when he joined that company as assistant to the master of transportation, being promoted to master of transportation in 1860, where he was in for a most difficult task ahead as the Civil War was about to begin. This was the ordeal that cost him his life very shortly, as pressures of his job became more and more severe.

Wm. Prescott Smith has been called the "good man Friday" of President J. W. Garrett of the B. & O. Actually he was much more than this, and only a failure of history to compile his works before this time under one cover shows now that his figure was indeed as important as that of the road president, and perhaps some will say more so; keeping always in mind that it was he who was really running the B. & O. Railroad and any failure on his part to do so would have resulted in his immediate discharge.

On July 1, 1866, he resigned from the B. & O. and was appointed a commissioner to examine the Pacific railroad by President Johnson, after which he was made collector of internal revenue of Maryland's Third District by President Johnson.

In May of 1867 he made a tour of Europe to try to regain his failing health. Returning to the United States, he resigned from government service and on July 1, 1868, he was appointed general manager of the New York & Washington Airline Rail Road. He remained on this job until he was unanimously recalled by the board of directors of the B. & O. Railroad Company on September 1, 1872, to again become master of transportation of that line. A few days later he was taken ill and was confined to his bed September 15, 1872, where he reached the end of life on October 1, 1872.

Wm. Prescott Smith left a wife, Margaret A. Smith, and three children, one of whom was already married. His wife was to live on until February 2, 1905, when she too followed her husband in death.

The family grave site today holds the bodies of Wm. Prescott Smith, his wife, Margaret, and a grandson, Wm. Prescott Smith II. The author has been able to locate only one name of the original three children; that one son of Wm. Prescott and Margaret Smith was J. Van Smith. J. Van Smith married Charlotte E. Smith, and the trail of the past disappears from view. Perhaps some living relative of Wm. Prescott and Margaret A. Smith will now come forward to aid in completing the family tree.

Records today show that Wm. Prescott Smith married Margaret A. Smith in Baltimore and was issued license No. 151 on December 3, 1846. His wife was the former Margaret A. Vansant, daughter of Hon. Joshua Vansant, Mayor of Baltimore, President of the Maryland Institute and Director of the Baltimore & Ohio Railroad.

Wm. Prescott Smith's widow was voted a sum of $5,000.00 of its 6% stock for her benefit, and friends in Baltimore began a subscription for a fitting monument to his memory. It was begun at a

13

public meeting with an anonymous subscription of $1,000.00 to which $165.00 more was added that one evening alone.

Wm. Prescott Smith was buried in Greenmount Cemetery, which today is fairly large and very old and is located a few blocks from Penn Station. Until November 3, 1963, streetcars passed close by. The Penn main line goes under the cemetery in twin tunnels.

Wm. Prescott Smith's friends commissioned Wm. H. Rinehart, 1825-1874, to make the monument for his grave. Rinehart made only a sketch but died before any further work was done. Later, in 1876, Frederick Volck of Munich, Germany, completed the memorial which is now located above Smith's grave. Certainly no better resting place could have been selected for this veteran leader of the American Rail Road, and today his statue stands, briefcase in hand, as though he is ready to step aboard the Washington City train for another visit with his friend, Mr. A. Lincoln. By our standards today his short 47 years of life were far shy of achieving the final success of being President of the B. & O., a goal that he undoubtedly was very much in line for.

At the time of his death Wm. Prescott Smith was president of the famous Wednesday Club of Baltimore, one of the first men's business groups to meet Wednesday noon hour over lunch, a type of group so very popular today.

He worked closely with President Thomas A. Scott of the Penn. Railroad and Col. David A. McCallum, Military Director of Railroads during the Civil War.

Included in his works we must observe Wm. Prescott Smith as an author. He published a *History and Description of the Baltimore & Ohio Rail Road in 1853*. Today this is a rare book. It contains 200 pages and was published by John Murphy & Co. of Baltimore. This work can be found today in the library of the A.A.R. in Washington; and it is one of the very best records of the earliest years of the B. & O., including much information on Charles Carroll of Carrollton, a signer of the Declaration of Independence and then later a charter member of the B. &. O. Railroad Company. Wm. Prescott Smith wrote *The Book of Great Railway Celebrations of 1857,* published in 1858 in New York by D. Appleton.

During the writing of this work, Wm. Prescott Smith records his own position as that of Asst. Master of Transportation appointed 1853.

This book deals with a grand tour in which Smith took part on the first rail tour of the "nation's greats" from New York to Saint Louis via Baltimore, Washington, and Cincinnati. This account is actually a form of "Golden Spike" observance east of the Mississippi River.

The old woodcuts of depots, trackage, and shops are from Wm. Prescott Smith's own book on the railway celebrations of 1857. These structures and locations of trackage changed little or none up to the time of the Civil War and the messages Mr. Smith saved for us today.

BALTIMORE AMERICAN
October 2, 1872

William Prescott Smith.
The record of a busy life.
A great railroad man.
From obscurity to fame.
A death to be lamented.

Wiilliam Prescott Smith, Esq. died last night at 45 minutes after seven o'clock at his residence on the corner of Parkin and Hollins streets. This will be sad news to the people of this city, and many throughout the United States will receive it with unfeigned regret. For several weeks he had been indisposed and at times confined to his house, but no serious result was apprehended. His ardent temperament and resistless energy led him to disregard those precautions which were advised, and his longing to realize the improvements which his fertile mind had suggested as necessary on the Baltimore and Ohio Railroad induced him too soon to resign the couch of sickness for the path of duty.

To this, perhaps, in a measure, his death was due. He was attacked by a violent hemorrahage of the bowels, and on Monday morning a painful rumor forced its way through all the avenues of the city to the effect that Mr. Smith was at the point of death.

The most skillful medical practitioners were consulted, and nothing left undone to save his life to the community. The hemorrhage was stayed at eight o'clock yesterday morning, but the utter prostration of his system gave but little encouragement to the thousands who were eagerly awaiting tidings of his condition.

Professor Nathan R. Smith a gentleman in whom Mr. Smith reposed the utmost confidence was summoned to his bedside yesterday morning as consultating physician.

Mr. Prescott Smith did not realized his danger until that moment, but at the sight of the Professor his countenance suddenly fell, he appeared to abandon all hope and gradually sank unto a lethargy from which he was released by death at the hour named above.

Mr. Smith's Life

Mr. Smith was born in Baltimore about 1822. His family were in humble circumstances, and he received merely a common school education. He was apprenticed to a trade, and served his time with credit to himself and profit to his employer. He evinced at an early age a taste for letters, and lost no opportunities for cultivation of it.

His passion for literature led to the establishment of numerous debating societies in which he was always the life and soul, and to which is probably due much of the varied learning and information he displayed in after years.

He was an enthusiastic Old Line Whig of the Henry Clay school, and during the exciting days of the "Hard Cider," and "Log Cabin", campaign though scarcely out of his teens, he fear-

16

lessly mounted the stump in advocacy of his principals and never ceased to regret the dissolution of the old Whig Party.

In 1846 Mr. Smith was married to the daughter of Honorable Joshua Vansant, the present Mayor of Baltimore, and through the influence of his father-in-law, who was then a Director of that road, he was created an assistant in 1850, to Mr. L. M. Cole, at that time General Superintendent of the Baltimore and Ohio Railroad.

Governor Swann was President of the road, and very soon discovered in Mr. Smith the talents which have since proved of so much benefit to the company.

Shortly after his appointment he was made Assistant Master of Transportation under Honorable John H. Done, and at his death in 1855 Mr. Smith was elected to succeed him.

He resigned his position in 1865 and accepted from President Johnson the office of Collector of Internal Revenue for the third District of Maryland.

In 1867 he visited Europe, and subsequently accepted the position of General Superintendent of the through Line between Washington and New York.

Recently he was recalled to the position of Master of Transportation on the Baltimore and Ohio Railroad with a salary nearly double that which he received when he formerly filled that office, and his sphere of usefulness greatly enlarged. He held this office at the time of his death.

William Prescott Smith was a wonderful man even in these days of remarkable phenomena. Whether we consider him as a scholar, a wit, a gentleman or a rail road magnate he was simply admirable. His early opportunities were few, but he made the best of them.

Perhaps no man in the community was better informed or had a happier faculty for imparting what he knew to others. For many years he was an indefallable correspondent and the old files of the Baltimore American give the clearest evidence of their indebtedness to his facile pen. His wit was inimitable not that which cuts like a knife but a gentle flow of humor which furnished as much amusement to those who were its object as to the spectators and listeners. As a mimic he was natural and could at his pleasure "set the table on a roof."

He was born a gentleman. Courtesy was ingrained with him, and needed not the promptings of set rules, to give it play. He loved his fellow creatures and instinctively appreciated their natures and their wants.

As a railroad man he had no superior on this continent, and his untimely death leaves it a matter of speculation to what position he would have arisen had his life been spared but a few years longer. To find the key to his success it is only necessary to bear in mind certain gifts which he possessed and combined in a greater degree than is usually accorded to any single individual.

A beautiful fancy, coupled with great and well digested information, a knowledge of human nature, its better and therefore weaker features, a courtesy which sprang from the native kindness of his disposition, and a faculty which he never abused for entwining himself around the hearts of those with whom he came in contact, were the materials with which he worked upon his fellow creatures.

These were the "open sesame," to every circle and through these he was enabled to bend to his purposes every one, from the President in his official state to the humblest laborer upon the railroad.

During the troubled times which attended the late civil war the services of Mr. Smith were invaluable.

The Baltimore and Ohio Railroad was in bad order at Washington and the Confederates in Virginia were constantly tearing up the track, blowing up the bridges, and spiriting away the rolling stock. Mr. Smith was ubiquetous. He softened the prejudices of the officials arranged the passage of the trains when it seemed an impossibility and at the same time preserved its connections, throughout the entire length with such accuracy as at no time to

18

suffer more than twenty-four hours delay whatever may have been the obstruction which the rude jars of war produced.

But it was as a member of the community that the loss of William Prescott Smith will be most keenly felt. He was an, "Admirable-Criehton" in the truest sense of the terms. The asthetic features of his character were always foremost. He liked letters, music, art, for their own sake, and he infused into all about him and around him some portion of his enthusiastic devotion.

Nor was his the love which contents itself with simple admiration. He was always ready to extend a helping hand to mend whenever he discovered it, and his infinite tact in assimilating people and characters of opposite dispositions would of itself have won for him a reputation.

Art, though in its infancy in this city is indebted to him for its, "swaddling clothes". Music by his efforts, has been exalted in Baltimore to the position of a science and a community of sentiment has been created amongst its lovers despite the disparity of their circumstances, which it is to be hoped will be coextensive with his memory. In his social relations he was as gentle as a woman and as courtly as a Bayard. The recollections of his delightful reunions will not soon die out of the minds of Baltimoreans, and their beneficent influence will be perpetual.

His worth is amply attested by the profound sorrow which has swept like a pall over all circles in the community at the announcement of his danger, and certainly the loss of no citizen will be more deeply deplored, nor the void made by his death more difficult to fill.

His Family

Mr. Smith leaves a wife and three children, one of them married, to mourn his loss. His whole souled generosity and lavish hospitality had prevented him from amassing a fortune, but it is understood that they are abundantly provided for by a large amount of insurance on his life.

Local Matters

Death of William Prescott Smith—Sketch of his life and career —Last illness, etc.

Mr. William Prescott Smith, master of transportation of the Baltimore and Ohio Railroad, whose dangerous illness was announced yesterday, died last evening at 7:55 o'clock. Mr. Smith was probably one of the most widely known citizens of Baltimore, and equally popular at home and abroad. He was only forty seven years and seven months of age, having been born on the 22nd of February, 1825, at Georgetown, D. C. removing at a very early age to Baltimore where he has remained ever since, always identified with the best interests of the city, and always one of its most progressive and active citizens.

In 1846 at the age of 21, he married the daughter of Honorable Joshua Vansant, and was soon after appointed to the custom-house under George P. Kane, the collector of this port.

Mr. Smith was at this time an active Whig, and an ardent admirer of Henry Clay, distinguishing himself on the rostrum as an eloquent speaker.

He was several times nominated for local offices by the party to which he belonged, and once ran for the city council in the ninth ward, but was of course defeated. About this time also he was prominent as one of the organizers and members of the Ringgold Light Infantry. He was a member of the original board of managers of the Maryland Institute, which started in 1847, under the presidency of Mr. Vansant. During the number of years he was identified with this institution, Mr. Smith imparted to its management all the energy, address, and tact for which he was noted, doing more to establish and spread its usefulness in the community, probably, than any other individual.

In his early career, Mr. Smith was at different times connected with the press, for which he had a strong predilection. In music and the arts he was a rare connoisseur, and though not a wealthy

20

man his dwelling was a treasury of art and articles of virtue, as well as the abode of hospitality. In 1850 he went into the service of the Baltimore and Ohio Railroad Company, and remained continuously in the employ of the company for sixteen years. He entered the service during the presidency of Honorable Thomas Swann as assistant to Mr. Lewis M. Cole, then master of transportation, now the general ticket agent.

At this time Mr. William Parker was general superintendent of the road.

Mr. Smith remained assistant master of transportation under Mr. John H. Done and Dr. Woodside until 1860, when he succeeded to the office of master of transportation. This important position he held all through the trying and critical period of the late war, developing extraordinary capacity for railroad matters which added to his remarkable social qualities, made him known everywhere in the country.

As the executive officer of one of the main arteries of travel upon which so much depended during the war, he passed through as terrible ordeal of sleepless nights and constant responsibility in the transportation of vast bodies of troops and immence stores of munitions of war without a single accident.

On the 1st of July, 1866, he resigned his post as the master of transportation of the railroad and was appointed by President Andrew Johnson as commissioner to examine the Pacific railroad, then in process of its construction as required, to determine the payment of the government bonds to that work, and soon after was made collector of internal revenue for the third district of Maryland by the President, his nomination being confirmed without opposition by the Senate, which position he held for about a year.

In the meantime in May, 1867, he went to Europe making an extended tour for the benefit of his health. On his return he resigned, and on the 1st of July, 1868, was appointed general manager of the New York and Washington air line. This position he held up to the 1st of September last when he was unanimonsly recalled by the board of directors of the Baltimore and Ohio Railroad Company to again become master of transportation of that road, in place of John L. Willson, the past master of road. Mr. Smith had therefore reoccupied his old post but a month when removed by death.

It is understood that he accepted his old place at the earnest solicitation of Mr. Garrett.

During his connection with the Washington and New York air-line, Mr. Smith was appointed commissioner from Maryland to the Philadelphia Centennial Exposition to be held on July 4, 1876 —an honorary appointment, which gave a great deal of satisfaction to his many friends in Philadelphia, as well as in Baltimore. Mr. Smith had not been in very good health for more than six months past, having during the early part of the summer experienced vertigo in Philadelphia, besides debility at various times during the trying summer through which we have passed.

He was not taken ill however until the 12th of September, and did not go to bed till three days afterwards when be began to suffer from neuralgia and rheumatism. He was confined to his room until Friday last when he became so much better that he rode out in a carriage, but on returning complained of chilliness.

On Saturday his condition became rapidly worse, the disease apparently changing and on Monday he had severe hemorrhages which though temporarily checked, left him utterly prostrated and unable to rally though everything was done that the best medical skill could suggest to restore the sufferor.

He remained conscious up to noon yesterday; his physicians however were not without hope until 3 o'clock P.M., when it became evident that he was dying, though he did not breathe his last until 7:55 P.M. During the latter years of his life Mr. Smith's continuous mental activity and travel had overtaxed both brain and body, producing torpidity of the liver and morbid blood diseases, which even the strongest vitality could not resist.

During the whole course of his illness he received the kind

22

attention of numerous friends, and at the critical period he was constantly watched by Mr. Walter Wilkinson.

During yesterday many telegrams were received from New York, Philadelphia, and Washington, from inquiring friends solicitous to learn the truth about Mr. Smith's condition. At night after his death, the flag at Camden Street Depot of the Baltimore and Ohio railroad was placed at half-mast in respect to the menory of the deceased.

The funeral will take place from his late residence, No. 2 Parkin street, at three o'clock P.M. tomorrow and the remains will be interred at Greenmount.

Mr. Smith leaves a widow and four children.

BALTIMORE AMERICAN
Wednesday, October 2, 1872

A Good Man Gone

In the very midst of a busy and useful life one of the most tireless workers of our day has been stricken by the hand of death. If it is true that the self-made man is the model American, then William Prescott Smith had earned the right to be taken as an exemplar for every one who would conquer the circumstances that surround his entry on the stage of the world, progress continually onward and upward from his starting point, and gather to himself honor and credit with the increase of his years.

The record of his days can be crowned with no prouder tribute than the simple truth that of his own bent and energy he won each of the promotions that he gained in life. The sphere in which manhood found him was too small for his fertile brain and industrious bent.

Taken into the service of one of the greatest railway corporations of the country at a time when it was struggling for existence and the fulfilment of the destiny which had been fashioned for it by its early founders he became by the force of his active mind and never flagging disposition to plan and work a necessary aid towards the consummation of its aims.

The history of the Baltimore and Ohio Railroad could not be truthfully written without doing honor to the administrative ability of the man who lies with his face upturned to the rising sun of this bright October morning.

His ordering of the vast forces of so mighty a corporation, the perfection of detail and the symmetry of a system of government of which he was the head, and the impress of his powerful will upon each of the subordinates who under him were entrusted with duties, the proper performance of which never failed of the reward of his kindly approval, are the best testimonials to his abilities.

In these days when great railroads enlist so much of executive skill it is no small thing to say of one of their chiefs that he was pre-eminent in the trust given to him.

Yet this is of Mr. Smith. The transportation of thousands of troops over the road during the war called all his abilities and energies into play, and how well he then discharged his duties is best attested by the close friendship established between himself and President Lincoln and Secretary Stanton, and which continued warm and unbroken until death severed the ties that were so close during life.

When placed in the position of managing that railway route over which thousands are transported daily, the line between the commerical and political centers of the country, the grand character of the man was no less prominent in making of it the perfection of highways for the travel of a nation.

Socially Mr. Smith was too near and dear to the hearts of many who will read these words to need a tribute from us. His kindly humor never failed, a pleasant word was never lacking from his lips, and the sunny geniality of his nature won him friends among all with whom he came in contact. He was sociable in the best and truest sense of the term.

Men instinctively opened their hearts to him, and women

leaned upon his arm with a pride in their prenz chevailler. He was as great in social as in business life, and from those who knew him in either capacity there will come today many an honest and earnest regret that a life so full of honor and so fair in promise has been ended. While the memories of his happy and prosperous existence crowd thickly beside his tomb, it may truly be said of him that he died—

"Like one who draws the drapery of his couch,
About him, and lies down to pleasant dreams."

PARTIAL LIST OF PERSONS MENTIONED

Barker, E. W.—
Blair, Montgomery—U. S. Postmaster General
Boehm, L. C.—Agent at Cumberland
Brown, J.—General Supervisor Trains on the Road
Cofran, L. R.—Agent at Parkersburg
Cole, L. M.—General Ticket Agent, Baltimore
Curtin, Andrew G.—Governor of Pennsylvania
Darby, Darius—Agent at Martinsburg
Dawson, James W.—Supervisor of Track
Diffey, Alexander—Supervisor of Trains East of Piedmont
Donohoo, J.—
Du Barry, J. N.—General Superintendent Northern Central Railway, Harrisburg
England, J. T.—Agent Camden Station
Fairbank, A. J.—Agent Mt. Clare
Felton, S. M.—President Philadelphia, Wilmington & Baltimore Railroad
Fessenden, W. P.—U. S. Secretary of the Treasury, July, 1864-Feb., 1865
Flowers, A.—Agent at Annapolis Junction
Ford, J. B.—Agent at Wheeling
Garrett, John W.—President Baltimore & Ohio R. R.
Gay, Sidney H.—Editor New York Tribune

Hardenbrook, Dr.—Correspondent New York Tribune
Harvey, C. W.—Agent at Sandy Hook
Heskett, Thomas—Supervisor of Bridges
Hicks, Thomas H.—Governor of Maryland, 1858-1862
Hillery, A.—
Hoblitzell, Oliver C. G.—Chief Clerk Transportation Office
Kelley, Gen. Benj. F.—Union Commander of Railroad District in
    Northwestern Virginia
Killdow,—Carpenter, Bridge Repair Work
King, John, Jr.—Auditor B. & O. R. R. Later President Winchester
    & Strasburg R. R.
Koontz, George S.—Agent at Washington, D. C.
Letcher, John—Governor of Virginia
Lewis, E.—Superintendent Pennsylvania Central R. R.
McAlister, Jas.—Assistant Supervisor Transportation
McCallum, Col. D. C.—Director of U. S. Military Railroads
McKean, J. D.—Operator at Locust Point
Mantz, F.—Agent at Monocacy
Murray—Operator at Grafton
Noyes, C. S.—Editor Washington Star
Perveil, C. W.—
Pierpont, Francis H.—Governor of West Virginia, 1861-1868
Porter, Wm. E.—Assistant Master of Road
Quincy, Walter C.—Assistant Master of Road
Quynn, J. T.—Agent at Frederick
Randall, L. E.—Agent at Piedmont
Riley, J. J. G.—Superintendent of Telegraph
Scott, Col. Thomas A.—Assistant Secretary of War, and Supt. of
    all U. S. Telegraph and Railroad Lines, 1861-1862. Vice
    President Penn. Railroad 1859-1874. President Pa. R. R.
    1874-1880.
Scott, Lt. Gen. Winfield—General in Chief U. S. Army until Nov.
    1, 1861
Seward, Wm. H.—U. S. Secretary of State, 1861-1869
Sharpe, Thomas R.—Special Agent Confederate States Army.

26

After close of War Master of Transportation of B. & O. Railroad.

Shock, W. A.—

Showacre, John W.—Dispatcher B. & O. R. R.

Shutt, A. P.—Passenger Train Conductor

Sinn, J. T.—

Smith, C. W.—Agent Harper's Ferry

Smith, J. R.—Supervisor of Machinery of Road

Smith, Wm. Prescott—Master of Transportation

Spurrier, John—Operator Plane #4

Stanton, Hon. Edwin M.—U. S. Secretary of War, 1862-1868

Stoddard, G. W.—

Sullivan, J. H.—General Western Agent B. & O. R. R.

Swinton, Wm.—Correspondent New York Times

Walling, H. J.—

Warner, E. R.—

Ways, C. E.—Telegraph Operator, Hagerstown

Welles, Gideon—U. S. Secretary of Navy, 1860-1869

Westbrook, C.—Superintendent Telegraph

Whiton, W. H.—

Williams, J. P.—Supervisor of Road

OUTLINE OF HISTORICAL EVENTS

The following memo of historical events to which the papers of William Prescott Smith have reference is extracted from *The Soldier in our Civil War*, edited by Paul F. Mottelay, and from the *Annual Reports* of the Baltimore & Ohio R. R. Co.

1861

April 18—Arsenal at Harper's Ferry burned and abandoned by Federal forces.

April 19—Riot in the streets of Baltimore over passage of the 6th Mass. State Militia and 26th Penn. Volunteers enroute to Washington. Connecting railroad bridges near Baltimore

27

destroyed. Troops were then sent by boat from Havre de Grace to Annapolis and thence to Washington.

May 5—Routes between Philadelphia, Harrisburg, and Washington, via Baltimore, were reestablished. Gen. Butler sent two regiments to occupy the Relay House.

May 13—Baltimore garrisoned by Federal troops under General Butler.

May 14—Seizure of a train of cars at Harper's Ferry.

June 2—Opequan Bridge destroyed and more than fifty loaded coal cars run into the chasm. These burned for two months with heat so intense that wheels and axles were melted.

Sept. 23-25—Engagements at Rommey, W. Va.

Sept. 24—Skirmish at Point of Rocks, Md.

Oct. 11—Skirmish at Harper's Ferry.

Oct. 16—Skirmish at Bolivar Heights.

Oct. 21—Operations on the Potomac near Lessburg, Va.

Oct. 22—Brig. Gen. Kelley assigned to command of the Department of Harper's Ferry and Cumberland.

1862

Jan. 4—Skirmishes at Great Cacapon Bridge and Sir John's Run, Capt. Hooker, Federal commander.

Jan. 5—Attack on Hancock. No trains running east of Green Spring. Great Cacapon trestling burned, also two houses adjacent belonging to the Company.

1863

April 26—Raid into western Maryland and Virginia by Jones' and Imboden's men. Stock train captured at Altamont, adjacent bridges and track destroyed. Attack upon guards at Cheat River Bridge was repulsed.

April 27—Machine shop, engine house and sand house at Newburg burned, and Raccoon Iron Bridge No. 2 blown up. Raiders passed through Kingwood and Morgantown.

April 28—Conferate forces arrived at Fairmont and, after capturing the guard at the Monongahela bridge, blew it up. This bridge consisted of three spans of 205 ft. each, and was the largest iron bridge upon the Road. Five other bridges of wood and iron were burned and the telegraph lines destroyed. The Confederate force, estimated at 6000, was under Gen. W. E. Jones.

May 1-4—Battle of Chancellorsville, Va.

May 1—Federal attack under Hooker stopped by Confederates under Lee.

May 2—At dawn Gen. "Stonewall" Jackson after a brilliant flank movement attacked Hooker in the rear and routed his troops. Gen. Jackson was accidentally wounded the night of May 2, dying from his wounds on May 10.

May 3—Gen. Hooker retreated across the Rappahannock at night.

May 15—Capture of a company of Federal Cavalry at Charles Town, recaptured by Federals the next day.

Nov. 19—Consecration of National Cemetery at Gettysburg, Pa.

The Messages

April 19, 1861
4:00 P.M.

S. M. Felton,
Philadelphia.

This day will be historical. It is evident that whatever our Authorities may want in Maryland or at Washington, the people of this state will fight to prevent any Northern troops passing through. I never risked my own life so sadly before. The first regiment got off with greatest difficulty, our street tracks were obstructed in every form, and also for five miles out of town, through all which the troops had literally to fight their way.

We could not return our teams for your second train, and its troops while remaining at President Street were attacked violently while in cars there—the greater part of police being yet on western border of town with Boston regiment.

Some of troops hurt with stones and other missiles, and as they fired on the crowd repeatedly at different points, from five to ten Citizens of Baltimore are killed and many others wounded.

We consulted the Authorities, and Governor Hicks and Mayor Brown jointly advised that troops at your station be returned northward beyond borders of Maryland. They also telegraphed Mr. Lincoln to let no more troops come through our state as excitement was fearful, and uncontrollable unless cause was thus removed. Our local military are called out and martial law is about being proclaimed. A general town meeting being held in

Monument Square. In this state of things, we cannot undertake to carry any more Northern troops over any part of our road.

W. P. Smith

Private

April 19 - 1861
6 P.M.

J. H. Sullivan,
Bellaire
J. B. Ford,
Wheeling
Today will be marked in history for events at Harper's Ferry and here. A perfect revolution seems raging over both Maryland and Virginia. Northern troops driven back from Baltimore in large numbers. We can take no more troops even to Washington.

W. P. Smith

By B. & O. R.R. Telegraph
Wheeling, April 20, 1861
Rec'd 10:00 A.M.

W. P. Smith,
The following has just been put in circulation in Wheeling. It looks like a special design upon our Road—viz:—

"Narrative of the Special Reporter of the Philadelphia Inquirer. The Special Reporter of the Philadelphia Inquirer has just reached here from Washington by Harper's Ferry and has telegraphed the following information to Washington and the principal cities. He also states that when he left Washington orders had been given for the stoppage of all mails over the B. & O. Railroad as they had refused to allow the Federal Government the use of the road for carrying troops and had tendered it to Virginia and Maryland. The most intense excitement exists in Washington.

The wires are so obstructed that no reliable information can be received from the South or Harper's Ferry.

(Signed) Ed. Inteligencer

The Reporter's Statement

Left Washington at 2:46 P.M. Friday afternoon. On reaching Junction of B. & O. Rd. we there learned of the riot at Baltimore and from passengers who had seen it learned that the United States Volunteers had been attacked by a mob and returned fire. The report of killed varied from 6 to 13 citizens and 4 to 7 volunteers. A perfect panic was reigning. Maryland troops were ordered out, the firemen are ringing the bells and the Railroad Company refused to carry the troops and turned them back. About 800 had got through before the riot. Those will get through to Washington and make the force there five thousand. The balance, said to be about four thousand, are retained north of Baltimore.

Left Junction of B. &. O. R.R. at 4 P.M. on Friday. Train cars full. Along the route I found business stopped. All was excitement at Ijamsville. There was a crowd around the flag pole with the American flag. Cheering at Point of Rocks for the Confederate flag. On reaching the bridge at Harper's Ferry the train was stopped by Virginia soldiers with loaded cannon planted in front of the cars. On the conductor assuring them that no United States Agents or soldiers were on board or any reporters, the train was allowed to cross the bridge there. We were again stopped by loaded cannon pointed obliquely at the cars so they could demolish the whole train, with men at the touch-holes ready to fire. As soon as the train stopped the soldiers rushed to the sides of the cars and commenced to search them. The conductor was told to ask no questions, that orders had been given to allow no one to land, and men with drawn swords and loaded muskets asked what is the news from Baltimore. A member of the Richmond Convention stepped on the platform and shouted "Go on, boys, first blood for Baltimore. The United States troops have fired into an unarmed crowd of citizens and killed thirteen of them. Four soldiers were killed, and every man in Baltimore was now going to stand by his state and shed his last drop of blood sooner than have abolition hordes come down there to murder them." The mob cheered him and the conductor finding nothing could be done told them the road would carry none but Southern men and started the train. Men followed the train with swords as long as they could keep up, to prevent any one getting off.

On the armory flag staff floats the Virginia flag and over the remains of the arsenal a piece of the U. S. flag. About 3000 men are in and about the arsenal, mostly armed and equipped. The arsenal and a part of the factory are burned to the ground. Several volunteers had got on the train. I asked one what all this means. He said he had orders not to tell. On going into another car and talking secession I found from them that the news that Virginia had seceded reached them Tuesday and that Letcher had ordered the arsenal to be seized as the property of the State. Men were mustering and on Thursday night the United States Artillery Company set the arsenal on fire and fled for Carlisle. The citizens rallied and put out the fire, but not until the arms were all burnt. Then a party had started after them to capture them.

The wildest excitement rages there. Troops are pouring in from all parts of the surrounding country and are told that Gen. Scott had resigned and would head the Southern army at Alexandria, where they would start for today. The panic is so great that it is crushing out the Union men, who are charged with being traitors to their state. At Martinsburg we stopped for supper. Here there was a great crowd, a repetition of the speech the member of the Virginia Convention (Armstrong) had made at Harper's Ferry and assurance given that the railroad would carry none but Virginia and Maryland men. A number of Union men are here, but will soon be gagged.

A Lieutenant of the Hedgesville Blues and ten men got on the cars here and came to North Mountain saying they would not fight against the United States flag till Maryland seceded. At Cumberland cheers were given by a crowd for the Union and groans for the traitors. At Wheeling orders were received from Governor Letcher to seize the custom house, but Wheeling is strong for the Union and last night it was guarded by the Mayor for the United States. The citizens in Wheeling are in great excitement for the news and the announcement that the mail will be stopped on the Baltimore & Ohio Rail-road."

The above is copy of extra issued by the Inteligencer.

J. B. Ford

Baltimore, May 14, 1861
Midnight

General Shriver,
Frederick.

No relief can reach you tonight. Hold the bridge if possible, and send word if attacked. If possible I will relieve you in force.

B. F. Butler,
Brig. General Commanding.

Baltimore, May 15, 1861
12:30 A.M.

Lieut. General Scott,
General in Chief U. S. Army,
War Department, Washington.

I have just received the following telegram:—

Frederick, May 14, 11:10 P.M.

Danger is apprehended at the Monocacy Bridge tonight. An engine and cars east was seized at Harper's Ferry at 2 o'clock today. All connections west are cut off since 8 o'clock tonight. We are guarding the wires as far as our forces enable us. Please send us immediate relief. Answer quick as possible by telegraph.

Edward Shriver,
Brigadier General.

What instructions have I upon this point which is not within my department? Please answer immediately. Ross Winans is now in Annapolis under arrest.

B. F. Butler,
Brigadier General Commanding.

June 2, 1861

Hon. M. Blair,
 Post Master General, or
Hon. Mr. McLellan,
 2nd Asst. P.M. General,
 Washington.

I have to advise you that the Southern forces at Harper's Ferry took the Mail matter from our Mail train, bound east from Wheeling for Baltimore, during the night. This is the first instance, as far as my reports advise, wherein the Mail has been disturbed at any point on our lines, and I hasten to inform the Department of it, as a matter of duty. The quantity thus seized was very small, being but some six to ten bags from local points, and doubtless of little relative importance.

Another bridge upon our line was destroyed at nine o'clock this morning, near Martinsburg, but as four of those previously destroyed have been restored already, and as we are determined to continue working the road to fullest extent wherever it is all safe to do so, we hope the Department will understand that we are not disposed to suspend our operations for any cause whatever that we can possibly control. The road is now entirely clear again between Cumberland and Wheeling and Parkersburg, and the local Mail service there fully resumed.

W. P. Smith

June 6, 1861

T. A. Scott,
 Washington

I find it necessary to report the improper conduct of four privates of the 71st New York Regiment named T. J. Duncan, James Board, Thomas H. Grant and John Hewlett. They came from Washington on our 7:10 train this morning, without a ticket or pass of any kind authorizing us to take them, and they positively refused to pay fare. They also refused to get out of train, and threatened the life of Conductor if he attempted putting them off. We have had considerable trouble of this kind, our Conductors inform me, and several cases especially with the men of the 71st. What do you advise under such circumstances? You know the tendency of such conduct towards deranging our operations in every way.

W. P. Smith

Copy.

(Pencil notation says:—
Rec'd Oct. 4, 12 noon,
Mailed Grafton, Oct. 2nd)
Head Quarters District of Grafton
Grafton, Va., Sept. 29, 1861

Wm. P. Smith, Esq.
    My Dear Sir:
        Yours of a recent date was received whilst I was on my back from effects of a surgical operation. I am happy to inform you, however, that I am now rapidly recovering my usual health and strength, and hope in a few weeks to "be as good as new".
        In regard to the change of time of running trains so as to avoid night travel on the east or Cumberland end of the road, I fully concur with you in the policy; in fact, I consider it as a necessity.
        I am constrained to say to you frankly, that in my judgment the property of the B. & O. R.R. and the road itself, has never been in greater danger than it is at this time,—that is, between Piedmont and Cumberland. My information is, that a large Rebel

36

force is concentrating at or near Romney,—say four or five regiments. What their object is, we are left to conjecture; but my own judgment is, that it is to destroy the B. &. O. R.R. and thereby prevent us from transporting troops and munitions of war. My force is now small at New Creek and Camp Pendleton,—only one regiment at each place, and but very few men to reinforce either place,—General Rosecrans and General Reynolds having withdrawn all of the available troops from my district, leaving me only sufficient force to guard the bridges. I cannot, therefore, strengthen my position at New Creek, without endangering our communication between Grafton and the Ohio River, which of necessity must be kept intact, or our army in the mountains must retreat for want of food.

I have requested Gov. Pierpoint to telegraph Gov. Curtin for two regiments, to be sent to Cumberland by way of Bedford or Hagerstown. I have also telegraphed Col. Bruce of Cumberland to dispatch a messenger to Gov. Curtin for aid. I wish you would go yourself and see him, and show him the necessity of protecting loyal Western Maryland from the Rebels. I understand there are several regiments now in camp in Pennsylvania and ready to march. With two regiments at Cumberland, I think we would be perfectly safe, and our communication over the B. & O. R.R. kept open and unmolested.

Shall be glad to hear from you
I am, Sir, your most obd't servant,
B. F. Kelley,
Brig. General.

RESOLUTIONS OF BOARD OF DIRECTORS
JANUARY, 1862

WHEREAS, upwards of 650,000 soldiers of the Armies of the United States have been transported over the Baltimore and Ohio Road and its Branches since the commencement of the War, without killing or seriously injuring a single soldier confided to the Care of the Company; and Whereas, the immense supplies and munitions required under sudden and pressing exigencies have been forwarded with remarkable promptness, success and reliability, thus deserving and attracting the commendation and marked approval of all the leading Military and other Officers connected with the Government who have operated and are operating within the 520 miles of territory embraced by the lines of the Road and its Branches; and Wheras, the good faith, energy and loyalty of the Officers and employees of the Company have been signally tested and manifested in the accomplishment of these great results, whilst in many instances surrounded by circumstances of grave peril and unprecendented difficulty.

THEREFORE, RESOLVED, that the faithful and effective action of the Officers and Employees of the Company entitle them to the highest confidence and regard of the Board.

RESOLVED, that the appreciation by the Government of the great services of the Company and the vital importance of the road to the interests of the whole country exhibited by its present vigorous and decisive action on re-opening the Line is viewed by the Board with profound interest and gratification and that it hails a re-construction of the bridges at Great Cacapon River, Sleepy Creek, Cherry Run and Back Creed and the recent opening of the Road to the latter point combined with the protection proposed for the entire line as the precursor of the early restoration of the full use of the Baltimore and Ohio Road for the maintenance and promotion of all the vast interests connected with the route.

RESOLVED, that the display of the American Flag as heretofore at prominent stations of the Company, be approved and that as the Company regains possession of its Road the National Flag shall be displayed at its principal Stations and shall so continue until otherwise ordered by the Board.

Head Quarters R. R. District
Cumberland, June 11, 1862

Sir:

I have the honor to forward herewith General Order No. 4 from these Headquarters relating to oath of allegiance to be taken by the Agents and Employees of the B. & O. and N.W. Va. Rail Roads serving within the limits of this military District. The General Commanding has given the matter careful consideration and believes that such an order is proper and advisable. He hopes that those to whom the order relates will promptly comply with its provisions.

By order Brigadier General Kelley,
I am very respectfully
Your Obedient Servant,
Thayer Melvin,
A.A.A. Genl.

W. P. Smith, Esq.,
Master of Transportation,
Baltimore & Ohio R.R.,
Baltimore, Md.

OATH OF ALLEGIANCE

I, the undersigned   of   County, State of   do hereby solemnly swear before Almighty God, that I will bear true allegiance to the United States of America, and support its Constitution; that I will at no time and in no wise aid or abet, by counsel or act, directly or indirectly, any of the enemies of said Government; but that I will at all times conduct myself as a peaceful, loyal and obedient subject of the same, and faithfully discharge my duties as its lawabiding citizen; all of which I swear of my free will and accord; so help me God. Subscribed and sworn to, on this   day of   1862, at   before me.

In the event of any of the parties herein mentioned failing or refusing to comply with the conditions of this order within a reasonable time, the parties so failing or refusing will cease to be employed by any or either of the said Companies within the boundaries of this Military District.

By order Brigadier General Kelley.

Thayer Melvin, A.A.A.G.

Unsigned memorandum

Dated: May 1, 1863.

The train that has gone was to take three companies of 14th Mass. Artillery (or Infantry) to Martinsburg, and to take from Martinsburg west the 12th Regiment Penn. Cavalry—say 500.

Another train must take the 14th Regt. Pa. Cavalry (say 500) from Harper's Ferry west, and take also 580 men of 14th New Jersey Infantry to Martinsburg.

Mem: If the three companies Mass. troops did not go to Martinsburg in train today they must go in train tonight.

May 1, 1863
11:20 A.M.

C. Smith,
Harper's Ferry

A regiment of cavalry (800 horses and 800 men) are to go from the Ferry to Grafton, besides another of 500 from Martinsburg. Mr. Fairban has sent cars enough for nearly all the men both places, and 35 cars for horses from Mt. Clare. You must get cars from Weverton or Plane No. 1 for the balance of the horses. Give this earliest attention.

W. P. Smith

May 1, 1863
11:51 A.M.

D. Darby
Martinsburg

A regiment of 500 cavalry (horses and men) are to go at

40

once from Martinsburg to Grafton. 35 cars for horses, and troop and passenger cars for men have left Mount Clare for Harper's Ferry and Martinsburg. A regiment of 800 horses and men goes from Ferry, besides your 500. The remainder of the stock cars will have to be got from Sandy Hook and Plane No. 1. Give thorough attention to this. Let me know when cavalry will be ready at both places.

W. P. Smith

By B. & O. R.R. Telegraph
New Creek, May 1, 1863
Received: 11:54 A.M.

W. P. Smith

Send cars to Harper's Ferry to move 14th Pennsylvania Cavalry to Grafton. I presume they will not have over 500 men and horses.

B. F. Kelley
B. G.

May 1, 1863
12:15 Noon

C. Smith

Harper's Ferry

L. I. Kelley telegraphs that the 14th Penn. cavalry will start from Ferry, not over 500 men and horses. How is this? Gen. Schenck said the regiment at Ferry was about 800, and that at Martinsburg 500. Be careful not to take all the cars that go up for your regiment but *send to Martinsburg promptly enough for the men and horses there.* Use house cars for men, if you have not enough with seats.

W. P. Smith

By B. & O. R.R. Telegraph
Harper's Ferry, May 1, 1863
Rec'd:—3:48 P.M.

W. P. Smith

There will be 700 horses in the 14th Pa. Regiment. The 35 stock cars from Baltimore with those at Weverton not reach more than about 40 cars suitable for stock. The 700 horses here will require about 56 cars, consequently there will not be enough for this place and no stock cars for Martinsburg. Answer to Sandy Hook.

C. Smith

(Pencil notation: Have ordered.)

By B. & O. R.R. Telegraph
Willard's Hotel, May 1, 1863
Rec'd: 5:07 P.M.

W. P. Smith

How much will you charge the New York Times for use of locomotive to New York tomorrow? Reply immediately.

Samuel Wilkinson.

May 1, 1863
5:10 P.M.

C. Smith,
Harper's Ferry

At what time will the regiment be ready? The 500 for Martinsburg will be there at 5:30 P.M. If your regiment is not ready, send cars for 500 to Martinsburg at once without fail. You will have to have second floors or plank put in to house cars to make up the requisite number. This must be done at once.

W. P. Smith

May 1, 1863
5:15 P.M.

F. Mantz,
 Monocacy
 At least 40 more stock cars for horses will be wanted at Ferry and Martinsburg at once. Can you raise them at Plane No. 1? If not, send house cars to have second floors put in them.

W. P. Smith

May 1, 1863
5:15 P.M.

Spurrier,
 Plane No. 4
 You must go over to No. 1 at once, and get every car there fit for horses, and take to Harper's Ferry. Also all the empty house cars. Please be quick.

W. P. Smith

May 1, 1863
5:20 P.M.

C. Smith,
 Harper's Ferry
 General Schenck says three companies of infantry are to go from Ferry at once to Martinsburg, to march to Winchester. You can send them up in the cars that go to Martinsburg for the cavalrymen.

W. P. Smith

By B. & O. R.R. Telegraph
Monocacy, May 1, 1863
Rec'd: 6:12 P.M.

W. P. Smith,

43

There is no stock cars at Plane No. 1. What was there was moved to Baltimore last P.M. No empty house cars on road west of Baltimore except what few is at Sandy Hook. I think I understood Mr. Harvey to say today there was some 20 empty cars at Hook.

F. Mantz

May 1, 1863
6:45 P.M.

J. H. Sullivan
J. B. Ford
　　Wheeling
　　Your dispatch about troops wanted from Pennsylvania received 2 P.M. Friday. Our advices since noon represent enemy at Bridgeport, same force believed to have been at Fairmont. Large forces are moving quite near from our side, which must have effect of driving them entirely off the line. Further arrangements are also made of a peculiar character for this. Porter was at

Fairmont at noon. Main stem believed to be clear. Telegraph repair going on from Grafton to Wheeling effectively.

W. P. Smith

May 1, 1863
6:50 P.M.

W. Crawford,
President St.
W. Stearns,
Wilmington
We want to borrow 30 cars fit for horses for special government movement promptly. Can't you let us have them, and by what hour?

W. P. Smith

May 1, 1863
7:10 P.M.

A. J. Fairbank:
Can you raise any more cars from Washington, P.W. & B. Road or Locust Point fit for horses? We want say 40 more. How many empty house cars can you raise about Mt. Clare all told? We may have to plank the floors of some to take horses.

W. P. Smith

By B. & O. R.R. Telegraph
May 1, 1863, 8 P.M.

C. Smith
and
C. W. Harvey,
Harper's Ferry.
How many cars fit for horses will you have after sending the 33 to Martinsburg for the first 500 cavalry there? How many

empty house cars can you raise in all besides those for horses and troops?

Answer fully. This is most important.

W. P. Smith

May 1, 1863
8:12 P.M.

A. J. Fairbank,
Mt. Clare:
Send Hoppers and Gondolas west in A.M. as fully as possible

W. P. Smith

May 1, 1863
8:15 P.M.

L. C. Boehm, Cumberland
L. E. Randall, Piedmont
Large number Hoppers and Gondolas go west in A.M. Urge miners to load with promptness and fully. Don't let the cars be idle. As other business is light, we can do very large coal trade.

W. P. Smith,
per H.

By B. & O. R.R. Telegraph
May 1, 1863, 8:40 P.M.

C. Smith,
and
C. W. Harvey,
Harper's Ferry or Sandy Hook:
Have the cars for 500 horses and 500 men gone to Martinsburg as ordered, and did they take up the three companies 14th Mass. with them? The 14th New Jersey Infantry is to go from

Ferry to Martinsburg in same cars, 500 men, if the trains have not yet gone.

The 500 men and horses from Ferry are to go in A.M., when we hope to have cars enough for them from Baltimore. Do you understand all this? Don't send over 33 cars to Martinsburg for the 500 horses there and 14 for the 500 men, all to go west.

Answer fully.

W. P. Smith

By B. & O. R.R. Telegraph
May 1, 1863, 8:50 P.M.

A. J. Fairbank,
   Mt. Clare:

Get out a first class engine for Harper's Ferry at once. I am on may way up to see you at your office at once.

W. P. Smith

By B. & O. R.R. Telegraph
Mt. Clare, May 1, 1863
Received: 8:58 P.M.

W. P. Smith:

We have two B. & O. House, no Horse Cars. There are now in the Yard 12 P.W.& B. House Cars and 2 P.W.& B. Stock Cars. I doubt whether it would be safe to load horses in any of the House Cars now here.

A. P. Fairbank

By B. & O. R.R. Telegraph
Harper's Ferry, May 1, 1863
Received: 9:15 P.M.

W. P. Smith:

Commanding officers here demand transportation for the

47

14th Cavalry Regiment, 700 men and horses, which takes all the Stock Cars we can get hold of, even by using all the House Cars with heavy bottoms. We have 10 Passenger and Troop Cars left to send to Martinsburg. None of the trains have gone west yet. No application has been made here for transportation for the 3 Companies of the 14th Mass. nor 14th New Jersey Infantry. The 14th Penn. Cavalry now loading.

C. Smith

By B. & O. R.R. Telegraph
May 1, 1863, - 9:30 P. M.

C. Smith,
Harper's Ferry:

Why have you not obeyed my order at six P. M.* to send cars to Martinsburg for the 500 cavalry there first. It is by General Schneck's command. Send 30 cars for the 500 horses and the cars for men at once, getting the three companies 14th Mass. to go in the troop cars.

Answer quick, sending message for Mt. Clare.

W. P. Smith

* (Penciled note interpolated:
"12 M. and before")

By B. & O. R.R. Telegraph
Martinsburg, May 1, 1863
Received: 9:45 P.M.

W. P. Smith:

We have not cars sufficient to load more than 100 horses. They have 364 horses and men. They will use all the stock cars they have at Sandy Hook. We will have to get cars from Cumberland or Baltimore tonight. We will want fifteen (15) from Baltimore tonight if possible.

D. Darby

By B. & O. R.R. Telegraph
Harper's Ferry, May 1, 1863
Received: 9:50 P.M.

W. P. Smith:

The best that can be done under present circumstances will be to let cavalry at Martinsburg wait until cars arrive from Baltimore in A.M. for horses.

C. Smith

By B. & O. R.R. Telegraph
May 1, 1863, 10 P.M.

C. Smith, Harper's Ferry
D. Darby, Martinsburg

I have ordered the train of fourteen large Horse Cars to go from Baltimore to Martinsburg direct instead of Ferry. The 3 Companies of 14th Mass. will not go to M. from Ferry, but the New Jersey Regiment will go.

W. P. Smith

By B. & O. R.R. Telegraph
May 1, 1863, 10:50 P.M.

C. Smith,
Harper's Ferry

Do you now not understand that the three companies of 14th Mass. do not go, but the 14th New Jersey Infantry, 580 about, do go to Martinsburg. As the run is so short they can go in any kind of cars you have, after getting off the Cavalry.

When will Cavalry go? Have you all the cars and engines needed? They go to Grafton. Notify all parties west by telegraph of your starting.

W. P. Smith

By B. & O. R.R. Telegraph

May 1, 1863, 10:55 P.M.

D. Darby,
    Martinsburg
    Get Cavalry off in A. M. as soon after cars from Baltimore arrive as possible. They go to Grafton. Notify all agents by telegraph west of you of starting.

W. P. Smith

By B. & O. R.R. Telegraph
Grafton, May 1, 1863
Received: 11 P.M.

J. L. Wilson,
    The Rebels have gone south of the Parkersburg Road, burning as they went the 18th trestle work, one 25 ft. span west of Bridgeport and the bridge which R. Gary was rebuilding for Col. Wilkinson. Also burned 2 Gondolas, 1 flat car and the bridge car with all the tools. Mr. Gary and all his men was captured and taken south except one man.
    Killdow reports that the bridge guards were all drunk.

W. E. Porter.

Master of Transportation's Office
Baltimore and Ohio Railroad Co.
Baltimore, May 1, 1863, 11 P.M.

Major Genl. Schenck:
    We have cars at Harper's Ferry for 700 men and 700 horses to be taken to Grafton and have arranged also to take the New Jersey Regiment to Martinsburg when it offers. The 700 Cavalry at Ferry are now loading as I understand and ought to be ready to start during the night.
    At Martinsburg we will have by 7 A.M. the cars for the 500 other horses and men for Grafton.

50

Very respectfully your
obdt. servt.
W. P. Smith,
M. of T.

By B. & O. R.R. Telegraph
Sandy Hook, May 2, 1863
Received: 3:30 A.M.

W. P. Smith:
    1st   engine with Cavalry Reg't left 9:40
    2nd engine with   "   " left 12:30
    3rd engine with   "   " left 1:40
and engine 48 with N. Jersey Infy. left Ferry 2:15
Engine 97 left Hook 2:25 with about 17 empty stock and 2 passenger cars for Martinsburg.
    14th Pa. Cav. fell short of first order about 200 horses and men. They were not quite 500 strong, though they first demanded transportation for 700 horses and men. [*]
                               C. Smith
[*] Penciled note:
    This demand is what deranged the plans.

May 1, 1863
7:10 P.M.

A. J. Fairbank:
    Can you raise any more cars from Washington, P.W.& B. Road or Locust Point fit for horses? We want say 40 more. How many empty house cars can you raise about Mt. Clare all told? We may have to plank the floors of some to take horses.
                      W. P. Smith

By B. & O. R.R. Telegraph
May 1, 1863, 8:40 P.M.

C. Smith,
and
C. W. Harvey,

Harper's Ferry or Sandy Hook:

Have the cars for 500 horses and 500 men gone to Martinsburg as ordered, and did they take up the three companies 14th Mass. with them? The 14th New Jersey Infantry is to go from Ferry to Martinsburg in same cars, 500 men, if the trains have not yet gone.

The 500 men and horses from Ferry are to go in A. M., when we hope to have cars enough for them from Baltimore. Do you understand all this? Don't send over 33 cars to Martinsburg for the 500 horses there and 14 for the 500 men, all to go west.

Answer fully.

W. P. Smith

By B. & O. R.R. Telegraph
Harper's Ferry, May 1, 1863
Received: 9:15 P.M.

W. P. Smith:

Commanding officers here demand transportation for the 14th Cavalry Regiment, 700 men and horses, which takes all the Stock Cars we can get hold of, even by using all the House Cars with heavy bottoms. We have 10 Passenger and Troop Cars left to send to Martinsburg. None of the trains have gone west yet. No application has been made here for transportation for the 3 Companies of the 14th Mass. nor 14th New Jersey Infantry. The 14th Penn. Cavalry now loading.

C. Smith

By B. & O. R.R. Telegraph
Wheeling, May 1, 1863
Received: May 2, 9:07 A.M.

W. P. Smith:

General Lightburn moves tonight. Important to know where the troops are that should have left Harper's Ferry this morning, and when they will reach Grafton, as near as you can give it.

J. B. Ford,
Genl. Agent, B. & O. R. R.

(Notes on back:

All the Cavalry left both Harper's Ferry and Martinsburg in night early.

W. P. S.

How avoid the error of sending cars by *special* train from Baltimore which are reported not wanted? How hurry? What order? Can we get certificate and pay?)

By B. & O. R.R. Telegraph
Martinsburg, May 2, 1863
Received: 9:39 A.M.

W. P. Smith:

First train left here at 11:30 last P.M. with 12 loads horses and 9 cars of commissary. Second (2nd) train left here at 5 A.M. Third (3rd) train left at 6 o'clock. Fourth (4th) train left here at 8:20. Fifth and last train left here at 8:30.

D. Darby

By B. & O. R.R. Telegraph
Martinsburg, May 2, 1863
Received: 2:26 P.M.

W. P. Smith:

The cavalry companies from Winchester reported here about 5:30 yesterday. They would have commenced loading by 6 o'clock if we had had the cars. We had the cars by 6 o'clock this A.M. and they commenced loading and we were finished and ready to start at 8:30. They reported as having 364 horses and men, they loaded but 294 horses, 300 men. The New Jersey Regiment arrived here at 4 o'clock this A.M.

D. Darby

By B. & O. R.R. Telegraph
Grafton, May 2, 1863
Received: 6:00 P.M.

W. P. Smith:

I have just returned from Monongahela Bridge. The telegraph wires are connected through. While there Mr. Ford and Sullivan telegraphed me if we could not transfer freight while the river is being trestled. I replied that we have not the first facility for such business. No boats suitable and no side track on either side of bridge, and a heavy bank of considerable height to climb each side, and besides it will interfere with trestling operations and delay. We can get one small boat and Benton's Ferry that will transfer passengers and baggage until trestling is completed. On receiving Mr. Ford's dispatch I consulted Messrs. McMurphy and Porter. They both decided that it would be attended with more expense than profit.

If possible, come out on first train. Mr. Porter has timber here and will commence work at Monongahela Bridge tomorrow A.M. McMurphy and Willard are with workmen trestling the bridge between Barracksville and Fairmont and will get through tomorrow P.M.

A. Diffey

By B. & O. R.R. Telegraph
Martinsburg, May 2, 1863
Received: 8:45 P.M.

W. P. Smith:

Tonnage trains of this P.M. all made in and stock trains

from Baltimore in. One more due. Three of the troop trains with horses, etc., that left Harper's Ferry last P.M. are ordered back to Harper's Ferry. Last one left here at eight o'clock.

D. Darby

(Note with reference to last two sentences:
What does this mean?   )

By B. & O. R.R. Telegraph
Grafton, May 2, 1863
Received: 9:20 P.M.

W. P. Smith:

Grafton is again in a state of excitement. Information has been telegraphed here that Jones and Imboden's forces combined would attack this place within twelve hours. Reinforcements are ordered here from Fairmont and cavalry are coming west by rail tonight. Col. Mulligan does not altogether credit the report, but is preparing to meet them should they attack. We have cars all coupled up and engines ready to leave at a moment's notice. I was in hopes our troubles were over, and that we could resume operations as far as condition of bridges would admit. Yet this may only be rumor and no truth in it.

A. Diffey

(Note at bottom of page:
President: It *can't* be that they are strong enough to attempt this. They *must* know of the present strength of Roberts, etc. W. P. S.

By B. & O. R.R. Telegraph
Received: 9:55 P.M.
May 2, 1863
War Dept.

W. Prescott Smith,
Genl. Supt.,
B. & O. R.R.

Private

The Secretary of War directs me to say to you that he does not deem it advisable to run any special trains tomorrow for the transmission of military news unless sanctioned by that Department.

Very respectfully,
E. S. Sanford,
Military Supervisor.

By B. & O. R.R. Telegraph
Grafton, May 2, 1863
Received: 11:25 P.M.

W. P. Smith:

Our information of attack is from General Roberts and he has ordered General Lightburn from Fairmont here to reinforce Colonel Mulligan. Not much confidence in the report here, at same time preparations are made to receive them. I fear an attack on Rowlesburg more than this place and have telegraphed Colonel Webster the reports and that perhaps it is to draw attention while the enemy attacks him for the purpose of destroying bridges and trestle work in the Cheat River region, and asked him to keep sharp lookout tonight for the enemy. All quiet up to eleven o'clock.

A. Diffey

By B. & O. R.R. Telegraph
Philadelphia, May 2, 1863
Received: 11:40 P.M.

W. P. Smith:

We have been notified by the Secretary of War tonight not to run any special tomorrow, Sunday, for the transmission of news, unless sanctioned by the Department. If we get an order from the Department, we will run the Times man from Baltimore to Philadelphia for one hundred (100) dollars, and Mr. Gutzner says they will run him from Philadelphia to New York for one hundred (100) dollars. Please let us know as soon as possible.

Wm. Stern

By B. & O. R.R. Telegraph
Cumberland, May 3, 1863
Received: 7:10 A.M.

W. P. Smith:

The 12th Pennsylvania Cavalry left Martinsburg yesterday at 9:30 in the morning, arriving at this station at 5:30 P.M., left at 6 P.M. We know of no other cavalry coming, at least have not been apprised of it.

L. C. Boehm

By B. & O. R.R. Telegraph
Barracksville, May 3, 1863
Received: 4:20 P.M.

W. P. Smith:

We will have the bridges all done to Fairmont so as to pass trains to that point tonight. Will through passenger train be run from Baltimore to the east side of Fairmont bridge to connect by transfer with trains to and from Wheeling? During the last twenty-four hours I have heard nothing but vague and variable reports. I think it is safe for the resumption of through travel. If the trains will be run, when will they commence, so that I can have a train in readiness at Fairmont to commence operations. 44.

J. P. Willard.

(Pencil note on back:

I see no reports of progress of repairs on N. W. Va. Road. How soon can you get through freight?)

By B. & O. R.R. Telegraph
Cumberland, May 3, 1863
Received: 5:24 P.M.

W. P. Smith:

Willard informs me bridge will be trestled and road all right from Wheeling to Fairmont this P.M. Will you start express train from Baltimore tomorrow night to go through to Wheeling? I have arranged for passenger trains between here and Grafton and return tomorrow morning. Let me hear so we can have train west of Fairmont to transfer to.

A. Diffey.

By B. & O. R.R. Telegraph
Martinsburg, May 4, 1863
Received: 8:29 A.M.

W. P. Smith, Esq.,

Dispatched east on Stock time engines 117. 236. with 7 house cars, 6 hoppers, 3 passenger cars.

D. Darby

(Penciled note at bottom:
Why not held for full loads—coal, etc.?)

By B. & O. R. R. Telegraph
Grafton, May 4, 1863
Received: 11:20 P.M.

W. P. Smith:

All quiet at this station and all parts on line of Road as far as I can learn. We have rumor about every hour of an attack about being made at different points on Road. We are busy moving troops from one point to another in small numbers. All the bridges were completed to Fairmont at one o'clock today. Mr. Porter is pushing the Monongahela trestling as rapidly as possible. Workmen are busy in repairing track and putting up trestles on Branch.

We expect to be able to cross Monongahela in about ten days from Sunday last. We are prepared for transfer tomorrow, have a boat which will accommodate about 60 passengers. Col. Mulligan thinks we are safe from further interruption by the enemy providing troops are not moved from the most important points while the enemy is within striking distance.

A. Diffey.

By B. & O. R.R. Telegraph
May 4 (Date noted in pencil)

W. P. Smith, Esq.,

Dear Sir:

I have just learned from a gentleman who professs to be posted, and I think he is, that Hooker telegraphs the department that he has them surrounded and that they must either surrender or be cut to pieces.

Am going up town tonight and anything I hear will telegraph you, so that you will understand.

Yours most respectfully,
Geo. S. Koontz

PUBLIC NOTICE

Office Provost Marshal General
Wheeling, May 4, 1863.

Having such intelligence as to make it certain that the bridges on the Baltimore and Ohio Railroad, near Burton, were destroyed by persons in sympathy with the present rebellion against the Government of the United States, general warning is hereby given to all such, that if the road is again damaged in any particular, all well known secessionists in the immediate locality where the damage is done, will be held directly responsible;

and such punishment will be inflicted upon them as will put an effectual stop to all depredations of this character.

Joseph Darr, Jr.
Maj. 1st Va. Cavalry,
Provost Marshal General.

By B.&O. R.R. Telegraph
Washington, May 6, 1863
Received: 3:30 P.M.

Wm. P. Smith,
Master of Trans., B. & O. R.R.

Asst. Quarter Master James Aikin telegraphs from Indianapolis under date of April 30th as follows:

A train of artillery horses was sent to Washington today. The train of Cavalry which left on Friday, on arrival at Columbus I ordered to Steubenville and Pittsburg. These horses have not arrived. Please direct your agents to use every possible means to forward these and other horses coming forward for the Government. It is of vital importance. *Answer.*

D. C. McCallum,
M. D. & C.

(Penciled note on back:

Advise your thorough and prompt attention as they reach you. Watch and urge forward all these movements.)

May 6, 1863

W. P. Smith, Esq.,
Dear Sir:

I learn from persons who profess to have just come from Falmouth, that we have suffered a disastrous defeat. One individual, who *I know* arrived from there *last night*, says that we have been *driven* across the Rappahannock, and that when he left the enemy was shelling us vigorously at that place. He says, further, that the Rebels have taken many more prisoners than our side has and that they — the Rebels — have captured immense lots of stores and a great many guns. Our side, too, burned large lots of stores to prevent their falling into hands of enemy.

I saw a man from Acquia Creek who says that when he left everything there was being removed, that even the locomotives had been placed on vessels.

Rumor says that General Peck has come up from Suffolk and that he is now in river on transports.

Another rumor, Hooker is to be relieved. One thing is certain, and it is, Hooker is on this side of the Rappahannock.

There is nothing whatever encouraging, on the contrary everything is discouraging, what the papers say to the contrary.

I send you Morning Chronicle. Read Editorial!

In haste,
Geo. S. Koontz.

By B. & O. R.R. Telegraph
War Department, May 6, 1863
Received: 10:02 P.M.

W. P. Smith,
Supt. B. & O. R.R.

There are three thousand prisoners with one thousand guards to be sent by railroad from this point to Philadelphia. Please answer me the earliest possible moment when the transportation for them will be ready. It is important that they leave here as soon as possible.

D. H. Rucker,
Q. M. Col. & Co.

By B. & O. R.R. Telegraph
Mt. Clare, May 7, 1863
Received: 1:12 A.M.

W. P. Smith:

We can raise 15 empty house cars at Mt. Clare, 14 passenger and 9 troop cars at Camden Station, total 38 cars, which will leave about 2:30 this morning for Washington. Parties are instructed to run as extra. Road has been duly notified.

A. J. Fairbank.

Head-Quarters, Middle Department
Eighth Army Corps,
Baltimore, Md., May 7, 1863
Received: 9:10 A.M.

W. P. Smith, Esq.,
Master Transportation,
B. & O. R.R.

Dear Sir:

I have just ordered two regiments of infantry from Winchester to Martinsburg, Va. Will you have transportation ready for them, to take them to Grafton, and at what time?

I am very respectfully,
Your obedient servant,
W. H. Chesebrough,
Lt. Col. & A. A. G.

By B. & O. Telegraph
Grafton, May 8, 1863
Received: 2:57 P.M.
C. Westbrook:
McAfee arrived at Clarksburg this A.M., reports wires along the road all right as far as Cornwallis. Operator gone, three bridges burned across Hughes River, two between Cornwallis and Cairo, one west of Cairo. Tunnel No. 18 fired at both ends. No rebels there this A.M. This came via West Union to Clarksburg.

Murray,
Operator.

By B. & O. R.R. Telegraph
Benwood, May 8, 1863
Received: May 9, 12:03 A.M.
W. P. Smith:
Just received following.

J. B. Ford.

Parkersburg, May 8, 1863
J. B. Ford:
Wharf boats loaded on opposite side river. Cars all loaded and as well under cover of gunboats as possible. Loaded all cars we could as only chance of saving freight in case of depot being fired. Situation of enemy uncertain. Reported to be about ten miles out. Cannot say certainly what number of men.

Jas. McAlister

Head Quarters, Middle Department,
Eighth Army Corps,
Baltimore, May 9, 1863
W. P. Smith, Esq.,
Master of Transportation,

63

B. & O. R.R., Baltimore, Md.

Sir:

An other regiment, the 12th Va. Infantry, 750 men, will arrive at Halltown from Winchester tonight. The General desires to know if you can have a train ready for them at Harper's Ferry or Halltown tonight or very early in the morning, and at what hour?

Very respectfully, etc.,
Maxwell Woodhull,
Capt. & A.D.C.

By B. & O. R.R. Telegraph
Harper's Ferry, May 10, 1863
Received: 11:20 A.M.

W. P. Smith:

Sixty (60) freight cars are wanted here immediately by order of Brig. Gen. Kelley.

Wm. Golde,
Capt. & A.Q.M.

(Note at bottom:

Answered at 11:50 asking what it meant and what *kind* of cars, if hoppers would not do, as others are exceedingly short. No response at 5 P.M.)

By B. & O. R.R. Telegraph
Monocacy, May 10, 1863
Received: 1:00 P.M.

W. P. Smith:

I have here now 4 empty stock, 1 empty gondola and 1 flat car, this is all.

F. Mantz

(Notes at bottom:
House - Stock - Gondolas

(Continued Page 73)

Grave of Wm. Prescott Smith in Greenmount Cemetery, Baltimore, Maryland.

On these facing pages, two views of the statue erected in honor of Wm.
Prescott Smith.

Briefcase in hand, Wm. Prescott Smith looks ready to board the Washington train to see his good friend A. Lincoln.

Inscription at base of the statue.

Grave of Margaret A. Smith.

Grave of grandson of Wm. Prescott Smith in Greenmount, alongside the grave of his grandfather.

THE CAMDEN STATION BUILDINGS, being a Front View of the new General City Depot of the BALTIMORE & OHIO RAILROAD, Camden Street, between Howard and Eutaw Streets, Baltimore. The entire buildings will front on Camden Street 388 feet. The centre tower is 188 feet, and the corner towers will be 80 feet in height. *Dimensions and Uses.*—The centre building, which is now entirely completed, has three stories—its wings will have two stories. It is occupied by the President, Treasurer, Masters of Transportation, Road, and Machinery, and other general officers of the Company. The entire premises, when completed, will cover a space of 350 by 1,110 feet, and will constitute one of the most complete structures of the kind in the world.

MARTINSBURG STATION,

100 Miles from Baltimore, and the Dividing Point between the First and Second Divisions of the Road.

1	4	2	Monocacy
1		13	Cumberland
22			Washington
8	5		Harper's Ferry
4	6		Piedmont
2			
--	--	--	
37	15	15	
15			
15			
--			

67 cars and no report from Mt. Clare or Martinsburg.)

> By B. & O. R.R. Telegraph
> Cumberland, May 10, 1863
> Received: 1:45 P.M.

W. P. Smith:

We have here 8 empty gondolas, 1 empty house; 5 empty gondolas, and 191 empty hoppers coming on tonnage west today.

> L. C. Boehm

> By B. & O. R.R. Telegraph
> Washington, May 10, 1863
> Received: 2:05 P.M.

W. P. Smith:

We have 22 empty house and 9 troop cars, 10 hoppers which are in course of unloading. We sent up 5 gondolas, 3 empty Philadelphia house and about 12 Philadelphia flats on No. 1 Tonnage.

> Geo. S. Koontz

> By B. & O. R.R. Telegraph
> Piedmont, May 10, 1863
> Received: 3:10 P.M.

W. P. Smith:

We have but 6 cattle cars empty, 4 house cars and 2 rock cars now on hand and 110 hoppers. Sent 30 empty cars from here for the Ferry last night. All the cars for the past two or three days moving west of this are yet at Grafton and vicinity, none returning. Sent forward all the loaded cars last night we had on hand containing perishable goods, etc., to be transferred at Fairmont bridge. Soldiers passing west are committing numerous depredations on loaded cars here despite all our efforts to prevent it. Have no military guard stationed here to keep order.

L. E. Randall

By B. & O. R.R. Telegraph
Cincinnati, May 10, 1863
Received: 3:35 P.M.

W. P. Smith:

Had the Commission better come by the Baltimore & Ohio Railroad from Wheeling to Baltimore? Answer immediately. We leave tonight.

Donn Piatt
Judge Advocate

(Note at bottom:

Answered:—Safe, as far as we know.

W.P.S.

Second note, probably by Pres. Garrett:

You should have advised it by Wheeling.)

By B. & O. R.R. Telegraph
Mt. Clare, May 10, 1863
Received: 4:10 P.M.

W. P. Smith:

We have at the station the following cars:—

8 empty B.&O. house
11   "   "   gondolas

2	"	"	hoppers
3	"	"	long flats
2	"	"	rack cars
6	"	"	stock
3	"	P.W.&B.	house
7	"	"	flats
1	"	A.&E.	gondola

43 Total

A. J. Fairbank

By B. & O. R.R. Telegraph
Martinsburg, May 10, 1863
Received: 4:45 P.M.

W. P. Smith:

Shall we send what empty gondolas and house cars we have to Harper's Ferry?

D. Darby

(Penciled note as follows:

Telegraph General Kelley the necessity for a military guard at Cumberland. Boehm should have called at once on nearest officer for guard to protect against military depredations.)

Apparently above note is by Pres. Garrett and is intended to refer to telegram from L. E. Randall at Piedmont, received at 3:10 P.M., May 10.

By B. & O. R.R. Telegraph
Washington, May 11, 1863
Received: 11:10 A.M.

W. P. Smith:

The City Council of Washington are about to proceed to New York tomorrow afternoon with a few invited guests to present to Genl. McClellan a sword. A Committee has called on me to learn whether we will issue round trip tickets good for five (5) days at a reduced rate. I have promised them an answer at half past five this P.M. at which hour they will call on me. Please answer before that time.

Geo. S. Koontz

By B. & O. R.R. Telegraph
Sandy Hook, May 11, 1863
Received: 12:46 P.M.

W. P. Smith:

I think we will have stock and gondolas enough to supply present demands at Ferry. The large number of gondolas required is owing to so many wagons to be sent. We are now loading wagons and horses belonging to 17th Ind. Battery. 12th Va. Regiment was started yesterday at one o'clock P.M. in train of 25 cars. Quarter Master of the same has ordered his wagons and horses to Martinsburg to be carried from there, which will require 5 stock cars, 10 gondolas and 1 house car at Martinsburg for the 12th Va. Reg't, baggage train, etc.

C. Smith

By B. & O. R.R. Telegraph
Wheeling, May 10, 1863
Received: May 11, 1:45 P.M.

W. P. Smith:

All quiet this P.M. Mulligan's Regiment left Fairmont at 6 this A.M. Stop at Moundsville. Gen. Barry meets them there. Learn from some of our men just from Parkersburg that 9 bridges in all have been destroyed on Parkersburg Road and the wood filling of one tunnel east of Cairo was on fire. Engine 220 started out from Parkersburg on Thursday to bring in Company stationed at Ellenboro, was stopped by obstruction on track west of Cairo. Watchman told them track was torn up in several places between there and Cairo. Engine 91 started from Parkersburg yesterday to Petroleum, was stopped by the enemy's pickets one and a half miles west of that point and had to return. There is no apprehension of enemy's doing more damage to Road at any point. With General Kelley's prompt attention we can now go to work and repair damage and get freights forward.

J. B. Ford

By B. & O. R.R. Telegraph
Sandy Hook, May 16, 1863
Received: 9:27 A.M.

W. P. Smith:

Some citizens from Charles Town and Halltown report a small Rebel Cavalry force in and about Charles Town. Have captured a part of Capt. Summers' Company of Federal Cavalry.

C. Smith

October 1, 1863
Sent 11:32 P.M.

Hon. E. M. Stanton
Sec'y of War, Washington.

Your despatch of inquiry received.

As the move ment is now entirely completed on our line, except a small remnant of horses about starting from the Manassas road, and as all the reports continued of a uniformly successful character, I thought it would be tedious to send you more bulletins, unless some change occurred, which I am happy to say is not the case. The only place where any real impediment has been threatened is Indianapolis; and I am more than ever satisfied of the correctness of my judgment, when I advised you and General Hooker this day a week ago that the troops should have gone to Cincinnati direct by rail, and taken steamers for Louisville.

The change of cars at Indianapolis, with the march of over a mile across the town, has been very tedious and difficult, because there was no track room, or other facilities, for such an occasion; nor were they familiar in that quarter with the details of such things, on such a scale. Under all the circumstances, however, wonders have been achieved even there,—the average delay at that point being only about six hours.

Up to 12 o'clock noon yesterday (Wednesday) 14 out of the 20,000 men had passed Indianapolis, and by dark last evening, that number had reached Jeffersonville. The last trains of troops proper crossed the Ohio River at Bellaire yesterday afternoon, and are now nearly due at Jeffersonville. Some of the batteries are following closely, but even they have all crossed the Ohio River, and are on the way to Indianapolis. I hope to send you the final report tomorrow morning.

In summing up results, I find over twenty thousand men, 10 batteries and their horses — besides other horses — and more than 100 cars of baggage, etc., have gone, being, in the whole movement, an average of 35 per cent beyond the requisition and our expectations; and we only wonder, that under such circumstances, such results have been secured.

I am glad to say, however, that even without previous notice, we feel ready to undertake it again, with all the anxiety and constant effort involved.

W. P. Smith

By B. & O. R.R. Telegraph
War. Dept., 10:30 A.M., Nov. 3, 1863
Received: 10:55 A.M.

W. P. Smith:

General Halleck informed me yesterday afternoon that he would immediately order the troops to be forwarded by rail to Cincinnati. I cannot agree with you that it is safe to risk the river at the present stage. It seems to me exceedingly hazardous and unwise to send troops from Wheeling on three feet of water. You will, therefore, forward by rail without delay. If there should be a rise the later divisions can go by water.

> Edwin M. Stanton,
> Sec'y War.

> By B. & O. R.R. Telegraph
> War Dept., Nov. 7, 1863, 11:55 A.M.
> Received: 11:55 A.M.

J. W. Garrett, Pres., B. & O.

Please have an engine in readiness to haul special train from Baltimore to Washington on its arrival from Philadelphia at an early hour tomorrow morning. Secretary Seward leaves New York at 7½ o'clock this evening and a special train has been ordered to bring him from Philadelphia to Washington.

By order of the Secretary of War.

> Anson Stager,
> Col. & A.D.C.

> By B. & O. R.R. Telegraph
> Philadelphia, Nov. 7, 1863
> Received: 3:15 P.M.

W. P. Smith:

Please send one of your special cars to Philadelphia on our No. 20 train tonight to return to Washington upon our 12 o'clock train tonight with Hon. Secretary Seward and party. Please answer.

> Wm. Stearns

> By B. & O. R.R. Telegraph
> Philadelphia, Nov. 7, 1863
> Received: 4:10 P.M.

W. P. Smith:

There is 43 prisoners on our No. 7 train and they wish to go through to Washington tonight.

Wm. Stearns

Copy of Telegram

Baltimore, Nov. 8

J. N. Du Barry,
 Harrisburg:

Mr. Lincoln and a portion of the Cabinet expect to go to the Gettysburg Consecration, and have sent to me making inquiries as to the route and facilities.

Will you take them up in our private cars, through from Washington, if we will deliver to you at Bolton? How near to Gettysburg can you take them by rail? Which is the best route — by Hanover or Westminster?

Please answer promptly. I will confer with you further about details, after route is determined.

(Signed) W. P. Smith

By Northern Central Railway
Company's Telegraph Line
Harrisburg, Nov. 9, 1863

W. P. Smith:

Message received. Will be most happy to make arrangements to take your cars with party mentioned. Route Baltimore to Hanover Junction by Northern Central Railway thence to the town of Gettysburg by Hanover Branch Road. Westminster is not on the route. Advise me fully of time, etc., early as possible to make all necessary arrangements.

J. N. Du Barry

(Penciled note:
So advised Gov. Chase.)

By B. & O. R.R. Telegraph
Washington, Nov. 16, 1863
Received: 10:55 A.M.

W. P. Smith:

On what terms will you run an Excursion train to Gettysburg from Washington on Thursday? At how much per head? I running all risk of advertising posters, tickets, etc. Also how many hours travel is it from Washington and what is regular fare?

W. R. Hooper

(Penciled note at bottom:
No.)

By B. & O. R.R. Telegraph
Washington, Nov. 16, 1863
Received: 10:09 P.M.

J. W. Garrett,
    Prest. B. & O. R. R.:

Will you be kind enough to furnish car for three (3) o'clock train from here tomorrow, Tuesday, and inform me by telegraph if arrangements can be made with other roads so as to get into Gettysburgh without delay? What time will train leave on Northern Central?

Ward H. Lamon,
Marshal

(Penciled note on back:
Mast. of Trans.
Will you arrange this fully and telegraph the Marshal promptly.
Monday, 10:30 P.M.   J. W. G.   )

Office of The Press
Nov. 16, 1863

Dear Sir:

The bearer of this, Mr. McDevitt of *The Press*, goes to Gettysburg to attend the celebration. He will accompany the President for the purpose of recording the incidents of his journey, — and we should esteem it as a great favor if you could arrange his journey that he might have that advantage.

Thanking you for other kindnesses, I am

Very Truly Yours,
Jno. Russell Young,
Ed-in-Chief

Wm. Prescott Smith, Esq.

Head Quarters, Middle Department,
Eighth Army Corps,
Baltimore, Nov. 17, 1863

Wm. P. Smith, Esq.,
Master of Trans.
Dear Sir:

General Schenck and staff, a party of about 12, are to go to Gettysburg tomorrow on the Presidential train at 1½ from Calvert

Station. But the General is unwilling to impose this party upon the cars of the President, fearing there may not be room.

The Northern Central R. R. Co. is so much pressed for cars that they could with difficulty furnish one. I therefore request that a special car may be supplied by your Company to be attached to the President's train. A small car is sufficient.

If you furnish the car, it would be better that the General should take the car at *Camden Street* instead of at the Calvert Station, if agreeable to you. Please answer.

Respectfully yours,
Alexander Bliss,
Lt. Col & Q. M.

North Central Rail Way Co.'s
Telegraph Line
Harrisburg, Nov. 17, 1863
Received: 5:12 P. M.

W. P. Smith:

It is understood that Northern Central will have all arrangements made to leave Bolton at 2 P. M. Wednesday, Nov. 18th. I have ordered the two cars to Camden and will go through street this P. M. I will advise you of departure, etc., from Gettysburg and return.

I have advised Howard Street kept clear from Wednesday A. M. till 5 P. M., orders for passage of special train. Please order this on your end of street.

J. N. Du Barry
Genl. Supt.

Baltimore and Ohio Railroad,
President's Office,
Baltimore, Nov. 18, 1863.

Sir:

Supt. DuBarry's telegram of 17th nst. indicates a design to attend thoroughly to the President and Suite. You will of course see fully to having Howard Street clear, and that all arrangements upon our line are as perfect as possible for the comfort, safety, and rapidity of movement of the party.

Be very vigilant regarding an understanding for their return. Have this point understood as early as practicable, and be specially careful to have the street track clear for them, and your arrangements so made that there will be no cause of complaint.

Respectfully yours,
J. W. Garrett
President.

Wm. Prescott Smith, Esq.
Master of Transportation.

By B. & O. R.R. Telegraph
Cumberland, Nov. 18, 1863
Received: 8:55 A.M.

W. P. Smith:

As Engine 232, express west this morning, was passing Paw Paw some explosive machine bursted under it and caused a great concussion on the whole train, breaking head light and house light of engine and some of the glass in the passenger cars. The marks on the engine show it was none of our torpedoes. We find dents in the driving wheel, the brass binding on foot board is broken in two, the shield over the driving wheel has a piece broken out and bent. The track was not injured as the extra train with iron rails passed there without any interruption after Express west. I believe the attempt was made to stop the Passenger train, perhaps for the purpose of robbery.

L. C. Boehm

By B. & O. R.R. Telegraph
Cumberland, Nov. 18, 1863

Received: 10:10 A. M.
W. P. Smith:

Further examination of Engine 232 shows the explosion of a shell under the engine. A piece of shell is found sticking in the boiler casing.

L. C. Boehm

(Penciled note on back:

The telegram E. Dorsey, etc., is probably a canard. Carefully avoid all publicity re this case. Knowledge of it would be very damaging.)

Copy

By B. & O. R.R. Telegraph
No. 12, Nov. 18, 1863
Received: 12:30 P.M.

W. C. Quincy:

The rebels were on the track last night and night before at Paw Paw. They attacked the Express west last night.

I. W. Dawson,
Supervisor.

By B. & O. R.R. Telegraph
Cumberland, Nov. 18, 1863
Received: 3:43 P.M.

W. P. Smith:

There was three shells on the track at Paw Paw this A.M. Two of them were found unexploded. They were placed along the rail just sufficiently projecting above for a wheel to strike.

L. C. Boehm

By B. & O. R.R. Telegraph
Washington, Nov. 18, 1863

W. P. Smith:

The following telegram has been sent to Supt. Du Barry:

"The President and party wish to leave Gettysburg for Washington as soon after the close of the Ceremonies tomorrow as possible, probably about 5 o'clock P.M. Please make arrangements to have them brought through by special train. Inform W. P. Smith time of departure of train from Gettysburg and when it will be due in Baltimore, so that he will have a train in readiness to bring them through. Please answer. Please do all you can to facilitate prompt return of the President and party to Washington and oblige

Yours,

D. C. McCallum

(Penciled note on back, probably by J.W.G.:

Attend to this very thoroughly. When do you expect the President here?   )

By B. & O. R.R. Telegraph
No. 12, Nov. 18, 1863
Received: 10:10 P.M.

W. P. Smith:

I have succeeded in getting a company of 60 men at Paw Paw to guard the tunnel and the covered bridge east of the tunnel. From what I can learn there was only four or five men engaged in placing the obstruction on the track for express west of this morning. There was three shells placed under rail, fixed so as to explode as soon as the engine came in contact with them, but fortunately only one of them exploded which damaged the engine slightly; but if the other had exploded it would have been a serious matter. I will send you one of the shells on mail train in A.M. You will discover a wooden screw in the shell with a hole entirely through it which was intended for a torpedo to set in, and as soon as the engine would come in contact with the torpedo it would explode the shell. The shell I send you is not loaded. I will write you full particulars.

Geo. W. Stoddard

Master of Road's Office
Baltimore & Ohio Railroad Co.,
Baltimore, Nov. 18, 1863

W. P. Smith, Esq.,
  Master of Trans.
Sir:

The following just received by telegraph:—

Dated, No. 12, Nov. 18, 1863

"The Rebels were on the track last night and night before at Paw Paw. They attacked the Express west last night."

(Signed) I. W. Dawson, Superv.

I have before stated there are no troops at Willett's Run, Rockwell's Run, No. 12, and Paw Paw. These are all exposed points and should be guarded. Large convoys of trains — say 10 engines and 250 cars — "lay off" at Rockwells and No. 12 both day and night. They are at the mercy of any roving bands. This matter demands immediate attention.

Truly yours,
W. C. Quincy,
A.M.R.

By B. & O. R.R. Telegraph
No. 12, Nov. 19, 1863
Received: 11:50 A. M.

W. P. Smith:

I send you a copy of dispatch addressed to me and found at Paw Paw tunnel and near where the shells were placed on track for Express West of yesterday morning. Mr. Stoddard got it at Paw Paw Station and handed it to me this morning.

"Head Quarters, C. S. Forces
Paw Paw, Nov. 18
To Abraham Lincoln, Prest., etc.,
    Washington, D. C.
    I arrived here early this morning with the expectation of meeting you. Sorry you were not aboard. Hope better luck will attend our efforts next time. Kindest regards to all.   .
                             Robert S. Todd,
                                C. S. Army
P. S. Operator will please send the above dispatch and collect, as I have no greenbacks convenient. Evan Dorsey of Baltimore accompanied this expedition.
                        (Signed) R. S. Todd, C. S. Army"
                             Riley, Operator.

OUTLINE OF HISTORICAL EVENTS

The following memo of historical events to which the papers of William Prescott Smith have reference is extracted from THE SOLDIER IN OUR CIVIL WAR, edited by Paul F. Mottelay, and from the Annual Reports of the Baltimore & Ohio Railroad Company.

1864

July 4 — Engagement at Point of Rocks. Attack on Bolivar and Maryland Heights, July 4-7.

July 5 — Occupation by Confederate forces of Hagerstown and Pleasant Valley, Md.

July 6 — Confederate attempt to destroy trestling at Great Cacapon River prevented by troops in iron-clad train. Confederates driven from Sir John's Run after burning depot and water station. Action at Hagar's Mountain and Middleton, Md.

July 7 — Action at Solomon's Gap and Frederick, Md.

Head-Quarters, Middle Department
Eighth Army Corps
Baltimore, Md., June 3, 1864

W. P. Smith, Esq.
Dear Sir:
If you have at hand transportation sufficient for two thousand convalescents now at Frederick, I would be obliged to you if you would have it ready to move to that place upon receipt of an order.
Please answer.

Truly yours,
Lew Wallace
Maj. Gen. Commanding

(Penciled note on back: 9 P.M.
Answered. Could be done, and I am arranging it.)

By B. & O. R.R. Telegraph
Harper's Ferry, June 4, 1864
Received: 4:12 A.M.

W. P. Smith:
I have just received information from General Sigel that he is with his troops from Leetown and Martinsburg at Shepherdstown. Genl. Sigel will cross the river tonight and march to Harper's Ferry. The enemy took possession of Martinsburg at one o'clock P.M. yesterday. The rebel cavalry is under command of Maj. Gen. Ransom. They are now reported to be marching on Williamsport. Our small force fought well but were outflanked on every side. I regret to say that great damage will be done to the railroad.

Max Weber,
Brig. Genl.

Head Quarters, Maryland Militia
Baltimore, July ...., 1864

Temporary leave of absence for .... days from military service
is granted to ....
enrolled under the enrollment of 1862, he being now necessarily
engaged in the service of the Baltimore & Ohio Railroad Co.

Private

July 2, 1864
9:15 A.M.

H. F. Kenney,
Philadelphia
On what day do you expect the President and Mrs. Lincoln
to return in your car to Washington?
W. P. Smith

By B. & O. R.R. Telegraph
Martinsburg, July 3, 1864
Received: 8:05 A.M.

W. P. Smith
and
J. W. Garrett:
Express East and West passed this A.M. nearly on time.
The stock trains from Cumberland have made in. They contain
house cars, stock and coal.

We are now sending them East. We are now loading sick soldiers for Frederick. The Q. M. is loading all their stores as fast as possible. There is no signs of the enemy quite near us yet. Cannonading is heard in the direction of Winchester this A. M.

D. Darby

Copy sent to J. W. Garrett, Esq.

July 3, 1864

W. P. Smith
Mt. Clare:
    We have at Camden Station after 3:30 leaves:
      10 Passenger Cars
      9 Empty House Car
      1 Iron Car.

J. T. England,
Agent.

Middle Dept., 8th Army Corps,
Medical Director's Office,
Balto., Md., July 3, 1864.

Sir:
    Intelligent has just been received that 2000 patients must be moved *immediately* from Frederick City to this point.

    I am telegraphing the War Dept, to know if they shall go to Camp Parole or this city. Have you the cars which can be sent right up?

    I will communicate with you when I get word from Washington which will be in about an hour.

Your respectfully,
Your Obd. Servt.
C. R. Greenleaf
Mr. Smith
Supt. B. & O.
Asst. Surgeon U. S. A.
Asst. Medical Director

Head-Quarters, Middle Dept.,
8th Army Corps,
Balto., Md., July 3, 1864.

W. P. Smith, Esq.
Master of Transportation,
Balto. & Ohio R. R.
Sir:

I am directed by the General Commanding to inform you the late dispatches fix the number of patients to be moved from Frederick, Md., under existing orders at 1000 men. I am therefore instructed to inform you that the train you have sent with accommodations for that number will be sufficient transportation.

I am, Sir,
Very Respectfully,
Your Obd. Servt.
Max Woodhull,
Captain.

By B. & O. R.R. Telegraph
Sandy Hook, July 3, 1864
Received: 1:15 P. M.

W. P. Smith
and
J. W. Garrett:

Last Engine and cars arrived at Sandy Hook at 1 O'clock

all safe. There is 8 cars left at Cherry Run. All the other cars on this side of the Run. I started an Engine to Cherry Run this A. M. They went as far as Myers Water Station when they came in contact with Rebel Cavalry and returned. What disposition shall be made with the engines here? The men can get nothing to eat here.

D. Darby

By B. & O. R.R. Telegraph
Mt. Clare, July 3, 1864
Received: 2 P. M.

J. W. Garrett, Prest.

I find Fairbank has about 60 cars at Mt. Clare, including the 30 for the 1000 men from Camden. We sent east last P. M. 17 loaded House, 18 empty house, 18 empty stock, 17 empty gondolas and 128 Hoppers. We will get ready as early as possible 3 engines to take troops and empty cars to Monocacy and Harper's Ferry.

W. P. Smith.

By B. & O. R. R. Telegraph
Monocacy, July 3, 1864
Received: 3:39 P. M.

W. P. Smith:

The latest accounts that I can get are that one of our engines was started west this morning and when they got as far as Myers Water Station found that the enemy was on the road. The train then returned to Martinsburg. The amount of force is estimated 3000 and upwards.

F. Mantz

By B. & O. R.R. Telegraph
Baltimore, July 3, 1864.
Received: 3:50 P.M.

J. T. Quynn,
Frederick.

We have 35 good troop and house cars to go from Camden to Monocacy with 1000 men and you can use them as far as they go for sick, and use hoppers for the stores to be removed.

I hope the sick are not being moved from any immediate fear of enemy. Not a sign of them any nearer than Leetown, four miles south of Kearneysville, where an outpost of 300 men are keeping them at bay since daylight.

W. P. Smith

(Pencil note at the bottom:

If Sigel has retreated may not the enemy cross river, move down National Road if, which is still doubtful, their force is large.)

By B. & O. R.R. Telegraph
Mt. Clare, July 3, 1864
Received: 4:02 P.M.

W. P. Smith
and
J. T. England.

I will send 2 engines to Camden with 35 empty troop and house cars for the 1000 men to Monocacy. The engines and cars will be around by 4:30. I will not send the third engine out.

A. J. Fairbank.

By B. & O. R.R. Telegraph
Harper's Ferry, July 3, 1864
Received: 4:45 P.M.

J.W. Garrett:

The General Commanding has just seen a telegram to T. N. Heskett from W. C. Quincey and desires me to say that at the worst the iron work of your bridge will not be destroyed. The trestle work at the most will be sufficient and that will not go unless a heavy force of infantry and cavalry attack us.

H. M. Burleigh
A. A. G.

By B. & O. R.R. Telegraph
Monocacy, July 4, 1864
Received: 1:45 A.M.

W. P. Smith:

Your dispatch to me is the first of my knowing anything about wanting cars to move the sick from Frederick, the only cars being ordered from parties at Harper's Ferry. All the cars that went into Frederick with sick and wounded today I learn have been preseed and are being loaded with government freight which will consume all the cars that went into Frederick today with sick and wounded. Out of the number of sick and wounded that went into Frederick today four hundred were found to be able bodied and not sick and were ordered to be sent back. We have no cars empty here now that we could make up a train of the sick to be moved at Frederick. Had of known that the stores were to have been loaded up and moved away from Frederick other cars could have been furnished for this purpose and house cars used for sick.

I understand late this evening no sick were to be moved, moving stores only; not knowing that any of the sick were to be moved until I just received your dispatch. There were about 450 sick that came down from Martinsburg. It seems that Harper's Ferry is expecting to receive some 35 cars from Baltimore tonight.

F. Mantz

By B. &. O. R.R. Telegraph
Relay House, July 4, 1864
Received: 4:30 A.M.

W. P. Smith:

Engine 72 with 28 loads sick soldiers from Frederick for Annapolis left here at 10:05.

W. E. Vernetson.

By B. & O. R.R. Telegraph
Washington, July 4, 1864
Received: 7:30 A.M.

W. P. Smith:

I have not yet received a single car from Whiton. Will be short of cars for the troops. Have only 25 cars for the 1800 or 2000men. Will start at about 7:30. Six hundred and fifty troops for Harper's Ferry and very shortly after a train with Battery. Both engines will be supplied with sufficient coal to go up Main Stem. May I load Philadelphia cars with troops?

G. S. Koontz

By B. & O. R.R. Telegraph
Mt. Clare, July 4, 1864
Received: 2:51 P.M.

W. P. Smith:

I will be able to start ten wheel engine about 3 o'clock this P.M. with 25 empty cars for Frederick. This takes all the empty house and troop cars we have at this station.

A. J. Fairbank.

By B. & O. R.R. Telegraph
Monocacy, July 4, 1864
Received: 4:28 P.M.

W. P. Smith:

Sick train has arrived and will leave in a few minutes. Just as soon as the engine gets coal.

F. Mantz.

By B. & O. R.R. Telegraph
Point of Rocks, July 4, 1864
Received: 9:10 P.M.

W. P. Smith:

The rebels under Moseby, numbering about 150 men, crossed the river about half mile west of this point under cover of 1 piece of artillery and forced our troops to retreat towards Frederick. This was about 12:45. They have robbed and plundered all the soldiers, etc., it seems, of this place, even taking from them their watches and pocket books. They captured about 4 privates and one Lieutenant. They showed no quarters to prisoners even after they had surrendered. They fired into our mail train bound East about a half mile or more west of here, but the train succeeded in returning to Sandy Hook, but I have heard with loss of engineer, who it is said was killed. They destroyed all Government property and had it not been for a lady friend of mine would have burnt my office. They have broken everything to pieces in the office. They cut the telegraph lines in several places, but I repaired them. I saved all my instruments, but at great risk to my life. They left here about 6 P.M., but a number of them are yet lingering about here. About 20 on opposite side of river looking over. We look for the whole force to come over again tonight. They took our agent, Mr. Means, prisoner after taking all his moveable property. I will have to go to Mountain again. I have been eye witness to all that has transpired and will stay here until they starve me out. I fear they have captured the train of ammunition which left here about 12:30 today for Sandy Hook. No one killed that I have heard of.

Yours Etc.
W. W. Shock.

By B. & O. R.R. Telegraph
Monocacy, July 5, 1864
Received: 8:35 A.M.

W. P. Smith:

The raid of yesterday has proven to be Moseby. He crossed the River at Mocks Ford near Dents Lock about one mile west of Point of Rocks. The crossing was protected by two pieces of artillery. The crossing had not been long made before it was time for our Mail Train East. The first attack was made on an excursion boat with a lot of men on excursion from the Treasury Department going to Washington from Harper's Ferry. This attack was made at Dents Lock. The boat was burned and all valuables that could be got hold of taken. The burning of boat caused our Mail Train to slacken, and when the engineman got sight of the enemy, they made every effort to stop, at the same time the enemy opening fire from across the river with the artillery. There was shots fired at the train from the time it stopped until it commenced retreating. The enemy's cavalry followed the train some distance. A Good number of persons jumped off the train to make their escape. It is represented that the fireman was killed. The enemy then advancing on Point of Rocks when our Military there gave up the Point to the enemy without a struggle and commenced a stampede. There was much property taken from private persons. The Warehouse at the Point represented as burnt. After robbing stores and burning the camps the enemy advanced in the direction of Poolesville, their artillery remaining on South side of River, and when our cavalry pickets saw the enemy's cavalry advancing they left. One company of infantry also which came in here this morning, the enemy then crossing the river below Point of Rocks. Some of the Treasury Excursionists supposed captured. There has been a large wagon train passing through by Frederick from Harper's Ferry that I can hear of. Firing still going on in that direction this A.M.

F. Mantz

By B. & O. R.R. Telegraph
Monocacy, 10:30 A.M., July 5, 1864
Received: 10:31 A.M.

100

W. P. Smith:

Mr. Warner, Mr. J. P. Williams, Mr. Ludwig, telegraph operator, and myself left Sandy Hook this A.M. about 8 o'clock on yard engine 31 for the purpose of ascertaining the true condition of affairs along the road east. Had to do this not being able to get any information from the Military. When we arrived at Point of Rocks we were fired at from the Loudon side. I return at once to bring mail east of yesterday and also all the engines and cars down. Will do this carefully. Will run ahead with engine 31 so that if we meet trouble we can return to Sandy Hook. Mail of yesterday was fired into, fireman badly wounded and baggage master captured. No injury was done to the train. Track all right yet. Harper's Ferry was evacuated last night about 8. Genl. Sigel's forces arrived about 9 last P.M. The wood work of the bridge has been destroyed. Harper's Ferry now garrisoned by the enemy and I am told the Union forces have notified the citizens to leave the town as they intend to shell the place. I will telegraph you again if I get down all right with the engines from Sandy Hook.

J. Donohoo

Head-Quarters, Middle Dept.,
8th Army Corps,
Balto., Md., July 5, 1864.

W. P. Smith, Esq.,
    Master of Transportation,
       B. & O. R.R.

Sir:

A train is wanted at once to convey a Battery of Artillery with their horses, guns and caissons to Monocacy Junction.

Please state when the train will be ready.

By command of Major General Wallace,
Saml. B. Lawrence
A. A. G.

Received: 5:56 P.M.

Baltimore, July 6, 1864

W. P. Smith, Esq.,
    Master Transportation,
      Balto. & Ohio R.R. Co.

Dear Sir:

I left Baltimore on the morning of the 4th in charge of Mail train west as far as Harper's Ferry. Left in charge of Mail Train East on Mail Train time, and when near the Point of Rocks my train was attacked by an armed band of Confederate soldiers or Guerillas and fired into, severely wounding the fireman of engine 234. When the first discovery was made by Mr. Darby, my engineman, it was by the burning of a canal boat, and the whistle of engine was sounded for brakes, and the engine was reversed, and as the train was moving towards the west the parties made their appearance and called upon us to stop; but this we did not deem prudent under the circumstances, and we beat a very hasty retreat back towards Sandy Hook, arriving there safely. There was quite a number of my passengers who jumped off my train, but from what I can learn they all made their escape to the Mountains and I believed arrived safely in Frederick. There was none of my passengers wounded or hurt as I could learn. The Fireman was left at Sandy Hook in the care of the Widow Mocabee, who is giving him every attention. I left Sandy Hook yesterday with a guard in advance and arrived in Baltimore on the 5th inst., at 9 o'clock P.M. 15 Min.

Thomas A. Wiley
Conductor

P.S. Mr. Williams, the Supervisor of Road, has furnished one of his men to nurse the Fireman, as it will be too laborious on Mrs. Mocabee to attend to him all the time, but from what the Dr. told me on yesterday I am afraid he will not live.

Thomas A. Wiley

By B. & O. R.R. Telegraph
Monocacy, July 6, 1864
Received: 11:06 A.M.
W. P. Smith:
Your telegraph operator at Monrovia has deserted his post.
Please send him back or supply his place with another man.
Lew Wallace
Maj. Genl.

By B. & O. R.R. Telegraph
Sandy Hook, July 6, 1864
Received: 5:05 P.M.
W. P. Smith:
From the most reliable sources I have no reason to doubt
the truth of my last dispatch. I want to get the engine and cars
now here away. An orderly just from Head-Quarters says the
advance has already attacked Sigel and he has repulsed them. If
I can get away the Company's property I will try and take care of
myself afterwards. If I am caught the Lords' will be done. I will
not show the white feather. We have too many men of that sort.
Military dispatches are all sent from this office. I will transmit to
you all information I can obtain. Engine 31 with 3 cars left here
at 3:40 for Monocacy.
E. R. Warner
By B. & O. R.R. Telegraph
Sandy Hook, July 6, 1864
Received: 9:50 P.M.
J. King, Jr.:
Nothing new since my last to Smith. We hope however
that every vestige of the Confederate army will be driven out of
Maryland tomorrow. Facts seem to warrant this. A Mr. Grover,
who is well known here and was taken prisoner by Moseby at
Point of Rocks and today released, says Moseby had 350 men
ready to tear up the road and destroy everything belonging to

the company at Point of Rocks; but when he saw our engine and us leaving troops there he remarked reinforcements were coming and they better be getting away; and when the trains came down he threw three or four shells at them and has retreated into Virginia; and Grover says but for our running down with the 31 the road would have been destroyed and the trains still here. We have nothing at all here of the Company's except 17 cars loaded with ammunition under government order to remain. I told Mantz to hold engine 31 at or near Monocacy that we could easily get her again if the storm passes over. Capt. Gardner tells me he has ordered stores and forage from Baltimore and they intend to send a force to Harper's Ferry in the morning to bring away forage that is there yet undisturbed. There are only 75 of the enemy reported at Harper's Ferry. No fighting except at long range since the 4th.

Warner.

Baltimore & Ohio

RAILROAD,

CONNECTING

ALL PARTS OF THE EAST

WITH

ALL PARTS OF THE WEST,

AND

THE SHORTEST ROUTE

BETWEEN

NEW YORK, PHILADELPHIA, BALTIMORE & WASHINGTON,

AND

COLUMBUS, CINCINNATI, LOUISVILLE,
DAYTON, INDIANAPOLIS, ST. LOUIS,
CAIRO, MEMPHIS and NEW ORLEANS.

☞ This Great Railroad is located nearly upon the line formerly traveled by the NATIONAL ROAD, running between the Cities of *WASHINGTON* and *BALTIMORE* and the Commercial Cities of the OHIO AND MISSISSIPPI VALLEYS.

Through Tickets

FOR THE WESTERN CITIES, AND

BAGGAGE CHECKS,

By the Baltimore and Ohio Railroad and its various Connecting Lines, may be had at

NEW YORK, PHILADELPHIA, BALTIMORE & WASHINGTON.

☞ FREIGHT OF ALL KINDS, ☜

In any quantity, will be carried by Through Receipt, in the Quickest Time, and at the Lowest Rates.

☞ *For Particulars, see Newspaper Advertisements and Handbills.*

HARPER'S FERRY,

From the Maryland Side of the Potomac, Showing the Confluence of that River with the Shenandoah, the Baltimore & Ohio Railroad Crossing the Potomac by the Extensive Covered Bridge.

106

POINT OF ROCKS,

BALTIMORE & OHIO RAILROAD, SEVENTY MILES FROM BALTIMORE.

CHESAPEAKE & OHIO CANAL and POTOMAC RIVER

ARE SEEN IN VIEW.

VIEW OF THE CENTRAL PORTIONS OF BALTIMORE CITY,

From the Rear of the Washington Monument, Looking Due South.

108

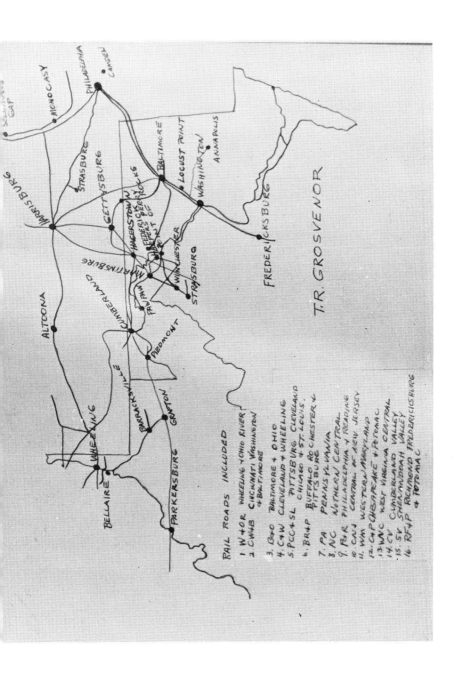

RAIL ROADS INCLUDED

1. W+OR   WHEELING + OHIO RIVER
2. CWWB CINCINNATI WASHINGTON + BALTIMORE

3. B+O   BALTIMORE + OHIO
4. C+W   CLEVELAND + WHEELING
5. PCC+SL PITTSBURG CLEVELAND CHICAGO + ST. LOUIS.
6. BR+P BUFFALO ROCHESTER + PITTSBURG

7. PA   PENNSYLVANIA
8. NC   NOTHERN CENTRAL
9. P+R   PHILADELPHIA + READING
10. CNJ CENTRAL OF NEW JERSEY
11. WM   WESTERN/MARYLAND
12. C+P CHESAPEAKE + POTOMAC
13. WVC WEST VIRGINIA CENTRAL
14. CV   CUMBERLAND VALLEY
15. SV   SHENANDOAH VALLEY
16. RF+P RICHMOND FREDERICKSBURG + POTOMAC

T.R. GROSVENOR

109

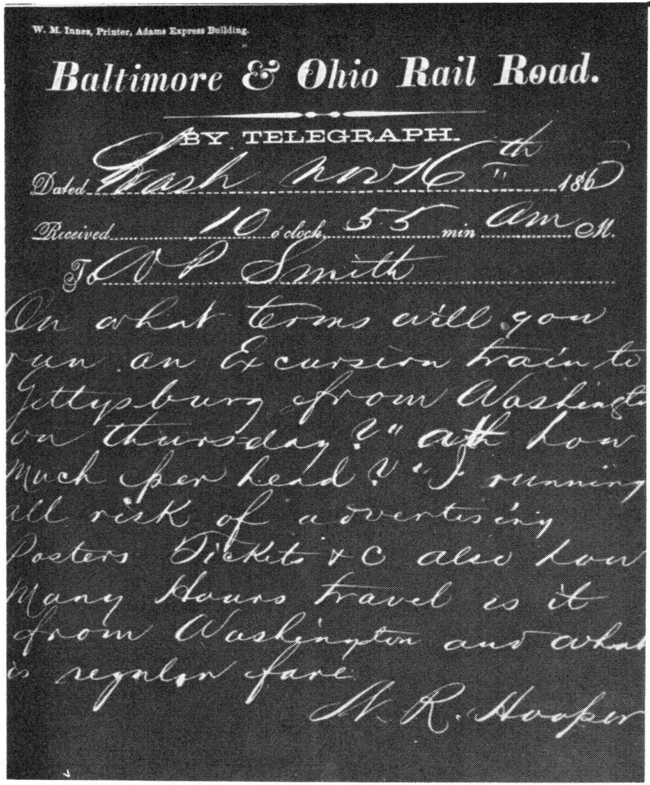

W. M. Innes, Printer, Adams Express Building.

Baltimore & Ohio Rail Road.

BY TELEGRAPH.

Dated Wash Nov 16th 186

Received 10 o'clock 55 min am M.

To W P Smith

On what terms will you run an Excursion train to Gettysburg from Washington on thursday 19th & at how much per head? & running all risk of advertising Posters Tickets &c also how Many Hours travel is it from Washington and what is regular fare

N. R. Hooper

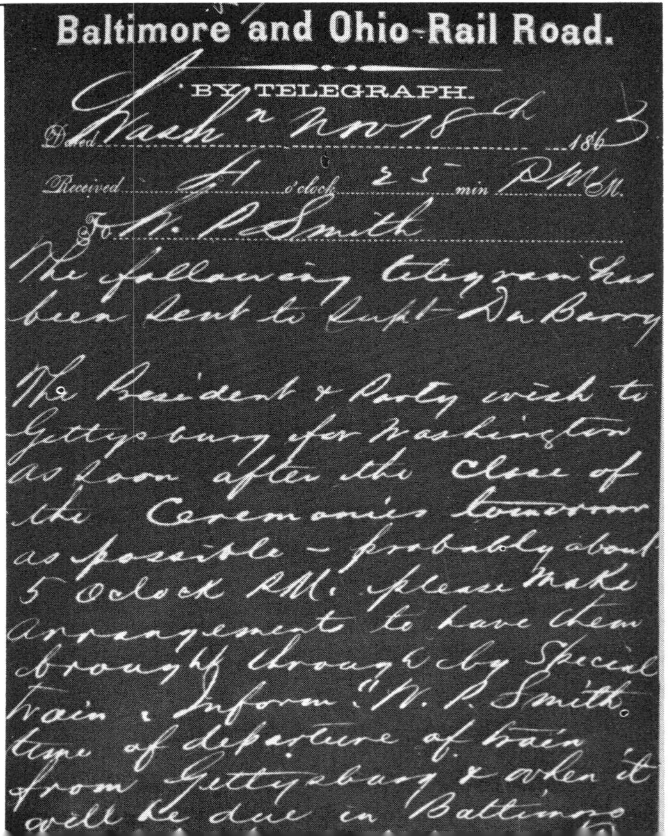

Baltimore and Ohio-Rail Road.

BY TELEGRAPH.

Dated Wash n Nov 18th 1863

Received 4 o'clock 25 min PM M.

To W. P. Smith

The following telegram has been sent to Supt Du Barry

The President & Party wish to Gettysburg for Washington as soon after the close of the Ceremonies tomorrow as possible — probably about 5 Oclock PM. please make arrangement to have them brought through by Special train. Inform W. P. Smith time of departure of train from Gettysburg & when it will be due in Baltimore

Baltimore and Ohio Rail Road.

BY TELEGRAPH.

Dated 186

Received .... o'clock .... min .... M.

To .... (2)

In readiness to bring them through — please answer.

Please do all you can to facilitate prompt return of the President & Party to Wash'n & oblige

Yours

D. C. McCallum

Photostats of two more messages.

[Copy of Telegram.]

Baltimore, Nov. 8.

J. N. DuBarry,
Harrisburg:

Mr. Lincoln and a portion of the Cabinet expect to go to the Gettysburg Consecration, and have sent to me making inquiries as to the route and facilities.

Will you take them up in our private cars through from Washington, if we will deliver to you at Bolton? How near to Gettysburg can you take them by rail? Which is the best route — by Hanover or Westminster?

Please answer promptly. I will confer with you further about details, after route is determined.

(signed) W. P. Smith.

PIEDMONT STATION, B. & O. R. R.,
AT THE "FOOT OF THE MOUNTAIN," 207 MILES FROM BALTIMORE, AND THE DIVIDING POINT
BETWEEN THE SECOND AND THIRD (OR "MOUNTAIN") DIVISIONS OF THE ROAD.

OUTLINE OF HISTORICAL EVENTS

The following memo of historical events to which the papers of William Prescott Smith has reference is extracted from THE SOLDIER IN OUR CIVIL WAR, edited by Paul F. Mottelay, and from the Annual Reports of the Baltimore & Ohio Railroad Company.

1864

July 9—Battle at Monocacy Bridge, Md., between 9000 Federal troops under Gen. Lew Wallace and 20,000 Confederates under Gen. Jubal Early.

July 11—Baltimore cut off from the North by destruction of bridges on P. W. & B. and Northern Central Railroads.

July 12—Attack on Fort Stevens, Washington, by Confederates under General Early repulsed by Federal troops under General Augur. Confederate cavalry reached the line of the Washington Branch at Beltsville, destroying a camp train.

July 20—Battle at Winchester, Va., between Federal cavalry under Gen. Averill and Confederate cavalry under Gen. Early.

July 24—Battle at Winchester, Va. 10,000 troops of Federal Army of West Virginia under Gen. Crook defeated by Gen. Early.

July 25—Confederate attack upon Martinsburg.

July 27-30—Engagement and explosion of mine at Petersburg, Va. Generals Burnside and Meade under Gen. Grant opposing General Lee. Confederate advantage, Federal losses very heavy.

July 29—Engagement at Clear Springs, Md.

Aug. 1—Attack upon Cumberland by Confederates under Johnson and McCausland successfully resisted by Federal forces under Brig. Gen. B. F. Kelley.

Aug. 2—Skirmish at Green Springs Depot, W. Va., near Old Town, Md.

By B. & O. R.R. Telegraph
Washington, July 7, 1864
Received: 4:40 P.M.

W. P. Smith:

I have no orders for movement of troops except the wounded of which I have already telegraphed you. I have sixty-five empty house cars, included in which are 37 government cars which are here subject to my disposition. I have two camel engines, one of which I might send you with the sixty-five (65) cars, and hold the other to take up any that Whiton may send us. I wait your directions.

Geo. S. Koontz.

By B. & O. R.R. Telegraph
Washington, July 7, 1864
Received: 7:55 P.M.

W. P. Smith:

We sent on No. 1 tonnage 15 Pennsylvania, 7 Philadelphia, and 3 B. & O. cars all empty. Engine 120 with 37 U. S. cars and 28 B. & O. cars all empty left at 6:55 o'clock. Could not get her off sooner because No. 7 south was late arriving. I have an engine here to take up any cars Whiton may send us.

Geo. S. Koontz

By B. & O. R.R. Telegraph
Annapolis Junction, July 7, 1864
Received: 11:13 P.M.

W. P. Smith:

Engine 172 with 7 loads wounded men from Frederick for

Annapolis arrived here at 11:10 P.M. I have had not notice of these men and I cannot now get the operator at Annapolis. The wounded men will have to remain here till morning. We can send no engine from Annapolis for them.

A. Flowers.

Car No. 37—

47 Boxes Medical Stores
10 Bundles Litters
1 Bundle Splints

Surgeon Blaney Medical Director
Sandy Hook

July 8th.

By B. & O. R.R. Telegraph
Monocacy, July 8, 1864
Received: 11:07 A.M.

W. P. Smith:

Engine 165 with General Howe arrived in good time, laid by until morning and then started for Sandy Hook. Engine 48, first engine with ammunition arrived and delivered her load at Frederick. Engine 119, first troop train, arrived and unloaded at Frederick. Engine 178, second train with troops, has arrived and now at Frederick unloading. Engine 234, second train with ammunition, has arrived and gone to Frederick to unload. Frederick train east late, caused by getting a car badly off the track at Y switch on Frederick Road.

F. Mantz

By B. & O. R. R. Telegraph
Locust Point, July 8, 1864
Received: 2:40 P.M.

W. P. Smith:

Send special train immediately. I desire to leave here as soon as possible. When may I expect the train. Answer quick.

Genl. Ricketts
Commd'g 3rd Div.
6th Corps.

(Pencil note at bottom—Passenger car was sent to Bailey's and was attached to troop train, leaving there at about 4:30 P.M.)

By B. & O. R.R. Telegraph
Locust Point, July 8, 1864
Received: 4:03 P.M.

W. P. Smith:

I shall start a train of 24 cars in 10 or 15 minutes. Please have the passenger car for Genl. Ricketts at Bailey's. He will ride up to that point in your car and then change to passenger car.

By B. & O. R.R. Telegraph
Parkersburg, July 8, 1864
Received: 7:46 P.M.

W. P. Smith:

Troops are all being moved as fast as they arrive here. Three trains of troops that arrived last P.M. and were detained some three or four hours by slip on Silver Run grade, were again delayed one hour by mail train which was detained by engine 28 with trains east getting driving wheels off near 6th section. Trestle running over that section of the track. Nothing else has worked well. Genl. Hunter and staff left here this P.M. at 8 o'clock. Some 4700 troops and 300 cavalry have already gone forward. The number of troops to ship has been changed from 8000 to 14,000, they have not all left Charleston yet.

L. R. Cofran.

Philadelphia, Wilm. & Balto R.R. Co.
By Morse Telegraph

W. P. Smith,
Camden Station.

You telegraphed me last night and again this A.M. that the wounded men would leave Washington today and I sent you 24 of our troop cars.

We have detained a train since 10 o'clock this morning for them and can hear nothing from you. Can you give me any information. We want our cars in Philadelphia and want the engine and men that have been waiting here all day.

W. Crawford

By B. & O. R.R. Telegraph
Mt. Clare, July 8, 1864
Received: 9:50 P.M.

W. P. Smith:

I have about 40 loads of subsistence and forage for Sandy Hook, Frederick and Monocacy. I will send it forward as soon as possible. I sent the four loads west by Mr. England's extra train this P. M.

A. J. Fairbank.

Head-Quarters, Middle Dept.,
8th Army Corps,
Baltimore, Md. July 8, 1864

Mr. Garrett,
Pres't B. & O. R. R.
Sir:

A subsistence train was loaded last night and ready this A.M. at five (5) o'clock to go to the Monocacy.

Another train with 100,000 rations was ready at about noon to-day.

I am just informed that neither train has been moved yet. Notwithstanding I have written five orders today on the subject and gave most definite instructions last night to all officers concerned as to the importance of the subsistance being forwarded at once.

General Wallace has sent four telegrams from Frederick today. It appears they are entirely out of rations. Will you please give orders that the trains depart at once.

It was agreed with Genl. Rickett that he should be able to draw rations on his arrival at Monocacy.

By B. & O. R.R. Telegraph
Washington, July 8, 1864
Received: 10:10 P.M.

W. P. Smith:
Engine 38 with 49 empty cars and 3 loads ammunition left at 9:20 A.M.

G. S. Koontz

By B. & O. R.R. Telegraph
Monocacy, July 8, 1864
Received: 11:07 P.M.

W. P. Smith:
Things now begin to look unhopeful West of us. Communication appears to be cut as we have no circuit West. We have a bad affair on Frederick Road. Engine 47 has got off the track between Monocacy and Frederick. I have ordered all force that can be got to go to the assistance of getting engine on. This blocks the train of sick and wounded.

F. Mantz.

Master of Transportation's Office
Balto. & Ohio R.R. Co.
Baltimore, July 8, 1864

Wm. P. Smith, Esq.
Sir:
I have ordered through Mr. Fairbanks from 35 to 40 tons of coal from Piedmont but it has not arrived. Now as you have coal on the cars at Mt. Clare, I desire you to sell me the same amount and I will pay you the money or return the coal when the road

opens. My brick kiln is set and ready to burn. I have sold part of the bricks to Mr. Gearey and part to Mr. Markland for Lawrence Reed's house and I will fail if I do not get the coal asked for. Please accomodate me if possible and oblige,

Yours etc.
Cyrus Gault.

(Answer attached: "We cannot part with a ton of coal under present circumstances.

The importance for being prepared for all emergencies, requires us to hold all the coal we can control.

July 3/64   J. W. C.)

Ordinance Office,
Head-Quarters, 8th Army Corps
Baltimore, July 8, 1864

Mr. Garrett,
    Pres't B. & O. R.R.
        Camden Station
Sir:

A special train is required immediately to carry sixty thousand (60,000) rounds ammunition to Frederick for Genl. Lew Wallace. Will you please inform me by bearer if train can be at Fort Avenue switch by 12 o'clock to-night. If so, this will be your order for the same to proceed immediately to Frederick when loaded.

Very respectfully,
Your Obd. Servt.
Chas. L. Issacs
Lieut. & Ord. Office
8th Army Corp.

(Note at bottom:
    Weight about 6000 lbs.)

By B. & O. R.R. Telegraph
Plane No. 1, July 9, 1864
Received: 2:06 A.M.

W. P. Smith:

I directed conductor of engine 165 to leave two large cars at Elysville for Mr. Gearys. Engine 165 left Plane No. 1 after the Frederick train west arrived. We have been getting along very well all day with trains except engine 128. She lost some time tonight on account of heavy train. She passed here at 12:22 o'clock.

J. R. Smith

By B. & O. R.R. Telegraph
Monocacy, July 9, 1864
Received: 6:18 A.M.

W. P. Smith:

I am nearly or quite broken down from a stretch of one week's day and night's labor without rest. For this I am not ready to complain, but I must complain of some of the operators on the line. Early this morning after I had moved all trains from Mariottsville, I went to give some trains east but have not been able to do so from the fact that the operator at Marriottsville could not nor cannot be got to arrange with to move these trains. Consequently they are kept laying at Plane No. 1 for want of an arrangement with Marriottsville to get them away.

F. Mantz

By B. & O. R.R. Telegraph
Plane No. 4, July 9, 1864
Received: 7:00 A.M.
W. P. Smith:

The two troop trains started west about 4 o'clock. They stopped to get 3 days rations. Got one train of commissaries ready and had it brought back from No. 1, and when it arrived here there were two scouts came up the road and ordered the train stopped, stating that our army was sadly whipped and was falling back over the Railroad and Pike, enemy following up. Things look very badly indeed. I ordered Wilson to get the two troop trains back from Monrovia as soon as possible. I really think that there is some credit to be given to the report that the scout brought in, because he delivered it in writing to the Col. of the 6th Md. and was particular in timing. His horse had been ridden very hard. A very fine large barn of Mr. Wails was burned. The large bridge over the Monocacy on Georgetown.

By B. & O. R.R. Telegraph
Locust Point, July 9, 1864
Received: 7:20 A.M.
W. P. Smith:

Engine 113 left here at 6:45 o'clock with 23 cars of troops 950 men.

A. Hilleary

By B. & O. R.R. Telegraph
Locust Point, July 9, 1864
Received: 7:30 A.M.

W. P. Smith:

Engine left here at 7:30 with 13 cars of stock and baggage and 100 men. All the troops are gone forward.

A. Hilleary

By B. & O. R.R. Telegraph
Plane No. 1 July 9, 1864
Received: 7:35 A.M.

W. P. Smith:

Dispatched East from Plane No. 1 this A.M. as extras, the following engines with trains. Engine 47 in place of engine 26. The 47 broke spring hanger and the 26 took her place on Frederick train. Engine 235, 179, 178, and 80. The 80 has some sick and wounded soldiers. First train left at 6:04 o'clock and last at 7:06 o'clock.

J. R. Smith

By B. & O. R.R. Telegraph
Mt. Clare, July 9, 1864
Received: 8:40 A.M.

W. P. Smith:

24 empty P. W. & B. troop cars arrived last night from Washington. Mr. Lee informs me that those cars were intended to bring 900 sick and wounded soldiers from Washington. Please let me know what is to be done with those cars. We have a large number of U. S. empty cars and more to arrive from the West. What is to be done with them. Are they to be sent back to Washington or held over at this station?

A. J. Fairbanks

Answered.

COPY

Frederick Junction, July 9, 1864
9:45 A. M.

Sidney H. Gay,
  Tribune, N. Y.
      Early Friday morning Brig. Genl. Tyler, under orders Genl. Wallace, went to front at Frederick and took command. Col. Clendenin with cavalry commenced and continued skirmishing with enemy all day in mountains back to city. In afternoon Genl. Wallace went to front with reinforcements. Learning that the enemy's position on our front was merely a feint to cover his movement on Urbania and thence toward Washington, Genl. Wallace withdrew his forces and evacuated Frederick City at 10 o'clock Friday night. Early this morning rebels were in line of battle and advanced on Frederick, which they reoccupied. We removed everything possible from the city, sick, wounded, stores, etc. Two citizens were arrested by our returning skirmishers making signals to rebs last night from the city. General has headquarters here this Saturday.

By B. & O. R.R. Telegraph
Ellicott's Mills, July 9, 1864
Received: 11:15 A.M.

W. P. Smith:
      Troops arriving slowly. We propose to load them as they arrive, as there are no officers here in charge of troops. We will not wait altogether for Military, as it will be too much delay. There is now firing going on in the rear in two different directions. Enemy pushing the rear slowly.

F. Mantz.

By B. & O. R.R. Telegraph
Plane No. 4, July 9, 1864
Received: 11:25 A.M.

W. P. Smith:

The line is not working from here West and the conductor of troop train has reports fighting between Frederick and Monocacy. Do you think it safe for me to go on? If so please instruct me.

A. P. Shutt.

By B. & O. R.R. Telegraph
Plane No. 1 July 9, 1864
Received: 12:40 P.M.

W. P. Smith:

We have made a safe retreat with all property. Enemy close on to us. I have ordered the instruments of this office to be put away. I will let you hear from me at Marriottsville.

F. Mantz

By B. & O. R.R. Telegraph
Philadelphia, July 9, 1864
Received: 12:42 P.M.

W. P. Smith:

C. & A. R.R. reports they have advices of 3000 men to leave tomorrow. Do not know the time. Will give you promptly when they leave Philadelphia.

H. F. Kenney.

125

By B. & O. R.R. Telegraph
Annapolis Junction, July 9, 1864
Received: 2:00 P.M.

W. P. Smith:

Engine 82 with wounded from Frederick for Annapolis arrived here at 1 o'clock 45 minutes A.M. I was not notified of their coming until they arrived. Detained here until 1:30 P.M. Waiting on engine from Annapolis.

A. Flowers

By B. & O. R.R. Telegraph
Plane No. 4, July 9, 1864
Received: 1:35 P.M.

W. P. Smith:

I have worked all trains back this far. Enemy opened on us heavy this morning with artillery and pressed hard on our forces to get position. They seem determined. I think the force is larger than has been estimated. We did not leave until the very last moment. I fear they have too much artillery for us. I think my house is burned, the station house or the large wood bridge over the Monocacy on Washington Road. The troops ought to be sent forward.

F. Mantz.

By B. & O. R.R. Telegraph
Monocacy, July 9, 1864
Received: 2:16 P.M.

W. P. Smith:

I have started all empty cars East that could be got hold of. 4 trains now which will soon be at No. 1. Last train had some 10 loads of sick and wounded. I have received no instructions where to send them. Officers in hurry getting them away. No cars left back except such as had commissary stores in them. They are now standing in Gambrill's switch on East side of bridge.

F. Mantz

(Note on back:

With the appearances in the vicinity of Frederick it is desirable to get all your equipment returned to Baltimore as quickly as possible. Mantz should be instructed to have commissary stores, etc., unloaded and the cars returned.

It should be explained to the military authorities that as we are making very heavy movements to Washington, etc., it is important to unload, and give us the control of the equipment at the earliest practicable moment.

J. W. G.

July 9, 1864

By B. & O. R.R. Telegraph
Washington, July 9, 1864
Received: 2:40 P.M.

W. P. Smith:

I want cars early Monday morning for 250 horses.

G. S. Koontz

By B. & O. R.R. Telegraph
Washington, July 9, 1864
Received: 7:10 P.M.

W. P. Smith:

The Secretary is on 6:30 train in car next to our Green sleeping car. I have informed that private car is at Philadelphia depot for him.

G. S. Koontz

By B. & O. R.R. Telegraph
Mt. Clare, July 9, 1864
Received: 7:50 P.M.

W. P. Smith:

I have over one hundred probably 125 cars for troops and am now prepared to load 800 head of horses. They must load at the platform at the junction.

A. J. Fairbank

By B. & O. R.R. Telegraph
New York, July 9, 1864
Received: 8:40 P.M.

W. P. Smith:

Quarter Master notifies us to be ready for over 3000 troops tomorrow by way of Amboy. Destination not known yet.

Ira Bliss.

By B. & O. R.R. Telegraph
Annapolis Junction, July 9, 1864
Received: 8:45 P.M.

W. P. Smith:

Nine empty cars, taken to Annapolis with wounded this

morning, have just been returned. Shall I send them to Baltimore by No. 2 tonnage North this P.M.?

A. Flowers.

By B. & O. R.R. Telegraph
Plane No. 1, July 9, 1864
Received: 8:50 P.M.

W. P. Smith:

I have dispatched all the engines East except the Frederick train. They started to Mt. Airy and were met by soldiers and told to return that the Federal troops were retreating down the pike pursued by Confederates.

C. W. Harvey

By B. & O. R.R. Telegraph
Plane No. 1, July 9, 1864
Received: 8:59 P.M.

W. P. Smith:

I can hear nothing from Mr. Mantz or the troop trains that went to Monrovia and fear they have all been captured.

C. W. Harvey

W. P. Smith, Esq.
  Master of Trans.
Sir:

We loaded to-day with government stores for Frederick cars 1106, 1173, 1333, 1007, 1222 and 1450, and for Sandy Hook cars 1202, 1494, and 1745. These cars have been sent round to Mount Clare and I have notified Fairbank government wants them sent up at once.

Yours respectfully
J. T. England

July 9, 1864

By B. & O. R.R. Telegraph
Philadelphia, July 9, 1864
Received: 9:26 P.M.

W. P. Smith:

I learn there will be no troops leave New York tonight. Three thousand are expected to leave New York tomorrow. Will advise you.

H. F. Kenney.

Cipher

By U.S. Military Telegraph

*Rohrersburg, Md.

July 9, 1864, - 10 P.M.

W. P. Smith:

Have shipped up to this time about five thousand seven hundred troops, three hundred and fifteen cavalry horses, twenty six horse wagons and horses, all Head Quarters horses and baggage. No more troops here, nor none expected tonight. None have had to wait a moment on transportation. Everything working well on this branch today.

L. R. Cofran,
Agent.

*Pencil note-corrected to Parkersburg.

By B. & O. R.R. Telegraph
Plane No. 1, July 9, 1864
Received: 10:23 P.M.

J. W. Garrett, Esq.
Prest.

I did as I promised. Held the bridge to the last. They overwhelmed with numbers. My troops fought splendidly. Losses fearful. Send me cars enough to Ellicott's Mills to take up my retreating columns. Don't fail me.

Lew Wallace
Maj. Genl. Cmdg.

By B. & O. R.R. Telegraph
Parkersburg, July 9, 1864- 10 P.M.
Received: 10th, 10:30 P.M.

W. P. Smith:

Have shipped about twelve hundred (1200) troops today. Everything works well, no more troops here. What are shipped today cleared up Gen. Sullivan's Command. Gen. Crook's command is on the way. It will be coming for a week. About sixteen hundred (1600) cavalry are expected to arrive here some time tonight. Have arranged to commence loading them at daylight in the morning. We have but 40 stock cars on hand to commence with. The others having all gone east with horses and not commenced returning yet. I think we will be able to send them away as fast as they arrive. Have telegraphed to Mr. Willard to hurry the stock cars back as fast as possible.

L. R. Cofran.

Bordentown, July 25, 1864

W. P. Smith, Esq.
Baltimore,
Dear Sir:

The following is a list of trains moving north, of which I have received no reports.

July 12th	7:30 A.M.	July 7th	11:15 A.M.
July 13	7:30 A.M.	July 12	11:15 A.M.
July 14	7:30 A.M.	July 13	11:15 A.M.
July 15	7:30 A.M.	July 15	11:15 A.M.
July 10	6:30 P.M.	July 11	8:30 P.M.
July 11	6:30 P.M.	July 12	8:30 P.M.
July 12	6:30 P.M.	July 13	8:30 P.M.
July 13	6:30 P.M.	July 14	8:30 P.M.
July 14	6:30 P.M.	July 15	8:30 P.M.
July 15	6:30 P.M.		
July 16	6:30 P.M.		

July 17   6:30 P.M.
July 18   6:30 P.M.

No doubt many of these trains were interferred with or prevented altogether from running by the recent invasion. I would like to be informed which they are so that I can account for the gap in my consolidated statements. I have written twice to Mr. Koontz for this information but have received no reply owing doubtless to his pressing duties, which I am aware are arduous and constant. Cannot this statement be made from the memorandum of your Mr. Showacre?

I regret to say that I have no little difficulty in obtaining answers to my letters and telegrams which often proves a hinderance to the efficient performance of my duties.

Your obd. Servt.
W. C. Murphy

Private and Confidential

Harper's Ferry
July 25, 1 P. M.

W. P. Smith, Esq.

Crook is at Martinsburg, we are falling back towards Williamsport. Hill and Longstreet said to be in the Valley advancing.

Things look very gloomy. We will make a fight here. Col. Mulligan was killed yesterday.

Respectfully,
R. L. Shelley

P.S. Please send the enclosed by telegraph and much obliged. The enclosure is key is decoded as follows:

Crook has fallen back to Martinsburg and is going to Williamsport. Hill and Longstreet said to be advancing. We will make a fight here.

E. W. B.

By B. & O. R.R. Telegraph
Wheeling, July 27, 1864
Received: 12:46 P.M.

W. P. Smith:

*"Othello" reports road safe to Back Creek and wishes particularly to know condition of things at Harper's Ferry. Answer immediately.

J. B. Ford.

(Penciled note on back by J. W. Garrett:

See my telegram of yesterday to Major General K.)

*"Othello" is code name for Maj. Gen. Kelley, as shown in other dispatches.

By B. & O. R.R. Telegraph
Point of Rocks, July 27, 1864
Received: 2:15 P.M.

W. P. Smith:

I do not deem it safe for trains to run to-night between this point and Monocacy. I have reliable information of the presence of several small squads of White's rebel command being in the vicinity of Buckeystown. Do not think it is sufficient to do any damage in daytime to road but under cover of darkness they may commit some damage to road. There are no troops stationed on road between here and Monocacy.

W. Shock

By B. & O. R.R. Telegraph
Monocacy, July 27, 1864
Received: 3:48 P.M.

W. P. Smith:

Capt. Snyder informs me that Collins, the man that acted as Supervisor to the appointment of Wm. Morris, that he Collins saw some ten or eleven cavalry this A.M. between Adamstown and Point of Rocks. He says that he knew some of them before they went in the Army. Snyder says he saw a Mr. Bosh (I think is the name) from the neighborhood of Dunnington or Kearneysville, who informed him (Snyder) that he had a conversation with one of the Confederate officers, who informed him that the track was not torn up, that it was not their intention to tear up the road at present. Did not know what might be done hereafter, that their intention was to go to Pennsylvania. From all the rumors I have heard today there appears to be no doubt that rebels hold Martinsburg. John Horneworth.

By B. & O. R.R. Telegraph
Sandy Hook, July 27, 1864
Received: 3:20 P.M.

W. P. Smith:

Mail and extra train arrived here regularly. Engine 234 with five car loads of clothing, etc., has arrived. Cars were unloaded. Engine 234 with the five empty cars left here about 2:02, Mail East flagging her. Can get nothing from Martinsburg or vicinity. Crook's Command now arriving here.

C. Smith

By B. & O. R.R. Telegraph
Sandy Hook July 27, 1864
Received: 5:15 P.M.

W. P. Smith:

It has been reported to me by Mr. Collins one of Norris'
foremen that it is not safe to run trains at present between Sandy
Hook and Point of Rocks at night. Collins had some conversation
with one of the rebels.

C. Smith

By B. & O. R.R. Telegraph
Sandy Hook, July 27, 1864
Received: 9:25 P.M.

W. P. Smith:

Would it not be well to instruct agent at Monocacy not to
allow anything to pass that place until after daylight in A.M.? Mr.
Fairbank reports one engine from his station for this place which
left 7:10. From the information we have it would be very unsafe
to run anything between Monocacy and this place tonight.

J. Donohoo.

By B. & O. R.R. Telegraph
Harper's Ferry, July 27, 1864
Received:

W. P. Smith:

The Major General Commanding requests that the lumber
be forwarded to this point.

R. S. Gardner,
A. Q. M.

By B. & O. R.R. Telegraph
Cumberland, July 27, 1864
Received: 28th 9:05 A.M.

W. P. Smith:

From information received today there is no doubt *that
Back Creek bridge was burnt this A.M.* Road all right to Cherry
Run. All quiet here.

J. P. Willard

W. P. Smith:

Genl. Tyler has received following from Col. Clendenin at Frederick and repeats it to Mr. Garrett:

"Patrol has just returned from Williamsport. No rebels have crossed. Genl. Averell is near Hagerstown with Division. Genl. Crooks has moved down to Sharpsburg on route to Harper's Ferry. His train also. We have cavalry and artillery at Williamsport. 18,000 rebels are reported opposite Clearspring. The rebels are running threshing machines and gathering the harvest. Mulligan is killed.

Dr. Clendenin.

Nothing more.

Respectfully,
J. J. E. R.

Private & Confidential.

Harper's Ferry,
July 28, 1864

W. P. Smith, Esq.

Dear Sir:

I wrote you two or three hurried lines on the 25th giving you some information which I had just received from General Averell's Adjutant General.

I went out to Williamsport the next day to investigate matters and found our men in a very demoralized state, straggling all over the country, a great many of them having thrown away their arms, and all telling the exagerated and absurd stories.

I had an interview with Crook, and he thinks that the enemy's forces number at least thirty thousand, while ours scarcely number ten thousand effective men. Their "Line of Battle" extended two miles beyond ours on the right flank and caused a stampede of the cavalry who were guarding our flanks and train. Prisoners captured represent that they belong to Longstreet and Hill's corps, but their stories may have been prepared for them before we caught them.

Our command are all encamped on Maryland Heights. The men look tired and worn out after their *hard* and *incessant* marching of the past two months. The infantry have all marched some six hundred, and the cavalry nine hundred miles. All military men competent to judge concur in the opinion that it will take at least *three weeks* to organize this force, and get it into any kind of shape to take the field with a probability of success.

Crook's infantry and Duffie's cavalry arrived here at noon yesterday.

Averell is at Hagerstown picketing the Fords all the way down the river to Antietam Ford.

The Sixth corps was expected at Frederick yesterday evening. I am confident the Rebels are determined to hold the Valley at all hazards until they have harvested the crops.

They have been very quiet since Monday morning, in fact too much so. There are rumors that they have sent a force westward towards Cumberland, but I do not credit them. I think the bulk of their force is at Winchester.

Very Respectfully,
Richard L. Shelby.

Mount Clare, July 28, 1864

W. P. Smith,
Master of Trans.
Dear Sir:

I regret that I have to report to you that I have good reason to believe that car 1047 loaded at Locust Point for Benwood was robbed at this station some time during yesterday. This car had been used for hauling troops and the weatherboarding has been knocked off and partly boarded up with rough boards; and on one side of the car there was an opening nearly large enough for a man to get through. Just at this place there are boxes containing canned peaches. Two of the boxes have been opened. They are marked to contain two dozen cans. One of them is empty while the other is nearly empty. This car stands in the middle of the yard. I have had an extra watchman over the western loading during the night, but had not in daytime, as I did not suppose for a moment a car could have been robbed in the yard during the day. I have put a watchman day and night over those cars, and I do not think the like can occur again.

Respectfully,
A. J. Fairbank,
Agt.

July 29, 1864

W. P. Smith,
    Master of Trans.
Dear Sir:
    On the night of the 27th I was ordered by Mr. England to send cars to Washington to bring 1000 wounded to Baltimore; also to send 2 cars to Relady to take troops to Elysville. Those orders left us without a single house car, hence we could send no cars to Locust Point yesterday. I have sent 15 cars to Locust Point this A. M. and will continue to send 15 daily whenever we can raise them.

Respectfully,
A. J. Fairbank
Agent.

Baltimore, July 29, 1864

W. P. Smith, Esq.,
    M. of Trans.,
Sir:
    I got a note from you saying there were 1000 sick to come

up from Washington in the morning and that you had notified
N.C.R.R. to send to Camden Station 30 cars by 11 o'clock. These
cars did not come. Mr. Barker saw me and I told him I had 8
troop and 2 house cars I could send round to Mr. Fairbank, which
I did and notified him what Mr. Koontz wanted. Mr. Koontz had
only 730 sick and sent 31 cars. Gen. Tyler ordered two cars on way
train to take troops from Relay House to Elysville which he said
must go before passenger train time. We got no cars from
N.C.R.R. after waiting for them. I had to load night before last
6 troop cars with bread for Frederick to go out on morning tonnage. We have very few cars and have today 3000 boxes bread
and 5 or 600 barrels meat, etc., for Sandy Hook. I sent 8 troop
cars to Washington this morning with troops and have 9 troop
cars at the station.

> Your respectfully,
> J. T. England

> Head Quarters, Middle Dept.
> 8th Army Corps,
> Baltimore, July 29, 1864 7:30 P.M.

(Original by telegraph.)
W. P. Smith, Esq.
B.&.O.R.R.
There is no telegraph operator at the Relay House or Ridgeville. It is very important that one should be at each place. Can
you do anything to put one at each place during the present
emergency?

> (Signed) Lew Wallace
> Maj. Genl. Vols.

A true copy
James R. Ross.
Major A.A.A.G

Maj. Genl. Wallace:

I have sent an operator to the Relay who is now on duty.

There is an office at Plane No. 1 about 2½ or 3 miles from Ridgeville and the nearest point on our line to Ridgeville is Mt! Airy. Do you wish an office opened there? I think there is an operator in one of the companies at that point named E. Fulton who would do. Can you detail him for this service?

Please reply quick.

J. J. G. Riley
Supt. Teleg.

Copy

By B. & O. R.R. Telegraph
Point of Rocks July 29, 1864
Received: 8:00 P.M.

Comdg. Officer Relay
Comdg. Officer Monocacy:
Genl. Wallace and J. W. Garrett:

"The report that Moseby had or is crossing the river at Edward's Ferry is incorrect. Our operator at Poolsville reports to me that some of our cavalry passed through Leesburg this P. M. and reports all quiet about Edward's Ferry.

W. Shock
Operator

Frederick, July 29, 1864

W. P. Smith, Esq.
Sir:

Our colored scouts came into Hagerstown last night reporting rebels crossing at Falling Waters. Everything belonging to government left Hagertown. Driver of stage reports Genl. Averill gone to Chambersburg. Difference of opinion as to numbers, some place high figures, others about the same when here. There is no communication between Martinsburg and Hagerstown. Rebels hold Martinsburg.

There is great excitement from Boonsboro to Hagerstown. Farmers taking their stock off. I cannot find for a certainty if any of the enemy have crossed, but the driver believes they have. *Mr. Baughman and Norris's family will be sent over the lines in the morning.* This is a damn shame. If the stage should return here any time tonight I will telegraph you if I can. This is for your private use. Show it to no one.

Thomas Sinn.

By B. & O. R.R. Telegraph
Mt. Clare, July 30, 1864
Received: 7:45 A.M.

W. P. Smith:

There are some ten (10) or fifteen (15) men here who claim to be in charge of Capt. Uray's cars, which were sent from Harper's Ferry for safety. They are ransacking every car about the place and it is almost impossible prevent it. I hope you will have a guard placed over these cars and have these men now here sent away.

A. J. Fairbank.

(Pencil note at bottom:
Telegraphed Genl.
Follow up and get rid of them).

By B. & O. R.R. Telegraph
Sandy Hook July 30, 1864
Received: 9:15 A.M.

W. P. Smith:

Have just returned from Head quarters. I proposed to send an engine up the road towards Martinsburg to examine condition of road and etc. But was informed that it would not be prudent to do so at present, consequently the trip was postponed for the present.

C. Smith

By B. & O. R.R. Telegraph
Point of Rocks July 30, 1864
Received 9:44 A.M.

From what appears to be a reliable source I learn that Moseby is to concentrate all his forces at Taylortown, Va. about 3 miles from here and make a raid into Maryland sometime during the day. He will be likely to strike at Berlin or this point. His forces are supposed to number about three or four hundred (300) or (400). I will report to you any information I can gain.

W. Shock.

By B. & O. R.R. Telegraph
Monocacy, July 30, 1864
Received: 1:55 P.M.

W. P. Smith:

Way train west has just returned from Adamstown. They report rebels on line of road cutting wires down. They were stopped at Lime Kiln by 2 of our Pickets and ordered back but conductor went forward and when he reached Adamstown the people were all leaving, running in every direction. One of our repair men stopped the train and said he saw them cutting poles down. Mail west and engine 174 with sixteen (16) loads of freight, 2 loads soldiers have gone west and cannot find out anything about them, whether they arrived at Sandy Hook or not.

H. J. Walling

Cumberland, July 30, 1864

W. P. Smith, Esq.
　　Master of Trans.
Dear Sir:

The delay to the Mail train West of the 21st that arrived at Wheeling five hours late as reported by Mr. Cofran, was delayed at Sandy Hook until 3:45 P.M. waiting for mail train east. The cause of the delay to Mail train east was all the culverts between Duffields and Harper's Ferry had to be restored before the train could reach the Ferry, which was not accomplished until 3:30 P.M. I reported the time that Mail trains east and west left Sandy Hook immediately after they left to you from Sandy Hook. There is nothing new to communicate in regard to the situation of military matters here. Genl. Kelley stills holds the road as far east as Sleepy Creek. Back Creek bridge is certainly down and from information I received at Hancock I fear the track and everything of any use to us at Martinsburg is utterly destroyed. I commenced yesterday running a train to Hancock and will continue it as long as it is safe to do so. It was believed yesterday that a large force of the enemy were near McCoy's Ferry getting ready to cross into Maryland. Yesterday there was a small force of cavalry on the Maryland side ten miles east of Hancock.

We are running no trains from here west but the express train, and the way train which runs west one day and east the next which is ample for all the business doing.

Very truly yours,
J. P. Willard

By B. & O. R.R. Telegraph
Cumberland, July 31, 1864
Received: 1:45 A.M.

W. P. Smith:

Great excitement here this P.M. The enemy occupied Hancock this A.M. The Ironclads gave them fight at Hancock. But withdrew from fight after having the smokestack of engine knocked off. Averill is said to have driven them from Hancock, and that they were advancing on Cumberland. Sleepy Creek bridge and station house at Alpine said to be burned. Do not think report of the burning reliable.

J. P. Willard

By B. & O. R.R. Telegraph
Washington, July 31, 1864
Received: 11:35 A.M.

W. P. Smith
    and
J. T. England:

Engine 182 with 30 loads troops left at 7:30 and engine 120 with 31 loads troops left at 7:30. Had all loaded by 4:15 but could not get them off on account of telegraph failing to work.

G. S. Koontz

(Penciled note at bottom:

Our telegraphs are all doing badly.

Note in pencil, probably by J. W. Garrett:

Why is that? Especially on Washington Road?

If necessary we must use another wire. Superintendent of Telegraph confer.)

By B. & O. R.R. Telegraph
Relay House, July 31, 1864
Received: 12:16 P.M.

Lt. Col. S. R. Lawrence, A.A.G.:

Just received the following dispatch: General Tyler has gone up the road with reinforcements.

"Monocacy, 11 A.M.

To Gen. Tyler:

Information just received from a signal officer that three heavy columns of rebels are moving up towards Emmittsburg; 19th Corps in pursuit; Hunter moving through Middletown Valley; 2nd Division 6th Corps holding the Gaps in South Mountain; one division moving up, which will pass through Frederick.

(Signed) D. R. Clendenin,
Lt. Col."
Wm. H. Weigel, A.A.G.

By B. & O. R.R. Telegraph
Washington, July 31, 1864
Received: 1:41 P.M.

W. P. Smith:

From what I learn I think we may have another movement to make probably as heavy as the one made last night. I think it advisable to have equipment of last night returned as speedily as praticable.

Geo. S. Koontz

By B. & O. R.R. Telegraph
Point of Rocks, July 31, 1864
Received: 10:30 P.M.

W. P. Smith:

Your dispatch received. According to instructions I will give you what little information I am in possession of. The main column of the rebels who crossed the river at Williamsport and advanced into Pennsylvania have recrossed the Potomac into Va. This is the most reliable information I can gain from that quarter.

The news in this immediate vicinity is quite conflicting. Many rumors as to the whereabouts of the enemy, their intentions and etc., but as yet nothing reliable. But I think by ten A.M. tomorrow I will be able to give you some reliable information. At present there appears to be no other Confederate forces in this vicinity or for many miles around excepting Moseby, with his guerrilla band, a portion of whom report says, are still lurking on this side of the Potomac near Poolsville, but their force is so small they will hardly attempt anything desperate. We have sufficient force here to protect us from attack from Moseby. We are about adopting measures by which to discover the strength, whereabouts and intentions of the enemy. As soon as we ascertain these facts I will immediately report the same to you by telegraph and if necessary give immediate warning to "Dispatchers."

My telegraphic communication to Washington via Poolsville, Nolands Ferry, etc., are uninterrupted and working through all right.

You will hear from me soon again.

Your obedient servant,
W. W. Shock.

Monocacy, Aug. 1st, 1864
Wm. P. Smith,
M. of Trans.
Sir:

The troop trains from Washington which arrived here yesterday were all unloaded promptly and safely. At once the engine and empty cars were sent back to Baltimore with as little delay as possible with the exception of one train which was kept at the bridge by order of Genl. Tyler, that was engine 120 with 31 empty cars, are held here subject to Military orders. The troop trains were detained yesterday on the road unusually long on account of some of the engines being over loaded. Engine 72 which was the leading engine had as many as 37 cars. That is certainly too much for any engine to drag to make any time. That was the cause of detaining the rest of them. It also detained Mail train East at Plane No. 1 much longer than it ought to have done. In order to get them up I had to order Spurrier to go down cautiously to meet them to get them up to Plane No. 1 where he met them, I believe, near Woodbine, as I understand.

I have from reliable information that there were four hundred rebels across the river near Poolsville yesterday and but seventy of them came up to Adamstown doing no damage to the road only cutting the wires. After leaving Adamstown were going towards the river, where they met the balance of their force. When they came in contact with a detachment of the 8th Illinois cavalry, a small skirmish ensued when they killed one and captured a Lieut. with 17 men, also took with them about two hundred horses. They have not been heard of since. We have here now a pretty strong force of about 7 or 8 thousand, I should suppose. Whether they will remain here or not I cannot learn. The main body of the rebel army that crossed the river above a few days ago were passing through Emmittsburg on yesterday afternoon, that portion of the 8th and 19th army corps that were near Harper's Ferry were passing through Frederick on yesterday afternoon in hot pursuit of them. It is now a general belief that they are making their way towards Pennsylvania and if overtaken we expect to hear of a battle in a few days.

Yours respectfully,
H. J. Walling.

Quartermaster General's Office,
Washington City, 2d Febry, 1865

W. Prescott Smith, Esq.,
    Master of Transpn., B.&.O.R.R.,
      Baltimore, Md.

Sir:

The transportation of the Twenty-third (23rd) Army Corps, numbering twenty thousand (20,000) men, with all its artillery and eight hundred (800) animals from Tennessee to the banks of the Potomac, a distance of nearly fourteen hundred (1400) miles has been completed.

This movement made amid the multiplied difficulties, dangers and severities of mid winter without disaster or accident in the unprecedented short time of eleven (11) days forms a remarkable incident in this eventful war, the like of which cannot, I think, find its parallel in the history of warfare, and well illustrates the vast importance for the protection of our country of such means of communication as you control.

Having communicated in my report to the Secretary of War the distinguished part which yourself, and the officers and employees connected with your Company, have borne in the movement, and that is mainly owing to the sleepless vigilance and earnest efforts of the managers of our Rail Roads that his orders have been so successfully executed, I am directed by him to return to you his thanks and full recognition of the valuable services you have thereby rendered to the country in these days of its peril.

> I have the Honor to be,
> Very Respectfully,
> Your Obt. Servt.,
> Lewis B. Parsons,
> Col. & Chf. R.&R. Transpn.

> War Department,
> Washington City,
> February 2nd, 1865.

Dear Sir:

I have to thank you very sincerely for your successful and devoted exertions in the transportation of the 23rd Army Corps over the Baltimore and Ohio Railroad. So vast a movement, accomplished with such rapidity in the midst of circumstances of difficulty so extraordinary, is something unknown in the history of warfare, and a great part of its success is to be attributed to you.

> I am, dear Sir,
> Yours very faithfully,
> C. A. Dana.

William Prescott Smith, Esquire,
Master of Transportation,
Baltimore.

Copy

Baltimore, Md.
Feb. 9, 1865

Dear Sir:

Ever since the receipt of your highly-esteemed favor of the 2nd inst., thanking me for my exertions in the transportation of the 23rd Army Corps over our railroad, I have designed responding to it in a becoming manner, either in person or by letter.

The first being denied me, I can only now express to you the deep gratification I feel in receiving such a testimonial as you have conferred. It is a sufficient compensation for all the efforts I made in the recent movement, which you have very properly characterized as having been "accomplished with such rapidity, in the midst of circumstances of difficulty so extraordinary", and to which you are pleased, as I think, with great propriety, to add, "as something unknown in the history of warfare."

Permit me to say further, in this acknowledgement of your very graceful compliment, that the success of my own exertions was heightened, if not entirely secured, by the cooperative efforts of the officers and men in my own and other Departments of our Company's service.

I understand that your immediate Agent supervising this movement, Colonel Parsons, of the Quartermaster General's Department, is about making a report to you, in which he proposes to enumerate briefly such general officers of our Road as can most properly share the satisfaction of duty well performed in this connection.

Again assuring you that your appreciation is a source of the highest satisfaction to me, personally and officially, and will prove an incentive to further efforts when occasion requires,

I remain,
With great regard,
Obediently yours,
Wm. Prescott Smith

149

(Signed)
Hon. Charles A. Dana,
   Assistant Secretary of War,
    Washington, D.C.

WAR DEPARTMENT
Office of
Director and General Manager of Military Rail Road, U. S.
Washington, Feb. 10, 1865

W. P. Smith, Esq.,
M. of Trans. B. & O. R.R.,
Dear Sir:

I have the honor to tender you the position of General Superintendent of Government Rail Roads in the Military Division of the Miss. Headquarters at Nashville, Tenn.

Should you conclude to accept the same, your compensation will be at the rate of Four thousand five hundred (4500) dollars per Annum. In addition thereto, a suitable dwelling and rations will be furnished you. The position is an important one, and I trust you may be induced to oblige me by responding favorably.

        I am, Sir very respectfully
        Your Obedient Servant,
        D. C. McCallum,
        Brev. Brig. Genl. Etc.

        Washington, Jan. 26, 1869.
Hon. J. M. Brodhead,

        Comptroller U.S. Treasury.
Sir:

My attention has been called to some papers in the case of a claim of the B. & O. R.R. Co. against the United States, for its services in the great proposed and partially executed movement of Genl. McClellan from Washington on Manassas via Harper's Ferry, in February, 1862.

In these I find a decision from your office, signed by yourself, and dated September 19, 1867, addressed to the Hon. John Wilson, 3d Auditor, in regard to the items of this claim.

As I was, at the date of these transactions, not only the chief transportation officer of the Road in question, but personally and intimately cognizant of the whole proceeding, I may express my very great surprise at the totally inadequate conception, shown in the papers before me, of the important events to which they refer.

Your decision states that "the orders of Genl. McClellan contemplated the moving of 16 guns and caissons, 4 battery wagons, 280 artillery horses and 550 artillery men, 750 cavalry men and horses, and 10,000 infantry from Washington to Sandy Hook, Md."

You further say "that the order for the movement was given on the 26th and abandoned on the 27th," and all that "in the meantime the General and Staff were transported the entire distance," etc. Now, will you please permit me to state herein some facts connected with this matter, which could not be properly disclosed in my sworn statement of November 3, 1863, for obvious military reasons—the war then still pending.

This movement, to my certain knowledge (obtained from the then Secretary of War, Maj. Genl. McClellan, and his Chief of Staff, Genl. Marcy) contemplated nothing more nor less than a grand flank advance, to open the spring campaign against the enemy at Manassas Junction with 75,000 men, mainly drawn from Washington by way of Harper's Ferry and Winchester. 25,000 of the proposed force was embraced in Banks' corps, forming the right wing of the great army of the Potomac that had wintered at Frederick, Md., and had been moved by the B. & O. R.R. between the 23d and 26th of February, in cars from Frederick and vicinity to Sandy Hook, opposite Harper's Ferry, at which point the road was yet interrupted by the original destruction of Harper's Ferry bridge by Genl. Johnston's forces on the 10th of June, 1861.

The Secretary of War and General McClellan had consulted

the Company a week or more previous to this movement, as to its ability and readiness to move 50,000 men, of all arms, with their accompaniments, from Washington to Sandy Hook, and they were informed that we should require fully 48 hours notice to effect such a movement in the time desired, so that we could gather our cars and engines at Washington, obtain additional equipment from other railroads north and east of Baltimore, and bring around, by way of Wheeling, Pittsburg and Harrisburg from West Virginia, a number of our most valuable train men, extra telegraph operators, and others in service there. This we deemed essential to our success in the movement, as its extent and character was then altogether unprecedented in the transportation experience of our country, and our facilities then at command, east of the break in the Road, was regarded as inadequate.

No notice was given to us, however, as expected, and we had concluded that this proposed flank attack was abandoned. We received orders at midnight on the 25th of February, to provide at Washington a special train at 6 o'clock the following morning, to carry Gen. McClellan with his Staff, mounted body guard of the Sturgis rifles, with horses and baggage for all of them, to Sandy Hook. (I may here remark that for this item the Railroad Co. has furnished a bill, as for a special train, at so much per mile, instead of charging per capita for the passengers, and according to the freight tariff for passenger or first class freight trains for the horses and baggage. They had the right, under agreement and practice, to charge in that way, when the amount would have been very much larger.)

I accompanied the train myself from the Relay Junction, and we reached Harper's Ferry about noon on the 26th. After pontooning the river for Banks' army to cross, and after making a personal survey as far as Charlestown, 12 miles southwardly, Genl. McClellan reoccupied his quarters on the train by 6 o'clock P.M. Nothing further occurring, I started about 9 o'clock that night on my return to Baltimore, leaving Gen. McClellan and Staff at Sandy Hook upon their train. As I was about taking my leave of him, and supposing there was nothing further to be done, I was greatly surprised to receive his oral requisition to move the heavy forces from Washington to Sandy Hook contemplated in the consultation alluded to, and which he required us to begin at daylight on the following morning, or in about 9 hours from the moment of his order.

He wanted at first, or within 24 hours of the time he gave the order, if possible, some 2 to 3000 cavalrymen and horses, 16 guns, caissons, equipage and the horses and men accompanying them, and say 10,000 infantry, with their equipage and supplies. He wanted us to follow that very heavy work with some 20 to 25,000 infantry and supplies on the following day, or as rapidly as possible.

I represented to him our difficulties in doing this most extraordinary task, practically without notice, and that it would absorb the equipment of the Road, including that diverted from the daily use of the public in working the regular passenger, mail and freight trains, and also oblige us to obtain additional cars from other roads, etc.—all of which he said he desired us to do, and would sustain us in doing.

I left him at about 10 o'clock, promising to do our best towards his great object; and I at once telegraphed to all quarters from Sandy Hook, and afterwards from the Point of Rocks, Monocacy and other stations during the night, as I advanced upon a locomotive to Baltimore. The whole operating force of the Road at Baltimore, Washington, Sandy Hook and all intermediate points, was aroused and kept at work through the night, in preparing for this unexpected emergency; and all the business of the line and branches was deranged, or set aside in greater or less extent, to provide for executing such an unparalleled demand.

No effort or expense was spared. By examining the accounts rendered the Government by the railroad company, I am surprised to find them so moderate and meagre; for I do not hesitate to declare, that in my judgment the effort made by the company in this case, and the extent, variety, promptness and effect of its

153

preparations, exceeded those of any movement of the war; and the outlays and losses, direct and indirect, involved on its part, would not be compensated by double the whole amount charged by the road on this account.

It is clear to me that the Government officers are not aware of the difficulties encountered, expenditures incurred, and really extraordinary service rendered by the Railroad Co. in their efforts to meet this great requisition. Over one half of the first cost in labor, material, etc. required of the Company to perform the entire movement of the 45 to 50,000 men, horses, equipage, etc. for which they would have received considerably more than $100,000 was actually incurred, and, if the troops had been furnished us at Washington as promptly as promised for loading, and the order to suspend had not come upon the Company with even more suddenness than the order to begin, the whole large force would have been moved to Sandy Hook by from two and a half to three days, and would have constituted the largest operation, all in all, within so short a time, that the whole war anywhere witnessed.

The distance from Washington is 102 miles, with a transfer involved from the branch to the main line at the Relay, with a long grade of 90 feet to the mile to overcome.

The Quartermaster's Department, I may remark, is singularly in error in the idea that the Railroad Company should have had at Washington, or in easy call, stock cars sufficient for such a really heavy movement of horses. This may be better understood when I mention that the whole freight equipment of the Company, for both its roads east of the break at Harper's Ferry, was not over 800 cars, and that 3000 cavalry and 500 artillery would take fully 250 cars for horses alone, beside those for the guns, forage, subsistence, ammunition, equipage and the men.

This paper is already too long for a business document; but I might readily amplify the particulars yet further, to show the utter inadequacy of the amounts proposed to be allowed for the very extraordinary efforts required of, and made by the Railroad

Company, and the outlays incurred, losses sustained, and services actually rendered, as well as preparations matured for yet greater service, required but remitted after such effort and preparation for its rapid and effective execution.

Very respectfully,
Your obdt. servant,
W. P. Smith.

Explanatory Note:

The Mr. Sharpe introduced in the following letter is the man who, during the Confererate occupation of Martinsburg in the summer of 1861, engineered the removal of 14 locomotives from the Baltimore & Ohio shops 40 miles over dirt roads for use of Southern lines. He later became Master of Transportation of the Baltimore & Ohio Railroad Company.

Quartermaster's Office,
Strasburg, Aug. 10, 1861

Col. Angus McDonald:
My Dear Sir:

I introduce to your acquaintance and particular attention my friend, Mr. Sharpe, the "Special Agent of the Confederate States." I have no doubt you are fully aware of the important services Mr. Sharpe has rendered in his prompt and successful removal of a large number of locomotives to this place from Martinsburg for the use of the Southern Confederacy. He has just returned from a most remarkable and eminently successful enterprise, viz., the removal of two splendid engines from Leesburg to Piedmont Depot on the M.J.R.R., the accomplishment of which has attracted the attention and elicited the admiration of all in that section of the country and the congratulations and thanks of the officers of this R.R. Company. Mr. Sharpe now only needs your protecting wing to complete his valuable labours in another direction, the importance of which, I feel confident you will fully appreciate, and after his explanation and evidence of his authority to embark in the matter, will elicit your full approbation and protection. Knowing your own eagerness to "prey upon the enemy" and engage in all that would add to our cause and their discomfort, I leave Mr. Sharpe to explain everything to you himself.

Very Sincerely and Respectfully Yours,
W. T. Jones.

DATE DUE